SOUTH AFRICA'S YESTERDAYS

Reader's Digest

SOUTH AFRICA'S YESTERDAYS

Published by The Reader's Digest Association South Africa (Pty.) Limited,
130 Strand Street, Cape Town 8001.

ISBN 0 620 05019 5

EDITOR: Peter Joyce   ART DIRECTOR: John Meek

RESEARCH EDITORS: Frances Howard, Patricia Kramer

ASSISTANT EDITOR: Alan Duggan

EDITORIAL/PRODUCTION CO-ORDINATOR: Ros Lavine

ASSISTANT TO THE ART DIRECTOR: Susan Hart

RESEARCHERS: Yvonne van der Walt,
Jane Askew, Lizanne Barnett, Judy Beyer, Lynne Bryer, Renée Durbach, Jill Ledingham,
Sandra Moran, Rodney Odlin, Beverley Opperman, Wilma van Biljon

MAJOR CONTRIBUTORS:
Lynne Bryer, Alan Duggan, Brian Johnson-Barker, Roger Kenyon,
Jim Penrith, Nic Slabbert, Paul Tingay

This book is designed to provide an intriguing glimpse, largely through the windows of contemporary comment and illustration, of our recent past. The time span is about a century; the subject matter is social rather than political; the issues are reported rather than argued.

In conceiving the volume we did not set out to tell the full story of South Africa, to describe in any detail the great and often controversial events in this century of turbulence and change, but instead to create a kind of national family album, one which reflects the day-to-day preoccupations of the parents, grandparents and great-grandparents of today's South Africans. So our objective in choosing the subjects we cover was threefold: to tell a good story, to trigger memories, and to evoke the mood of the times.

SOUTH AFRICA'S YESTERDAYS is a journey back in time, a diversion down nostalgic byways to a world that many of us never knew, or have forgotten. It will, we hope, provide a brief escape from the cares and strains of today's world.

A great many people helped in the preparation of this volume. The publishers, however, acknowledge their special indebtedness to the Chief Librarian and staff of the South African Library, Cape Town; the management of the Star newspaper; the City Librarian, Johannesburg Public Library, and the staff of the Africana Museum.

The Editors

'Presenting addresses to Lord Selborne at Pretoria.'
Lord Selborne came to South Africa in 1905 as
High Commissioner and Governor
of the Transvaal and Orange River Colony

Contents

Birth of a Nation

New Year's Day 1900 saw a divided South Africa, a country scarred by war. The Anglo-Boer conflict would last a further two-and-a-half years and result in many thousands of deaths, but from its fiery anvil the Union of South Africa would be forged.

Towering above all the millions who built the nation were two giants: Cecil Rhodes and Paul Kruger. Rhodes, the self-made millionaire who dreamed of extending Britain's Imperial domain from the Cape to Cairo, was a shrewd businessman, politician and empire-builder. 'Oom Paul' Kruger, the Transvaal patriarch, was already a tired old man at the start of the Anglo-Boer War. He was unbending and conservative, and enormously respected by the people. Both were to die early in the century without realising their ambitions — perhaps appropriately, for they were men of an earlier, different world, and their passing coincided with the end of one era and the birth of another.

Thirty-first of May 1910. Four hundred and twenty-two years after Bartolomeu Dias coaxed his storm-lashed caravel around an unseen Cape, and two hundred and fifty-eight years after Jan van Riebeeck landed in Table Bay to pioneer a victualling station for merchantmen of the Dutch East India Company, united South Africa was born.

The Act of Union fused together the vast and beautiful land between the Cape of Good Hope and Kipling's 'great, grey-green, greasy' Limpopo River, 2 000 kilometres to the north. Bounded by the tropical waters of the Indian Ocean in the east and the chilly Atlantic to the west, the Cape Colony, Natal, the Orange Free State and Oom Paul Kruger's beloved Transvaal became one nation.

Under Louis Botha and Jan Smuts, Union was consolidated, and thus South Africa was better equipped to survive the great upheavals of the century: two world wars and the Great Depression of the 1930s. The Anglo-Boer War had, however, left bitter memories which periodically bedevilled relations between Afrikaans- and English-speaking South Africans.

For the black man, the first eight decades of the century brought material reward but increasingly few political bouquets. In 1948, with the National Party electoral victory, the era of apartheid and the Social Engineers was launched. It reached full maturity with the proclamation of the Republic of South Africa in 1961.

Much has been forgotten; much has yet to be told. To some, the events that heralded South Africa's stormy passage into the modern era will explain a little about the country today. And the story is far from over.

A typical Boer family at the turn of the century. The bitter fighting and harsh conditions of the Anglo-Boer War often wrenched them apart

A people at war

'IT IS OUR COUNTRY YOU WANT'

To stunned Victorians throughout the Empire, Britain's very presence in South Africa seemed in the balance in the closing days of December 1899. In 'Black Week', her soldiers suffered disastrous defeats against the Mauser rifles of the Transvaal and Orange Free State at Stormberg, Magersfontein and Colenso — defeats that had Russia, Germany and France applauding none too silently.

What began as a simple military exercise to bring to heel a rag-bag force of rustic Afrikaner horsemen had become a shattering national crisis. Doggedly determined now, Tommy Atkins took the Queen's Shilling, donned the new khaki, sang a brave good-bye to Dolly Gray and, cheered on by rapturous London crowds, steamed south to do serious battle with 'Brother Boer'.

The grievances of the voteless British immigrant uitlander community of the Rand provided the trigger for the Anglo-Boer War of 1899-1902. 'The case for intervention is overwhelming,' dispatched Alfred Milner, High Commissioner to South Africa in July 1899. '. . . The spectacle of thousands of British subjects kept permanently in the position of helots . . . does steadily undermine the influence and reputation of Great Britain.'

But the seeds of conflict had been sown long before. To Jan Smuts — Transvaal State Attorney turned Boer general — nineteenth century South Africa was a 'century of wrong'. It was also a century of war, in which Boer, Briton, and tribesmen from Zulu to Bushman

Boers at Spionkop ready to warn of the barrage of British naval guns from nearby Mount Alice

were locked in a deadly and almost continuous struggle for land. And for survival. By the 1890s the most powerful nation to survive the wars, the Afrikaners, had entrenched themselves in the northern republics of the Transvaal and the Orange Free State.

Britain had annexed the Transvaal in 1877. Four years later the Transvalers, bitterly resentful of their new colonial status, went to war with the 'mother country', and won. A British army under Sir George Pomeroy Colley suffered humiliating defeat on the bloody slopes of Majuba Hill and a form of independence was restored.

For a while after that Britain was content to leave the troublesome little state alone — until the discovery of the golden treasure house of the Witwatersrand in 1886. Englishmen poured in to profit from the new wealth, and soon there was a popular outcry for voting rights. Kruger refused to extend the franchise, and Dr L. S. Jameson's quixotic raid to rescue the allegedly imperilled citizens of Johannesburg in 1896 ended in fiasco. The German Kaiser sent a telegram to Kruger congratulating him on his handling of the military side of the affair, and hinted that if he should need foreign help in the future, Germany would be sympathetic. The

KRUGER   STEYN   JOUBERT   DE WET   SMUTS   BOTHA   DE LA REY

Men of war. Paul Kruger and Marthinus Steyn, leaders of the tiny republics of the Transvaal and Orange Free State, took on Britain's Imperial might on 12 October 1899 in a brave effort to preserve their independence. The brilliance of such generals as Louis Botha, Koos de la Rey, the youthful Jan Smuts and Christiaan de Wet, the enterprising guerilla commander, compensated for the over-cautiousness of some of the Boer leaders, notably the aging Piet Joubert

CHAMBERLAIN   MILNER   ROBERTS   KITCHENER   BULLER   BADEN-POWELL   WHITE

British Colonial Secretary Joseph Chamberlain and arch-schemer Alfred Milner started the war ostensibly to protect the uitlanders of the South African Republic, but in reality for gold, territorial expansion and Imperial glory. Their leaders suffered quick and surprising reverses in the field: Baden-Powell locked himself up in Mafeking; George White in Ladysmith, which Redvers Buller eventually managed to relieve. Harsh in war, the British proved generous in victory

Jameson Raid, and Transvaal's flirtation with an ambitious and powerful Germany, intensified the mutual distrust of Boer and Briton.

And then there was that most provocative of elements, British arrogance. 'Every Englishman is born with a certain miraculous power, that makes him master of the world,' Bernard Shaw caricatured in 1896. Architects of war Milner and Joseph Chamberlain, Secretary of State for the Colonies, would have agreed. It was Milner in particular, that 'finest flower of culture', Balliol scholar and arch-Imperialist, who ardently believed in Britain's 'civilising influence'. He had determined on British paramountcy over all South Africa. Paul Kruger, President of the South African Republic (Transvaal) and President Marthinus Theunis Steyn of the Orange Free State were equally determined to maintain their independence.

To Rudyard Kipling and readers of the London *Times*, Kruger was 'Cruel in the shadow, crafty in the sun . . . Sloven, sullen, savage, secret, uncontrolled', but to his *volk* this father of 16 children was a Solomon-wise and granite-firm patriarch. They would follow where he led.

Milner insisted that 'There is no way out except reform in the Transvaal or war'. Protested Kruger: 'It is our country you want.' And, on 12 October 1899, war it was.

At the start of the war the Republics were able to put 35 000 men into the field against some 15 000 British troops. The Boers seized the initiative and invaded Natal on 12 October. Cape Prime Minister, W. P. Schreiner (whose sister, Olive, wrote *The Story of an African Farm)*, strove to remain neutral. But on 1 November 1899 Free State commandos crossed the Orange River, and drew large numbers of Cape Afrikaners to their ranks.

The brutal reality

To young Deneys Reitz, son of a former President of the Orange Free State, the imagined dignity of death in battle was soon replaced by the brutal reality of '. . . ashen faces and staring eyeballs'. But Reitz and his compatriots, despite their inexperience, took easily to warfare.

Morning Post correspondent Winston Churchill wrote: 'We must face the facts. The individual Boer, mounted in suitable country, is worth from three to five regular soldiers.' Armed with the modern clip-loading Mauser rifle, provisioned with rusks and biltong, the Boer was a formidable adversary. His marksmanship was superb, and his horsemanship and mobility an unnerving revelation to the ponderous columns of British infantry.

Republican artillery pieces were more modern and longer-ranging than those of the British. Men of the Staats Artillerie handled their guns with the skill of experts, often deploying them with a flair unknown at Woolwich.

Boer generals, though, tended to be overcautious. Joubert in Natal and Cronjé in the Northern Cape, especially, wasted time and manpower besieging towns instead of thrusting for the coastal ports. Of a different calibre was 'Koos' de la Rey — 'a striking model for some warrior prophet of the Old Testament' — who rolled up the railway for 500 kilometres on the

Image and reality. Left: 'Tommy's welcome to Cape Town' — British troops arrive in South Africa to teach Brother Boer a short, sharp lesson. Right: What began as a punitive expedition soon became a national calamity for Britain. Picture shows dead soldiers of the Queen in their trenches at Spionkop

western border of the Republics and who devised the ingenious trench system at the foot of the range of hills at Magersfontein. Had the younger breed — De Wet, Smuts and Botha — come into their own early in the war, the course of events might have been very different.

British generalship during the first phase was also poor. Blunders by Buller in Natal and Gatacre at Stormberg gave rise to a Boer joke that it would be regarded as a capital offence to kill a British general. Indeed, Buller's vacillation and the succession of defeats led to his replacement as Commander-in-Chief by Lord Frederick Sleigh Roberts of Kandahar. Roberts, who had spent 41 military years in India, had lost his only son in the battle of Colenso. He chose as his Chief-of-Staff 'that molten mass of devouring energy and burning ambition', General Sir Horatio Herbert Kitchener, hero of Omdurman. 'From Khyber Pass to the Upper Nile the earth had trembled where they stood,'

wrote one contemporary of the two new leaders. Boer reaction was somewhat more reserved.

As the new century began, 85 000 British troops were in or on their way to South Africa. Ultimately, almost half a million would fight there, against an absolute total of 88 000 on the Republican side, of whom no more than some 40 000 were in the field at any one time.

For the British, wealthy and well-meaning patriots raised and equipped special units of irregulars: Strathcona's Horse, Paget's Horse and Lord Lovat's Scouts were just a few. In Natal, former uitlanders formed, at their own expense, the Imperial Light Horse, which played an important part in the defence of Ladysmith and relief of Mafeking.

The delightfully jingoistic ditties of a host of lyricists stirred many a patriotic heart. One character in an H. G. Wells novel confessed: 'The prevailing force in my undergraduate days was not Socialism but Kiplingism . . .' Royalties from performances of Kipling's *Absent-minded Beggar* were paid into a fund to provide help for the families of the plucky lads who flocked to the colours:

When you've shouted 'Rule Britannia',
When you've sung 'God save the Queen',
When you've finished killing Kruger with your mouth,
Will you kindly drop a shilling in my little tambourine
For a gentleman in khaki ordered South?

The loyal 'Cubs of Empire' — Canada, New Zealand and Australia — sent troops; a unit of European planters came from Ceylon, and Natal Indians volunteered for the medical service. Mohandas K. Gandhi was a 'bodysnatcher', as the stretcher-bearers were known, at Colenso and Spionkop. 'They are sons of the Empire after all,' The *Natal Advertiser* graciously declared.

There was no shortage of bravery. Said an observer of the British: 'I have seen these clean-faced, long-limbed "Lion's cubs" leading charges, going to certain death without flinching, as though they were but cheering a cricket match . . .' Others were equally admiring of the Boers. An English clergyman's son, in a letter home after the battle of Spionkop in January 1900, wrote: 'To see those great bearded warriors charging up a mountain, taking death as nothing . . . there was something god-like in those men: their faces change to iron and they seem like Fate itself.'

And so, tragically inspired by conviction, race, rhetoric and revenge, the battle rolled on.

Sieges and shrapnel

THE MYTH OF MAFEKING

The London newsboys had something to shout about. On 20 October 1899 a bayonet charge cleared the Boers from the summit of Talana Hill in Natal. The next day, British infantry and cavalry dislodged the Boers from their position at nearby Elandslaagte. Britain was winning the war. True, losses had been heavy (fatal casualties included a general, Sir W. Penn Symons), but there was no doubt in the public mind that Kruger's burghers were about to be taught a sharp lesson.

And then, unaccountably it seemed, the British were on the run. The Boer forces closed around the Natal army at Ladysmith, Kimberley was invested (Cecil Rhodes was among those trapped) and a Boer army surrounded a third town: Mafeking. At the time few people in England had ever heard of the place, but its name was to become a legend, and even a part of the English language.

Baden-Powell waits it out

'One or two small field guns are shelling the town. Nobody cares.' So went a typical, nonchalant message from beleaguered Mafeking's commander, Colonel Robert Baden-Powell, whose defence of this 'small, tin-roofed town of small houses plumped down upon the open veld' was to make him Britain's hero of heroes.

The wily and irrepressible Baden-Powell, with 1 183 troops, had tucked himself inside Mafeking just before the outbreak of war. He waited to be besieged, and for 217 days did very little to get out again. On 12 October, General De la Rey captured an armoured train at nearby Kraaipan. There was 'a dull booming noise which almost froze the blood in my veins', said Lady Sarah Wilson, daughter of the Duke of Marlborough and sister to Lord Randolph Churchill. Lady Sarah, who was hovering

Blacks in Mafeking starved while Lady Sarah Wilson entertained officers and other notables in her well-furnished dugout. Soup kitchens such as this one barely kept alive the estimated 7 000 men, women and children who crowded into a motley collection of mud huts known as the Native Stadt. Baden-Powell executed by firing-squad some blacks caught stealing food, had 115 others flogged, forbade them to buy bread, and drastically reduced their supply of grain. Emerson Neilly of the Pall Mall Gazette wrote: '. . . words could not portray the scene of misery'

around the Boer lines at the time, eventually talked her way into the town.

Bombardment began in a half-hearted way and little damage was done. It was all like a 'gigantic picnic', wrote Angus Hamilton of The Times. Eventually 6 000 burghers, under General Piet Cronjé surrounded the town. On 24 October a 'Long Tom' Creusot 94-pounder, nicknamed 'Creaky', was first used to shell the town. The more blasé residents reckoned they had enough time to take cover once they saw the puff of smoke on the horizon.

The Boers made only two serious efforts to take the town, and these were never resolutely carried through. Baden-Powell arranged a good system of trenches, dugout shelters and earthworks so that everyone, in B-P's words, could 'sit tight and wait for them to go'.

Baden-Powell occasionally organised night raids, or 'demonstrations', against the Boer camps, but at other times there was no action for anything up to seven weeks. He and Cronjé indulged in regular, polite and sometimes indignant correspondence, always ending with the formal 'Your obedient servant'. Stamps and bank-notes were printed as the normal supplies ran out, and a newspaper, the Mafeking Mail, was 'Issued Daily, Shells Permitting'.

Cricket, pony-racing, polo and football matches were regular events in the besieged town. Baden-Powell himself awarded the prizes, and it was obvious he was enjoying himself. He took a leading part in the Sunday concerts (there was a Sunday truce), and one of his favourite revue acts was an impersonation of the pianist Paderewski 'with a mop of false hair and many high-pitched shrieks'. But Sunday polo eventually had to be cancelled because J.P. Snyman, who took over from General Cronjé, 'disapproved' and threatened to shell the field. The Boers rather enjoyed the siege, too. Stage coaches arrived regularly with comforts and visiting womenfolk, who were sometimes allowed to pull 'Creaky's' firing lanyard.

In England the siege was played on the public stage, and Baden-Powell's 'jolly messages had the nation in an orgy of admiration'.

But the blacks of the town starved. Even the dog cemetery was raided for its bones and other remains. Emerson Neilly of the Pall Mall Gazette wrote: 'I saw them fall down on the veldt and lie

Lord Baden-Powell, founder of the worldwide Boy Scout Association, greets the South African contingent attending a 'Jamboree' at Wembley, London. The movement was inspired by the Mafeking siege, when Baden-Powell used boys as runners. In a message to 'loyal Britishers' in 1904, he wrote: '. . . but we ought really not to think too much of any boy, even though a cricketer and footballer, unless he can also aim and shoot, and will be therefore useful as a soldier . . .'

The relief of Mafeking provoked a surge of patriotic fervour that approached hysteria. The Natal Mercury brought the glad tidings to its readers in this colourful 'souvenir special'; the London Daily Express headlined its front page on 19 May 1900: 'When Shall Their Glory Fade?' Crowds went wild in the streets of London, young men wore Union Jacks as waistcoats, and Baden-Powell, quite undeservedly, became the most popular English hero since Nelson

THE WRATH OF LONG CECIL

American engineer George Labram leans on Long Cecil, the gun he designed during the siege of Kimberley. He had noticed a billet of steel lying in the De Beers workshop yard, and it occurred to him that it might be used for a large-calibre artillery piece. He read articles in an old engineering journal, a few paragraphs of the *Encyclopaedia Britannica,* a War Office 'Treatise on Ammunition' and a gunnery textbook, and built the gun and carriage in 24 days. Mrs Pickering, wife of the Secretary of the De Beers Company, was invited to pull the ring lanyard for the first time, and seconds later the shell burst in a hitherto safe Boer laager 7 200 m away, causing considerable alarm. Labram died shortly afterwards in tragically ironic circumstances. He was dressing for dinner in Kimberley's Grand Hotel when a shell from one of the Boers' Long Toms burst on the second floor, killing him instantly. The Long Tom had been brought to Kimberley to counter the threat of Long Cecil.

Ladysmith's main street during the siege of 1900. Food was scarce, the water supply polluted, and enteric fever and dysentery accounted for 2 000 patients in a hospital built for 300. One resident, Dr James Alexander Kay, described the town as '. . . an awful hole, celebrated for heat, dust, storms, wind and insects'

The rosette worn by Charles Smythe, premier of Natal, to celebrate the relief of Ladysmith

Left: the telegram that informed a delighted Smythe that the siege had been lifted

---

where they had fallen, too weak to go on their way. Hunger had them in its grip, and many were black spectres and living skeletons . . .'

When at last a relief force set out for Mafeking, the Boers felt obliged to make a final effort. On the night of 11 May a party of them rushed the town, entered it unnoticed, started fires and fought furiously before surrendering to Baden-Powell's overwhelmingly superior numbers. 'It gives a pleasant finish to the siege,' wrote one officer. 'It just wanted a finishing touch to make it satisfactory.'

The relief column arrived near Mafeking on 16 May and the garrison spent the day taking group photographs. When the column entered the town that night, Baden-Powell was asleep.

An unusual trade sprang up in Kimberley during the siege. Portraits like this became common as souvenir-hunters exchanged and bargained for shells and put them on display. A complete, unexploded shell sold for £5; a shell casing cost a sovereign

KIMBERLEY: SOUP TICKETS, AND QUEUES FOR HORSE MEAT

Life was hard and often dangerous for the beleaguered residents of Kimberley. The infant mortality rate rocketed, and 1 500 people were to die — most of them from enteric fever. Theresa Stevenson wrote to her sister on 23 February 1900: '. . . the worst is standing waiting for your meat turn in the mornings. You stand two by two on the market square and the first morning Netta and I stood 3½ hours before our turn came — then if you don't take horse meat — you get a soup ticket and have to tramp up again and get the soup at 11.30.

'Louie, we are like skeletons here — over 200 children have died in the last two months. I am thinner now than after the typhoid fever and Jack is just a frame.' The shelling made life even more uncomfortable:

'All the food starvation was bad enough and the small shells — but worse was to follow — a fortnight ago — the devils started shelling us with 100 lb shells. I went quite mad and had to go to Dr Smith. He said my nerves were all gone and I wanted medical comforts. He gave me a permit for 1 lb bacon a week but I told him to give me something to make me sleep. He gave me two sleeping draughts. They started shelling us Wednesday 7th and on the 9th killed Mr Labram.

'He was buried on the Saturday night at eight and as the funeral left the hospital a rocket went up from some Dutch spies in Camp and the devils started shelling and kept up till 11.30. Can you imagine anything more dreadful — shelling the dead. On Thursday night we went down the mine to the 1,500 ft level and thank God we were alive to go down there out of the sound and noise of that gun. Over 1,000 were at the station under the carriage and the bridge for four days and nights. I can't tell you now about the killed and wounded with the shells. I feel too bad . . . we have been relieved a week now but are not getting better food yet. If we don't get more food in a few days we shall go to Cape Town as Jack can't work here on the goods we are getting . . . love to all, more next time — my poor head is gone soft and Jack has gone off his sleep again with all this worry . . .'

This was typical of the many shelters built to protect residents from 100 lb shells during the Kimberley siege

The guerilla war

HIT AND RUN, BLACKENED RUINS AND TRAMPLED FIELDS

By the winter of 1900 many burghers, their spirits low, had accepted Roberts's offer to surrender their weapons and return to their farms. But Christiaan de Wet's successful raids in the Free State revived their spirits and once again they began to join the commandos of Louis Botha in the South-Eastern Transvaal, Ben Viljoen in the North East, De la Rey in the West and De Wet in the O.F.S.

Centrally co-ordinated under Botha, but operating independently, these highly mobile commandos, nourished and aided by their kinsfolk and living off the country, attacked British units, cut railways (155 incidents between December 1900 and September 1901), seized supplies, prepared to invade the Cape and generally harassed the frustrated British. The 'Great De Wet hunts' were launched. They involved tens of thousands of British troops, and they did not succeed.

Scorching the earth

The British reacted viciously to the new Boer tactics. Smuts, in the western districts, wrote to Louis Botha on 22 December 1900: 'Wherever the enemy now appears, he carries out indescribable destruction. All houses are burned down, all fields and gardens utterly destroyed, all cattle and foodstuffs carried off and all males taken prisoner ... In some cases where an attack by us is expected, even the women and children are carried off to their camps as a protective measure.'

Thirty thousand farmsteads and 20 villages would eventually be destroyed in Roberts's, and more particularly Kitchener's, scorched earth policy and their great 'drives' to capture the

British troops entering Johannesburg. The arrival of Roberts and Kitchener in January 1900 had injected fresh optimism into the British troops. By 15 February Kimberley had been relieved, and two weeks later Cronjé, with 4 000 burghers, surrendered at Paardeberg. On 3 March Buller finally made his triumphal entry into Ladysmith, and some of those who had been besieged there took part in the relief of Mafeking on 15 May. Two months before that, Bloemfontein had fallen, Johannesburg was occupied on 31 May and Pretoria on 5 June. President Kruger left Lourenço Marques aboard the Dutch cruiser Gelderland — to die in exile four years later at Clarens in Switzerland. The republics were annexed as Transvaal Colony and the Orange River Colony, and by December 1900 Roberts, convinced that the war was over barring minor mopping-up operations, was ready to return to England. But the Boers, heartened by Christiaan de Wet's hit-and-run successes, took to the field again, and the fighting went on for another eighteen tragic months

Boers. In *Commando*, Deneys Reitz described a 'driven' area he passed through en route to join Smuts in the Cape: ' ... leaving behind it only blackened ruins and trampled fields, so that our course lay through a silent unpeopled waste, across which we navigated our wagon like a lonely ship at sea.'

At first there was some British heart-searching about the burning of homes, though Louis Botha, in his Roos Senekal instruction of 10 October 1900, threatened to do the same himself to burghers who laid down their arms.

Elements in the Boer leadership, including brothers of De Wet and Cronjé, believed it was pointless to continue the war and, through the Burgher Peace Committee, were prepared to persuade their compatriots in the field of its futility. They were regarded as *hensoppers* or 'hands-uppers' — traitors — by the fighting burghers. But the peace-makers went further: encouraged by Roberts, A. P. Cronjé was influential in forming the National Scouts, a force which actively helped the British. It was partly to protect the families of these men that the

Jan Smuts, the brilliant young Boer general, seated centre, with some of his officers. His commandos invaded the Cape, and reached the sea at one point

This photograph, originally reproduced in The Sphere *in 1900, carried the caption: 'Characteristic types of the men we are fighting.' Even young boys fought the British — De Wet claimed a seven-year-old was among his battle casualties*

WINSTON CHURCHILL: WAR CORRESPONDENT

A young Churchill addresses a meeting outside Durban's Town Hall (now a post office) after his escape from Pretoria.

Winston Churchill had sailed to South Africa with some qualms. The *Morning Post* correspondent appeared afraid that the war would be over by the time his ship docked, and wrote to his mother: 'Fourteen days is a long time at war . . .' Chamberlain wrote to Milner that Churchill had a reputation for bumptiousness and suggested that Milner 'put him on the right lines'. His fears were well-founded, for it was only a month later that Churchill was captured by General Botha's men in an ambush on an armoured train in Natal.

In his book, *The Boer War*, Thomas Packenham said it appeared that Churchill's 'burning desire to see battle' helped to persuade the train's commander not to turn back when they first spotted the signs of a trap. It was not long afterwards that the war correspondent made a daring escape from Pretoria prison and returned to the front — as brash and irrepressible as ever.

The Boer guerillas were expert saboteurs. Typical of the havoc they wrought was the destruction of the Pienaars River Bridge, north of Pretoria. The railway line was a vital artery for the supply and movement of British troops

'It was the most beautiful display of fireworks that I have ever seen,' De Wet wrote of the capture of an English supply train at Roodewal in June 1900. After helping themselves, the burghers set light to the contents which included mail and ammunition

British, in the second half of 1900, initiated the concentration camps.

Kitchener, contrary to his ferocious image, was prepared to talk terms. But Milner's directive was unconditional surrender. He also urged the incarceration of the burghers — to prevent them returning to their farms, recuperating, and then rejoining their commandos. As to the concentration camps, what had started as an unofficial refugee scheme under Roberts became, under Kitchener in December 1900, a deliberate policy of wholesale internment.

Drives and deportation

'May the 20th century bring forth a new period of peace, and blessing for our sorely tried and martyred people,' Smuts wrote to De la Rey on Christmas Day 1900. But it was not to be.

In January 1901, De Wet organised the second Cape invasion by commandos under Gideon Scheepers, Kritzinger and J. B. M. Hertzog. Kitchener's answer — for the guerillas: massive drives and a system of blockhouses (linked by trenches and barbed wire); for the women and children: concentration camps; for prisoners: deportation to St Helena, Bermuda, Ceylon and India.

There were tales of atrocities, which the Cape opposition newspapers took up. Champions of the cause included Olive Schreiner and Marie Koopmans de Wet. The editors were tried and their papers suppressed.

Boers caught wearing British military uniforms were sometimes executed — but as often as not they had no choice. Some were even reduced to wearing grain bags.

The Middelburg peace conference between Botha and Kitchener, 29 February — 16 March 1901, was abortive. Both sides wanted too much at a time when neither side had reached exhaustion. Kitchener was inclined to modera-

tion but his proposals, scarcely acceptable to the Boers (who insisted on full independence for their republics), were whittled down even further by Milner and Chamberlain. 'The cause is not yet lost,' Botha decided, 'and since nothing worse than this can befall us, it is well worth while to fight on.'

And the fight did go on. Smuts's invasion of the Cape was a particularly dramatic event in the guerilla war. Through valley and mountain range his troops were hounded by the British, and they were often starved, tired and cold.

Sometimes, though, they received their kinsmen's sympathy and assistance. The Boers were proud of having at one point ridden their horses to the coast and into the sea — a novel experience for the highveld burgher.

'Show me the road!' Deneys Reitz demands of one Hottentot fisherman.

'What road, Baas?'

'The road to England . . . we are crossing tonight to capture London.'

'My God, Baas, don't do it; the water is over your head here, and you will all be drowned.'

Troops in the field were remarkably self-sufficient, operating efficient commisariats, field telegraphs (right) powered by crude batteries and even printing presses for the production of banknotes. The Boer guerillas, harried by tens of thousands of British troops, ran a soap factory, a tannery that turned out boots and leather clothing and a telephone system linking the laagers. They made salt (using acid and soda), horseshoes and nails (from fencing wire), and even established a State Mint which produced gold coins — the 'Een Rand, ZAR, 1902'. But probably their greatest talent lay in their high degree of mobility: they could pack up a well-organised camp and be on the move within minutes. Left: P.J. Kloppers, Mint Master in the field, with hammer and die (he cast it himself at Pilgrim's Rest) and his team of craftsmen

Peace with honour

THE BOERS SIGN, AND TOMMY GOES HOME

The vast open spaces the Boers loved and exploited so well were eventually denied them. Kitchener, with his 8 000 blockhouses, each garrisoned by seven soldiers, his drives and barbed wire, parcelled up the land. The British had the men, the money and the organisation. And they eventually won.

In early 1902 the Free State had 7 000 burgher guerillas left in the field. The countryside looked as if a massive veld fire had ravaged it. In the Cape, 3 000 invaders and rebels criss-crossed the mountains and valleys, but there was no general rebellion. In the Transvaal 12 000 fighting Boers were still at large — but the war of attrition was taking a terrible toll.

On 9 April the Boer leaders met in Klerksdorp, decided they would talk peace with Kitchener, and entrained for Pretoria.

Kitchener listened and then asked, surprised: 'Must I understand from what you say that you wish to retain your independence?'

'Yes,' President Steyn of the OFS replied, 'the people must not lose their self-respect.'

For so long both sides had fought for just that on the battlefield and now, a little wiser perhaps, they fought for it in the council chambers.

Allegiance to Edward

The Boers wanted to consult their burghers. The British agreed. The Boers called their leaders together at a convention on 15 May at Vereeniging to decide between peace and war. Sixty delegates met. Each leader reported conditions in his area, and they were divided on the issue.

Nine days were then spent in negotiation with the British in Pretoria — the word 'surrender' had to be avoided at all costs.

A huge crowd looks on as the Peace of Vereeniging is formally announced on 2 June 1902 in front of the Raadsaal, Pretoria. The historic document had been signed at Pretoria's gracious Melrose House on 31 May. Sheer numbers and superior wealth had won Britain the war; the Boers were eventually to win the peace

After much heated and bitter debate, the British terms were finally accepted 55 minutes before midnight on Saturday, 31 May 1902. The war had lasted two years and eight months. Some of the Boers broke their guns and refused the oath '. . . to testify . . . allegiance to King Edward VII, his heirs and successors . . .' They were deported. But most agreed, and so Tommy began to go home. Kipling, of course, had the last word:

> But now, discharged, I fall away
> To do with little things again . . .
> Gawd, 'oo knows all I cannot say,
> Look after me in Thamesfontein!

The irony of Vereeniging is that although it brought the two Republics back to colonial status for a while, it actually promised them self-government. The Dutch language was safeguarded and it was ensured that Africans in the two Republics were excluded from the political process. The British, having won the war, handed the spoils to the Boers.

For the pro-British blacks, though, there was scant sympathy. In his book, *The Boer War*, Thomas Packenham quotes Canon Farmer, a leading British missionary in the Transvaal: 'Of all who have suffered by the war, those who have endured most and will receive least sympathy, are the Natives in the country places of the Transvaal . . .'

THEATRES AND GRAVEYARDS IN CEYLON

Many Boers came from afar to return to their homes. The Vereeniging peace proposals included 'a free gift of three million pounds', loans, district commissions to assist resettlement and 'provide necessities lost in the war'.

Twenty-seven thousand Boers became prisoners of war and exiles. They were divided into three groups: POWs who were concentrated in places like Green Point in Cape Town and Bellevue in Simonstown, or sent to the Bermudas, St Helena (Broadbottom and Deadwood camps), India and Ceylon (now Sri Lanka). The second group, the 'internees', were burghers and their families who had crossed the Transvaal/Portuguese East Africa border ahead of advancing British troops. They were interned in Caldas Da Rainha, Penibe and Alcobaca in Portugal. The third group were the 'undesirables' — Cape Colony men and women who sympathised with the Boer Republics. Most of these were sent to Port Alfred, near Grahamstown.

Boer prisoners of war marching through Jamestown, St Helena, en route to Deadwood camp

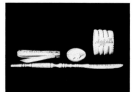

Above: Boer prisoners of war occupied their time by carving curios. The wooden cannons were later exhibited at London's Crystal Palace

Life for the exiled Boers wasn't too bad. The Deadwood and Broadbottom camps on St Helena had a string quartet, piano trio, brass band, minstrel group, home breweries and even an anti-smoking club! Curio-making and newspaper-printing, particularly in Ceylon and on St Helena, were two popular occupations. In Ceylon *De Strever*, organ of the Christian Endeavour Society, appeared every Saturday from 19 December 1901 to 26 July 1902. One advertisement read:

> Here in Kerneels van Schalkwyk's cafe a Boer
> Be he rich or be he poor
> For money so little its spending not felt
> Can have his tummy press tight on his belt.

Churches were built, and also graveyards — 131 Boers lie buried in Diyatalawa camp in Ceylon, another 146 on St Helena. Stamp dealers, photographers, bakers, tailors set up shop. Sports, theatres, choral and debating societies flourished. Schools were established. Joubert Reitz's *Searchlight* was written in the camp:

> When the searchlight from the gunboat
> Throws its rays upon my tent
> Then I think of home and comrades
> And the happy days I spent . . .
> . . . And of scenes I'll never forget . . .
> . . . And only then I realise
> How much my freedom meant

Several men escaped — one group swam out to a Russian ship in the port of Colombo and eventually arrived home via Russia, Germany, the Netherlands and Walvis Bay. Others stayed on after the war and married.

Prisoners were not allowed to return to South Africa unless they swore allegiance to the British Crown and promised not to assist 'His Majesty's enemies'. On signing they were issued with a permit (right)

St Helena prisoners — all men — put on a stage show called The Bells of the Town

Far from the sound of gunfire: Boer prisoners of war at St Helena relaxing with their guardian

TWO MEN, AND AN ERA, PASS AWAY

One of the great protagonists, Cecil John Rhodes, was dead; the other, President Paul Kruger, was soon to follow. 'Everything in the world is too short. Life and fame and achievement . . .' Rhodes said at the end. He died in his cottage at Muizenberg on 26 March 1902, bequeathing much of his vast wealth to the service of the public.

A de luxe train (which he had helped to de-sign) on a railway from the Cape-to-still-hoped-for-Cairo (that was largely his creation) chugged north, carrying his body to a new country (named after him) and the lonely, brooding hills of the Matopos. The 'immense and brooding spirit' was finally laid to rest in the grave of his choosing, on a hill he had called 'World's View'.

Like Rhodes, Paul Kruger had stood astride his nation and his people: a colossus. When the British occupied Pretoria in June 1900, he moved east with Louis Botha and the remnants of the main army. He was never to see his wife again. Machadodorp and Water-val Onder were his headquarters for a while, but with the advent of guerilla war there was no alternative but to go into exile.

The French, the Germans and the Dutch received him hospitably but gave him no material aid. He remained in Holland for the rest of the war. Later he moved to Clarens on Lake Geneva, where he died on 14 July 1904. His embalmed body was brought to Cape Town on board the *Batavier VI*. On 16 December, the Day of the Covenant, his body was interred in the plot now known as Heroes' Acre in Pretoria.

Two giants of their time were home at last.

President Paul Kruger's body is taken from Cape Town harbour in 1904

The train carrying Rhodes's body to the Matopos pauses at Beaufort West

By-products of conflict: an Anglo-Boer War miscellany

The three years of conflict from 1899 produced a size-able crop of subsidiary industries on both sides as manufacturers and merchants cashed in on patriotic fervour. In Britain, every other windowsill sported the red, white and blue 'Union Jack', while in South Africa people rushed to buy Anglo-Boer War games, song sheets and other miscellania.

Both sides produced their own banknotes and even newspapers — sometimes under almost impossible conditions. In the Transvaal De Staatscourant (government gazette) was published by the Transvaal 'flying press'. The editorial staff and printing press were installed in a railway carriage! Jong Transvaal, a handwritten newspaper which devoted its pages to articles on war and peace gave its head office address as Het Vlakke Veld (The Open Veld).

The Cossack Post, produced by British POWs on General De la Rey's farm in the Lichtenburg district, appeared from February to May 1901.

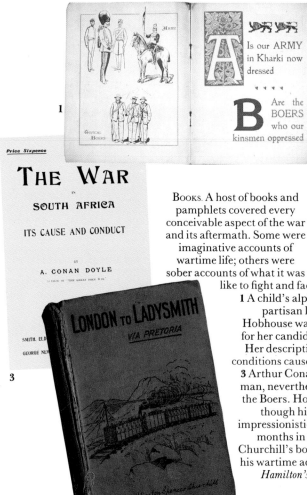

BOOKS. A host of books and pamphlets covered every conceivable aspect of the war and its aftermath. Some were imaginative accounts of wartime life; others were sober accounts of what it was like to fight and face death in the trenches.
1 A child's alphabet book with a distinctly partisan look at the war. **2** Emily Hobhouse was both admired and reviled for her candid accounts of women at war. Her descriptions of concentration camp conditions caused a furore in Britain. **3** Arthur Conan Doyle, a staunch Empire man, nevertheless respected and admired the Boers. However, his book on the war, though highly readable, was very impressionistic: he wrote it after only three months in South Africa. **4** Winston Churchill's book, a widely-read account of his wartime adventures. He published *Ian Hamilton's March* in the same year

TOYS AND GAMES. The Anglo-Boer War saw the emergence of many toys, games and puzzles featuring the two sides and their leaders.
1 *Transvaal* was a popular game played with counters on a board portraying battlefield scenes. **2** *Boer- en Rooinekspel* was manufactured in Holland. Players had to reach their objectives without succumbing to pitfalls such as Majuba (site of the British defeat in the first Anglo-Boer War) and Ladysmith (where the British held out against besieging Boer forces for 118 days). **3** A London firm made *The Great Transvaal War Puzzle*, in which the object was to get the red balls (representing British soldiers) into the Pretoria slot by manoeuvring around the blue balls (Boers). **4.** These playing cards, made in Germany, depict the leading characters on both sides in the war, as well as battle scenes. The German government's tax stamp has been made on the ace of spades

SONG SHEETS. Sieges, battles, farewells to sweethearts and similar wartime events were immortalised in song sheets that found thousands of ready buyers in the warring nations — both during and after the fighting. **1** The siege of Ladysmith, the Natal town occupied by a garrison of 13 500 officers and men under Sir George White, was the subject of a rousing 4/- song sheet composed by Theo Bonheur. **2** Even the disastrous Jameson Raid was featured. **3** Winifred M. Newberry's *La Liberté Waltz* was published by Ivan F. Haarburger of Bloemfontein. **4** One of the more flamboyant song sheets of the time was *The Last Goodbye*, a song written and composed by Murray and Leigh and 'sung with the greatest possible success' by statuesque Miss Florrie Forde. Miss Forde's costume was in sharp contrast to the mood engendered by the song's chorus: *'Tis the last goodbye, you must take your place in the line, Go and do your duty, Jack I'll do mine, I'll work for the Children as a Soldier's wife should do, And while their father is fighting the foe, I'll be Mother and Father too*

CHOCOLATE. British commerce got into the act too. *South African Storekeeper* reported in January 1900: 'Messrs Cadbury's first consignment of chocolate for the troops arrived by the *Mexican*, 40 000 boxes were ordered from them by her Majesty, and 30 000 each from Messrs Fry and Rowntree'

TOBACCO. Manufacturers plastered their labels with pictures of soldiers, Union Jacks and the indomitable British lion. One brand, 'British Pluck', had a label portraying sword-wielding troopers scattering hordes of Boers — they were loyal if not always accurate!

CURRENCY NOTES. Both sides issued emergency paper money during the war. The *Gouvernements Noten* of the Republic were printed by the Government Printer in Pretoria, later at Pietersburg, and in the field in the final stages of the fighting. Probably the best-known of the British notes are the 'good-fors' issued during the siege of Mafeking on the authority of the garrison's commander, Colonel Baden-Powell. **1** One of the rarest Anglo-Boer War banknotes. This £5 note was issued by the Commandant at Koffyfontein (now Koffiefontein), Major G.W. Robertson. The town was besieged by a large Boer force from 25 October, and it is obvious that Major Robertson expected it to last a long time: the £5 notes were valid only 'if presented for payment before January 1st 1901' (in fact the siege lasted only nine days). **2** The British banknotes were more ornate affairs and printed on superior quality paper. **3** A £1 *Gouvernements Noot* printed at Pilgrim's Rest. **4** and **5** Crude 'banknotes' issued to the Border Scouts at Upington in March 1902. **6** Even prisoners had their own currency. This note was valid only for prisoners at the Green Point camp

Repairing the ravaged land

MILNER'S BRAVE NEW ANGLO-SAXON WORLD

'Loyal! Of course you are loyal; it would be monstrous if you were not.' Thus spoke Lord Milner to the Afrikaner Bond in reply to their address of welcome to him at Graaff-Reinet in March 1898. It summed up Milner the Imperialist — and his desire for British control over the whole of South Africa. There had been a bruising, bitter war; he had achieved his objective. Now he had to rebuild the nation and consolidate the peace.

Milner relied on economic recovery to win over the Transvalers and Free Staters. For the phoenix to rise from the ashes of war, the gold mines had to be brought to full production, the farmers resettled on the land, their farms restocked. Attempts to form a full customs union, suspended during the war years, needed to be renewed. A loan of £35 million under Imperial guarantee and a ten per cent tax on mining profits helped to get things started.

Milner was now Governor of the Transvaal and Orange River Colony. To assist him, as Lieutenant-Governors, were Sir Arthur Lawley and Sir Hamilton Goold-Adams, each with an Executive Council. The year 1903 saw the first sessions of the newly appointed Legislative Councils. In June 1903 an Inter-Colonial Council of four (later twelve nominees) and fourteen officials came into being. Certain agencies — the Central South African Railways, Baden-Powell's South African Constabulary, schooling and repatriation — were all controlled by the Council, the idea being to reduce regional authority and widen loyalties.

The Kindergarten

As administrators, Milner imported Oxford graduates, a talented if controversial 'Kindergarten' of expertise. They included Philip Kerr, Marquis of Lothian, who eventually became British Ambassador to Washington; Geoffrey Robinson (Dawson) who later edited the Johannesburg *Star*, and then *The Times* of London; the Hon. Richard Feetham, who became a judge of the Appellate Division of the High Court of South Africa. They were all bachelors and several lived together in Moot House in Johannesburg.

Patrick Duncan, formerly Milner's private secretary, was perhaps the most important of Milner's team. He became Colonial Secretary of the Transvaal and later Governor-General of the Union of South Africa. John Buchan, the writer *(The Thirty Nine Steps)*, was responsible for repatriation and reconstruction in country areas. Lionel Curtis was the author of the Selborne Memorandum, which played a major role in the unification of South Africa. These young administrators dreamed up and launched scientific farming projects and irrigation and forestry schemes, new roads and railways. They indeed proved to be a powerhouse of talent and energy, and the ravages of war, if not the memories, were soon healed.

Although criticised in some quarters, Milner devoted enormous energy to reconstruction. He was determined that it would be a 'British' South Africa, but he had a firm ap-

A group of Milner's 'Celestials' — Chinese labourers brought in to help re-open the gold mines after the war (the original request for Ugandans had been turned down). Rumour and controversy, accusation and counter-accusation characterised the issue: as a result, the Tories lost the 1906 General Election in Britain

THE BOER LEADERS IN EUROPE

Soon after the Peace was signed, the 'Glorious Trio' of Louis Botha, Christiaan de Wet and Koos de la Rey set off for Europe to raise funds for their stricken countrymen. The tour, to Britain, Holland, Belgium and Germany, turned into something of a triumphal cavalcade. To Continentals, and even to Englishmen, these men were heroes, and were tumultuously welcomed as such. To all this they responded with dignified reserve, refusing invitations to the Coronation Review and from London society hostesses. Botha (whose entry in one hotel register was 'Begger for a people oppressed, but proficient') remarked that 'A man whose father, sons or brother have been killed in a quarrel may agree to forgive the slayer . . . to become his fellow-countryman in a good cause . . . but can be expected to do no more than that before the first blades of grass have sprung

General De Wet, General Botha and General De la Rey leave Cape Town on their fund-raising tour

up on the graves . . .' Financial donations, though, were less than expected, and when their visit to Germany provoked anti-British demonstrations, the threesome decided to return home. The tour ended with dinner at Buckingham Palace, and offers of knighthoods — also politely declined.

During their tour the Boer generals joined exiled Paul Kruger at a service in the Groote Kerk in The Hague, Holland. Front row from left: De Wet, Botha, Kruger, Hermanus Bredell (Kruger's secretary) and De la Rey

preciation of the people he was working with, the Afrikaners. In a letter of 22 May 1903 to Eugene Marais, he praised '. . . their patriotism, their courage, their resourcefulness, their endurance, their dignity and self-restraint in victory and their stoicism in defeat'.

The coming of the 'Celestials'

African workmen were slow to return to the mines after the war, and there was a shortage of 130 000 labourers. 'Everything is at a standstill, owing to the lack of labour,' wrote Violet Markham in her *New Era in South Africa*. 'Industrial development and mining development are checked and crippled, and the State finances, which naturally reflect the general prosperity of the country, are crippled in turn.'

Milner decided on indentured Chinese labour, the 'Celestials', who started to arrive in 1904. They were a highly controversial issue in both South Africa and England. '. . . Chinamen have been brought into this country against the wish of the public and . . . the people who are suffering now are the unprotected people living outside in the districts . . .' claimed one Transvaler. Horrendous (and invariably false) tales of Chinese banditry and savagery swept the Reef, while more sophisticated accusations of Chinese 'slavery' were levelled at the mine managers and British Government by the political opposition in England. 'The Transvaal is fighting its own peculiar yellow peril,' a correspondent of the *Rand Daily Mail* wrote on 25 September 1905. 'For the moment it is a land under the shadow of the Chinese danger . . . in the country districts men manufacture weapons of defence and barricade their houses by night, and women dread to be left alone. . .'

The British General Election of 1906 was fought on the issue. (Specifically, on the question of the flogging of the Chinese. Milner received the green light for his plan provided the labourers were treated well — but news of brutalities soon reached England.) The Government fell, and steps were taken to halt the flow of Chinese workers and repatriate those that had arrived. In March 1910 the last of the labourers sailed home.

Meanwhile, there was progress on the economic front. The railway from Kimberley to the Rand, and another linking the Natal and Orange River Colony systems between Ladysmith and Kroonstad, were completed. The capacity of the line from Lourenço Marques to Witbank was doubled. A trial pan-South African Customs Union was set up in 1903, and all internal customs dues abolished. Although most people were back on the land by the end of 1902, rural recovery was delayed by the drought conditions that lasted from 1903 to 1908.

Afrikanerdom and discord

'I no more want to exterminate the Dutch than I want to exterminate the British,' Milner wrote, but there was no doubt he wanted the British element, both political and cultural, to be dominant. In government schools 'Dutch should only be used to teach English, and English to teach anything else'.

The weekly cleaning in an Aliwal North concentration camp. In August 1901 there were 710 confirmed cases of measles in the camp: 166 of the patients died. This was one of the worst camps

During the war over 40 concentration camps had been established for whites, most of them in the Transvaal and Orange Free State. Initially run by the military, they were transferred to civilian control in November 1901: Milner was worried by the public scandal they were creating. The English liberal writer, Emily Hobhouse — 'that bloody woman', Kitchener called her — had visited the camps in January 1901 and returned to stir the British conscience. To Liberal Party leader Henry Campbell-Bannerman, they were 'methods of barbarism'. Lloyd George prophesied that 'A barrier of dead children's bodies will rise up between the British and the Boer races in South Africa'.

The death rate was high: 344 per thousand in October 1901. Altogether 26 000 died, of whom 20 000 were under the age of 16. Between June 1901 and May 1902 the camps held an average total of 190 000 Boer women, children and old men.

An enormous amount of propaganda and prejudice was generated at the time and later by stories of poisoned food and 'blue things' in the sugar. There was no truth in them: the camps were designed to intern, not to exterminate.

Sickness killed the internees — measles, amoebic dysentery, pneumonia. Bad organisation (especially in the early days), inadequate food, the poor health of those entering camps from the war-ravaged land — all these contributed to the appalling number of deaths from disease.

By war's end there were 107 344 Africans, mainly women and children from the Boer farms, in 29 camps, of whom 13 315 died — officially. The real death rate was probably much higher. Neither Emily Hobhouse nor Dame Millicent Fawcett's Ladies Committee had time to publicise the issue. But in time, conditions improved, and the mortality rate dropped dramatically.

In 1977, the Johannesburg *Star* published an interview with Mrs Lillian du Preez who, as a child of seven, was in the Standerton concentration camp. 'There are many stories about ill-treatment,' she recalled, 'but I don't believe them. There just was not enough food. The people died of sickness and hunger . . . I think the children suffered most . . . when they saw the children buried, the bitterness became terrible.' Mrs du Preez added: 'The whole war was a mistake . . . just because of the gold mines.'

Also 'A good world history would be worth anything . . . Everything that cramps and confines their views to South Africa only . . . makes for Afrikanerdom and further discord'.

Milner failed. His brave new Anglo-Saxon world refused to materialise. He managed to get only 1 300 English-speaking heads of families on the land instead of his 10 000 settlers 'within a twelvemonth'. The Afrikaners were deeply offended by Milner's programmes and, with funds from the Netherlands, opened Christian National schools for their children. They were determined to retain their language and culture.

Milner's ideas on race, too, were hardly liberal. He appointed a South African Native Affairs Commission, an almost exclusively English-speaking body, which managed to formalise even further the existing tendency to segregation. It approved of 'locations' for urban blacks and the separation of black and white in political life. A future federal legislature should have blacks represented by whites.

Coming together

Het Volk, the Afrikaner political organisation led by Generals Smuts and Botha, came into being on 28 January 1905. They objected particularly to the importation of the Chinese,

but also criticised the administration of relief funds and the curbs on the public use of Dutch. The Second Language Movement was reborn. With writers such as Jan F.E. Celliers and Eugene Marais backing it, Afrikaans eventually (in 1925) became an official language of the Union, replacing Dutch.

Gradually there was conciliation — between the *bittereinder* and the National Scout; between Afrikaans and English-speaking South Africans (both Het Volk and the Orangia Unie Afrikaner parties opened their doors to the latter), and between South Africa and Britain.

A movement for responsible government grew in the Transvaal, linking, to a degree, Afrikaner and English-speaking whites. In 1907 an elective Legislative Assembly of 69 members was constituted, Het Volk winning 37 of the seats.

Self-government came to the Orange River Colony in June 1907: the election of 1908 gave Orangia Unie 30 of the 38 lower house seats.

Railways, Customs and other regional differences provoked first a campaign for political federation, and then for total unification. In Smuts's words: 'What we want is a supreme national authority to give expression to the national will of South Africa, and the rest is really subordinate.'

United South Africa

FINALLY, THE TWO WHITE TRIBES COME TOGETHER

'Was it possible for the Boers ever to forget such generosity?' Louis Botha asked when the Transvaal and Orange River Colony gained responsible government.

But there was a greater goal: unification of the whole country. 'I have the fullest faith that I shall be able . . . to make of those two great races of South Africa one solid, united and strong race,' he said at the 1907 Colonial Conference in London.

The powerful alliance

The Afrikaner movements; J.X. Merriman, M.T. Steyn and J.C. Smuts were all in favour of unification. These three men, their respective parties dominant in the Cape Colony, OFS and the Transvaal, accelerated and controlled the movement towards unity. Milner's Kindergarten acted as expert advisers and propagandists. Had the Natal leadership thought they could go it alone, they would have done so but a referendum voted 11 121 to 3 701 in favour of union.

Between 12 October 1908 and 11 May 1909 the National Convention, charged with the task of uniting South Africa, sat variously in Durban, Cape Town and Bloemfontein. The governments and opposition white parties of the four colonies were represented in almost equal proportion. There was no black, coloured or Asian representation.

The South African National Convention took a year to complete its job (compared to the decade spent by Australia on a similar task). The composition of the House of Assembly, the allocation of seats among the provinces, the interests of town and country in the distribution of seats all took much debate. The Cape's W.P. Schreiner and Gandhi, the great Indian, tried hard to speak up for non-whites, but without success: Briton and Boer was the key issue, not white and black.

'The National Convention was the co-operation of many of the greatest names in our history,' General Smuts said, 'and from their common statesmanship the new South Africa was born.' To keep most people happy, the

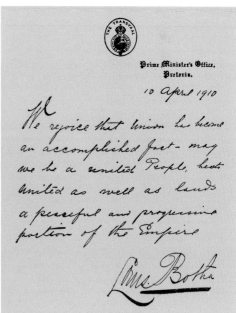

Louis Botha arrives at Waterloo Station, London, for the 1907 Colonial Conference. Three years later he became South Africa's first premier. Above right: His message to the new nation. Botha was a superb (though at first rather a reluctant) general during the Anglo-Boer War, and became a great 'Empire Man'

Mother City became the seat of Parliament, Pretoria of administration, and Bloemfontein the judicial capital. Natal lost out altogether.

Die Taal

In 1904, when Milner was trying his hardest to anglicise the country, Smuts had written: 'South Africa is on the downward grade in every sense, and at present I see no ray of light in the future.' But a movement was launched to rediscover Afrikaner identity. Led by the *predikante*, it centred on the language. A simplified spelling of Dutch was adopted in 1904 by the Zuid-Afrikaansche Taalbond. Lord Selborne, who replaced Milner in 1905 as High Commissioner, could afford to be tolerant towards the new Taal; it was not a written language and possessed little literature. 'Consequently,' he said, 'although in my opinion the Taal will be a language of affection and patriotism in South Africa for centuries to come, from the political point of view there is

no reason for any jealousy between English and the Taal.' How wrong he was!

Section 138 of the Draft Constitution established the equality of English and Dutch. They '. . . shall be official languages of the Union, and shall be treated on a footing of equality, and possess and enjoy equal freedom, rights and privileges . . .' Malan, leader of the Transvaal Progressive Party, diarised on 20 October 1908: 'Truly this is a good sign,' while Barry Hertzog, war hero and future Prime Minister, exclaimed in his diary: 'Great Victory.'

The finishing touches

On 31 May 1910, South Africa was united. Herbert Gladstone, the fourth son of the great Liberal Prime Minister, became Governor-General. He had been neither pro-Boer nor Imperialist during the war, and his appointment was well received. Merriman and Louis Botha were the only real contenders for the

Union is debated, hotly, in Natal. Above: Two contemplative delegates — C.J. Smythe and T. Hyslop — stride towards the Durban Town Hall, venue of one of the sessions of the National Convention (the hall now serves as the city's main post office). Left: Rival posters argue economics and appeal to the sentiment. Right: Polling day

Coming together. Above: The Union of South Africa is proclaimed from the Raadsaal, Pretoria, on 31 May 1910. The first Parliament was to have been opened by Edward VII, but the King died earlier that year. His place was taken by the Duke of Connaught, pictured left on his arrival in South Africa. Right: Britannia launches the new ship of state on the cover of the Cape Times *special Union Supplement*

office of Prime Minister. But Botha was by far the stronger, and on 21 May, Gladstone asked him to form a government.

Because of the death of King Edward VII on 6 May, Union came into being with only moderate ceremony. A gathering of 10 000 schoolchildren at the Wanderers in Johannesburg was one highlight. Another was the swearing-in of the Governor-General in Pretoria. 'Glorious weather ushered in Union Day in the capital,' the *Star* wrote. 'The town was astir early . . . flags and bunting draped the chief stores and the public buildings . . .' In Johannesburg a bilingual thanksgiving service was held in Market Square. Canada sent warm wishes '. . . from their brothers and sisters across the seas'.

The *Friend* of Bloemfontein, on 31 May 1910, wrote: 'At midnight last night . . . one of the greatest revolutions ever effected in South Africa . . . took place.' On that day church services were held in villages, towns and cities all over the country.

The first general election was held on 15 September 1910. Botha's South African Nationalist Party won 67 seats against the 59 of Leander Starr Jameson's Unionist Party of South Africa.

In spite of Botha's good intentions, the election developed into a Boer-Briton contest. In the constituency of Pretoria East, Sir Percy FitzPatrick, pre-war Reform Committee member, author of *Jock of the Bushveld* and leader of the Transvaal Unionists, actually defeated Botha, who later entered Parliament via a back-door by-election.

The entrée to South Africa's first Parliament

POMP, PAGEANTRY AND THE SWASTIKA

South Africa's cities, and some of their citizens, dress up for the Union celebrations

Even more impressive than the Union Day celebrations was the Pageant held in Cape Town at the end of October. Sir Frank Lascelles, who had organised Canada's tercentenary festival, was commissioned to oversee the arrangements; the Government contributed £15 000. There were firework displays, gymnastics and variety concerts. And, on the Foreshore, historical pageants illuminating the main events of South Africa's history. These were lavish spectacles (23 000 metres of material went into the costumes; 2 000 metres for the Royal Portuguese Court alone). The Swastika, symbolising the four colonies, had been adopted as the overall emblem. Cape Town's notorious south-easter obligingly disappeared for the splendid occasion.

Present at the celebrations were the Duke and Duchess of Connaught, who had arrived on *Balmoral Castle* to represent the King and to open the first Union Parliament.

The search for national symbols

THE UNION FLAG: COLOURFUL MIX OF HISTORIC ENSIGNS

The new Union of 1910 had four provinces and three capital cities — but no national flag. The Ensign of Great Britain, with the Union coat of arms in a roundel in the lower corner, served as a temporary and not very popular expedient.

In 1926 General Hertzog formally announced his government's intention to seek a purely South African flag. The South African Party insisted that the design should include the Union Jack, while the National Party wanted a 'clean' flag, with no reminders of a divided past. The Cape sensibly said that 'the Flag should represent the part which both races have played in the work of civilising South Africa and contributing to the structure of the nation'. A long, acrimonious controversy ensued. Smuts told his biographer shortly afterwards: 'Public opinion was worked up until the pot almost boiled over. The state of feeling in the country was such as I have not seen since the Boer War.' The quarrel subsided temporarily when the Labour Party suggested that on State occasions two flags, one being the Union Jack, might be flown together from separate poles.

Historian Eric Walker's design appealed to the Cabinet and to Afrikaans-speaking people, but it looked too much like the old Transvaal *Vierkleur* and raised a storm of protest among English South Africans. Predictably, Royalist sentiment was strongest in Natal. The *Mercury* described it as 'a nondescript rag, inspiring no patriotism nor recalling any great exploit'. Union Jacks appeared all over the province — as car pennants, lapel buttonholes, and even on the rostrums used by traffic-directing police.

At the beginning of the 1927 parliamentary session the issue was still unsolved. Interior Minister D.F. Malan's proposal for what the *Mercury* called the 'Hot Cross Bun Flag' (it had red and white crosses on a green field) incensed Durban's citizens, 15 000 of whom gathered outside the town hall to 'rededicate' themselves to the Union Jack. Several people who were vocal in their opposition to its retention were hurled down the front steps.

Professor Blommaert of the Central Flag Committee came up with the answer. He proposed the flag of the oldest administration in South Africa — the orange, white and blue *Prinsenvlag* flown at the Cape in 1652 — with a central design comprising the flags of the old Transvaal and Orange Free State republics and the Union Jack. It was, said the *Rand Daily Mail*, 'an amicable gesture'.

On Union Day 1928 the new flag was flown, together with the Union Jack, for the first time, at ceremonies performed by the Governor-General, the Earl of Athlone, in Cape Town and by his wife, Princess Alice, in Pretoria. In 1957 the dual system was abolished, and the national ensign became the only flag of the Union and, from 1961, of the Republic.

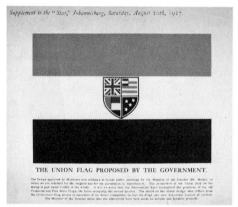

THE UNION FLAG PROPOSED BY THE GOVERNMENT.

In the mid-1920s the issue of a national flag was hotly debated in Parliament (Members almost came to blows) and around the country as pro- and anti-British factions gave free rein to their sentiments. Natal, predictably, was fiercely Royalist almost to a man and was determined to keep the Union Jack. Hundreds of designs were submitted (right, top and bottom) and an 'amicable' compromise was reached in 1927 when the Government accepted the design pictured bottom left. The colourful flag at top left was proposed as early as 1910

DID A NEGRO SLAVE SONG INSPIRE 'SARIE MARAIS'?

It was 1901. In a farmhouse near Vryheid, soldiers of General Louis Botha's commando gathered round a piano. At the keyboard was one of the few women allowed in the war zone. The troops sang lustily to her accompaniment, picking out popular tunes from an album which contained American slave songs.

The words of one song told of the girl left behind because of the cruel war that had divided the American people. To the homesick commandos, it was a poignant reminder that they were cut off from their own loved ones in the Transvaal. Then someone suggested that they should compose their own song in Afrikaans and not in *die Rooinek se taal*. The idea was received enthusiastically.

The pianist, Ella de Wet, wife of Louis Botha's military secretary, was soon prompting suggestions for the song. Slowly it took shape, and eventually became:

> *My Sarie Marais is so ver van my hart,*
> *Maar 'k hoop om haar weer te sien.*
> *Sy het in die wyk van die Mooirivier gewoon,*
> *Nog voor die oorlog het begin.*

And then the chorus:

> *O bring my terug na die ou Transvaal,*
> *Daar waar my Sarie woon,*
> *Daar onder in die mielies by die groen doring-boom,*
> *Daar woon my Sarie Marais.*

Who was this Sarie Maré (the name was later changed to Marais, possibly by the printer or publisher) who was so far from their hearts?

She was the mother of Paul Nel, much-beloved minister of Jeppestown, Johannesburg, the home of many of the Boer commandos who stood around that farmhouse piano in 1901. In bringing spiritual comfort to the Boers on the Transvaal and Natal battlefronts, Dominee Nel told the story of how his mother, Sarie Maré, from Uitenhage in the Eastern Cape, had in her youth fallen in love with a young man of Voortrekker stock, Vaal (blond) Louis Nel. She married Nel shortly after her 17th birthday and settled on the Nel farm, Welgegund *in die wyk van die Mooirivier*.

Which of these two ladies inspired the song Sarie Marais? *Left: Sarie Maré Nel, mother of Jeppestown's popular minister, married at 17, bore eleven children and died in childbirth in 1877. Right: Susara Margaretha Maré Toerien. Mrs Nel has the edge*

Sarie bore eleven children in 20 years of marriage before dying in childbirth at the age of 37. The story of Nel's mother and father and their youthful love touched the boisterous singers, and they were unanimous in dedicating their song to the memory of the dominee's mother.

However, when *Sarie Marais* first appeared in print in 1937 — *in orde deur* [arranged by] *Ella de Wet* — there was another claimant for the origin of the title role. Susara Margaretha Maré, wife of one of the champions of the Afrikaans language, J.P. Toerien, was said to have admitted to an enterprising young reporter of Bloemfontein's *Volksblad* that the song had been written by her husband and inspired by her.

Before her story was printed, Susara Margaretha retracted her statement, but her initial claim provoked a dispute about Sarie's true identity that has not yet been settled.

What isn't in doubt is the origin of the music. The words of *Sarie Marais* were set to the negro 'slave ballad' *Carry me back to Tennessee*, also known as *Ellie Rhee*. The lyrics of the original song were written by American Septimus Winner — best known for his *Listen to the Mocking Bird*.

The striking similarity between Winner's words and the first two verses of *Sarie Marais*

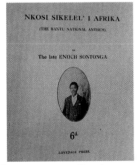
Enoch Sontonga never lived to see his song become the unofficial anthem of the blacks of South Africa. A gifted schoolteacher from the Mpinga family of the Tembu tribe, he was constantly composing music and words for his pupils, writing them down in tonic-solfa on odd sheets of paper. For the ordination of the first black Methodist minister at Nancefield in 1899, Sontonga wrote a special song, *Nkosi Sikelel' iAfrika* — God bless Africa. Sontonga had hoped to publish his collection of songs, but he died at the turn of the century without realising his ambition.

The words of *Nkosi Sikelel' iAfrika* did not appear in print (the original Xhosa version was lost at Sontonga's death) until 1927, when the Johannesburg weekly *Umteteleli wa Bantu* published them. And in 1963 the song became the national anthem of the Transkei — the land of Sontonga's origins. That same year the newly independent state of Zambia also adopted the music, and a local version of the words, as its official anthem.

GREEN AND GOLD, SPRINGBOK AND PROTEA

Left: in 1965 Dr Lyall Watson, director of the Johannesburg Zoo, together with wildlife artist P. Rose, produced a new emblem depicting the now-famous, gracefully leaping springbok

The changing face of our national animal. Top: the original was based on a drawing of a mounted springbok made during the 1906 South African rugby tour of Britain. Right: the 1906 cap with emblem

The first South African rugby team to tour Britain, in 1906, arrived without any insignia but returned as the first 'Springbok XV', wearing dark-green gold-edged blazers bearing the first golden springboks as pocket-badges.

Over the years the name was applied more generally, to players representing the country in other sports, and the springbok was eventually accepted as a national symbol. The name was extended to South African soldiers fighting 'Up North' and elsewhere beyond the national boundaries in the Second World War; and the springbok itself appeared on army badges, aircraft, and railway coaches.

Almost as well-known as the springbok is the giant protea, officially selected by the SA Association of Botanists as the national flower in 1976. The flower, unique in its variety, form and beauty, had in fact been incorporated into the Union Coat-of-Arms in 1932.

In 1960 the distinctive and graceful blue crane was adopted as the national bird, and in 1975 the yellowwood as the national tree.

seem to bear out the story of the Boer soldiers extemporising around the piano:

> *Sweet Ellie Rhee, so dear to me,*
> *Is lost for ever more.*
> *Our home was down in Tennessee*
> *Before this cruel war.*
> *Then carry me back to Tennessee,*
> *Back where I long to be,*
> *Amid the fields of yellow corn,*
> *To my darling Ellie Rhee.*

The original melody was adapted to fit the Afrikaans lyrics and provide a more lilting tune. During the Second World War, South African troops popularised it in North Africa and Italy. It was taken up by other Allied soldiers and spread throughout Europe. Americans who started whistling the catchy tune found it hard to recognise one of their country's popular folk tunes. Versions were also sung in Italian, French and even Russian.

DIE STEM: CALL OF SOUTH AFRICA

To Cornelis Jakob Langenhoven, Afrikaans was a 'precious pearl' for which he would have gladly sacrificed all his wordly possessions. And it was this passion for the language of his people that he felt when, one May afternoon in 1918, he sat at a table in his Oudtshoorn home and, in his beautifully-formed script, began to write:

> *Uit die blou van onse hemel, uit die*
> *diepte van ons see, Oor ons ewige*
> *gebergtes waar die kranse antwoord gee,*
> *Deur ons ver-verlate vlaktes met die*
> *kreun van ossewa — Ruis die stem van*
> *ons geliefde, van ons land Suid-Afrika.*

In *Die Stem van Suid-Afrika* the Union had

found a national anthem, although it was not to be officially accepted as such until almost 40 years later — in May 1957.

Anthems old and new

The search for a South African national anthem began even before Union. *God Save the King*, obviously, was unacceptable to most Afrikaans-speaking people. A *Volkslied*, composed by C.E. Viljoen and set to music by Dr J.H. Meiring Beck, was published in the official programme of the pageant of Union, but its final couplet killed its chances of survival:

> *With loyal hearts we'll render thee*
> *Great Britain's proudest prize.*

After the First World War, various attempts to establish an anthem for the Afrikaans-speaking people came to nothing, mainly because the melodies were too contrived. Then Nico Hofmeyr wrote *Afrikaners, Landgenoten* set to Haydn's *Gott erhalte Franz den Kaiser* (the Austrian national anthem) or — its other title — *Deutschland, Deutschland Über Alles*. The stirring tune gained popularity and was tipped to become the Union's official anthem until Langenhoven wrote *Die Stem* and, a year later, the Reverend M.L. de Villiers scored the music for it. Ironically, if Hofmeyr's song had been adopted, South Africans would have marched to war in 1939 to the same tune as their enemy.

An English translation was approved in 1952 — after the selection committee, chaired by poet H.A. Fagan, had rejected 226 entries and produced a composite of its own. *The Call of South Africa* was sung at the ceremonial laying of the foundation stone of Cape Town's 'Gateway to Africa' in April of that year.

In 1957 *Die Stem* became the country's official anthem.

A day in the life of 1910

LIVING WELL ON £160 A YEAR

Gordon Murray is a typical white-collar worker in the Durban of 1910. He is a chief clerk in an insurance company and, in mid-career, earns £160 a year.

Gordon lives in a brick villa in the Berea — just a double-decker tram stage (fare 1d) from his office in the city. The villa has sanitation and electric light (he is one of 5 000 out of the city's population who enjoy this luxury), four bedrooms, kitchen, pantry and bathroom, and for this he pays a rental of £3.5s. a month.

In the bathroom hot water spouts erratically from the wood-fired copper boiler into the heavy, roll-rimmed cast iron bath standing on claw feet. Gordon strops his hollow-ground 'cut-throat' razor and dips his beaver-hair brush ('Guaranteed Free From Anthrax') into a heavy porcelain shaving mug. The new-fangled 'safety razor' has not yet found general acceptance among the more conservative.

His wife, meanwhile, is grilling his breakfast sausages in the kitchen on a wood-fired stove. There is a zinc-lined oak ice-chest, and Sparks and Youngs' 'pure crystal ice' is delivered once a week. The Murrays pay a coloured servant £3.10s. a month to do the family wash — in a zinc bath set up on planks in the back yard.

From the light fitting above the breakfast table hangs a fly paper, a curling strip impregnated with melted resin and golden syrup. It is studded with flies. Gordon deluges his sausages and eggs in Worcestershire sauce and washes them down with two cups of strong, sugary Mazawattee tea. He promises to ring his wife if he has to work late — he is one of the 1 763 telephone subscribers in Durban (yearly subscription: £12.10s.). Warns the slim directory: 'It is dangerous to touch the apparatus while there is a heavy thunderstorm in the vicinity.'

Then he takes his round-crowned hard hat from the hallstand and sets out for the office. A gold chain, less massive than the 'Albert' of former years, spans his waistcoat: from one end hangs his gold watch. The waistcoat is an indispensable badge of respectability. Even in the privacy of his office, on a sweltering summer day, he might be tempted to shed his coat — but his waistcoat must stay on.

There are quite a number of motor cars in

A typical middle-class family early this century. Their position usually called for a double-storey house set in spacious grounds (right). They would employ at least four servants indoors and probably one or more gardeners

Gordon's Durban (speed limit 12 mph within city limits, 20 mph outside), but horse-drawn vehicles are still very much in the majority. The main streets of the city and its suburbs have been hardened, in some cases asphalted as well, and West Street has a splendid 'Tarco' surface.

West and Smith streets are the main shopping area: Gordon's wife patronises John Orr's and Bon Marché, where smart summer dresses go for between 5/11 and 12/11 at clearance sales.

Gordon's interests centre on his family, but he has others. His favourite spectator sport is cricket, and he likes to spend the occasional summer Saturday afternoon at Lord's ground, venue of Currie Cup matches (in 1910-11 the Currie Cup soccer and the South African Athletic Championships were also held in Durban). Cricket bats cost 10/6 at A.G. Knox's in West Street.

Sometimes he takes his family for a stroll along the beach front and the semi-circular pier, from which they can watch more adventurous spirits in the safety bathing enclosure. Durban's first permanent cinema, 'The Electric Theatre', had been opened the year before, and the Murrays have been twice to see the silver screen.

Mater and pater

Several notches up the social scale is the manager of Gordon's insurance company. He is a portly man who unfailingly leads his family to its own church pew every Sunday. His two-storey house is set in spacious grounds, has a

panelled billiard-room, a conservatory and a coach-house for carriage and the newly-acquired motor car. His children, five of them, call him 'Pater'. The household maintains four servants — cook earning £7 a month, a general servant earning £4 a month, a house-maid £2.10s. and a nursemaid £1.10s. a month.

His wife, 'Mater' to the children, is a 'lady', never a woman. One afternoon each month she is 'at home'. On that important day — perhaps the first Monday or the second Thursday, as announced on her engraved copper-plate visiting card — she 'receives' in her immaculate but cluttered drawing room, dispensing tea from a silver pot, cakes from a three-tier silver stand, and genteel conversation to her genteel callers — ladies, of course.

Calling is an essential and rigid social ritual. The visitor seldom stays more than an hour, and on departing, leaves *her* card, with its implied invitation, on the embossed silver salver in the hall. It is a sort of social chain-letter system.

Neither 'Mater' nor her grown-up daughters use lipstick, although a discreet application of face powder is acceptable. None of them smokes, though they know that there are 'fast girls' who do. None ever uses such words as 'sex', 'contraception' or 'pregnancy', although they talk (in lowered voices) of 'expecting' and being 'confined'. They know more about the workings of their sewing machines than about their own bodies. The daughters, even when in their twenties, are not allowed to be out at night without a chaperone.

Mazawattee tea (left and centre), a popular beverage during the early 1900s, was sold in a variety of brightly-coloured tins. Right: Even pharmaceutical products were attractively packaged. This huis apotheek (a small medicine box) was typical. Many early printed 'tin' containers have since become collectors' items

Opzitting, *one of a series of sketches on Boer life by the artist and illustrator Heinrich Egersdörfer*

CANDLELIGHT IN THE KAROO

The roof creaks and cracks as the iron sheets contract in the cold of the Karoo evening. The kitchen is the warmest room, where a low fire burns in the three-metre wide hearth, slowly curing the hams suspended out of sight high in the chimney and gradually warming the brown, *brak* water in the large oval pot. The zinc bath stands on the dung-smeared floor before the hearth: tonight it is Hendrik van Rensburg's bath-night.

But now, with his wife and their two eldest daughters, he is busy with one of the chores of home. Anna, the mother of the family, has noticed that the supply of candles in the chest is low, and a ball of cotton yarn on the little table with the three ox-horn legs is within reach of all. The cotton threads are being twisted into candle wicks by a practised flick and roll along the thigh, left hands maintaining the tension until the right twist and length has been reached. Then the loose end is knotted, and the other end, looped, is slipped over the dipstick.

From the sitting room *(voorkamer)* the American clock, with its stained and pressed-pattern plywood front, strikes nine. There are perhaps 150 wicks prepared, and it is the girls' bedtime. The candle flame gleams on the small panes of their uncurtained window as they pour water from the patterned jug into the matching basin on the marble-topped wash stand. Their faces tingle with the chilly splash of the water. Pinafores are neatly folded — because tonight it is cold, they will sleep in their calico bodices and petticoats, under crocheted quilts stuffed with down which they spent hours collecting in the poultry yard.

Anna walks softly from the kitchen. As she goes down the passage, the shadows of kudu and buffalo horns leap in the candlelight. She pushes aside the curtain to her young son's bedroom and tenderly feels his forehead. He is still hot, but the infusion of *slanghoutjies* — snake root — she gave him earlier is reducing the fever.

She unlocks the pantry door, and takes down a cake of soap. She makes this herself, once a year, from the rendered-down fats of the animals they slaughter, boiling this with lye in a great three-legged pot on a corner of the hearth. From the thick, creamy layer of soap which rises to the surface, bars of some

ten centimetres in length are planed smooth. Some will be exhibited at the next agricultural show, but the best have been carved with the initials of her children, and will be presented only on their wedding day.

Hendrik is filling his pipe with wafers of tobacco cut on his small guillotine-like carving block. The tobacco is cheap, only two-pence a pound, but he finds it too strong, so he soaks it in water to reduce the nicotine content, dries it, and then cuts it into flakes which he crumbles in his hand. It burns well.

He takes the soap from his wife, who fills the zinc bath. When she has gone to bed, snuggled under blankets and the warm jackal-skin kaross, he undresses, close to the fire. The soap lathers well, not like the soap that the shop sells for threepence a pound, or will exchange at the rate of eight pounds of soap for three pounds of fat and tallow.

In his nightshirt, he gets into bed. It is a bedstead with a stinkwood frame, originally made for slinging beneath a wagon. Its comfortable, feather-stuffed mattress (made by his wife) is supported on a latticework of leather straps.

The family is at breakfast before sunrise. *Moskonfyt*, a syrup prepared by boiling down fresh grape juice, is liberally spread on thick slices of bread baked in batches of 20 loaves in the big oven at the back of the hearth. There is coffee, drunk black from thick china mugs bought last year from the *smous*: the itinerant peddler.

Father hitches up his corduroys and goes out. It is November, but the wind is chill, and light frost crunches beneath his *velskoene* as he walks to the threshing floor.

It is a hard day of work, spent among the

STAR TURN OF THE YEAR

HALLEY'S COMET
Photographed at the Transvaal Observatory.

Halley's Comet photographed from the Transvaal Observatory in 1910. There was no need to be alarmed, the *Cape Argus* told its readers in May that year. Quoting an article by Professor S. A. Mitchell, 'the well-known American Astronomer', the newspaper pointed out that although the earth would pass through the comet's tail, there was no possibility that particles could penetrate to the earth's surface because it was covered by 'a shell of atmosphere thousands of times denser than the comet's tail'.

Added the *Cape Argus*: 'While nothing is known absolutely of how bright the comet will be, astronomers are generally agreed that it will be a splendid object, readily visible to the naked eye, with a tail at least 50 degrees in length . . . the modern theory of the tails of comets tells us that though their size is enormous their weight is excessively small, and as a result the number of particles per cubic mile in the comet's tail is almost vanishingly small.'

Halley's Comet is due to reappear in 1986.

golden sheaves in the company of his white overseer, his two labourers and the four-horse team.

He is home again by seven in the evening. Anna has been busy kneading and pummelling whole grain meal for another batch of loaves which will be put into the oven with the long-handled bread scoop. For supper there is mutton soup, followed by roast goat — and again *moskonfyt* and bread.

Then, peering through the lenses of the spectacles bought from the *smous*, Hendrik reads from the yellowing pages of the family Bible. A psalm is sung to the accompaniment of the Chicago-made harmonium played by the eldest daughter; and, as starlight glints on the roof, one by one the lights are extinguished.

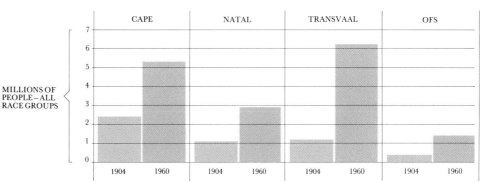

In 1911 an official census set the total population of South Africa at 5,972 757. By 1960 this figure had climbed to 16,002 797. This graph shows the population (all race groups) in each of the provinces in 1904 and 1960

29

Notes, coins and stamps

A SHOCK FOR KRUGER

In 1890 De Nasionale Bank van Zuid-Afrika was granted a bank concession which provided for a State mint to be established in Pretoria. Arrangements were made for trained staff and equipment to be imported from Germany, and the engraver, Otto Schulz, produced dies protraying the bust of President Kruger on the obverse face.

In 1893 a special consignment of gold coins and five-shilling pieces arrived from Germany and were put into circulation. An outcry erupted. The designer had used a German wagon as a model instead of the single-shafted Voortrekker wagon. Worse still, the designer's initials, O.S., had been placed on Kruger's bust on the obverse of the gold coins: they spelt the Dutch word for ox. The presidential campaign was in progress, and General Joubert's supporters made gleeful references to this 'os', Kruger! The design was quickly changed.

The mint produced coins for the Transvaal republic between 1892 and 1900, when it was closed. It re-opened in 1923 as a branch of the Royal Mint, under the control of the Master of the Mint in London. In 1941 the direct link with the Royal Mint was severed.

During the Second World War, the mint (which already possessed much of the necessary equipment and trained staff) also manufactured bullets and other munitions.

The commercial banks issued their own notes from the early part of the 19th century until 1922, when the Currency and Banking Act of 1920 gave the South African Reserve Bank sole right to issue banknotes for the Union. Until then, a few of the more important business houses also issued their own notes as well as 'good-fors' and 'token coins'.

The first Reserve Bank notes were dated 17 September 1921, but were not issued until 1922. They were in sterling denominations and all notes carried a date until decimalisation in 1961. Except for the 10/- note, a predominantly blue ornamental design, all the other denominations were to the Pilkington design (after the designer). The Reserve Bank imported all its banknote forms from England until 1962, when it established its own printing works in Pretoria.

South Africa changed from pounds, shillings and pence to rands and cents on 14 February 1961, the day known as R-day (Rand-day) or D-day (Decimalisation-day). The Union took the logical step of splitting the pound into two for its basic unit. Gone for-

In 1898 President Kruger allowed his friend Sammy Marks to use the mint for a day, and Marks struck 215 of these gold tickeys. They were not legal tender

In 1891 the Bank Note Act was passed, providing security for all future notes issued by Cape banks (centre), and a stock of uniform-type notes was printed by a London firm for the Cape Treasury. The Natal Government never issued paper money, but left it to private enterprise. In 1910 there were six banks of issue in South Africa

PROOF KRUGERRAND TENDER No. 6

CLOSING DATE JUNE 22nd 1976

First minted in 1967, Krugerrands (they do not have a denomination) each contain one troy ounce of fine gold. In 1967 a Krugerrand was worth approximately R28; by 1980 (the year the ½ oz, 1/4 oz and 1/10 oz coins were introduced) it could fetch over R750. Krugerrands have already earned South Africa billions of rands in foreign exchange

STAMPS THAT NEVER WERE

Some stamp designs never made it to the printer. After the Anglo-Boer War, stamps of the four colonies were valid only in the colony of issue, but after 1910 they could be used throughout the country. The government intended issuing the first Union stamp on 31 May 1910, and 11 designs were submitted, but there was disagreement between the Cape and the Transvaal. Instead, a commemorative stamp was planned to coincide with the opening of Union Parliament just over five months later.

ever would be the half-crown and humble tickey.

Some suburban train commuters noticed that a 2/2 fare became a 24c fare — an effective 2/5. But for the majority of South Africans, rands and cents were introduced with little upset. The newspaper boy rattled off machine-gun-like 'Two-and-a-half-cents-a-tickey, sir.' Bus passengers who still asked for a 'sixpenny to town' were corrected as the conductor flipped out his new 5c tickets.

The biggest controversy involved the English pronunciation of the main unit — the rand — and its plural. 'The pronunciation,' said the *Star* on R-day, 'is so fluid you could drown in it . . . runt, rarnt, rarnd and rent.' But to thousands of South Africans it was to be pronounced 'ten bob' for a long time.

'Making do' with the Boer stamps

The legendary Cape of Good Hope triangular stamps, introduced in 1853 and now much prized by collectors, remained valid until 1900 — a year of war, and of confusion in South African philately. In beleaguered Mafeking, for example, Baden-Powell issued two stamps, one of which bore his own portrait, and in the newly-occupied republics of the Transvaal and Free State, the British made do with the existing Boer stamps but overprinted them with the Royal cypher.

On 4 November 1910 a special stamp was issued to commemorate the opening of the first Union Parliament. The name of the country was printed in English and Dutch and each corner bore the heraldic insignia of a province. In the centre was a portrait of King George V.

The first series of stamps, bearing the King's profile, appeared in 1913, and airmail stamps, printed in Cape Town, were issued 12 years later. The next definitive issue, which appeared in 1926, remained in use until 1954 with only minor alterations. These were pictorials, with a range of designs that included the head of a springbok, the Union buildings, Groote Schuur and a trek wagon.

The 50th anniversary of Union in 1960 was marked by an issue of special designs, and 'Decimalisation Day' on 14 February 1961 by a decimal indication on some of the existing designs in sterling values. There was no commemorative issue to mark the inauguration of the Republic on 31 May 1961, but collectors scrambled to buy Republican 'first-day covers', which featured a new, definitive series of stamps in decimal values.

Another issue of note was a 3d (later changed to 2½c) stamp showing the heads of the Union's six prime ministers up to 1960 — generals Botha, Smuts and Hertzog, Dr Malan, Mr Strijdom and Dr Verwoerd.

The number of special issues increased after the Second World War. Between 1910 and 1945 only 11 specials or commemoratives appeared. From the year of the Royal visit, 1947, to 1979 there were close on a hundred.

The stamp issued to mark the opening of the first Union Parliament in 1910. The first series of stamps, bearing a profile of King George V, were printed in London and appeared in South Africa in September 1913

'Decimal Dan' (far left), decimal converters and information pamphlets gave South Africans ample warning of the change to decimalisation in February 1961. Top left: The Pretoria Mint staff worked overtime to produce the new coinage

Royal connections

A PLAYGROUND FOR THE BRITISH

South Africa had a century of close Royal connections before becoming a republic in 1961. Prince Alfred arrived as a 16-year-old midshipman in 1860: he inaugurated Cape Town's new breakwater. During the 20th century there were several visits by members of the Royal family before 1925, when the Prince of Wales arrived to take the country by storm. The Duke and Duchess of Cornwall (later King George V and Queen Mary) visited South Africa in 1901 on their world tour; Princess Christian (one of Queen Victoria's daughters) came to South Africa in 1904 to visit the grave of her son.

Mothers groomed their daughters and mayors in small towns throughout the country prepared speeches, bunting and cornerstones as the 30-year-old Royal ambassador ('South Africa's loved and honoured guest') launched into one of history's most exhausting official tours. But he would cheerfully quote the advice of a wise old courtier: 'Only two rules really count. Never miss an opportunity to relieve yourself; never miss a chance to sit down and rest your feet.'

This advice stood him in good stead as he swept through the overwhelmingly attentive and almost embarrassingly affectionate South Africa of 1925. Elders were hurriedly consulted on questions of protocol, *boere-orkeste* began frenzied rehearsals of *Land of Hope and Glory*, and the Prince was given a welcome he would never forget.

The day of his arrival in Cape Town (1 May 1925) was typical of the hectic schedule he followed throughout his tour. Included on his

Government bodies and local authorities went to considerable lengths to transport, feed and entertain their Royal visitors. These official programmes regulated their activities with meticulous accuracy

This commemorative arch was one of a series built in Adderley Street for the visit of the Duke and Duchess of Cornwall and York in 1901

programme was: official welcome on the Pier; inspect guard of honour at Pier; drive to Grand Parade to be presented with address of welcome and to make a speech; drive to Government House to meet more dignitaries; civic luncheon at City Hall; visit to cycle track to review ex-servicemen, Boy Scouts, Girl Guides and school children; visit Green Point Common for welcome from coloured section of the population; formal dinner; State Ball (for over 1 000 guests).

Edward, Prince of Wales, made thousands of friends as he crossed South Africa with his ever-present ukelele and a seemingly inexhaustible supply of stamina.

A little gift for the Prince

The Prince's aplomb was occasionally challenged, though. One night, when the Royal train had drawn up at a lonely siding, he was approached by an elderly black man who explained that he would like to make a gift of his teenage daughter. After hurried consultation it was decided that the Prince would first accept the gift, but immediately repay it by presenting the father with six oxen and returning his daughter. The scheme suited everyone ex-

A cheerful General Smuts with the British Royal family in the Drakensberg during their 1947 tour

From left: The Duke and Duchess of Cornwall and York about to take their seats on the white thrones in Durban; the Prince of Wales used one of the thrones a quarter-century later; the Duke of Kent takes his seat during the interminable speeches (note his straw boater propped against the throne); King George VI and Queen Elizabeth — and those thrones again! They seated Royalty for nearly half a century

cept the daughter, who promptly burst into tears.

Two decades later, when the entire Royal family visited South Africa, Queen Elizabeth (the Queen Mother) handled equally awkward situations with the grace and humour that has made her popular throughout the world. An anti-British farmer accosted her at a reception one day and said sternly: 'I'm sorry, but I really hate the English.' Whereupon Her Majesty replied: 'I do sympathise — you see, I'm Scots.'

When HMS *Vanguard* berthed in Cape Town harbour on 17 February 1947 the streets of South Africa's oldest city were crowded to bursting point. On board were King George VI, Queen Elizabeth and their two daughters, Princess Margaret and Princess Elizabeth. It was the first visit of a reigning British monarch to South Africa.

Jukskei and bulges in the right places

Princess Elizabeth celebrated her 21st birthday in Cape Town. Her broadcast to the Commonwealth on that occasion carried all the grave sincerity of a young woman who knew she was destined to be Queen: '. . . I declare before you all that my whole life, whether it be long or short, shall be devoted to your service and the service of our Great Imperial Commonwealth to which we all belong.'

If the Royal family expected antagonism and distrust, they were pleasantly surprised. If His Majesty's subjects expected icy dignity, they too were wrong. Queen Elizabeth tackled the peculiar and peculiarly South African game of jukskei: Princess Elizabeth prompted newspaper reports on 'bulges in the right places' when she went swimming at Port Elizabeth, and King George actually faked a drowning incident to test the abilities of local lifesavers.

General Smuts, in turn, swallowed his pride and accompanied the Royal party in the

In 1901 the Durban Town Council had two heavy wooden thrones made to seat the visiting Duke and Duchess of Cornwall and York, later King George V and Queen Mary, at various civic functions.

The two thrones were painted white, with gold touches to carved designs on the back rests. Red velvet cushions made the seats a little more comfortable. After the visit, the chairs were put into storage until 1925, when the dashing 30-year-old Prince of Wales (later King Edward VIII) visited Durban during the course of his South African tour. One of the white thrones was installed in

cablecar to the top of Table Mountain (he had always insisted on walking up) and, when a gust of wind blew Queen Elizabeth's hat off, he quickly recovered it and confiscated a feather for his own hat.

The Prime Minister knew just how much South Africa owed to the Royal connection. While the descendants of the Voortrekkers were opening up the hinterland with farms and towns, British engineers, craftsmen and businessmen were establishing a system of administration, roads, mines, harbours and industries that still exists — as does the institution of Parliament itself.

'A wayside inn'

It was probably the last occasion on which South Africa could express its devotion and affection for the monarchy. The colonial spirit had been alive and flourishing for more than a century, but there was no denying the republican drive. The signs had been there for a long

front of the garlanded Town Hall.

Nine years later, a white throne was brought out again — this time for the Duke of Kent, who was later killed in an air crash. The two thrones made their final appearance for a royal occasion when King George VI and the Royal family spent several days in Durban while on their tour of South Africa in 1947.

After this visit the two thrones were placed in the care of the MOTH organisation at its memorial centre in Durban's Old Fort Road, where they were displayed for some time before being relegated to a storeroom.

time. As the Marquess of Crewe told the House of Lords over 70 years ago, South Africa was considered 'a wayside inn' on the great highway to the east. From the time South Africa became British in 1814, he said, there had been more than one movement to escape from the 'somewhat uninformed' control exercised over the country.

'The most famous of those movements was what is known as the Great Trek of 1836. I am afraid, my lords, it must be admitted that the domestic virtues of Downing Street have sometimes been imperial vices . . .'

One of history's mightiest empires finally relinquished control. In 1960 a small boy leaned across a school desk and whispered to his best friend: 'Who will you vote for; the Queen or the republic?' His question was answered in a referendum among 1,8 million white voters in October of that year, and the royal connection was severed at last in 1961.

The Royal family arrives in Pretoria's Church Square in March 1947. Right: One of the Royal tour programmes

The middle years

THE CHANGING FACE OF THE NATION

The five decades from Union in 1910 to the coming of the Republic in 1961 were some of the most eventful in South Africa's history. It became apparent to the world that the once-disparate and troublesome collection of colonies and republics was evolving into one of the wealthiest and most powerful nations on the African continent.

Inevitably, however, there were growing pains. Just four years after Union, Prime Minister Louis Botha went to war with the Kaiser's Germany, but there was a rebellion to quell at home before his troops could set out to conquer South West and East Africa and go on to distinguish themselves in the European theatre.

The euphoria following the Armistice of 1918 was soon dissipated as the country battled to survive a post-war depression. The Rand Revolt, an armed uprising that followed the miners' strike of 1921-22, was symptomatic of these difficult years: people were hungry, and they were anxious about their jobs. The revolt was crushed after fierce clashes had paralysed the Witwatersrand and badly damaged the economy.

Came the Thirties, and South Africans were plunged into a decade of crippling depression, droughts that decimated crops and livestock and confusion on the political scene. This decade saw the start of the Second World War, one of the most horrific conflicts in modern history.

The 1933 general election was an election with a difference: for the first time women were exercising their right to vote. Much of the credit for this innovation was due to Bertha Solomon, a petite, dignified woman with curly white hair and alert eyes. Born Bertha Schwartz in Minsk, Russia, in 1892, she had come to South Africa at

Flags fluttered from poles and every other shop window when thousands gathered at the Johannesburg City Hall to celebrate the Armistice of 1918

Fordsburg's Market Square after the showdown between troops and strikers in the Revolt of 1921-22

A farmer views the results of 'sheet' erosion, caused by overstocking and veld burning, in the drought of 1933

Votes for the Women of SOUTH AFRICA

The local Suffragist Society, known as the Women's Enfranchisement League, have under consideration a scheme whereby the Society will provide meals for the starving Husbands, and for the care of the neglected Homes and Children of Ladies (not being members of the said Society) who reprehensibly leave the sanctity of their Firesides and Stoeps to drink tea with their Friends, to play in Bridge, Croquet, Tennis, Golf, or other degrading Tournaments; to attend Theatres, Concerts, Dances, Recruiting Meetings, Committee Meetings of charitable organisations, etc., to the danger of the welfare of their said Homes and Families.

For particulars apply to the "Secretary," Women's Enfranchisement League, of this town.

Fees moderate. Attendance prompt. Staff attractive and charming. (An extra charge will be made for the President's or Vice-President's attendance.)

MEN OF SOUTH AFRICA!

Enfranchise the Women

Let them work WITH as well as FOR you.

South African suffragettes did not mince words in their campaign

About 250 000 attended the unveiling of the Voortrekker Monument in Pretoria on 16 December 1949

Prime Minister Hertzog and Mrs Hertzog are presented with the newly-authorised Afrikaans Bible in 1933

South Africans went to war for the second time in September 1939. Smuts's troops fought well in East and North Africa and in Italy, where they experienced some of the bloodiest clashes of the Second World War

This replica of Jan van Riebeeck's Drommedaris *was specially built for the tercentenary in 1952*

Rescue workers lower sound equipment down a shaft in an attempt to pick up sounds from trapped miners after the Coalbrook mine disaster of January 1960. Hundreds of men died when the mine collapsed

Harold Macmillan delivers his 'wind of change' speech to the Houses of Parliament in February 1960

A large crowd at Cape Town's D.F. Malan airport awaits the return of Dr Verwoerd from London in 1961

the age of four; became one of the first women in the country to be called to the Bar; fought energetically for the woman's vote and served as a Member of Parliament for 20 years.

Opposition to the women's movement had been formidable, and sometimes ludicrous. In the Senate it was presented as 'a scientific fact' that female brains did not develop to the same extent as those of men. Even Senator C.J. Langenhoven, composer of what was to become South Africa's national anthem, expressed concern. The enfranchisement of women, he said, was part of a 'world-wide movement against authority and discipline'.

'Bertha's Bill', the Matrimonial Affairs Bill which became law in 1953, was the crowning achievement of Mrs Solomon's long campaign to improve the legal status of married women.

During the Thirties, too, Afrikaners found fresh pride in their language and traditions.

The centenary of the Battle of Blood River was marked, in 1938, by the laying of the foundation stones of the Voortrekker Monument in Pretoria, and of a monument on the battlefield itself, in Natal. The descendants of the trekkers were deeply moved as ox wagons, some of them 100 years old, followed 14 routes across the country to converge on the two celebration sites by 16 December. The Pretoria monument was unveiled in 1949: it was a massive symbol of Afrikaner identity.

The century has witnessed some spectacular disasters. One of the most tragic of all occurred on the afternoon of 21 January 1960, at the Coalbrook North Shaft of the Clydesdale Colliery near Sasolburg. When the mine collapsed, hundreds of people were working underground: 435 men died

Nineteen-sixty, too, was the last year that South Africans celebrated Union Day.

British premier Harold Macmillan told a stunned Union Parliament that a 'wind of change' was blowing through Africa. The message was clear: Britain wanted to rid itself of its colonial past; black nations were emerging; South Africa could expect little support in any forthcoming confrontation.

Prime Minister Hendrik Verwoerd led South Africa out of the Commonwealth and, in 1961, into the republican era.

Politics and protest

THE MIXED SOCIETY: PROBLEMS WITHOUT SIMPLE SOLUTIONS

The triumph of Dr D.F. Malan's National Party at the 1948 polls introduced a new and troubled era — the era of the social engineers.

It was also the constitutional climax of a struggle that properly began more than a century before, when Piet Retief's trekkers set out for the great interior, armed with musket, Bible and faith in their destiny, in search of *lebensraum* and the right to live their own lives.

Afrikanerdom never did find the peace and isolation it was looking for. Nor, given the country's ethnic mix and its enormous potential wealth, could it have done so.

Historians have referred to the almost Darwinian inevitability of events — of action and often violent reaction — that has been South Africa's story ever since the Boers established their vulnerable republics north of the Orange River in the mid-nineteenth century. On the one side there were the indigenous peoples, the threat their sheer numbers posed to the tiny white communities, and competition for land. On the other was British Imperialism, at its best a 'civilising influence', at its worst greedy for power, prestige — and for gold.

This was the background to the war that erupted between Boer and Briton in 1899. The death and destruction and the brutalities left a legacy of bitterness that neither a generous peace nor the statesmanship of Louis Botha and Jan Smuts managed to eradicate. To a hard core of Afrikaner nationalists these men were 'traitors' to the cause, and the war had to go on, although now it would be fought in the political arena.

The rapier and the broadsword

The years between the two world wars were dominated by two powerful political figures — both Afrikaners, both heroes of the guerilla campaigns against Kitchener's regiments, but otherwise totally dissimilar. Jan Smuts was the ascetic intellectual, advocate of peace, friend of Winston Churchill, Empire man. His opponent for most of the time: Barry Hertzog, rugged, uncompromising, determined to preserve Afrikaner identity, forge Afrikaner unity, engineer Afrikaner political power.

In the end it was Hertzog — or rather, his natural successors — who won.

In the 1920s and 1930s political parties came and went; there were alignments and re-alignments; and at one point, in 1933, the two men actually came together to create a coalition government. They formed the United Party the following year. Significantly, though, the more conservative of the white nationalists rejected this reunion and established their own Purified National Party under the leadership of Dr D.F. Malan, a former Cape cleric and editor of *Die Burger*. It was this movement which, 14 years and a world war later, was granted — and kept — the reins of power.

Smuts, striding the world stage, had not fully recognised the increasingly powerful ap-

When Mohandas Gandhi (extreme left) returned to India in 1914, Smuts wrote: 'The Saint has left our shores.' The two leaders had a mutual respect

peal of apartheid to the voters of both white language groups, and in the general election of 1948 he paid the price.

The man from India

Meanwhile, often pushed into the background but always there, inseparable from the central political issue, smouldering ominously and occasionally flaring into fiery prominence, was the question of 'non-white' rights.

The British and South African architects of the Union constitution of 1910 made little provision for 'non-white' representation (the Cape electorate was the exception).

In 1893 a bright young lawyer named Mohandas Gandhi, destined to become the father of modern India, came to South Africa and soon became a champion of the Indian people's cause. In 1907, three years before Union, he launched his 'passive resistance' cam-

These pictures show the Israelites' 'temple', sect members rounded up after their clash with police, arrival of the Israelites' envoy before the fight, the 'Prophet' Enoch (bottom centre), and the interrogation of prisoners

The conservatives come to power. Dr D.F. Malan (left) and his National Party government launched a new era after their electoral victory in 1948. Separate development was the cornerstone of their policy. Malan's successor, J.G. Strijdom (right), the 'Lion of the north', presided over the removal of the coloured people from the voters roll

Demonstrations of the Torch Commando, headed by war hero 'Sailor' Malan, recaptured the camaraderie of former years but failed to divert the government

'The turning point at which nobody turned.' After Sharpeville, attitudes on both sides hardened

paign. This unique approach to achieving social and political reform, and Gandhi's campaigns against the immigration laws, led to his arrest on a number of occasions — the last one in November 1913, after he organised strikes in the coal mines of northern Natal. There was an outcry; the government appointed the Soloman Commission to investigate the Indian question; the Indian Relief Act was passed the following year and this, together with the Smuts-Gandhi agreement of June 1914, effectively ended the first Indian passive resistance movement in South Africa.

Gandhi returned to his native land that same year, asserting in a letter to Smuts that 'Complete satisfaction cannot be expected until full civic rights have been conceded to the resident Indian population'.

Law and disorder

Malan's post-war Nationalists forged aggressively ahead with their policy of separate development and, inevitably, racial confrontation intensified.

This was not, however, a complete break with the past — at no time in South Africa's history had blacks enjoyed the full rights of citizenship. In 1923, for instance, the Union Parliament passed the Natives (Urban Areas) Act — a measure which would be amended many times and which, according to Professor T.R.H. Davenport in his *South Africa — A Modern History* 'grew into one of the most complex pieces of control legislation ever devised anywhere'.

Well before that, black political consciousness had emerged to tax the integrity and expertise of the country's leaders. As early as 1906 Smuts had complained that he felt 'inclined to shift the intolerable burden of solving this sphinx problem to the ampler shoulders and stronger brains of the future'.

Soon after Union, in 1912, blacks began to organise themselves, forming the South African Native National Congress, which, in 1923, became the African National Congress (now banned in South Africa). Among its aims were direct political representation, the abolition of the colour bar and (after 1913) the repeal of the Natives Land Act.

Their hopes consistently frustrated, some began to find an outlet in independent church organisations. A sect known as the Israelites settled illegally at the Bulhoek location near Queenstown in 1920.

Local Fingo tribesmen, ensconced in the area for generations, protested. The Israelites defied government orders to move — the law of their God, they said, was above the law of the state.

Under orders not to shoot, a 100-strong police detachment was sent to evict them, but withdrew when confronted by an armed and hostile mob. Six months later the police returned, heavily reinforced and supported by artillery. In the ensuing melée 163 Israelites were killed and 129 wounded. A government commission of enquiry reported 'a growth of race consciousness with its natural outcome of social and political aspirations among the Natives of the Union'.

In the years that followed, that consciousness grew to immense proportions.

Sharpeville rocks the country

The 1950s was the decade of unyielding legislation. It brought, among others, the Unlawful Organisations Act; the Riotous Assemblies Act; the Suppression of Communism Act; and the Separate Registration of Voters Act. This last measure removed the coloured voters in the Cape from the common voters roll, a right which had been entrenched in the constitution at Union. Second World War fighter ace 'Sailor' Malan and his Torch Commando, a pressure group composed of ex-servicemen, were among those who fought long, hard, and ultimately unsuccessfully, to keep government hands off the constitution.

The Nationalists continued to consolidate both their authority (their parliamentary majority became unassailable) and their policy, amending existing laws and creating new legislation to control the black population.

Then, in 1960, there occurred an incident which jolted millions of South Africans. In the township of Sharpeville, near Vereeniging, thousands of demonstrators began to gather around the police station in an anti-pass law demonstration organised by the Pan-Africanist Congress. Four Saracen armoured cars were sent in, and a call went out for police reinforcements. Matters rapidly deteriorated; stones were hurled.

At 1.15 p.m. Colonel A.T. Spengler, the commandant, was thrown to the ground in a scuffle with one of the demonstrators. The security fence around the police station began to give way — and suddenly the situation was out of control. Police opened up with .303 rifles and sten guns, bringing down dozens of people. The final toll was 67 dead and 186 wounded.

In the years that followed there were further outbreaks of violence, the most tragic occurring in 1976 when black schoolchildren took to the streets and clashed with police in bloody encounters across the country.

The government recognised and sought to accommodate some black political aspirations. Whether its measures will provide a solution to South Africa's acute and complex racial problems remains to be seen.

Senator Robert Kennedy meets Chief Albert Luthuli, winner of the Nobel Peace Prize in 1960 and former leader of the African National Congress

The coming of the Republic

HATS OFF TO THE PAST;
JACKETS OFF
TO THE FUTURE

A gusting drizzle swept across Pretoria's Church Square on the morning of 31 May 1961. Among the huge crowd, several hundreds rubbed stiff limbs after a night spent camping out on the square.

A procession approached, escorted by mounted police and motorcycle dispatch-riders, and there was a burst of cheering. Charles Robberts Swart, newly invested with the Presidential sash of office by Chief Justice the Honourable L.C. Steyn, stepped onto the covered rostrum. Prime Minister Dr H.F. Verwoerd was among the dignitaries with him, and moved to the microphone to present to the nation the first State President of the new Republic of South Africa.

'For South Africa it is a momentous day,' said Dr Verwoerd. The rainy weather, he believed, was a blessing, a condition of nature always associated in South Africa with prosperity, joy and life-giving growth.

'The statue of President Paul Kruger, wet and glistening, seemed to look down benignly, and to listen intently,' reported the *Natal Mercury*. President Swart moved to begin his address. The rain stopped, and weak sunlight bathed the square in a gentle glow. It was exactly 59 years since the death warrant of the last republic had been signed at Melrose House, Pretoria.

Putting it to the vote

On 20 January 1960, Dr Verwoerd had announced in Parliament that legislation would be introduced during that session to provide for a referendum on whether South Africa should become a republic. The Referendum Bill was passed by the House of Assembly on 2 May that year by a majority of 78 to 44, and 16 days later the Prime Minister said the Government wanted South Africa to remain in the Commonwealth, whether or not it became a republic.

Political parties lobbied fiercely for votes in the 1960 referendum. This National Party stand enticed Durban voters

Political parties immediately launched their campaigns: the National Party was emphatically in favour of a republic, while the United, Liberal and Progressive parties were equally emphatic in their opposition to the idea. Newspapers devoted their columns to opinion polls and interviews with people expressing widely-varying views.

The Minister of Transport, Ben Schoeman, told a meeting in Brits that South Africa should look for unity so great that even the events in the outside world would be unable to break it. In Johannesburg the Progressive Party asserted that if the Nationalists won the referendum, it would be interpreted by extremists as a mandate to 'run roughshod over the Constitution in a way they have never dared to in the past'. On 7 September 1960 the *Cape Times* quoted the Minister of Lands, Paul Sauer, as saying it was South Africa's 'urgent wish' to remain in the Commonwealth when a republic was declared.

The *Cape Times* of 4 October reported a speech by Sir De Villiers Graaff, Leader of the Opposition, in which he expressed his fears

that communist forces opposed to the South African way of life were hoping that the country would become a republic. 'They would like to see the country blunder into isolation and become weak,' he warned. Dr Verwoerd, in turn, accused the anti-republican parties of fighting together, though in different ways, for a change of constitution in the dangerous direction of multiracialism. The time was more than ripe for the launching of a republic, he said.

Came 5 October 1960, and 1,626,336 white South Africans cast their votes. The counting took two days, and Natal was the only province in which more votes were cast against the republic than for it. The final figures: 850,458 for the republic and 775,878 against. March 1961, and Dr Verwoerd rose to tell the assembled Commonwealth Prime Ministers in London that he 'thought it better for South Africa and the Commonwealth to withdraw [South Africa's] application for re-admission to membership'. It had become apparent that most of the Commonwealth members were vehemently opposed to South Africa's racial

Posters, pamphlets, car stickers and a host of other gimmicks urged the electorate to make the 'right' decision in 1960. Left: The anti-republic campaign intensifies. Mrs Helen Suzman and Mr Lionel Margo examine a poster outside the polling tent in Killarney on the day before the referendum. Top right: Voting slip for the Sea Point constituency. Countrywide, the pro-republicans won with a majority of fewer than 80 000 votes

Paul Kruger's statue overlooks the large crowd which gathered in Pretoria's Church Square to welcome the Republic

The front pages told of the Republic's birth

policies, and pressure was applied in attempts to make her modify the controversial legislation. Dr Verwoerd said later: 'The proceedings at today's meeting, which have obliged me to take this regrettable step, in my opinion mark the beginning of the disintegration of the Commonwealth.' The move left many South Africans embittered: the Government had earlier declared itself in favour of continued membership, and it was felt that foreknowledge of South Africa's withdrawal could have influenced the voting.

The last Governor-General of the Union, Mr C.R. Swart, resigned on 30 April 1961, to be nominated as the National Party's candidate for State President ten days later. On 20 May, Cape and Natal Citizen Force units were called up, and the Government imposed a ban on meetings 'held for a specific or common purpose', without a magistrate's written permission.

A country-wide three-day stay-at-home by blacks was planned to coincide with the Republic's inaugural festivities. Nelson Mandela, leader of the African Action Council,

emphasised the 'peaceful intentions' of the campaign, which turned out to be only partly successful in the Johannesburg area, and a total failure elsewhere.

On 24 May, Empire Day was celebrated for the last time in South Africa. At a wreath-laying ceremony in Durban, Perla Siedle Gibson — 'The Lady in White' — led the singing of *Land of Hope and Glory* and *God Save the Queen*. One week later the Republic was born.

The day dawns

From all over the country, cars streamed towards the focus of the Republican celebrations — Pretoria. Dust-streaked vehicles jammed the streets as the new arrivals hunted for accommodation. Many spent an uncomfortable night in their cars. Hardier souls braved the chill and, with blankets, sandwiches and coffee, slept out in Church Square.

'Twins born States apart,' announced the *Star's* front page. A Johannesburg woman had given birth to a girl shortly before 11 p.m. on 30 May, and to a twin boy at 12.20 a.m. on 31 May. Her new daughter, said the *Star*, was

born in the Monarchy, and her son in the Republic. Mr Swart took the oath of office in the Groote Kerk; his wife listened to the broadcast from her hospital bed in Bloemfontein. From a rostrum in front of the Palace of Justice, he made his first speech, interrupted from time to time by the singing of patriotic songs and enthusiastic cries of '*Vrystaat!*'. 'Hats off to the past,' he said, 'but jackets off to the future. . .'

THE STATE PRESIDENT'S GUARD

The funeral of the State President designate, Dr Eben Dönges, in January 1968 saw the first public appearance of the South African Defence Force's newest and most prestigious unit — the State President's Guard. Officially established in May the previous year, the unit's distinctive green and gold uniforms and befeathered caps soon became a familiar sight.

This showpiece unit, led by officers and N.C.O.s from the Permanent Force, is drawn from the top national servicemen in the country. And the requirements are strict. A candidate must be a bilingual South African citizen of irreproachable character. The rules specify height, build, state of health, education . . . and a talent for parade-ground work.

The new State President addresses the nation from Church Square. He is flanked by Mrs Verwoerd and Dr Verwoerd

Growing Up

In 1880 South Africa was little more than a loosely-knit collection of towns and peoples at the southern tip of the continent. Although Kimberley was booming, attracting hopefuls from all over the world with its immensely wealthy store of diamonds, there was little evidence of civilisation in the hinterland. Johannesburg did not yet exist.

Then, in 1886, a surveyor named J.E. de Villiers began laying out a town on the farm Randjeslaagte. The first plots were auctioned in December that year (some sold for only three shillings) — and so was born Johannesburg, centre of the West's largest gold mining industry.

South Africa grew ... and grew. By 1904 there were over five million people of all races in the four colonies. By 1946 this figure had more than doubled, and by May 1970, the total population was 21,448 169. Towns and cities also grew apace, and with them came the essential services that make up a modern country.

The 20th century had dawned over a decidedly unhealthy South Africa. In 1901 the plague killed hundreds of people, and women and children were dying by the thousand in British concentration camps throughout the country as enteric fever, typhoid and other diseases took their toll. In the field, conditions were hardly any better: disease killed more British soldiers than Boer bullets and shells.

Although there were sporadic attempts to establish an awareness of public health hazards, progress was slow. Many people relied on folk medicine to remedy everything from whooping cough to aching backs. Sometimes it worked, but sometimes they killed those they were designed to cure. Came 1918, and the epidemic of Spanish Influenza. Over two million South Africans contracted the disease; nearly 140 000 died. And finally there was action. Sir Thomas Watt was appointed as first Minister of Public Health under the Public Health Act (No. 36 of 1919), and soon hospitals and clinics began to spring up across the country.

Universities established medical schools, children were taught the basics of hygiene, and South Africa's health service was on its way.

Education in South Africa had an equally shaky start. In 1900 there were 144 340 pupils enrolled at Cape schools (58 471 of these were white). By 1905, when the School Board Act was passed, the number had grown by almost 20 000. At that time it was estimated that over 60 000 white children of school-going age were not in school.

The authorities had to take notice. When Union came in 1910 the Cape was spending £440 000 a year on education. Within a decade this figure had climbed to £2 million and in the years that followed the number of schools expanded dramatically. So, too, did the number and size of training and technical colleges. By the middle of the century South Africa's system of education — for all races —was probably more advanced than that of any other African country.

Captain Robinson's adult art class in Cape Town. Not all South Africans had the opportunity to better themselves: early education was often a haphazard affair

Johannesburg is born

'I THINK IT IS A PAYABLE GOLDFIELD'

'My name is George Harrison,' the prospector declared in an affidavit to Pretoria's Mines Department, 'and I come from the newly discovered goldfields Kliprivier, especially from a farm owned by a certain Gert Oosthuizen. I have a long experience as an Australian gold-digger, and I think it is a payable goldfield.' With that understatement of the century, made on 24 July 1886, Johannesburg, the Golden City, was born.

'And what are we going to call this new dorp?' Paul Kruger is reported to have asked Johannes Rissik, Acting Surveyor-General of the South African Republic and his colleague, Christiaan Johannes Joubert.

'As both Joubert and I are called Johannes, Mr President,' Rissik replied, 'we thought of suggesting "Johannesburg" as the name . . . and I would point out that Your Honour's name is also Johannes.' That sealed it; Johannesburg it was. Or so the legend goes.

The town was laid out on the five farms of Braamfontein, Turffontein, Langlaagte (where Harrison discovered the 'Main Reef'), Doornfontein and particularly Randjeslaagte, an unwanted *uitvalgrond* waterless and rocky outcrop owned by the government. The original surveyor's beacon still stands on Randjeslaagte, 'the dale of little ridges', at the corner of East and Louis Botha avenues. The southern boundary of the farm lay along to-day's Commissioner Street.

By October 1886, the population of the new goldfields was 600, divided between Turffontein's 'Ferreira's Camp' and Doornfontein's 'Natal Camp'.

The first camp leader was the flamboyant 50-year-old diamond digger, frontier policeman and adventurer, Colonel Ignatius Philip Ferreira. He headed the Diggers Committee, later renamed the Sanitary Committee: an indication of the mining camp's priorities.

As the golden message spread throughout the world and the diggers flooded in, Johannesburg mushroomed. The contours of the ground were ignored by Surveyor J.E. de

Rissik Street in the 1890s was a profusion of pillars and the cast iron decoration so beloved of Victorian architects

The old Johannesburg Law Courts, about 1900. The building stood between Eloff and Rissik streets

'Between the Chains', Johannesburg's famous open-air bourse, where shares were bought and sold

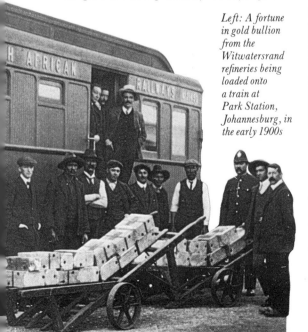

Left: A fortune in gold bullion from the Witwatersrand refineries being loaded onto a train at Park Station, Johannesburg, in the early 1900s

Pritchard Street was already one of the city's busiest thoroughfares in 1910. It was named after W.H.A. Pritchard, one of Johannesburg's pioneers. In 1936 (the city's 50th anniversary) he staged a tableau of Ferreira's Camp with himself and others dressed in diggers' costume. Right: Pritchard remembered the early days in this 1936 article

THE OUTSPAN

Next Tuesday the Rand officially celebrates its Fiftieth Birthday with a Public Holiday and a Gala Day

When Johannesburg Was Born...

I WAS A YOUNG MAN OF 25

By Wm. H. Auret Pritchard, J.P.

A Mr Gallagher owned the 'Cafe-de Move-On', Johannesburg's popular and unusual mobile food shop

Left: The Old Arcade, between Commissioner and Market streets, was built in 1893 (the ironwork was imported from Glasgow) and rebuilt in 1962. Above: The suburb of Houghton viewed from the top of Munro Drive in the mid-1920s. Today it is the densely-populated heart of affluent Johannesburg

Triumphal arches were built at the major approaches to central Johannesburg for the Jubilee in 1936

In 1968 this truck was lifted half-way up Standard Bank Building to pour concrete into a huge beam

water tanks were emptied every second day by 800 horse-drawn wagons.)

Johannesburg, whose rebellious, disenfranchised uitlanders helped spark off the Anglo-Boer War, was ironically untouched by the conflict. The mines were abandoned but remained unharmed, although many a Transvaal burgher called for their demolition.

On 1 June 1900, the Vierkleur came down and the Union Jack was hoisted in its place. In The Johannesburg Story, F. Addington Symonds tells how one man in the crowd was seen to keep his hat on; another tried to knock it off. He was stopped by a fellow-Englishman who said: 'Leave him alone! He's got as much right to his own feelings as we have!'

The end of the Anglo-Boer War revived Johannesburg's skittery optimism. It was business as usual and much talk of a coming boom. The financial houses promised Milner a £30 million loan for reconstruction and accepted his ten per cent profits tax on gold. The gold magnates, rich in country estates, yachts, racing stables and London town houses did much to boost their golden city with their chunky office blocks and somewhat tasteless town houses.

From September 1936 to January 1937 Johannesburg staged the Empire Exhibition to mark her first 50 years and Golden Jubilee. Visitors came from all over the world and two million paid for admission. The first four months of 1937 saw a stock market boom.

Shorthand typists, office boys and lift attendants pooled their savings in 'syndicates' to buy shares. On the floor of the Exchange the stockbrokers literally tore the coats off each other's backs in their eagerness to buy. Then the bubble burst; West Wits shares, for example, dropped from 325/- to 45/- in 24 hours. Black Friday. Thousands of Johannesburgers went bust. That's Jo'burg for you.

Villiers; all streets simply ran north-south or west-east. The early architecture of Johannesburg was soulless and not at all solid.

Wood and iron buildings were erected in preference to more enduring structures in spite of official exhortations that ' . . . we may be here still when our children have grown up'. Claims were furiously bought and sold, companies and syndicates formed. The opening of a new mine or engineering workshop was almost a daily occurrence.

The cyanide gold-recovery process revolutionised the now deep-level workings and the great companies emerged: Consolidated Mines Selection, Barnato Mines, General Mining and Finance Corporation and the Goerz Group. The last was to become the Union Corporation. The mines attracted thousands of immigrant uitlanders to the Reef, created a food market for farmers and stimulated railway construction. If you had guts, it was all gold and go.

Joseph Benjamin Robinson arrived from Kimberley with £20 000 which he had borrowed from Alfred Beit. Barney Barnato, the Cape Colony MP, ex-cigar salesman, ex-kopje-walloper, Kimberley diamond magnate, conjuror, stage, ring and racing enthusiast — came in 1888 in his check suit and

straw hat, and ten months later stated that ' . . . Johannesburg will soon be one of the greatest and most prosperous towns in South Africa'. At the time it was a bold prophesy. The first mines, including the Ferreira, Robinson, Village Main Reef, City Suburban and Crown Mines, went into production. The first theatre, the Globe, was opened in 1888, as were a school and hospital.

The gold attracted desperadoes, too. One of the most notorious was F.B. Deeming, swindler, fake mining expert and murderer, who arrived in 1889. In the unlit streets of Johannesburg, six people were killed. Arrested and released for lack of evidence, Deeming made his way to England where he married, then murdered and buried (in concrete) his wife and family. Not content with this, he repeated the procedure with a second wife in Melbourne, Australia. Only this time his luck ran out: he was caught, tried and hanged in Australia on 23 May 1892.

By 1892 Johannesburg had a population of 40 000: a veritable Gomorrah on Pretoria's doorstep. (By 1905 it had grown to 150 000 — and it was only in that year that flush sanitation was introduced. Up till then buckets were removed nightly from each house by hundreds of mule-drawn carts, while bath and slop

SANDTON CITY

Sandton City, the shopping and office complex about 13 km from central Johannesburg, is one of the biggest and most successful decentralisation projects of its kind in South Africa. The first stage of the project cost R20 million, and the final cost is likely to be about R140 million. The complex features art galleries, cinemas, banks and many restaurants, and when completed will accommodate over 200 shops. The siting of the complex solved some of the biggest problems associated with latter-day shopping.

Diamonds... and an ox named Bloem

A FEW SHINY STONES

Fleetwood Rawstorne and his fellow diggers, known as the 'Red Cap Party', were annoyed when their servant, Damon, had too much to drink. They had staked their claim on the northern Cape farm, Vooruitzicht, in the hope of making themselves rich — and the last thing they needed was a drunken servant. So, as a punishment, Damon was sent to a nearby hillside and told not to return until he had found a diamond.

A few days later he returned — sober. He brought with him a few shiny stones that were to give birth to the richest diamond mine in the world. The date was 16 July 1871, and the course of South Africa's history was about to be changed.

Rawstorne's group rushed to stake their claims on the hillock (they named it 'Colesberg Kopje') and soon the area was a frantically busy mining community: hopefuls arrived from all parts of the world. Their claims were divided and subdivided; cables and pulleys criss-crossed the working area until it began to resemble a huge spider's web. The site became known as De Beers New Rush (it was named after the brothers who owned the farm Vooruitzicht), and in 1873 the community was named Kimberley in honour of the British Colonial Secretary, Lord Kimberley.

Colesberg Kopje disappeared as more and more diggers (eventually there were 1 600 separate claims in the mine) delved deep into the 'blue ground' (kimberlite) surrounding the diamond-bearing volcanic pipe. Although roadways had been laid out across the site, these were gradually eroded by the miners, and most had collapsed before the end of 1872.

In his book, *South Africa* (1878), Anthony Trollope described Kimberley as 'one of the most interesting places on the face of the earth'. Yet he found some aspects of the town distasteful in the extreme, commenting: 'I sometimes thought that the people of Kimberley were proud of their flies and their dust.'

Trollope was highly disapproving of the diggers' singleminded pursuit of wealth: 'This feeling runs through even to his wife and children, teaching them that dirt thrice turned may yet be turned a fourth time with some hope of profit. Consequently ladies, and children, do turn dirt instead of making pretty

Kimberley, 1905. Separating diamonds from gravel after the concentrates have come off the grease table

A De Beers employee armed with tweezers and magnifying glasses classifying a pile of diamonds

In 1934 the children of the Newton Dutch Reformed Church began to collect pennies for their Sunday school fund. By 9 June they had gathered enough coins to spell out the words above and below the whitewash 'Bible'

By 1874 Kimberley Mine was criss-crossed by a vast network of ropes linking claims with the surface

This building was once a bar attached to the old Crown Hotel, where many diamonds changed hands

A panoramic view of Dutoitspan in the late 1800s. Merchants and tradesmen frequently doubled as diamond buyers: the pickings were too good to miss

Three nonchalant workers ride a wire-suspended aerial trolley down the Kimberley Mine in 1903

needle-work or wholesome mud pies.'

But the miners cared little for sentiment — they did not have the time. For them, life was digging out the blue ground, sifting it for diamonds, and guarding their finds from the rich profusion of scoundrels that flocked to the diamond fields by the score.

They dug at Bultfontein and Dutoitspan too, where diamonds had been found years earlier. The town appeared to be built on a veritable sea of gems.

'Mansions of tarpaulins and props'

Conditions in the diamond fields were primitive and dangerous. Miners lived in tents, roughly-built 'homes' of wood and corrugated iron, or simply huddled beneath tarpaulins. Sanitary services were non-existent and nobody appeared to care about health and hygiene.

Describing early Kimberley, the *S.A. Handbook* (1905) recalled the 'canvas age': 'One gentleman of our acquaintance spent six months in a big tub. He was very proud of it as an ideal residence, because if a "dust devil" was blowing, or there was a storm at night, he could just head it round to the wind, curl up cosily inside and defy the elements. Others made mansions of tarpaulins and props . . . It was a very jolly, happy-go-lucky life, full of excitement, whisky, champagne in buckets, and sudden departures for the hereafter . . .'

Meanwhile digging continued apace. Cecil Rhodes got a foothold in the Kimberley Mine, enlarged his holdings with characteristic shrewdness, and in 1888 the amalgamation of his interests with those of Barney Barnato led to the creation of De Beers Consolidated Mines Limited. Colossal fortunes were being made, and Kimberley was booming.

In those days illicit diamond-buying flourished to an incredible extent, said the *Handbook*, and the profits were large: 'One of the most awful sights in the Kimberley of those days was the departure of an open wagon laden with chained White men, singing a dolorous song, for the Cape Town breakwater.'

The Kimberley Mine, or 'Big Hole', was closed down in August 1914 at the outbreak of the First World War. In its 43 years of life, it had yielded 25 million tons of soil and rock and 14,504 375 carats of diamonds (about three tons!) valued at £47,139 842.

AN ADVENTUROUS OX

Bloem, an ox with a wanderlust, often spelt trouble for pioneer farmer Rudolph Martinus Brits, who in 1840 had settled on land fed by a strongly-flowing spring near the Modder River. Bloem had a habit of wandering off after jumping the walls of his kraal. Finally he paid the penalty for his insubordination: he was taken by a lion lurking near the spring.

Farmer Brits, so legend has it, thereupon called his new farm Bloemfontein, never imagining that he was giving the name of his adventurous ox to a thriving city.

Another version is that the future capital of the Free State got its name from a roguish old Koranna chief named Jan Bloem, who lived near the spring at the end of the previous century with a band of marauders. More prosaic historians, however, are inclined to believe that it was so named simply because the spring was surrounded by flowers.

However it got its name, the farm was bought by the British Agent in 1846, and when Britain annexed the territory two years later, it became the administrative centre. The discovery of diamonds in the Sixties boosted the growth of the little town in the middle of nowhere, and the finding of gold in the Transvaal provided another stimulus. In due course, Bloemfontein became the capital of

---

A TORRENT OF DEATH

The area had been in the grip of a drought so severe that the military had been reduced to bombarding the clouds with dynamite in a vain effort at rain-making. The situation was critical when the drought ended — with a vengeance. Disaster struck Bloemfontein on Sunday, 17 January 1904.

That morning, a farmer to the west of the town heard 'a sudden report like a cannon' from three different places. 'Then an enormous body of water was seen to fall from the heavens and, striking the ground, rushed round and round like the water in a boiling cauldron, and then shot out like the smoke from a rifle . . .' The torrent thundered into the town, sweeping away 175 homes, drowning at least 28 people, and leaving hundreds homeless.

Once a row of shops, Fountain Street, in Bloemfontein, after the disastrous floods of 1904. At least 28 people were drowned

---

the newly constituted Free State, and with the coming of Union, it was made the judicial capital of South Africa.

Anthony Trollope, who visited Bloemfontein just over a hundred years ago, wrote in his book, *South Africa:* 'I found Bloemfontein a pleasant place . . . but one requiring much labour and trouble both in reaching and leaving . . . It stands isolated in the plain . . . with as clearly defined a boundary on each side as might be a town built with a pack of cards . . .'

'After travelling through a country ugly, dusty and treeless for many weary hours the traveller at last reaches Bloemfontein . . . wondering at the fate which has led him to a spot on the world's surface, so far away, apparently so purposeless, and so unlike the cities which he has known.'

Bloemfontein escaped the worst of the Anglo-Boer War because the Boer forces left the town at the approach of General Roberts, and the municipality continued to function after the British take-over.

Bloemfontein is now notable principally for its fine government buildings, its wealth of monuments to a past rich in history, its statues of many of South Africa's greatest sons, its museums and its schools. Its central position in the Republic has made it an outstanding venue for national conferences. It is believed to be the only city in the world to have a game park at its centre; it has spread over the years to surround Naval Hill, site of the Franklin Game Reserve and an astronomical observatory.

It also has the dubious honour of being the first town in South Africa to introduce parking meters.

The old Market in Bloemfontein. Moved in 1925, the area is now Hoffman Square, a garden

The fourth Raadsaal, Bloemfontein, completed in 1893. In the Anglo-Boer War it was a military hospital

Pretoria: corridors of power

DEEP MUD AND BLOOMING ROSES

'Pretoria . . . is a little town,' wrote Anthony Trollope in *South Africa* (1878). The town that would by 1910 become the Washington of South Africa was then not noted for its jacarandas and fine buildings, and in fact appears to have been rather ordinary. 'The streets,' the writer remarked with conscious superiority, 'lie in holes, in which when it rains the mud is very deep. In all such towns as these mud assumes the force of a fifth element.'

But Trollope conceded that 'in spite of the mud . . . Pretoria is both picturesque and promising'. He was thinking of its abundant roses, which inspired another Victorian novelist, Rider Haggard, to describe Pretoria in *Jess* as 'the prettiest of the South African towns, with its red and white houses, its tall clumps of trees, and pink lines of blooming rose hedges . . .'

The heart of Pretoria, then as now, was Church Square, site of the town's first church (a mud-walled edifice rebuilt after a fire in 1882) and its first bar, Brodrick's Hole-in-the-Wall. Market days, auctions 'under the oaks' and regular nagmaal gatherings transformed the wide square into a sea of ox wagons. But this was late 19th century Pretoria, a Boer capital named after Andries Pretorius, hero of Blood River. It was also the Pretoria of Oom Paul Kruger, the irascible Boer president.

Church Square: saga of a statue

The story of Church Square sums up the changes in Pretoria as it grew from a remote ivory clearing-house to the capital of a Boer republic rolling in gold, and finally to the administrative capital of South Africa. Even in President Kruger's time the new wealth made itself felt: an imposing Palace of Justice rose on the square, dwarfing the nagmaal wagons. The Palace was ready by 1898, but its first use was destined to be as a hospital for the British when they occupied the town in 1900.

One of Kruger's trusted friends was Samuel Marks, the Lithuanian Jew who had risen from *smous* to millionaire industrialist. In 1895, grateful that he had been allowed to build Pretoria's first synagogue two blocks from Church Square, Sammy Marks commissioned a young Anton van Wouw (his fee was £10 000) to sculpt a statue of President Kruger. Kruger returned the compliment by allowing Marks to strike souvenir gold 'tickeys' in the Mint. The statue, cast in bronze in Rome, was completed in 1899, and arrived at Lourenço Marques just as the Anglo-Boer War began. The pedestal already waiting on Church Square was to stand vacant for many years.

Deneys Reitz tells in his Anglo-Boer War book, *Commando*, of the time Mrs Kruger showed him a picture of the forthcoming statue: 'The President was shown dressed like an elder of the Church in a top hat, and the old lady suggested that the hat should be hollowed out and filled with water, to serve as a drinking-fountain for the birds. My father and I laughed heartily on our way home at her

Church Square in 1893. Families sometimes travelled hundreds of kilometres to attend the quarterly nagmaal

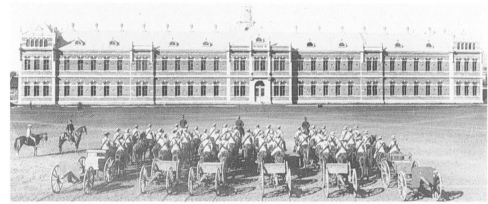

Gun teams at the imposing Artillery Barracks in Potgieter Street, Pretoria — photographed in 1890

Old Lion Bridge (then called Arcadia Bridge) on Church Street East. The bridge spans the Apies River

The Volksraad in session in the historic Raadsaal, Pretoria, at the turn of the century

The Palace of Justice, Pretoria. It was used as a military hospital during the Anglo-Boer War

Church Square in 1905. The fountain was donated by Sammy Marks, friend of President Kruger

Kruger's statue is transferred to Church Square in 1954. It was unveiled that year by Dr D.F. Malan

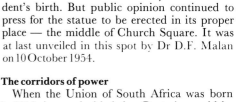

The old South African Reserve Bank. It was established in 1921 and given the sole right to issue notes

Church Street in the early 1900s. The town was already large — and it was growing fast

of the station on the centenary of the President's birth. But public opinion continued to press for the statue to be erected in its proper place — the middle of Church Square. It was at last unveiled in this spot by Dr D.F. Malan on 10 October 1954.

The corridors of power

When the Union of South Africa was born in 1910, it was decided that Pretoria would be the site of its administrative capital. It was at this time that the streets were planted with avenues of gracious jacarandas (the city's first two trees are said to have been grown by J.F. Celliers in his Sunnyside garden from seed brought from South America). And it was now that a grand building was needed, both to symbolise the union of the four provinces and to house its administrators. The architect chosen was Herbert Baker, Rhodes's protégé, whose distinctive style was already to be seen in Cape Town, Johannesburg and Pretoria itself.

'I was given a free hand in suggesting sites in and around the city,' Baker said in *Architecture and Personalities*. 'I was shown the block of land which the Government had bought in the centre of the city ... But with the high ideals we all had at that time I thought this site unworthy of the capital buildings of a United South Africa. So I explored the surrounding kopjes ...'

Baker settled on Meintjeskop, 'a natural site for an acropolis'. Below it stretched a natural amphitheatre which he incorporated into his grand, semi-circular colonnaded design inspired by memories of Greek and Roman temples. Though the open-air amphitheatre drew much criticism, Baker found his vision justified during the First World War, when both Botha and Smuts were welcomed there, after victorious campaigns, by vast crowds, 'all of whom could hear'.

Yet Baker's dream had not been realised in full. A comparison between his idealised drawings and the finished Union Buildings of 1913 show a discrepancy. Though he used many local materials — stinkwood panelling, Rhodesian teak, Vereeniging tiles — Baker wanted imported stone. Instead, he got locally-quarried stone on a base of rough Transvaal granite, and the result has been labelled 'ponderous and stony'.

simplicity, but we agreed that it was decent of her to have thought of such a thing.' The laugh may have been on Reitz after all, because after the war, when the British authorities refused to erect Kruger's statue, Sammy Marks gave the city an elaborate cast iron fountain instead. The fountain, which had been a feature of the Glasgow Exhibition, was put up in the middle of Church Square in 1905.

In 1910 the square, now denuded of the church owing to its unsafe tower, was totally redesigned. Sammy Marks's fountain was banished to the Zoo and neglected until its restoration in 1970. Kruger's statue, still lying

in store, was ignored (as were the pleas for flowers and fountains). Instead, Church Square became a terminus for the new electric trams. Kruger's ill-fated statue was finally allowed out of store and onto a plinth — but only in Prince's Park, where it was unveiled by General Schalk Burger in May 1913. The four figures of burghers designed to surround the plinth were missing. Two were found later on Lord Kitchener's estate in England; the other two had been incorporated into the war memorial at Chatham's Military College.

The burghers took their rightful place at Kruger's feet on 10 October 1925, when the much-travelled statue was moved to the front

Church Square in 1951. The Raadsaal is on the right and the Standard Bank building on the left

October is jacaranda time. They were planted by the Town Engineer, 'Jacaranda Jim', in 1906

Union Buildings. Architect Herbert Baker selected Meintjeskop as 'a natural site for an acropolis'

The gateway to Africa

LAWRENCE GREEN'S CAPE TOWN

'Away from Cape Town I live in exile . . . I fell under the spell of Cape Town soon after I became conscious of this world. For me it would be an evil turning of life's wheel if I were forced to end my days elsewhere.' So wrote Lawrence Green in *Tavern of the Seas*. No other writer has succeeded in so evocatively and affectionately recalling Cape Town's past.

As a schoolboy, Green developed a great love for the sea, and spent hours at the docks, where he saw the last of the American whalers coming in. 'They were the square-rigged "spouters" out of Nantucket and New Bedford, sails darkened by blubber smoke, stumpy masts and swift boats at the davits.'

Early 20th century Cape Town had a spirit which no visitor could forget. The hawkers, buskers, evangelists and flower-sellers were more numerous and colourful then.

There was the familiar 'praa, praa, praa' of the fish horn, too, lovingly remembered today, but greeted with mixed feelings in the city of 1904, when the Mayor and Corporation were petitioned: 'The undermentioned ladies and gentlemen, belonging to the musical, literary and theatrical world of Cape Town and Suburbs, beg to request you, in the interest of the nerves, general health and good temper of the community in general, to pass a law prohibiting the appalling and terrible noise caused by the use of that barbaric instrument, the fish horn!'

The great storms of 1904

The winter of that year saw massive floods in the streets of Cape Town. The face of Table Mountain at times resembled the Victoria Falls as incredible quantities of rainwater poured down into the city. Every shop on one side of Adderley Street was damaged, railway platforms were submerged, and in St George's Street a man was forced to swim for his life. One entrepreneur even turned out a book entitled *A Series of Realistic Photographs*, with a *Complete Description of the Effects of the Great Storms of June 23 and 25, 1904*. Disaster has always been good business.

In the early 1900s Cape Town's main streets were macadamised, and the city's growth began to accelerate. During William Duncan Baxter's year as Mayor in 1907-08, the Cape Peninsula Publicity Association was formed — one of the first in the British Empire. Not all, however, were in favour: councillors thought the organisation would attract 'riff-raff' and lead to overcrowding. The Publicity Association proposed a cableway up Table Mountain and a 'pleasure lake on Green Point Common with water pumped in by windmill power'. It also took over the running of the city's Municipal Orchestra.

The municipalities of Cape Town, Green Point and Sea Point, Woodstock, Mowbray, Maitland, Rondebosch, Claremont and Kalk Bay were assimilated by the Mother City just before the First World War, and the City of Greater Cape Town was born (Wynberg was absorbed in 1927).

A parade of fire tenders featuring horse-drawn and steam-powered vehicles is led by the fire brigade's newest acquisition — powered by an internal combustion engine. Note Cape Town's famous Tivoli Theatre

A view down Wale Street early this century, with the original tower of St George's Cathedral on the right

Darling Street photographed from the Grand Parade which today is only half its original size

Left: In May 1885 a bazaar was held on Robben Island to raise funds for the erection of a recreation room for the use of resident officials, 'harmless lunatics' and patients. There was no jetty then, and visitors had to be carried ashore. In 1929 a cablecar carrying the Mayor of Cape Town, the Reverend A.J.S. Lewis, made the inaugural ascent of Table Mountain. In their book, Oos, Wes, Tuis Bes: Distrik Ses: Poesie, photographer Chris Jansen and poet Adam Small captured the authentic flavour of this once bustling community:

'Wat willie mooi mêrim hê?
Kôs mêrim, mêrim moet ma net sê!
Ag nai, mêrim, plies, moenie hyl vi ons nie
kôs onse motto, mêrim, is
sorrow is for tomorrow!'

Constructed in 1912, the Pier at the end of Adderley Street gradually lost its popularity, and was demolished to make way for harbour development. Inset: The tower at the end of the Pier comes down in 1940

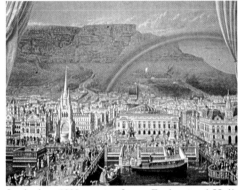

In the late 1800s, artist James Ford painted Holiday Time in Cape Town in the 20th Century

A landmark for many years, Grand Hotel at the corner of Strand and Adderley streets in 1949

Although cars had been seen in Cape Town's streets for some time, it was still customary to deride this new-fangled form of transport. Cape Town at this time was a city of 200 hansom cabs whose drivers fought a losing battle against the motor car. At a 1908 protest meeting called by the Cab Owners' and Cab Drivers' Association, a spokesman declared: 'Like all innovations, the motor car will be patronised at first, but it will soon wane in popularity, for it is always getting out of order and causing accidents.'

The vanishing past

But the city was changing. Ian Colvin, as-sistant editor of the *Cape Times*, wrote in the newspaper's 1906 Christmas issue: 'Old Cape Town is vanishing away. The pleasant stately white-washed houses of which the city used to be composed remain only here and there, forlorn relics of an age long past . . . How noble and simple they are . . . Their generous doorways . . . great teak doors, their quaint fanlight, their many-paned and green-shuttered windows, their stoeps with corner seats of stone, the glimpse of the courtyard behind . . .'

The growth of the Mother City was particularly noticeable on the foreshore, or Rogge Bay. In *Grow Lovely, Growing Old*, Lawrence Green recalled it as it used to be: 'Cape Town lost the liveliest corner of its waterfront when the last fishing boat departed from Rogge Bay and the famous beach vanished beneath the reclamation scheme . . . I remember it as a beach covered with the familiar open boats, all with their bows turned seawards, all left ready for launching at a moment's notice.

'A beach of oars, tackle boxes and snoek kerries, anchor ropes and stone anchors. It was a memorable sight when the whole fleet put to sea under spritsails and jibs, and the scene on their return was even more vivid. For then all the old Malay priests and grey-bearded hadjis in Cape Town, all the bright-skirted Malay womenfolk and fezzed small boys seemed to be waiting on the sand. Then the fish carts were piled high and the fish-horns sounded triumphantly. Boats were washed and scrubbed, canvas covers lashed over spars and sails. Yet when the tired fishermen had departed Rogge Bay remained alive and raucous — alive with eager, greedy black-backed gulls screaming over the offal.' But development was inevitable and in *Tavern of the Seas* Green described the changing shoreline with some regret: 'The modern view may be cleaner, but the fascinating scene of Rogge Bay has been buried.'

The 'burial' of the Rogge Bay shoreline took a long time — and a lot of money. The Foreshore scheme was first outlined in 1935. The Duncan Dock, named after Sir Patrick Duncan, the Governor-General of the Union, was so planned that it required the reclamation of the land between the old sea wall and the new quay-wall. With its development came a solution to the overcrowding of the city's central business area. The contract for the reclamation was awarded in December 1937, and rapid progress was made in pushing back the sea.

An article in the *Outspan* of 14 October 1938 devoted several pages of pictures and text describing the man-made island in Table Bay, the new 2 080 metre long mole (or wall) across the bay, and how much would be spent (£9 million): 'In fact, it is confidently expected that the *Empress of Britain* may be berthed in the new basin next March.'

Left: Three Anchor Bay in the 1900s. There was no wall to contain the sea, and waves would lap at the railway lines during storms. The railway station may be seen in the left background, and the level crossing booms on the right. The Sea Point Railway was built in 1899 and operated until 1929

Durban: South Africa's playground

SUN, SAND AND SKYSCRAPERS

A coast desolate, dangerous and remote, fringed by dunes, mangrove swamps and rushy marshland, backing onto bush and dense jungle teeming with elephants, lions and lesser game. Hardly a promising site for one of the great holiday playgrounds of South Africa, able to supplement the golden gifts of sun and sand with just about every pleasure, simple to sybaritic, that sophisticated living can provide.

But this is the fairytale story of Durban (or 'Durbs' to the more familiar). The transition of this resort city from swampy wilderness to dazzling metropolis of skyscrapers and flickering neon has fascinated writers and observers from all parts of the world. In his book, *In Search of South Africa*, H.V. Morton says of the sub-tropical port: 'There is an air of musical comedy or of a film set about this place. The light is just a little too strong and white to be sunlight, the flowers are a little too bright to be real, the flamboyant trees seem too exotic to be genuine . . .' He wrote that in 1948, when Durban was only an architectural skeleton of what it is today.

In his autobiography, *Light on a Dark Horse*, poet Roy Campbell recalled how he and other children would be driven down 'to the deserted "back beach"', now the ornate Marine Parade, where amidst the ribs of an old, wrecked sailing-ship we could safely paddle, bathe, and play about without fear of sharks or backwash . . .' In 1944, Campbell recalled, there was no wartime blackout: 'I could see the new "Marine Parade" receding like a more flashy super-Brighton, lined with glittering skyscrapers and luxury hotels.

'I can remember playing there when it was the old "Back Beach", a mass of dunes . . . with only one tin shanty of a so-called "Hotel" made of wood and iron. I must confess I liked it better like that.'

But even in 1937, the roamings of lions and elephants in Durban were within the personal recollection of a well-known figure in the city, 83-year-old Colonel Harry Sparks. He wrote in *Outspan*: 'When I was a boy lions visited the

Durban's North Beach in the late 1930s. It has always been one of the city's most popular beaches

Berea and elephants occasionally crashed through the bush . . . How well I remember a fright I had when walking from the Umgeni River to my home at Sydenham. In a thick part of the bush I heard a pack of wild dogs give tongue. There was a crash in a thicket and an exhausted bush buck rushed out. Within a few yards of me the pack caught up with the buck and tore it to pieces. I took to my heels and ran home with the speed of fear.' That same part of Durban is today the sprawling and exclusive suburb of the Berea.

The grand design

The Cinderella-like transformation of Durban was not accomplished by a benevolent fairy godmother. It was the result of hard work and great expense. In a 1927 issue of

A 1903 view of Durban docks showing early stages of construction alongside the Bluff — then virtually uninhabited

'The Water Chute', once a major attraction, featured on this 1908 postcard

The Bay Esplanade — another favourite view. Today it is one of the city's busiest roads

Left: Victorian cast iron charm. Centre: Macrorie House. Right: The bandstand in Alexandra Park

'Pietermaritzburg is a fine-looking city which wears its air of grace and quality with becoming ease.' H.V. Morton's book, *In Search of South Africa* (1948), summed up the appeal of this architectural treasure-house.

Railings, shop-fronts and chandeliers of cast iron can still be seen all over the city: the late Victorian and Edwardian years produced a feast of ornamental castings, mostly from Macfarlanes of Glasgow. After the mid-19th century many buildings featured the soft-textured, salmon-coloured bricks that inspired some of the finest architecture of the late Victorian era, and which still characterise the city today.

Visitors in the late 1800s generally appeared to like Pietermaritzburg's air of serenity. Wrote A.F. Hattersley in *Pietermaritzburg Panorama* (1938): 'Visitors appreciated the aspect of a quiet country town . . . the even tempo of Pietermaritzburg life, the luxuriance of the gardens, and, in the main streets, the Victorian quaintness of the older shops. Within their demure interiors, customers still expected to be served in cone-shaped paper containers.'

Early publicity material displays some of the attractions that made Durban the most popular resort

Outspan, a former Mayor of Durban, Councillor Tom Burman, gives some hint of the determination of the Durban people to compete against other parts of the country in attracting tourists: 'In 1905 the Durban beach was as primitive as when Natal was first discovered . . . In 1907 the Natal Legislature handed over to the Durban Corporation the beach from Rutherford Street to the Umgeni Lagoon with the proviso that the Corporation had to spend £100,000 on developing it within a few years . . . We have built a music pavilion for the orchestra . . . and we have the finest and biggest swimming bath in the world . . . All what is now wasteland will be built upon . . .' In a few years' time, predicted Burman, 'the whole of the beach north of Durban to the Umgeni Lagoon will be transformed and be the playground of the people from the interior.'

Councillor Burman knew what he was talking about. Over the years, the 8 km stretch of golden beach hugging the Indian Ocean became one of the most popular resorts for inland South Africans — and particularly those living in the Transvaal. Its reputation was born in the 1890s when a railway line was opened to Charlestown in the interior, bringing Johannesburgers to within reach of a playpen they were quick to make their own.

Fours years later, the railway line was pushed through to Johannesburg, and the trickle of holidaymakers from the city to Durban during the holiday season became a flood. The trip took 27 hours; today it is made by rail overnight and in less than an hour by air. One of the city's fascinations is the inimitable mixture of East and West. The Indian community, which grew from a core of labourers brought to South Africa for the sugar cane industry, imported a culture that contrasted sharply with that of the colonial die-hards.

Although Durban is now South Africa's busiest port, it once had a reputation as a 'ship killer' among the world's sailors. British novelist Anthony Trollope said of it in his book, *South Africa:* 'South African harbours are not good and among those which are bad Durban is one of the worst.' The harbour's problem was a sand bar which varied in height with the changes in season. Until it was dredged, ships had to anchor well out in the bay and could cross only at high tide. Colonel Sparks had written in *Outspan:* 'In those days the outer anchorage was a treacherous one. Strong currents swept along the shores and, when the gales blew, the ships would drag at their anchors. Many a vessel was blown ashore to be pounded to pieces by the heavy surf.' From 1845 to 1885, 66 large ocean-going ships were wrecked on Durban beach.

Changes had to be made — and they were. A lighthouse was built and piers constructed to make a safe channel for the entry of ships. The harbour was dredged, and kilometres of sheds and quays were erected. By the 20th century, Durban had become a safe haven, capable of handling some of the largest ships.

Durban agrees with me splendidly, the people here vie one with the other in giving one a real good time.

Left: Visitors found Durban warm and friendly. Right: Coin-operated film machines on the beachfront

A view of Durban's Smith Street, looking towards the Berea, photographed about 1909

The Eastern Cape: settler country

Colourful Port Elizabeth, viewed from the jetty around 1910. By this time the port was a flourishing commercial centre and the biggest town in the Eastern Cape

THE FRIENDLY CITY

Port Elizabeth has been called many things, from 'The Bay', 'Little Bess' and the 'Liverpool of the Cape' to modern alternatives: the 'Friendly City' (favoured by the inhabitants) or, as its detractors insist, the 'Windy City'. Named after his wife Elizabeth by the bereaved Acting Governor, Sir Rufane Donkin, the port was little more than a military post (Fort Frederick) when the British settlers arrived in Algoa Bay in 1820. Although they first went inland, some later came back to the Bay to make their fortunes.

The port thrived on shipments of ivory and sales of ostrich feathers (to the value of £304 393 in 1875), wool, mohair, 'hides, skins, horns, karosses, etc', as the 1893 *Guide to Port Elizabeth* reveals. The feather market slumped, but wool, mohair, hides and skins are still part of the city's trade today, along with motor cars and related industries, chocolates and leather.

Port Elizabeth's merchants formed a chamber of commerce as early as 1864, ensuring that the 19th century town became 'the premier port of the Cape Colony'. Civic pride prompted the building of a splendid Renaissance-style town hall (1862); Victorian novelist Anthony Trollope thought the town put 'its rival and elder sister Cape Town quite to shame'. He approved heartily of the Port Elizabeth Club, which he also described in his book, *South Africa,* as 'a pattern club for all colonial towns', declaring his was 'the nicest bedroom I was ever invited to occupy'.

Whatever the town's comforts and facilities by the early 1900s — an opera house, ornate library, concert hall and the novelty of electric trams (since 1897) — Port Elizabeth had its disadvantages. Gales and floods were a regular scourge, with ships driven from the busy bay to be pounded to matchwood on the shore. The *Guide to Port Elizabeth* (1893) noted: 'The ravines which once scarped the hillsides have been turned into account and are now wide streets.' Unfortunately, these streets, so steeply inclined, were prone to turn back into rushing ravines after a storm. Severe damage resulted in 1867, 1897, 1908 and on Sunday morning, 1 September 1968 when nearly 431

Colour postcards of Port Elizabeth around 1905. Left: Obelisk in Market Square. Right: Main Street

Some of the 20 ships which went aground on Port Elizabeth's North End Beach after the storm of 1902

Ostrich feathers on sale in the Feather Market Hall during Port Elizabeth's feather boom in the late 1800s

Main Street, Port Elizabeth, in the 1920s. The Mutual Arcade Building is in the right foreground

The Old Pontoon at East London was a familiar landmark for many years. It was originally pulled across the Buffalo River by hand, and switched to electricity in 1906. It was slow, but it was the only way across

mm of rain fell on the city in a very short time. Eight people lost their lives, roads were washed away, cars 'bobbed like corks' on the raging Baakens River, and the swans of Settlers Park were washed out to sea.

Until a modern enclosed harbour was completed in 1933, landing from a ship at Port Elizabeth was a rigorous experience. Passengers were passed from ship to tug in a cylindrical basket which swayed and bumped against the hull in rough weather. Somewhat more relaxed in atmosphere was the sea-bathing at Humewood's 'Canvas Town', where a cottage tent cost 7/6 a week in 1911. That year's *Guide* sang the praises of this 'truly Arcadian' life where 'he or she may saunter in dressing-gown and slippers for the morning dip'.

Port Elizabeth's growing popularity as a resort was accompanied by sideshows: the famous Snake Park where venomous fangs were bared at daily shows until overshadowed in the 1960s by the performing dolphins at the Oceanarium. Even the city's best-known monument is something of a curiosity: the Horse Memorial depicts a soldier kneeling to water his mount, and was erected to honour the horses who suffered during the Anglo-Boer War.

THREE VILLAGES, ONE CITY

South Africa's only river port, at the mouth of the Buffalo (originally Port Rex, but renamed 'Port of East London' in 1848 by Sir Harry Smith) was once divided by more than its river. Until 1873 there were three villages: East London West, on the west bank, East London East on the east bank, and Panmure, described by Anthony Trollope as 'an unpromising assemblage of stores and houses which declares of itself that it means to snuff East London altogether out'.

In 1873 the three villages were formed into one municipality. The pontoon linking them continued to ply back and forth until 1908. Although it had already run for two years on electricity (instead of being pulled across by hand) the pontoon was finally replaced by a 'temporary' bridge. It remained 'temporary' until 1935, when it made way for the first 'double-decker' bridge in South Africa. It carried rail traffic on the lower deck and vehicles and pedestrians on the upper.

The German settlers of the 1850s gave East London's hinterland distinctive place names such as Stutterheim, Berlin, Frankfurt and Potsdam. In the city, street names such as Quanza, Brighton and Cadwallon, as well as the name of East London's most popular recreation spot, Orient Beach, commemorate a different feature of the past: the numerous wrecks of sailing ships driven ashore in the 19th and early 20th centuries. The *Orient*, wrecked on 29 July 1907, created a particular stir when its cargo of wheat fermented — to the disgust of sensitive townspeople.

For a long time, East Londoners regarded mixed bathing with horror, writing to the newspaper indignantly about each 'flagrant

East London's Market Square in the 1930s was a mixture of ox-drawn wagons, shoppers and cars

case of promiscuous ablutions'. In 1892 the town council constructed a public bath for 'Ladies and Children', and in 1905-06, two new tidal pools went up — with a wall segregating the sexes. But the barrier, removed only in 1923, did not appear to have affected East London's reputation as a pleasure town. Camping grounds, complete with electricity, the fashionable promenade of the Esplanade, several fairgrounds and a Pagoda tearoom vied with the pleasures of boating and picnicking on the Buffalo River to bring summer guests flocking to East London in the early decades of the century.

FRONTIER TOWN

The Settler City of the Eastern Cape still possesses what was referred to by H.V. Morton in his book, *In Search of South Africa*, as 'the cosy look of a solid, early 19th century British town'. The 1820 Settlers ensured Grahamstown's growth as they gradually left their unprofitable and dangerous frontier farms for the town's more welcoming streets.

1938. Professor J.L.B. Smith with 'Old Fourlegs', the 'extinct' coelacanth caught near East London

Grahamstown's alternative title, City of Saints, is held by some to derive from an incident in which a trooper was sent from an outlying fort to order a carpenter's vice from the town. He returned empty-handed, explaining: 'There is no vice in Grahamstown.' But the title is more likely to refer to the 40-odd churches (including chapels at the numerous schools) in the city.

Prominent on the Church Square is the imposing stone Cathedral of St Michael and St George, begun in 1824. Only the south wall of the original building remains. The graceful spire which replaced the original squat tower was designed by Sir Gilbert Scott, Victorian architect of St Pancras Station and the Albert Memorial in London, and was completed in 1878.

As champion of the English language in South Africa, Grahamstown is, fittingly, an important educational centre, well endowed with schools of the calibre of St Andrew's College (a private school dating from 1855), often called 'the Eton of South Africa'. From its senior classes evolved Rhodes University, opening its doors in 1904 to 50 undergraduates.

Bathurst Street in Grahamstown in the late 1800s. Right: The 1820 Settlers Monument, completed in 1974. The annual Grahamstown Festival, which features art, literature, drama and other cultural activities mostly centred on the heritage of the English language in South Africa, was first staged in that year

The health of a nation

FIGHTING DISEASE AND PREJUDICE

South Africa made an unhealthy entry into the 20th century. Tuberculosis was killing people like flies, enteric fever was cutting swathes through the inmates of British concentration camps, and hundreds more were about to die from the plague. In 1899 Dr W.J. Dodds, president of the Cape of Good Hope branch of the British Medical Association, warned: 'Imperfect as our knowledge is, I think we may fairly conclude, even on the most roseate view, that this country has no right to lull itself into the belief that little needs to be done here to save life and to prevent disease.'

While doctors were highly respected members of any community, their lives were not easy. Their fight against germs was only half the battle: distrust, prejudice and plain carelessness appeared to be killing almost as many patients as diseases were. Specialisation was unknown in South Africa — at least outside the big cities — and patients demanded all-round competence (this included both major and minor surgery) from their family doctor.

Afrikaners in rural areas were reluctant to accept help, even medical help, from a government they saw as hostile to the Boer cause. In April 1919 the *Medical Journal of South Africa* reported that a Dr Spencer had arrived at a Transvaal village during the influenza epidemic of 1918 to inoculate the residents. He found that political feeling in the district had resulted in an appalling death rate: patients had to be dragged to hospital for treatment, where they would cry until released.

A country doctor had to play father confessor, psychiatrist, surgeon — and even dentist. In his book, *Every Man Must Play A Part*, Isadore Frack wrote of his encounter with an old farmer in Helfontein. Before stating his problem the old man wanted to know where the doctor had come from, why he was in Helfontein, why he was so young, whether he was married, what he hoped to do there, whether he was a proper doctor — and finally, could he draw teeth?

A Johannesburg General Hospital nurse of the early 1900s. One of the best-known hospitals in South Africa is the Kimberley hospital, established in 1882 by the amalgamation of the Diggers and Carnarvon hospitals. Its matron was Henrietta Stockdale, who in 1879 established the first training school for nurses and midwives in the country, and in 1891 was responsible for the first registry of nurses in the world

Giving away disinfectant fluid at the Cape during the plague of 1901. Right: The authorities did what they could

THE MUNICIPALITY
OF
STELLENBOSCH.
NOTICE.
Gratis Inoculation Against
Plague.

DR. HAMMANN, Health Officer for Stellenbosch, will continue Inoculating Gratis against Bubonic Plague all Residents of the Municipality of Stellenbosch and District on Mondays and Thursdays (forenoon), from 10 to 12 o'clock, at his residence, Masonic Hotel.

By order of the Councillors,
D. P. MOSTERT,
Town Clerk.

Stellenbosch,
17th April, 1901.

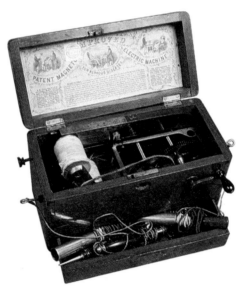

Workers gather for their vaccinations in 1897. Left: An apparatus advertised as a 'Patent Magnetic Electric Machine'. This machine was said to have been used by Queen Victoria to ease her rheumatism

The thoroughly demoralised doctor was about to administer a local anaesthetic when his patient announced that he did not believe in *doodspuiting*, that none of his family believed in it either, and any man who created that much fuss could not be much of a doctor. 'He commanded me in a voice of thunder to pull and be done with it,' recalled Frack. 'I pulled, and strange to say, the tooth came out — whole. He turned and looked at me, squirted out about a pint of blood, tobacco juice and saliva on to the floor, and in tones of great condescension complimented me on not being a bad tooth-drawer.'

In an age when illness was still often attributed to God's judgement, and cures invoked the supernatural, merchants and peddlers of patent medicines found the South African public gratifyingly gullible. 'It is a generally accepted fact,' stated an advertisement in the *Cape Times* in 1901, 'that smoking is a great protection from the plague. That being the case, the public are strongly advised to smoke Taddy's Myrtle Grove cigarettes.'

Yet although the get-rich-quick brigade cheated and sometimes even killed their 'patients', the serious advocates of home cures were often no better. The 'Ladies' Commission' reported after visiting concentration camps during the Anglo-Boer War: 'One woman in the Krugersdorp Camp, whose children were ill with measles, painted their bodies with common green oil paint, and in the case of one of them, added a plaster made of American leather thickly daubed with the same paint ... Both the children died of arsenical poisoning.'

The ignorance of early medical practitioners was often just as crippling as the administrative inadequacies and primitive health controls. Although hospitals and clinics had been increasing in size and sophistication since Van Riebeeck's day, it was only in June 1912 that the first Anatomical and Physiological Laboratories of the South African College (later the University of Cape Town) were opened. Even then only pre-clinical training was available, and students had to go abroad to complete their studies. But there *was* progress: the South African Institute for Medical Research was created in the same year through an agreement between the Government and the mining industry. It was a major step in combating the tragically high incidence of serious illnesses among black mine workers.

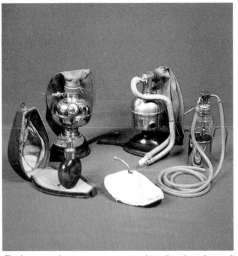

Early anaesthetic apparatus used in South Africa. It includes a mask and a bottle of chloroform

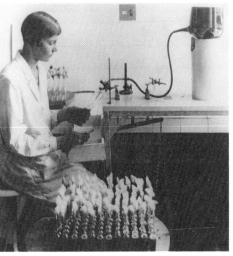

Filling serum ampoules at the South African Institute of Medical Research in 1930

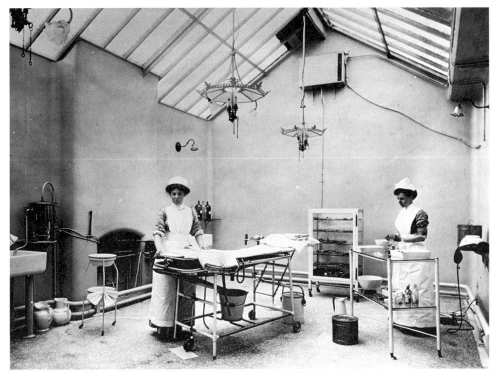

An operating theatre in the Johannesburg General Hospital, about 1902. Note the use of natural light

what had happened, staggered to his feet to seek a doctor. At the inquiry he was to be exonerated from all blame: he was the mine's first victim of Spanish Influenza.

The guns of the First World War were soon to fall silent, only to be replaced by a virus as deadly as a sniper's bullet. Believed to have started among German and Austrian troops, the 'flu quickly spread to Spain, where eight million people were infected (surprisingly, only 700 died). The Moscow newspaper, *Pravda*, dubbed the disease 'Ispanka' (Spanish Lady) — and the name stuck. Her kiss spread fear across the world.

The first case of Spanish Influenza in South Africa was reported in Durban on 14 September 1918. The total population then was just over six million: of these over 2,6 million contracted the disease, and within a few weeks 139 471 had died.

At first the disease affected mainly the ports and larger towns: it was reported in Kimberley on 23 September and in Johannesburg and Cape Town two days later. Then it spread rapidly. Factories and shops closed their doors; trains and trams operated spasmodically, and food grew scarce.

Hospitals overflowed, doctors collapsed from exhaustion and people were buried in mass graves after the supply of coffins ran out. There was no safety in the country, either: refugees were spreading the disease to every corner of South Africa.

'Take a good dose of Epsom salts . . .'

Men were more frequently affected than women, and the group between 25 and 45 years of age seemed particularly vulnerable. They were dying in their thousands, many of them without ever seeing a doctor. Makeshift explanations and medical advice were freely given, though. The *Cape Times* quoted 'a high medical authority' in Cape Town as saying the Germans' use of poison gas in the war was to blame as it 'favoured the growth of a germ previously unknown in medical science'.

Then, almost as suddenly as it had spread, the epidemic ended. In the Cape alone, 87 108 people had died. Of the nearly 140 000 victims in South Africa, over 127 000 were black.

THE KISS OF THE 'SPANISH LADY'

William Hill was an experienced man with nine years' service on East Rand Proprietary Mines. He was sitting at the controls in the engine-room, coaxing up the cage carrying the night shift to the surface. It was routine work, but Hill was alert. His eyes caught the notice that had been pinned up in the engine-room ten days earlier: 'Spanish Influenza: In the event of a driver feeling indisposed, he is to stop hoisting immediately and inform the banksman.' It was 3 a.m. on 1 October 1918, and Hill was feeling fine.

In his book, *The Plague of the Spanish Lady*, Richard Collier describes how, without warning, an icy sweat drenched Hill's body. His limbs seemed lifeless. As he groped for the brake lever, 'a multitude of lights' exploded before his eyes. Banksman Carl Calitz watched helplessly from outside as the cage rushed upwards towards the headgear. Bells rang frantically — but the only man who could prevent the cage from smashing into the headgear was lying comatose in the engine-room, his hands resting uselessly on the brake

lever. Seconds later, the cage was ripped apart by the impact, plunging 30 metres to smash against the timbered rim of the shaft's mouth. Nineteen men were killed instantly and another 19 lay broken and bleeding. Collier tells how Hill, dazed and only dimly aware of

An 'iron lung' built in South Africa during the Second World War, now preserved in the Adler Museum

This full page advertisement for the Caledon Baths appeared in Motoring in South Africa *in 1912. The resort featured over 100 bedrooms and even had a concert hall. The tariff ranged from 10/6 to 15/- a day for 'Accommodation, Board and the ordinary Hot and Cold Mineral Baths'*

Miracle under Table Mountain

THIS THING CAN START ROLLING

At ten o'clock on the evening of 2 December 1967 a 44-year-old doctor was wakened by the shrill ring of a telephone. He dressed quickly, strode to his car and within minutes was turning into the driveway at Cape Town's Groote Schuur Hospital. Christiaan Neethling Barnard had an appointment with a patient — and with fame.

For years Barnard had been researching a technique that would revolutionise cardiac surgery. While open-heart operations had given thousands of diseased hearts a new lease on life, for many patients there was no hope. If the disease had progressed too far, then that was it — they died. Barnard did not accept this, nor did Professor Velva Schrire, the physician who was head of the Cardiac Clinic and a key man in the future transplant team. Barnard gradually built up a team which he hoped would perform the first human heart transplant, and finally they needed only two things — a recipient and a donor.

A man with only one hope

Louis Washkansky had lived with death for a long time. From an active and vibrant man, a veteran of the North African and Italian campaigns of the Second World War, he had been reduced to a bed-ridden cripple. Four heart attacks since 1960 had left him with a heart so weak that he could barely move when admitted to Groote Schuur Hospital on 14 September 1967. In *The Transplanted Heart*, Peter Hawthorne recounts Ann Washkansky's description of one of her visits: "'His colour was so grey it was almost black. He was on the point of collapsing . . .'"

Then one day Washkansky told his wife that 'the big noises' had spoken to him, 'And they're giving me a brand new heart!'

There were frustrating delays. On 22 November Ann Washkansky was summoned to the hospital and told there was a likely donor. But when she got there the operation had been called off. Louis Washkansky was furious, then despondent. Early in December he told his wife: 'Look, now it's Saturday. They all came in to say goodbye to me for the weekend. They'll all be going fishing and having a good time and I'll be forgotten for another week. You know they never operate on Saturday or Sunday.'

But he was wrong. That Saturday afternoon a young woman set out with her family to visit friends. They parked in Main Road, Observatory, to buy a cake at a shop only a short distance from where Louis Washkansky struggled with his breathing. The young woman and her mother started to cross the busy road. There was a screech of tyres and a dull thud. The impact left the mother dead and the daughter barely alive.

Her life was supported by a respirator and it was clear to the surgeons that her brain was damaged beyond repair. Her father said to doctors: 'If there's no hope for her, then try to save the life of this man.' The call went out to Professor Chris Barnard.

Newspapers, television and radio stations kept the world informed of Louis Washkansky's progress

The first heart transplant team. Professor Chris Barnard is fourth from the right and his brother, Dr Marius Barnard, on the extreme right. The brothers were later to work as a team (and individually) on several heart transplant operations. Theatre Matron Kingsley is in the blue uniform and on her right is Professor Jannie Louw

Some South African heart transplant patients. From left: Dr Philip Blaiberg, who received his new heart in January 1968; Miss Dorothy Fisher, the longest-surviving recipient; Mr Pieter Smith and Mr Dirk van Zyl

Right: Professor Christiaan Barnard in 1968. The surgeon had a brilliant academic and medical career and was respected by his colleagues for his inquiring mind. In 1963 he successfully transplanted a heart into a dog, and on one occasion he attached a second head to a dog, which was then capable of using either head to sip milk. Far right: Professor Barnard in 1980 with his second wife, Barbara, and their children

For any human transplant to succeed, the new organ has to be compatible with the body which is to receive it. Dr M.C. Botha, an immunologist at Groote Schuur Hospital, had spent a long time studying the latest techniques in the typing of body tissues. By the time he responded to the urgent call from the hospital, samples of Denise's blood and Washkansky's white blood cells were waiting. At 2 a.m. Botha called Dr Siebert 'Bossie' Bosman, one of Barnard's registrars, with the fateful words: 'Bossie, as far as I am concerned this thing can start rolling.'

In fact the operation had already begun. Thirty doctors, sisters and technicians had scrubbed up. Washkansky was linked to a heart-lung machine and the team prepared him for the receipt of Denise Darvall's heart.

Barnard turned to his patient, and the operation was under way. A young intern afterwards described the atmosphere in the theatre to the *Cape Times:* 'This was the most exciting experience I have ever had. It was like watching a bullfight. There were the classical manoeuvres — beautifully executed —that always precede the grand finale.'

Everyone sensed that the operation was drawing to a magnificent conclusion, said the intern, and even the nurses in the gallery were so tense that their fists were clenched. He went on: 'Most of the time was taken up by the anastomosis . . . the suturing of the main arteries and veins of the patient to those of the donor heart.

'They clamped the tubes leading from the heart to the pump. This was the moment of truth. Everybody leaned forward . . . Professor Barnard muttered; "It's going to work."' An electric shock was administered to Washkansky's new heart, and it began to beat. The anaesthetist called out the blood pressure as it rose slowly, so slowly, to a safe level . . . and suddenly it was done.

Just after six on that Sunday morning the heart of a young woman started a new life in the body of a 54-year-old man. Ann Washkansky saw her revitalised husband for the first time on 7 December, and said with tears in her eyes: 'He looked so beautiful . . . just too beautiful.'

The news flashed around the world. Reporters descended on Cape Town from newspapers, radio and television stations with one burning question: 'How did you do it?' And Barnard, in an unprecedented news conference, told them.

Controversy was inevitable, and discussions on the ethics of heart transplantation went on for years. When was a person really dead, people asked, and who had the right to decide?

Louis Washkansky was to live only 18 days. A post-mortem examination attributed his death to respiratory failure due to pneumonia. Though dispirited, the Groote Schuur Hospital heart team still retained their faith in the transplant technique, and soon another patient was being prepared for a new heart.

Today heart transplants are carried out in several big hospitals abroad, and doctors and scientists are already studying the possibility of brain transplants.

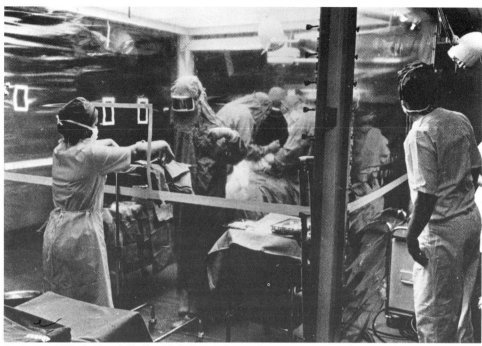

In August 1971 the Rand Daily Mail *described a revolutionary operating theatre in Pretoria's H.F. Verwoerd Hospital (above) which provided a sealed environment in which the surgical team could work. The air in the plastic-sided enclosure was changed 400 times an hour, drastically reducing the risk of infection. These surgeons are implanting an artificial hip joint in a crippled woman — a particularly delicate operation*

Left: The Johannesburg General Hospital in 1896. Its official opening six years earlier was attended by 4 000 people. Above: Johannesburg Hospital complex. Its design and construction were commissioned by the Transvaal Provincial Administration in 1968

THE FAMOUS SIX OF SUPERDAD ROSENKOWITZ

To the rest of the world, Colin and Susan Rosenkowitz were just another ordinary, happily-married South African couple. Then Susan Rosenkowitz began taking a fertility drug.

The news began to filter through to newspapers in early January 1974: an ultrasound scanning technique had revealed the presence of at least four foetuses in her womb. Later, startled doctors discovered that Susan Rosenkowitz was expecting *six* babies.

A team of specialists stood by as Mrs Rosenkowitz's condition was monitored hour by hour in Groote Schuur Hospital. On the morning of 11 January she was wheeled to the theatre, where she was met by two surgeons, six paediatricians, six specialist nurses, two anaesthetists and four sisters. By 8.30 a.m. the group had been joined by David, Nickie, Jason, Emma, Grant and Elizabeth — born by Caesarean section. Their combined mass was 11,04 kg, and all were perfectly formed.

Colin Rosenkowitz, a 39-year-old salesman and newly dubbed 'Superdad' was grinning with relief: 'Words cannot express how I feel about this miracle which has happened to us.' No other hospital in the world could have done better, he said.

The public went wild. The family was showered with gifts and invitations — and contracts. Pressmen struggled to circumvent a deal between the father and a South African magazine publishing company, a deal which gave it the exclusive story on the world's only living sextuplets. Newspaper appeals for information were met with a bland 'no comment', and reporters debated wild schemes to smuggle themselves into the hospital wearing borrowed stethoscopes and white coats.

The sextuplets became six years old on 11 January 1980 — and by a curious quirk of fate a Florentine woman gave birth to sextuplets the very same day.

Educating our children

Education in South Africa was something of a haphazard affair before the Anglo-Boer War. The many thousands of children living in remote rural areas were often taught in makeshift schools and in some communities their teacher's sole qualification was the ability to read and write.

Many school-goers remember the disturbing and distinctly painful frequency of corporal punishment — still a feature today, of course, but now administered with a great deal more moderation. In his story, *Concertinas and Confetti*, Herman Charles Bosman wrote of a little whitewashed schoolroom and a certain bush which grew 'within convenient reach of the penknife of the Hollander schoolmaster, who went out and cut a number of thick but supple canes every morning just after the Bible lesson'.

A pupil who ultimately became a school inspector recalls his harassing introduction to a 'large' village school after an initial grounding by a governess in a five-pupil farm school: 'All the kindergarten pupils were seated on long benches of eight or ten seats each. One youngster next to me misbehaved himself. The bearded principal immediately grabbed him by the neck, flattened him over the edge of the bench, and gave him a good few lashes with a contraption consisting of a wooden handle and a broad thong attached to it.'

The Anglo-Boer War of 1899-1902 had a devastating effect on schooling in the Boer republics: for a time all schools were closed and education ceased. When it became apparent that the war would last more than a few months, the Boers themselves launched Christian National (C.N.O.) schools in the less troubled areas of the Transvaal with the help of funds from Holland. These were later to play a powerful part in the resistance to the colonial government's attempts to anglicise education after the war.

The British, intent on herding women and children from the Transvaal and Free State into concentration camps, at last awoke to the problem they had created — and to the opportunities it presented. Edmund Beale Sargant, appointed Acting Director of Education for

The class of '98. Pupils and their teachers pose outside Schietfontein farm school, near Pretoria. This photograph formed part of an exhibition which won 12 gold medals at the World Fair in Paris the following year

The interior of a unique school on wheels, built at Ermelo in 1932 to combat the shortage of classrooms

Getting to school sometimes posed problems. Above left: These children travelled to schools between Zeerust and Mafeking in 1914 with the help of slow-plodding oxen. Above right: 'Government donkeys' were supplied from 1909, bringing an improvement in school attendance in the Transvaal. Sometimes, however, the scheme went awry. School log books of the time reveal that 'Piet was late for school because the donkey could not be found', and 'John was absent because the donkey died'. Each animal was branded DOE to ensure that Education Department donkeys were easily identifiable. Some donkey transport schemes remained operative right up to the 1940s. Left: Children board a school bus — the first in the Transvaal and possibly the first in South Africa — in early 1927

'A Knotty Problem' in 1908. The class at a mission school, run by Trappist missionaries, look on intently

the two republics in November 1900, was inspired by the sight of Boer prisoners of war who had started their own school at the Green Point camp in Cape Town.

Noting their 'eagerness ... for instruction in the English language' in his 1901 Annual Report, Sargant perceived an opportunity for larger-scale anglicisation of the future Boer population, and camp schools were hastily established.

'An inch of twist tobacco'

School conditions in the poorer country areas remained harsh and primitive well into the twentieth century. In *Bushveld Doctor*, the poet and author C. Louis Leipoldt, who took up the post of Medical Inspector of Schools in the Transvaal in 1914, described the rudimentary bushveld schools he encountered.

Ragged children would trudge barefoot along rough tracks or spend as long as two hours getting there by donkey cart — often without having had any breakfast, and with only a crust to look forward to for lunch. Questioning one undernourished boy, Leipoldt discovered that 'When he left home in the morning his father gave him an inch of twist tobacco which he put into his mouth and chewed on his way to school ...'

The lack of facilities was also a problem. In 1905 there were 67 798 white pupils registered at Cape schools, but nearly the same number were still out of school.

'READING AND WRITING WERE ALSO INCLUDED'

The history of black education in South Africa is inseparably linked with that of the missionaries who penetrated the remotest regions in their evangelical and educational crusades. In 1917 Dr C.T. Loram wrote in *The Education of the South African Native:* ' ... it is due entirely to the efforts of the missionaries that the Natives of South Africa have received any education at all, and to this day all but three of the several thousand Native schools are conducted by missionary agencies.'

Only a few years had passed since the introduction of a new curriculum in the Transvaal

— a system based on the 'possibilities, needs and aspirations' of the black people.

The curriculum provided for moral and religious training, and aimed at the cultivation of habits of cleanliness, obedience, punctuality, tidiness, orderliness, honesty, self-dependence, self-restraint, temperance and charity. Such practical subjects as reading and writing were also included.

The Inter-departmental Committee on Native Education, appointed in July 1935, reported that the overwhelming majority of black schools were state-aided mission schools; about 35 per cent of the black teachers possessed no professional qualifications. The committee also found that the average school life of black pupils was less than three years and that over 70 per cent of blacks of school age were not at school. The problem remained for many years, and yet another factor was introduced in 1948 when the National Party came to power.

Separate education

The party's policy of apartheid, or separate development, was to make far-reaching changes in the patterns of South African education. In January 1949 the government appointed a commission on 'Native Education' under the chairmanship of Dr W.W.M. Eiselen. This report, which appeared in 1951, was one of the most important and controversial documents on education to appear in this country: two years later its recommendations were embodied in the Bantu Education Act, which was followed, in 1954, by the transfer of the control of black education from the provincial administrations to the central government Department of Native Affairs. In 1958 the Department of Bantu Education was created.

By 1974 there were some 3,5 million black children of schoolgoing age enrolled at South African schools (representing about 20 per cent of the total black population).

Tobacco and a tot of brandy

Pieter van der Stael, Jan van Riebeeck's brother-in-law, enticed pupils to his Dutch Reformed school for slaves in 1658 by offering each of them a small piece of tobacco and a tot of brandy daily.

From this humble beginning grew the country-wide system of schools for coloured people which, in 1969, had an enrolment of nearly half a million. Apartheid has affected coloured education since the late 1800s, and formal legislation was passed in 1911 to prohibit coloured children from attending white schools in the Cape — home of the majority of South Africa's coloured people.

WITS END

In June 1925 the citizens of Johannesburg were delighted (though some were shocked) by an elaborate hoax in which a local policeman impersonated the visiting Prince of Wales at an official ceremony.

It began when Saul (Pete) Suzman, vice-president of the Students' Representative Council at the University of the Witwatersrand, noticed a strong resemblance between the Prince — who was due to open the new Main Block and receive an honorary degree — and Constable Coetzer, a Johannesburg policeman. It was a perfect opportunity.

The students' plan received official approval, and they went ahead. The bogus Prince received the Royal salute and inspected cadets at the university with great solemnity before making a dignified ascent to his seat. The hoax was a resounding success (the authentic ceremonies passed off without incident!). Above left: The bogus Prince, accompanied by Professor O.G. Backeberg, inspects the guard of honour. Right: Two early *Wits' Wits* rag magazines. Artist Walter Battiss, then a student at Wits, designed the cover for the first issue in 1931.

House and Home

Eight decades ago, middle-class urban South Africans lived in suburbs that were a jumble of architectural styles and whims, most of them imported without regard for differences in climate or local needs. Regency elegance clashed with Victorian primness and verandahs abounded with wrought iron curlicues. Wealthy settlers arrived from Britain to build grand mansions better suited to the stockbroker belt of Surrey than to mountainous Cape Town, subtropical Durban or stony-ridged Johannesburg.

Architect Herbert Baker was one of the first to recognise the absurdities and actually do something about them. His designs before the First World War, still partly English but incorporating many traditional Cape features in acknowledgement of the bright, sunny climate, were to have a profound influence on local architecture.

With the 1930s came a startling new approach. Rex Martienssen led the movement that produced the first houses of the International Style: cubism was king and houses were blocky and strictly functional. Although the stark designs of 'modern' architecture were a little too radical for many, they helped to sweep away the cobwebs. Soon a distinctive South African home began to appear: long, low and large-windowed, with shady eaves and low-pitched roof.

The vast, double-storeyed Edwardian houses, outmoded and impractical to run without their teams of servants, suffered conversion — into boarding houses, hospitals, student hostels. The grounds of many were subdivided to accommodate a host of small, modern homes.

After the Second World War, the demands of returning veteran and immigrant settler transformed many gracious old suburbs into towering, impersonal flatlands.

South Africa has a rich and diverse architectural heritage, stretching back hundreds of years. The fight to preserve the best is continuing.

The front stoeps of early South African homes were idyllic havens shaded from the summer sun by vine-covered pergolas. But opinions and architectural styles changed, and stoeps were often abandoned as old-fashioned and impractical

Victorian hangover

THE TASSELS AND TINSELLED BOBBLES OF RESPECTABILITY

In 1900 the drawing-room of a middle-class South African home was invariably a dim, stuffy, crowded conglomeration of massive furniture, heavy curtains and endless bric-a-brac. The centrepiece was the hearth, with its cast iron fireplace glorified with decorative tiles and a gleaming brass fender. The whole was an ornate monument to respectability.

Everything in the room that could be was fringed, draped or upholstered. The wallpaper, embossed and often gilded or flocked, rejoiced in a patterned or flowered frieze. As if a plain surface were an affront, tables, chairs, piano and every other possible item of furniture were covered with plush. Buttons and tassels secured the swatched velvet on stiff, horsehair-stuffed chairs — impossible to clean and difficult to sit on in comfort. These were still further burdened by cushions tasselled in chenille, and by lovingly crocheted antimacassars.

Blinds wore fringes of tinselled bobbles (even the cords carried tassels), while the heavy, bordered curtains might be held aside by curtain-chains of brass. Brass was in fact a common feature of a 1900s room, providing the base for the oil lamp, hooks for blind cords, rings and solid rods for curtains, and picture hooks to support the heavy gilded frames of the day.

And if the home-owner didn't like too much brass, there were curtain rods faked to resemble bamboo and even tortoise-shell. Indeed, copies were so prevalent that as late as 1913 the author of *The South African Household Guide* deplored the continuing vogue for 'imitation everything from fruit and flowers to imitation marble on the papers, and imitation wood grain on the doors'.

The elegant and the massive

'Let all things be frankly what they *are*,' she pleaded, adding: 'A piano is a piano, so do not disguise it till it looks like a badly-draped, ill-assorted shop counter.' But in 1900 few would have appreciated her plea for greater simplicity.

The potted palm was an almost mandatory feature of the home in the early years of the century. This Johannesburg housewife went further, though, festooning her dining table with potted plants and flowers

It was a time when 'elegant' (meaning elaborate) and 'massive' were much-favoured words in the catalogues of furniture dealers. 'Elegant' came up most frequently in connection with the drawing-room, where a richly-carved suite in mahogany or walnut, upholstered in tapestry with plush borders, would cost about £28. The suite consisted of couch, two easy chairs, two occasional chairs and four small chairs (upright and armless). The same suite in inlaid rosewood and Genoa velvet rose to a princely 55 guineas.

'Massive' came into its own in the dining-room, where an enormous mahogany table 'with Massive Legs' (£11.15s. from Stuttafords, Cape Town) would be accompanied by a huge Renaissance-style carved sideboard (£6.15s.) crowded with the family silver; a three-shelved dinner wagon (£5) for the dishes; a walnut chiffonier (£6.15s.) and if possible not only the dining chairs but another suite of upholstered easy chairs which included a buttoned and uncomfortable-looking chaise-longue.

Hallways were no less crowded, with hallstand, hatrack, palmstand and umbrella stand,

The typical Victorian drawing-room. Above the fireplace hung an elaborate overmantel decked with shelves, mirrors, fluted pillars and as many ornaments as it could hold. The mantelpiece itself bore not only a handsome clock of marble, or of wood imitation-marble, but also velvet or plush 'mantel bordering' bought by the yard complete with bobbles, tassels or fringe. Left: the Oriental influence in a turn-of-the-century Durban home

This 'very massive, artistically carved' solid walnut sideboard cost an expensive £50

but in the privacy of the master bedroom nothing less than a 'Massive Black Brass Bedstead' (£4.7s.6d.) was needed to match the carved and bevelled acreage of the satin walnut wardrobe, sold in a suite (from £17 upwards) with a tiled washstand and a 'toilet table' (dressing table today), or the more solid 'dressing chest' topped with numerous mirrors. A floral china toilet set of basin, jug and soap-dish would grace the marble top of the washstand (bathrooms were still a rarity), while the swing mirror of the toilet table reflected an array of silver-mounted brushes, cut-glass, silver-topped scent-bottles, puff jars, powder pots, hair tidies and hat-pin stands; and a silver button-hook, 'shoe lift' and manicure set.

In 1904 Mr Caleb Keene opened a showroom in Lloyd's Buildings, Long Street, Cape Town, which reflected, according to the *South African Architect and Builder*, 'a growing taste for what has been described as the "Modern Individualistic and Historical" styles of furniture and general house decoration'. The display included 'relief decorations for walls and ceilings, specially designed and selected wall papers and friezes, furniture from the best house firms and of Mr Keene's manufacture at his own workshops, oak panelling, parquet flooring and Mosaic panelling for oriental decoration'. The showroom, said the journal, would be welcomed by architects who had been trying for a long time to introduce to South Africa 'something more of the artistic effects which are to be found in so many of the homes of England and the Continent'.

Lighter and brighter

Despite the Victorian hangover, which lasted in some homes until well into the 1920s, the changing styles of the Edwardian days did gradually catch on with the middle class South Afri-

South Africa's oldest city — Cape Town — was a gaslit city until the last decade of the 19th century. But in the outlying suburbs, like Claremont and Wynberg, there were no gas mains, which meant no gas lighting for the many houses there.

People simply went on using the oil lamp, as they did in the country, until electricity became generally available, which it did quite quickly in the early years of the 20th century.

Catalogues of the time reveal a vast choice of oil lamps (one Cape Town firm advertised 300 different designs in 1900): chain-hung, glass-shaded 'suspension' lamps; tall table lamps with a brass or china base; tiny night lamps; bracket lamps for the wall; and wrought iron

can. In *A Cape Childhood* Norah Henshilwood recalls that by the time she was seven, in 1910, 'heavy furniture and dark curtains had given place to something lighter, though the taste for knick-knacks had not disappeared entirely'. Her own mother's Claremont drawing-room, for all its congestion of chairs and ornaments, she nevertheless remembers chiefly as a sanctuary graced by fresh muslin curtains, delicate cream wallpaper and a constant profusion of fresh, scented flowers.

And the author of *Natal Homes — how to furnish them*, published in 1914, declared that 'much of the present-day drawing-room furniture is founded on light Sheraton, Hepplewhite or French models — light, graceful and beautiful in design'.

Certainly brown woodwork did give way slowly to white. Wallpaper, curtain and carpet colours lightened from crimson, maroon and olive to grey, rose, cream or blue. Mrs Yvonne Miller, describing her grandmother's Durban

'floor standard lamps of incredibly fussy appearance'. Fancy shades of ruched and flounced silk, lace and even crêpe paper — all looking highly unsuitable and inflammable — rivalled ladies' hats in their extravagance.

Gas lighting, when it was available, had one disadvantage: unlike the oil lamp, it couldn't be carried around. The new 'Surprise Pendant' of 1895 offered to meet 'a long-felt need', since it could be drawn down close to the table for reading or sewing without its brilliance hurting the eyes. Where electricity's smokeless light was available — and by 1900 wealthy citizens in Cape Town and Johannesburg had already begun to instal their own private plants — the Surprise Pendant could still fit the bill.

home, said: 'The downstairs rooms had wallpapers with small, neat patterns, but the upstairs rooms were revolutionary. They had colourwashed walls, then called "distempered", in pale green or blue.'

Plush tablecloths yielded to lace, velvet upholstery to chintz, and stiff-backed chairs to more comfortable wicker and cushions. In the bedroom, ash and fumed oak replaced walnut and mahogany with simpler lines, the heavy carving giving way to copper plaques worked with stylised tulips and lilies of Art Nouveau influence. A further innovation was 'French twin beds'.

The result was a lighter, brighter house gradually becoming easier to clean and simpler to furnish: a boon both to servants and housewife, and to young couples setting up home. Like Victorian clothing, the fads and furnishings of a Victorian home had for too long been highly unsuitable to the warm, sunny climate of colonial South Africa.

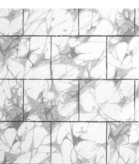

A selection of ornate Victorian wallpapers. But, said the South African Architect and Builder *in 1904, 'Nervous people should dispense with all decorations'*

Mansions of the magnates

TURRETS, CORNICES, CHANDELIERS — AND A MINSTREL'S GALLERY

Gold created South Africa's richest concentration of opulent homes: the mansions of youthful Johannesburg's premier suburb, Parktown.

Laid out in 1893 by the Braamfontein Estate Company on some bare and unproductive quartzite ridges, the new suburb at first attracted the big pre-Anglo-Boer War mining financiers. Lionel Phillips's Hohenheim was the first to command the skyline; Sir Llewellyn Andersson's Dolobran, Sir Thomas Cullinan's The View and R.W. Schumacher's Pallinghurst followed soon after, their imposing red-brick facades bulging with bow windows and crisply outlined by white wooden verandahs. Turrets, half-timbering and a forest of chimneys enhanced the stately air of wealth still projected by the few such houses that have escaped the demolition hammer.

The end of the Anglo-Boer War in 1902 brought a new rush: administrators, judges, lawyers, bankers and newspaper men, mostly British in background and taste, flocked to the Reef — and to Parktown. The spaces between the magnates' homes would have filled up with still more red-brick English-style houses had not Herbert Baker, a young and prominent architect, also arrived in Johannesburg in 1902.

British High Commissioner Lord Milner, anxious to prevent the threatened post-war sprawl of poor-quality housing, had requested Baker's move from Cape Town. Soon he was doing fine work on city buildings and housing estates — and was busy designing a village of homes for the very rich in Parktown, where his own Stone House, built in 1902, is now a

Sunnyside, built in 1896, on an eight-hectare site, was home to British High Commissioner Lord Milner after the Anglo-Boer War. In 1906, five years after this picture was taken, it was serving as a hostel for students of the University of the Witwatersrand. By 1930 it had become the Sunnyside Residential Hotel; in the early 1960s the building was leased by the Southern Suns group and now forms part of the Sunnyside Hotel

national monument. White-gabled Marienhof (1904), later renamed Brenthurst, today houses the Oppenheimer family. The Moot House (1904) was the scene of many historic meetings of Milner's 'Kindergarten'. Mining magnate Lionel Phillips commissioned the vast white Italianate Villa Arcadia (1909), an extravagance of arches, loggias, a beamed medieval hall hung with tapestries, and somewhat incongruous barley-twist chimneys.

Inside, Baker's grand houses were orna-mented with elaborate plasterwork and ceiling detail: moulded cornices, garlands, brass chandeliers. George Ness's delicate wrought iron work graced the Villa Arcadia staircase; Northwards boasted a minstrels' gallery; Jacobean timber and inglenooks gave sombre, antique elegance to many a room.

Where ladies lit the staircase

But it was not only Baker's houses that were filled with such a variety of features and fur-

Dolobran, built for Sir Llewellyn Andersson, son of explorer and ornithologist Charles Andersson. It remains the property of Andersson's descendants

The age of opulence: drawing room of Andersson's Dolobran, soon after the house was completed in 1905

Hohenheim, the home of Sir Lionel Phillips, a friend of Rhodes, mining baron and politician (he was sentenced to death for his involvement in the Jameson Raid; the sentence was commuted to a heavy fine). The house was occupied by fellow politician and author Sir Percy FitzPatrick in 1898. In due course it became the Otto Beit Convalescent Home and, in 1970, it was demolished to make way for the new Johannesburg Hospital

Northwards, pictured soon after it was built, in 1904, for J. Dale Lace. The house was bought by Sir George Albu, who had made a fortune on the Kimberley diamond fields. Northwards was demolished in 1972

Sir Lionel Phillips' first Parktown house, Arcadia. He replaced it in 1909 with Villa Arcadia — 'an extravangance of arches, loggias, beamed medieval hall, barley-twist chimneys'. It was built at a cost of £28 000

nishings. The prevailing style of the day in wealthy, upper-class homes tended heavily towards the ornate, the densely detailed and cluttered room.

John Wentzel, son of a Rand magistrate, was brought up in a large 16-roomed Parktown mansion, The Towers. Built in 1904 for a couple who immediately lost their fortune, The Towers had been designed by London architects who had never seen a South African *koppie*; they sent an exact copy of a red-brick Surrey stockbroker's house. It had been furnished from Maple's in London in solid rosewood and mahogany furniture, right down to the grand piano. Impressive panelling and carved overmantels vied with dark wallpaper and red plush curtains to dim every room. Two bronze ladies 'with small electric globes in their hair' were needed to light the enormous staircase.

It was, remembers Wentzel in *A View from the Ridge*, a 'solid rather than beautiful' house, but typical of its time and place. The most sumptuous rooms were on the ground floor: breakfast room, drawing-room, study and mahogany-panelled diningroom — plus a turreted conservatory of stained glass 'like a rather rakish bathing box'.

Upstairs were the family's bedrooms, the nursery and two bathrooms 'with ornate brass taps'. In the top storey under the roof lived the cook, nurse and two parlourmaids. Far below, the garden fell in terraces to tennis court and croquet lawn; behind the house the stableyard, converted to garaging, sported a white pigeon loft 'imported complete in a packing case from England'.

The Towers, with its effortless air of luxury, space and security, was typical of the kind of 'expatriate Englishman's' castle' that dotted the Empire during the years of Pax Britannica. It was demolished in 1968 — a fate shared by so

many of those grand edifices. In its later years it had served as a retreat for Dominican nuns.

Today Upper Parktown is 'a bankrupt principality . . . decayed, invaded and scarred', mourned only by those inhabitants who, like Arnold Benjamin, still remember its brief moment of glory. Benjamin, in his book *Parktown 1892-1972*, wrote: 'At Northwards the musicians' gallery is boarded off to make offices for school inspectors, Arcadia looks bedraggled, its gardens tangled and overgrown, North Lodge has lost its fairy tale spires. Most poignant of all is Hohenheim, Parktown's first house, untenanted now for several years as it waits for the hammers. Its rooms are thick with dust. The garden over which Lady Phillips took such pains has gone back to bush.'

THE DANDELION DAYS OF OUDTSHOORN

Among the most flamboyant of all Edwardian mansions in South Africa were the celebrated Ostrich Palaces of Oudtshoorn. Today, though the biggest have been turned into student hostels, they remain as imposing reminders of the sudden flood of wealth which startled Oudtshoorn from its slumbers in the late 19th century. Fed by fashion, the feather boom lasted until 1914. (In 1913 more than a million pounds weight of feathers, valued at £3 million, was exported from the area.)

Farmers who, almost overnight, became fabulously rich men of the world, built for themselves luxurious marble-floored farmhouses — or else moved into town and constructed mansions.

Gert Olivier, M.P. for Oudtshoorn and foremost ostrich farmer (so he claimed) in the world (at the height of the boom he owned no less than

5 000 birds) built The Towers in 1905 for his beautiful second wife Helena. She became the acknowledged leader of the town's often brilliant social life: banquets, balls, Gilbert and Sullivan operas, charades, 'At Homes', picnic trips to the Cango Caves (illuminated by magnesium flares) and, in later years, the never-to-be-forgotten visit of the Prince of Wales.

With its 20 lavishly-decorated rooms, The Towers was the show house of the town, featuring white-and-gold rose-festooned French wallpaper, cream ceilings studded with gilded *amorini*, and acres of costly teak panelling. Externally its extravagance included turrets, gables, a belfry and a great deal of cast iron trimming.

Pinehurst, built by E.T.L. Edmeades at a cost of £10 000, was another imposing 20-roomed pile raised in limestone from nearby quarries. A daughter-in-law remembers feeling 'like a queen' as she descended its sweeping staircase to the ball in progress below. Both Pinehurst and Olivier Towers became student hostels some time after the Second World War and today retain only their external splendour. Panelling still rises as high as two metres from the floors, but gone is the magnificence of French wallpaper, silk drapes and Persian carpeting, the imported tiles and the sunken marble baths.

Pinehurst was declared a national monument in 1963. Other fine examples of the ostrich-feather building boom can be seen all over Oudtshoorn and its surrounding districts, distinguished by fanciful turrets, thick teak doors with fanlights, and the icing-sugar glories of much intricate cast iron lace.

More than 600 guests attended the wedding of Olivier's eldest daughter Maggie in 1907. The picture was taken on the steps of The Towers; Olivier stands at left. The grounds, reported the magazine South Africa, *were 'bright with flags and bunting and with floral decorations, among which the arches of arum lilies were a striking feature. The Prototype Band played an excellent selection during the afternoon. . . The bridegroom's presents to the bridesmaids were gold bangles and to the flower girls pearl brooches and pearl pendants'*

Fads and fashions

THE SUBURBAN HOME, 1900-1930s ... RED-BRICK AND IMITATION

When famed travel writer H.V. Morton wrote *In Search of South Africa* in the 1940s, he remembered the suburbs of Johannesburg as 'covered with expensive houses, each one an example of Spanish Colonial, Cape Dutch, Tudor, or what Mr Osbert Lancaster has called "Brewers' Gothic" and "By-pass Variegated"' — thus pinpointing the largely imitative nature of early South African suburban architecture.

Allister Macmillan, in his book *Homes of the Golden City,* writes: 'A new class of wealthy industrialists arose who lacked the social and cultural background of the former wealthy classes and as a result were unable to exercise good judgement in architecture and the allied arts. Furniture, pictures and other works of art were purchased at home and abroad according to the tastes of the individual who demanded a suitable setting for them and we have the beginning of what has been termed "the battle for the styles".'

On the other hand the locals seemed quite happy with their suburban designs: a supplement to the *African Pictorial* in 1903 boasted of 'the picturesqueness' of Johannesburg's new residences, and added, sniping at Durban, that 'a walk round their lovely Berea fills the mind of the man of culture with dismay on beholding the deadly dullness and the monotony of the commonplace — aye, even vulgarity — in their [Durban's] bungalows and villas'.

Around the turn of the century the Cape alone was fortunate in having a long-established tradition of fine indigenous buildings — but even there, red brick and neo-Gothic were running riot in houses made up haphazardly from prefabricated ingredients: imported fanlights, mouldings, verandah columns and cast iron filigree.

But styles changed. In the first two decades of the 20th century popular taste was slowly swinging away from what were seen as fussy, overdecorated facades. Herbert Baker's influence

Herbert Baker adapted traditional Cape styles with imaginative effect; his imitators carried the ideas to almost comical extremes. Gables were stuck haphazardly onto suburban homes big and small

A large percentage of South African houses in the early years of the century were an extraordinary mix of borrowed styles. Left: Ionic columns and Chinese pagoda; right: unconvincing Tudor

was considerable, both for his insistence on the use of good local materials, and for his re-introduction of elements from the old Cape style: gables, white columns, shutters, slate or tile roofs. These he combined with traditional English features (beamed ceilings, inglenooks, high chimneys) and Mediterranean loggias and arches, to produce a mixed-origin but distinctive style.

Baker took his ideas to Johannesburg when he moved to the Transvaal in 1902. There, white plastered walls or local dressed stone gradually won the day against encroaching British red brick, a style which had achieved a true harmonious unity in only one South African town: Pietermaritzburg.

But the average South African style prevail-

NOTHING CHANGES

Getting a house designed and constructed seemed to have been as frustrating a business eight decades ago as it is today. The *African Pictorial* published this lament, entitled 'An Architectural Alphabet', in 1903:

A was for architect, old in his prime.
B was for builder, who took his own time.
C was a client who had his own views.
D were the details no one would use.
E the erection he tried to excuse.
G was the ground plan exceeding the site.
H the half timber he had to reveal.
I was the ironwork, hard to conceal.
J was the joinery, mostly of deal.
K was the kingpost that ought to have stood.
L the stone lintel that proved to be wood.
M the mullion that blocked the light.
N was the newel too thin for its height.
O the oak sill that was not water tight.
P was the price on the contract agreed.
Q were the quantities down to a bead.
R was the rage that the client displayed, and
S the sarcastic remarks that he made — when
T was the total that had to be paid.
U was the umpire called on to decide.
V was the value the client denied.
W stands for the words that he said.
X were the extras for which he was bled.
Y-Z the young zealot who wished he was dead.

ing in the 1920s was still an architectural patchwork: steep-pitched red-tiled roof with overhanging eaves; a central pillared porch; small teak casement windows; white walls. Inside, the house was dim, often with beamed ceilings and red-tiled fireplace. The whole echoed the traditional English home with a few South African features — the white walls, here a gable, there shutters — tacked on, probably as a concession to Herbert Baker's influence.

In 1930, when the *Outspan* ran its 'My Home' competition, arousing intense interest among its country-wide readers, a Sea Point home in Cape Town called La Roche was finally voted the winner. An odd amalgamation of Mediterranean and English features, the double-storeyed house was especially praised as being 'devoid . . . of artificiality'. It had obviously been chosen as a modern South African home of great desirability (its sale value was estimated at a high £2 900), yet it still sported all the old-fashioned elements so soon to be swept away by the revolution of the 'International Style'.

Spanish Mission and Mediterranean

A Natal architect could still say, in 1906, that 'The two great classes of style upon which we can draw our inspiration may be said to be Classic and Gothic. The Classic division has been taken as including Halian, Greek and what is known as Queen Anne or free Classic — and Gothic on the other hand may be taken as including pointed styles such as early English, Decorated, Perpendicular, Tudor, Elizabethan and Jacobean'.

But Natal's tropical climate was difficult to ignore for long, and by the 1920s there was great interest in Spanish and Italian architectural styles. Arthur McKinlay, another Natal architect, wrote in the *Outspan* in October 1927: '. . . I suggest that the sunny Mediterranean types are most suited to us here in Natal . . . The simplest forms are brought out in their full values by the wonderfully clear and vibrant atmosphere. The deep purple shadows induced by the vivid white sunshine make unnecessary any elaboration of wall surfaces.'

He cited the example set by California, where architects had been quick to adapt 'Spanish Mission' features for a similar climate, and pleaded that 'Spanish, Italian, Moorish, Byzantine and Indian should not be kept segregated'. It became a popular, recurring style in Natal

Winner of Outspan's 'My Home' competition. The Cape Town house belonged to architect Hubert Roberts

A 'Spanish Mission' house in Johannesburg features distinctive arched porch, curved tiles and grille-work

and elsewhere in South Africa. Typical features include curved roof tiles, paved patios, striped awnings, heavy teak doors and shutters, and bright tropical plants in pots, lending 'their quota to the riot of colour against the verdant green of the grass and the white tinted stucco'.

Pretty enough, though a pity that most of the features served only to decorate. The true Mediterranean house, with its thick walls, cool courtyard and flagstone floors — ideally suited to South Africa's climate — is still a rarity in this country.

EVERYTHING INCLUDING THE KITCHEN SINK: COMPLETE KITS FROM OVERSEAS

In the 1880s and 1890s an enormous volume of cast iron and other ready-made components were imported into South Africa. It was off-the-peg building carried to extremes.

Walter Macfarlane and Co of Glasgow, the biggest supplier, issued a 2 000-page catalogue offering designs for anything from entire edifices to city arcades (Johannesburg's came from Macfarlane's), bandstands, lamps, fencing, gates, skylights, panels, gratings, balconies, stairs, columns, lavatory ranges, baths and drinking fountains. In 1890 the company employed 1 200 skilled workmen, its foundry covered four hectares, and its products were swiftly and efficiently dispatched to the colonies from the company's own wharf.

The popularity of cast iron, prized today by collectors and home owners with a taste for Victoriana, began to decline after the turn of the century, although journals like *The South African Builder* were still carrying advertisements for cast iron items as late as 1930.

Intricate Victorian-style filigree cast iron fences and gates still lend charm to many South African homes in the older suburbs of South African cities

Towards a South African style

REX MARTIENSSEN AND THE MODERN MOVEMENT

In the 1920s South Africa stood on the threshold of Modern Architecture — a style which was to strip away all the superfluous decoration and re-assess the house as a 'living unit'. The leader and inspiration of the small group of pioneering architects who whole-heartedly adopted the new ideas was a young and brilliant man from Johannesburg: Rex Martienssen.

Born in Queenstown in 1904, Martienssen made an unimpressive start to his career by failing his first-year course at the University of the Witwatersrand. But he quickly rallied, and from then on there was no looking back. He received a Bachelor of Architecture degree in 1929, and straightaway left on his second overseas tour. His trips to Western Europe had a profound influence on his designs. His approach was, essentially, cubistic; the emphasis on maximum economy and efficiency. In 1932 he wrote: 'When a man confuses beauty with structure, when he is convinced that beauty and floridity are synonymous, then it is time he played with bricks and studied the cube.'

A plan for living

Martienssen and his two friends, Norman Hanson and Gordon McIntosh, introduced the first Modern houses to South Africa with designs based on function rather than appearance. The sensible starting point, they argued, was 'a plan for living' which would be based on cubism, yet retain a modern beauty. In 1931 Martienssen became joint editor of the *South African Architectural Record*, and the following year was appointed sole editor. It proved a golden opportunity to spread his ideas.

To some, the effect of flat roofs and long horizontal windows set flush into white walls came as a shock; others welcomed the bold experiment in light and shadow.

The interiors of these new houses carried innovation to further extremes: black ceilings, walls in lime-green, red or blue; flush doors and fireplace surrounds of sand-blasted glass. Furniture, light fittings and even door handles were specially designed and made locally for individual houses. Problems did arise, but these were due less to public disapproval of 'shoebox architecture' than to practical difficulties presented by the flat roofs, which were inclined to leak and to make the houses uncomfortably hot. The next generation of flat-roofed houses was built with parapets to conceal low-pitched roofs of ordinary galvanised iron: to purists like Martienssen this was sacrilege.

Martienssen's sudden death in 1942, at the early age of 37, was a blow to South African architecture. It ended one of the most exciting and fruitful careers in the history of the profession.

A revelation in the art of living

Norman Musgrave Eaton was born in Pretoria on 11 October 1902. He studied archi-

House Stern in its original form. Martienssen was an idealist who dreamed of a world where 'architecture is one with contemporary life', and his designs reflected his preoccupation with unrelieved functionalism. By the 1960s, House Stern, below right, and the other two prototypes, Hanson's House Harris and McIntosh's House Munro, all had pitched roofs — resembling peaked lids added to boxes. However sensible the change, the effect was to reduce the original distinctive, prophetic designs to the sadly commonplace

tecture at the University of the Witwatersrand, where he qualified in 1928, and won the Herbert Baker Scholarship with his design for a conference centre. The scholarship took him, in 1930, to the British School of Architecture in Rome. He was enchanted by the ancient city and declared himself 'fully and obsessively prepared to be influenced and inspired by the factual and creative impulses of a great occasion in architecture — the Roman occasion'. His work in Rome deeply affected his later work in South Africa. Eaton

Rex Martienssen, founder of the Modern school in South Africa. He was awarded a Master of Architecture degree in 1940 for a thesis on 'Constructivism', and became a Doctor of Literature the following year for a thesis on 'The Idea of Space in Greek Architecture'

By the early 1930s Martienssen and his two friends, Norman Hanson and Gordon McIntosh, were firm converts to the Modern school. Together they launched this magazine in 1933 and, although there was only one issue, it provoked a lot of comment

A thatched rondavel guest-house is linked to a servants' village at Eaton's House Greenwood. With its wall of local stone, it displays a kraal-like unity which has been compared, in its essence, to the ruins of Zimbabwe

Probably the most striking of all Norman Eaton's designs was his country-built House Greenwood (1950) near Pretoria, where glass, random stone and natural wood blend to create a timeless elegance. Right: architect Norman Eaton. Close friendships were rare for this brilliant man, and he never married

grew to love simple, basic earth materials such as bricks, marble, travertine, ceramic and terracotta.

In 1933 the young architect returned to South Africa and established a private practice in Pretoria.

His first commission was for a small double-storeyed house to be built on a sloping hillside in Brooklyn, Pretoria, for a Miss L. Boyes. The design he produced was thoroughly contemporary — seemingly a contradiction of his training and background. The house, com-

pleted in 1934, was a flat-roofed cubic affair, its angularity offset by two cylindrical forms: those of a stairwell to the east, and a curved end to the projecting verandah to the west. A critic wrote of his work many years later: 'It is apparent that Norman Eaton was able . . . to design solely in terms of good architecture, unfettered by the precepts of style and fashion. These early houses express an individual talent, in work that was contemporary and yet independent of fashion and prototypes.'

Each of the houses he designed in the 1940s and 1950s was the unique response to a particular site and need. Wide terraces, plant-filled verandahs, pleasing façades of brick or local stone, and a naturalness which scarcely disturbed the landscape — these were the hallmarks of an Eaton design.

THE IDEAL HOME

Two Ideal Home competitions — one in 1934 and the other three years later — introduced the public to modern architecture. The 1934 competition, organised by the *Rand Daily Mail*, was opened by the Governor-General, the Earl of Clarendon, and proved a phenomenal success. It was a huge exhibition, mounted in the Transport Hall at the Milner Park showgrounds, and the winning house — the result was kept secret until the opening — was actually built in the grounds. The winning entry was designed by a Liverpool-trained South African architect, Douglas Cowin.

His house was basically modern but not as stark as those of the Modern Movement. Cowin himself said of it: 'Huge sheets of glass are all very well in Germany, but they are not suitable for this country; the direct rays of the sun are too strong and the light is too intense.' It was, said the *South African Lady's Pictorial*, 'a conscious attempt to create a house suitable to the country and climate'.

The competition and the winning entry were widely covered in the press, and long queues formed outside Cowin's house every day. It was estimated that about 35 000 people saw it during the show, and it was not long before diluted versions of the design began to appear in the suburbs. Commented the *Star*: 'The winning design may be described as modern as opposed to the traditional style, but it is not alarmingly so.'

Three years later, the same newspaper said of the results in the Ideal Homes contest run by the Argus group: 'The South African house is slowly developing; a low, light, cool-looking building, with a dark, flat-pitched roof, large, unobstructed windows sheltered by the deep eaves, and an enclosed yard with the native rooms.'

Among the flood of designs submitted by South African architects were some 'Spanish mission' houses and a few nostalgic gabled cottages, but a significant proportion of homes were decidedly modern. Already the International Style of Martienssen and his group had made its impact.

Tremendous public interest was shown in Douglas Cowin's winning design in the Ideal Home competition in 1934. The outstanding features of the house were its flat roof and black bathroom

The Edwardian domestic

AND SO THE DAYS WENT BY...

Faced with her dust-trap of a drawing-room — all that fussy carving, velvet, bobbles and ornamentation — the ordinary white colonial housewife of 1900 might have banished its fashionable clutter sooner had she not been able to rely on the help of a servant.

The work of a 'general maid' in an Edwardian middle-class home added up to a stupefying list of tasks tackled room by room, on a rota. Once a week she moved the heavy drawing-room and diningroom furniture, scattered wet tea-leaves on carpets to minimise the dust raised by her stiff broom, cleaned hordes of ornaments, waxed floors, and, as Norah Henshilwood describes in *A Cape Childhood*, polished all the furniture with a 'sweet-smelling mixture of vinegar and oils'.

Fireplaces had to be cleaned out daily in winter, while all year round the brass of door-knobs, the glass of lamp-chimneys and the silver of cutlery needed constant attention to maintain a gleaming standard. Bedrooms with their washstands and chamber-pots were the cause of more 'work that was taken for granted'. But the kitchen demanded perhaps the greatest amount of drudgery: its board floor had to be scrubbed to whiteness, coal stove laboriously cleaned and blackleaded, and endless piles of pots, pans and plates washed.

Hildagonda Duckitt, in her 1902 *Diary of a Cape Housekeeper*, wrote that the ordinary suburban housewife in Cape Town could afford one servant only, and warned that 'the days have to be carefully mapped out to get all done'. She urged an early start — the maid cleaning the diningroom and preparing breakfast while the people of the household took their morning baths.

'Then we have prayers and breakfast,' she went on. Next, while the maid washed up, the mistress dealt with calls from the butcher and various hawkers, and 'then the ferns are watered and flower-stands attended to in summer'. Miss Duckitt added that 'hosing the flower-beds takes quite an hour'. Meanwhile the maid 'did' the bedrooms, and the mistress retired indoors

The Rees family of East London with their servants in the garden of Park House in 1898. The household staff comprised a cook, housemaid, parlourmaid, chauffeur, gardener and his assistant

to tackle a little home dressmaking or preserving — 'and so the days go by'.

Luckily for most Cape housewives and their maids in the early 1900s, laundry was traditionally taken away by Malay washerwomen, who drove picturesque open Cape carts piled high with baskets of snowy fabrics. Other South African households weren't so lucky. Few tasks were as well documented as the dreaded washing: not only of clothes and the many layers of Edwardian underwear, but of all the bed and table linen, tray cloths, lace mats and those fine lace or muslin curtains. These, A.R. Barnes's *Household Guide* cautioned, needed to be folded into three and tacked with thread, soaked overnight, boiled in hot soap-suds, rinsed in cold water and lastly in 'slightly blued water'. Then they were

dipped into hot starch, wrung, pulled back into shape, pinned to a clean sheet and hung on the line. Finally, as if all this was not enough, the *Guide* insisted: 'Muslin curtains should always be ironed . . .' No mean task when the heavy flat-irons had to be heated in droves on the stove and wiped before use in case blacklead or soot stuck to them, in which case the whole routine might have to be repeated.

There were domestic washing machines of a kind, but they made little difference to an arduous task. They still called for manual effort to turn or pump the handle, and the *Guide* advised that 'an assistant to rinse, blue and hang up the clothes' would speed up the operation. Wringing was also a manual business, while table-top mangles (intended for pressing clothes and linen when dry — in short, early ironing machines) required skilled handling and physical effort to do the job well.

In rural areas the business of washing often went on in the age-old way — beside the river, with boulders for rubbing-boards. Plentiful sunshine ensured well-bleached linen without the need to boil it in coppers ('the English method'). But readers of the *Guide* were cautioned: 'If living in the country, and your clothes are spread upon bushes, take care the bucks, kids or ostriches do not tear or devour them.'

The servant problem

'Servants are not plentiful or good,' Hildagonda Duckitt warned her readers. Speaking of the Cape, where Malay and coloured people, rather than blacks, made up the bulk of the working population, she advised anyone with patience to hire a young white or coloured girl from a 'nice home' and train her.

Wages should, she indicated, start at £1 a month for the first half year, rising afterwards to the usual £1.10s. or £1.15s. Upper limit for a

Left: a young South African servant in 1884, the time when the 'kitchen boy's' uniform made its appearance

Cleaning the coal stove, right, was one of the most hated and time-consuming jobs. After being thoroughly scrubbed, it was coated with blacklead, which had been dissolved in water, and 'vigorously polished to a good shining black'

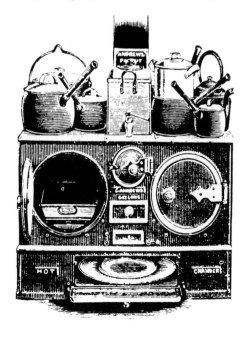

general servant in Cape Town appears to have been £2 monthly. In Natal, Transvaal and the 'Orange River Colony', households commonly employed 'native "boys" and coolies', the latter indentured for five years from India. By the law of supply and demand, wages in towns, and especially in the new city of Johannesburg, were higher than farm wages, which averaged only 10/- a month, though mealie-meal rations were an extra.

In Johannesburg the 'boys' who filled the posts of cook, house servant and gardener, wore 'cotton tunics and trousers ending just below the knee, white or blue and edged with red braid'.

Bringing help from 'Home'

However good or bad the local help, though, it was seldom considered enough. As Miss Duckitt told new colonists: 'Where there are children, bring an English nurse with you!' It was common practice for middle-class families in South African towns to import their nurses, or nannies, from Britain. The wealthier homes also imported lady's maids, parlourmaids, butlers, head gardeners, coachmen and, later, even their chauffeurs from 'Home'.

Jan Juta writes in *Background in Sunshine* of those 'stiff superior white nurses' from England, who, like his mother's personal lady's maid, came to South Africa on a three-year contract and were invariably 'condescending, even rude to the other domestics'.

The Jutas were a prominent and wealthy Cape family (Sir Henry at one time served as Attorney-General of the Colony). Their large, luxurious home, Mon Desir, had a special servants' wing to house their many domestics —which, apart from the lady's maid, included a coachman called Taylor, a coloured cook and housemaid, a coloured butler called John, and a coloured gardener. The Basuto groom lived over the stables; Malay washerwomen took away the laundry; and once a year six women arrived to weed the spacious lawns.

That the imported servants were not without their problems is borne out by John Wentzel's slightly later but equally Edwardian-flavoured memory, in a *A View from the Ridge*, of white nan-

An Edwardian Middelburg family with their young servant in standard dress of cotton tunic and trousers

A governess, probably brought out from England, attends to her charge. In 1903 the Daily Telegraph, *in an article about domestic vacancies in the Cape Colony, advised applicants to 'produce a medical certificate of sound health and physique, undeniable references as to honesty, sobriety, and character generally'. For some curious reason the would-be South African employer had to recruit through the Ministry of Agriculture in Cape Town and 'at the same time pay £3, the Government undertaking the balance of the cost of passage'. The newspaper pointed out that a magistrate had the power to annul a contract if an employer was cruel or if the servant was incurably lazy*

nies from overseas. In their comfortable Johannesburg mansion 'French Nanny' was succeeded by 'a brassy redhead whom I remember well . . . She used to parade the nursery in cami-knickers and long well-boned stays up to her armpits while, like Alice in Wonderland, she sipped alternately from two bottles — the one in her right hand containing what I now realise was gin, and another in the left hand containing eau-de-cologne or some other breath camouflager'.

Parents seem to have been blissfully unaware of the strange habits and unfriendly aloofness of their English servants. What chiefly concerned them was the eagerness of the nanny or maid to return home to civilisation, despite what Jan Juta calls 'their much happier, freer position' in the colonies. An article in the January 1903 issue of *African Pictorial* throws a more impartial

light on the causes: 'Good servants, imported from England, can command high wages,' it ran, 'but, even in England, girls prefer factory life to service because of the freedom they have after the working hours.' When the same article deplored that 'the old prejudice that a servant should work from 6 a.m. to 9 p.m. still exists', it is easy to see why working girls were beginning to shun domestic service. Nor did anyone mention the simple homesickness which surely lay behind many an English maid's longing to go home.

Certainly they would never have felt themselves to be 'part of the family', tucked away as they so often were in spartan attic or outer rooms, and while on duty compelled to wear the uniform of their trade: black dress, starched white muslin apron and lace cap with long muslin streamers.

MAKING A CLEAN SWEEP OF THINGS

Hearth Brush.   Dusting Brush.   Soft Sweeping Broom.   W.C. Brush.

Saucepan Brush.   Scrubbing Brush.   Floor Polisher   Hard Sweeping Broom.   Yard Broom.   Hard Sweeping Brush.   Shoe Brush.

Housecraft: Principles and Practice described the types and uses of household brushes in the early days. Servants worked hard. A recommended timetable for a housemaid: '6.30 a.m.: Rise. 7.0-8.0: Call family, collect shoes for cleaning. Pull up blinds and ventilate house. Attend to stove in kitchen, fill kettle with fresh drinking water (after allowing water to run a few minutes), and put it on stove to begin heating. If necessary, attend to sitting-room grate, lay fire, and fill coal box. Sweep step, cleaning it if necessary. Do daily work in dining-room, and lay breakfast table. Prepare and cook breakfast. 8.0: Serve breakfast. Have own meal; and when finished clean shoes. 8.40: Empty slops, and make beds, which have been left airing by the respective members of the family. Do daily work in bedrooms, bathroom, lavatory, landing, stairs, and hall. Prepare

vegetables for dinner, and get ready any pans that may be required for cooking that meal. 10.0: Do special work for the day, during which dinner must receive attention from time to time if the mistress is not in the kitchen. At 10.30 a pause of ten minutes for a cup of cocoa. 12.30: Lay the table for dinner, and dish up. 1.0: Serve dinner; have own meal. 1.45: Clear dinner table. Wash up dinner things. Fetch fuel sufficient to stoke boiler for the evening and next morning: and get ready paper and wood for laying sitting-room fire next day. Do daily work in kitchen, and leave service wagon prepared for tea. Lay dining-room table for supper; fill kettle for tea, and put to begin heating on boiler. 3.15: Change dress. 4.15: Serve tea.' Evening chores included the preparation of bedrooms, cooking and serving dinner, and washing dishes.

Six decades of furniture

JAMES, ANNE AND VICTORIA: A PROFUSION OF FAKES

Imported oak, mahogany and walnut graced most South African rooms in the Edwardian era, but these distinctive, if cumbersome, suites were to give way to 'colonial made' furniture after the First World War. This uncertain style was castigated in *Outspan* in 1929 by a writer who exclaimed: 'Everything must have spiral twisting, cabriole legs, claw and ball feet, linenfold fronts and a profusion of inlaying and carving . . . I have seen sets of chairs in stinkwood with Jacobean backs, early Victorian skirts and seats, and Queen Anne legs. Everything was wrong with them, yet they sold like the proverbial hot cakes.'

This incongruous mixture complemented the architecture of the time: a watered-down English look complete with 'fake antique' interiors. Antique oak was one of the most popular woods, either in the two-tone shading of 'rubbed oak' or so darkly stained as to be practically black — except, that is, in the bedroom, where there was a vogue for painting furniture white and, sometimes, even a daring silver-grey.

Beige or 'fawn' was the rage for walls, carpets and upholstery, with notes of orange and royal blue added by cushions and rugs. Desert scenes framed in dark oak hung from the picture rails, companions to another Arabic item: the almost indispensable brass Moorish tray on its folding stand.

The open-plan Thirties

In the 1930s a boom in flats and small, economical houses brought a need for 'easy living' and 'labour saving' furniture. Two features of the trend were open-plan living and built-in furniture. *Home Talk* was a magazine which gave its readers a taste of the latest in home decoration, promoting simpler lines for furniture and emphasising space-saving and storage. Built-in cupboards, breakfast nooks and wall seats were among its useful new ideas, along with dining recesses in the living room and that American invention, the built-in cocktail cabinet.

Home Talk's ideal kitchen contained wood-

The 1920s' claw-and-ball furniture was much more ornate in South Africa than in England. The local design was usually a heavily-carved chunk of wood with many ledges and corners which were difficult to keep clean. One of the more popular pieces of furniture on the South African market was this claw-and-ball 'displaygram', a radiogram disguised as a sideboard with the radio hidden behind the louvred doors. A visiting British manufacturer noted, with admirable restraint, that 'the South African market is more prone to these temptations than we are at home . . . We doubt if the British housewife would look forward to dusting all those ledges'

work 'enamelled pale green', but in the living-room beige and off-white were favourite background colours, here and there outlined in crispest black. Curtains, mirrors and light shades reflected the influence of Art Deco's geometric designs: zig-zags, steps, segmented fans and that popular motif — the rising sun. In fact, South Africa so loved this symbol that it also appeared on innumerable wrought iron gates — a distinctively South African sight.

But during the Thirties clean modern lines were the exception rather than the rule in this land of varying tastes. A rash of enormous Chesterfield suites disfigured many a suburban lounge, their massively sprung chairs hideously upholstered in a combination of

tapestry and the new plastic material called Rexine. Plastic-padded wardrobes and bedheads extended the theme to the bedroom — though sometimes the alternative here was woodwork with a veneer of the highest possible sheen. Shiny too were the teak 'Step Arms' and 'Wide Slope Arms' of the heavy lounge suites produced by Frye's in Port Elizabeth and designed with the smoker and his ashtray in mind.

Claw-and-ball

'Good' furniture remained in the claw-and-ball rut berated in *Outspan* as early as 1929. Stinkwood was too rare and expensive; it was the light-and-dark markings of imbuia which,

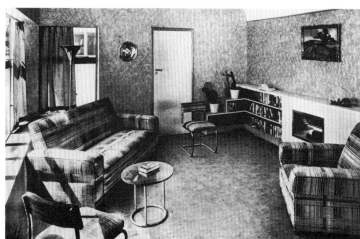

Mrs Roberts' home, left, prizewinner of the 'My Home' competition, 1930, contrasts with the winning interior, right, in the Ideal Home competition, 1934

in the 1940s, emerged in the form of stiff, cane-backed claw-and-ball settees, vast gleaming linen-fold kists and barley-twist lamp stands.

A German immigrant who arrived in South Africa in the late 1940s remembers searching without success for an alternative to these solid but unattractive imbuia styles. She saw them as monstrous — especially the elaborate glass-fronted display cabinets. But they were items that had long been held dear in South Africa, persisting until well into the 1950s, when quality modern pieces of Scandinavian design finally became available in this country. Their laminated curves, slender legs and pale wood tones have since become as familiar as imbuia once was, opening the way for the trend, in the 1960s, toward the lighter 'natural wood' look in floors and furniture: cottage pine, stripped oak and an upsurge of interest in old Cape yellowwood, favoured for its rich and mellow tones.

In recent years movable wall units, room dividers and interchangeable modular lounge chairs have become as common in South African homes as once were the *wakis* and the *kartel* in the trekker's wagon, indicating, perhaps, how modern families must often transfer from one town to another.

John Tabraham's furniture was typical of the clean and uncluttered shapes that emerged in the 1960s — a decade when young designers drew inspiration from Scandinavian countries. A distinct South African style began to appear in the country areas, too, where the slender Swedish fashions clashed with old homesteads. A solid, simple design was developed with the use of timber such as kiaat and saddle leather for seats

SETTING UP A TWENTIES' HOME — FOR £200

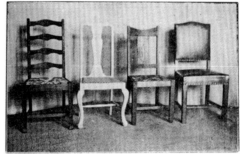

The cost of a home and its furniture was as pressing a problem to newlyweds in the 1920s as it is now. But an *Outspan* in 1927 provided some hope when it explored the possibility of 'Marriage on £200', recommending a low £8 for the honeymoon (in a farmhouse, for economy); £50 for the deposit on a four-roomed house ('Do not be *too* ambitious and want a mansion'); and just over £95 for furnishing the four rooms and kitchen. This included a rather sparse and curtainless £8 lounge containing two chairs (£5), and a mat (12/6) and sundry brass ornaments and pictures; a £39 diningroom more opulently furnished with table and chairs (£10), as well as a 'Chesterfield and club easies' (£16); a £23 best bedroom; £19 for the kitchen, and a somewhat mean £6 guest room. Left over was £47, optimistically earmarked by Mrs Beggs, the author, 'for a rainy day'. But readers wrote in, hotly challenging her figures. Some insisted it could be done for even less: 'X' of Brackpan started his home with only the 'bare necessities' — they cost £56.14s. and excluded the comfort of carpeting (except for linoleum in one room). Another insisted on a figure of £350 as more realistic — she was horrified by Mrs Beggs' spartan spare bedroom.

20s' furniture. Clockwise from above: diningroom chairs ranging from £2.19s.6d. to £5.10s.; luxury settee costing £28.10s.; dining table £14.10s.; teak sideboard £18.10s.; table £8.15s.; occasional chair £5.17s.6d. and, below left easy chair £16.10s.

From icebox to fridge

THE ALL-ELECTRIC HOME COMES TO SOUTH AFRICA

It was only in the 1920s that what *Outspan* termed 'The Electrical Home' became a genuine possibility for the ordinary white South African housewife. Electricity had long been the preserve of the mansioned rich, who were able to afford their own generators, and when it finally became available to the average suburban homeowner soon after the turn of the century, it was used almost exclusively for lighting. By the 1920s electric lighting was the general rule in South African city houses.

Then, in an effort to entrench the all-electric home, Cape Town launched an ambitious 'Cook by Wire' campaign: cheaper rates for cooking and heating were coupled with showrooms selling and demonstrating the swift, clean wizardry of electricity in everything from stoves, toasters, kettles and irons to waffle-makers and heated shaving mugs.

Public response varied. *Outspan* published its readers' views on 'whether modern inventions were likely to replace "Jim" and "Maria" in their homes'. A Dundee, Natal, housewife opted unhesitatingly for the help of servants, explaining: 'No electrical appliance has yet been perfected that will "mind the baby", nor is there anything that will automatically reproduce the complete effect of shouting for Jim to "enza tea".' But according to an advertisement in the *South African Lady's Pictorial*, 'Electricity is the ideal servant.'

A Durban woman was ecstatic about her experience of electricity. Beginning with iron and kettle, she soon bought a small stove and found that 'My most expensive month for current was July of this year, £1.15s.' (Visitors and marmalade-making accounted, she said, for this unusual expense.) The same housewife looked forward to buying that modern miracle, a vacuum cleaner, among whose attachments she was confident of finding 'one

The first primitive vacuum cleaners were made in the late 1850s. Many of the early cleaners had bellows which were worked by hand, but in about 1908 the first electric model appeared in America. The cleaners had obvious advantages in homes made dusty by coal fires and furnished with heavy, dust-gathering curtains, chairs and carpets. A typical bellows-type machine illustrated here in the book Housecraft: Principles and Practice

An early General Electric advertisement in Good Housekeeping *advocated an all-electric kitchen. By 1936 many homes featured electric stoves, toasters, kettles and irons*

which will clean the windows at one operation'. Not content with this Utopian dream, she also envisaged 'some miraculous implement which will wash the dishes and place them on a rack which will dry them'.

But most South African housewives were simply unable to afford the freedom promised by these enticing magazine advertisements. A 1927 article in *Outspan* drew attention to the major drawback of electrical appliances: their high initial cost. Running expenses certainly did offset the disadvantage — they were calculated at £21 a year (for electric current and a charlady) as against £75 for the 'old methods' (coal stove plus fulltime servant and her food). But initial outlay was the problem:

Old Methods

Coal stove	£15. 0. 0.
Pots and pans	£ 2.10. 0.
	£17.10. 0.

Kinnes's patent automatic ant-proof cooling safe was advertised in 1917. It would keep meat fresh and milk cool, claimed the manufacturer, and 'The Hotter the Day the Greater the Difference'

Electrical Methods

Electric range, including pots and pans	£25. 0. 0.
Kettle	£ 2.10. 0.
Iron	£ 1. 5. 0.
Radiator	£ 2.10. 0.
Toaster	£ 1.15. 0.
Vacuum cleaner	£15. 0. 0.
	£48. 0. 0.

However, a number of municipalities (Cape Town, Ermelo, Vereeniging, Pretoria, Johannesburg) were eager to promote the extensive use of electrical appliances in order to make full use of the electrical plants they had established.

Dutch oven to Defy

Although most white South African housewives were aware of the advantages of electric stoves by the start of the Second World War, many were obliged to cook on old-fashioned, smelly 'monsters' because they simply couldn't afford the more sophisticated models. Their stoves — while not as primitive as the outside Dutch oven that farmers' wives still used for baking — were either the wood-burning 'Dover', the coal-fed 'Aga' (which in 1940 consumed 7/6 worth of anthracite monthly) or the oil-burning 'Perfection'.

When she could afford one of the new electric stoves, either imported (from Britain and America) or, from 1932, made locally by Defy (then the Durban Falkirk Iron Co) she was often nostalgically regretful at losing an old friend. In *Rondebosch and Roundabout*, Adèle Naudé mourns the good old days of her mother's huge coal-burning stove, polished with Zebra blacking compound and Brasso for the handles: 'All she did was to hold her hand in the oven to gauge the heat, testing her cakes afterwards with a long hat pin if she could not trust her practised eye.'

The nostalgia extended to other old-fashioned methods and gadgets. Katherine Heywood, in *Cape Hills in Sunlight*, records the arrival of electric power on the family's Cape fruit farm in 1935. Immediately they bought refrigerator, an iron and kettle, a 'Columbus polisher and Canadian wash-machine', and 'We seemed suddenly to become too civilised after living the simple life of pioneers. Goodbye to our oil lamps and candles, our black smoothing irons, our home-made sacking cooler dripping outside the kitchen door, our black iron kettle steaming away on the Dover wood stove!'

In the early days it wasn't only the farmers who managed to contrive primitive meat-safes and butter-coolers. In Cape Town in the early 1900s Norah Henshilwood's family relied on a home-made 'larder' of wood and wire standing on legs in the coolest part of the garden. 'Because of the uncertainty of keeping food fresh, one had to shop every day,' she recalls in *A Cape Childhood*.

The *South African Domestic Monthly*, in 1910, gave instructions for the care of the hanging meat-safe: 'It must be emptied and wiped out with a clean wet cloth twice a week at least in summer . . . As soon as the butcher delivers the meat, examine it, and remove any flaw,

KEEPING IT FRESH

Housewives developed methods of storing perishable foods before the advent of refrigerators. A book entitled *Housecraft: Principles and Practice* offered this advice in 1929:

THE LARDER. The larder is a place for storing perishable articles of food, and should therefore be as cool as possible in order to retard the growth of moulds.

MEAT. Uncooked meat is best hung up . . . in the meat safe, which should be well ventilated, but impervious to flies, a hook is usually found in the roof for this purpose.

FISH. This can be kept on slate or marble, and in very hot weather in a butter-cooler, which may be bought for a few shillings.

MILK. This keeps best if placed in shallow vessels which are scalded daily, kept covered with muslin and stored in the coolest part of the larder.

CHEESE. To prevent hardening, cheese should be kept wrapped in grease-proof paper, and placed in a cheese dish with a ventilated cover.

The contents of the larder should be inspected daily.

Every week all the food should be removed and placed on fresh plates, after which 'all dust should be removed from walls, shelves and floor, and any stone or wooden parts washed and scrubbed thoroughly'.

Above: The meat-safe was usually kept in the coolest part of the garden. Right: a 1927 Outspan advertisement showing the 'Mod-N-Ice' which only cost a penny a day to run. This model, claimed the manufacturers, could produce up to 75 lb of ice in 24 hours. Far right: Thos. Barlow & Sons showed the housewife how electric appliances could make her work much easier

and immediately hang it in the safe . . . Do not admit any flies.'

Mrs Yvonne Miller describes the domestic arrangements in her grandmother's house in about 1909: 'When we first lived in the house we had no refrigeration of any sort; food was kept in a meat-safe in the pantry. Milk had to be boiled as soon as it was delivered (twice a day). Meat was delivered daily, everyone had a butcher's book in which the order for the next day was written down and handed back to the butcher's boy. The Sunday joint was cooked as soon as it came on Saturday, put in the safe and heated up on the next day. Jellies were impossible except in cold weather.'

Slightly more sophisticated than the meat-safes were the domestic ice chests made of oak and lined with zinc. The ice was delivered by an ice man complete with awesome grappling hook (he was still delivering as late as 1937), and the large blocks lasted for up to a week.

By the late 1920s, electric fridges were becoming increasingly common, backed by claims that 'proper refrigeration means proper health', 'costs a penny a day to run', and 'keep all your perishable foods perfectly fresh and wholesome every day, and for days and weeks on end if necessary'.

In hot South Africa a luxury like ice cream presented a few problems without a refrigerator. John Wentzel paints a vivid picture in *A View from the Ridge* of preparations for his sister's twenty-first birthday party in Johannesburg, involving 'a mountain of ice' and borrowed ice cream machines: ' . . . Cyril and I did our bit by turning the handles on the machines . . . which had to be filled with finely chopped ice. It was team-work and whilst we turned the handles Aunt Alice, sitting stiff-legged on the ground, attacked each ice-block with a chopper, like an alpine climber making free with his alpenstock.'

A far more powerful lure than the refrigerator was that of the labour-saving electric washing machine. But even here prices were a serious obstacle, and South African housewives and their servants generally remained slaves to the washboard and the mangle until well after the Second World War. The electric washing machines they were able to buy at the time still had mangles on top: washed clothes were fed through these into the bath for final rinsing and a second round of wringing.

Twin-tub machines, where one tub washes and the other rinses and spins dry, were a relatively recent 1950s luxury, but it wasn't until the fully automatic, programmed washing machine came into widespread use in the 1960s that the South African housewife, or her domestic servant if she had one, was finally freed from the enormous burden of blue Mondays.

One of the earlier electric refrigerators, manufactured in 1932 by BTH, with cooling unit on top

Electric stove dating from the early 1930s

1937 Hotpoint electric washing-machine, with mangle

An insulated icebox from the turn of the century

Housing the increasing thousands

HOMES FOR THE HEROES

The Johannesburg *Star* announced the news with some satisfaction: 'Homes for Ex-Volunteers On Very Easy Terms. Strong Recommendation By National Conference.' South African servicemen were returning to their homeland in their thousands at the end of the Second World War, and they had nowhere to live. So much money and manpower had been invested in the war effort that very few homes were built between 1939 and 1945 — and there had been a serious housing problem even before the war.

Ex-servicemen's associations, municipalities and other organisations launched themselves into the housing effort with enthusiasm, and a Transvaal newspaper reported at the end of 1945: 'The Accommodation Section of the Johannesburg Discharged Soldiers' Demobilisation Committee has been in a state of siege for ten days. Unable to cope with the demand for houses and flats, and hopelessly behindhand with the work involved in the 2 408 applications already received, the overworked officials have been compelled to put up "temporarily closed" notices.'

In search of a roof

Thousands of returned soldiers walked the streets in search of temporary accommodation for themselves and their families. Householders were urged to take them in and not to think it beneath their dignity to receive payment for board and lodging. *Outspan* observed

In early 1946 the first batch of ex-servicemen and their families moved into the 'African Star' flat complex in West Turffontein, Johannesburg. The Johannesburg Ex-Servicemen's League built eight blocks of flats, a communal laundry, children's playground, servants' quarters and garages — all within a year. Mr J.J. Wedderburn, left, explains the plans of the project to Major-General Evered Poole, Commanding Officer of the Sixth S.A. Armoured Division, and Mrs Poole during their visit to the site in 1945

in January 1946: 'One reads of homeless soldiers seizing empty houses in Johannesburg and elsewhere and of two and even three families sharing one house, with the parents sleeping in bathrooms, corridors and on open verandahs, and of families living in different parts of the same town or even in different towns . . .'

The Van Eck Committee on Housing estimated in 1946 that the Union's requirements in the next ten years would be 440 000 houses — about 180 000 of these for whites and the rest for blacks. It was a massive challenge. The National Housing and Planning Commission launched a building programme aimed at producing 6 000 houses in the first year, and

SANDRINGHAM: CIVVY-STREET COMFORT

A model township was constructed in Johannesburg at the end of the Second World War in a highly successful effort to house some of the returning veterans. The scheme, sponsored by the S.A. Legion of the British Empire Service League (B.E.S.L.), was launched with the co-operation of sympathetic architects, surveyors, builders and finance houses, and the first batch of 51 houses was allocated by ballot at the end of 1945. The new suburb was named Sandringham.

On his first day back in Civvy Street, reported *Outspan*, Mr Basil Benjamin, a former shuttle-service pilot, drew the first house. It was the first thing he had ever won in a draw, he said afterwards, and it was the prize he wanted most. Announcing the start of work on a further 114 houses, the magazine commented: 'This, of course, will not solve the city's housing problem, but it will be a substantial contribution towards it . . .'

Houses sold for between £2 250 and £2 750, including the ground, and loans were repayable at moderate rates over 30 years. To prevent speculation, buyers were precluded from selling within a certain period — except back to the company at cost. All the financial risk was taken by public-spirited Johannesburg citizens, most of them veterans of the First World War. There were no profits.

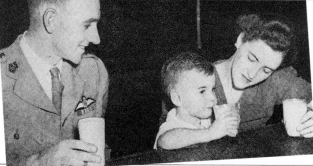

Left: Mr Basil Benjamin and his family were the first of 51 families to draw houses in the ballot for homes at Sandringham. A building society agreed to advance money to the ex-servicemen at a reduced rate of interest.
Above: One of the twenty different designs provided by the Transvaal Institute of Architects for Sandringham

In 1939 the Johannesburg City Council decided that all houses for blacks would in future be built on a pattern designed to meet the needs of a family. It specified a separate kitchen and a bathroom in the houses. Overwhelming demand soon forced a reversion to austere economy of design. Pictured is a double unit in Pimville

appointed officials to keep careful control of standards and building materials. The Commission also lent money to municipalities in an effort to broaden the campaign.

Empty houses were commandeered, buildings used by wartime personnel were subdivided and converted . . . and the waiting list kept growing. An independent investigator into the Rand's housing problem wrote in 1947: 'Despondency is registered daily on the faces of the long queue of homeless people who besiege the offices of the Johannesburg Letting Controller. Husbands and wives with families literally beg officials to help them to find a home . . .'

But the Government was determined to solve the problem. The *Cape Times* announced in February the same year that 22 583 dwellings had been constructed by the Government or Government-sponsored agencies in the 28 months that the National Housing and Planning Commission had been in existence. Two months later it reported that the housing allocation had been increased from £22,5 million to £29 million. Meanwhile building costs had been rocketing. W.A. Yeld, an official with the Commission, told the *Cape Argus* in 1949 that 3 788 subsidised dwellings could be built for £1 million before the war. In 1949 the same sum would cover only 949 subsidised units. The road to recovery was to be long and hard: the problem of accommodating war veterans was massively compounded by the post-war influx of immigrants. In 1947 the country had a net gain of 21 000 whites, the following year a gain of 28 000.

A SPRAWLING METROPOLIS OF MANY CONTRASTS

Soweto. To many the name represents merely a large black township 'somewhere near Johannesburg'. In reality it is a huge city — home, at the end of the 1970s, to an official population of one million (unofficial estimates put this figure much higher). A few are rich, and many live comfortably, but most are very poor.

When Soweto (South-Western Townships) came into being soon after the Second World War, it was regarded as a great slum clearance scheme. Township development had stopped when war broke out. The post-war era was one of rapid industrialisation. Johannesburg became the economic hub of South Africa, attracting hundreds of thousands of blacks from the rural areas — and the city's meagre housing resources simply could not cope. Eleven squatter camps mushroomed in the veld: 'Hovels pieced together with scraps of rusty corrugated iron, lengths of hessian, bran and coal bags, boxwood, cardboard and odds and ends for blocking up gaps in walls and roofs. Shin-deep mud in the rainy months and in winter incessant screens of blinding dust. Bugs, disease, gangsters . . . ' Peter Becker's description of life in the camps in his book, *Tribe to Township*, did not exaggerate. Life in the crowded communities was harsh indeed.

Prefabricated houses, such as this one in Dobsonville, were once thought the answer to the housing problem

This imposing house belongs to a prominent Soweto personality, 'Uncle Dutch' (in front of house)

Luxury is often found side by side with poverty in Soweto as the growing black middle class sets down its roots

The first of these camps was established when war veteran James ('Sofasonke') Mpanze erected his own canvas shelter near Orlando. Others followed his example, and Tobruk — later known as Amasaka ('sack shelter') — was born. A storm destroyed the settlement, and in 1946 Moroka was laid out to take the homeless. It came none too soon: gangster bosses had been openly flouting the law, imposing levies on the population and handing out savage punishment for default in payment.

Oppenheimer steps in

The Johannesburg City Council began its work. Serviced sites were made available in 1953 and blacks were encouraged to erect temporary structures until finance could be raised for permanent housing.

Real help came in 1957 when Sir Ernest Oppenheimer, chairman of the giant Anglo-American Corporation, arranged a R6 million loan with the Chamber of Mines for black township development, repayable over 30 years. This was the injection of capital the city needed. In one year 11 074 homes were built, and hostels, schools and other facilities sprang up all over the township. The Government contributed R11 million. Soweto grew . . . and grew . . . and grew.

Although Soweto's outer boundary is 12 km from Johannesburg's city centre, the two complexes are today linked in a symbiotic relationship. Soweto is almost entirely dependent upon Johannesburg for its livelihood, and Johannesburg is equally dependent on Soweto for the manpower to keep its businesses and factories operating.

Witchdoctors and technology

The Soweto of the 1980s is a microcosm of black Africa. It houses the grand mansions of the wealthy and the soulless rows of brick and asbestos homes occupied by the rest. Its streets teem with pacifists and militants; witchdoctors, diviners and herbalists who practise their ancient skills in defiance of progress and ever-encroaching technology; manual labourers and bankers; shopkeepers and shebeen queens. In 1980 there was an average of ten people per house; rents ranged from R16 to R18 a month — but individual rooms were sometimes privately let to the homeless for as much as R25 a month — and the homeless numbered something over 175 000.

Author Ellen Hellman described it thus in *Soweto: Johannesburg's African City:* 'Sunny, sullen, scowling, soulful, soulless, swinging . . . pulsating, soccer-crazy, singing, laughing . . . Soweto is all of this and much more.'

A roof over our heads

GOODBYE TO STERN LANDLADIES

In 1927 *Outspan* summed up the decade's growing enthusiasm for the new style of accommodation: 'It is with no feeling of surprise that one observes the steady increase in the numbers of flats in South Africa, for this is undoubtedly an age of flat life . . . through sheer merit the flat is coming into its own.'

Flats were originally seen as the logical way of replacing the dirt-littered slums that had grown in almost every large town. As early as 1904 Cape Town's Medical Officer of Health appealed for 'large blocks of flats built around extensive courtyards' to house people from the unhealthy tenements which had mushroomed around the city. By the 1920s flats were beginning to become popular — particularly among young people who saw them as an alternative to impersonal boarding houses and stern landladies. They were also a boon to those who neither wanted nor could afford to live in a house.

The comparative advantages and disadvantages of houses and flats were hotly debated in newspapers and magazines. One devotee of flat life wrote in *Outspan*: 'It stands to reason that homes which are well above the level of the street below must be very much less dusty, and therefore more conducive to good health than the bungalow house which stands but a few feet back from the road itself. Most flats, again, are very modern, and the result of the most careful planning.'

Another reader later commented: 'We decided in favour of a flat solely for financial reasons. We were able to procure a small flat for £8 (no service), whereas a house in a nice locality would not be hired under £9 a month, with water and light running into £1, compared with 9s in the flat.'

Enthusiasts were quick to point out the fact that less furniture was needed for a flat, that water was usually free, and that it was often situated within walking distance of their workplace. Wrote Ernest Hope: 'Since living in a flat, I am constrained to admit that my former prejudices have entirely disappeared, and I am one of their most ardent sup-

Bantrycourt, one of Cape Town's most luxurious apartment blocks, built in the mid-1920s. The larger flats had individual balconies overlooking the sea, and every possible labour-saving device. Above left: This large tennis court was built on the steep slope between Bantrycourt and the sea. Other facilities included a swimming pool among the rocks at the sea's edge, gas outlets, telephones and luxurious fittings. There was even a circular dance floor near the pool. Above right: In 1926 the two-roomed apartments would have cost about eight guineas a month and 55 years later were being sold off by sectional title. The asking price: about R25 000

porters . . .' His wife was not troubled by that nightmare of the average housewife's existence, the servant problem. 'A boy provided by the owner of the flats does the floors, windows, polishes furniture and brass, and for the very modest gratuity of two shillings per month he even attends to the washing-up of the dishes.'

Enough to drive a man to drink

Rising land and building costs and the ever-widening urban sprawl, with its increasing transport problems, accelerated the growth of taller blocks. The young South African couple's dream of 'our own house on our own land' was becoming more and more difficult to realise, and the inevitable result was a high-rise boom that really became evident after the Second World War.

But even then there were dissident voices: 'D.I.' of Cape Town wrote in a letter to *Outspan*: 'No matter how handsome the block of

This row of terrace houses in Donkin Street, Port Elizabeth, was built in the 1870s and proclaimed a national monument in 1967. Once a drab, run-down row, it is being restored by individual owners. Right: Since restoration the value of the houses has rocketed

flats, or how up-to-date its fittings and gadgets, it is impossible as a real home for the average energetic, enthusiastic husband. I attribute the increase in unhappy marriages to modern flat life.' She believed that a healthy, virile young man would feel like a 'caged animal' if boxed up in a two-roomed flat. What would the husband do with his spare time? she asked. 'Husbands soon tire of continual love-making and look round for everyday pastimes . . . the life of a flat-dweller is enough to drive an energetic man to drink.'

But the lure of convenient, cheap living could not be denied. In the mid-1920s a three-roomed flat with kitchen, pantry and bathroom could be rented for between £10 and £12 a month; a bed-sitter — including hot water, electricity and every modern convenience — for as little as two guineas. Rent control was first introduced with the Tenants' Protection (Temporary) Act of 1920, followed, in the same year, by the Rents Act, which was amended over the years to provide security from greedy landlords by pegging the income from rentals to the 'value' of the block. Although these steps suited tenants, the legislation left many property owners embittered because the valuations on which their returns were based were purely arbitrary: the rent allowed did not necessarily have to coincide with market value.

In 1936 Johannesburg had 13 668 flats — more than Cape Town (4 821), Durban (4 909) and Pretoria (1 148) put together. By 1946 Johannesburg had 22 124 flats, and Durban had over 10 000. Today, Hillbrow is South Africa's best-known 'flat-land'. In 1970 over 84 per cent of its 19 027 people were living in flats, and even more blocks were being built. Its average population per acre was then 505, compared with 60 people per acre in an area of semi-detached houses and four people per acre in very affluent areas.

REVIVING THE TOWN HOUSES

As cities grew ever larger, roads became more congested and, later, fuel prices rocketed. The advantages of living in the neglected inner suburbs were discovered by thousands of South Africans in the 1960s. Houses which seemed doomed to demolition in the 1950s became highly prized — and highly priced.

The early 1970s saw a revival of interest in 'town houses' — a modern version of the terrace homes of the late 19th century — and speculators across the country made large profits by buying up rows of houses, restoring them and reselling at a big mark-up. Two or three town houses can be built in the space occupied by one detached house, and they are popular because they offer as much privacy as a detached house and avoid the institutional atmosphere of huge blocks of flats. Cluster housing, a scheme in which owners are levied for the maintenance of communal amenities such as swimming pool and tennis courts, gardens and playgrounds, is also catching on in South Africa.

BORED, AND LODGING

'The lady of the house . . . asked if I would like some bread and jam'

The idiosyncrasies of landladies and fellow tenants were the subjects of furious arguments among boarding house residents in the early decades of the century. *Outspan* readers told of the psychological warfare — and often warfare of a more open kind — in which prejudices and quick tempers were muted by circumstances to produce the kind of tensions that could be recognised only by those who had experienced it for themselves.

One young man wrote bitterly of his spartan diet: 'For instance I happened to be there over the New Year and thought that at least on New Year's Day we would have a good dinner. What we did have was cold corned beef (resurrected for the third time) and then the lady of the house, feeling a bit expansive in view of the festive season no doubt, asked if I would like some bread and jam.'

Another disillusioned veteran of coastal boarding houses was annoyed by the 'unearthly calm' that ruled in the lounge after nine every night. 'The lounge would by then be in darkness and I always had an awkward feeling that pointed questions would be asked if I had the temerity one night to invite a few friends and light up the lounge and indulge in a game of bridge.'

Yet there were some who found the companionship of a boarding house reassuring. A Johannesburg woman who had spent years in various establishments around South Africa wrote: 'There are boarders of all sorts, and I don't think one can really discriminate unless one marries them. And as we can't marry the lot we must take our chance and risks as well when Cupid comes along and transfixes two hearts that one never dreamt would meet.'

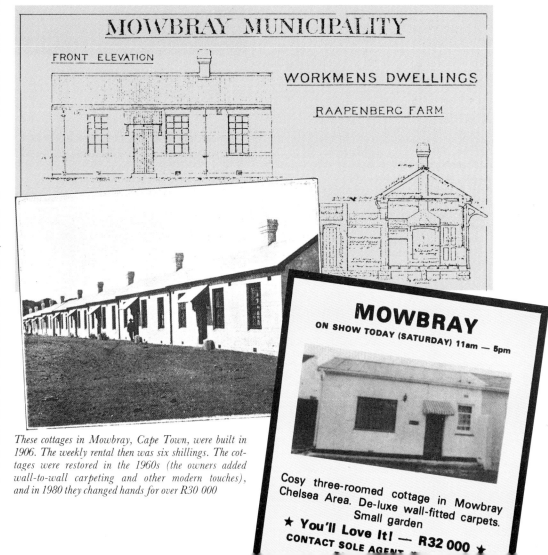

These cottages in Mowbray, Cape Town, were built in 1906. The weekly rental then was six shillings. The cottages were restored in the 1960s (the owners added wall-to-wall carpeting and other modern touches), and in 1980 they changed hands for over R30 000

Preserving South Africa's past

A HELPING HAND FOR HISTORY

Nobody paid much attention to the old Cape Dutch houses, with their crumbling walls and rotting thatch, until the beginning of this century. Then, on 18 February 1905, a small group of people met under the chairmanship of Sir Henry (later Lord) de Villiers, Chief Justice of the Cape Colony, and formed the South African National Society for the Preservation of Objects of Historical Interest and Natural Beauty.

In 1923 the Natural and Historical Monuments Act was passed, by which the Historical Monuments Commission was established.

Today the National Monuments Council (as it later became known) is a widely respected body with a proud record, working closely with local authorities, historians, architects and property owners in what must rate as one of the most successful programmes of its type in the world.

Big business offers a hand

At the beginning of the 20th century there were about 3 000 Cape Dutch houses and mansions in South Africa. Sixty years later, fewer than 500 remained, and of these relatively few retained their original character. But then some people took notice.

Historical Homes of South Africa Limited was registered in March 1966 with a nominal share capital of R1 million, and within five years the company — with the hefty backing of Sanlam, the Anglo-American Corporation and the Rembrandt Tobacco Company — had acquired 43 historic buildings, of which 29 had already been repaired or restored and put out to lease under contract.

'Oom Jochem's Place.' This elaborately-designed mansion was built near Pretoria at the beginning of this century by Jochemus Erasmus, son of a wealthy cattle farmer, in quasi-Victorian style, with fancy balustrades and tall turrets. Oom Jochem's son decided to restore the house in the late 1960s, and spent an estimated R30 000 on the project. Today it is in immaculate condition, and has even been used as a set for a ghost movie

A NIGHT OF TERROR AND DESTRUCTION

A few people felt a slight tremor in the late afternoon, but nobody took it very seriously. Some hours later, though, the earth shifted far beneath their feet — and suddenly the peaceful village of Tulbagh was shaken by an earthquake so violent that houses crumbled, fissures opened in the streets and huge boulders toppled from nearby mountains. In 30 seconds the village was a ruin, and 11 people lay dead or dying.

A newspaper reported on 1 October 1969: 'Tulbagh, the picturesque old village at the foot of the Witzenberg, will never again be the same. Within a very brief moment the devastating earthquake had so mutilated most of the old houses which give the village its peculiar character that they will have to be razed to the ground . . .' Historic buildings were particularly hard hit, and several old homesteads had collapsed into heaps of rubble.

It was a unique opportunity for conservationists: the entire length of Church Street could be restored to its 18th- and 19th-century glory. A national committee was quickly set up to coordinate the project and the Prime Minister at the time, Mr B.J.

The beautiful Old Drostdy, an historical monument destroyed on the night of 29 September 1969

Vorster, agreed to become its chief patron. Architects, engineers, historians and other enthusiasts from all walks of life combined their knowledge and talents. An extensive fund-raising campaign was launched.

Old photographs and sketches were studied for precise architectural details, restoration plans were produced, and the builders moved in. The result was an almost perfect replica of the original Church Street. The scheme has been hailed as one of the greatest triumphs for conservation in South Africa.

Church Street, Tulbagh, after restoration

Sans Souci, just outside Pietermaritzburg, was built in 1884 by a Mr A. Halder, who introduced a number of Neo-Classical concepts in what was essentially a 'verandah house'. The triple temple fronts are slightly at odds with its otherwise simple form

Nova Constantia was built sometime between 1793 and 1808 after the Groot Constantia estate was divided into three parts. The homestead had deteriorated into partial ruin by 1972, when it was purchased by a large company and restored with the help of conservation bodies. Left: before restoration, thatched roof rotting and façade marred by the addition of an ugly corrugated iron roof. Right: the geometrical purity of Nova Constantia's façade after restoration. Some believe the house was designed by the architect Louis Michel Thibault

The Simon van der Stel Foundation

Large-scale publicity drives and many years of sheer hard work have placed the Simon van der Stel Foundation among the foremost of South Africa's conservation bodies. Established on 8 April 1959, this national trust organisation has dedicated itself to the preservation of a wide range of squares, buildings and historical sites which might otherwise fall foul of demolition teams or simply neglect.

Funds are obtained from the contributions of its thousands of members (it is registered as a non-profit organisation), from a government grant-in-aid scheme, and from donations. Among its successful restorations are De Oude Bakkerij in Tulbagh, the English wool mill at Bathurst, Coornhoop in Mowbray, Cape Town, and Boekenhoutfontein near Rustenburg, an estate once farmed by President Kruger.

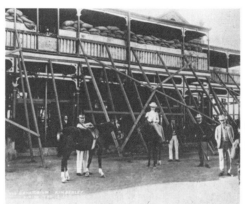

Left: Sandbags and shored-up balconies crowd the façade of the Sanatorium Hotel during the siege of Kimberley. Cecil Rhodes stands beside his horse in the left foreground. It was at this hotel that he received General French after the relief of the town in 1900. An advertisement in 1906 described the hotel as 'unsurpassed in South Africa for Comfort, Luxury and Style'. Right: The Sanatorium as it appears today. The building is now part of the McGregor Museum, and features displays on Kimberley's history and personalities

YOUNG MAN WITH A VISION

Jimmy Logan was a shrewd businessman. When he arrived in South Africa from Scotland towards the end of the last century, he had only £5 in his pocket. He started working for the Cape Colonial Railways as a porter for a modest 5/- a day, rose to become stationmaster of the newly-completed Cape Town Station, and by the age of 21 had moved to Touws River as a district superintendent.

Logan soon learnt that a good living could be made by supplying food and accommodation to the thousands of travellers on their way to the Kimberley diamond fields and, later, the gold mines of the Reef. He got the concession for the station refreshment room at Touws River, became lessee of the railways-owned Frere Hotel there in the same year, and obtained the Matjiesfontein refreshment room concession in 1884.

He built up the tiny settlement into a thriving health resort for people suffering from lung complaints, and very soon the 'Laird of Matjiesfontein' was wealthy enough to entertain governors, premiers, leading Cape political figures (including Cecil Rhodes) and members of the British aristocracy in his elegant house, Tweedside Lodge.

But the Anglo-Boer War intervened, and by the time James Douglas Logan died in 1920 his once fashionable resort was in decline, and when it was bypassed by the national road at the end of the Second World War, it seemed to be all over for Matjiesfontein. But then, in 1968, the entire village was bought by a Stellenbosch hotelier, David Rawdon. The 30-hectare property accommodated the hotel, town hall, police station, magistrate's office, a shop and 15 dwellings.

The Hotel Milner, renamed the Lord Milner, reopened its doors two years later and several more buildings were painstakingly restored over the years. Today Matjiesfontein is a top tourist attraction.

Lions, malaria and gold

An Australian named Alex Patterson is credited with the first discovery of alluvial gold in 'Pilgrim's Creek', in a mountainous area not far from the Kruger National Park. His discovery led to a rush of would-be millionaires from the Transvaal highveld and many other parts of South Africa, and soon a lusty, brawling shanty town began to grow beside the creek. Its name: Pilgrim's Rest. The date: 1874.

The Transvaal Gold Mining Estates Company, under the chairmanship of Lionel Philips, Percy FitzPatrick and Abe Bailey, took over the town's mining interests in 1895 and opened up mines such as the Theta, Clewer, Ponies Krantz, Jubilee and Beta. By the time the mines were worked out in 1970, some £20 million worth of gold had been re-moved. Pilgrim's Rest still exists, and its 3 000 inhabitants revel in its corrugated iron antiquity. Today the town's historic buildings are administered by the Transvaal Museums Service.

The famous Royal Hotel at Pilgrim's Rest. Established at the turn of the century by John McIntyre. Its corrugated iron walls enclose a bar-room which is said to have once served as a church in Lourenço Marques. It was hauled to Pilgrim's Rest after it became too small for its congregation

Matjiesfontein's main street in 1906. The Hotel Milner served as a convalescent hospital for British officers during the Anglo-Boer War, and its central turret became an armed lookout post. The hotel has been restored, and today it bristles with antiques

Leisure and Pleasure

When the 20th century was young, life moved at a leisurely pace. In the long autumn of the British Empire, the world was a safe and stable place for all who basked in the pomp, pageantry and protection of Pax Britannica. Wars came and went, but there was a contentment and serenity about everyday living that made people believe the foundations of society were as firm and unchanging as rock. Their tranquility was perhaps mirrored most clearly in the family: home was truly where the heart was.

In those days families did not depend on outside entertainment — they made their own. They spent pleasant evenings around the piano or pianola, singing sentimental ballads and raucous music-hall favourites. There were visits to the seaside and picnics in the country attended by mother and father, uncles and aunts, grandparents and grubby-faced infants. For those who disliked the rather smug cosiness of the Empire, the family was the centre of things. Families dined, sported, rebelled, prayed and grieved together. In the Afrikaner household, familial bonds were sacred and leisure was inextricably bound with hospitality to kinsmen and friends.

The thunder of war in 1914 shattered this complacency, bringing new maturity and introducing irrevocable changes to the people and their society. The country, and the world, was plunged into a convulsion of destruction and death. Its aftermath was a new, desperate gaiety. When the war ended, the formality and most of the reserve had disappeared. The music was livelier, attitudes to morals and etiquette had relaxed, and there was greater frankness and sophistication in the pursuit of enjoyment. Grandma was shocked by new courting customs and stared in disbelief at women who dared to smoke in public. We were introduced to peculiar dances and exotic drinks. Yet some things would never change. Friends still gathered at picnic spots each weekend. Families continued to stuff themselves with roast turkey and steamed pudding every Christmas, and children always laughed at the circus clowns and their age-old routines...

Camping has always been a popular pastime in South Africa. This group, photographed in the 1930s, parked their caravan and pitched their tents outside Potchefstroom. Note the 'Tudor'-style windows in the wooden caravan

Making their own fun

THE DELIGHTS OF MUSICAL EVENINGS AND HOME AMUSEMENTS

'Music in the home means happiness and contentment,' read an advertisement for pianos in the 1920s: it was a sentiment that had been around for a long time.

A Grahamstown lady born in 1902 clearly remembers how the large family she was part of used to 'get up concerts, the children the performers and the long-suffering parents the audience'. Everyone did what they could: her own first performance was to play *Jesus High in Glory, Lend a Listening Ear* — on the piano with one finger.

Edwardian mums were as often as not excellent piano players, leading the family in evening sing-songs or Sunday hymns and Christmas carols. The piano was the focus of the drawing-room, complete, as Adèle Naudé remembers in her book, *Rondebosch and Roundabout*, with 'fretwork front with pleated red satin behind the fretwork, and candlesticks'. It gave life to an otherwise formal, rather unwelcoming room, and many who were young in those days recall with nostalgia the long evenings singing lustily together songs like *Clementine* and *Campdown Races*.

Pianos and perforated rollers

Among the Edwardian home pleasures that have disappeared is the pianola. This instrument — a piano with a special attach-

The South African Musical Times *carried this advertisement in 1914 for the Pianola Piano. Rainy days were welcome if your home contained one of these instruments, it claimed: 'The ceaseless drizzle of an autumn night, the dripping, reeking dampness of the streets cannot mar your pleasure when awaiting you, in the cosy seclusion of your own home, is the best and most absorbing of all recreations . . . the Pianola Piano is alone in the possession of devices which enable you to play with as much sympathy and personal expression as if your fingers were actually playing the notes'*

ment — reached the country soon after the Anglo-Boer War and had a unique attraction: it could be played by people who had never learned music. John Wentzel, in *A View from the Ridge*, recalls: 'We were very seldom allowed to play the pianola except under strict supervision, because the perforated rollers which carried the music tore so easily. The instrument had to be loaded like an old Kodak with a roll of paper . . . punctured in the same

way as a computerised cheque by little slots, through which the air, laboriously pumped by the player into the bellows, was blown strongly enough to operate the particular note that was to be played.'

The rolls cost a few shillings and an enormous range of musical works, popular and classical, was available. Wentzel says, though, that once the novelty wore off the music became monotonous: it was impossible to

BEFORE THEIR VERY EYES: THE MAGIC LANTERN

Not all family entertainments revolved around music. Almost as popular was the Magic Lantern, forerunner of the modern slide projector. The images from the slides were projected through lenses with paraffin lamps acting as the light sources. Although originally regarded as toys, the lanterns were being used for adult entertainment by the 1860s (Stuttafords were still selling Magic Lanterns in 1901 as part of its large selection of toys). They were sold complete with a selection of slides at prices ranging from 3/11 to 32/6, and were still on sale in the late 1920s. Below: a selection of Magic Lanterns advertised in a 1905 photographic catalogue. Right: some of the hand-coloured lantern slides available in South Africa. The first colour slides reached this country in 1908.

'achieve light or shade' or alter the expression of a piece in any way. By the end of the Twenties pianolas had been relegated to museums, their place taken by the gramophone.

The popularity of the piano lasted a lot longer. The jazz era of the 1920s introduced a new technique: syncopation. The Billy Mayerl School in Johannesburg promised to teach you, through the post, how to be 'a brilliant syncopated pianist' and 'the envy of your friends'. People who could play at informal home dances were much in demand, and the vogue spread to other jazz instruments — banjos (an expensive £24 for the Orpheum model), guitars (63/-) and ukeleles (ordinary model with case selling at 25/-).

But few talents were as unusual as those of Florrie Hill, a relation Wentzel remembers for two startling musical accomplishments: '. . . She could whistle with her lips and teeth, trilling like a bird and sighing like a lover, or she could play a small version of the recently-invented Swanee whistle — a curious instrument with a mouthpiece, fingerhold stops and a piston that moved up and down inside the barrel to vary the notes.' Small wonder that 'even Father, who was inclined to shut himself up in his study' on Mrs Wentzel's musical evenings, emerged when Florrie came to play!

Many families of the 1900s went in for reading aloud, enough to warrant the establishment of the South African Home Reading Union in Pretoria in 1903. The union soon had branches in all four colonies and its own quarterly magazine which regularly appeared until 1914. The Kaiser's War brought an end to this charming occupation, as it did to so many others.

The games we used to play

What the war diminished, but not quite obliterated, was the enduring popularity of indoor games. At the turn of the century Stuttafords' toy department offered many still familiar today: Ludo, Snakes and Ladders, Snap, Happy Families and Tiddlywinks — all priced at 9d — as well as Ping Pong, Dominoes, Draughts and Chess. More dated are Table Croquet, Halma and the Planchette, or the 'Mysterious Talking Board'.

Nor is Spillikins (today known as 'pick-up sticks' and made of plastic) as common a game now, perhaps because others shared the experience of Iris Vaughan, whose Diary condemned it as 'a game Chinamen play, a truly horofic [sic] game . . . Thin little ivory sticks like birds or fishes, you throw on the table then you have a picker up stick and have to hook them out without moving even one. We had to sit around the table in the afternoon to play this . . . it was awful. I got the cramp in my leg with sitting still so long. Our hands began to shake and then Florence pinched Charles when he was picking up her spiliken bird and he said a loud swear word like Pop and there was a bad time for all of us then. But Charles said it was better to have a punishing than to sit there any more'.

Cards and chequers

For the more serious-minded there were plenty of skilful card games: The Enquirer's Oracle, which appeared in the early 1900s, gave space to Whist, Cribbage, Pope Joan, Loo, Bezique and sundry others not well known today, like Commerce, Commit, Speculation, Dumby, All Fours and Matrimony. Biritch, or Russian Whist (now called Bridge), wasn't listed — it became popular in the late 1920s.

Nor did Edwardian South Africans know about crossword puzzles — also introduced in the 1920s — but they did go in for Acrostics (a form of word puzzle). Draughts and chequers were especially popular among Continental immigrants.

One imported game, though, achieved an unexpectedly wide appeal: 'Fox and Geese', also known as 'Mühle' (Mill) in German, caught the fancy of the black community and its squared board and discs are a prominent feature of township life today.

Indoor games popular at the turn of the century. Above left: draughts was so popular that the Illustrated Star *ran a weekly column on the game. Above: many South Africans, however, preferred Lexicon — a word-spelling card game similiar to Scrabble. Left: Halma, which according to Hoyles's Games, 'is played on a board with 256 squares, each player having 19 men of distinguishing colours. The instructions for the various and complicated moves are always included with the apparatus which it is neccessary to purchase in order to play the game'*

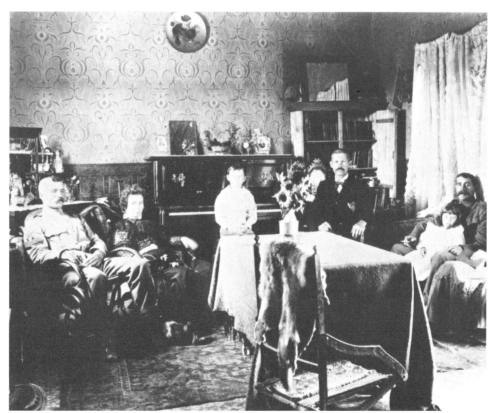

South Africans at home around the turn of the century. At this time the piano was a standard piece of furniture in the middle-class home — and most children were required to take lessons. The advertisers of Wichin's pianoforte 'Tutor' claimed in 1910 that over 200 000 copies had been sold

Party time

LAMPLIGHT REVELRY AND THE SCENT OF SPRING BLOSSOMS

Warm welcomes, lavish meals, hordes of relatives and friends, non-stop entertainment. These were what distinguished old-time parties — certainly until the Depression of the 1930s.

Juliet Marais Louw, in her book *Wagon Tracks and Orchards*, describing a mixed Afrikaans, English and German community on the Reef in the 1920s, writes that 'any one of the little houses was liable to burst suddenly into a party. The living-room furniture would be piled into an adjacent bedroom, while we smothered the cement floor in powder, fondly imagining that we were making it suitable for dancing. Pantry shelves were heaped with iced cakes and jam tarts and *koeksisters* and cooked chicken.

'On the back stoep the lady of the house made pancakes on a pressure stove, offering them to us on the point of her knife. We burnt our tongues eating them and then licked the grease off our fingers. The kitchen table was covered with coffee cups, while the farm labourers washed up and their wives did the drying, babies on backs.

'Few of us went visiting without taking with us everyone who happened to be in the house at the time, from great-grandfather to the newborn babe. There was no such thing as asking Mr and Mrs van der Merwe to dinner. One invited the Van der Merwes, which included Oom Frikkie, Tant Hanna, Mrs van der Merwe's sister from the Free State and all seven little Van der Merwes. We would arrive in families, shake hands individually with everyone already there...

'Someone would wind the portable gramophone and put on record after record, turning each one over on to the other side, winding the handle — over and over again — for hours on end. All the guests contributed records. I never hear "Side by Side" or "You are my Honeysuckle" or any of the revivals of the twenties without smelling again the dust and heat and stuffiness, feeling the scrape of work-hardened hands in mine, the swing of bodies under moist shirts, the exhilaration and the light-heartedness of the little, lamplit rooms. Sometimes too we went out into the garden, sweet with the scent of night, and walked under orchard trees amid flowering blossoms. It was spring and we were young.'

A buffet under the oaks

Country parties were a striking feature of life in Edwardian South Africa, guests coming from far and wide in Cape cart and ox wagon.

As the crowds gathered, there might be a watermelon feast ('Oh! The deliciousness of that ice-cream watermelon — and the quantities we ate!' an old lady recalls of a week-end on a farm near Stellenbosch); fruit-tasting tours of the orchard, tennis and croquet, and, as another old-timer puts it, 'a sort of perpetual buffet spread under the big oak trees'.

Adèle Naudé, in her book, *Rondebosch and*

One of the highlights of the 1928 'season' in the Cape was the garden party given at the historic Klein Constantia homestead. South African Lady's Pictorial waxed eloquent: 'Over six hundred people attended the delightful garden party which Mr and Mrs de Villiers gave in honour of Dr and Mrs Turnbull and their daughters, the Misses Harriet and Janet Turnbull (from Pittsburgh, U.S.A.), and several other visitors from the Laconia ... the pièce-de-résistance of this function was the roulette dance, which, needless to say, has its origin in Monte Carlo. This was danced on the croquet lawn which had been marked in numbered squares'

Roundabout, describes the vast repasts of family birthday gatherings: 'The parties were huge luncheons, adults at the family table, children at a separate one...' In the way of food there was *hoenderpastei*, without which no birthday dinner was complete, and occasionally tortoise pie too. 'The glazed sweet potatoes were almost transparent, the raisins in the yellow rice swollen like balloons, the crackling on the sucking pigs as no electric oven can achieve and the stuffed poultry tasting as no battery

hen or deep-freeze chicken can taste today.'

Afternoon tea followed the huge meal and its 'fluffy puddings with cream'. Then there was supper, and the dancing began.

Where there was no gramophone, there was sure to be a piano or concertina to provide music for vigorous rounds of waltzes, polkas and lancers. The more remote the area, the more uproarious the fun. Johannes Meintjes, in his book, *Frontier Family*, tells of such an occasion at his family farm near Molteno: 'The

Some of the ornate visiting-card cases used by ladies early this century. If no-one was at home the visitor would leave her card on the silver salver usually placed somewhere in the hall. The procedure was rigid and inviolate

diningroom at that time had a floor of dung, soot and milk polished with blood. Such a floor had a magnificient hard shiny surface, but it could hardly stand up to the rigours of lusty rural dancing, particularly when the hob-nails of those without dancing pumps lacerated the surface. The result was that the floor dissolved into fine powder, reducing visibility and coating everything, while lamps and candles attained a more and more ghostly radiance.'

In his book, *Twilight over the Tygerberg*, J.P. Duminy recalled the splendid parties and 'delicious old-time delicacies' which graced the long family dining table: 'Among the meats I remember were a whole roast sucking-pig with the traditional roast potato in its mouth, roast turkey and duck, as well as our favourite chicken curry and yellow rice ... finally the pièce-de-résistance, the three-tier birthday cake with its outer layers of marzipan and fancy icing, topped with tiny silvered "sugar pearls", was specially made by Attwells', the bakers of Strand Street in Cape Town, who usually added a few dozen extra-large petits-fours for good measure.' Although wine was seldom drunk in their home, said Duminy, a birthday celebration was not complete without the broaching of a bottle or two of Heidsieck or Mumm champagne.

The colonial style

Not all entertainments, though, were as cheerful and unselfconscious as these family gatherings. In English 'society' — the cliques of Natal, Johannesburg and Cape Town — formality was the order: banquets, balls and garden parties were the rule; every lady (Edwardian or later) wore her grandest outfit.

This was the world of colonial convention, where rigid etiquette and lace-capped maids in black frocks set a strict though gracious tone. Adèle Naudé's memories of this 'At Home' style of entertaining are in striking contrast to her country-party descriptions. Her mother's 'best' handbag, she recalls, 'was cluttered by an engraved silver calling-card case opening out into fanlike divisions.

'On these cards were not only her name and address, but, at the bottom, also the wording "Second Tuesdays", her afternoon for being at home to people wishing to call on her. If she herself went out calling, when taking leave after tea she would unobtrusively leave one of her own cards and two smaller ones of my father's in the silver salver in the hall, indicating that she had called on the hostess and my father had called on both hostess and husband. But there was more to this ritual of calling. On the first occasion, only cards were left. On the second, one stayed ten minutes, refusing tea although it would politely be offered. Instead, the caller would invite the new lady to her "At home" day; thereafter calling became normal.

'Tuesday morning was quite a serious business. Not only did the gold, mauve and black sitting-room have to be extra spotless, the candlesticks on the piano and the feet of the old Sheraton table shine as brightly as the Peerbooms could make them, but ... fresh flowers had to be arranged — carnations in

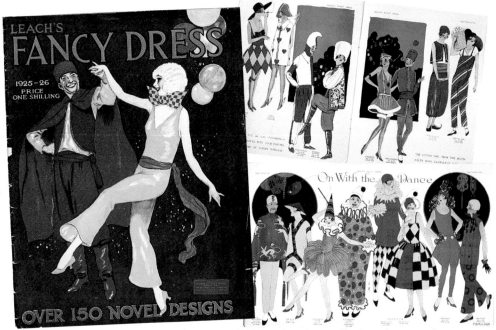

Fancy dress parties were all the rage in the 1920s amd 1930s, and catalogues offered a wide variety of costumes

tall, thin silver vases and Michaelmas daisies or agapanthas in front of the fireplace. These were made to look even more formal by the long, fluted crystal vase they were plonked into ...

'There was seldom any variation in the tea menu, at which both China and Indian were served, but in my mind I can still see the cucumber sandwiches, the lacy silver cake-basket with small cakes, and the silver-handled three-tier stand, its china plates decorated with bunches of violets and roses ...

'These formal tea parties, at four o'clock, were not lengthy affairs but during this period all children were banned from the front of the house, unless specially invited and dressed in our best to be presented to a newcomer.'

If the serving of tea was such a fussy business, a more elaborate entertainment involved something close to a social convulsion. In the 1920s a 21st birthday celebration in one of Johannesburg's wealthier homes called for an orchestra in the ballroom, champagne and punch in the study, and in the diningroom all the best silver and crystal to serve a 'light sup-

per' of chicken, asparagus and home-churned ice-cream. Between dances the guests could sit out on the shaded verandah or in that classical retreat, the fern-filled conservatory. Halcyon days.

'Plates of depressed sardine savouries'

Cocktail parties were all the rage in the 1930s. Although it started as a smart gathering for businessmen and their wives, it soon became the ideal way in which to return hospitality or simply get together with friends, and it was avidly adopted by college students, society hostesses and even working girls. Sometimes, though, the cocktail was treated too casually. Lamented *Pleasure Magazine*: 'Alas! How many dreary, shoddy drinking parties today pass under the name of a "cocktail party"? And the reason is that the host and hostess, thinking this form of entertainment is so simple, do nothing to add to the gaiety of the guests ... don't you know the type of cocktail party where the whisky runs out after the first half hour; where two plates of depressed sardine savouries are handed round ...'

Left: A large tea party at the old Carlton Hotel in Johannesburg. It became fashionable for such gatherings to have a theme. Thus a writer in the South African Domestic Monthly, *bored with 'book teas', 'flower teas' and 'author teas', proposed an 'emblem tea'. Outspan published this cartoon (right) in December 1929 together with a selection of readers' letters revealing their secrets for 'thawing' guests at a party. The guest is shown planting a tree with his own name on the label*

CARD COLLECTING
FOR THE FAMILY ALBUM

In 1865 a German post official, Dr Heinrich von Stephan, caused some consternation when he proposed that a small card be introduced to replace the more expensive letters — which he believed were too long and full of quite unnecessary flourishes. Germany dithered, fearing that social upheavals would ensue when servants and postmen read the mail of their betters. But Austria took the plunge, and in 1869 it introduced the world's first postcards. Three million were sold in the first three months, and yet there was no revolution!

Cigarette cards appeared in the late 19th century, when they were used as stiffeners between layers of cigarettes. Although they were blank in the beginning, manufacturers were quick to recognise their potential as a promotional medium, and soon they were being collected by thousands of South Africans.

SPEED THROUGH THE AGES
Edited by Sir Malcolm Campbell
Max Virginia Cigarettes

MISS MARIE LLOYD
Muratti

H. B. CAMERON and B.L. OSLER from 'Springbok Rugby & Cricket Teams 1931'. The United Tobacco Cos. (South) Ltd

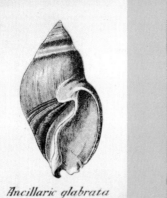

HANDMAID from 'Types of Sea Shells'
African Tobacco Manufacturers

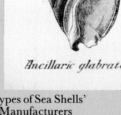

SWEET AND SLOW and EASY TO TAKE
Flag Cigarettes and Springbok Cigarettes

ANTI-AIRCRAFT GUN and GAS MASK
United Tobacco Company

WHITE RHINO from 'Our South African National Parks' and
BLACK SUNBIRD from 'Our South African Birds'
United Tobacco Company

EARLY POSTCARDS represented a wide range of people, places and moods.
Some were humorous, such as animals dressed
as people, some were unashamedly sentimental, and others were devoted
to religious themes. It became the accepted practice to
send postcards to friends and relatives from virtually every stop
during a holiday. The message was the inevitable: 'Wish you were here'

POSTCARDS were used as we use telephones today. Many would carry
simple messages ('Meet me at 2 p.m.') sent
to acquaintances in the same town! Some cards were sent simply
to add to the collections of friends and relatives (right), and some enthusiasts even sent cards
to themselves. These cards were sent from France to a South African collector

Children's games and toys

In the days when children weren't surrounded by mass-produced toys nor lured indoors by the hypnotic eye of the television set, they had many traditional amusements that have since disappeared. A number of South Africans of various backgrounds remember how they played when they were children:

'Toys were very scarce indeed up-country just after the Boer War, so we made do with empty tins. Our fathers put wheels on them and we pushed them round as wagons. We played with bits of broken glass and china too — in fact with anything we could find.'

'Whatever playthings we had we made ourselves. The thing that sticks in my mind was how we'd imitate the horses at the Agricultural Show. We'd cut reeds from the river, four or five feet long, and cut deep so that we got a piece of the root — that would be the head of the "horse". We'd put it between our legs and prance around all over the streets. We took great pride in these horses and polished them up. Man, they were so dear to us that when we went to bed we'd line them up, four or five in a row, in our bedrooms — just as if they were real horses in the Showground stalls.'

'Mesgooi [knife-throwing] — now, that was a great game. You'd hold a knife and you had to twist it off your hand down into the sand. The chap that could throw his knife in the most unusual way was the champion. You did it from your elbow, from your shoulder, from your chest perhaps — and from different fingers in your hand. The knife had to spin and stick in the ground.'

'Motor cars weren't common then; you only saw one here and there in the streets. But already they took our imagination. The sardine tin cans came in useful there — we used to clean them out nicely, make little axles

Top left: dolls, books of fairy tales and hobby-horses were popular gifts for little girls in 1915. Top right: Fairy Tales in Wonderland was presented to Dorothy Radloff in 1910 in recognition of her neat work in Standard Two. Its stand-up pictures (above) portrayed the adventures of Goldilocks and other favourites

Above: early school slates were heavy affairs with wooden frames. Arithmetic and spelling exercises were performed with the aid of a crude slate pencil. Wax crayons (an early variety is seen here in its metal box) are still used by kindergarten children today. Right: toy wheelbarrows and young children have always been inseparable

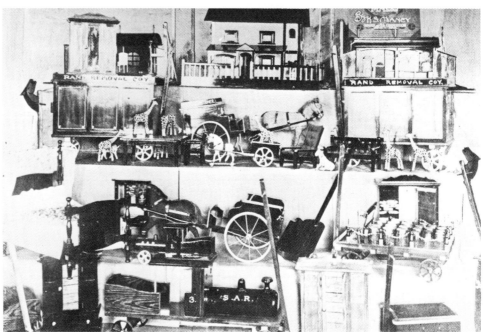

These toys were offered to Christmas shoppers in 1916. They were all manufactured in South Africa

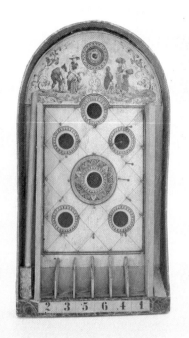

'Tivoli' was a popular 19th century board game and many families made their own versions

This papier-mâché doll, featuring a swivelling head and natural hair, was made in the early 1900s

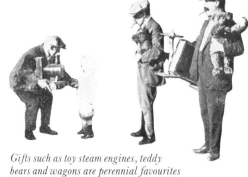

Gifts such as toy steam engines, teddy bears and wagons are perennial favourites

French-made lead soldiers in Boer 'uniforms'. One carries the 'Vierkleur' of the Transvaal Republic

Six different pictures could be built with this set of blocks — an early toy manufactured in England

French on to the English side without being caught and taken prisoner.'

The Depression of the 1930s brought a fresh crop of homemade amusements:

'A *woer-woer* was a wooden ruler you tied at one end to good strong fishing-line, then you spun it round your head: *woer! woer!*'

'My granny made me lappie [rag] dolls with stocking faces — she embroidered the features and crocheted the hair.'

'When we had sheep's trotters my mother would boil up the bones for us to play with; we called them *dolosse* ["play-oxen"]. The long bones were horses and cows, the small ones were sheep. Some children harnessed the small bones to the long ones to make wagons complete with spans of oxen.'

'You took a wooden cotton-reel and cut V's into its edges with a blade. Through the middle you put a piece of really strong red rubber, pinned on one side with a tack; on the other side you slit the rubber to stick a pencil through. You gave it about twenty twists till the pencil lifted its tail like a scorpion. Then you put it down and it climbed over everything in its way: handkerchiefs, socks, your school cap . . . Just like a real tank.'

Children who grew up in South Africa during the Second World War were not much different:

'One of my most precious possessions was a *draadkar* (wire car). It was made of wire fashioned to resemble the outline of a car, with wire axles and wire wheels. There was a long wire steering shaft with a steering wheel at the end, which you used to push and steer the car.'

'I was a tomboy and my earliest memories are of playing with tops — wooden tops with a metal tip. You wound the string round carefully and set it spinning, which was quite an art. I played marbles a lot too — the most precious were the "Ironies" which were old ball bearings.'

'Growing up in wartime, I can remember a gollywog my grandmother made me out of black stockings, and other stocking dolls with plaited wool for hair. When the war was over and I was eight, I got my first bought doll. She was beautiful, with eyes that opened and closed; she was dressed in tartan, with a red beret. Later paper dolls of the popular film stars were the rage. I remember that my favourites were Esther Williams, June Allyson and Jane Powell.'

from sticks and use empty cotton-reels for wheels. You pulled the cars with a piece of string: four or five joined together became a train. They amused us for days on end.'

'We were the lucky generation who didn't have toys as they have them today. But we did have dolls — dolls in profusion. They had porcelain heads and beautiful soft bodies. We made their dresses and we fed them — cooked them proper little meals on an open fire outside. And washday for the dolls was a very big thing: I remember a little line strung on tiny poles — we were very proud of that. But often when the clothes were out in the sun to dry, we'd get bored.'

'We boys played tops and marbles and *kennetjie* — you took a little stick, say four inches long, and you cut down the ends to sharpen it, so that if you hit it on the side it jumped up. You hit it with another stick and away it went. We'd see who could hit it furthest in a certain direction. No, there were no prizes. We did it only for the glory of it.'

'The doctor had the first car in town, so we got his round petrol drums and we'd stand on them and roll right down the street on those drums — what a feat! The streets were so quiet we could roll right from the doctor's house to the Victoria Hotel. People used to stand and watch us in amazement.'

'We weren't given toys — the only things we might have got were doll's teacups or a mirror, something for the doll's house. Every girl had a doll's house. Mine wasn't so marvellous, only a few wooden cases with curtains in front. I had three rooms: a bedroom, a living-room, a kitchen. You know, you'd put in a little bottle, arrange a flower . . .'

'We didn't play cowboys and Indians then. Our great outdoors game was French and English: two opposing teams standing in front of a pile of stones. The game was to get the stones from behind the

A working model of a steam locomotive and tender. A small spirit burner provided heat for the steam

The festive season

YULETIDE CUSTOMS FROM ACROSS THE SEA

Christmas in Edwardian South Africa was a varied affair. For old-fashioned Afrikaners it was a sober day with a long church service (like their Dutch forebears, they exchanged gifts on St Nicholas's Day, 15 December). But in the Cape Colony, many Afrikaners had adopted English customs: Christmas Day was an occasion for presents, turkey, flaming plum puddings and trinket-bearing crackers. And, of course, cranberry sauce.

In Cape Town, Norah Henshilwood recalls, in *All these under a Summer Sun*, Christmas was characterised by 'the comfortable sound of the turtledoves, the drone of the Christmas bee and heat waves over the fields'. Stuttafords department store offered a wide array of decorations: little artificial Christmas trees (10/6 for the 29-inch model), Chinese lanterns (3d to 2/6 each), boxes of paper crackers at 1/- a dozen, fairy lamps, candles and intricate glass balls.

Christmas trees were not yet common. A German custom popularised by Queen Victoria's consort, Albert, they were first seen in South Africa at parties like those given by Rand millionaires. Mrs C.J. Jordi remembers one such party with its 'superb Christmas tree and staggering presents and — can my

Left: Children loved to collect the brightly-coloured stickers from Christmas crackers. Top: Christmas shopping in Johannesburg. Above: Father Christmas and entourage

Mothers and their children head for home with a bounty of Christmas gifts after a hard day's shopping

A Johannesburg shop window draws wistful gazes. For some, the toys on display were only a dream

SNOWFLAKES AND ROBINS

Some people *did* try to introduce Christmas cards which featured indigenous subjects: as early as 1902 the *African Pictorial* ran a competition with a prize of £25 for 'something original in the way of a Christmas card', which it was felt was badly wanted in South Africa. 'This prize is for the best and most appropriate card emanating from this coun-try at Christmas time.' But it took a long time before local designs were accepted.

In 1933 a writer in *Outspan* pointed out that cards with South African designs were poorly patronised, and even today many people still select cards with illustrations of robins, snow, yule logs and distinctly exotic mistletoe.

memory be at fault or were there really pow-dered footmen in knee-breeches?'

Some quite unsuitable English customs continued in South Africa. Writing in *Outspan*, Mrs Jordi recalled Christmas in Johannesburg around the turn of the century as being 'a familiar friend trapped out in unfamiliar gar-ments; roast turkey, plum pudding and mince pies, Christmas trees and stockings, decora-tions — blue gum and wattle branches instead of holly and mistletoe — in the unaccustomed setting of thunderstorms, dust, hot sultry days . . .'

Fay King Goldie, a young Durban writer, told in a 1933 issue of *Outspan* about her pre-Depression Christmases: 'With the traditional English Christmas in our minds we draped cotton wool over prim little fir trees standing in painted tubs, and decorated them with glit-tering knick-knacks . . . we hung little bunches of artificial mistletoe above our doors in antic-ipation and crowned our Christmas puddings with sprigs of artificial holly . . . like happy foolish martyrs, we ate great helpings of stuffed turkey, Christmas pudding and mince pies, while the thermometer registered 97 de-grees in the shade.'

However she continued: 'The absurdity of our English-cum-South African Christmas had been troubling me for some time, and . . . we decided that we would no longer suffer the old order to things, but would see what we could do in the way of a real, honest-to-goodness South African Christmas for a change . . . because we South Africans are so essentially an out-of-doors people, we decided that our Christmas would be an alfresco affair.'

Her family would rise early on Christmas morning, don khaki shorts and shirts, eat a light breakfast consisting of toast and coffee, and fresh fruit, and shoulder light rucksacks packed with bathing costumes, towels, and dainty 'surprise' lunches. 'We make an early start, and arrive at our chosen camping-place . . . and spend the day swimming, and lazing in the sun and shade, and eating . . .'

Christmas stamps were introduced to South Africa by the wife of the Danish consul in Durban, Mrs Maja Christiansen, in 1929. Revenues from the sale of the stamps have helped to build and maintain institutions for young tuberculosis patients for over half a century. In the first year the fund raised only £786, but by 1979 the figure had climbed to R124 468. The woman sel-ling Christmas stamps is still a familiar sight

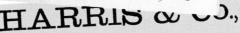

Merchants have always recognised the need to adver-tise at Christmas. Their gift suggestions included such items as war souvenirs (advertised early this cen-tury), the usual selection of hats and clothing, and bottles of perfume packed in containers shaped like oysters, hotel doors and even wheelbarrows

PEACH BRANDY AND CONCERTINA MUSIC

When it came to New Year, though, all South Africans were, for once, agreed. The Afrikaner now entered wholeheartedly into the festive mood, enjoying peach brandy, concertina and much dancing. New Year's Day was for pic-nics and folk gatherings, *volkspele* and *jukskei*. For the English, New Year's Eve dances, com-plete with champagne, balloons, streamers and a mass singing of *Auld Lang Syne*, had be-come an established custom by the 1930s.

In Cape Town the big New Year's event was the Coon Carnival. This focus for Cape coloured revelry is said to have started in the 1890s, when a baker named Cole organised his workers into an American-style Christy Minstrel troupe as an advertising gimmick. Thus began an annual street parade that grew rapidly in popularity.

By 1910 there was a league of troupes. The *Cape Argus* held competitions at the Green Point Stadium, awarding trophies for the best-dressed troupe, best marching, best sing-ing and even the 'best losing troupe'.

Colour and noise reigned supreme: men and boys in satin costumes, striped, checked or polka-dotted, paraded the streets singing, dancing, cavorting. A stiltwalker led a vast procession flourishing batons, umbrellas or musical instruments ranging from cellos to tambourines. But in time, over-organisation and problems such as traffic control (there were often jams as the troupes paraded through the streets) killed the spontaneity of the carni-vals, and the version that remains today only echoes the exuberance of the old days.

Weekend fun in the early 1900s

PROMENADE, PEEPSHOWS AND BANDSTAND REVELRY

Edwardian weekends were treasured times for outings: Saturday was for shopping and amusements that carried on far into the evening; Sunday for a tram- or train-ride to a beach, park or pier, to paddle, see the ships or listen to a band. Promenading crowds, sporting their weekend finery, were a feature of South African cities.

Cape Town was especially notable for its colourful, lively crowds. In 1880 Charles Duval, a travelling actor, described the Good Hope Gardens, graced with shining gas jets among the trees and seething with evening merrymakers despite the strong Cape wind: 'Cape people are so well acquainted with the South-East wind that they conceded that it was all right, and enjoyed themselves with a hearty goodwill that left nothing to be desired. The Gardens were crowded, the band crashed away; some people promenaded, others skated in the rinks; the lessee of the place discharged a few half-hearted squibs from very unorthodox Roman candles, and about a dozen semi-paralysed rockets, which he was pleased to call a "Grand Fireworks Display"; and amid roaring wind, rustling branches, laughter, cheers and general good humour, I bade adieu to the public of Cape Town . . .'

By 1911 Capetonians seeking a sea breeze could head for the Promenade Pier — a graceful new addition to the foreshore, with a minaret-like Observation Tower, benches and shel-

Crowds thronged the bandstand in Pietermaritzburg on summer afternoons to hear Strauss waltzes

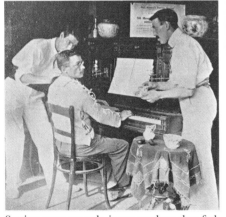

KEYBOARD CAPERS

Setting new records is no modern-day fad. Back in 1905, Mr Karl Mueller established a world record for continuous piano playing when he set a new time of 50 hours. Playing at the academy of a Professor Sparnon in Braamfontein, Transvaal, he broke the previous record of 48 hours with apparent ease. As he passed the old mark, eight-year-old Miss Isabella Hutson presented him with a silver-mounted pipe. It was reported at the time: '. . . at 11.25 p.m. the musician started playing "Auld Lang Syne", the audience joining in, and finished his remarkable feat by rendering "God Save the King".'

'Messing about in boats' had a wide popular appeal. These enthusiasts were boating at Boksburg Lake

ters, a café, and an open-air theatre where evening concerts were held.

For many years there was a miniature fair close by, while the Pier itself offered penny-machine peepshows of the 'What the Butler Saw' variety. Alongside, at Roggebaai, rowing boats could be hired for a shilling an hour.

The street of many colours

Trips further afield beckoned — you could go by single-decker bus to Camps Bay and back over Kloof Nek, or by train to Sea Point. But it was Adderley Street that drew the people and continued to do so for many years, as *Outspan* testified in 1927: 'On a Saturday morning [the street] is so flamboyantly splashed with colour that it might be a picture out of the "Arabian Nights". There stand the coloured flowerwomen with blooms of a myriad hues, pink nerine, red-brown protea, dainty pastel-shaded painted ladies, rosy crassula . . .' Family outings to town would invariably finish up in one of the famous tea-rooms; like Cartwrights and Markhams where, as Norah Henshilwood remembers in *A Cape Childhood:* 'Always we had tea, or ices,

Taking tea on the balcony of Stuttafords in Cape Town in 1907. It was a favourite rendezvous

on one of the balconies overlooking Adderley Street. From this height we watched the motley crowd in the street.' It was much the same in the 1920s when, reported the *Outspan*, 'Malays dressed up in all their finery and wearing an oriental smile, parade the streets; there go their maidens whose exotic, eastern beauty is accentuated by their menfolk capped with fez — all making themselves seen and heard as they elbow their way along, banded together, adding to the fascination of this ever-changing panorama.'

And there was music in the streets, too. George Manuel, writing in the *Cape Times*, recalls how the city rang to the 'praa-praa' of the fish-horns, hawkers' cries, loud 'oompa' music from street-corner bands, and the carnival sounds of 'an extraordinarily large crop of buskers . . . acrobats, violinists, harpists, even Continental organ-grinders with fez-wearing monkeys on chains, or mere ragged bands of "unemployed" itinerant musicians'.

Elephants ride the Reef

Johannesburg in its early days had a share of the same bustling street-life. Writer Alice

M. Ralls, in *Daughter of Yesterday*, has sketched the raw, vivid life of those years: Chinese hawkers complete with straw hats and baskets on poles; 'old Jews in long frock-coats or caftans and high black hats' (they traded in old bottles, newspapers and clothes); Armenian women with 'exciting trays of bright trinkets, brooches, cottons, tapes and beads'; and 'well-dressed men who played at street corners . . . with shining brass instruments'.

Children were drawn to the 'Hokey-Pokey' men, who sold ice-cream: 'They tinkled the usual small bell to call to children to cluster about their little carts.' Later they were attracted in droves by the Sunday pleasures of Johannesburg Zoo, with its ornate bandstand. John Wentzel tells in *A View from the Ridge* how 'in white peakcaps and serge uniforms covered in braid, the members of the Old Comrades, the Salvation Army and various military brass bands sat on small wooden chairs and puffed and sweated their way through selections from *Iolanthe* and *The Merry Widow* or played rousing Sousa marches in the hot afternoon sun.

'Near by, excited children — some of the boys in sailor suits and the girls in white organdie dresses, cartwheel hats and black sashes — queued for the elephant and pony-cart rides . . . On their backs the elephants had saddles topped by a row of back-to-back seats like a jaunting car. On each side four or five children were clamped into their places by an iron bar that was locked across their laps.

'When both elephants were fully loaded, the head Mahout gave the splendid gentleman in full regimentals who led the band a pre-arranged signal. With his little ebony stick the bandmaster tapped the music stand in front of him and immediately the band struck up waltz music such as "The Blue Danube" or "The Skater's Waltz" played in slow time. This was the signal for the elephants to start. Like heavy freight trains leaving a station they began to move majestically out of the concrete loading bays . . . and lurched and ambled twice around the outer perimeter of the arena under the admiring gaze of mothers and nannies who lined the bank and waved to their charges as they passed.'

Bustle of the bazaar

Durban also had its elephant rides, and a seaside promenade enlivened by the tropical light and the vivid African note of its 'ricksha boys'.

Even the smallest village, *Outspan* said, made a festival of Saturday: 'Every other day in the week the dorp looks deserted but on Saturday there is animation, briskness, bustle . . . The farmers arrive from outlying places in Cape carts, ox wagons, buggies, spiders.'

Upcountry 'promenading' was rather more static: 'Their womenfolk stand about in groups in the street retailing all the family news of the last year or two; they look at each other's dresses until they know every stitch by heart, discuss the latest sermon on the Hereafter, praise Dr Well-being's new pills for dyspepsia. Pleasant, savoury gossip!'

But those rural wives knew how to move when it came to the annual church bazaar or

The Durban amusement park drew thousands of visitors every year. The ever-popular Ferris wheel made women scream, as it still does, and other attractions such as roller-coasters and fortune-tellers survive to this day

Zoos and museums were a favourite weekend visiting spot in the early 1900s. This respectful little group watches Peter the tortoise, a large specimen of legendary age who once roamed the grounds of the South African Museum in Cape Town

the local agricultural show — both firmly entrenched features of South African life. Norah Henshilwood tells of stalls groaning with 'fruit, vegetables, dressed poultry and milk tarts. Sometimes there were pancakes, tossed before our eyes as we waited to buy them'.

Country church bazaars were famed for their cakes and *koeksisters*, their brawns, *boerewors* and bottled jams and preserves. Often, too, as Adèle Naudé writes in *Rondebosch and Roundabout*, there were sit-down lunches for sale 'at 2s. 6d. a head, served in the side halls — real South African dinners of the highest quality and not a bredie in sight. Rather, a great deal of crackling sucking pig and turkey and *hoenderpastei* [chicken pie], salads of every kind and exquisite, mouth-watering puddings oozing cream'.

A First World War 'Japanese Fête' held in the Johannesburg Town Hall 'in aid of the Overseas and German-East Dependents, and the Wounded Belgian Soldiers Fund', offered a host of stalls, sideshows and concerts. Produce, perfume, dips and dolls, tea served by Geishas, shooting galleries and fortune-telling must have had a hard time competing with 'Biffing the Kaiser' (held on the roof garden by one Mrs Trevail).

Children were entertained by Wardley's Royal Punch and Judy Show; a banjo, mandoline and guitar band played in the evening, and the grand carnival ball promised exhibition dances of the Fox-trot, Maxixe and L'Hesitation Waltz. And through it all, the programme urged: 'Don't forget to *straf* the Kaiser — *biff him!*'

ROLLER SKATING WITHOUT ROWDYISM

Roller skating was a popular leisure activity early this century. Rinks sprouted all over the country — even Jagersfontein had its own rink — and people of all ages took to the sport with alacrity. There was a Rink Football League and the journal *South African Wheels* (1909) was published monthly in the interests of motoring, cycling and roller skating (it lasted for only two issues). Skating rink operators were offered these tips on running their businesses: 'Under no circumstances should employees use cigarettes or tobacco from the time they come into the rink. How disgusting it is for women to engage instructors and be annoyed by tobacco (not to speak of alcoholic odours — ed.)

breezing by her continually.' Fast skating and rowdyism should be eliminated entirely, was the advice, and there should always be something on the bill to interest patrons.

'Do not let them skate their heads off and reach that point where skating becomes monotonous. Carnivals of every description, skating exhibitions of the refined order, thrillers and novelty attractions, skating races . . . an absolute tone of refinement must at all times exist.' Above: skaters link arms for a leisurely roll around the Capital Rink in Pretoria. A two-day fancy dress carnival at the Capital drew an audience of 4 000 and 270 'winged-footers' actually took part.

The pleasures of the picnic

STARCHED TABLECLOTHS AND LAZILY BUZZING BEES

Flip through almost any Edwardian family's photograph album and you will find a faded picture of mother, father, children and perhaps Aunt Mary at a picnic. They will be formally dressed, of course, and their cold chicken and sandwiches will be laid out on a white starched tablecloth. The sunlight of 70 years ago is almost tangible as the picnickers, lulled by hock and the lazily buzzing bees, pull their straw boaters over their eyes and drowse away the afternoon . . .

Like the Victorians before them, the Edwardians loved picnics — and the longer and more lavish the better. Said the Reverend James MacKinnon in his book, *South African Traits*: 'There is perhaps no other land where picnicking forms such a frequent pastime as at the Cape.' Certainly picnics were popular: South Africans have always loved the outdoors. They would order picnic baskets from any one of several hotels and cafés and head for their favourite spot. Klusmann's of Pritchard Street in Johannesburg advertised 'picnic baskets prepared on the shortest notice' and the Craighall Park Hotel announced: 'Picnic parties specially catered for in any number.' There was music, too. A 1927 advertisement for His Master's Voice gramophones pointed out that the portable model was ideally suited to picnics (the 'popular portable model' sold for £9.15s.).

Hildagonda Duckitt's *Diary of a Cape Housekeeper* describes the cooking of potatoes and freshly-caught fish over driftwood fires after 'an eight-mile drive over a very rough road (but no-one seemed to mind that!)'. Some of the picnickers went on horseback, while others would pile into a farm buck-wagon 'turned into a comfortable conveyance by soft seats made of bags filled with straw'.

Cold frikkadels and 'moss bolletjies'

In her opinion Christmas was the best time for picnics, and she describes the food taken on a week-long camping trip to Cape Point: a piece of corned beef, a leg of mutton made into sosaties, cold roast chickens, cold frikkadels, fish (to be caught locally), a few dozen mutton patties (which, says she, should keep

This Esperanto picnic at Derdepoort in the Transvaal was attended by members of the local Swiss community. Picnics were often rather formal

Cooking pots are suspended over a fire by the characteristic tripod and chain at this group's camp in January 1908. By today's standards, untensils are huge

Smiling contestants and undisputed winner of the ladies' race. Families eat, drink and play together at the works picnic of Wright, Boag & Co Ltd, engineers, early this century. Employees and their families were encouraged to enter such events as egg-and-spoon and potato races before sitting down to a huge lunch

for a few days if home-made), sponge cakes in tins, buns, 'moss bolletjies', turnovers and fruit, home-made bread, a few pounds of fresh butter and coffee essence (milk was to be purchased from farmers).

A day picnic for a party of 12 people would require two cold roast chickens, a loaf of bread, ½ lb butter, salad dressing, lettuces, ½ dozen tomatoes, two dozen tartlets, cakes, fruit, coffee essence and milk. In those days much emphasis was placed on the purchase of fresh produce from local farmers. And some rules never change: Hildagonda Duckitt recommends that picnickers check carefully to

see they have everything they will need; otherwise they are bound to arrive at their destination only to find they have left some vital piece of equipment behind.

But not everyone had halcyon memories. A Natal sugarmill worker recalled ruefully: 'The Tongaat Sugar Company used to lend us an ox wagon and the whole family would go down to the beach. It used to take us all morning to get down there, and by the time we had outspanned the oxen and got the food ready, it was almost time to inspan and go home again. We drank smokey tea, sat under the casuarinas which drop nobbly pellets all the time,

The stiff and voluminous dresses worn by early women picnickers must have made their leisure time slightly uncomfortable. The men were hardly better off: they wore ties even in the hottest weather

With its 13 cm high vented container, the famous Primus paraffin stove was a boon to early picnickers. Many years later the cleaner, more convenient, gas stove was introduced

An early Stuttafords catalogue offered a neatly-packed 'Luncheon Basket' for six people (above) at 90/- and a smaller 'Marvel Tea Basket'. Most baskets came with all the necessary crockery and even a compact spirit stove. In 1919 the South African Lady's Pictorial advertised a selection of vacuum flasks to ease the burden of picnickers, travellers and housewives. There was even a baby version (above right) with rubber hose and teat attached!

A hamper with aluminium cups and containers. In 1980 a similar basket could cost R200

Crowds of picnickers at the Maselspoort pleasure resort in the Free State in 1956. Ties and stiff collars had given way to shorts and open-necked shirts, and the women were far more comfortable in light, brightly-patterned frocks. The traditional picnic baskets had almost disappeared

and ate sandwiches after brushing off the ants. We were always very pleased to pack up and go.'

The males of the party at such a picnic did have one great advantage: they could at least swim or paddle. The ladies and girls, trapped in their voluminous petticoats, skirts, stockings and firmly-laced boots, had to remain envious onlookers. Occasionally a lady's attempts to preserve her dignity in the country would come lamentably adrift, as described by Charles Scott Shaw in his *Stories from the Karkloof Hills*: ' . . . one town-bred governess caused much mirth when she put her cushion on top of a partridge. As she settled down, the bird rose up with frantic whirring of wings and unearthly screeches. Our guffaws brought forth a severe reprimand from the lady.'

A feast for thousands

Factories, mining companies and other firms often organised large-scale picnics for their employees. Families were invited to compete in such events as egg-and-spoon races and tug-of-war. But few picnics could have matched the event arranged by the De Beers mining company shortly before the Anglo-Boer War: the logistics of the affair must have been formidable. *South African Handbook* described the day: 'The sports included foot races, wrestling competitions and other athletic contests. There were boats on the big dam, and two bands of music. Children's races, for handsome prizes, too, were run, and there was dancing.

'Then, of course, there was the important business of refreshment, which was lavishly provided. In the marquees were long tables, absolutely creaking, if not literally groaning, under the weight of the eatables and drinkables . . .' Cecil Rhodes himself attended this Christmas picnic for 4 000. It was a gargantuan feast, boasting '350 turkeys, 1 200 fowls, 500 chickens, 200 geese, 100 hams, 1 000 meat pies, salads, fruits and cakes, besides fancy dishes of all kinds'.

Champagne and beer (2 400 bottles of each) predominated over the whisky and brandy, and De Beers managed to produce a staggering 12 000 bottles of mineral water — ranging from the popular ginger beer to 'pop', or carbonised colddrink.

The plum pudding, we are told, was so vast that it had to be boiled in four trucks lined with bricks. The result was 'wonderfully good', and the picnic was one that Kimberley would never forget.

THE BRAAI — 'A TASTE FOR COLD CHARCOAL'

Meat has been cooked over open fires in South Africa for a long time — but as a necessity, since there was no other way of cooking it. The centenary celebration of the Great Trek in 1938 did a lot towards transforming the braaivleis from a chore into a social function, and it has since become an institution. The *Dictionary of South African English* mentions that one of the earliest references to a braaivleis as a social event was a report in the *Cape Times* of a braai organised to raise war funds in 1942.

Today's braaivleis is a sophisticated form of entertainment. Many homes have built-in barbecues and elaborate systems of grids, shelves and cabinets, and those not bound by tradition sometimes opt for the gas braai: 'If a sudden downpour surprises the party, a gas operated braai is going to be the ideal thing. Gas is foolproof, instant, clean and pollution-free, so you taste the food, not the fire.' An imported model actually features a lid with a temperature gauge — all of which seems to defeat the whole point of a braai in the first place!

Some people, however, view the braai with trepidation. Writing in the *Star* in 1973, 'The Man on the Reef' commented: 'My enthusiasm for this form of catering is as lukewarm as the chops, steaks and appalling sausages invariably served up out of the smoke on these occasions. Simple persons with self-contained breathing systems, fire-proof eyeballs and a taste for cold charcoal will tell you that noth-

ing else tastes quite like the meat of a braaivleis.'

The highest peak the braaivleis can attain is the Braaivleis Contest. The first contest was held in Montagu, Cape, in the 1950s and has since grown into an enormous event, attracting over 300 teams each year from all over the country. The rules are strict: if the entrant says his steak will be medium-rare, then it must be just that.

Points are also awarded for side dishes such as *stywe pap* (literally 'stiff porridge'), *roosterkoek* and *askoek* (griddle and ash cakes) and sosaties — curried kebabs of Malay origin.

A reflection on his manhood

Families have observed the old rituals of braais for many years. The men (who actually do the cooking) stand around the fire, drinking beer and discussing such manly subjects as rugby, the consistency of the *stywe pap* and the origin of the firewood. The women are responsible for the buttered rolls, salads, marinades — and the occasional interjection ('Can't you talk about something *nice*?') when the conversation turns to politics. Woe betide the person who suggests to the man in charge that the coals don't look right: this grievous insult is a reflection on his manhood as well as his ancestry.

Rawbone Malong's (Robin Malan) account of a *bra-flace* (braaivleis) in his book, *Ah Big Yaws?* can be truly relished only by those attuned to South African English as she is spoke: ' . . . everyone forgathers in some sandy, often quite unpleasant spot outdoors. Invariably there's a strong wind blowing, or it's dusty-hot. The men all gather twigs and *Parnkerns* [pine cones] and logs, while the women prepare the raw *Tjopps* [chops] and *Booravorce* [boerewors]. Some time later, say four beers later, when everyone is half choked to death by the smoke, the meat is then thoroughly charred over the fire, well-sanded by being dropped several times, and consumed with apparent relish . . . everyone goes home saying they've enjoyed an invigorating outing. Oh, the great South African outdoors!'

The nationwide braai contest produces some appetising dishes. Competitors take the contest very seriously, sometimes rising at dawn to prepare their sites. At one stage the more enthusiastic entrants were decorating their braai areas with shrubs and false lawn; their tables groaned under the weight of silver cutlery, crystal glassware and fine china plates. This was later discouraged by the organisers

In camera

History in limbo. This photograph, taken during an outing of the Cape Town Photographic Society in 1893, shows Percy Lindup, age six, holding tightly to his father's hand. Seventy-five years later, Colonel Percy Lindup (now 81) donated his father's camera to a museum: this picture was found undeveloped inside it

LADIES AS WELL AS GENTLEMEN

It was the medium that captured everything we ever wanted to see in ourselves — and much that we did not. We dressed in our finest clothes, adjusted our stiffest and most uncomfortable collars, and adopted our sternest expressions as the man buried his head beneath a black hood. Magnesium powder flared and died, and suddenly we were immortal.

Photography has wooed and won many thousands of people since its introduction to South Africa in the mid-1800s. Daguerreotype (photographs produced with iodine-sensitised silver plates and mercury vapour) and collodion (wet plate) methods gave way to the more convenient dry plate process in the 1880s, launching the era of the amateur photographer. George Eastman's small hand-held cameras were a product of this era.

There were still many professionals, but the ranks of the home photographers were growing rapidly. South Africa's first camera club — with a membership of 18 — met at Kimberley's Gresham Hotel on 9 May 1890. A special feature — unusual for this time — of the Port Elizabeth club was that ladies as well as gentlemen could become members. The club was very active. In 1892 its committee organised a New Year picnic at Knysna. The *Eastern Province Herald* reported that it linked up with the Naturalist Society, and hired two steamers for the 260 kilometre journey. One hundred and fifty people went on the trip at the inclusive cost of £2.10s. each. The following year they went by wagon to Van Staden's Pass. There were combined outings, and exchanges of group photographs at Christmas were typical. A national salon was held for the first time in 1896.

Theatres and scotch

Photography in Johannesburg thrived from the very beginning of the city's life. When the *Diggers News* first came out on 24 February

Left: A photographic society in action around 1910. By this time there were many clubs and societies dotted about the country. They were friendly associations, and members were fond of organising outings. Right: A novel invention for the mobile enthusiast of the 1880s was this bicycle with a camera on the handlebars

This Kodak bellows-type camera was typical of the Edwardian era: the whole family participated

1887, three photographers advertised in it. In his book, *Silver Images*, Dr A.D. Bensusan records that Miss Rose Bell, actress, was photographed after her first professional performance in Ferreira's Camp. One photographic gem shows a crowd in 1887 gathered around a huge sign labelled 'Scotch': obviously the supplies had just come in.

Sir Percy FitzPatrick, politician and author of *Jock of the Bushveld*, was the inaugural president of the Johannesburg Photographic Society, which was founded in 1899. The town's enthusiasts had special problems, and one was the lack of water. The *South African Photographer* of 1898 recorded that 'year after year comes the order, returning like a bad penny, to the effect that till further notice, anyone using the water for his garden or for anything but household use is liable to have it cut off'. That was one regulation the enthusiastic camera community discreetly ignored.

An important international exhibition — the first of its kind in the country — was held in Cape Town in 1906, when 629 prints were

South Africa has produced some great photographers. Among them was Arthur Elliott, who was born in New York in 1870 and arrived in South Africa in the late 1880s after working as a chemist's assistant, billiard marker, watchmaker, stationmaster and at many other jobs. He finally became a photographer in 1900.

In his lifetime he produced five major photographic exhibitions and took many thousands of pictures which are today regarded as a unique cultural asset to the country. Harold Smith was another innovator: his evocative colour photographs were the first produced in South Africa.

A 1908 photograph by pioneer Harold Smith

The Sandpipers, *Arthur Elliott's most famous photograph, was published in almost every country in the world*

Mountain Hamlet, *by Will Till, was exhibited in London in 1938. Till bought his first 'decent' camera in 1926, and was a top amateur photographer*

In 1978 a staff photographer on the Argus *newspaper, Les Hammond, won the annual World Press Photo award with this picture, entitled* Teargas Terror

displayed in the City Hall. The exhibition, described as the finest collection south of the equator, also featured a selection of pictures taken by Queen Alexandra.

The scope for professional photographers, too, kept growing. By 1962 there were reported to be over 650 professionals in South Africa, and millions of rands were being spent every year on equipment and sensitive materials. South Africans photographed wild animals, birds, landscapes — and each other. The results of their efforts are preserved in albums throughout the country, but some pioneers left large, entrancing collections to posterity.

Among the better ones are the Arthur Elliott Collection in Cape Town, the David Barnett Collection in Johannesburg and the Duggan-Cronin Collection in Kimberley. In Johannesburg the Bensusan Museum of Photography boasts a fine collection of historic photographs, old cameras and other equipment illustrating the growth of photography in South Africa.

Left: A Kodak box camera. Its simple construction (the casing was mostly of cardboard) and equally simple operation (it had a fixed focus) made it the ideal family camera. In 1926 a Kodak box camera cost 13/6. Right: A vest pocket Kodak 'Autographic', manufactured from 1915 to 1926. A metal stylus was used to inscribe details of the photograph on the actual negative (a small flap was lifted at the back of the camera)

DUGGAN-CRONIN'S CHILDREN

In the final years of the 19th century a young Irishman named Alfred Martin Cronin gave up a calling to the Jesuit priesthood and sailed for South Africa. Settling in Kimberley as a night-watchman with the De Beers Company, he began photographing the African mineworkers with his ten-shilling box camera — thus launching a career that was to win him international acclaim and even a tribute from the Pope.

His hobby soon became a serious life study as the enthusiastic photographer (he later changed his name to Duggan-Cronin) travelled around the country, capturing the essence of African tribal life on 'Imperial Sovereign' plates. He was determined to preserve a rec-

ord of tribesmen in their natural habitat before they were overwhelmed by civilisation, and by the start of the Second World War he had photographed virtually every important tribe in the Union and adjacent territories, travelling over 120 000 km in the process.

A lesser-known side of Duggan-Cronin's work was his collection of child studies. He spent many hours of his spare time photographing children of all ages, managing to capture much of the high-spiritedness, spontaneity and sometimes poignancy that continues to elude many photographers today. General Smuts said after viewing Duggan-Cronin's work in the gallery at Kimberley: 'You can die now, Cronin, for your monument is raised.'

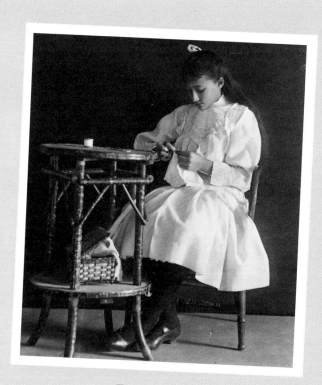

Dancing feet

SWIRLING TO THE WALTZ AND CAVORTING TO THE POLKA

'In my day everything was very proper,' says one old-timer, remembering pre-First World War days in Zululand. 'We did the polka and the barn dance and the quickstep and even the waltz but there was always a space between the dancers.' It was not the done thing to dance with a man who smelt of drink, either, nor to go outside alone with a man for a look at the moon. Those were the days when, in dancing as in everything else, formality was the name of the game.

Formal dances and fancy dress balls were the spice of society life during the first two decades of the century, and received much coverage in the press. Hampered by the lack of photographs, social writers poured out columns describing such things as 'creations of hydrangea chiffon and black lace over white silk with a glimmer of jet beads and frills of white chiffon at the bodice'.

Chaperones were a must, men wore white gloves and always bowed to their partners before making even remote contact, and people who could reverse were in great demand. Dance cards had to be filled in and strictly followed, and wallflowers gathered in the retiring room to pinch their pale cheeks and wonder if anyone would ask them for the Supper Dance.

In the *Outspan* in 1930, Olive Bruce voiced these recollections of dancing twenty years earlier. 'To begin with, we did not dance night after night and all the year round until we were satisfied. We had perhaps half-a-dozen big "balls" during the winter and a few flannel dances in the summer at the seaside . . .

'Well do I remember a dance given in honour of my coming-of-age.

'We practised steps on every conceivable occasion, teaching and helping those of our number not too proficient. One girl of twenty-six did not sleep for two nights beforehand — it was her first real dance!

'At last the great day dawned. There was a little rest in the late afternoon, to be quite fresh, though no sleep was possible for excitement, then a bath and at last came the moment when one could begin to dress. Our evening dress and best undies would have been laid out in good time, and oh the excitement of getting into them . . .

'As one dressed one was full of excitement as to whom one would meet, for dances then were decidedly sociable affairs, not the cliquish affairs they are today. We did not go in a crowd, meet the same crowd and dance with the same crowd wherever we went.

'There were always appointed M.C.'s who had very definite work to do and one met many new people and danced with many and varied partners. I think it was this very element of surprise that made each affair a wonderful adventure, for I suppose, sub-consciously, the thought was always there that one might meet Mr. Right.'

In spite of this conviviality, strict conven-

LOW CLASS STYLE

HIGH CLASS STYLE-RECOMMENDED

NO STYLE

In the late 1800s dancing styles were much debated. In his book, Dancing, *Edward Scott emphasised that a girl 'properly and scientifically' taught to dance could render it impossible for a man to hold her too closely*

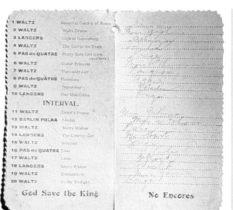

Left and centre: The cover and inside of a 1911 dance programme. Right: A list of forthcoming dances in Johannesburg, in October 1936. Commented Murray Leslie of the Savoy Hotel in London: 'Since arriving in sunny South Africa I have been very much impressed with the great interest shown by nearly everyone in dancing and the desire to improve . . . I would not describe dancing as a craze. It is more than that; it is a habit'

VOLKSPELE — FROM SWEDISH SONGS TO A SOUTH AFRICAN INSTITUTION

On 28 February 1914 a picnic was held at Boshof in the Orange Free State. The revelry was enhanced by a very special performance: a display by a group of schoolchildren of four dances imported from Sweden, together with Swedish songs translated into Afrikaans. In spite of their Scandinavian origin, those dances and songs marked the beginning of South African *volkspele*.

The youthful dancers at the epoch-making picnic, who had also performed traditional Afrikaner dances such as *Vanaand gaan die volkies koring sny* and *Pollie ons gaan Pêrel toe*,

were pupils of headmaster Dr S. Henri Pellissier. Two years earlier he had visited Sweden and been impressed by the awareness of national identity that he had found there. He set out to establish a similar spirit in South Africa by promoting folk-dances and songs that had grown out of simple picnic games.

The 1938 centenary of the Great Trek sparked off new interest in traditional Voortrekker dress and customs, and enthusiasm for *volkspele* increased. Formal courses were held in various centres and a national council for folk singing and dancing was formed in 1941. When the Voortrekker Monument was inaugurated in 1949, 2 000 dancers took part in a giant, colourful display, and 3 000 dancers performed at the celebration of South Africa's tercentenary in 1952.

Since then bands of dancers in their brightly-hued dress — based on the *kisdrag* or best clothes of the Voortrekkers — have continued to enliven South African festivals.

tions governed the selection of partners for many years. In *Cape Hills in Sunlight* Katherine Heywood says of the Twenties: 'We dared not be so bold as to invite a young man personally in those days. Fathers did that. We did not necessarily go in couples. Those were the days of programmes with dainty pencils attached by silken cords of rainbow colours, and each girl depended on her personal charm to attract the desired partners to fill her programme. What heartburnings if her programme had gaps and she was a wall-flower!

'We always made our own frocks and evening coats and it was with utter satisfaction that I beheld myself in my first evening dress of shell-pink Chinese silk-crepe trimmed with tiny blue crystal buttons running all the way from neck to hem, together with a glorious blue satin evening wrap lined with pink silk, long pink silk gloves, pink satin shoes and pink silk stockings. A freshly picked pink rosebud in the hair completed the picture of sweet seventeen who devoutly hoped she'd fill her dance programme in a very short time! It was entrancing to have your partners, wearing white kid gloves, hold your silk-gloved hand as you waltzed and hopped around in the polkas and lancers while the chaperones, studded around the room, looked on approvingly or otherwise.'

Bunny Hug and Turkey Trot

The old-style formality eventually had to give way, albeit gradually. New, livelier dances, staunchly resisted by the older generation at first, were becoming entrenched. During the First World War (when it was reported that 'the young people have found the evenings very monotonous due to all the dancing men serving their country') the masses sang the plaintive *Roses of Picardy* and *If You were the Only Girl in the World*, but already their feet were beginning to tap out the tango and thump to ragtime. The 'wild abandon' of the tango was followed by the equally hectic Bunny Hug and Turkey Trot, causing one prim South African dancing mistress to advertise that 'Madame teaches the Foxtrot, Hesitation and Boston, but no vulgar freaks'.

In the Twenties the correct dancing hold was a common subject of conversation and letters to editors. The first national ballroom dancing competition was organised in 1928 by Polliak and Sons, with heats in various centres and a final in Johannesburg — the winners were a Cape Town couple, Bunny Croneen and Edith Franklyn. By 1930 chaperones were a giggle of the past and dance cards were being treated with a levity that soon abolished them altogether.

In 1937 Bob Garganico, a top British ballroom dancer, visited the Union to judge the national championships and commented afterwards: 'Speaking generally, I found a number of good dancers in South Africa, but it seemed to me that they lacked what I call "flair" — that is, they did not move as naturally as they should, nor look as pleasant as they might. Many were stiff. . .

'The foxtrot is, perhaps, the most popular of all the dances out here in South Africa, but I think the quickstep rivals it closely . . .

The Tangorilla.

Left: Professor and Mrs Sparman demonstrate the Tango. The dance caused a sensation all over the world in 1914. The English newspaper, the Daily Graphic, *noted that 'no self-respecting woman of the world dances the Tango since the Church forbade it'. The* South African Musical Times *gave their own impression of the dance (above). In the 1920s an even more daring and decidely more energetic dance hit the headlines: the Charleston. Hems were higher by then, and women's knees were clearly visible*

C.E. Turner's painting of a 1930s New Year's Eve ball at the Wanderers ballroom in Braamfontein. Not everyone enjoyed these affairs; many felt the new dances were undignified. Lamented a writer in Outspan *in 1930: 'Oh! What sad and sorry affairs are these much-vaunted jazz-filled nights to us of the Old Brigade! To those of us who knew the joy of a "ball" fifteen or twenty years ago, the dance of today is boredom inexpressible'*

Dancing at Ferndale Hotel, Margate, in the 1930s

'The tango, of course, is the ideal dance for this climate. It does not need a much greater sense of rhythm than any of the other dances, and yet its smooth rhythmic steps and lazy movements are the very thing for a warm climate.'

In later years the Latin-American rhythm of the cha-cha, rumba, samba and bossa nova ousted the foxtrot and tango in their turn. But it was rock 'n roll in the 1950s that shook the world of ballroom dancing, perhaps because it could not compete with the youthful ease and informality of the new dances.

Rock 'n Roll took the western world by storm in the 1950s and helped change the face of modern dancing

The circus comes to town

THRILLS AND SPILLS UNDER THE BIG TOP

In August 1887 an extravaganza of colour and dazzling excitement came to Johannesburg. Some say that it was the real beginning of the world of entertainment on the Reef. The show was presented in a tent on Marshall Square and presided over by a Mistress of the Ring, Miss Rosa Bell, who is described by writer Joy Collier in *The Purple and the Gold* as a 'nymph with an hour-glass waist'. There were equestrian feats and a panorama of other spectacular delights, both human and animal, which proved irresistible to a public hungry for diversion.

Frank Fillis's circus had come to town.

The proprietor, Fillis, sailed to South Africa from Britain in 1880 to join what was then Bell's Circus, which he took over when the owner died. His success with it was such that in the 1890s he was able to house his show in permanent buildings in Johannesburg, Cape Town and Kimberley.

Fillis was a showman in the grand style. His wife, Vincenta, was equally famous, both as the world's first human cannonball and as a skilled equestrienne. Extravagant tableaux, pantomimes and re-creations of historic rides and battles were the reasons why, on gala nights, boxes at Fillis's Circus could cost a staggering 10 guineas. And the performers received their share of the wealth. Clowns earned £30, the high-diver £75 and the trapeze-flyer Diavolo a cool £175 a week — excellent money for those days.

The big dive

Another crowd-pleaser is described by the clown Tickey in T.V. Bulpin's biography, *Tickey:* 'The most spectacular water act I have ever heard of, but never managed to see, was performed in Fillis's Circus. For this act, a flap was cut into the top of the tent. An American performer named Gurney Speed climbed up a ladder and disappeared through this flap. Above it there was a special platform on which he stood, 40 m above the floor of the ring. In the ring there was a tank of

The lavish programme for Fillis's Circus and, right, the ever-popular elephant act, one of several which featured animals. There was also a travelling zoo

water 5 m square. After a build-up from the ringmaster and mounting tension among the audience, he suddenly dived through the flap and hurtled into the tank with a prodigious splash. His wife would always be standing next to the tank, holding a dressing gown. This was for the sake of decorum — apparently every time he hit the water his tights split.'

For Queen Victoria's Diamond Jubilee, Fillis staged a parade through Johannesburg with a band and a tableau of the Queen as Empress of India, attended by the Viceroy, slaves, ladies of the harem and five elephants bejewelled from head to tail.

But Fillis, with his fondness for lavish overseas tours, was often in financial straits. Soon

German-born Wilhelm ('William') Pagel, one of South Africa's most notable impresarios, was an immensely strong man. In his youth he could lift a dray horse into the air; as an adult, in the circus ring, he would wrestle with a full-grown lion

Pagel's Circus in the 1930s. Mr and Mrs Pagel are seated in the centre, surrounded by troupers who helped to keep the circus at the top of the popularity poll for decades

another circus appeared on the scene, and it was to become a household name: Pagel's.

William Pagel was born in Pomerania, where, as a blacksmith's apprentice, he could lift huge dray horses into the air. He brought to South Africa not only his own astonishing strength, but a favourite lion called Hopetoun with whom he would wrestle in the ring, and a wife whose show-business flair matched his: Mrs Pagel regularly startled South Africans by driving about in an open car with the full-grown Hopetoun lounging at her side.

By 1914 Pagel's had ousted Fillis's Circus completely. But it wasn't the only one on the circuit: Bostock's Circus from Britain was a frequent touring visitor, bringing its famous clown Spuds; and soon the Boswell brothers, left stranded when Fillis's Circus was finally disbanded, started their own show.

The Boswell boom

Business boomed for the Boswells, who offered a fast, flashy show crammed with animals and entertainment. Mrs Pagel's death in 1939 removed much of the competition. By the 1940s Boswell's dominated the South African scene, not least through Tickey the midget clown.

Tickey recalls the Boswell's first show, which gave delighted audiences a taste of the magic to come: 'The programme started with a lion act. Then came the house clown, Tony Murell, with Walter Boswell assisting him under the name of Pickles; next was Alberto doing her juggling act; then came the Gay Gordons in a pyramid act; Jim Boswell with his horses; more clowning; the St Moritz skaters in a tableau roller-skating act; our trampoline act; Buck and Chic doing "western pastimes": lariat spinning, shooting and knife-throwing; the clowns again; and finally the Gay Gordons with their bagpipes and drums to provide the show with a good, flashy, noisy ending. We would all go into the ring for the finale, we would bow, one of the Boswells would make a short speech, and, if the operator could find the right groove in the record, there would be "God Save the King". If he found the wrong groove it would turn out "Land of Hope and Glory".'

Madame Pagel chats to one of the liger cubs — offspring of a Bengal tigress and an African lion — who captured the imagination of the world. Bella the tigress, and Prince the lion met in Pagel's Circus in the 1930s and fell in love. In December 1935 Bella gave birth to the three liger cubs that were to make the Bloemfontein zoo famous. But in February 1942, tragically and for no apparent reason, Prince fatally mauled Bella in their cage at the zoo

Jim Boswell and his family built up their £200-a-night road-show into a £1 000-a-night spectacular

Frank Fillis was one of South Africa's greatest ever showmen. In 1899 he chartered the liner Goth *to take him to England with 'Savage South Africa', a spectacular entertainment featuring 500 'Zulus' (actually Shangaans from Portuguese East Africa), hundreds of Basuto ponies, buck, lions, tigers and elephants. Featuring episodes from the Matabele and other wars, the show ran for six months until the outbreak of the Anglo-Boer War. He returned to South Africa and toured with his usual circus until 1904, when he sailed for the United States with yet another 'war' show — this time featuring the Boer generals Pieter Cronjé, whose forces had invested Kimberley and Mafeking; Viljoen and '1 000 veterans'. Picture shows the site of Fillis's Boer War Show in St Louis, Missouri*

THE BEST-LOVED CLOWN OF ALL

Originally recruited as a trampolinist, the diminutive Eric Hoyland was rechristened Tickey, by Syd Boswell, after the smallest coin in South Africa. Dressed in the costume of an *auguste* — the tramp-clown with baggy clothes, red nose and enormous mouth — Tickey described his terror as he stumbled into the ring, picked himself up and blinked in the glare of the spotlights: 'There was a horrible moment of silence and my heart stopped beating. Then the crowd roared. They laughed and laughed, and something happened inside me. It was suddenly marvellous fun to be laughed at when you wanted to be laughed at. It was more wonderful to be a clown, out on your own, than a trampolinist. This was my life: Tickey the idiot; Tickey the fool; Tickey the *auguste;* Tickey the clown — and very proud of it!' South Africa's most lovable clown had come to stay.

'Music was provided by what was then known as a panatrope, a rather primitive electric gramophone. A drummer named Mickey Haycock accompanied the panatrope's melodies and provided the sound effects for all acts . . . electricity came from a dynamo driven by an old, tired-looking McCormick Deering tractor. The belt connecting the dynamo to the tractor was very neurotic . . . the thing would get temperamental right at the climax of some act and slip off . . . and some artist would be left balancing on his nose in pitch darkness.'

Competition arrived in 1954 in the shape of Wilkie's Circus from England, and South Africans could now enjoy a double selection of the best artistes in the world. Wilkie's also had a midget clown, JoJo — a symbol of the intense rivalry between the two companies. Eventually, in 1963, they merged, which brought the combined show under the control of I.W. Schlesinger's entertainment giant, African Consolidated Theatres. Other circuses took to the road: Chipperfield's from England, and the short-lived Doyle's Circus, which opened in 1965 but ran out of money in De Aar in 1967.

South African performers have also won international honours: in 1968 Charlie Bale took the 'Clown Oscar', awarded every five years for outstanding circus performance.

The show goes on.

Holiday time

Left: a castle-building contest at Port Elizabeth's Humewood Beach in 1904. Right: Humewood Beach photographed from roughly the same position in 1937

BATHING AND DABBLING, GAZING AND PADDLING

'Little more than a year ago the Beach was, perhaps, one of the most deserted and inhospitable spots in Durban, and a single visit seemed to suffice for such as wandered there experimentally. The tea-rooms have effected a complete change, and the beach is now a most popular resort, the place at times swarming with visitors. Ladies in particular seem to find the rooms a great attraction . . .'

So wrote J. Forsyth Ingram in 1899 in his *Story of an African Seaport*. 'Connected with the tea-rooms are a number of bathing tents for ladies . . .' he went on. 'Each of these tents is provided with a long rope . . . and the ladies have gladly availed themselves of the opportunities thus provided of a safe dip.'

The three-year-old Anglo-Boer War more or less brought to an end holiday travel, but as soon as it was over, South Africans once again headed in cheerful droves for the seaside.

AROUND THE WORLD ON £300

In 1927 *Outspan* printed an account of a traveller's journey around the world on a budget of only £300. His marathon trip took him from Cape Town to Sydney (fare: £26), where he spent a week at an average of 15/- a day, and on to Hong Kong via Brisbane, Thursday Island, Zamboanga and Manila. This stage cost him a modest £50.

He sailed from the Far East to Vancouver on the west coast of Canada, crossed that country and parts of America by rail, and travelled second class on a 25 000-ton liner to England — all for £80. He completed the entire journey in only five months.

In the same year *Outspan* described a three-month overseas trip by one of its readers who had managed to enjoy herself immensely on as little as £100. She emphasised that it was not an impossible holiday for the ordinary working girl or young man earning only £16 or £18 a month.

Once there, Edwardian families were content with rather primitive arrangements: the Duminy family, who farmed where the Cape's Bellville sprawls today, spent an annual four-week holiday in simple thatched fishermen's cottages at Blaauwberg Strand. 'There were no shops there,' records Katherine Heywood in *Cape Hills in Sunlight*, 'so the baggage wagon carried great quantities of meal for bread, butter and eggs salted down in barrels, together with the endless requirements to feed a large family.'

Further along the coast, Mossel Bay was a favourite among Afrikaans families from the Little Karoo. A.R. Burton in *Cape Colony Today* (1907) described there the 'great numbers of country people, who travel long distances by road and rail, and camp out, till the whole shore often looks like a great Boer camp'.

Improvements to South Africa's several railway systems made holidaying a lot easier and more comfortable. Until the mid-1890s there was no such thing as on-train catering so that holiday-makers were dependent on *padkos* — home-made and home-packed supplies — unless they could rush to Mr J.D. Logan's refreshment counters at places where the trains only-too-briefly stopped. Long after the coming of increasingly luxurious mobile refreshment coaches, South Africans continued the *padkos* habit. Some follow the tradition today. In the early 1900s, though, they couldn't have known what they were missing. A typical pre-First World War breakfast menu on the Cape Railways:

Quaker Oats,	Sauté Potatoes.
Fresh Milk.	Poached and Fried
Fried Fillets	Eggs.
Stockfish.	Savoury Omelette
Finnon Haddock.	(to order).
Curry and Rice.	Cold Ham.
Fried Sausage.	Ox Tongue.
Grilled Mutton	Dry Toast.
Chops.	Preserves.
Broiled Ham/and Bacon.	Tea. Coffee.

Natal was slower than the Cape in building its resort rail links. In 1902 the South Coast

Railway Line ran only as far as Isipingo, 16 km from Durban, after which holiday-makers depended on the post-cart or wagons to reach Umkomaas, Scottburgh and — if they were very enterprising — Port Shepstone. No one had yet heard of any places beyond and it was not until after the First World War that Margate came into existence. The Natal North Coast told the same story — there, for many years, the railway stopped at Verulam, just 28 km from Durban.

Some parts of the Eastern Cape coast also developed slowly; even in the 1920s, holidays at a place like Bushman's River near Port Alfred were casual, economical affairs. In her memoir, *Bloomie*, May O'Shea tells of renting an 'unfurnished cottage' there for a mere £5: you could stay as long as you liked, and the price included the hire of the wagon to take you and your baggage from Grahamstown to the coast. The cottage turned out to be a wood-and-iron shack with a floor of black sand and crude wooden boards for windows (you propped them open for air). But,

Motor coaches pause for a tea break at the Hotel Drummond in the Valley of a Thousand Hills — one of Natal's famed beauty spots

THE MAN WHO CHANGED EVERYTHING

On 26 March 1898 the *Official Gazette* proclaimed. that a large area in the northeastern corner of the Transvaal Lowveld was to become a nature reserve, and that the destruction, hunting or wounding of game within the area was prohibited. President Kruger's wish was fulfilled and the Sabie Game Reserve was born.

In July 1902, Lieutenant-Colonel James Stevenson-Hamilton of the 6th (Inniskilling) Dragoon Guards was appointed chief game warden: he held the post for 44 successful years. Determined to enforce the no-shooting law that was being ignored by hunters, he showed he meant business when he prosecuted a senior police officer for shooting a wildebeest. The man was convicted and fined £5.

Determined lobbying and negotiation enabled Stevenson-Hamilton to increase the original Sabie Game Reserve to 36 260 km², and he laid the foundations of the Kruger National Park, which now covers an area of nearly two million hectares. The first tourist cars entered the park in 1927 (tourists were allowed to carry firearms and made their own camps among the thorn bushes) and by 1968 the park was drawing over 300 000 visitors a year.

needless to say, the O'Sheas loved their rough-and-ready holiday and often went back in later years.

Once at the seaside, Edwardian holidaymakers enjoyed much the same amusements as we do today, although in the early 1900s there were few who swam well. Recalls Katherine Heywood of her family: 'No one could swim, but we bobbed up and down in a circle, holding hands and shouting loudly as the cold Atlantic waters embraced us.'

A.R. Burton vividly described how, in 1907, the holiday crowds of Muizenberg 'bathed and dabbled and gazed and paddled and boated and fished and crabbed'. At the Kowie, as Port Alfred was then popularly called, golf was a thriving holiday pleasure before the First World War, while at Muizenberg and Durban surf-bathing — with old-style wooden boards — challenged the stronger swimmers to an invigorating new sport.

The establishment of South African Railways in 1913 not only encouraged the up-country holiday-maker who wanted to visit the seaside, but the coastal resident who yearned for a holiday inland. There was now a Railway Publicity Department, which issued posters exhorting people to entrain for the Drakensberg to see the scenery, go trout fishing, climb mountains.

Although it was eventually to revolutionise holiday travel, the motor car had little impact until the 1920s. The 1906 *Guide to South Africa for Tourists, Sportsmen, Invalids and Settlers* pronounced: 'Until the roads in South Africa have been improved, the highclass touring car must be restricted in its movements. For cross-country work all cars must give a good clearance between wheels, because of the deepness of the ruts and the hummocky character of the road centre, where the soil is soft and sandy. As so many water-courses, are unbridged, the carburettor, magneto, commutator etc. must be placed as high as possible. A car that will not stand rough usage will not be of much use. As regards power, great speed can rarely be indulged in; therefore about 16 hp with three speeds forward, should meet all reasonable requirements . . .'

Snapshots from a typical family photograph album taken after a coastal trip in the 1930s. In those days the accepted route for the more adventurous holiday-makers was Cape Town, Port Elizabeth, East London, Durban, Lourenço Marques and Beira. Sometimes they made excursions by rail to the Victoria Falls

EARLY HOMES ON WHEELS

The 1920s and 1930s saw an enormous increase in the popularity of caravanning, and manufacturers produced some ingenious designs. A novel 'road yacht' was introduced in 1927 and sold, said *Outspan*, at the price of 'an ordinary well-formed touring car' Its lozenge-shaped body accommodated a large 'living room' which could seat five people. It was fitted with a radio and gramophone compartment, a 'galley' complete with electric oven and even a shower cabinet! Pioneer airman Dr John Weston, one of the country's first caravanners, spent several years travelling abroad in his 'road yacht'.

The 1927 'road yacht' was 5,5 m long, and had two single-berth cabins, lounge, galley and shower-bath

'Mr and Mrs Dotter are touring the country in their motor caravan,' reported the *South African Lady's Pictorial* in 1924. The couple's mobile home was built on a one-ton Ford chassis, and the body was of wood covered with canvas, giving it the appearance of a Romany caravan. Their motor caravan featured three electric lights (powered by the caravan's battery) and a 20-gallon water tank mounted beneath the body. Today caravanning is one of South Africa's favourite leisure activities: there are an estimated 120 000 caravans on the road and they are catered for by about 800 parks.

Mr and Mrs Dotter's motor caravan with teak interior and electric lights charged from the battery

Staying at hotels

ELEGANT OUTPOSTS OF EMPIRE

In the early 1900s there were some South African hotels that compared favourably with the best in the world. The world's rich (as well as the bored, adventurous and crooked) flocked to these elegant outposts of the Empire to revel and relax in an atmosphere of obsequiousness and quiet splendour. It was said of Durban's Royal Hotel that if you sat on the verandah for long enough you would see everyone who was anyone in Africa pass by. Rider Haggard, Mark Twain, Rudyard Kipling and H.G. Wells all stayed there, and the hotel — Durban's first — owed its name to a visit in 1860 by Queen Victoria's 15-year-old son, Prince Alfred. Previously it had been called the Masonic, and later the Commercial. Through these changes of name it remained a low, thatched wattle-and-daub building with a shady verandah, more like a cottage than an hotel.

In 1879 the Zulu War brought a minor boom, and scarlet uniforms thronged the Royal. A noteworthy guest was the Prince Imperial of France, soon to be killed in a Zulu ambush. The courtyard round which the Royal's many buildings clustered was renamed Ulundi Square, to commemorate the final battle. Its cool, tiled floor formed a peaceful colonial oasis and remained for many years the heart of the building — even when the hotel was modernised in the 1890s.

In 1902, one year after a second royal visit — this time by the Duke and Duchess of York (later King George V and Queen Mary) —the hotel was sold for £46 000. By then it boasted 100 bedrooms, and a 200-seat diningroom offering the best cuisine in Durban. The tariff was 15/- a day.

Rebuilt again in 1909, and then amalgamated with the next-door Marine Hotel in

Barney Barnato's Carlton Hotel in 1920. Its opulence was legendary and its clientele included the rich and famous from all over the world

An invitation to the opening of the Carlton in 1906. The original is now in the Africana Museum

The staff of Messrs Norman Anstey gathered at the Carlton Hotel for a dinner in 1914. The Illustrated Star *noted that a presentation was made to the head of the firm (Anstey was also Mayor of Johannesburg)*

A 1926 receipted account from the Carlton. Lunch for twelve — with drinks — a nostalgic £12.13s.

1928, the Royal was completely reconstructed as a five-star glossy skyscraper in the 1970s.

The inimitable Nellie

In the heyday of the mailships, those firm links with Empire, the Mount Nelson in Cape Town represented more than an hotel to seasoned travellers: it was a way of life.

Opened only six months before the Anglo-Boer War began in 1899, the Mount Nelson quickly became the headquarters of the English. The scores of rich young officers instantly christened it the 'Nellie' — a name that stuck. But wealthy refugees from the Reef, chafing at their enforced idleness, gave it a less attractive nickname: 'Helot's Rest'.

Famous people flocked to the hotel. Kipling came — and H.G. Wells and Conan Doyle. Buller, Roberts and Kitchener in turn established their headquarters in the Nellie. Cecil Rhodes entertained there, and Winston Churchill's mother enjoyed the strawberries. (Many women followed their fighting men to South Africa during the war but seldom, it seems, ventured further than the comforts of the Mount Nelson.) Churchill himself, after his spectacular escape from the Boers, retired

to one of the luxury suites to continue issuing his war reports.

The Castle shipping line, which built the Nellie to rival the Union Steamships' Grand Hotel, had the rich and leisured class very much in mind when they created its 150 bedrooms, grand salon with Chippendale tables and chairs, domed diningroom, acres of oak panelling and polished oak floors. The *Cape Times* of the time rhapsodised: 'For the more gregarious, there is the beautiful verandah running along the entire frontage, in close touch with the garden and vineries, where the easy chairs tempt to a lengthy after-dinner stay in the company of a good cigar.'

The imposing columns which still dominate the entrance today were built in 1924; they combined with the avenue of tall palms to create a fine air of colonial ease. By this time the hotel had its regulars, Britons who came year after year to escape cruel northern winters, and who continued to come as long as the mailships sailed. Extensions and modernisation have continued, yet the hotel has managed to retain its essentially Edwardian atmosphere of grace, spaciousness and leisure.

The captain's table from the Windsor Castle was inherited by the Mount Nelson Hotel in 1977

A miniature city

'Meet me at the Carlton' was once a phrase so common that Eric Rosenthal used it as the title for his book about this famous Johannesburg hotel, which was a South African landmark for more than half a century.

The Carlton was the brainchild of Barney Barnato, although the magnate was destined never to see the hotel he had dreamed of as the biggest and best in the land. When it opened in 1906, the first issue of another Rand newcomer, the *Sunday Times*, raved: 'It isn't merely a hotel — it's a miniature city, insofar as it contains within its four walls the whole of those comforts which the luxury-loving modern desires.'

There were over 300 bedrooms; a vast, cool Rotunda as entrance hall; opulent carpets in every corridor; a white-and-gold glass-roofed Palm Court; a Grill Room panelled in oak (and a Smoke Room panelled in pigskin); a handsome, soon-to-be-famous Ball Room, complete with orchestra gallery.

As for tariffs: 'Single bedrooms at from 8s, double bedrooms at from 12s, and a self-contained suite of three rooms at from 35s, per day.' By 1920 prices had risen to 23/- per day (full board included) and 45/- for the suites.

Famous guests included Lily Langtry, Marie Tempest, Pavlova; after the First World War: Sybil Thorndike, Gracie Fields, and in 1925, the Prince of Wales. Ivor Novello, Danny Kaye, Margot Fonteyn, Yehudi Menuhin and Nelson Rockefeller were among those who followed. In 1947 the whole fifth floor was reserved for King George VI and his family.

The Carlton's Palm Court offered the first *thé dansants* of the Ragtime era. Its Grill Room, oyster bar, hairdressing salon, flower stall and Turkish Baths — mornings reserved for ladies, afternoons for gentlemen, with 'ordinary Turkish Baths' at 7/6 and 'Turkish Bath with Scientific Massage' 21/- — attracted a constant flow of people.

Pre-First World War Carlton manager, Mr Morelli, in Rosenthal's book on the Carlton, recalls the Edwardian extravagance of it all: 'Some idea of the scale of operations may be gained from the fact that every three months we needed four hundred cases of champagne.'

But the flow of champagne and money could not disguise the fact that the Carlton was running at a loss. Millionaire I.W. Schlesinger took over the hotel in 1923 and introduced sterner economies. In the 1930s private bathrooms were introduced (in place of the bedroom washstands); brass bedsteads were replaced by divans, and costly coal-fires banned from the bedrooms. For the Empire Exhibition of 1936, the basic tariff rose to 30/- (single).

In 1962 came the shock: the Carlton was to be demolished to make way for a 20-storey skyscraper. Despite public sentiment, which ran to a mourning ode in the *Star* ('Mutely the Carlton waits the loud machines . . .'), demolition began in 1964 after a fortnight of auctions to which the nostalgic swarmed to buy its relics; everything from crockery to bar counters. The Golden City had lost its premier monument to luxury.

Today a skyscraper, this is Durban's Royal Hotel at the turn of the century. Left: In 1903 the Commercial Review and Southern African Storekeeper *announced the signing of a £35 000 contract for the erection of King Edward's Mansions — which became Port Elizabeth's newest and grandest hotel. The three-storey building had a frontage of 150 metres*

HOSPITALITY IN THE COUNTRY

The young Iris Vaughan, staying at an hotel in the small Karoo town of Maraisburg at the turn of the century, wrote in her *Diary:* 'It is not a nice hotel. It is worse than at Pearston. The floors are of mud. Every week the floors are smeared with mis which is cowdung made soft like mud with water. It has a nasty smell. There is room where men are sitting and laughing loudly and spitting into white basins on the floor.'

Candles lit the spartan bedrooms, and 'in the dining room are three tables and a big clock. At one table a man was eating and doing much belching and never excuse me please'. She probably had a point. Many travellers were confronted by primitive accommodation and few, if any, of the facilities they enjoyed in their own homes.

In 1927 a traveller, writing in *Outspan*, asked why country hotels — which were generally little more than 'low-roofed corrugated-iron shanties' — had such pretentious names as 'Palace' or 'Royal'. Surely, she suggested,

the Springbok and the Outspan would be more appropriate?

By the late 1930s, the situation seems to have improved. An Englishwoman who toured South Africa later wrote in the *Outspan:* 'I have no hesitation in saying that the standard of comfort, cleanliness, food and service is high. The hotels in the large towns are second to none in the world where these attributes are concerned and lack that atmosphere of weary sloth which I personally find distasteful in London and on the continent.' Even in remote dorps she found 'adequate comforts' provided behind 'what is necessarily a most unpromising exterior'. Although she admitted that in a few 'exceptionally dried up places . . . the humble banana is the only fruit offered', she did point out that the free baths (if there was water) were acts of tremendous generosity.

In the early 1900s prices ranged from 12/6 or 15/- a day (all inclusive) to 35/- for a suite at hotels like Cape Town's International, or the newer Grand; Johannesburg's Grand Hotel; or the fashionable luxury of the hot-springs spa at Caledon, where the price included 'hot and cold mineral baths'.

THE NOT-QUITE-SO-GRAND HOTEL

Coxford's Victoria Hotel in Ladybrand had 'the reputation of being one of the best in South Africa'

The Central Hotel in Dordrecht, Cape, boasted every convenience for commercial travellers

The Royal Hotel in Ladysmith

The smaller country hotels of the early 1900s were hard put to find features attractive enough to draw customers for more than an overnight stay. In 1911 the Central Hotel in Dordrecht, Cape, was advertised as 'the most up-to-date Hotel on the Frontier'. Carts met all trains, it was stated, and the hotel was lit throughout with acetylene gas. Ladysmith's Crown Hotel (the names were grand but the establishments were distinctly modest) offered new-fangled electric lights and the best liquors, and proudly advertised that 'Traps can always be arranged for to visit the Battlefields' [sic].

Wining and dining

CLUBS AND CAFÉS OF THE 1900s — A MAN'S WORLD

Edwardian South Africans rarely dined out as a family unless attending formal banquets — which were rather daunting affairs. One served at the National Hotel, Caledon, in 1902, to mark the opening of the local railway, ran to no less than 24 courses, including two soups, four fish dishes, ten entrées and eight sweets. Those who sat through this culinary ordeal, cheered by sherry, chablis and champagne, had to listen to eight different toasts.

It was the Edwardian gentleman who upheld the English tradition of dining out — at clubs, hotels and grill rooms. This was essentially a masculine preserve: the business or professional man's luncheon where he could discourse freely without the restricting presence of ladies. Parliamentarians in Cape Town favoured the Royal Hotel in Plein Street — General Botha liked its snoek — while the city's oldest restaurant, the Café Royal (still flourishing in 1980), was also patronised by many notables.

General Smuts, as Lawrence Green has recorded, was 'fastidious, an epicure in his own way. Grilled snoek with brown butter sauce, new potatoes and rice formed one of his favourite dishes' at the Café Royal. General Hertzog enjoyed traditional food, too, the *boboties* and *bredies* for which the Cape was famed. Tielman Roos favoured *geelbek* with mayonnaise; Paul Sauer fried *perlemoen* with lemon sauce.

In the 1880s, the Café Royal could offer pea soup for 6d, roast beef and Yorkshire pudding or lamb cutlets and green peas for 1/-, and tea or coffee for a penny. Prices had since risen, but for those who wished to eat well *and* cheaply in the 1900s, there were still bargains to be had. Again, it seemed to be the single male who benefited most. In his Cape Town schooldays, Green frequented the Café Diane in Long Street for its 1/3 lunches: 'I ate as only a schoolboy can. French onion soup, a *cassoulet* of haricot beans, pork and mutton and other ingredients, and a fruit jelly . . .'

That great South African poet and gourmet, C. Louis Leipoldt, also wrote with nostalgia, in 1946, of his turn-of-the-century meals: 'I have, as a boy, sat down at Haylett's White House in the Strand at nine o 'clock of a morning to consume not cereals and Melba toast . . . but turmeric scones, *soesaties* [sic] with fried bananas and fried eggs, long, much-spiced sausages deliciously fried over wood coals, and a buffet of cold game and fowl and gammon ham.' Equally well-remembered midday dinners at Poole's Hotel consisted of thick soup, two kinds of fish, stews, roasts and vegetables, with 'a couple of sweets to follow'.

The best houses in town

South Africa's other towns also witnessed a burgeoning of Edwardian eating places. Mrs Favill's in Durban; the Glasgow Restaurant in Port Elizabeth; and — where the diggers and nabobs introduced a strong Continental note — Kimberley's Café Français and the Criterion; Johannesburg's Vienna Café de Beurs.

Johannesburg's Café Royal (left) was one of the city's smarter restaurants in the early 1900s. Diners could enjoy an intimate tête-à-tête in a private booth. Top right: Frascati's Café in Cape Town offered a grilled rump steak for only 9d. Right: Early this century people flocked to this tearoom on the jetty at Durban

'PERSONALLY I PREFER THE JOHANNESBURG CAFÉS'

The attractions and deficiencies of cafés in South Africa's major cities was the subject of enthusiastic debate in the late 1920s. A writer in the *Outspan* of 22 July 1927 suggested that someone could make a fortune by introducing an American-style 'cafetaria' to South Africa, commenting: ' . . . there is something very jolly and sporting about the atmosphere of the average American cafetaria, and this might distinctly appeal to a jolly and sporting people like South Africans.'

Another writer felt that if a 'cafetaria' was to be successful, it would have to be in Johannesburg, as 'the people up there are more "sporty" '. Cape Town was too dignified, the writer told *Outspan*, 'and as the tray affair in the cafetaria is very embarrassing Capetonians will not readily condescend'.

A Bloemfontein reader, placing Johannesburg cafés as the best and cheapest in the country, had a suggestion: '. . . a café to cater specially for business girls as the business girl as a rule objects to take lunch in a café crowded with men.'

Said another reader: 'Very few of the cafés in this country are fitted with ladies' or gents' toilet rooms and these, I think, are a great asset to a café. In Britain all the cafés have the most beautifully-equipped toilet rooms attached for both ladies and gentlemen, and if we had more of such places in this country fewer ladies would be seen using the powder puff and rouge box in public.' The same reader proposed that instead

of the large creamy cakes ('the cream of which is often sour') which were served with afternoon tea, some of the cafés might serve a daintier cake with more icing instead of cream. 'After all, one doesn't usually want to make a meal of afternoon tea . . .'

A Pretoria man, writing of his experiences in Cape Town restaurants, described an establishment where one could buy a sole for a shilling: 'It was some sole; it hung far over on each side of the plate and wagged its tail up and down as it was brought in. I once took a lady there. She ordered sole, but when she saw the size of it she nearly fell off her chair.'

To his mind, said the writer, one of the greatest attractions a café could offer was an open air balcony. However he didn't like the idea of 'cafetarias': 'Personally . . . it savours too much of army methods.'

High standards in Continental cuisine were set by a crop of luxury hotels, beginning with Cape Town's Mount Nelson in 1899 (it promised Swiss chefs and 'high-class French cooking'); the expanded Royal in Durban (where, after the Anglo-Boer War, a steep 5/- was charged for dinner); and Johannesburg's glittering Carlton Hotel of 1906, which advertised: 'Recherché Cuisine; Choice Wines; Spacious Grill Room; Magnificent Restaurant; After-Theatre Suppers; Rooms for Private Dinners, Banquets Etc.'

During the First World War its restaurant offered a quick lunch at 3/- or the Carlton Lunch at 4/6, a Theatre Dinner (4/6) or the Carlton Dinner (6/-). Other restaurants opened in Johannesburg to siphon off their share of the smart 'Carlton Hotel trade': the Francati, the Continental, the Grand National and the Trocadero, whose waiters wore tails and where the atmosphere was one of international sophistication.

MUSIC WHILE THEY ATE

It was in the years between the two world wars that eating out became a truly fashionable occupation. By the 1930s, the vogue for evening wining and dining was well established.

But the dinner-dance was the real attraction. The connection between music and food had first been established, immediately before the First World War, by the enormous popularity of *thé dansants* and Tango Teas. Then the Jazz Age — the 1920s — brought resident orchestras to noted restaurants like Johannesburg's Corner Lounge and the Madeleine. From now on very little eating was to be accomplished in silence. Even tearooms boasted orchestras or modern jazz bands. In Cape Town in the 1930s and 1940s, it was the done thing for young people to meet on Saturday mornings at fashionable restaurants like the Waldorf and consume strawberries or *spanspek* and icecream, tea and tiny cakes to the tinkle of spoons and the strains of popular tunes.

By the time the Second World War broke out in 1939, nightclubs were the rage — and they stayed popular throughout those feverish, exciting years. Couples would spend vir-

Ciro's Restaurant Club in Johannesburg in the mid-1950s. The restaurant abounded with heavy drapes, huge columns and crystal chandeliers. Right: A dinner-dance menu from 1946

tually whole nights out — at the Stardust in Cape Town, His Majesty's in Johannesburg, or that specially well-loved spot, also called the Stardust, in Port Elizabeth.

Recalls one former habitué: 'You never went before ten or eleven; often you went on to the Stardust from a ball at midnight. Then you danced till four or five in the morning. It was all subdued lights and soft music, very "glam". The men wore white tuxedos, the women always the sexiest long dresses. By three in the morning the air would be blue with cigarette smoke, the music would grow dreamier and smoochier — it was divine! We danced till our legs wouldn't carry us, then we went home in the dawn with the sun rising and the milkmen on the streets.'

By the 1950s what one club addict called 'a rush for life' had diminished and it was not until the 1960s that eating out became high fashion again — this time less for music or atmosphere than for the food. Rising prices (compare today's with the 5/- paid for a mixed grill at the Stardust in the 1940s) were a major cause of the change. So was the increasing opportunity for international travel — South Africans abroad learned to appreciate Continental cuisine.

New Year's Eve
Souper Dansant
31st December, 1946

THE COMING OF THE TAKE-AWAY

At the turn of the century, many bars offered the informal diner snacks and counter lunches; some of Cape Town's taverns were known as 'Sosatie and Rice' houses.

Cafés were the next rung up the casual-food ladder. Providing cheap, filling meals at first, these gradually changed to become the popular tearoom: the place to meet and to listen to live music. Shoppers could also retire to balcony cafés, like Cartwright's in Cape Town, or the roof garden of Anstey's in Johannesburg.

Hollywood films between the wars introduced fashionable late-night snacks: toasted sandwiches, hot dogs and hamburgers. Drive-in restaurants became the thing — in Cape Town in the late 1930s, for instance, the Spotted Dog was a landmark for revellers returning from naval dances at Muizenberg.

Fast foods rapidly gained in popularity over the next decades. Not all city workers wanted to sit down to the solid, square meals provided so cheaply by cafés in the pre-war years Take-away foods became a feature of the 1950s, and the hamburger a symbol of the quickening pace of modern living. In the 1960s, chains of casual American-style fast-food and take-away establishments sprang up all over South Africa: Wimpy Bars, steak houses and Kentucky Fried Chicken kiosks. American soft-serve icecream, dispensed by machines, replaced many of the leisurely old-style Italian icecream parlours.

The opening of the Del Monico in Cape Town was the social highlight of the year, drawing an estimated 800 guests to the inaugural cocktail party in September 1936. Right: The ornate main entrance to what the Pictorial *described as 'the finest and most up-to-date restaurant in the Southern Hemisphere'. The Del Monico, probably one of South Africa's most famous dining spots, has now been demolished*

The smoking habit

CIGARETTES COME OF AGE IN THE GLAMOROUS THIRTIES

In the 1930s, Hollywood stars puffed away elegantly on the movie screen and lent enormous glamour to smoking. Advertisements for sheer stockings depicted long-legged women who waved their cigarette holders nonchalantly among the cocktail glasses. This super-sophisticated new image signalled the growing popularity of smoking among women as well as men — and the coming of age of cigarettes.

At the turn of the century, it was thought 'fast' for a woman to smoke in public, and South African men were mostly pipe-smokers. The farmer was especially addicted: in the Magaliesberg and the Little Karoo around Oudtshoorn, he grew and cured his own tobacco, making sharp guillotine cutters to shave each day's fresh ration. An early cigarette card series on 'Riders of the World' included a Boer on horseback, his pipe firmly clamped in his mouth. In the world's eyes, it seemed, a Boer and his pipe were inseparable.

Sophisticated city gentlemen often preferred the luxury of a cigar, especially after dinner when the ladies left the room before the English ritual of port and masculine conversation. Dinner jackets could then be exchanged for quilted smoking jackets, which were also favoured for all-male diversions such as billiards.

In 1922 Smokers' Stores in Port Elizabeth ('the well-known rendezvous for smokers who display good taste in their choice of Cigars, Cigarettes, Tobaccos and Smoking Equipment generally') stocked not only a wide

An Edwardian lady (beneath open window) pauses for a few languid puffs on her cigarette before lunch

range of cigars, pipes, tobaccos and cigarettes, but also ashtrays, cigarette cases, cigarette holders, pipe racks, smokers' cabinets, tobacco pouches, walking sticks and canes.

At this stage, the milder flavour of cigarettes appealed mostly to women. Rich-scented Turkish tobacco was more popular for cigarettes than Virginia, reflecting the origin of the cigarette smoking habit — British soldiers learnt it from the Turks during the Crimean War of the 1850s. By the end of the 19th century, cigarettes were well-established: in South Africa, their manufacture began, by

hand, in Port Elizabeth in 1875. Cape Town soon followed suit. Mechanization came in the 1890s, followed by a proliferation of new factories after the Anglo-Boer War.

Puffing in public

Public smoking for men had been sanctioned in Edwardian times by 'smoking concerts', though there were a few restrictions — the Empire Palace of Varieties in Johannesburg, for instance, advertised special 'Ladies' Nights' when no smoking was allowed in the front stalls.

Left: A programme for a 'smoking concert' — once a popular form of entertainment. This concert was launched with a pianoforte solo, followed by a toast to the King and several other musical items. Above: Displaying cigarettes collected for soldiers at the front in 1914

QUALITY renowned throughout the world

WILLS'S
Gold Flake
FILTER TIP CIGARETTES

A 1939 cigarette advertisement. Left: By 1950 smoking was more 'ladylike'

This pyramid of cigarette box fronts represents more than 3,25 million smoked cigarettes, and illustrates one of the methods employed by manufacturers early this century to promote their brands of cigarettes. The 334 000 Needlepoint cigarette box fronts in the picture were those returned in a 1906 competition

Some early tobacco and cigarette packs. Brand names often reflected a South African preoccupation with the military

In Edwardian years the habit was very much a masculine one. A few women did smoke, but in most cases only in the privacy of their own drawing rooms, where they were less likely to cause offence.

The First World War created a freer society, and by the 1920s, women were smoking openly, though not without comment. The *South African Lady's Pictorial* asked in 1923: 'Should a woman smoke?', warning that excessive smoking led to blotchy skin, indigestion and lassitude. *The Family Magazine* pointed out that 'a strong desire to smoke is the first evidence of "tobaccomania" which ultimately is bound to lead to disaster'.

Fatal to his wind

In the 1930s, too, the Anti-Smoking League of South Africa marketed a vigorous campaign. Boxer Willie Smith warned that 'excessive smoking is extremely injurious to the general health and a real hindrance to all those who go in for any sport. In my own profession, particularly, over-indulgence in tobacco would prove absolutely fatal to my wind'.

This warning was echoed by other famous sportsmen: but the habit continued to spread. Few people seemed worried about the health hazards or nuisance element of smoking, and a blue-grey haze became an established feature of nightclubs and other public venues. Some found it curiously comforting.

Some idea of the popularity of smoking can be gleaned from the following statistics, provided by the *Standard Encyclopaedia of Southern Africa,* on cigarette smoking in this country. Cigarettes consumed in millions:

1920	1930	1940	1950	1968
1 517	2 651	4 625	9 089	15 400

A MEDICAL OPINION

Opinions on the hazards of smoking have been debated for many years. In 1903 the *Commercial Review and S.A. Storekeeper* announced with some satisfaction:

'An American medico has been well employed in shattering one of the cherished traditions about the toxic effect of tobacco. The talk one hears of nicotine saturating the system of smokers, he declares, is "mostly rot". Nicotine is a deadly poison, and one drop, if injected subcutaneously, would make a big mastiff turn up his toes, and but very little of it would kill a man much quicker than many a Mauser bullet. The truth is that even the most confirmed smokers absorb very little nicotine. Nobody ever died through smoking tobacco.' However the periodical did make one concession: 'It must be admitted, however, that indulgence in the soothing weed stimulates the heart, especially of cigarette smokers, who commonly inhale the fumes.'

Seventy-six years later, the *Reader's Digest* magazine published figures which revealed that the most popular cigarette brands contained the highest levels of 'tar' and nicotine, the substances which may cause malignant tumours and contribute to heart and other circulatory diseases.

Packing C to C cigarettes at the United Tobacco Company's factory in Cape Town in the days before mechanization

Changing trends in drink

CAPE SMOKE AND PEACH BRANDY

In the early 1900s South Africans had two strong preferences in drink: brandy, the local 'Cape Smoke' (described by Birkby in *Thirstland Trek* as 'the fiercest brandy that ever came from a still') long respected for its potency; and that unmistakably masculine beverage, beer. English gentlemen might sit on their club verandahs sipping whisky (so Olive Schreiner characterised them in her *Thoughts on South Africa*), but the average man in South Africa's taverns opted for the less pretentious tipple.

In rural districts, brandy-making was a popular home industry, and many families quaffed glass after glass of vile-tasting liquid with apparent enjoyment. A young visitor to Jonkershoek, near Stellenbosch, in 1906, described the casual trampling of the grapes whereby most of the skins went into the wine too: 'Brandy is made when they take all the skins and put them into big kettles with a lot of *wyn sop* (wine which is too weak for wine) and then they close the kettle and make a big fire underneath and then the steam is caught by it rising to the top and then flows out by a pipe wound in a snake in a tub so as to get cool . . .' The description was completed by a sketch of a typical brandy still. Similar copper stills may still be found in museums and occasionally on farms in various parts of South Africa.

Herman Charles Bosman's story, *Willem Prinsloo's Peach Brandy*, has immortalised the effects of those powerful, home-distilled liquors variously known as *mampoer*, *witblits* and *withond*. They vary in quality (the basic ingredients range from grapes and peaches to potatoes, sugar-cane, prickly pears and karree berries),but all have one thing in common: a nasty habit of putting the unwary to sleep in a remarkably short time. They are still made — albeit discreetly — on some farms today.

Left: An early bar scene. Some bars were incredibly ornate, featuring a profusion of mirrors, pillars and fancy woodwork. The bar counters were of massive proportions. Right: George Hackenschmidt, the famous strongman, lifts barrels of beer in an advertising stunt emphasising the manliness of South Africa's favourite drink

Producers went to some lengths to shake off the old image of brandy as the drink of the rough, tough, hard-boozing he-man. The July 1908 issue of the *Cape Magazine* stated that they were 'happy to think that Mr Malan is mistaken in saying that the man who goes into a Capetown bar and calls for Colonial brandy is "looked down upon".' An advertisement for Perfection Brandy before the Second World War described it as 'the favourite beverage and stimulant of cultured people'. Picardie was praised as 'a safeguard in the home in case of emergency or illness' and Chateau offered 'that deep and satisfying goodness'.

Great improvements in the quality of South African brandy followed the establishment of the KWV (Co-operative Wine Farmers' Association) in 1918, when strict control was introduced in the production of wine, brandy and other fruits of the vine.

Clear, sparkling lagers

At the turn of the century, though, the most widely appreciated drink in South Africa was probably beer. The ale-drinking habit was an integral part of Cape life in the early days of the Dutch occupation and was twice reinforced — first by the English with their

Mementos of early brewing in South Africa. At one time ashtrays, jugs and unusual beer mugs such as these were displayed in thousands of South African homes

Top: A pre-First World War beer advertisement. Above: Chandler's beer wagon. The firm was founded by George and Charles Chandler in 1884

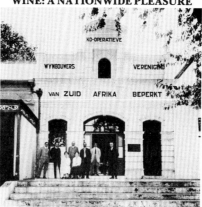

The KWV building at Paarl in 1918, the year the co-operative was launched. Its growth was phenomenal

As the 19th century drew to a close, Cape wine farmers were still suffering from the effects of phyloxera, the disease which attacks the roots of the vines. South African wines were few and poor.

But the industry began to find its feet again, and by 1904 there were an estimated 78 million vines in the country. Ironically, the farmers next had to contend with over-production on a large scale, and in 1909 representatives from all the wine districts marched to Parliament and presented a resolution to the government calling for immediate action to bale out the industry. Their plea had little effect.

The turning point came in 1918 with the registration of the 'Ko-operatiewe Wijnbouwers Vereeniging van Zuid-Afrika Beperkt' (KWV). Wine farming was revolutionised, and by 1925 South Africa had a firm foothold in the Dutch and British markets. But then came another problem: farmers were so enamoured of fixed prices for their produce that they abandoned other crops in favour of vines. It became clear that price control without production control would lead to disaster.

In 1940 Parliament passed an Act authorising the KWV to limit Cape wine production (the Act was later amended to extend the authority to the other provinces). Farmers were allowed to produce wine on a quota system, and their product could be sold only through the co-operative. In 1919 the KWV had paid farmers an estimated R1 million; within half a century the figure had climbed to over R28 million. By 1980 the organisation was paying its approximately 5 700 members about R140 million a year for their wine.

It was only in the 1960s that wine-drinking really caught on as a nationwide pleasure, starting with popular picnic wines such as Lieberstein and graduating to quality reds and whites produced in the rich valleys of Paarl and Stellenbosch.

watery 'bitter' and dark stout, and later by the German element, which preferred clear, sparkling lagers of the type brewed in South Africa today.

In the 1870s a German visitor named Ernst von Weber, visiting the mining camp of Pniel, complained that 'no decent-tasting drink' was to be found. All he was offered was 'warm English ale, bitter as gall'. To call this miserable concoction beer, he maintained, would be heresy. But by 1900 Von Weber would have had no cause to complain. Beer brewing had become big business in South Africa — particularly in the vast digger populations of Kimberley and Johannesburg. The Reef, crowded with thirsty uitlanders, was particularly rich in breweries and German beer halls.

'Their Bier Hall is to them what the tea-shop is to us,' declared a writer in the *South African Handbook* series. 'Round the bar men stand discussing the latest thing in politics, sport or society, each with his glass of bier, and a plateful of his particular fancy in the food line. But generally it is the one thing — long, juicy, steaming pretty-nearly-raw sausages, with plenty of ice-cold potato salad. At the tables inside are the family men with their sweethearts, beating time with their glasses to the strains of the orchestra . . .'

The same writer mentions a 'sparkling lager', a brew that was to emerge as the firm South African favourite. Requiring temperatures of freezing point and below to mature, the commercial development of lager beers was made possible in the 1890s by the advent of large scale refrigeration plants. Castle Breweries opened their first lager beer plant in Johannesburg in 1898, urging:

> 'Taste its brilliancy! Taste its flavour! Absolutely pure beer at 6d a glass.'

Pretoria's Lion Brewery, closed during the Anglo-Boer War, re-opened in 1902 to offer 'Lager Beer, Bock Beer and Stout'.

Beer had become an important part of South African life. Strongmen George Hackenschmidt and William Pagel (of circus fame) lent their muscular frames to advertising campaigns for Castle and Lion beer. For many years the South African Breweries competed vigorously with two other brewing giants: Chandler's (dating from 1884 in Kimberley, and from 1887 in Johannesburg) and the famous Ohlsson's Brewery in Cape Town — formed by an amalgamation of smaller breweries in 1889 and run by a man styled as 'Prince of Colonial Brewers'.

In the early 1950s a heavy excise duty was imposed on beer, and this, combined with the increasing cost of production, persuaded the three giants to merge in 1956 under the banner of the South African Breweries. Although no longer a cheap drink, well-chilled lager remains an indispensable part of South Africa's indoor and outdoor life.

In 1978 the per capita consumption of beer in South Africa was 20,4 litres — ranking it 38th in the world.

Women who liked an occasional tipple had a difficult time in early South Africa. It was, like smoking, considered unladylike — and dangerous to boot. Women were often the prime activists in the Temperance Union, an anti-alcohol league which put out propagandist literature, provided non-alcoholic recipes and sent lecturers into the field. Iris Vaughan's *Diary* records the visit of the 'Temperence lady' to her school shortly after the Anglo-Boer War:

'All school children had to come in big room to listen to this lady talking about strong drink. She said it is the food of Satan. She put two pictures on the blackboard. One was a great fat red heart and one was a small pink heart. The fat heart was the brandy drinkers and the pink heart the water drinkers. The lady said Now all look at these hearts and then you can tell me what heart you would like to have. And Lindsay . . . stood up and said I would like to have that nice fat heart and teacher put him down and Frances stood up and said I want the nice pink small heart and everyone was releaved [sic] . . .' The message was clear: brandy drinkers had fat red hearts!

Many homes were fitted with cocktail bars during the surge of popularity of cocktail parties in the 1950s

The Performing Arts

South Africans have at least one thing in common with people all over the world: they love to be entertained. In the early 1880s, Charles du Val travelled throughout the country with his little theatrical company, performing in stores, warehouses and any other place large enough to accommodate an audience. Came the 20th century, and theatres, some primitive and others plushly-decorated in red and gilt, sprang up in every centre.

Dramatic companies and music hall artistes were imported from England and America, and vaudeville flourished. The first cinemas appeared, and South African audiences were introduced to their first 'epics' by courtesy of Thomas Edison's amazing invention, the Bioscope machine.

I. W. Schlesinger stepped in, and in May 1913 created the conglomerate which later became African Consolidated Theatres. Vaudeville and music halls were now a thing of the past; the silver screen rapidly took over. There was music, too. Jazz made its appearance, and some of us did not understand it. Radio stations beamed out news and songs from the early 1920s, and by 1932 there were 161 767 licensed sets in the Union. The South African Broadcasting Corporation was created in 1936.

By this time, the thirty-year era of silent movies was over. Sydney Hayden had successfully exhibited his 'phonofilms' in Cape Town in February 1927, and when he opened in Johannesburg, crowds flocked to every performance. We saw statuesque Mae West in *She Done Him Wrong*, and blushed at Marlene Dietrich in *The Blue Angel*. Clarke Gable's rugged good looks won thousands of female hearts.

In 1950, a young schoolteacher spent £170 on filming equipment for his first film. It was *Daar Doer in die Bosveld*, and the producer was Jamie Uys. Thirty years later, he was still making South Africans laugh at themselves with films such as *Funny People* and *The Gods Must Be Crazy*.

South African Theatre was also growing up. André Huguenet, winner of the Suid-Afrikaanse Akademie's gold medal, was a magnificently successful actor, manager and writer who helped to put Afrikaans drama on the map in more than three decades of hard work. Brian Brooke was repatriated to South Africa in 1946, and after a bad start, was soon touring the country with *The Boy Friend*, a nostalgic and highly successful musical by Sandy Wilson. Taubie Kushlick produced *Jacques Brel is Alive and Well . . .*; actors, actresses and playwrights — such as Yvonne Bryceland and Athol Fugard — won international acclaim.

Then, in January 1976, came a development that Dr Albert Hertzog had fervently hoped we would avoid: South Africans switched on their television sets. Home entertainment was revolutionised, and the country's social preoccupations would never again be quite the same.

Thelma Versveld has mixed feelings about the lure of the footlights. The diminutive artiste is thought to have been taking part in the celebrations marking the end of the Anglo-Boer War in 1902

117

Vaudeville and music hall

Anything for publicity. In 1912 'Illusionist' Nicola has himself manacled to the tramlines at Camps Bay, Cape, and is then covered by a blanket

Houdini-like, Nicola slips the bands just in time to escape the onrushing tramcar. The onlooking crowd is gratifyingly impressed by his daring

THE TRAVELLING SHOWMEN OF YESTERYEAR

It was the year 1880, and the few hundred souls of the Cape town of Middelburg had waited expectantly all day for the 'performers'. And then, late in the afternoon, a four-wheeled cart was seen raising the dust as it trundled into the dorp. The inhabitants deemed it impossible that between 5.30 and 8 o'clock a grand performance of *Odds and Ends* could be assembled from the mass of debris unloaded.

But, as Charles du Val tells in his memoirs, entitled *With a Show through Southern Africa*, 'all hands to work; span in all the spare Africans available to carry seats and for platform building . . . and carry a piano, and you shall have as much Cape brandy as you can soak your woolly heads in'. And, as the town hall clock struck eight, to the amazement of Middelburgers, the curtain was ready to go up on the show — a pot-pourri of songs, dramatic readings by Du Val himself and magic lantern slides.

By the following day, Du Val's company would be back on the cart, leaving a better-informed audience behind (though there would be fulsome sermons delivered by the

Dopper minister on the evils of the theatre). Ahead lay a trek of perhaps 20 hours to the next small town. Du Val, the first of the travelling showmen, was to claim that he visited every town and village in South Africa during his hectic two years in the country. He was caught up in the Transvaal War and left in 1881.

At about the same time, another pioneer of the early theatre was touring the colonies and Boer republics. With his wife, and son Frank, Benjamin Wheeler loaded an ox wagon with actors and actresses and hampers of costumes, and travelled the country. The young Frank was later to become famous as an energetic impresario who brought out whole West End theatrical companies to enthral South African audiences.

And there were others — Captain Disney Roebuck, for example, who built the Theatre Royal in Cape Town, and the famed Luscombe Searelle, and Frank de Jong who, with the Wheelers, presented overseas talent in dramas and light opera. All had a common bond: a love for the stage and the ability to take financial risks, most of which were to pay off.

No reviews of risqué shows

In the early years of this century, theatre

managements went to great pains to tell prospective patrons that they only put on 'polite vaudeville' or 'refined music hall'. In a review of the World's Entertainers at the Empire Theatre, Johannesburg, in 1902, a critic used half his column to stress that there was 'nothing of a vulgar nature, nor anything approaching what is termed the "music hall" form of amusement, nothing on the programme that could offend good taste or which could offend the most fastidious in these matters'.

Newspapers remained fairly muted on the risqué performances of 'music halls', choosing to ignore them completely rather than popularise their vulgarity. The non-coverage of a new show clearly indicated disapproval — and brought in the crowds.

Music hall had been the fount of entertainment for the raucous miners of the Witwatersrand before the Anglo-Boer War. Cornishmen would change their pay cheques at the bars of the Old Empire. Americans would shoot up the bars, tossing handfuls of notes to the well-endowed barmaids. Inside the theatre, the audiences enjoyed a good singing comic and whistled noisily at the show-girls. Classical music would combine with burlesque.

Jack Stodel, son of the great impresario Harry, recalls that W.C. Fields, who was

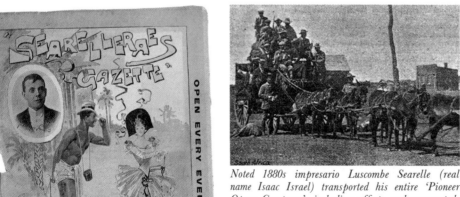

Noted 1880s impresario Luscombe Searelle (real name Isaac Israel) transported his entire 'Pioneer Opera Company', including effects and corrugated-iron Theatre Royal, by ox wagon from Durban to Johannesburg. Many of his ventures failed, and he was often in debt. Above: Searelle's troupers on the road; left: the front cover of his 'Gazette', published every Saturday; right: some of the costumes they wore (now museum pieces)

to achieve fame in both silent and talking movies, was first billed in South Africa as 'the greatest of all American jugglers' when he appeared in a gala Christmas performance at Johannesburg's Empire Palace of Varieties in 1903. By 1914 his fame had grown and, when he returned to the Empire, a splash advertisement announced 'the world's grotesque [sic] juggler W.C. Fields, the silent humorist (direct from Metropolitan Starring Engagements). Straight from Triumphs in Three Continents'. In 1911 Harry Stodel paid £300 for only one performance by Sir Seymour Hicks — an astronomical figure for the time.

Music from the boys' room

Apart from Harry Lauder, Jack Stodel says, 'there was the other great Scottish artist, the late Will Fyffe. In spite of the tremendous gap in ages, we formed a wonderful friendship.

'Now there's a story about Will Fyffe that can be told in this day and age. But I'll come to the story in a moment. I was assigned to him because he was a great fisherman, a lover of fishing. Salmon on the River Tay and all that kind of thing. His dresser was a ruse, he was really a gillie Will brought with him to put on the bait and look after the tackle. I used to take him to the fishing spots around the Cape. We forged a fine friendship which lasted for years until he passed on as the result of an accident.

'The story — he was caught one day with a bout of constipation and he went to the boys' room and that's where he spent nearly the whole afternoon, so what did he come out with? He came out with the words and the music of a song that wherever English is spoken in the world, I swear is sung every day, and that song was "I belong to Glasgow".'

Some of the artistes brought to Cape Town's Tivoli by Harry Stodel. Acts featuring midgets (top left) were a special attraction. More extravagant was Tiny Town, a travelling Liliputian village, which caused a national sensation when it toured South Africa in 1913. With its midget citizens, no more than 90 cm tall, the town boasted its own shops, fire brigade, police force and even its own mayor. At each centre Tiny Town performed vaudeville and circus acts with a trained string of ponies only six to eight hands high. A midget couple touring the world on honeymoon delighted audiences by appearing in full bridal regalia to the strains of the Wedding March. Top right: the Jester Follies; left: the Crocodile and the Lizard and, above, the Gilley Sisters

The elaborate interior of the Tivoli, Cape Town. Opened in 1903, it was described by the Commercial Review and South African Storekeeper *as 'a charming little house . . . The stalls are seated with the latest form of tip-up chair upholstered in blue velvet, and the whole floor is covered with a Wilton carpet of the same colour'. The theatre was electrically lit ('gas has been laid on should the electric light fail') and fire-proofed. Its cream, blue and gold auditorium had a ceiling of painted panels, its handsome smoking lounge a mural of Dutch canal scenes, and the circle 'a lantern roof made to slide open, the latest idea in this class of building'. Walls and columns bore fussy reliefs and carvings, and cherubs simpered at the audience from all sides*

THE KING, HIS PALACE AND HIS PLAYERS

For late-Victorian and Edwardian Capetonians the great centre of entertainment was the Tivoli, where Harry Stodel, immigrant from the East End of London and an experienced vaudeville performer, turned what had been a white elephant into a splendid palace of varieties.

In 1889, when he was 20, he took passage to South Africa, travelled to the Rand, and returned to Cape Town to take over — and make an institution of — the Tivoli Theatre.

Stodel brought out all the greats of entertainment while he ran the Tivoli — Marie Lloyd, Ada Reeves, Julian Rose, Sir Harry Lauder, Betty King, George Robey, Little Tich, Wilkie Bard and, as he puts it, 'a host of those good companions of the stage who made the music halls of the "Nautie Nineties" and the gay Edwardian days, the meeting place of all who loved a good joke and a hearty laugh'.

His son, Jack, who was to become one of the leading figures in entertainment in South Africa, joined Harry Stodel when he was ten years old, selling tickets and watching the chorus girls from the lighting gantry. And, as Jack says with a wink, 'they often had to change costumes in the wings not knowing of the small pair of eyes above them'.

The ghosts of the old Tivoli

When the demolishers moved in to take apart the old Tivoli in Cape Town in 1932, a reviewer wandered around its tomblike interior looking for the ghosts of long-forgotten music hall artistes. Flipping through old undated programmes he remembered 'the heavy plush drape swung up to disclose the Flying Banvards . . . the first and greatest exponents of the trampoline and trapeze'. And Daisy Wood, 'singer of provocative songs and a dancer of sorts'. Then there was Captain Woodward and his seals and Millie Payne arriving to sing about the adventures of her father's pudding. Wilkie Bard, accustomed to colossal salaries in the West End of London, came to South Africa to 'sink to the depths of impecunious despair'. And, of course, the immortal Marie Lloyd. 'Who could forget that husky voice, the inimitable wink and the leer with which she used to tick-off the chucker out before making her entrance? High-heeled diamond studded shoes, preposterously befeathered hat, moth-eaten skunk tippet or cotton shawl, there was only one Marie Lloyd, and there can never be another.'

Stars of the early stage

'THE GUV'NOR' – A LEGEND OF SOUTH AFRICAN THEATRE

In the post-war Johannesburg of 1902, theatregoers thirsted for long-deprived entertainment, and curfew permits were issued to see Harry Miller's Comedy Company in *The Arabian Nights* at the Standard – a performance dedicated to the 'elite of Johannesburg'. At the same time the 'clever child actress' Miss Myrtle Howard was wooing Pretorians in the title role in *Little Lord Fauntleroy* at the Empire.

In October 1902, the opening night of the new Gaiety Theatre – now thoroughly renovated – was graced by the celebrated London actress Miss Kate Vaughan in *The Dancing Girl* by Henry Arthur Jones. The glittering evening was under the patronage of High Commissioner Lord Milner himself, which guaranteed that the four-guinea boxes went as soon as bookings opened. All Johannesburg society wanted to be there in its fashionable finery for what was to be reported as a theatrical occasion 'which has not, for a long time, if ever, been equalised in Johannesburg'.

'If the recuperative powers of a nation may be to some extent gauged by its capacity for amusement,' wrote the *Star's* critic, 'then we have turned the corner.' Unlike the two other shows playing in town at the time, *The French Maid* at Frank de Jong's Standard and *The Shop Girl* at B. & F. Wheeler's Empire, both lightweight musical plays, *The Dancing Girl* offered legitimate theatre. And the man who gave it to them was Leonard Rayne who, in the next quarter of a century, was to become a legend of the South African stage.

'The Guv'nor', as he became affectionately known, had first visited South Africa in 1895, having started in the London theatre as a call-boy at the age of nine. His company had then presented *Othello* to an audience in a fever of anticipation – the Jameson Raid was but three days away. Even so, the house was full each night. Amy Coleridge played Desdemona, and Rayne the title role.

Three years later, Rayne returned to South Africa, but his plans to open a theatre in the Golden City were thwarted by the Anglo-Boer War, and he played at the Opera House, Cape Town, instead. In spite of bad news from the north, audiences flocked to performances of *Hamlet*, *Virginius*, *A Message from Mars*, *The Three Musketeers* and *Rip van Winkle*. When the siege of Kimberley lifted, Rayne took his company to the town in an armoured train and played a six-week season.

Fumbling for their handkerchiefs

Rayne had faith in himself. He refused to compromise standards for 'colonial' audiences. His reputation for excellence reached London – *Elthorne's London Programme of Amusements* said of his production of *The Prodigal Daughter*: 'The crowded house went delirious with excitement over the realistic steeplechase.' His productions of Shakespeare – in which he appeared in all the principal male parts – proved that first-class drama could succeed in South Africa. But it is as Napoleon in *The Royal Divorce* that he is best remembered.

The father of South African theatre. Left: Leonard Rayne clutches Freda Godfrey in a scene from The White Man. *Above: Rayne's lavish* Julius Caesar *at Cape Town's Opera House. His Shakespearean productions proved that serious, legitimate theatre could succeed in what was generally regarded as a cultural backwater. Top: Rayne's repertory company, a happy band that stayed together for many years. Rayne is seated fourth from right, with Freda Godfrey at his feet. Superimposed is 'the Guv'nor' in his best-known part: as Napoleon in* The Royal Divorce

A.P. Cartwright, in his book *South African Hall of Fame*, tells how Rayne's portly figure was held erect, 'the rich, husky voice rang through the theatre as he said his farewell. The women in the audience fumbled for their handkerchiefs and put them to their eyes'.

This giant among South African actor-managers was adept at spotting talent. One of his more successful finds was the elfin-like girl playing the title role in *Little Lord Fauntleroy* in London. She was Freda Godfrey, who was to captivate audiences as 'the Mary Pickford of South Africa'. She played opposite Leonard Rayne in all the Shakespearean dramas and become the Union's first Peter Pan. Sir James Barrie persuaded her to play the role of Wendy in his play during a visit to London.

Rayne tried to resist the encroachment of bioscope in the second decade of the century by importing the West End's latest plays. But it was still an uphill struggle. Outside the oasis of Johannesburg, only music hall and cinema, it seemed, could bring in audiences. The entertainment monopoly of I.W. Schlesinger's African Consolidated Theatres provided what they said the masses wanted: bioscope – then

revelling in vulgarity and sensationalism – and vaudeville.

To counter this, Leonard Rayne sent two companies on tour: Freda Godfrey starring in *La Poupée* and Amy Coleridge in *Henry of Navarre*. He imported Ada Reeve and a London vaudeville company featuring Wee Georgie Wood. If serious drama palled, Rayne would fall back on hardy favourites such as *East Lynne* or *The Story of the Rosary*.

It was Freda Godfrey who, towards the end of Rayne's life, kept the company together at the Standard in Johannesburg. By the 1920s Rayne had retired to the Cape, an infrequent performer. Then one winter's night in 1925, a call-boy popped his head round the door of Freda Godfrey's dressing room. He announced: 'Miss Godfrey, the Guv'nor's dead; just heard it on the wireless.' Freda shunned suggestions that *Sleeping Partners*, in which she was appearing, should be stopped. 'No,' she said, Leonard would have hated that.'

Rayne's stature could be measured by the 60 and more cars that wound their way to Woltemade cemetery in Cape Town on 21 June 1925.

HIGH DRAMA IN THE RAIN

In 1895 Leonard Rayne and his wife Amy Grace joined Amy Coleridge, William Haviland, William Holloway and a company of picked London actors to open at the Standard Theatre, Johannesburg, described in *Outspan* in 1939 as 'a primitive building with a corrugated iron roof. At the back of the theatre the post office was in the course of construction, and raw Natives, engaged in the building operations, wearing little more than loin cloths in the African heat, chanted rhythmically in unison as they wielded their picks or heaved bricks. Their hammering and singing formed a "musical" background to the rehearsals taking place in the theatre'.

The company brought with them all their props and sound effects. One night they were playing *King Lear* and the rain was pelting down on the tin roof, accompanied by loud thunder and vivid lightning. There was no need to use their own sound effects, though the storm almost succeeded in killing the play: 'It was almost a nightly occurrence for the electric light to fail, being newly installed, and the "thud-thud" of the donkey engine could be plainly heard all over the building . . . The audience were very good-natured, taking everything as it came, and indulging in community singing during unavoidable "accidents".'

Amy Coleridge and Freda Godfrey were the two most noted and best loved of early actresses in South Africa. London-born Amy, an intimate of such greats as Sir Henry Irving and Ellen Terry, first came to South Africa before the Anglo-Boer War, when 'the bare veld extended right up to the back of Johannesburg's Standard Theatre'. She eventually settled in the city, where she started a drama school (right). Above right: studio portrait of the actress. Above: two of her sumptuous costumes

ENTERTAINING THE NEW UNION

In 1910 the first citizens of a united South Africa were offered a wide range of theatrical entertainment. In Johannesburg, theatregoers thronged to the opening night of Stephen Black's all-South African play, *Helena's Hope, Ltd*. On the eve of Union hundreds were turned away at the door. This 'mirror of Rand life' produced infectious laughter from an audience that behaved well: 'the usual hissing, eggs and bottles' were noticeably absent.

For those unable to get to the Standard Theatre, the Empire Palace offered family entertainment, with Captain Fred Woodward's wonderful performing seals and sea lions being the main attraction. Miss Daisy Jerome, who captivated music hall audiences in the following years, was way down the bill, coming after the 'celebrated Anglo-French impressionist' Foot-Gers.

In Cape Town Leonard Rayne's company was playing in repertory: *The Silver King* starred Miss Amy Coleridge as Nellie Denver and Mr P.A. Gawthorn as Wilfred Denver. Prices ranged from 1/6 to 6/- – surprisingly high compared with Wolfram's Bioscope in Cape Town's Adderley Street, which showed Charles Dickens's *The Mystery of Edwin Drood*, a rather melancholy offering for Union Day.

Ever popular, the city's Tivoli Theatre presented Julian Royston and Company in *Mrs Tempest's Telegram*, starring Leonard Stephens and Miss Frances White. The drama, which could be seen from the best seats at 4/- or in the gallery for a shilling, was played by 'the regular crowd' – Leonard and Leighton, Phil and Nellie Peters, Harry Stodel (who ran the Tivoli) and Jennie and Annie Stodel. For those who felt Union should be celebrated with less timidity, a Grand Auxetophone Recital was held in the Dutch Reformed Church Hall, Madame Clara Butt singing patriotic songs, including *Land of Hope and Glory*. Entrance cost 1/–, and 6d for children.

Players in the audience

Special guests of honour at Kimberley's Theatre Royal on Union night were members of the touring English football team that had been playing Griqualand West that day. Miss May Edouin and Mr Fred Edwardes starred in *In Honour Bound*, a comic tragedy, supported by a short play called *A Bachelor's Dream*.

The Charles Howitt Comedy Company packed the house with *Raffles* at the Theatre Royal, Durban, while down the road at the Beach Theatre there was vaudeville and 'bioscope'.

Most dorps offered a concert, together with church services of thanksgiving, on Union Day. In Grahamstown a 'Grand Patriotic Concert', which featured leading tenor Bernard Streatfield, filled the Town Hall at a shilling a seat. The 'Sleepy Hollow', Pietermaritzburg, lived up to its name by offering little in the way of live entertainment. Wrote 'Thespian' in the *Natal Witness*: 'Maritzburg just now exists upon Union Days and bioscopes, and neither can be called exciting fare. After all, it's about as much as we can expect,' noting that if any touring professional troupe of actors visited the city, the manager usually had to borrow the fare for the trip home.

Port Elizabeth revellers made their way to the Electric Theatre to see 'best moving pictures', which included 'Picturesque Devon' and 'Natal Sugar Industry'. Others were drawn to a Grand Concert – oratorios and madrigals – in the Feather Market Hall.

Freda Godfrey, 'the Mary Pickford of South Africa', in Two Orphans, 1912 (left). She first appeared on stage, at the age of ten, in the title rôle of Little Lord Fauntleroy. A close friend and long-lasting colleague of the 'the Guv'nor', she held Rayne's company together in his later years, struggling to resist the encroachment of the bioscope in the 1920s by importing, and starring in, the latest West End hits

DIAMOND BRACELETS AND STAGE-DOOR JOHNNIES

In the first few years of the century vaudeville was in decline; the 'electric theatre' ascendant. Legitimate theatre in South Africa competed against the flickering screen by importing some of the best West End shows — and the big stars of the stage. Most of the actresses came from England: the soulful, the statuesque, the histrionic and the erotic — and South Africa adored them. 'Stage-door Johnnies' waited at Johannesburg's Empire 'with a bouquet of orchids in one hand and a diamond bracelet in the other'. Gone were the days of the Pekin Palace of Varieties in Cape Town, where the seats were said to be coated with either beer or blood every night. The audiences had drama, romance and beauty.

Colour postcards featuring the period's favourite stars were much treasured. This selection is from the prized collection of Daisy Stodel, daughter of Harry Stodel — owner of Cape Town's old Tivoli Theatre. Some of the actresses shown here appeared in South Africa.

MAUD JEFFRIES

GABRIELLE RAY

OLIVE MAY

ZENA DARE

ETHEL OLIVER

LILY BRAYTON

GRACE STOHL

PHYLLIS DARE

MAUD ALLAN

VIOLET VANBRUGH

BILLIE BURKE

Playing to the audience

HOME-GROWN DRAMA

In 1910 a former boxer and sports writer named Stephen Black won widespread critical acclaim with his first satirical play, *Helena's Hope Ltd*. The play was performed 600 times in theatres across the country, and Black was on his way to introducing South Africans to the talents of an indigenous cast.

In the years just before and during the Second World War there was a serious attempt to organise a bi-cultural National Theatre. Afrikaners André Huguenet, Mathilda and Hendrik Hanekom and P.P. Breytenbach got together with Marda Vanne and Gwen Ffrangcon Davies, collectively and individually drawing large audiences with their productions – even though live theatre was in decline.

Getting it organised

In 1947, the National Theatre Organisation was formed — the first such state-subsidised body in the Commonwealth. They had just £1 500 to spend, and had to cover a bilingual country. Financial disaster hit their production of *Hassan* in 1952, but shortly afterwards, with *Summer of the Seventeenth Doll* a sell-out in every major centre, success seemed assured.

By 1958 the National Theatre Organisation had travelled nearly a million kilometres and played to nearly two million people during 6 524 performances. They had engaged top-class producers and artistes: Margaret Inglis, Anna Neethling-Pohl, Lydia Lindeque, Berdine Grunewald, Leontine Sagan, Pikkie Uys, Anna Romain-Hoffman, Ina du Toit, Frank Wise, Hendrik Hanekom, Leon Fagan, Philip Theunissen, David Saunders and Henri van Wyk.

The body was not an unqualified success, largely because it was hamstrung by its terms of reference — it had to play, on a shoestring, to small rural audiences. But the company

'André Huguenet en Geselskap'. Huguenet joined Paul de Groot's touring dramatic company in 1925, playing the juvenile lead in Huistoe *and other plays, and five years later played the lead in Stephanie Faure's pioneering production of indigenous drama,* Ampie. *From left: Siegfried Mynhardt, Johan Piek, André Huguenet, Ena du Toit, Bettie Reitz, Dewald van der Merwe, Lydia Lyndeque*

Far left: Margaret Inglis, who helped to create the National Theatre Organisation in 1947. Centre left: Anna Romain-Hoffman in 1935, when she played Mabel in Dear Brutus. *Centre right: A pensive Berdine Grunewald. She was equally at home in English and Afrikaans. Far right: Anna Neethling-Pohl. In 1965 she became a professor at the Institute of Acting and Elocution (now Drama Department) at the University of Pretoria*

Left: Hendrik Hanekom, the former town clerk of De Aar who resigned to form a professional theatrical company. He and his wife, Mathilde, dedicated their lives and talents to Afrikaans theatre. Far left (top): A scene from Onskuldig Veroordeel, *a detective drama produced by the Hanekoms in 1929. Far left (bottom): The Hanekom 'Geselskap'. From left: Mathilde Hanekom, Willie Beckman, Sann de Lange, Hendrik Hanekom, Kalman Postma, Johan Lubbe, Elsa Fouché. The man in front is Jan Lochne*

heralded the foundation of the provincial performing arts councils: relatively well-endowed spearheads of a South African stage renaissance.

Spreading the word

South African actors and actresses won considerable international recognition over the years, and among the best-known was Leontine Sagan, who achieved worldwide fame in the 1930s with her production of the play *Mädchen in Uniform* (she also produced the film version). In 1933 she returned to South Africa to produce and star in the play.

Another popular South African to 'make it' abroad was Margaretha van Hulsteyn, who assumed the stage name of Marda Vanne. Her acting career was interrupted by an ill-fated marriage to J.G. Strijdom (later Prime Minister), but she went on to fill many leading roles on West End stages between 1924 and 1939, when she returned to South Africa to launch more theatrical ventures.

Johannesburg's Moira Lister travelled to England during the Second World War and quickly became a star of the West End stage.

Far left: Leontine Sagan in 1915. She returned to South Africa from England in 1939, providing a vitally-needed spark in the ailing South African theatre world. Centre left: Gé Korsten, one of the most popular singers to emerge from South Africa. Centre right: Brian Brooke, the accomplished actor and theatrical entrepreneur, with Olive Bodill in a scene from the play Harvey. Far right: A poster for The Boy Friend

Far left: Sid James's parents were touring South Africa's music halls when he was born. He is probably best known for his roles in the 'Carry On' series. Centre left: Moira Lister, the Johannesburg actress who became a star of the West End Stage. Centre right: Lawrence Harvey was educated in South Africa. He was a leading Shakespearean actor before turning to the films which made him famous. Far right: Juliet Prowse. She trained as a ballet dancer in Johannesburg before moving to the United States. She made a film with Elvis Presley, was once engaged to Frank Sinatra, and became a top performer at Las Vegas nightspots

Latter-day success stories include those of Janet Suzman, who became a leading Shakespearean actress on the English stage; Hildegard Neil, a former Cape Town librarian who also earned a reputation with her performances at Stratford-on-Avon, and the versatile Cape Town actress, Yvonne Bryceland.

The most significant writing for South African theatre has been produced by a body of superb Afrikaans playwrights, including Louis Leipoldt, N.P. van Wyk Louw, Uys Krige, Bartho Smit, Adam Small, Chris Barnard, André P. Brink and P.G. du Plessis (the latter's award-winning play, Siener in die Suburbs, set a South African attendance record).

The Fifties saw the emergence of Athol Fugard, the former student, merchant seaman and journalist whose first major play, The Blood Knot, opened in Johannesburg in 1961 and later received critical acclaim in both Britain and America.

Fugard followed this up with a series of successes, including Hello and Goodbye, in which Janet Suzman played the lead; Statements After an Arrest Under the Immorality Act, a disturbing dramatisation of a peculiarly South African situation, which had its world première in New York; Sizwe Banzi is Dead (devised with John Kani and Winston Ntshona); Boesman en Lena, in which he and Yvonne Bryceland played the two leads; A Lesson From Aloes and The Island (another collaboration with Kani and Ntshona). The famous New York Times critic, Clive Barnes, described The Island as 'probably the most terrifyingly realistic play of prison life I have ever seen'.

Arts councils to the rescue

'Good, bad or indifferent, when does opera ever fail to attract bumper houses?' wrote Beatrice Marx, for 30 years music critic of the Cape Times. 'And when does it ever happen that expenses do not swamp most of the profits — costumes, scenery, lighting and a hundred other items?'

The National Theatre Organisation had been a failure and its only legacy was a few hundred rands and a clear indication that theatre on a national scale would be a disaster. Help, however, was on the way.

The Department of Education, Arts and Science was charged 'to provide our perform-ing artists with a fixed income, to present operas and ballet performances, to perform music and plays — in English and Afrikaans'. In creating performing arts councils in each of the provinces, the government insisted on the highest standards: 'It must no longer be necessary for people to go overseas to see the best.'

A decade later each council was able to report success. From small beginnings, often lacking experience in acting, singing or dancing, let alone theatrical technicalities, they brought drama, grand opera and ballet to cities and dorps alike. The councils continue to flourish and grow today.

Above: 'The 3 Hugos' in 1944. Hugo and Lucy Keleti and their daughter, Eve, were hard-working troupers of the old school. Left: Eve Boswell at the height of her fame. She even had the Queen beating time to her Suiker-bossie at the 1953 Royal Command performance

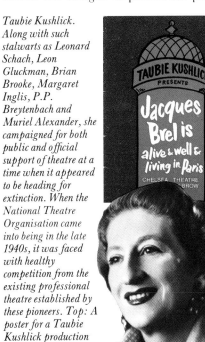

Taubie Kushlick. Along with such stalwarts as Leonard Schach, Leon Gluckman, Brian Brooke, Margaret Inglis, P.P. Breytenbach and Muriel Alexander, she campaigned for both public and official support of theatre at a time when it appeared to be heading for extinction. When the National Theatre Organisation came into being in the late 1940s, it was faced with healthy competition from the existing professional theatre established by these pioneers. Top: A poster for a Taubie Kushlick production

Mimi Coertse, South Africa's renowned opera star. As a child, Maria Sophia 'Mimi' Coertse used to sing Sarie Marais in church when everyone else was singing hymns. She became famous almost overnight as 'Queen of the Night' in Mozart's opera, The Magic Flute, and by 1960 she was being acclaimed as one of the world's top four coloratura sopranos

125

Music in the home

MR EDISON'S TALKING MACHINE ARRIVES

The 'Talking Machine' burst upon an astonished world in the last years of the 19th century. Invented by Thomas Alva Edison in America, the brass-horned phonograph enabled anyone to record and reproduce sound on wax cylinders. It was a scratchy, tinny sound, but magical nevertheless.

Not long afterwards came the gramophone. Although it could not record, its ability to reproduce sound from discs amazed and delighted the first listeners. In 1903 a gramophone cost between £3.10s. and £5 in Cape Town. Seven-inch records cost 2/- and the 10-inch discs sold for twice that price. An Edison phonograph with six records cost £5.15s. Edison Moulded Records — 'by far the most musical record on the market' — sold for 3/- each, which was quite expensive when one considers that at that time rice cost 2d a pound, milk 2d a pint and sugar 3d a pound.

The jazz generation

Although public concerts of recorded music were regularly performed in Johannesburg and other centres around 1910, South Africans did not immediately flock to buy the new machine: the piano remained the more popular instrument for some years. But the Zonophone Company made recordings of local musicians in Cape Town and Johannesburg as early as 1912. The musicians included Connie Thomas, Joey Stamrood, Kate Opperman and Willem Versfeld (they recorded his popular sketch *Die Voetbal Match*). It was only after the First World War that the portable wind-up gramophone became a common feature of the South African home.

Then came the Jazz Age, and a dance-crazy

In 1910 South Africans could buy a gramophone like this one for as little as £5. Then came the radio-gramophone (radiogram), and by the early 1920s they were very much part of the South African home

generation indulged itself in a new social custom. John Wentzel recalls it in his memoir of Johannesburg: '*The Jazz Singer, The Singing Fool, Rio Rita, The Web of Love, The Desert Song* and other musicals meant, for the young people, hours spent in Mackay Bros. or Polliacks listening to and selecting fragile 78 r.p.m. shellac records, most of which were made by H.M.V., Columbia, Brunswick or Parlophone.'

By the end of the 1920s the cylinder-playing phonograph had disappeared from the scene.

Gramophones had won the day and were very much part of the furniture, coming in a variety of smart cabinets.

The 'Chime-o-Phone', claimed a 1928 *Outspan* advertisement, was 'South Africa's Premier Gramphone', available in a choice of locally-designed cabinets: the 'Durban', the 'Aliwal', the 'Kimberley' and the elegant 'Parktown' (in figured walnut). The advertisers boasted that 'every Cabinet is fitted with a British-made motor . . . the latest design of Tone Arm and scientifically construc-

Fordsburg's town hall was lavishly decorated in October 1907 for the launch of Messrs Rose Brothers' gramophone rental company. In 1910 Henry Godfrey of Tarkastad, Cape, won the village's annual shooting contest and received as a prize an Edison Triumph phonograph with 100 cylinder records. For years afterwards he generously offered his machine for use at parties and other festive occasions, and even dances at the town hall were made possible by the music issuing from his stoep nearby

Singer's 'Afrikaanse Plate' (Afrikaans records) brought foot-tapping enjoyment to thousands of South Africans until well after the Second World War. Because of complicated agency rights, these early records were pressed overseas (left). The introduction of the electric turntable, right, revolutionised the recording industry

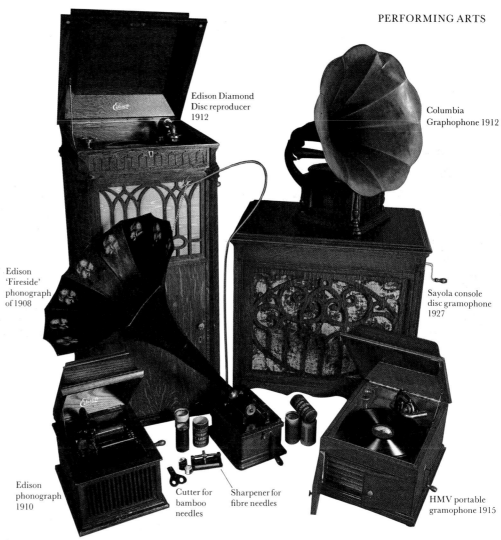

Edison Diamond
Disc reproducer
1912

Columbia
Graphophone 1912

Sayola console
disc gramophone
1927

Edison
'Fireside'
phonograph
of 1908

Edison
phonograph
1910

Cutter for
bamboo
needles

Sharpener for
fibre needles

HMV portable
gramophone 1915

Some of these machines provided surprisingly good reproduction for their day. The best sound came from machines using Edison's Diamond Discs, recorded with a 'hill-and-dale' groove. Edison made discs and cylinders until 1929. Centre left is the 'Fireside' model, and his diamond reproducer is mounted in the tall cabinet

ARTIST DOGGED BY SUCCESS

In 1899 an artist named Francis Barraud offered the Gramophone Company a painting which showed a small dog listening, his head slightly cocked, at the horn of a wax cylinder phonograph. It had obvious appeal, and the company bought the painting after asking Barraud to change the phonograph into a disc-playing gramophone (above).

The company launched its new symbol the following year — a trade mark which was to become one of the most famous in the world. Barraud called his picture *His Master's Voice,* and spent the rest of his life making copies of it.

ted Amplifier. Not a feature is left to chance, but is the result of careful study. The beautiful mellow tone . . . has been brought to a state of perfection by individual attention to each instrument, and not by mass production methods'.

John Hecht's triumph

The South African recording industry was born in the early 1930s, when many overseas recording companies had been shattered by the Wall Street crash and its aftermath.

In 1924 the British Edison-Bell Company had aroused interest by making a number of recordings in Cape Town. Then, in 1931, John Hecht, a sound-recording engineer imported from the Metropole Company in London, achieved something of a national triumph when he produced the first records for the Singer Gramophone Company in President Street, Johannesburg.

When Hecht accepted the offer to come to South Africa, he did not know what he was letting himself in for. He was used to working with the best artistes and best equipment of the age. In Johannesburg he had to transfer onto a disc the sounds produced by a happy-go-lucky band of men with concertinas and guitars — musicians accustomed to playing at parties and not the easiest people to work with in the relatively formal, demanding atmosphere of a professional recording studio. The ordeal was not made any easier by the type of disc then in use: a wax tablet from which mistakes could not be erased. An error meant starting all over again. But it was a beginning.

South Africa's record industry was greatly expanded after the Second World War, and records of high quality were produced. Long-playing records were made by such performers as Albie Louw, Dan Hill, Mimi Coertse, Arnold van Wyk and Lionel Bowmann.

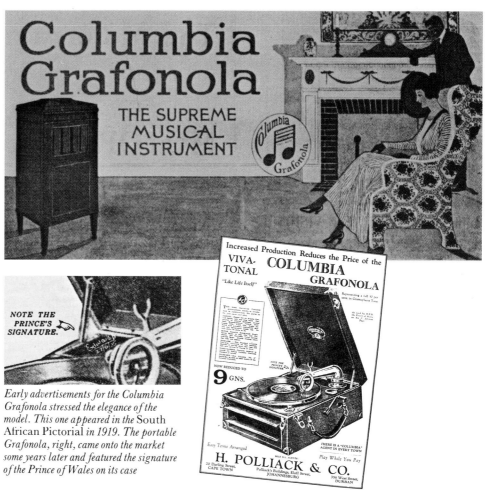

Columbia
Grafonola

THE SUPREME
MUSICAL
INSTRUMENT

NOTE THE
PRINCE'S
SIGNATURE.

Increased Production Reduces the Price of the
VIVA-
TONAL
COLUMBIA
GRAFONOLA

"Like Life Itself"

NOW REDUCED TO

9 GNS.

Easy Terms Arranged

THERE IS A "COLUMBIA"
AGENT IN EVERY TOWN

Play While You Pay

H. POLLIACK & CO.
20 Darling Street,
CAPE TOWN

Polliack's Buildings, Eloff Street,
JOHANNESBURG

356 West Street,
DURBAN

Early advertisements for the Columbia Grafonola stressed the elegance of the model. This one appeared in the South African Pictorial *in 1919. The portable Grafonola, right, came onto the market some years later and featured the signature of the Prince of Wales on its case*

Born to dance

A 1975 CAPAB production of Swan Lake. The renowned French dancers, Christianne Vlassi and Attilio Labis, danced the leading roles with the company in 1971

PAVLOVA: A SYMPHONY IN MOVEMENT

They started queueing outside Cape Town's Opera House just after lunch for a show that did not start until after eight. But for Rozilda, social columnist for the *Cape Argus*, it was worth the visit for that magical moment when, in the ballet, *The Fairy Doll*, a curtain was drawn aside to disclose 'a wonderful scintillating vision, the Fairy Doll — the peerless Anna Pavlova'. For ballet lovers of South Africa, a new vista opened on the evening of 29 December 1925.

'This famous dancer, together with her ballet, has revealed to the people of this country that dancing is an art as important as music itself,' wrote the *Argus's* critic, W.J. Makin.

Pavlova, accompanied by 40 dancers, a few key musicians and technicians, had arrived to a typical south-easter welcome in Table Bay at the end of 1925 for a season at the Cape Town Opera House and the Johannesburg Standard Theatre. Hundreds of balletomanes formed long queues, that wound round the block, for the pits and gallery. They were kept amused by an itinerant musician playing on a remarkable 'instrument' comprising a petrol tin, a mustard tin, and an old gramophone horn, with just one string that produced a wonderfully rich and mellow tone.

With patience they waited. Sounds from inside the gallery galvanised them, pressing forward until, twenty minutes later at 7.30 p.m., the doors swung open and the rush up the winding staircase began.

Pavlova, accompanied by 40 dancers, a few key musicians and technicians, had arrived to by the magnetism of her personality. Enthused Rozilda: 'Motionless she stood there — a figure in a poet's dream shimmering and lovely. Then bursts of applause thundered round her — such applause as Cape Town seldom gives.'

Wrote Makin: 'Pavlova was wafted on to the stage like a wisp of thistledown in the wind. Yet in that wisp of thistledown was inherent the whole art and expression of dancing and Cape Town was roaring its rapture.

'Pavlova's delicacy, her superb grace, the exquisite manner in which she seems positively to float into the air claims for her

Anna Pavlova dances in Cape Town's Opera House in 1925. The ballerina was already 45 years old

the true meaning of that much-abused word —incomparable.'

Pavlova's secret, Makin learnt in a backstage interview later, was 'Never be satisfied with your art; keep on working, keep on improving,' and he went on to recount: '"Been at it since 9.30 this morning," growled a scene shifter in my ear, "Had her lunch and dinner on stage. Done nuffink but rehearse. Gawd what a life!"' It was a lesson that the critics were eager to put across to the dancers of Cape Town. 'The ordinary toe-exercises that our children have been taught,' wrote Makin, 'the self-satisfaction of our ballroom accomplishments, all have been rendered naught by the magic of this lithesome figure in ballet skirts and white tights.'

Anna Pavlova in fact paid something of a tribute to the teachers of the city. For her last two performances in Cape Town she had created a special dance to display the huge fan of ostrich feathers they had presented to her. The music was Beethoven's *Rondo*, reported the *Argus*: 'It was no longer the pale, dead

Top: Helen Webb, who taught ballet in South Africa from 1913. A few years later she staged the first of her annual ballet performances with the Cape Town Municipal Orchestra. Centre: Dulcie Howes, one of the major figures in South African ballet. Bottom: Nadia Nerina was born in Cape Town in 1927. She was eight years old when she took her first dancing lesson, and later became one of the world's best-loved dancers

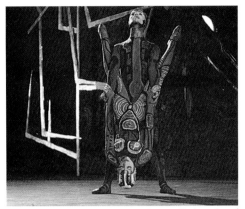

Veronica Paeper and Juan Sanchez in Raka, *based on the Afrikaans poem by N.P. van Wyk Louw*

PACT ballerina Dawn Weller. The company has produced some of the country's best dancers

John Cranko, the brilliant South African choreographer. He died in an airliner in 1973

Keith Mackintosh and Linda Smit with the CAPAB company in The Nutcracker. *The partnership won frequent critical acclaim. Top right: A souvenir of Dame Margot Fonteyn's visit to South Africa in 1973*

white dancer whose movements one has come to know and to marvel at, but a Pavlova in a gauzy, filmy mauve with golden wig, a living, breathing, happy woman delighted to display a present which has delighted her.'

Pavlova added fuel to a fire that was already burning brightly. Here, under a southern sun, people delighted in dancing to 'an almost preposterous degree', said the *Cape Argus* arts critic. 'It may be the sunshine, the atmosphere or something else. Yet the desire to express themselves in dancing is certainly inherent in South African children. There should be no difficulty in developing the art of the ballet in this country.'

This love had been given impetus by the arrival in Cape Town, in 1912, of the daughter of Captain Matthew Webb, the first man to swim the English Channel. Helen Webb had joined the South African College of Music, a year later setting up ballet tuition for young Capetonians. From 1916 she gave regular ballet performances with her pupils. And in 1923 she formed the Helen Webb Ballet Company.

South African ballet, though, was in its adolescence and career-minded dancers still made their way overseas. One was Dulcie Howes, trained by Helen Webb, who joined the Pavlova Company in 1928. It was Pavlova's inspiration that helped the young Mossel Bay girl gain confidence and skill, and to return to South Africa as a leading ballerina. In 1934, at the invitation of the imaginative Professor W.H. Bell, she transferred her recently-opened ballet to the College of Music, a department of the University of Cape Town. Through the Dulcie Howes Ballet Trust she was able to establish a company that toured widely throughout the Union, South West Africa and Rhodesia, performing both classical and modern works.

Formed by Cecily Robinson in 1938, the Cape Town Ballet Club (called the South African National Ballet from 1946) was also encouraging local talent. John Cranko was one of its principal dancers: he joined Sadler's Wells in 1946, built himself an international reputation as a choreographer, and was

appointed artistic director and choreographer of the ballet school and company at the Wurtenberg State Opera in Stuttgart in 1961. David Poole's was another success story: he became a principal dancer at Sadler's Wells, returned to the Union to teach in 1959, and took over from Dulcie Howes as Artistic Director of CAPAB Ballet (successor to the UCT ballet).

After the Second World War, South Africans were to feature prominently in European ballet companies: Nadia Nerina; Desmond Doyle; Northern Rhodesian Peter Cazalet, who made his name as a designer; Johaar Mosaval, the Cape Town-born dancer trained by Dulcie Howes. In 1962 he became principal dancer of the Royal Ballet. Another principal at Sadler's Wells, Patricia Miller, joined the Orange Free State Ballet and her husband, Dudley Davis, was appointed ballet master and later artistic director of Ballet Natal. Alfred Rodrigues, also one of Dulcie Howes' pupils, has choreographed ballets for the British Royal Ballet and La Scala, Milan.

The explosion of black talent

KING KONG
SWEEPS THE WORLD

It was a vibrant world of music and fear, of laughter and poverty and violent crime. From it came gifted players and singers. Township life in South Africa — a kind of living few whites knew about. Yet it produced the first South African theatrical venture to be internationally acclaimed — *King Kong*. The show not only revealed the immense talent buried in the black ghettos: it also made a world-renowned star of Miriam Makeba.

Jazz, with an African beat, had been developing in South Africa from the 1920s when an imaginative black schoolteacher, Griffiths Motsieloa, gathered together singers and instrumentalists to tour small towns with groups like Hiver Hivas, the African Darkies and De Peach Black Follies. Most of the musicians were self-taught, their mentors Duke Ellington and Louis Armstrong, whose distinctive sounds they heard only on gramophone records.

Songs such as *Mbube* by Solomon Linda, *Skokiaan* by August Msarurgwa, *Kilimanjaro* and *Lovely Lies* by Mackay Davashe made the hit parade overseas as well as in South Africa. Solomon Linda's *Wimoweh* was adapted in the United States and reached the top of the pops. Lyricists and performers got little financial reward — Linda's group, for instance, was paid £5 for the first recording of their smash hit. It was sheer exploitation. Only with the foundation of the Union of Southern African Artists in 1953 came some measure of control and organisation.

The gangster hero

Township ballads echoed the voices of black city life: they told of the pass laws, of bus boycotts, of shebeens — and of heroes. Boxer 'King Kong' was such a hero.

'Ezekiel "King Kong" Dhlamini,' wrote journalist Nat Nakasa in *Drum*, '... that rugged, ever-unkempt giant with the iron muscles of a Durban rickshaw puller — is

Children's ragtime band. Early township jazz, known as Marabi, *was a vibrant mix of Western and tribal music. It was played everywhere*

A scene from the 1979 revival of King Kong, *the story of the legendary black boxer. Eddie Tagoe, foreground, played the lead in the action-filled musical*

Miriam Makeba, who played the shebeen queen Joyce in King Kong *and went on to international stardom. She was 15 when she sang her first public solo*

Welcome Msomi in the lead role of uMabatha at Cape Town's Maynardville open-air theatre. The highly successful production had an all-Zulu cast

Two productions of the Eoan Group. The group was formed in 1933 to promote cultural interests among coloured people. Classes were held at the Zonnebloem Training College in Cape Town's District Six

back in the limelight. Within two years a legend has emerged round the man who threw himself into a dam rather than face the grey sameness of prison life.'

The legend started with a song about him that swept the townships. From this came the idea of a jazz opera. The originators were Harry Bloom, noted writer and a lawyer; musician Todd Matshikiza, a one-time journalist and razor-blade salesman, who composed the music; Pat Williams, who wrote the lyrics, and Arthur Goldreich, an architect who designed the scenery and costumes (Goldreich was later to feature in a sensational jailbreak after the Rivonia raid). The only person with professional theatrical experience was the producer, Leon Gluckman.

The female lead was Joyce, the queen of the Back of the Moon shebeen. At the time Dolly Rathebe was the leading songstress, but was several months pregnant. As a number of other candidates were already committed elsewhere, a singer who had once performed

Lemmy Special Mabaso (pictured) and Spokes Mashiyane were the kings of kwela in the Sixties. Dorkay House in Johannesburg was the focus of the era's black theatre and music

The creators of Sizwe Banzi is Dead — *Athol Fugard, John Kani and Winston Ntshona. Kani and Ntshona, two of South Africa's best actors, won the coveted* Tony *award as Best Actors on Broadway, 1974-75*

The cast of Peter Sephuma's Survival — *a story of prison life — which successfully toured the United States and won widespread critical acclaim*

Dollar Brand has appeared at the Newport Jazz Festival, the Lincoln Centre and Carnegie Hall. The great Duke Ellington was among his admirers

Ipi-Tombi *opened at the Brooke Theatre, Johannesburg, in 1974 and was an immediate smash hit. The music and lyrics, written by Bertha Egnos and her daughter Gail Lakier, were criticised by the purists but the show has nevertheless proved to be one of South Africa's most valuable entertainment exports*

with the Manhattan Brothers was auditioned. Her name: Miriam Makeba.

From Jo'burg to London

Slowly *King Kong* took shape. Harry Bloom, in his foreword to the published play, recalled how snags hit them all the way: members of the cast were arrested on the way to rehearsals for pass offences; more troublesome, black performers found it difficult to master the English words. So they played themselves. In the road-menders' scene, for instance, the singers acted with accomplished ease. Most of them had at one time worked on a road gang.

Eventually, exuberant improvisation brought the sights, sounds and smells of the shanty town to the University of the Witwatersrand's Great Hall on 2 February 1959.

'*King Kong* is greatest thrill in 20 years of South African theatre-going,' headlined the *Star.* 'Here's the Township Spirit!' declared the *Rand Daily Mail. Dagbreek* suggested it was material for the Edinburgh Festival.

The show made South African theatrical history when it opened at the Princes Theatre, Shaftesbury Avenue, in London's West End on 20 February 1961. Its reception by British audiences was just as enthusiastic as that given by South Africans. Harry Bloom recalled Dame Flora Robson's comment: 'I found when watching a *King Kong* rehearsal that I was enjoying one of the most exciting experiences in South Africa — the birth of the theatre for African people.'

Songster of the world

In Johannesburg, during their 1947 tour of the Union, King George V1 and Queen Elizabeth listened intently to black singers. The female soloist was 15-year-old Miriam Makeba. It was her first solo. Makeba was to join up with the Manhattan Brothers, and later to form her own group, The Skylarks, before playing Joyce in *King Kong*. The musical launched her on the world stage. Audiences loved the famed click song, *Qungothwana.*

When she made her début in the United States, singing the *Back of the Moon* number from the show, the audience was so enraptured that she had to beg them to let her leave the stage. After her marriage to Sonny Pillay ended in divorce, she married the civil rights activist Stokely Carmichael, and in the course of her world travels became a citizen of Uganda, Tanzania, Algeria, Sudan and Guinea — and a Guinean delegate to the United Nations.

King Kong started the African musical ball rolling. Musicals and plays were written, mostly around contemporary life in the townships. The productions were lively and increasingly imaginative. There was a departure from this tradition when Welcome Msomi saw the parallels in Shakespeare's *Macbeth* and the tyrannical rule of Shaka, 19th century Zulu king. In *uMabatha* he created an exciting theatrical experience using Shakespeare's plot and contrivances as the basis of a fable of black authority, assassination and treachery.

The success of *uMabatha* was followed by another musical, *Ipi-Tombi.* Devised and produced by Bertha Egnos, it was criticised for not truly reflecting township life, but songs like *Mama Tembu's Wedding* and *Where are the Girls?* made it a smash hit both in South Africa and overseas.

Plays that do reflect township life run in townships all over the country. Most notable has been Sam Mangwane's *Unfaithful Woman,* which by 1980 had run for 15 years — the world's longest-running play after *The Mousetrap.* Significant black playwrights are Gibson Kente, who wrote *Laduma* and *Sikalo,* Zakes Mofokeng, who wrote *The Train,* Peter Sephuma, who wrote *Survival,* and latterly the political writers — young men like Reverend Mzwandile Maqina.

His *Give us this Day,* which has not been published, is banned in South Africa, but has had tremendous impact in the townships. It is partly based on the assassination of Black Consciousness leader Abraham Tiro, who died in Botswana when a letter bomb exploded in his hands.

Ben 'Satch' Masinga. He starred in Taubie Kushlick's production of Gershwin's Porgy and Bess

Birth of the 'bioscope'

THE GREATEST ILLUSION OF THEM ALL

Carl Hertz, a suave, moustachioed showman, brought his act of conjuring tricks and illusions to Johannesburg's Empire 'Palace of Varieties' in 1896. The *Standard and Diggers News* advertised the greatest of the illusions early in May:

THE PHOTO-ELECTRIC SENSATION OF THE DAY
First production of the Great London Sensation

CINEMATOGRAPHE
The latest Astounding Invention in Photography.

The most startling scientific marvel of the age.
Every scene in motion reproduced as in real life.
A marvellous reproduction of animated nature.
Impossible to realise that the
figures represented are not actually living.

The first public performance was on Monday, 11 May 1896, but a preview was held on Saturday. The newspaper comments were ecstatic: 'It is difficult to realise they are only photographs.' 'The pictures are so life-like in size and other respects that the spectator has difficulty in realising that the figures are mere representations.'

The extended peep-show

What they had seen, in fact, was not one of the 'Cinematographes' of the French brothers Louis and Auguste Lumière, but an ingenious copy of Thomas Edison's projecting 'Kinetoscope' or 'Vitascope'. A London scientific instrument maker, Robert Paul, had advanced Edison's invention. The original Kinetoscope did not project pictures, but was similar to the fairground peep-show. Paul could see the advantage of getting the pictures 'out of the box' so a wider audience could view them. He devised a projector which could throw the pictures onto a screen. Edison tried to bar him from scooping his invention, and eventually refused to supply films. Paul went out into London streets and made his own.

Paul's 'Animatograph' was an immediate success at the Alhambra Palace of Varieties, and it was here that Hertz realised what an impact they would make on his forthcoming tour. He bought one of Paul's two projectors for £100, and a number of the films which Paul had made around London.

The success of the 'Cinematographe' was its complete novelty. The films themselves gave little hint of the art form cinema was to become. Robert Paul's London scenes, though evoking memories for expatriates, showed little more than people walking about the city. Hertz's programme, on the other hand, included *A Highland Fling*, with Scottish couples dancing; *Tommy Atkins with his Girl in the Park*, a flirtatious episode; an excited crowd watching a sparring match; firemen rescuing children from a blazing house. Hertz had also bought some of Edison's films and adapted them to Paul's projectors.

Hertz's success in Johannesburg was repeated throughout the country: there were full houses everywhere. The era of the 'bioscope' had arrived.

A special film show was given for President Kruger in January 1899. The Empire's musical director, Dave Foote, travelled to Pretoria for the country's first command performance. Paul Kruger was impressed. Scenes of himself leaving for the Raadsaal were shown 'to the undisguised delight and astonishment of the President', according to local newspaper reports

Carl Hertz showed the first moving pictures in South Africa at Johannesburg's Empire Palace of Varieties. Early audiences were subjected to primitive and sometimes hazardous shows as the highly inflammable celluloid rolled off the reels and gathered in spirals over the floor. The projectors clanked and whirred and sometimes even exploded

The Pavilion Picture Palace in Cape Town in 1917. Then, as now, patrons were criticised for habits offensive to the serious cinema-goer. Said African Film News: *'A number of Capetown bioscopes put on their programmes a request to their patrons not to eat monkey nuts in the theatre and asking ladies not to stick hatpins into the backs of the seats in front of them.' Less than a decade before, most audiences were entertained to film shows in ramshackle halls, barns and warehouses. It was German immigrant Wilhelm Wolfram, a quality-conscious showman, who did most to establish the cinema theatre as a feature of South African cities and towns*

Flicker on the front line

Among the forerunners of the cinema newsreel were films of President Paul Kruger and Queen Victoria's Jubilee. Queen Victoria's funeral was shown a mere five weeks after she died. After the Anglo-Boer War crowds cheered and called for encores at the screening of the *Hoisting of the Union Jack in Pretoria and the entrance of Lord Roberts*.

The war in fact was one of the first military events in history to be extensively filmed, and William Kennedy Laurie Dickson, backed by the British Biograph and Mutoscope Company, was among the first of the modern day film war correspondents. Tipped off by army commanders, his camera followed the front-line troops and captured on film sensational and — to the audiences in Cape Town and England — horrific scenes.

Dragging his enormous camera on the back of a Cape cart, he risked shells and many other hazards to get his material. Despite all this effort, the films often did not reach England, and, when they did, were badly damaged.

Dickson's major rival was Joseph Rosenthal, cameraman for the Warwick Trading Company, then one of the largest distributors of films. They claimed that Rosenthal was the only accredited military correspondent operating the 'Cinematographe'.

The showmen

Many believed moving pictures were a seven-day wonder which, once the public tired of them, would disappear. But the novelty which had captured the imagination of the city sophisticates — enraptured by anything 'electric' —was highly successful in dorps where entertainment had been confined to a tuneless piano, a fretful melody squeezed out of a con-

South Africans are unique in calling their cinema entertainment 'bioscope'.

According to Thelma Gutsche in *The History and Social Significance of Motion Pictures in South Africa 1895-1940*, the Bioscope machine itself was Thomas Edison's invention, and was used very successfully in Durban by a Mrs James. When the advertisements claimed 'Absolutely steady!', 'Steady as a rock', they generally referred to the Bioscope. The name was further entrenched when Wilhelm Wolfram clung steadfastly to the Bioscope of the Warwick Trading Company and called his new picture house Wolfram's Bioscope.

Filming the Anglo-Boer War, 1900. The first exhibition of war films was held in Cape Town that year

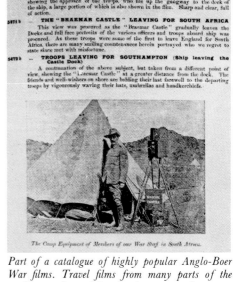

Part of a catalogue of highly popular Anglo-Boer War films. Travel films from many parts of the world were featured but few have survived

Selection of equipment marketed by Charles Urban's company during the 1900s

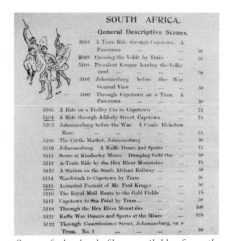

Some of the local films available from the Warwick Trading Company's catalogue

certina, or the skills of travelling entertainers. With projectors called 'Heliochromoscope', 'Vitagraph', 'Projectoscope' and 'Zeromettascope', the itinerant showmen became as much a feature of small South African towns as the *smous* ... but more dubious. He would often welsh on his audience: collecting their tickeys or sixpences, packing his cart and dashing off before his unsuspecting customers, sitting in pitch darkness, realised he had gone.

But a better class of showman, presenting better programmes, emerged. Foremost among them was Wilhelm Wolfram, a German immigrant who had tried his luck on the goldfields. His name was to become synonymous with 'bioscope' in South Africa.

It was not until the eve of Union that real picture palaces, or movie houses, came to replace the ramshackle variety halls, barns and warehouses that had been the early home of films in South Africa. Electric Theatres, as some of them were called, appeared in Durban, Germiston and Port Elizabeth. Cape Town had its Theatre-de-Luxe and then, in 1910, Wolfram opened his 565-seater 'Wolfram's Bioscope' in Cape Town. He presented films of quality (unlike the Electric group, who used worn-out British prints); avoided vulgarity, and was among the first to employ pianists to accompany the silent action. The content of the films themselves had improved immeasurably: fiction films like *Nero, or the Burning of Rome* and *The Trainer's Daughter*, a racecourse drama, played to capacity audiences.

The Stolen Favourite *was made in 1919 by African Film Productions and starred Miss Mabel May as Netta; and the cast included South Africa's heavyweight champion Jack Lalor, bottom left. The film was distinguished by an unbelievably intricate plot and some unusual names — Scrimjaw; Graggins; Little Sunlocks (top right)*

This 1918 South African production of The Bridge *starred Edward Vincent as 'Mad' John Moultry and Hilda Attenboro as his inamorata in a five-reel potboiler involving a love triangle, amnesia, a dramatic horse-ride, a spectacular rail crash, a lost ring, vengeance of the most diabolical sort and, finally, expiation of guilt through sacrifice*

When the 'bioscope' talked

SOUND COMES TO SOUTH AFRICAN CINEMAS

For more than 30 years the cinema was silent. In that time films had matured from hesitant flickers to full-length features of considerable merit. There were epics like *The Adventures of Tarzan*, a 14-reeler. And there were the greats of silent cinema: Mary Pickford, Douglas Fairbanks, Charlie Chaplin.

On the night of 28 February 1927, Capetonians flocked to a showing of *The Chinese Bungalow*, a silent picture starring Matheson Lang and Juliette Compton. A new company, Kinemas SA, had challenged the monopoly of African Theatres. But more interesting were the shorts shown after the main feature.

They talked.

The first full-length feature

The founder of Kinemas, Sydney Hayden, had imported 'phonofilms' — Dr Lee de Forest's first success at recording sound on celluloid and then reproducing it by means of a photo-electric cell. (Previous 'talkies' had relied on synchronised gramophone records.) Hayden then opened at the Johannesburg Town Hall in March 1927. The sound was metallic and harsh, but the synchronisation was fairly good. 'House full' notices went up immediately: there were 2 600 people at one showing. Encouraged, Kinemas set up a countrywide circuit, leasing halls in all the major cities and towns.

African Theatres countered with *The Jazz*

In 1926 African Theatres attempted to match the success of the rival Kinemas cinema chain by importing The Jazz Singer, *a full-length 'pseudo-talkie' starring Al Jolson. The film was singularly unsuccessful*

Singer, a full-length film featuring Al Jolson, his famous *Mammy*, other songs and snatches of dialogue. It met with only slight success. Unlike De Forest's system, it was presented on 'Panatrope', an electrical device working on the gramophone principle.

South Africans were well aware of and excited by the technical progress being made overseas; the race to bring the first full-length talking movie to the country was now on.

In 1929, advertisements proclaimed that it had arrived. On 6 July, at their newly-opened Astoria Kinema in Johannesburg, Hayden's group featured *Mr Smith Wakes Up*. Its syn-

chronisation was excellent, dialogue could be heard perfectly; it was a huge success. When it was shown in Cape Town a month later, the laughter drowned its sound. Kinemas had won the race — the boat carrying their film had arrived first.

On 13 September 1929, *Syncopation* was shown at the Astoria, Johannesburg. It started a craze for syncopated music, and among the lesser credits was Ian Hunter, a South African-born actor who played the villain. This widely-acclaimed film was followed by *High Treason*, the first full-length British talkie.

African Theatres came in almost four months later, in November, with Al Jolson's *The Singing Fool*, in which he immortalised the song *Sonny Boy*.

More than any other film, *Rio Rita*, released in early 1930, was to establish the sound cinema for ever. Though critics now write it off as an historical curiosity, it set new box office records in South Africa. In fact, so popular was this feature that it was generally remembered — mistakenly — as the first talkie. People journeyed from the country to hear its slick dialogue and see the novelty of Technicolor. It starred Bebe Daniels and John Boles.

Going to the talkies, in fact, became a weekly event in the lives of platteland families. Devoid of sound equipment in their local cinema or village hall, many would prefer a trip of 50 kilometres or more rather than miss the latest from the United States or Britain. Even so, the soundless bioscope lasted for several more years in the country areas.

The 1937 visit of Bebe Daniels and Ben Lyon created wild excitement among cinema-crazed South Africans. The couple were fêted and paraded through the streets

The immense popularity of cinema in the 1930s prompted a search for movie star material in the Union. Outspan *launched a nationwide search for South Africa's own film star. From among the thousands of aspiring actresses emerged Molly Lamont, right. In Hollywood she was given the usual screen test, short contract and the 'starlet' treatment that assured her small parts in several Hollywood films*

BIG FILMS, BIG STARS — AND MOVIE MADNESS

The 1930s was a cinema-crazed decade. Saturday night bioscope extended to 'fillums' on Tuesday and Friday nights as well. Customers paid their 1/9 (or 2/6 for the best seats) and programmes changed twice weekly.

Obvious romance, and sometimes blatant sex, gave way to a subtle suggestiveness, first seen in Mae West's *She Done Him Wrong*. 'At last we have a picture that men will enjoy more than women,' enthused African Theatres' publicist. This love story helped create the 'star' image. Marlene Dietrich was introduced in *The Blue Angel* (banned by the Cape Censor, which only whetted appetites in other provinces).

Of the great Swedish actress Greta Garbo, it was said: 'When Garbo talks the whole world listens.' Jean Harlow was a new kind of sex-symbol: peroxide blonde, with bright red lips, she managed to combine sophisticated provocation with a kind of childlike innocence. The men were also coming along, particularly a young crooner named Bing Crosby and a marvellous dancer, Fred Astaire.

In February 1933, The Pilgrim noted in the *Star*'s 'Stoep Talk': 'The Stock Exchange is not the only place in Johannesburg where there is a boom at the moment. Thursday night is usually a slack night for bioscopes but last night some people wandered from cinema to cinema only to be confronted with "house full" notices at the leading halls.'

Block-busting films

What had lured Johannesburgers out on their traditional 'maid's night off' were three block-busting films. At the Plaza, Marlene Dietrich was starring in *Shanghai Express*, a movie that was to set the pattern for innumerable train sagas. The Carlton had Chester Morris in an early talkie classic, *The Bat Whispers*, while at the Metro was a continuous performance of *Mata-Hari*, the spy classic starring Greta Garbo and Ramon Novarro. The censors had slapped a 'no 6-16' tag on it.

For those who were turned away, there was a choice of 13 other theatres, with such offerings as *Divorce Among Friends* at the Orpheum — 'where everybody goes' — or the thrills of big game hunting from *Congorilla* at the Standard.

THE FAIRY-LAND WORLD OF 'ATMOSPHERICS' AND WURLITZER

Palaces of make-believe. Left: Johannesburg's Bijou was typical of early picture palaces. The mighty Wurlitzer organ provided sonorous 'background' music. Right and below: Cape Town's Alhambra was South Africa's first 'atmospheric' theatre. Audiences walked on thick-pile carpets and sat in armchairs

The period between the two world wars was the golden age of the picture palaces, or 'atmospheric' theatres. The palaces, wrote Thelma Gutsche, 'endowed the showing of films with a wonder surpassing any they had previously possessed and their combination with the sound-film produced an effect almost of anaesthesia'.

Three of the most remarkable of these wonders were the Alhambra in Cape Town, Durban's Playhouse, and the Capitol, Pretoria. All three were the brainchildren of J. Rogers Cooke, a talented architect whom African Theatres had sent to the United States in 1927 to study cinema design.

By 1940 Cape Town had its Colosseum and Johannesburg its Twentieth Century. Although the latter, with its more modern décor, was not a true atmospheric, it was every bit as vast and opulent. The Union could now boast some of the finest theatres in the world. Patrons could walk on thick-piled carpets, sink into richly-upholstered armchairs, marvel at luxuriant and colourful decorations — twinkling stars, clouds et al. The Capitol, Pretoria, was designed in intricate and costly Italian Renaissance style (and this during the Depression). Others wafted cinemagoers into Roman villas, Spanish haciendas, Scottish castles and Tudor mansions.

The introduction of usherettes — small

armies of svelte maidens dressed in buckled shoes, silk stockings, tight satin knee-breeches and brightly coloured monkey-jackets — caused a minor sensation. Pride of attractions, though, was the mighty Wurlitzer organ, its booming resonance striking awe and wonder into the hearts of its first audiences. Metro-Goldwyn-Mayer opened their first super-cinema in Johannesburg with its £18 000 'Mighty Wurlitzer', played by Archie Parkhouse, who was to become South Africa's first cinema-organ 'personality'. The Metro could seat 3 000 and was decorated with French Impressionist prints, objets d'art and sumptuous 'cosmetic rooms'.

EVIL IN THE 'ABSOLUTE GROSS DARKNESS'

Once the silent cinema had become established, it quickly attracted its critics. One person complained to the newspapers of 'the evil passions aroused nightly by such degrading and semi-nude exhibitions'; another had taken his wife 'out of so poisonous a moral atmosphere'; a father was thunderstruck when he heard impressionable young girls in the audience asking 'What is B-E-T-R-A-Y-A-L, daddy?' as it was spelt out on the screen during a love story. There was demand for censorship; the Social Reform Association believed that the 'absolute gross darkness' encouraged indecent behaviour and the attendance of people of a low type, who molested women. Said the *S.A. Lady's Pictorial* in 1912: 'There is room enough and to spare in this hard world for good, healthy fun, and there is none for Kiljoys but surely fun is to be founded on something purer and less objectionable than the vulgar licence and exagger-

ated horse-play of the "comic" films in general use to-day. We all want to see pictures of "life" and "incident", but the glorification of bushranging as a profession, the "faked" representation of sordid tragedies, demonstrations of lawless personal revenge and vendetta, and reproductions of the worst features of the latest substitute for the prize-ring, are not among the sides of life or the class of incident which we desire to see illustrated in our entertainments . . . the time has come for an earnest protest against the flagrant abuse of an excellent source of entertainment and even of instruction.'

With the later silent film, in fact, came blatant sex, personified by Clara Bow in *The IT Girl*. The Cape was the first to introduce formal censorship. Cinema proprietors in the other provinces gleefully exploited the anomaly — a film banned there was guaranteed sell-out elsewhere. The absurdity of selective banning was apparent to everyone and, on 3 June 1931, the Entertainments (Censorship) Act brought films under the sharp and often over-zealous eyes of a Board of Censors.

Home-made movies

THE 'LITTLE MAN' LAUNCHES A BIG INDUSTRY

In 1913 the cinema and entertainment business was in turmoil. It looked as if over-competition and a general strike would bankrupt many theatres. Then a pint-sized giant stepped in. He was Isidore William Schlesinger — known as the 'Little Man' — who had arrived in South Africa in 1894 at the age of 17 to seek his fortune on the goldfields.

Penniless after paying his steerage-class fare from America, Schlesinger quickly learned he had a smooth way in insurance salesmanship. He travelled the country, policies in hand, and was soon earning £15 000 a year in commissions — a staggering income for those days. By the time he established the African Life Assurance Company, in 1904, he was a rich man.

But the former newspaper vendor is best remembered for his interest in the entertainment business. It began in 1913 when the proprietors of the Empire Theatre found themselves in debt to a bank for £60 000. Although not at all interested in theatres, Schlesinger could not resist a challenge. He told the bank that if it were prepared to risk another £60 000, he would take over the theatre and make it pay. The bank agreed, and within a short time Schlesinger had chalked up another success — becoming owner of the Empire in the process. He looked closely at the industry and decided it was in a shocking state, commenting later: 'When I took over, virtually every theatre owner in the country was insolvent.' He called owners to a meeting in Johannesburg and suggested they join a company which centralised the distribution of films and variety acts. They had little choice: they agreed.

In launching African Theatres Trust Limited he consolidated the majority of theatres showing films and vaudeville and put film dis-

Above: a poignant scene from the 1916 epic, De Voortrekkers. *From left to right: Holger Petersen, Edna Flugrath, Caroline Frances Cook, Stephen Ewart and M.A. Wetherell starred in the film that is said to have brought tears to the eyes of General Louis Botha. The massacre at Dingane's kraal, left, was one of the most exciting sequences in* De Voortrekkers. *The kraal was built in the grounds of the Killarney studios. The film cost £20 000 to make*

The man who put it all together. I.W. Schlesinger's hard work and superb business sense were responsible for the survival of South Africa's early film industry

Moedertjie, *a dramatic short, was the first Afrikaans sound film to be produced in South Africa. It won for director Joseph Albrecht a gold medal from the Suid-Afrikaanse Akademie vir Taal, Lettere en Kuns. From left to right: Pierre de Wet, Stephanie Fourie, Carl Richter, Jan Plaat-Stultjes and Joan du Toit*

African Film Productions Ltd produced their first 'talkies' in 1930. Here they are at work on their second production, a publicity film on Durban. The film proved to be highly successful both in South Africa and overseas

tribution on a more orderly basis. A spinoff of Schlesinger's take-over was something not immediately apparent: behind the hard businessman façade was a real love of show business, and especially of films.

African Film Productions Limited was founded with the intention of making South African films for South African audiences and produced a dozen short fiction films in 1915-16. Most had a topically local flavour, involving illicit gold buying and faithful servants. Schlesinger made sure that the talents of actress Mabel May were adequately displayed: he was to marry her and it was partly to further her career that he had founded African Film Productions Limited. In addition *African Mirror*, founded in 1913 and one of the oldest regular news-reels, covered actuality events — including the East African campaign, which brought the drama of the First World War to the relatively isolated towns of the Union.

South Africa's very first home-made film, in fact, had been the melodramatic *The Star of the South*, 'the story of a big diamond', produced by the Springbok Film Company. It was shown at Christmas 1911 by Wolfram and Africa's Amalgamated Theatres. The critics wrote it off as amateurish, but five years later they were unable to dismiss African Film Productions' next attempt: Harold Shaw's *De Voortrekkers*.

At the newly-erected Killarney Studios, then situated in an isolated tract of veld in the Johannesburg suburb of Killarney, production had started on what was to become an epic film, the first in South African cinema. The date: 1916.

Harold Shaw, a producer for the American Vitagraph Company, had been imported at a salary reputed to be £2 000 a year for the first 12 months, and £3 000 for the second, plus a percentage of the profits of any film he made. With him was his wife, Edna Flugrath, a popular film actress ('stars' had not yet been invented). Armed with a script by historian Dr. Gustav Preller, Shaw set to work on *De Voortrekkers*.

Though filming a momentous event and popular subject, Shaw met with hostility from the Afrikaans-speaking community. Many had been incensed by a jingoistic English film about the siege of Mafeking, which showed the Afrikaner as a dumb, witless backwoodsman. An indignant member of the Heidelberg branch of the women's National Party told how the film company arrived at *nagmaal* time and duped the unsophisticated farmers into performing. They were supplied with 'ludicrous costumes, wild beards and all sorts of ridiculous paraphernalia which would only serve to excite public contempt'.

In fact, Shaw and Preller went to enormous lengths to ensure authenticity in costume and props. They collected 500 rifles (including one used by trek leader Andries Pretorius), 20 000 assegais and other tribal equipment, and 40 trek wagons were made specially for the film.

Shaw was also up against a peculiarly South African problem when he filmed the attack at Blood River. The location was in fact Elsburg on the East Rand, and Dingane's

They built a Nation — Die Bou van 'n Nasie being filmed on the farm Schoongezicht at Stellenbosch. Production began early in 1937 and the Afrikaans version was first shown at a private exhibition in Pretoria on 12 December 1938. The English newspapers called it disjointed and 'charade-like', and a major row erupted over what some people maintained was pure propaganda against the Fusionist ideal

Zulus were drawn from the ERPM mine, with compound managers and other mine officials cast as trekkers. The Zulus charged the Boer wagons, but, instead of falling 'dead', carried on their attack. Police had to intervene to prevent what was rapidly becoming a real battle. Rushes of the film proved to be dramatically realistic — but inaccurate: the Zulus at Blood River never got within 150 metres of the laager. The scene had to be re-shot.

The first public showing of *De Voortrekkers* was on 16 December 1916, Dingane's Day (now the Day of the Vow), at Krugersdorp, where 40 000 Afrikaners had gathered at the Paardekraal Monument. It was acclaimed as 'the greatest film picture ever produced in the history of the cinema'. Running for nearly two hours, showings were continuous from ten in the morning to midnight.

EVERY RUBBER BALL IN JOHANNESBURG

Harold Shaw was a man who did not believe in cutting corners. His plans for the Killarney production of the Zulu war epic, *The Symbol of Sacrifice*, called for a huge cast and an array of sets and props that would have done Hollywood proud. *Stage and Cinema* described the undertaking in September 1917:

'5 000 shields are being made, at a cost of 2s each. To tip the shields, and to provide armlets and leg-pieces for the native warriors, 350 skins have been cut up. Thousands and thousands of assegais, knob-kerries, guns, swords and lances are being made. The knobs on the kerries are made of india-rubber balls, and for this purpose every rubber ball in Johannesburg, from 2¾ to 4 inches in circumference,

The Sunday Times *was highly enthusiastic about the new 'City of the Film' taking shape at the African Film Productions Ltd headquarters in Killarney: 'Pictures of all kinds will be produced in the city, and for that purpose it will contain handsome stone buildings and native kraals, an artificial river . . . it will be a scene of great activity, and the home of a busy, thriving population'*

was purchased.' Shooting began on 18 January under the watchful eye of Schlesinger, some sequences at Isandhlwana.

Two tons of paint were needed for the scenery and four van-loads of paper flowers were made to throw at the troops on their return from the wars. A kraal of 266 huts was constructed — only to be razed in one of the more spectacular scenes with the use of 180 litres of paraffin and two cartloads of straw. Commented *Stage and Cinema:* 'Sufficient has been said to indicate to the intelligent reader that the African Film Productions Ltd have inaugurated an industry the national importance of which to South Africa cannot be exaggerated.'

Miss Mabel May as Queen Nyleptha in a scene from the lavish production of Haggard's story of Allan Quatermain *in 1919: 'What, am I a Queen, and yet not free to choose the man whom I shall love?'*

On location

OSTRICH-RACING: 'SOUTH AFRICA'S FAVOURITE SPORT'

The growth of South Africa's film industry was slow and sporadic — the country was simply too unsophisticated to support professional, full-time performers and producers, and local talent tended to drift overseas. Many of the 'South African' feature films were produced by foreign studios.

Some of the early epics were the cause of both controversy and hilarity. One such was the ambitious *Rhodes of Africa*, launched in 1935 by Gaumont-British.

There were fears that the film would provoke still-simmering Boer-Briton resentments; Smuts himself vetted the script.

Walter Huston, in the title role, refused to come out to the Union and a double, Afrikaans actor Paul de Groot, stood in for the location shots — not an unusual practice then. Included in the cast were Basil Sydney (he also had a location stand-in for the part of Leander Starr Jameson); Ndanisa Kumalo, a tribal chief who played Lobengula (Kumalo subsequently joined Gaumont-British studios), Lewis Casson and Peggy Ashcroft.

When it had its first public showing on 18 May 1936, the English and Afrikaans press were united in their condemnation. The producer, Berthold Viertel, explained that in making a cinematic drama he had had to sacrifice accuracy and introduce fictitious events. Wrongly cast, Huston played a rough-hewn diamond-miner-cum-premier. The portrayal of Paul Kruger, slurping coffee and dipping his bread into it, was an insulting caricature. *Rhodes* established something of a pattern for inaccurate representation of South Africa in foreign-made films.

One of the most ludicrous locally-set films was called *Adventure in Diamonds*. Produced by Twentieth-Century Fox to satisfy a public interest in African settings, it was laughed out of 'bioscopes' in the Union. It ran for just one night at the Alhambra, Cape Town. Stock location shots had been blended with studio footage. The story had 'diamond barons' complete with topees driving a few short kilometres from Cape Town to Kimberley to watch ostrich racing, 'South Africa's most popular sport'.

Better was *We're Going to be Rich*, produced by Twentieth-Century Fox in the mid-Thirties and set in goldrush-Johannesburg. None of it was filmed in the Union but the studio scenes of the golden city were credible. It starred Victor McLaglen, a South African who had gone to England in childhood, and Gracie Fields, who toured the country in 1935.

After the Second World War, South African historical events were to be handled by overseas and local companies with varying success. In 1964, Stanley Baker produced and starred in his magnificent film, *Zulu*, the epic story of the defence of Rorke's Drift after the slaughter at Isandlwana. Also appearing was chief Gatsha Buthelezi, later Chief Minister of KwaZulu, who played Cetshwayo, Michael Caine, who played a British soldier, and Jack Hawkins as a missionary.

Hoor my Lied (1964), starring Gé Korsten and Min Shaw, was one of several pleasant but unexceptional 'family entertainment' features and musicals produced by Kavalier Films. Sentiment was the keynote: it told the story of a doctor who loses his wife in an accident which also leaves his daughter crippled. He then finds that he is going blind, sings for money to pay for the daughter's operation, becomes a successful opera performer, and all ends well. Right: Jy is my Liefling *(1968) was scripted in similarly melodramatic mould*

Veteran South African actor Siegfried Mynhardt plays the doctor searching for his lost son in Dr Kalie *(1968), one of the best of the Kavalier Films productions. Mynhardt gave some fine screen performances in the 1960s, but his star shone even brighter on the theatre stage*

KIMBERLEY JIM REEVES' RUSH

Reeves, left, Arthur Swemmer and Clive Parnell

In March 1963 American singer Jim Reeves arrived in South Africa to star in *Kimberley Jim*, a rumbustious musical set in the days when diggers still rushed for diamonds. Characters included slick American wheeler-dealers (Reeves) and con-artists, saloon girls, amateur boxers and the gamblers and roisterers of the small mining town of Mac-Mac. With Reeves in the cast were beauty queen and dancer Madeleine Usher, South African champion boxer Mike Holt, singer Webster Booth and Clive Parnell, an up-and-coming local actor. Director and writer Emil Nofal worked to a hair-raising schedule: Reeves' other commitments allowed him just 33 days on location, and he was still recording dialogue two hours before the return flight to the United States. Within six months, an entire village — including its electricity, sewerage and a two-kilometre road — had to be constructed in 1910 period style; the story scripted, the music scored and rehearsed; 1 300 extras costumed and drilled, and the shooting completed. Clive Parnell was also appearing on the Johannesburg stage at the time. He had to dress and make up for his part in the car that took him from film set to theatre, and reverse the process on his way back to the set for the nightshift. Shooting started at 5 a.m. and finished at one in the morning. *Kimberley Jim* was completed in five months.

Gert van den Bergh was the outstanding South African screen actor of the Sixties, and the first to be signed on for major roles by foreign film companies on location in this country. His output was prodigious

Among the more exciting South African-made films was Majuba, a British-Boer epic starring British actor Stanley Baker. The story tells of love, intrigue and sudden death in the stormy days preceding the Boer victory at Majuba. The large cast included such popular local stars as Brian Brooke, Siegfried Mynhardt, Michael Todd, Anna Neethling-Pohl, Esmé Euvrard and Dulcie van den Bergh

JAMIE UYS, A MAN OF MANY PARTS

In 1950 the South African film world was jolted by the appearance of the first Afrikaans production in colour. But even more startling was the method by which it was made: a young movie-mad schoolteacher had spent £170 on filming equipment, and then gone ahead to photograph, produce, direct and act in *Daar Doer in die Bosveld*. The man was Jamie Uys.

Judex C. Viljoen wrote in *Outspan*: '...

"Daar Doer" is a first-timer's film. This is the first time Jamie has written a story, the first time he has handled a ciné camera, the first time he has produced, directed, acted in or edited a film. Neither have any of his supporting players ever appeared before a camera or on the stage, in fact some of the actors had never *seen* a film before they started working on *Daar Doer*.'

Even as a schoolboy Jamie Uys was determined to produce films. He became a schoolteacher after graduation, but the lure of the film world was too strong: he finally decided to sell everything he possessed (except his old car) to finance his own production. Said *Outspan*: 'He had no money to spend on elaborate sets and expensive scenery, but he had the wonderful Bushveld landscape for his stage; and as for "props", well, there was an old jalopy, a bus that came once a week...'

It was only in the 1960s that the local film industry reached something resembling maturity. Although the output rose dramatically, films were unimpressive in terms of technique and only a few had all-round merit. But it was also the decade of the versatile and prolific Jamie Uys, who brought laughter to South African audiences with bilingual comedies such as *Hans en die Rooinek* (a tale of good-natured rivalry between Boer and Briton) and *Lord Oom Piet*. The following year he produced *Dingaka*, a more ambitious work portraying painful black adjustment to Western ways. The leading roles were filled by the British actor Stanley Baker, famed South African dancer Juliet Prowse and Ken Gampu.

And he didn't stop there. The 1970s saw the emergence of such internationally-successful films as *Beautiful People*, a series of delightful wildlife sequences, and *Funny People*, a candid-camera look at how ordinary people act in extraordinary situations. As he once told a *Sunday Times* reporter: 'When I'm moved I simply want to share the things I find beautiful and funny — the Bushmen, the desert, what makes me laugh. I can't write poetry and I can't paint...'

Jamie Uys produced Dirkie in 1969. The film, about a boy stranded in the desert after an air smash, pretended to offer nothing more than low-key charm and a little excitement. It succeeded admirably

Jamie Uys and Bob Courtney put their feet in it again in the comedy, All the way to Paris

Radio comes to South Africa

THE AMATEUR PIONEERS OF WIRELESS TELEGRAPHY

The South African Railways and Harbours made the country's first formal wireless broadcast from Johannesburg on 18 December 1923. Although there were already many amateur radio stations operating by that time, the event generated intense excitement. In July the following year, the Associated Scientific and Technical Broadcasting Company Limited started regular broadcasts from station JB in Johannesburg.

Almost three decades earlier, in 1896, 22-year-old Guglielmo Marconi had been granted the world's first patent for wireless telegraphy after two years of experiment.

In South Africa, at the same time, Edward Alfred Jennings, a skilled instrument maker who had emigrated from Britain in the early 1890s, invented wireless telegraphy independently of Marconi.

Working on an experimental telephone receiver at his house in Port Elizabeth in 1896, Jennings stumbled on the principle of the 'Coherer' — an apparatus which detected electric waves and which was used by Marconi and other inventors in the earliest types of wireless receivers.

At a crowded meeting in the Port Elizabeth Town Hall on 8 May 1899, the audience was told: 'Mr Jennings has been silently pursuing his studies for several years on the same important scientific subject and has arrived at results almost as satisfactory as those obtained by Professor Marconi. All the more credit is due to Mr Jennings as his pursuits have been carried out in his spare hours.'

WORKING IN A VACUUM

Dr Hendrik van der Bijl was one of South Africa's greatest radio pioneers. In 1914 he discovered the principle of the thermionic valve — on which all modern broadcasting and television depends — and produced a major scientific work, *The Thermionic Vacuum Tube*, which was considered fundamental to the study of radio. He also developed the first 'scrambling' device for radio speech, and engineered the transmission of the human voice from New York to Paris by short-wave wireless. This remarkable man later went on to found ESCOM, ISCOR and the Industrial Development Corporation.

Lady's earphone for crystal set

Five-valve radio with horn speaker. Round object below it, in the centre of the picture, is a loudspeaker for a radio, 1927

Crystal set, 1924

Radiair five-valve set, 1925–26. Standing on its cabinet is a Japanese portable valve radio

Westinghouse radio, 1937

Telefunken radio, 1928–29

Fisk Radiola, 1946

Atwater-Kent six-valve set, 1932-33

The oldest radio in this collection, a crystal set, dates from the early 1920s. It was tuned by moving a tiny piece of wire called a cat's whisker about the surface of a crystal of galena in search of a sensitive spot that detected the signal. The sets required earphones and very long aerials, and were popular until well into the 1930s. Enthusiasts often erected complicated systems of masts and other antennae over their houses in the early days of radio, while indoors, especially in the 1920s, the sets were dominated by large horn-shaped speakers. The batteries that powered the sets were also large — about the size of a modern car battery — and were usually stored in a cupboard under the set. At that time an effective portable radio was little more than a dream

From shore to ship

In July that year, Jennings erected a transmitter in the lighthouse on the Donkin Reserve in Port Elizabeth, and achieved a record transmission distance of 12,5 km. He also set up excellent communication between Port Elizabeth and a mail steamer 4,5 km out in Algoa Bay.

A formal request in the Cape Parliament for funds for further research was rejected by the Minister responsible, John X. Merriman. 'Life,' he said, 'is troublesome enough with ordinary telegrams. With wireless telegraphy it will be unbearable.' But Prime Minister W.P. Schreiner had been present at a display of wireless telegraphy in 1899 and was all in favour of the new science. An agreement to establish and work a signal station at Dassen Island, to communicate with Robben Island or the mainland, was finalised between Lloyd's of London and the Cape Government.

In 1902 the Cape Parliament introduced the

first radio legislation in the world: 'Electric Telegraph shall be interpreted as including any system or means of conveying signs, signals or communication by electricity, magnetism, electro-magnetism or other like agencies, whether with or without the aid of wires, and including the system commonly known as Wireless Telegraphy or Aetheric Signalling and any improvement and development of such system.'

The first wireless licences in the world were also introduced in South Africa, and by 1910 the country was producing its own radio equipment. 'Wireless telephones are already in a state suitable for application to commercial work,' reported the *South African Mining and Engineering Journal*.

Wireless soon became a proposition: in 1910 the Natal Government built an installation on the Bluff to operate at a range of between 400 km and 480 km; two years later the Cape Government erected a 5 kW Marconi transmitter with a 640 km daytime range and a 960-1 600 km night-time range at Kommetjie to serve one of the busiest shipping lanes in the world.

Before the First World War there were a number of amateurs in South Africa with experimental sets — among them Henry Lenton, subsequently a Postmaster-General — but their use was banned during the period of hostilities, and it was not until 1919 that broadcasting restrictions were lifted. Enthusiasts then revived their hobby, setting up transmitters in various parts of the country to broadcast weekly gramophone concerts and to exchange broadcast material.

Harry and his lassie

The first public demonstrations of broadcasting in South Africa took place in 1920 at the Western Province Agricultural Show in Cape Town, and at the Milner Park Show in Johannesburg. Audience reaction ranged from delight to disbelief as voices and music emerged through the ether by courtesy of the Wireless Agency Limited, official South African Marconi agents.

Later that year, visiting celebrity Harry Lauder sang *I Love a Lassie* into the Marconi Wireless Telephone Set. It was heard over the air by hundreds of South Africans. And in October, Reuter's undertook to supply a bulletin of South African general news to be broadcast every evening over recognised wireless stations for the special benefit of shipping.

The first official concert broadcast from Johannesburg took place on 18 December 1923. Broadcasting equipment and receiving sets were loaned by the Western Electric Company. Among the artistes was Billy Matthews, who recalled: 'In those days everyone stood on the same side of the mike. It was cosy but terrifying.' According to a spokesman from the South African Railways and Harbours, in whose headquarters the concert had been performed, reception was flawless: 'We feel that the occasion has given a tremendous fillip to interest in the cult of Wireless Telephony in South Africa.'

All the firsts

Regular broadcasting in South Africa officially started at 9 p.m. on 1 July 1924 when station JB broadcast speeches and a musical programme co-ordinated by Annie Manthey, South Africa's first radio announcer, from a studio crammed with government officials and important guests, on the first floor of the Stuttafords Building in Johannesburg.

Congratulatory telegrams — many addressed to Theo Wendt, general manager and studio director — arrrived from all over the country. With no previous radio experience, Wendt, formerly conductor of the Cape Town Municipal Orchestra, suggested schedules which were to become normal broadcasting procedure: time signals, news, reports on weather, sport and market prices.

'The wonder of wireless!' enthused the *Star*. 'All South Africa listens to Johannesburg; from Cape Town to Bulawayo. Postmaster-General besieged with application for licences.'

Amateurs from all over the country, who had been encouraged to build radio receivers (mostly of the 'cat's whisker' type with crystal

IT'S EIGHT O'CLOCK: DURBAN CALLING

Early broadcasts from Durban were limited to short programmes in the morning, afternoon and evening; Tuesdays were devoted to maintenance and repairs. Most of the musical backing was provided by the Durban Municipal Orchestra. Below right is the cover of the first weekly issue of Durban Calling — *the official programme. Below left: The Durban broadcasting studio in 1924. Situated in the Town Hall, it was the first municipally controlled radio station in the world. Above: A concert goes over the air*

It is a stifling summer night in Durban. On the top floor of the Town Hall over sixty people in full evening dress are packed into a small room which already contains a grand piano, a large gramophone, a pianola and a conductor's rostrum. More than half the people are musicians — members of the Durban Municipal Orchestra. The others are guests who make up the audience.

The room is not only small; it is also hot and close. The walls and ceiling are heavily draped with two layers of hessian and one layer each of blue and white casement cloth. Ventilation shafts provide the only supply of air which is circulated by ceiling fans. A window is partly open but this provides little relief because a storm is brewing.

The orchestra tunes up; men run handkerchiefs inside starched collars; ladies smooth their long skirts and flutter fans vigorously but no-one moves; no discomfort can dull the excitement of the moment. They are sitting in a broadcasting studio about to witness the first wireless programme to be transmitted from Durban. It is 10 December 1924.

There is a sudden quickening of interest. The heavy Marconi Round microphone is being wheeled across to the open window, and at exactly 7.57 p.m. it is switched on to pick up the voice of Durban — the hubbub

of humanity rising from the street below, the clanging tramcar bells and the blare of motor car hooters, and then the chimes of the Post Office clock as it strikes eight o'clock. The 'Durban Calling' signal has gone out loud and clear.

The window is closed; the microphone is returned to its central position; Mr H. Lyell-Tayler, conductor of the orchestra, takes his place on the rostrum and His Worship the Mayor, Councillor T.M. Wadley, J.P., declares the station open. The audience settles back for the musical programme, which commences with the *Overture Raymond*. The atmosphere is suffocating, but everyone agrees that the evening is a great success.

detectors, plus earphones) listened in.

In September 1924 the Cape and Peninsula Broadcasting Association began broadcasting in the J.N.X. Building in Greenmarket Square. Its studio manager was former clarinettist René Caprara — later director-general of the SABC and inventor of the Capraraphone (which made possible uninterrupted sound from transposed gramophone records).

The first complete church service was broadcast from Cape Town, and in 1925 the first-ever commentary in South Africa on a rugby match was made from Newlands. This was followed, in 1927, by commentaries on cricket, motor cycle racing and boxing and, a year later, on the first rugby test matches. In June 1926 the second anniversary of JB was celebrated with a link-up of musicians in Johannesburg, Cape Town and Durban, and within a year enthusiasts were predicting that the station would be heard all over Africa, and probably even as far as Europe.

But because of the limited coverage of the three separate stations, and inadequate licence revenue — wireless pirating was rife and there were only 15 509 paid licences in the entire country — JB was forced to close down in January 1927.

1927 news. English, one hour; Afrikaans, 5 minutes

Towards brighter broadcasting

POPULAR PILOTS OF THE AIR WAVES

On 1 April 1927 the wealthy Schlesinger Organisation, with Government permission, formed the African Broadcasting Corporation in Johannesburg. The independent Cape Town and Durban stations were incorporated soon afterwards. The ABC was granted sole broadcasting rights.

JB was on the air again, and within a few months the ABC was comfortably housed in Connaught Buildings, Bree Street, with increased power: an output of 5 kW from the aerial — comparable to New Zealand's Wellington Station, the most powerful in the British Empire.

Although technical improvements had been made, reception was erratic in the first few years. But by 1932 the ABC could confidently observe: 'The importance of wireless broadcasting — the romance of wireless: it is doubtful whether any application of science to the progress of civilisation has made a greater appeal to public imagination, or has so completely changed human outlook in matters of speed and distance.'

The number of licensed sets had increased to 161 767 in that year but there were still financial difficulties, and Prime Minister Hertzog ordered an enquiry into all aspects of broadcasting. This was followed by the creation of the SABC in 1936, with the stipulation that broadcasts, until then presented in English only, should within the following year also be made in Afrikaans.

Lourenço Marques comes on the air

In 1934, C.J. McHarry, a South African, started and ran broadcasting in Portuguese East Africa. Listeners in South Africa tuned in to the familiar Portuguese voices announcing: *Aquis Lourenço Marques — Radio Clube de Moçambique*. The station presented most programmes in English, with popular music and entertainment predominating. In 1935, when the Portuguese government gave McHarry the right to sell advertising on the air, Lourenço Marques introduced commercial radio in Southern Africa.

In 1947 Colonel Richard L. Meyer, previously associated with the International Broadcasting Company of London (which operated English stations, and Radio Toulouse, Radio Lyons and Radio Normandy in France) took over the management of Lourenço Marques in association with John Davenport — later an executive of the Reader's Digest Association — and beamed this highly successful commercial radio service into South Africa until 1972, when the SABC acquired control.

Sponsorship — and listenership

Interviewed in the *Outspan* on 14 June 1946, René Caprara announced: 'I have recommended to the Board of Governors that the SABC should start a chain of commercial stations in the Union for the benefit of broadcasting, listeners and the commercial community.'

With the creation of the third South African

Personality parade. Top left: Johnny Walker broadcasts Radio Juke Box *on Springbok Radio. The programme, still on the air in 1980, began in 1950. Top right: presenters Mervyn John and Esmé Euvrard. Above: Dulcie van den Bergh started presenting Springbok's* Hospitaaltyd *in 1956. The programme was one of the station's first hospital request series, in which music was played for patients*

service, the bilingual and commercial Springbok Radio, on 1 May 1950, romantic serials and audience participation shows gained enormous popularity. For the record: the first song to be broadcast that day was *Vat Jou Goed en Trek Ferreira*, which became Springbok's theme tune; the first broadcaster to speak was Eric Egan; the first commercial advertised Edblo mattresses. Among the programmes which began in 1950 and were still going strong 30 years later were *Radio Juke Box, Lux Radio Theatre* and *Hospital Time. Pick-a-Box* remained on the air for 17 years with the biggest listenership rating ever recorded on Springbok Radio — 600 000 people tuned in every week to a quiz programme whose sponsors offered £100 to the winner in 1950, R1 000 near the end of its run. Request and women's interest programmes produced personalities like veteran broadcaster Peter Merrill, who in 1980 was still associated with Springbok Radio.

In 1948 *Anything Goes*, one of the first South African-produced radio variety shows, was recorded by Charles Berman, produced and compèred by Peter Merrill, written by Monte Doyle to feature Dan Hill and his orchestra; Artemis; Al Debbo and Dennis Lotis. It was first recorded in front of an enthusiastic studio audience in the 20th Century Theatre in Johannesburg for broadcast on Lourenço Marques Radio. At one performance in 1949, 4 000 people, surging into the cinema, broke the large glass entrance doors.

Home-grown shows

Initially more than 60 per cent of all drama programmes on Springbok Radio were imported, mainly from Australia (they included *Mary Livingstone MD*, and *Portia Faces Life*).

But local shows quickly gained ground. The first all-South African English-language serial of note was *Brave Voyage;* the first Afrikaans: *Liefdeslied*, (1953 to 1959). One of the best

known local serials was *Stiefvader*, written in 1960 by Cyril Chosack and listed in the Guinness Book of Records as the world's longest running Afrikaans radio serial.

Audience response to thousands of episodes of *This is How*, first broadcast on Lourenço Marques Radio, was phenomenal: thousands of listeners contributed household hints. A similar programme, *So Maak Mens* on Springbok Radio, broadcast by Esmé Euvrard and Jan Cronje in 1956 was still on the air in 1979.

Actors, broadcasters and producers like André Brink, Michael Silver, Dean Herrick, Maggie Gordon, Stuart Brown, Dewar McCormack, Eric Egan, Bruce Anderson, Noreen Purdon, Ken Taylor, Barbara Cowan, Anne and Harold Freed, Leon Gluckman, Percy Sieff, Robert Griffiths, Simon Swindell, Bill Prince and Judy Henderson, all of whom made South African programmes in the early years of commercial radio, gained wide recognition for top class radio work.

And they did so against formidable odds: they had to compete against cheap imported transcriptions. Often they would be paid £1 an episode, and had to record 15-minute epi-

Leslie Green, the 'gentleman of radio', entertains Susy, a Russian bear from Wilkie's Circus, during one of his much-loved Tea With Mr Green *programmes, which ran from 1955 to 1968. In the later years he recorded in his studio at home. An outside microphone caught the authentic garden sounds of bird, bee and distant lawnmower, adding to the amiable informality of the programme. Green was also Springbok's* Do-It-Yourself This Weekend *man, the genial visitor in* Hospital Time *and presenter of* Pets' Parade. *In 23 years he found homes for over 300 000 pets — including a marmoset monkey, a sheep, snakes and silkworms*

Eric Egan's breakfast programme, which ran for 15 years, had a huge audience

Peter Chiswell was the presenter of the unconventional late-night programme, The 10.30 Club

Recording Intimately Yours *in 1948. Its signature tune was* I Got the Sun in the Morning

SNOEKTOWN CALLING

Left to right: Norrie Sowman, Cecil Wightman, Rosemary Barnard and Bernade van Alphen

Cecil Wightman convulsed South Africa with his satirical *Snoektown Calling*. A talented mimic and scriptwriter, he launched the programme in the mid-1930s (it was an extension of his earlier *Incredible Interviews*, in which he held imaginary conversations with famous personalities) and for 30 years he kept the country laughing at his myriad voices. It was broadcast from Cape Town.

Pick a Box's first presenter Jack Bryant (standing) with messily hopeful contestant. The forfeits were a highlight of the show

The pop era arrives. Radio Record Club, *launched in the mid-Fifties, was, said presenter Barry O'Donaghue, 'the first programme dealing with music ever to be broadcast in South Africa giving teenagers what they want'. It proved enormously popular*

sodes in just twenty minutes, sight-reading the scripts, improvising sound effects.

Three decades of delight

In letters to the *African Radio Announcer* in January 1948, readers' opinions of the SABC differed: 'I can find very little fault with the local broadcasting stations and I share my listening evenly amongst Durban, Joburg, Lourenço Marques and the BBC.' Commented a listener, in response to a Johannesburg reader who complained that the SABC needed a general spring cleaning: 'Their only asset is their charming musical programme arranger, Alan Mandell.'

One of the most popular early broadcasters on the English Service was Cecil Wightman, whose programme *Snoektown Calling — the Craziest Station South of the Line,* delighted listeners for thirty years.

On 17 July 1950 the SABC started its own news service and special correspondents were

appointed in various countries. Two years later regional news services were introduced. To improve reception, a short-wave transmitting station began operating at Paradys on 1 July 1956, followed by the introduction of a comprehensive FM network, which transmitted for the first time on Christmas Day 1961 from the Albert Hertzog Tower in Johannesburg.

By May 1967 three regional services — Radio Highveld, Radio Good Hope and Radio Port Natal — were on the air, and at the end of 1968 some 1 700 147 radio licences had been issued.

The external services, broadcasting in Afrikaans, English, Dutch, German, French, Portuguese, Tsonga, Swahili, ChiChewa and Lozi for a total of 156½ hours a week, were introduced on 1 May 1966. With the exception of the Spanish-speaking countries of South America, they reached every corner of the world.

The long wait for television

THE MINIATURE BIOSCOPE CHANGES SUBURBAN LIFE

On the night of Monday 5 January 1976, one million South Africans sat around what had been termed 'a miniature bioscope' to witness the Republic's belated entry into the television age. At a cost of R106 million the country was given the most technically advanced colour television service in the world. The quarter-million TV set owners at the official switch-on had paid anything up to R1 000 for a 66 cm colour model, in addition to a R36 licence fee — for 37½ hours of weekly viewing, half of each evening in Afrikaans, the other half in English.

Overnight, South African suburban lifestyles changed. Evening meals were taken early and hurried. The traditional 'sundowner' on the way home gave way to a TV-chair drink; bars emptied for the six o'clock switch on. Babies were bathed early, telephones taken off the hook, libraries lost subscribers. Restaurants and hotels tried to meet the challenge by installing television sets in diningrooms and bars. But favourite programmes became required home viewing. On the evenings they were screened, blockbuster series like *The World at War* and *Rich Man Poor Man* emptied restaurants, theatres and cinemas.

Bouquets and brickbats

Personalities were created by the TV screen and sustained by the Press. The professionalism of Michael de Morgan and Nigel Kane turned news readers into stars. The cheeky wink of presenter Mike Hobbs brought him a bulging mailbag. Viewers followed the increasingly obvious pregnancy of announcer Dorianne Berry with rapt interest.

The early days produced the first weekly series with which South Africans could identify: *The Villagers*, a story set on a Reef goldmine. Created by John Cundill and Noel Harford, its characters were ordinary, human and warm, and when Buller Wilmot was killed in a mine explosion, people in thousands of homes mourned and wept at his televised 'funeral'.

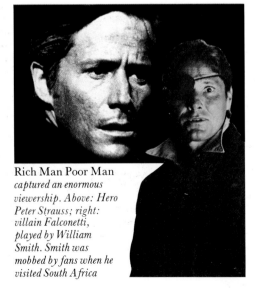

Rich Man Poor Man *captured an enormous viewership. Above: Hero Peter Strauss; right: villain Falconetti, played by William Smith. Smith was mobbed by fans when he visited South Africa*

In the first days of television the public, in what dealers called 'Switch-on madness', rushed to buy sets. By the end of 1975 — that is, before the formal inauguration of the service — a quarter-million had been sold. The windows of TV shops, with display sets tuned on to the test programmes, were magnets to passers-by

The verkrampte *(conservative) critics of television were a favourite target of cartoonists. The* Rand Daily Mail *ran this cartoon in 1976*

Prime Minister John Vorster inaugurates the SABC's television service on 5 January 1976. Test programmes had already beguiled viewers for months

The critics were as unanimous in handing out bouquets for good indigenous products such as *Willem*, a reluctant private eye with a zany girlfriend, as they were in their derision at series like *Quest*, which tried, and failed, to ape overseas crime programmes. *The Dingleys*, an uninspired attempt at situation comedy set in the 'sleepy hollow' of Pietermaritzburg, was more renowned for its signature tune, recorded by local pop group Rabbit, which went on to earn an international reputation.

The early pioneers

Television was not new to South Africa. In 1929, Lord Angus Kennedy headed a delegation to demonstrate the television, invented by Scotsman John Logie Baird, to the British Association in Cape Town and Johannesburg. Baird was then trying to get the BBC to inaugurate his system as the world's first public television service. He was to be disappointed. In 1936, a 405-line system of a rival company broadcast from Alexandra Palace in North London to an estimated 100 television owners.

A year later, thousands of visitors to the Empire Exhibition in Johannesburg watched in awe the pictures on the Marconi sets broadcast from a studio in the Milner Park showgrounds (just two kilometres from what is now the SABC's complex). 'It has come to stay,' said one writer. The studio was operated under TV licence No 1 issued by the Postmaster-

General to Mr L. Rhind, a local businessman. Receiving sets, which looked like radios with a blue-tinted screen, were dotted about the exhibition hall. Rhind's little daughter amused viewers by animating her face, laughing and telling jokes. Far from being 'here to stay', though, television broadcasting in South Africa was still 40 years away.

In 1947 René Caprara, director general of

DOCTOR HERTZOG'S TOWER

The man who had dubbed television 'the miniature bioscope' and who had warned that 'the effects of the wrong programmes on children, the less developed and other races can be destructive' was not one of the first-night viewers. Albert Hertzog had vanished from the Cabinet as Minister of Posts and Telegraphs long before the television service was launched. Each evening the TV news was introduced by a picture of the massive concrete mast at Auckland Park from which signals for the microwave network are sent. When it was first built to transmit FM radio to the nation, the tower, with its viewing platform at the top, was named after the then Minister — Albert Hertzog. With something approaching embarrassment, the 253 m mast was later renamed the SABC Tower.

A TELE VISION OF THE FUTURE

Almost half a century before the box reached this country South Africans were speculating on the prospects of a television service. The brilliant young British scientist John Logie Baird first demonstrated his invention in 1926. In 1928 TV pictures were transmitted from England to America, and in that year the magazine *Outspan* reported that I.W. Schlesinger, the South African entertainment tycoon, 'has been persuaded to go into the matter. If the prospects are favourable, television can easily be worked in conjunc-

tion with the existing broadcasting stations'. *Outspan's* predictions were impressively advanced for the time: 'There will be a service from individual to individual parallel in character to a telephone service. It might also be turned into a valuable educational asset such as lecturing when the face of a speaker in Cape Town with his examples and notes on the blackboard could be viewed by audiences all over the country.

'More ambitious still would be television as a means of world communication whereby events such as athletic contests, public ceremonies and theatrical performances would be broadcasted [sic] to South Africa from distant parts . . .

'Furthermore, think of the tremendous joy of watching from East London, Durban or from any of the towns or dorps the arrival and departure of friends or relatives on the majestic 'Carnarvon Castle' as it gracefully glides into or out of the harbour at Cape Town . . .' In 1949 British TV expert Sir Ernest Fisk told the *Cape Argus* that he thought a television transmitter would cost South Africa 'somewhere between £150 000 and £250 000'.

Television aerials, many of them home-made, sprouted in the most unlikely places

The first and one of the best local sagas was The Villagers. *Above left: Barman Cheesa Labuschagne (Stuart Brown) and miner Ted Dixon (Clive Scott); above right (from left to right): Buller Wilmot (Brian O'Shaughnessy), Hilton McRae (Gordon Mulholland) and Diana McRae (Val Dunlop)*

the South African Broadcasting Corporation, dampened hopes when he said television would not be introduced into the Union for 'some years yet'. One real problem facing any fledgling service in South Africa was the diversity of cultures, and especially the duality of official language. The Press claimed that the go-slow was largely an attempt to preserve Afrikaans culture. In the late 1950s, TV in America and Britain was slated — Minister of Posts and Telegraphs Albert Hertzog declared: 'It is the uneducated who possess TV sets.' Most viewers (he cited Britons) had an education level equivalent to standard four and five. He also felt that television would strain the eyes; and that it would cost too much.

Prime Minister Hendrik Verwoerd said: 'When a new discovery holds dangers, a gov-

ernment must be careful not to import it before they know how to ward off any dangers there might be.' The Press retorted that it was fortunate Verwoerd had not been around when the motor car was invented. Ironically, Verwoerd was to appear dramatically on television just a month later. An American TV crew captured for millions of viewers the sensational assassination attempt on the Prime Minister when he opened the Union Exposition at Milner Park.

Many a Third World country established its television service while South Africans were debating the issue. Newspaper editors taunted that the country would stand alone with Tibet in its isolation.

Then, in 1971, it was announced that television would be introduced nationwide, bilingual and in colour on the German 625-line PAL system.

Auntie Auk

On a 15-hectare site at Auckland Park, a new broadcasting complex was laid out — modern studios and equipment, and a massive 35-storey administration block. The country would be linked through the Post Office's microwave network and satellite transmissions would be received via the tracking station at Hartebeeshoek.

Though TV-Day was scheduled for 5 January 1976, the SABC started putting out hour-long test transmissions each day from 5 May 1975. When the test shows were repeated at lunchtimes, crowds gathered in store showrooms and pressed against shop windows. Two-hour test transmissions doubled the sale of sets.

Television antennae sprouted on roof tops, newspapers advised viewers on the position of their sets; the lighting required; how to prepare handy TV meals. Newspaper columnists pondered the effects on our social life. Though at least two decades behind the rest of the developed world, South Africans were determined to plunge across 'the threshold of a demanding but exciting era — a stage where for the first time we shall be able to witness and experience history as it happens'.

The Soweto riots in June 1976 and the street battles of Cape Town gave vivid reality to this prophecy. Television had arrived.

Katinka Heyns and Tobie Cronje, leading characters in Willem, *one of the most popular Afrikaans series*

Going Places

'One wonders whether those were indeed the good old days. But whether they were or not, there is this about them, that in those days we travelled at our leisure, stopped and chatted to acquaintances on the road, were welcomed to break our journey and over-night with wayside friends, or indeed with strangers; whence I am sure arose the tradition of South African hospitality.

'Who can forget the *kos-mandjie* with the roast chicken, not one of your skinny modern ones, but one fattened for the journey, hard-boiled eggs, biltong, fresh bread and butter, and other delicious tit-bits enjoyed at some wayside stream, or under a willow tree with the finches making music aloft?

'Yes: a plague on your moderns. Give us the old days with those unforgettable friendships made and enjoyed everywhere, anywhere and anyhow, swept away by your trains and motor-cars, not to speak of your aeroplanes.'

Ironically the man who wrote this, in 1955, was a former chairman of the National Roads Board. He had planned many of the highways that 'swept away' the leisurely modes of travel he had known in his youth.

Ox wagon and horse-drawn cart were the most common means of transport in South Africa at the turn of the century, but within a few years the roar of exhausts began to drown the clatter of hoofs. So, too, with sea-travel. Swaying masts and graceful sails vanished forever in the smoky clouds that belched from the funnels of steamships; themselves destined to give way to oil-fired vessels. Even the mailships are gone, their epitaph written in the jet-trails high above the waters they sailed for so many years.

And the jets themselves: their ancestors were those tiny wire-and-fabric contraptions that struggled into the air to fly, shakily, a few metres above the veld.

South Africa's first steam locomotive ran in 1860, on a track just a few kilometres long. From this modest beginning grew a mighty rail system that now reaches into almost every corner of the country. Today, in all but a few areas, electrification and diesel traction have replaced steam, and the old engines are silent, their once gleaming brasswork tarnishing beneath the sun in great locomotive graveyards.

A 1928 Auburn makes a cautious crossing at Port Elizabeth. Bridges were often something of a novelty in the early days of motoring

Days of the horse

Sensing journey's end, the horse team works up a sprint and a Zeederberg coach from the gold diggings at Barberton bowls along the dirt road into boom-town Johannesburg. Doul Zeederberg was one of the most famed of the mail coach pioneers: Cecil Rhodes once said of him that he had done more than any other man to open up Rhodesia. His coaches were replicas of those used in America's Wild West, and carried not only mail but passengers to the Kimberley diamond diggings

MAN'S COMPANION IN WAR AND PEACE

Fewer than one third of the more than half a million horses used by the British in the Anglo-Boer War survived. They had cost about £15 million, which was a lot more than the sum originally voted to defray the entire costs of the war. 'I never saw such shameful abuse of horseflesh in my life,' Major General Brabazon later told the Royal Commission of Enquiry into the war.

General Sir Ian Hamilton, however, praised the Boers as 'the only class of men I met who were constantly and eagerly on the lookout for a chance to ease their horses . . .' Most of the burghers had, literally, grown up with horses, but these too suffered grievously when Kitchener's scorched earth policy denied food and shelter to both men and animals. In his book *Commando* Deneys Reitz wrote movingly of the death of his 'Malpert' (the mad horse), who had carried him so long and so well: 'He had been game to the end — "puure paert" [all horse] — as the men called him, and my brother and I climbed down to pay a last visit to his poor emaciated carcass.'

The postman's melodious bugling

The horse was just as indispensable a part of life in the peace that followed. An old resident of the Southern Cape recalled: 'We had a tri-weekly postal service and conveyance of the posts was let to tender. What picturesque outfits some of these post carts were, some still embellished with the Royal cipher V. R. painted on the side-panels; interpreted by the unsophisticated country folks as "Vinnig Ry" [Go with speed]. There were two well-remembered drivers, Festus Klaasen and Hendrik Olieslager. Who of those days can ever forget the most perfect and melodious bugling of these two men at three o'clock of a morning, on their topping

the Gaol Hill and awakening the town to the fact that the Cape Post had arrived?'

The mail coach was not used in this area, and passengers on the open post carts had to tuck themselves as best they could among the bags of mail.

There were other 'picturesque knights of the road. The commercial travellers with their four-in-hands, well-groomed and splendid teams on their monthly circuits with their samples for exhibition in the sample room of the hotels . . . But without a doubt the crown of all the equine outfits were the equipages provided by Lalie Soeker, the Cape Town Malay livery-stable keeper. What spanking teams of eight conveyed the judges, followed by other teams conveying the advocates keeping circuit'.

Often, owners of private carts lacked the skill of the post cart driver. Iris Vaughan recorded this incident in her *Diary:* 'Mom is a good driver of horses. In East London when she was driving dog cart and a new horse Cecil bought and me sitting in seat with fat girl Truin and all going to fetch Pop at office. Then the new horse bolted running fast down the street and Mom said sit still and hold feet the child and she pulling on the reins and at last the new horse stopped at office and Pop came out being savige only becos he thought we could be dead and said it was the ticks made him to bolt.'

Last days of the coach

Only in parts of the Northern Transvaal did the stage coach survive into the new century. The steady advance of the railways diminished the lustre of such famed names as Zeederberg; George Heys; Cobb & Co, and the Gibson Brothers' Red Star Line, which used to cover the 960 kilometres from Cape Town to the Kimberley diggings in five days.

A newly-completed Cape cart awaits delivery in early 20th century Stellenbosch. It is thought that the cart's name may be derived not from its connection with the Cape but from the fact that because it had a fixed hood, it was originally called a kapkar — a cart with a cap. An early visitor to the Cape wrote that it was 'an invention for keeping the feet cold and the head hot'

The brothers Fred and John Gibson were among the first stage mail coach operators in South Africa, and in the early days their drivers had to travel across country that had no roads and ford rivers that had no bridges. On one occasion, mail carried by a Gibson brothers coach was eight days late, because the Vaal river was in flood. Pictured is a coach crossing the river

People in polite society kept their own carriages and grooms in the early 1900s. But a few years after this picture was taken, the elegant ladies in the brougham would be carried in motor cars

This cast iron horse-trough was erected in the Cape Town suburb of Rondebosch in 1892. It stands as a reminder of the leisurely days of horse-drawn transport

Resplendent and ready for any crisis in their brass helmets, the men of the Port Elizabeth Fire Brigade pose with their 'galloping cart' in 1904. Some are wearing medals of the recently-ended Anglo-Boer War. Their horse-drawn fire engine still had some years' service ahead of it

Country weddings were occasions just as grand: great gatherings of family and friends who came by cart, wagon or on horseback. The bride was swept up to the church in an open carriage drawn by four of the finest matched horses in the community. Again there were waving ostrich plumes, but this time they would be white.

Nagmaal, the three-day Afrikaner Communion, saw even greater concentrations of conveyances of all descriptions, from lumbering ox wagons to dainty traps. The people would camp out for three days, their animals grazing on the commonage. Communion was taken, friendships were formed or renewed, a lot of business transacted, and before light on the Monday morning the teams were inspanned for the homeward journey across the veld.

Riding to the party

A favourite Edwardian pastime was the riding-picnic. At holiday times, such as New Year, the young and eligible rode to nearby beauty spots to spend a few days in flirtation or showing off their equestrian skills. Tents and utensils, together with a suitable number of chaperones, were conveyed by spring wagon. The Fountains and Wonderboom were popular sites near Pretoria. In the Cape, those within reach of the sea would make for the beaches.

'The day being a holiday,' writer K.A. Carlson remembered of the early 1900s, 'we rode to the beach for a picnic.' A strenuous day's pleasure ended with an equally strenuous dance: 'Laughing and breathless we reined in after a last gallop up the carriageway. From within came the sounds of the band tuning their fiddles and accordians. Light from the windows streamed onto Cape carts and gigs, and glinted on the steel and nickel of harness.

'The girls slipped from their sidesaddles: dancing shoes and carefully-folded evening dresses were retrieved from spacious saddlebags as the hostess bustled out. The men tugged at their jackets, straightened their ties and flicked at the dust on their polished shoes.'

The dancing continued until daylight, and 'the ladies then dossed down all over the house anywhere and anyhow, while the men retired to the hay loft for a couple of hours' rest before mounting their horses and returning to their homes, some of them 25 or 30 miles away. I wonder how many of the present generation, young or old, would stand up to such a strain today.'

One of the guests was late for the dancing. Long after it had started, he was still struggling to replace the stiff cover on the wooden-rimmed wheel of his new motor. For the days of the horse, the writing was on the wall.

And it was underlined several years later by Christiaan de Wet, the great and elusive guerilla leader of the Anglo-Boer War. After the failure of the 'Armed Protest' in 1914, he retreated with his mounted rebels into the Kalahari — followed by a motorised column. He was captured. 'It was the motor cars that caught us,' he said.

The Gibsons had acquired the coach monopoly for the route in 1880. Fare per passenger was £12; the baggage allowance 25-30 parcels. By 1893 there were 16 major companies operating a total of 74 coaches on scheduled routes covering 2 830 km.

Most of the large, enclosed coaches, with a load capacity of two tons, were imported from England or America. A form of suspension was provided by slinging the body of the coach to the chassis with long straps, usually of buffalo-hide. Teams of up to 12 horses were needed to pull the coaches, which could hold 12 passengers inside, with another six clinging to straps on the roof.

In the larger towns, public transport included single and double-decker horse-drawn trams which, in Johannesburg, were replaced by electric trams only in 1906.

Cape Town's one-horse cabs lined Adderley Street for decades, their drivers perched on the high overhanging back seats. These drivers were more staid than the 'cabbies' of Johannesburg, who were renowned for their reckless driving. Most of Johannesburg's cabs were pulled by two horses, and one shaken passenger declared that the wheels 'touched the ground just three times in half a mile!'

Ostrich plumes, black and white

On the strength of the Durban Central Fire Station in 1906 were six horses ('though there is room for nine') which pulled, among other equipment, 'Galloping Escapes' with ladders, a two-horse Tender, and a one-horse Hose Cart.

In the country areas, horse-drawn hearses were in use right up to the 1940s. Elaborately carved and black-painted, with silver wreaths and designs picked out on their glass sides, they were drawn by two or four black-draped horses decked with swaying black ostrich feathers.

Stray dogs were a constant menace to man and beast on city streets in the last century. It is reckoned that there were some 3 000 of them in central Johannesburg alone. The man whose job it was to round them up was Supervisor Le Roux, pictured left with his team of dog catchers and the catchers' cart, in 1890. Their record catch was 56 dogs in a single day

The marvel of the century

GOODBYE TO RINDERPEST AND LAZY GROOMS

It was billed as the greatest thing in transport since the wheel. Carriages, cabs and ox-wagons would never be the same again. Farewell to problems of horse sickness, rinderpest, expensive forage and lazy grooms. Even the police would not dare to lay a hand on the Invention of the Age, the Wonder of the Century . . . the motor car, or horseless carriage.

At a time when progress was measured by the pace of the ox, it *was* a wonder.

On a bright midsummer's day shortly before

the turn of the century, hundreds of curious Transvaal burghers rolled up to Pretoria's Berea Park and eagerly paid 2/6 each to see the first demonstration in South Africa of this mechanical marvel. The guest of honour was none other than 'Oom Paul' Kruger, President of the South African Republic who, as a boy of ten, had travelled to the Transvaal the hard way — in a wagon, on the Great Trek. With him at the show were top Transvaal officials and a full military escort.

What the Pretorians saw that historic afternoon of 4 January 1897 was a spindly contraption called a Benz Voiturette, which had been specially imported from Germany by a leading city businessman, John Hess.

To most of those present, it must have looked little more than the familiar horse-drawn gig, but without the horse. Instead, a single-cylinder, 1½ hp motor drove the large, wire-spoked rear wheels through a system of chains and sprockets. Two people could sit side by side on the machine, guiding it by means of a tiller mounted on a vertical column protruding from the floor. Carriage candle lamps on either side provided illumination — not so much to see as to be seen. Low gear moved it along at wagon-pace. But in top gear, on the flat and with a wind behind it, speeds of up to 20 km/h were possible.

Memorable ride

Oom Paul and his party watched the Benz circle a cycle-racing track in the Park, with A.E. Reno, a newspaperman and business partner of Hess, at the helm. The passenger on that first memorable ride was the State Secretary, Dr Willem Leyds.

Oom Paul was offered a ride himself but declined, joking that dogs might bark at the car

and it would bolt. But he was impressed enough to give Hess a fitting memento, a solid gold medal with the Transvaal coat of arms on one side, and on the other, in Dutch, the inscription: 'Presented by His Honour Paul Kruger, President of the South African Republic, to Mr J.P. Hess on Monday, January 4, 1897, in commemoration of his having introduced the first motor car to South Africa.'

From Pretoria the car was taken by train to Johannesburg, where thousands paid 2/- a head to see it spin around the enclosure at the Wanderers' Sports Club. By now it had an additional claim to fame: the advertisements proclaimed it was 'patronised by His Honour, the State President; Mr Conyngham Greene (Her Majesty's Agent); Dr Leyds (State Secretary); the members of the Executive Council; and Chief Consular representatives, etc'.

Some cynics wanted to know why the car had not travelled from Pretoria to Johannesburg under its own power. The promoters retorted that it could have done so — provided the weather had been fine and the Yokeskei (a curious anglicisation of *Jukskei*) river not so deep as to flood the engine.

After the exhibition the car was bought for ' a substantial sum' by A.H. Jacobs, owner of a flourishing tea and coffee shop in Pritchard Street, Johannesburg. 'Coffee' Jacobs was soon advertising that anyone who bought a pound of his wares could see the car free of charge. One authority has it that he later used the Benz as a mobile billboard, and the public nicknamed it the 'Coffee Pot' — a name that was tagged onto other early motor vehicles on the Rand for years afterwards.

The little Benz had one final moment of glory. That same year was Queen Victoria's Diamond

Monday, 4 January 1897, was, as the notice had promised it would be, a Red-letter day for Pretorians. An admiring crowd, including President Paul Kruger, saw the Invention of the Age put through its paces in Berea Park. After the show, businessman John Hess leans proudly against his little Benz Voiturette, the first car seen in South Africa. At the controls sits Hess's partner, A.E. Reno; the passenger is the State Secretary, Dr Willem Leyds

Right from the start, there was no shortage of men eager to find fault with women at the wheel. As late as 1933, a correspondent signing himself 'Crusty' could write to The Motor: *'Taking them as a class, women drivers, like women voters, are irresponsible, erratic and a definite menace to the peace of the nation.' In Edwardian times it was even harder for a woman driver to be taken seriously. But this motorist and her passenger, in their 1906 French De Dion-Bouton, look self-possessed enough to reduce male critics to silence*

When the inaugural run of the Natal Automobile Club was held at Durban in 1906, the infant association had 35 members. Sixteen cars took part in the not-too-strenuous drive from the Esplanade to the 'charming residence of the Hon Marshall Campbell' and back. The Automobile Club of South Africa had already been in existence for five years when the Natal club was founded. It changed its name to the Royal Automobile Club in 1911, and in 1965 was taken over by the AA, the Automobile Association of South Africa

Jubilee. Her loyal subjects on the Reef organised a commemorative procession. At its head, leading the pageant through the dusty streets of Johannesburg, was the first car to run on South African soil.

Sadly the car did not survive for posterity. Later that year it and the shed in which it was stored were destroyed by fire.

Growling at the nuisance

In February of the same year three similar Benz vehicles were imported by Messrs Koenig of Cape Town, and South Africa thus possessed four of a reputed twenty cars in private ownership in the world.

William Alcock, a Port Elizabeth businessman, became the first car owner in the Eastern Cape. Said a writer to the *Eastern Province Herald* in August 1902: 'When we come in contact with the sickly odour of its oil and the deafening noise, we wonder what our streets will be like should their numbers increase, and we mentally ejaculate "Deliver us". Individually the public is growling at this infringement of the comparative quietude they have hitherto enjoyed, and it would be well for them to put their protest into definite shape before the nuisance becomes more general.' This heartfelt plea notwithstanding, Port Elizabeth eventually became the 'Detroit of South Africa'.

Opening for business

The first 'motor workshop' in South Africa was established in Cape Town in 1901 by the Rudge Whitworth Company, and a few months later a workshop devoted exclusively to the repair and maintenance of motor vehicles was opened by Malcolm Irving, also in Cape Town.

The first firm to enter the motor trade as dealers was that of Messrs Garlick of Cape Town, in the late 1890s. Immediately after the Anglo-Boer War, in 1902, the Johannesburg Motor Car Company, agents for the Cudell motor car, and the Continental Garage, with the De Dion franchise, opened for business. Progress was slower in Natal and the Orange Free State. It was only in 1907 that the South African Motor Company of Durban was established, and about the same time Lambon and Company, who had been firearms dealers, began selling cars in Bloemfontein. Shortly afterwards Rudge Whitworth opened another branch in the city.

South Africa's first motor show was held in 1908, at the Wanderers Club in Johannesburg. Among the now-vanished marques on display were Overland, Reo, Hupmobile, Franklin, Oakland, and the Adler motorcycle.

A reassuring feature of this 1910 motor car was the metal bar, or 'sprag', underneath the running board — an anchor-like device that prevented the car slipping backwards if it stalled on a hill

The MARKHAM MOTOR COAT.

DESIGNED with a practical knowledge of the Motorist's requirements, the "Markham Motor Coat" is an ideal wrap in which one may journey forth and defiantly brave the elements of wind and storm.

Made in dark grey Irish frieze weatherproof cloth, perfectly cut and tailored, it combines all the essentials necessary to the comfort and appearance of the motorist.

Convertible collar, wind cuffs, and lined tweed throughout body and sleeves.

Price 70/-
Exceptional Value.

Appointed Agents for BURBERRY'S Celebrated Coats.

MARKHAMS ADDERLEY STREET, CAPETOWN.

'Motor coats' were essential for Edwardian motorists as cars lacked windows and, sometimes, windscreens

East London's first taxi — a 1905 two-cylinder Panhard-Levassor. It had a wooden chassis

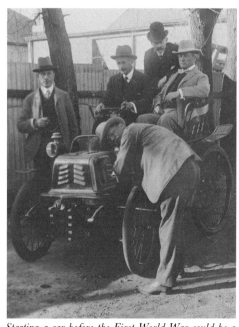

Starting a car before the First World War could be a somewhat hazardous business. It had to be cranked by hand, and the starting handle was liable to kick back viciously. Many a motorist nursed a bruised thumb or even a broken wrist as a reminder of his moment of carelessness

The pleasures of 'moting'

THE MOTORCYCLE COMES TO SOUTH AFRICA

'It seems strange that motor cycles have as yet not come into favour here in South Africa, considering they are so extensively used in England and on the Continent,' said the *Licensed Victuallers and Sporting Gazette* in January 1900. 'There are some ideal stretches of level roads in the suburbs, exactly what is required to enjoy "moting" to its fullest extent.'

The records show that Charles Mambretti of Cape Town imported South Africa's first motorcycle in 1902 (although one was rumoured to have been seen in Cape Town somewhat earlier). It was an Italian machine, but the make is no longer known. Two years later, Bert and Percy Hunt began bringing in motorcycle parts, which they assembled in their premises in Von Brandis Square, Johannesburg. Theirs was the first assembly plant in South Africa.

Among early models seen in the country were the British Royal Enfield, BSA, AJS and Ariel. A later arrival was the ABC, with its advanced design: including a transversely mounted flat-twin overhead valve engine, shaft drive and internal expanding brakes. At this time most manufacturers employed belt drive and a braking system, developed from the push-bike, operating on the rear wheel only.

Belgium exported the FN, including a 4-cylinder model. Popular among the American makes were the Henderson, Indian and Harley-Davidson. In 1912 a special twin-cylinder 8-valve Indian motorcycle was timed at a speed of 83 mph (133 km/h) on the Randfontein road.

Compared to the motor car, the motorcycle was cheap to buy and to maintain, although cynics claimed that this was offset by the high cost of hospitalisation. With unsprung frames and uncertain front fork suspension, they were certainly uncomfortable, but turned in creditable performances on the bad roads of early South Africa. Their popularity declined with the advent of the cheap 'baby' cars, but revived during the depression which followed the First World War.

Rider and pillion passenger on a motorbike made for two arrive for a picnic given by the manufacturers of the Indian motorcycle at Fountain Grove, Pretoria, in 1915. Motorcyclists were known as 'scorchers' in those days, and the fact that this dashing pair were both women drew from the Illustrated Star *the admiring headline: 'Preferable to the male scorcher'*

Edwardian family outing. The first imported sidecars were designed for right-of-the-road driving, so brothers Bert and Percy Hunt, who started the first motorcycle assembly plant in South Africa, produced their own for attachment to the left side of the machine. They built the frames and chassis in a shack in Johannesburg, and completed the bodywork in the backyard of the Hunt home. The finished 'high clearance sidecar' successfully negotiated that middle hump so characteristic of South African roads of the time

TRUE SPIRIT OF THE PIONEER

'Intrepid Wheelwoman to cycle 2 000 miles through the Union.' It was April 1912 and journalists could hardly contain their astonishment. Miss E.L.C. Watson from Elgin, northern Scotland ('from this land of heroes she no doubt inherits the pluck and endurance which show so plainly in her clear eyes and firm mouth') intended to make a solitary motorcycle ride from Cape Town to Johannesburg and on to Durban.

Her choice of vehicle was a '2½ hp motosacochi' and readers were relieved to note that she carried a complete set of tools and felt no anxiety.

An attitude not shared by reporters, one of whom said: 'She is certainly the first woman who had undertaken such a journey and to attempt to do it alone in a strange country where drifts are not unknown and roads are sometimes remarkable for their absence, shows the true spirit of the pioneer.'

Knee-length knickers

When photographed for the *South African Lady's Pictorial* she was wearing rather advanced gear for South African tastes: 'A neat and business-like costume, consisting of dark brown khaki (meaning the twill not the colour) overcoat reaching below the knee and met by brown leather boots. On her dark hair she wore a soft leather hat with a brim wide enough to shade her eyes from the sun.'

Miss Watson, it was pointed out lest her respectability be questioned, was a highly educated woman and had not only been a teacher of mathematics for some years but had even written a textbook on the subject.

Plucky, pint-sized Miss E.L.C. Watson, Scotswoman, maths teacher and motorcyclist extraordinary, with the 2½ hp machine on which, in 1912, she made a solo trip from Cape Town to Durban, via Johannesburg

... AND THE PERILS OF MOTORING

There were thrills and spills galore in the early days of motoring. Cars plunged into rivers, ran out of road, veered over mountainsides, were trapped under falling trees, even climbed to the top of Table Mountain. It was a crazy, harum scarum era with some drivers, unaccustomed to the power under the bonnet of this new-fangled form of conveyance, acting as though they had just arrived on the set of a Keystone Cops comedy.

South Africa's first serious motor accident happened on 1 October 1903, on a railway line in Maitland, Cape Town. Charles Garlick, member of a wealthy Capetonian family of department store owners, was driving his 24 hp Darracq from Mowbray to D'Urbanville. He had with him as passengers a Mr Harry Markham and a 'mechanician', Mr Snellgrove.

It was 9.30 at night, and dark. The first gate of the level crossing was open, and the car edged across the track. Then the occupants realised to their horror that the second gate was closed — and, suddenly, bearing down on them was the Johannesburg express. There was no time even to reverse. All they could do was try to scramble out of the car.

'All the occupants received more or less serious injuries,' reported the *Cape Times*. But a few days later it was able to inform its readers that Mr Garlick expected to be able to leave his bed within a few days; that Mr Markham, although his condition was still serious, was out of danger and 'bearing his sufferings with great fortitude'; and that 'Mr Snellgrove, the mechanician, is already out and about'.

The car, 'one of the finest in South Africa', also made a good recovery.

The wreckage after South Africa's first serious car accident, in October 1903. Surprisingly, the Darracq was successfully repaired and returned to the road

One of the disadvantages of driving in the days when the road system was still, in places, designed for the ox-cart was that cars tended to get stuck in swollen drifts

A sight to attract curiosity-seekers in Maitland Street, Bloemfontein — a car that seems to have decided to turn itself into a three-wheeler

Mummy, what's that car doing in a tree? The car was freed later, by sawing the tree into handy-sized logs, but it's doubtful whether it took to the road again

This time, there was a bridge over the river . . . but it wasn't quite where the driver thought it should be. Roads were rough in those days; mishaps common

Aftermath of a lucky escape on the Swartberg Pass, between Oudtshoorn and Prince Albert. Even today, the pass is not recommended for nervous drivers

In 1928 this Baby Austin was driven up Table Mountain, with a minimum of manhandling, in four hours. Its time for the descent — 40 minutes!

153

Henry Ford's Tin Lizzie

THE CAR THAT TOOK YOU ANYWHERE

The arrival of the first Model T Ford in 1910 ushered in a new era, not only in South African transport but in the South African way of life. Mass production meant more and cheaper cars; motoring was no longer the privilege of the sporty rich.

Seven years earlier Johannesburg's Arthur Youldon had imported a Model A, believed to be the first to leave the shores of North America (it survives today in the Heidelberg Transport Museum, Transvaal, after being rescued from obscurity in the basement of the Durban Technical College). A few other designs followed, but with the introduction of the Model T the words 'motor car' and 'Ford' became almost synonymous.

Nicknamed the 'Tin Lizzie' — although each Model T contained less than 250 g of tin — it was an instant success. By 1925 there were some 18 000 Fords on South African roads — almost three times more than any other make. In that year a five-seater Model T Tourer cost £165.

Not always black

With its spindly 30-in wooden-spoked wheels and exposed transverse springs at front and rear, the early model looked deceptively flimsy, but the vanadium steel used in its manufacture gave it strength. It could also clear the *middelmannetjie*, or central ridge, which was a feature of South African roads created by the eroding passage of countless wagons.

Apart from three oil lamps and a bulb horn, the first models came without 'extras', into which class fell the canvas hood, with its wooden framework, and the front-seat doors. Contrary to legend, not all Model T s were black. The early cars were painted bright red or grey; from 1909 to 1913 green with black trimmings and red striping, and black from 1913 to 1925 when buyers, for some extra cost, could have such options as 'Elephant Gray' and 'Moleskin'.

Ford's first South African assembly plant, in Grahamstown Road, Port Elizabeth, about 1925, with a Model T in the making. As well as putting the world on wheels, Henry Ford pioneered the modern techniques of assembly line production — and for its day, the Port Elizabeth plant, opened in 1924, was a miracle of productivity. It employed 70 workers who, in their first year, averaged an output of 12 cars a day

Proud trademark of the early Model T was its squarish brass radiator, changed in 1916 to one of black iron. The oil lamps were replaced by acetylene lamps, and finally by electric lights. Current was supplied by the magneto, so a Model T labouring uphill at night did so in almost total darkness, the lights blazing again only when it picked up speed.

Rear end up

In fact, hill-climbing in the Model T was something of an art — even by day. Petrol reached the carburettor by 'gravity feed' from the tank beneath the front seat, and the supply often cut off when the car was in a nose-up position. The answers here were either to drive at the hill at top speed — around 65 km/h — and hope

to reach the top before fuel-starvation stopped the engine, or, more popularly, to drive all the way up in reverse.

Before the electric starter was introduced to the Model T in 1919, the engine had to be hand-cranked. This had its hazards: a kick-back could cause a dislocated thumb or even a fractured arm. Before cranking, the driver had to climb up to his throne-like seat, set the ignition advance and throttle levers in the correct notches, and apply the handbrake fully. The choke wire protruded through the radiator next to the crank, and he had to pull it out to just the right length. He then gripped the crank-handle with his fingers only (to wrap the thumb around it was to invite injury) and gave an upward flick.

Back in the driving seat, he released the handbrake, depressed the left pedal to engage low gear and advanced the throttle lever to get Lizzie moving. Once his speed was up he released the pedal to its full extent and the car jerked into high gear. Neutral gear was 'somewhere between right up and right down'. There were two other pedals: the right hand one worked the rather inadequate brake band of the transmission; the centre pedal selected reverse gear.

The proverbial piece of string

As the car that would 'take you anywhere and bring you back', the Model T allowed for easy, and sometimes bizarre, repair techniques. More than one driver, stranded without oil, forced butter into the crankcase and drove home safely. It ran, protestingly, on benzene and even methylated spirits. Bits of wire, bent nails, scraps of copper sheet and inner tube rubber, lengths of string — all played their part in keeping the Model T going.

And, although the last Model T was manufactured in 1927, many are still going. Fifty years after the Tin Lizzie was introduced, the Ford Motor Company estimated that about 85 000 were still in service throughout the world.

The peace and quiet of sleepy Calvinia, in the Cape, was disturbed by the sputtering of this Model T. Its proud owner was an attorney named Yates, and it was built like a coach, with wooden bodywork. The steering and controls were, American-style, on the left hand side

By the mid-1920s, South Africa was well on the way to becoming a nation on wheels: between 1920 and 1928 car registrations leapt from about 24 000 to over 113 000. Scores of people drove to this Treasure Trove Proclamation in the Western Transvaal in 1926 in the hope of finding a diamond-rich patch of ground. In the background, drivers and hired runners wait anxiously for the signal to start the race for their stakes

A forerunner of the Model T was the even simpler Model N, seen here in front of a blockhouse — a relic of an Anglo-Boer War that was still fresh in people's memories. At the controls is Georges Chapart, who claimed to have given ex-President Steyn of the OFS and General Hertzog their first motor rides. Chapart drove the car round country shows, demonstrating it to farmers. The Model T arrived in 1910

FRUSTRATIONS OF A TWENTIES' DRIVER

With the 1920s came an astonishing boom in South African motoring. Car registrations climbed from 24 064 in 1920 to 113 360 in 1928.

Nevertheless, overland travel remained a frustrating business: lucky was the motorist who could enjoy a clear run of even a dozen kilometres of countryside. Farms were divided into grazing areas, pens, fields — and whenever the road passed from one enclosure to the next there was 'the gate, that object of hate'.

Lamented a British traveller: 'In a recent journey from Winburg to Bloemfontein, a distance of 100 miles, 73 gates had to be negotiated. Just think of it, the car had to be stopped and restarted 140 times that day!'

Those who neglected to shut a farm gate, whether or not they found it open, could be fined up to £10 or sentenced to several days' imprisonment. In spite of this, though, gates were often left open, or simply 'ridden down'. Some farmers retaliated by erecting heavy, chain-draped booms which threatened serious damage to any vehicle trying to barge through. One, in fact, managed to do just that and in splendid style. After a few frustrating trips between George and Knysna the burly driver of the mail-carrying Chalmers let it be known that he no longer considered himself responsible for the opening and shutting of gates. Farmers en route, somewhat alarmed, instructed their herdboys to be ready at the gates at the scheduled times. One was late. The petrified travelling mechanic sank into his seat as the driver stood up behind the wheel, bellowed 'Make way for His Majesty's mail!' and crashed through the offending obstacle.

In 1922, the *Handbook of the Port Elizabeth Automobile Club* published a list of essentials to be taken 'on tour'. Along with 'distilled water, spring repair clamps, *riems*, ropes and chains' were — 'pennies for gates'. Farm children had soon caught on to the financial possibilities of gate-opening. The going rate: one penny per gate. During the years of the Depression, white

adults were not above earning a few coppers in this way. Motorists, relieved of the maddening ritual of 'stop, alight, open, mount, forward, stop, alight, close, mount, forward', parted willingly with their pennies. In remoter areas, the children preferred to be paid in sweets, known as 'gate openers' and sold by country stores at two for a penny.

Eventually, divisional councils and other authorities began to install the cattle grid, with adjacent gate, and the happy motorist drove by his old enemy with only a slight bump and rattle of steel railings. The final disappearance of gates from major roads was mourned by nobody — save perhaps the wistful roadside urchin.

The Model T had not changed much by the time this advertisement appeared in 1924

FUELLING THE FIRST CARS — FROM METAL JUGS AND WOODEN CRATES

In the early days of motoring, petrol and oil were dispensed from metal jugs, which had to bear the seal of the Excise Department to certify that they contained the stated volume. Later, motorists could buy petrol in wooden crates, each costing £1.10s. and holding two four-gallon tins, which were clamped to the running boards of their cars.

Until the installation of mechanically driven pumps in 1924, Cape Town garages received their supplies in four-gallon tins, delivered by this gleaming Leyland, below, forerunner of the modern petrol tanker. Barnes Garage, East London, above right, offered a choice of three brands of petrol — Atlantic, Pegasus and Shell. But SATMAR, South Africa's 'own' petrol, above left, was available only in the Pretoria and Reef areas. SATMAR — the South African Torbanite Mining and Refining Company — produced petrol from torbanite, an oil shale found in the southern Transvaal in the 1930s.

After the deposits had been exhausted, the company converted to refining conventional crude oil at their factory in Boksburg, Transvaal.

Cars conquer the veld

THE ODYSSEY OF DE REVERTERA'S DE DION

By 1905, the motor car was a fairly common sight in towns and cities, and clubs were thriving. Though the more adventurous were prepared to test their new toys in endurance runs to outlying districts, for the most part the average driver rarely ventured much further than urban limits.

Dashes were being made from Cape Town to Houw Hoek over the gruelling Sir Lowry's Pass, and on the 225 km run from Johannesburg to Potchefstroom and back a Mercedes reached a creditable average of 70 km/h, covering the distance in 3½ hours. But these were the rarities. Distances between towns were huge; roads were little more than cart tracks; bridges were few and vulnerable to flood.

So it was with some amusement that Transvalers greeted the news that an Austrian nobleman, Count de Revertera – who farmed in the highveld – had taken a bet to drive to the Cape within a fortnight. More amazing was the car he had chosen for the expedition. It was a De Dion, a popular French make, but whose single-cylinder engine only rated 6 hp. He took along his chauffeur, though he intended doing most of the driving himself. He had just three months' experience as a motorist; neither of the men had any idea of the country they were to drive through.

The Count gave himself an exacting schedule, content to be on the road for over 12 hours a day, with rests for lunch. The De Dion, with a specially fitted 18-gallon fuel tank, set off from Johannesburg at 9 a.m. on Tuesday, 15 August 1905.

De Revertera was well pleased with his first day's run: a trouble-free 270 km that took him through Potchefstroom and Klerksdorp to

The little single-cylinder De Dion in which the Austrian Count de Revertera (at the controls) and his chauffeur, Fisher, made the first-ever car journey from Johannesburg to the Cape in 1905. The map at lower left shows their 2 000 km route, with some entries from the count's log

Wolmaransstad, following the path that only a few years before had seen the great stage coaches racing between the diamond fields of Kimberley and the new gold diggings on the Witwatersrand. The wager seemed safe.

And so it was: the De Dion covered the distance – 2 091 km – in eleven days, though the odyssey was not to be without its problems. After Kimberley the way was virtually uncharted: deep sand drifts gripped the narrow wheels of the car; roads became quagmires in heavy spells of rain; there were quick-running rivers to ford and precipitous hills to negotiate. The cold of the Karoo iced up the radiator (though surprisingly the single cylinder remained intact). Relying on the advice of townsfolk or of farmers who sometimes had sketchy ideas about the direction in which the next point lay, the party would lose itself. Leaving Fraserburg Road (now called Leeugamka) on the eighth day, they went full circle, found themselves back in the town two hours later, set off again in a snowstorm

and made Prince Albert Road at an average speed of 12 mph.

On the final day the Count swept through the Boland along a route taking in Villiersdorp and Houw Hoek, and descended to the Cape Flats to be met and fêted by the motoring fraternity of Cape Town. (Not so impressed, perhaps, was Capetonian Charles Rörich, who earlier that year had been fined for exceeding the city speed limit of 8 mph.)

Count de Revertera set a mark against which every other motorist could measure himself. For the next two decades, the record-breakers, driving more and more sophisticated cars, lowered the time between the two centres from days to hours. Manufacturers staked their products in eclipsing the speed of rivals.

Before the police and provincial laws halted races on public roads in the 1930s, the trip from Cape Town to Johannesburg had been brought down to a shade over 19 hours – an average speed of 78 km/h.

● JOHANNESBURG

'By far the best day's run of the whole journey'

● WOLMARANSSTAD

'A puncture was experienced at Bloemhof'

● FOURTEEN STREAMS

'Very sandy roads'

HONEY NEST KLOOF STATION

'Sand two feet deep'

FARM

'Two hours getting the car through a sand drift'

● RIETPOORT

'Lost the road . . .'

● THREE SISTERS

'Three hours through deep sand'

BEAUFORT WEST

'Snow storm'

PRINCE ALBERT ROAD

'Bad roads and compulsory stoppage'

● CONSTABLE

'A puncture'

● WORCESTER

● CAPE TOWN   'Cape Town was reached at 6.30 pm'

Entries from the log of Count de Revertera's journey

THE RECORD-BREAKERS

In the 1920s, it was the ambition of 'motor aces' to beat the Union Express train from Cape Town to Johannesburg. In October 1924 H.P. Rose, the Cape Town Hupmobile dealer, pulled away from the bottom of Adderley Street as the express steamed out of Cape Town station. His Hupp 6 had been stripped of mudguards, screen and roof.

Rose had contacted farmers en route to arrange for the opening and closing of hundreds of gates, and 38 hr 38 min after leaving Cape Town he arrived in Johannesburg, mud-spattered and with the Hupmobile's front wheels at a novel angle. A 'slight mishap' near Bloem-

hof had bent the front axle, wasting precious time and allowing the train to reach Johannesburg first. His time, nevertheless, was a record for the run.

Shortly afterwards Gerry Bouwer actually did beat the Union Express. Driving his Chrysler Six, described as 'standard in almost every respect', he reached Johannesburg in 26 hr 13 min. This time bettered that of the train by almost four hours. Bouwer set the final record for the route in 1932, when, forsaking his Chrysler for a Terraplane, he covered the distance in 19 hr 4 min. After this, record-breaking on public roads was banned.

German Army officer Paul Graetz takes a well-earned rest beside the mighty 40 hp Gaggenau during his 1907-09 journey across Africa

British Army Captain R.M. Kelsey (left) lounges against his Argyll at Johannesburg on his ill-fated 1913 attempt to be the first man to drive from the Cape to Cairo. But he underestimated the savagery of Africa, and the bid ended at Broken Hill, Northern Rhodesia, where Kelsey was killed by a leopard

ABE'S VISION OF THE GREAT TRUNK ROAD

Cape Town to Cairo overland. That was the great challenge, the pioneer motorist's Everest. There was more at stake than individual honour. Riding with the first safaris were national pride, and the prospect of vast economic development. The Kaiser publicly decorated Oberleutnant Paul Graetz of the Imperial German Army who linked German East and German West Africa by road in 1909. His epic trip, from Dar-es-Salaam to Swakopmund via Johannesburg, in a 40 hp Gaggenau, took almost two years.

Cecil Rhodes had long dreamed of a Cape to Cairo railroad, passing over British territory all the way. This remained a dream, but with the advent of the motor car, a great trunk road was seen as the next best thing. Sir Abe Bailey, mining magnate and financier, had a vision of a motor highway that would 'open up the dark spots of Africa for the light of progress to enter'.

A British officer and Anglo-Boer War veteran, Captain R.M. Kelsey, attempted the trip in 1913. His heavy Scots-built Argyll was plagued by breakdowns, and got no further than Broken Hill, Northern Rhodesia. There, while waiting for spares, Kelsey was killed by a leopard.

The First World War put a stop to further attempts. Then, in 1924, two expeditions set out, a French team heading south from Algiers, and a British expedition driving north from Cape Town. The Frenchman, Captain Delingette, travelling with his wife, a mechanic and a native servant aboard a sturdy 12-tyre Renault 'desert-car', reached Cape Town in July 1925. They were the first to cover the length of the continent and, according to a contemporary report, to have 'shown the banner of civilisation through the darkest spots of Africa'.

Taming the route

A party led by Major Court-Treatt, also travelling with his wife, followed an all-British route, and was the first to conquer the fabled Cape to Cairo journey. Their Crossley light lorries, built as Royal Flying Corps tenders during the war, took 16 months for the trip. Deserts and bushveld slowed but could not halt them. Where deep rivers lacked bridges or pontoons, the cars were dragged across under the water. Incredibly, after 4 800 km, they had suffered just two punctures.

Such adventures hardly meant that the route had been tamed. It was a South African team that really cut it down to size. In 1928 the *Rand Daily Mail* and the *Sunday Times* sponsored a motoring editor, Emil Mullin, and a well-known racing driver, Gerry Bouwer (a versatile man: six years earlier he had walked from Cairo to Johannesburg), in an attempt to slash the time to four months or less. Their tough 1928 Chrysler sedan pulled out of Cape Town in February. Just 93 days later it was in Cairo. Still not content, Bouwer stripped some excess weight off the Chrysler and, with his wife as passenger, roared back to the Cape in forty days.

But in 1930 a party of girl guides in a second-hand Morris capped these feats. Three members of the Rondebosch guide troop set out for a holiday jaunt through Africa. Their car reached Cairo, then chugged on to Oxford, England. The trip took six months.

There are no concessions to the heat and dust of South West Africa in the uniforms and stiff military bearing of these German soldiers. Their vehicle, though, is much better suited for the terrain. It is a specially built 45 hp Daimler, fitted with water reservoirs and four-wheel drive

The 12-wheeled Renault 'desert-car' of Frenchman Captain Delingette, who made the first north-south crossing of Africa in 1924-25. He is pictured at Nairobi with his wife and, leaning against the rear wheels, his Nigerian former batman, who had trekked hundreds of kilometres to beg to be taken along

Donkey power comes to the aid of horsepower during a newspaper-sponsored dash from the Cape to Cairo in 1928. Racing driver Gerry Bouwer and motoring editor Emil Mullin, in a Chrysler sedan, were on safari to survey a route that would realise Sir Abe Bailey's dream of a great highway down the length of Africa

She was only a second-hand, six-year-old Morris Oxford Tourer called Bohunkus. But in 1930 she took Miss M.L. Belcher and Miss E.C. Budgell, two Girl Guide officers from Rondebosch, Cape Town, on a 14 500 km jaunt to Oxford, England. A third member of the troop went with them as far as Nairobi

The new generation of cars

LONG QUEUES AND A LONG WAIT

After the Second World War endless streams of hopeful motorists besieged showrooms to put their names down for the latest models. But it was to be a long and frustrating time before the cars arrived.

For South African motorists, the 1940s had been a decade of austerity. General Motors' Port Elizabeth assembly plant stopped production for the civilian market in 1942; Ford turned out 60 000 vehicles during the war — all for military use — and car-owners nursed their aging models through years of petrol rationing and spares shortages.

The first post-war models which made their appearance in mid-1946 were disappointingly similar to their pre-war forebears. Ford's Prefect and Anglia had changed only in details of trim; the Austin and Vauxhall range seemed not to have changed at all. Solid front axles, side valve engines and shiny headlights mounted on top of flared wings were relics of a bygone age: factories were struggling to convert to the manufacture of private vehicles after years of war production.

The little Morris Eight showed pleasingly modern lines with faired-in headlights, but it too travelled on solid axles, until it was replaced by the Morris Minor and larger Morris Oxford. The Austin A40 Devon which appeared in 1949 was another representative of the 'new generation of motor cars'.

Arthur Barker entered his name on the list for a new car in 1946. Preference was given to doctors and others who performed 'essential services', and Arthur Barker was not a doctor. So it was only in 1948 that he took delivery of his new Austin Eight. 'My boys were delighted with it,' he says. 'They thought it was the finest car they had ever seen, with its shiny black Duco and leather bucket seats. The next year I managed to

1941 Packard 110 Convertible. This six-cylinder roadster had a top speed of about 136 km/h. The Packard Motor Co. merged with the Studebaker Corporation in 1954, and the Studebaker design gradually overtook the Packard lines. The new Studebakers, with their long, low, sporty lines, became classics

This advertisement for the new Austin A70 appeared in the British magazine Motor *in 1948. They were roomy, reliable cars and very popular in South Africa*

1949 Morris Minor. Today these little cars, with their simple lines and legendary reliability, are much sought after by enthusiasts

1947 M.G. TC. These two-seater sports cars are now worth many times their original value

SOUTH AFRICAN SPECIAL

In 1949, the *M.T.A. Bulletin* described an unusual car built entirely in South Africa: the 'De Jong Special'. It was built by Mr P.A. De Jong, a Philippolis garage-owner, and was powered by a Mercury engine mounted on a converted Ford chassis. Body framework was seamless steel tubing. 'He [Mr De Jong] used a converted air-riveting hammer for moulding the body. A 1/4 in. steel rod welded into the fender beading right round the car does away with fender stays and supports, and electric and gas-welded seams eliminate body bolts and nuts. Seats and door-tops are made of sponge rubber, and the reinforcing ribs of oil drums have become the radiator grill.'

DARTS AND BUBBLES

Left: In 1953 South Africans were introduced to the tiny Dart, a two-seater runabout believed by its makers to be the first motor car ever manufactured in this country. Said *Motor Age:* 'The manufacturers feel that a good potential market exists in Africa for an inexpensive, easy-to-drive, economical runabout. They predict that carrying only one person, running costs will amount to less than municipal busfare.'

The car's 5 hp engine was imported, but it was planned to manufacture the engine in South Africa under licence at a later stage. The Dart was designed by a Johannesburg engineering firm with the assistance of Italian and Czechoslovakian specialists. The operation of the ungainly-looking vehicle was simple but, sadly, it never went into production. Right: In October 1959, *Motor Parade* ran this cover picture of a bubble-car with a caption pointing out its 'economical all-weather mobility for thousands who do not favour two-wheelers and cannot yet afford full-sized motor cars'.

1958 Volkswagen Cabriolet. The Volkswagen works produced only the saloon version of the famous beetle, but several convertible versions were offered by various firms. The four-seater model by Karmann (above), one of Germany's oldest coach-building firms, and the Karmann-Ghia two-seater convertible and coupé versions became part of the official sales programme. The car shown here is an updated model with additional lights in the front and rear

buy a new Chevrolet De Luxe, with overhead valve engine, bench seat that took three in the front, with space for another three in the back. My youngest son, in particular, spent ages standing in front of the car and peering along the length of the bonnet. He just couldn't believe that a car could be so big, especially after the little Austin.'

The two-way look

The Americans were quicker to produce really new models. The Studebaker Champion, although still powered by a side valve engine, had a long, low bonnet and luggage boot that prompted one writer to observe that 'it looks as though it's going both ways at the same time'. By 1948 motor vehicles were again flowing into the Union, and of the 90 000 imported in that year, half came from North America.

Favoured for their comfort and power in covering the long distances between South African towns, the large American cars suddenly became an expensive proposition when Britain devalued the pound in 1949. The prices of popular six-cylinder cars like the Chevrolet, Dodge and Hudson were just short of £1 000 as against £378 for the less exciting but eminently serviceable Morris Minor. Imports from the United States dropped by half, with a corresponding doubling of the numbers from the United Kingdom.

Only General Motors and Ford had their own assembly plants in the Union, but other manufacturers competed by exporting their cars CKD – Completely Knocked Down – for assembly by local firms. Austins were turned out alongside Studebakers, with the Standard Vanguard and the Nash Rambler also emerging from a common shed. One company alone was assembling the products of four overseas manufacturers: Austin, Hudson, Peugeot and Willys Overland.

The first serious attempt to build a South African motor car was made by the Glassport Motor Company, whose GSM Dart, a two-seater sports car with fibreglass body, was highly successful on race tracks in South Africa and Britain.

In 1956 South Africans Willie Meissner and Verster de Wit met in England, discussed the project, and built the prototype in an old stable in London. The as-yet nameless car was entered in a motor race in England and led almost from start to finish. An excited race commentator, groping for words, called it 'that dart' – and the name stuck.

Later, a factory was established at Paarden Eiland, just outside Cape Town, where imported engines were modified and fitted to locally-made fibreglass bodies. In late 1961 the GSM Flamingo was introduced – a slightly more luxurious version of the Dart, and available with a choice of highly-tuned engines ranging from a four-cylinder to a powerful V8.

Local demand for the car, though, remained small and production stopped in 1965.

Another 'South African' motor car, along the lines of Australia's Holden, was General Motors' Ranger, a South African-designed body incorporating Vauxhall mechanical components, introduced in the late 1960s. But, with the move towards standardisation of model types, it too went out of production.

The fibreglass GSM Darts being assembled. In the centre the GSM Flamingo, a G.T. version. Right: Brochure advertising the Flamingo

The General Motors Ranger, described as South Africa's 'own' motor car, was launched in 1968

159

Crank-handles and great mechanical ingenuity

The attraction of polished brass, buttoned leather and spoked wheels has ensnared thousands of South Africans since the Second World War. Their love for vintage and veteran cars (cars manufactured from the beginning of motoring until 1918 are known as veterans; those between 1919 and 1930 as vintage) has produced a crop of immaculately-restored models. Today only the real optimist still dreams of finding a dust-covered Model T Ford in someone's barn.

There are four major clubs in South Africa: the Veteran Car Club of South Africa in Durban, the Crankhandle Club in Cape Town, the Vintage and Veteran Club in Johannesburg and the Free State Veteran Motor Club in Bloemfontein. Their members hold regular rallies and other events, and many put the cars to practical use. Spare parts are a headache, though, and some owners have to have them specially manufactured, or even make them themselves. This calls for real mechanical skill, as parts have to be cast, ground and polished to exacting standards.

Probably the biggest collection of veteran and vintage cars in this country was that of Mr. O.D. Inggs of Grahamstown, who sold all his models to a syndicate of Pretoria enthusiasts in 1968. They are still being used today. Smaller stables dotted about the Republic have such thoroughbreds as Bugattis, Rolls Royces, Armstrong-Siddeleys and Bentleys. Drivers often enter into the spirit of the thing and don voluminous cloaks, goggles, masks and rugs for their outings.

1928 CHRYSLER 72. In 1928 the *Rand Daily Mail* and the Johannesburg *Sunday Times* sponsored an effort to drive from Cape to Cairo within four months. The expedition left Cape Town on 8 February in a Chrysler 72 and reached their goal in 93 days. The lightened car made the return journey in less than half that time. The owner is Mr M. Cheminais

1928 BENTLEY. This model arrived in South Africa in 1946 and is presently owned by Mrs P.R. White, wife of the chairman of Cape Town's Crankhandle Club. The body is of wood, covered with a sturdy fabric, and has been totally rebuilt. Its 4,5 ℓ engine enables the car to cruise at an impressive 120 km/h

1904 DE DION BOUTON. South Africa's second petrol-driven vehicle was powered by the De Dion single cylinder air-cooled engine, a highly successful design by the De Dion company of Paris. This model was found in 1955 completely stripped: the engine was being used as a compressor and the rear portion of the chassis, with the gearbox and one wheel, had been adapted as a working head for a pump. The bonnet was serving as a chicken coop. The 6 hp engine (which had three forward gears and one reverse) could push the car along a level road at nearly 50 km/h. The owner is Mr G.H. Sheldrick

1901 ALBION 8 hp DOG CART. Spicer, Langley and Co of Long Street, Cape Town, established one of the first motor agencies in South Africa with the Albion franchise. This car was built on chassis No. 10 at the Albion Motor Car Company in Glasgow, Scotland, and is one of only seven 8 hp Dog Carts (of a total of 58 produced) which survives today. The present owner is Mr R. Blackwood Murray, grandson of Dr Blackwood Murray, co-founder of the Albion Motor Company

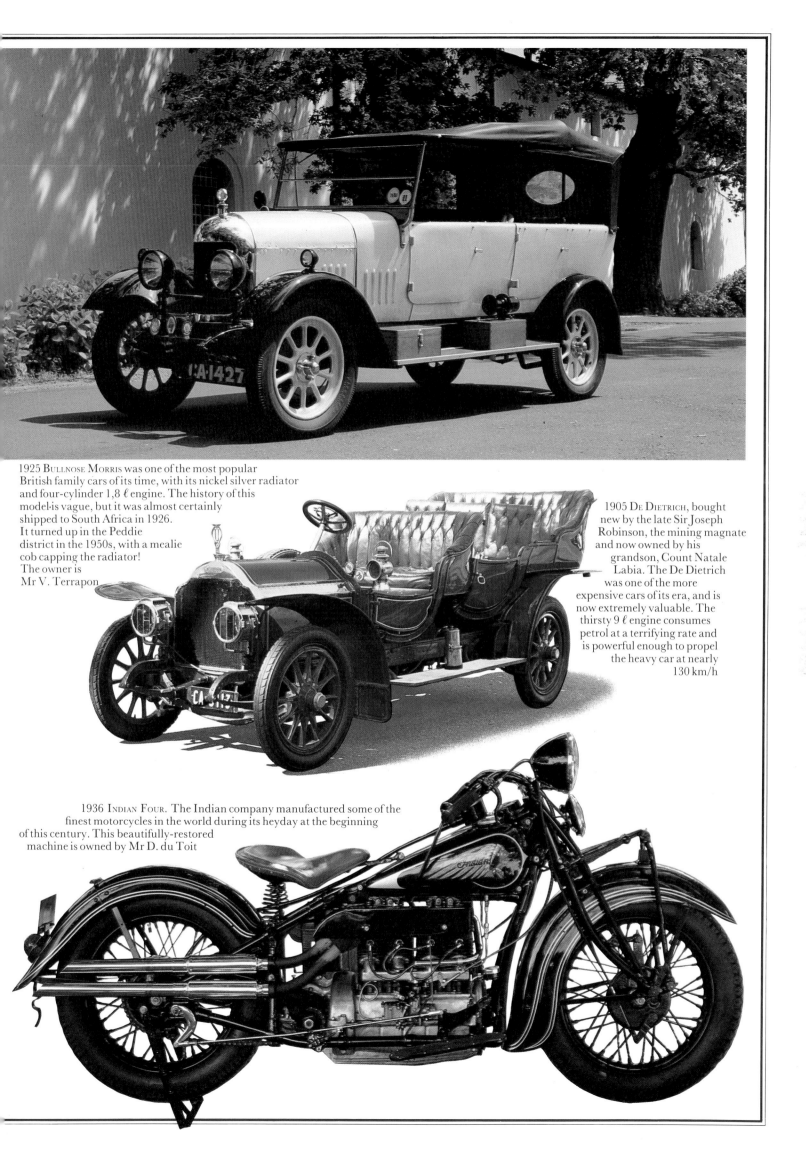

1925 Bullnose Morris was one of the most popular British family cars of its time, with its nickel silver radiator and four-cylinder 1,8 ℓ engine. The history of this model is vague, but it was almost certainly shipped to South Africa in 1926. It turned up in the Peddie district in the 1950s, with a mealie cob capping the radiator! The owner is Mr V. Terrapon

1905 De Dietrich, bought new by the late Sir Joseph Robinson, the mining magnate and now owned by his grandson, Count Natale Labia. The De Dietrich was one of the more expensive cars of its era, and is now extremely valuable. The thirsty 9 ℓ engine consumes petrol at a terrifying rate and is powerful enough to propel the heavy car at nearly 130 km/h

1936 Indian Four. The Indian company manufactured some of the finest motorcycles in the world during its heyday at the beginning of this century. This beautifully-restored machine is owned by Mr D. du Toit

Making tracks

The first locomotive to arrive in South Africa. It is now preserved in the foyer of Cape Town station

SPEECHES, A WHISTLE AND A ZULU HORDE

Rail travel came to South Africa after a series of false starts. On 25 October 1845, the London *Pictorial Times* reported on the first meeting of the Provincial Committee of the Cape of Good Hope Western Railway: '. . . this railway is calculated to be of immense benefit to this flourishing Colony; and as it is confined to the more populous districts in the neighbourhood of Cape Town, the enterprise is certain to return ample remunerative profits to its shareholders.'

But the promotion failed, and almost a decade was to pass before the citizens of London were invited to contribute towards a similar scheme. In 1853 the Cape Town Railway and Dock Company was incorporated in London with a registered capital of £600 000. It held a concession to build a line from Cape Town to Wellington in the Cape. Despite initial resistance to the railways, the Cape farming community soon recognised the advantages of direct and easy access to their markets. But they had to wait for it.

Construction finally began on 31 March 1859 when the Governor, Sir George Grey, turned the first sod with a silver spade. The first steam locomotive was landed in South Africa in September the same year and painstakingly assembled in a shed on the Parade in Cape Town by her Scottish engineer-driver, William Dabbs. Materials and equipment arrived, labour and financial problems were gradually sorted out, and the Cape railway began to take shape. But there were shocks ahead.

Pipped at the post

On 31 January 1859 the *Natal Mercury* published this prospectus: 'Natal Railway Company. To be incorporated by Special Act of the Legislature with Limited Liability. Capital £10 000 in 1 000 shares of £10 each with the power to increase. £2-10/- on allotment, £2-10/- thereafter and the balance as required giving three months' notice.'

The company was incorporated in June 1859 and a year later the same newspaper published the notice:

The Transvaal's first locomotive was preserved and put on display in Johannesburg station

Johannesburg's Park Station, about 1898. This large structure was once an exhibition hall in Holland

Three ladies take a break from the long Karoo crossing to pose aboard a locomotive

---

THE RACE FOR THE RAND

President Reitz of the Free State meets President Kruger in a ceremony marking the link between the Transvaal and Free State. They are standing beside a temporary bridge at Viljoensdrift

The discovery of gold on the Witwatersrand brought about wide-ranging economic and political changes in the colonies. As new wealth flowed into the coffers of the Transvaal Republic, neighbouring states competed to establish railway links with the source.

President Kruger was determined to be first to build an independent link between Pretoria and Delagoa Bay, in Portuguese territory. Both he and his Volksraad were distrustful of the Imperialistic ambitions of men such as Cecil Rhodes: they had to secure access to the sea without any reliance upon the Cape and Natal harbours.

In 1887 Kruger granted a concession to a Dutch group for the construction of the railway line from Komatipoort to Pretoria and Johannesburg, and the Nederlandsche Zuid-Afrikaansche Spoorweg-Maatschappij (NZASM)

was born. There were problems from the start: Kruger's presidency was under attack from several quarters inside and outside the Volksraad, the other states were building their own railways with frightening rapidity, and the Netherlands Company was running out of money (its financial relationship with the Government was so tortuous that even the Volksraad's finance committees were baffled).

After doing everything within his power to retard his competitors, Kruger at last acknowledged defeat. All his manipulations and tenuous alliances had been for nothing. The line to Johannesburg was open by September 1892, and on 1 January the following year the first train from a Cape port pulled into the city. The Netherlands Company's railway reached Johannesburg two years later.

NATAL RAILWAY
The Opening
of this
The First Railway in South Africa
will take place under the auspices of
His Excellency Major Williamson
the Acting Lieut-Govenor [sic]
On Tuesday, 26th June 1860

The Cape had been beaten to the post, and the massed populace of Durban turned out to rub it in. The Bishop invoked Divine Blessing on the enterprise, the Governor made his speech, train driver Henry Jacobs blew his whistle, and the country's first operational train steamed from the city followed by a horde of screaming Zulus.

Two years later, the link was completed between Cape Town and Eerste River, later being extended to Stellenbosch and Wellington. By 1875 the Cape boasted 246 kilometres of track (Natal had a mere 8 km) and the discovery of gold and diamonds promised even more rapid expansion. At the outbreak of the Anglo-Boer War in 1899, the country was criss-crossed by an impressive 6 860 kilometres of track.

Enamel chambers — for safety's sake!

In those days rail travel was an adventure. In his autobiography, *Worthwhile Journey*, the famous strong-man Tromp van Diggelen described a train journey in 1890: '. . . meals were only to be had when the train stopped long enough at some special station. When night came on, a guard would walk along the roofs of the carriages and put big oil-lamps through holes in the ceiling of each. For safety's sake, Metie carried an enamel chamber for our use; when needed, an open window made an easy means of disposal.'

Van Diggelen's train ran into a vast swarm of locusts and the rails became so slippery that they came to a stop. 'I lost my fear of those streams of fluttering locusts as I saw people standing all along the train, bending over and scooping handfuls of sand on to the crushed insects on the rails. We three children joined gleefully in the fun . . .'

The novelty of train travel appears to have overcome much of the reserve in the travellers of 1880. Georgina Lister was taken by her

father, Thomas Bain, in a train which formed part of the procession organised to celebrate the opening of the railway extension to Beaufort West. 'There were no washing facilities on the train,' she recorded, 'and we had to sleep sitting bolt upright, as the carriages of those days had no sleeping arrangements. The noisy and disorderly behaviour of some of the passengers was horrible and particularly distressed my father who hated drunkenness and scenes like those. Several men fell off the train and were injured . . .'

However conditions were to improve. On-train catering was introduced on the Cape Government Railways in 1885 and the first (civilian) dining cars appeared after the Anglo-Boer War (the Railways Catering Department was created in 1910). A traveller wrote of a journey by Cape Government Railways:

'How much less enjoyable a lounge in the observation car, a card party in the smoking room, or refreshments on one's specially reserved compartment would be without the intelligent and experienced attentions of the conductor and his staff. . . Here, for instance, is a writing room with a comfortable sleeping berth for one person. There is a smoking room quite as elegant as that on board the ship just left behind . . .'

The travelling bastions

The South African Railways and Harbours administration was established at the time of Union in 1910, and the former Government Railways of the Cape and Natal and the Central South African Railways functioned as 'systems' of the SAR central authority. Johannesburg became the centre of the network in 1916. Among the railways remaining in private hands were those of the Robertson-based New Cape Central Railways (whose initials NCCR were widely held to mean 'Never Can Come Right') and the Kowie Railway Company. The Natal-Zululand Railway company was in fact owned by the State.

Electrificaton had been considered in Natal in 1914, but its introduction was delayed by the First World War and it was only in January 1925 that a service of five electric trains a day was launched in the 70-kilometre track between Ladysmith and Estcourt. Three years later, the steam engines on the Cape Town-Simonstown suburban line gave way to electric units, and by 1938 much of the Reef mining area and Germiston-Pretoria sector had been electrified. The main line from Cape Town to Touws River was electrified in May 1954, and the bastions of 'the last stronghold of steam' began to tremble.

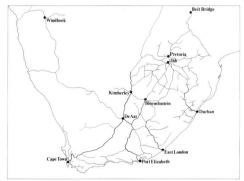

The South African railway network. In 1890 there were 3 844 km of railway line (shown in black) — most being in the Cape, with a short section south of Johannesburg. In 1902 7 500 km and, by 1936, the total was 21 885 km (shown in red)

This Ford motorised trolley, left, was seen at Port Elizabeth station. Note the brushes mounted in front. The motor rail coach, right, featured a separate cab for the driver and a four-wheel bogie mounted on leaf springs

Luxury travel

BELLS, TELEPHONES, AND A FIRE IN EVERY COACH

The Blue Train, one of the world's most famous passenger trains, owes its origins to the Union Limited and the Union Express, which linked Johannesburg with the mailships departing from Cape Town for England. Ordinary coaches were used until 1927, when articulated saloons were imported. Each had two complete coach bodies with bogies at the outer ends and a centred bogie common to both coaches. The two Union trains travelled the distance in 30 hours and introduced a new standard of luxury.

In July 1937 it was announced that 12 air-conditioned, all-steel sleeping coaches had been ordered from the Birmingham firm of Metro-Cammell at a cost of some R19 000 each. A later order called for all-steel lounge coaches and dining-cars, kitchen-cars and a baggage van. The coaches were delivered at the start of the Second World War, but the service was suspended in 1942 (as were other express trains) and was only resumed in February 1946. During this period it was used for a few State journeys.

Memories of blue and cream

In *Full Many a Glorious Morning*, author Lawrence Green wrote of his travels in the trains that captured the imagination of many thousands: 'I remember the first articulated saloons with an observation car giving an unusual view of the rails at the rear of the train. A blue and cream dining-car named Protea came in the early 1930s and this was followed by the Union Limited, a complete blue and cream train.

'This express left Johannesburg every Thursday for Cape Town to link up with the mail steamer departing next day. It was a fine train at that time with heaters and fans in every compartment. In each coach a bedding attendant kept a fire going under a cylinder for hot and cold water in basins and showers. The Union Limited had bells and telephones to the dining-car. Tea and drinks were served in a lounge-car, card-tables and easy chairs were provided.'

The original Blue Train, world-renowned for the excellence of its cuisine and comfort, was last hauled by steam power on the De Aar-Kimberley section behind a Class 25 NC locomotive in 1972, when the new (South African-built) Blue Train was taken into service. The original Blue Train still operates — now in green livery — as the Drakensberg Express on the Johannesburg-Durban route.

A train fit for a king

But the last word in luxury train travel came in the 1940s, when work began on the famous White Train. The *South African Railways and Harbours Magazine* reported in January 1947: 'The White Train of the Governor-General, brought up to date and enlarged by a number of specially-built coaches, is being placed at the disposal of the Royal visitors. After the tour is over two saloons used by the King [George VI] and

The Royal Train used by the Duke of Connaught on his trip to Cape Town to open Parliament in 1910

Queen [Elizabeth] will become a permanent part of the White Train while the other coaches will be added to the stock of the Blue Train.'

When completed, the train of 14 ivory-coloured coaches was indeed fit for a king.

The opulence of its interior surpassed anything ever seen on South African Railways. Richly embroidered furniture rested on hand-woven woollen carpets; mouldings and carved panels gleamed richly against silken curtains.

From his study the King was in radio contact with the entire Commonwealth — the

first time a South African train had been fitted with such a facility. For the King, Queen and two princesses, as well as the ladies-in-waiting, equerries, secretaries and other officials, the White Train was 'home' for 42 days of the nine-week tour.

The railways' magazine of February 1947 described some of the features of the luxury train which the SAR hoped would ease the Royal journey: 'The staterooms [for the princesses] are both identically panelled and furnished and their bathrooms have similar fittings. The furniture is of sycamore and

STATELY HOME FROM HOME

The interior of the coach used by President Paul Kruger. It originally consisted of two four-wheeled wagons joined by a concertina-like coupling, but the two sections were later welded together. A large reception room also served as a meeting place for the Government of the South African Republic (Transvaal), and there were two bedrooms (with built-in cupboards), a bathroom, a kitchen and a staff compartment furnished in the most expensive materials. There was even a refrigerator in the coach — of the type that was cooled with blocks of ice — and such facilities as electric lights and hot and cold water.

The railways' magazine of December

1951 reminded its readers of 'that historic and tragic night' when Kruger, persuaded by his advisers to leave Pretoria, stood on the balcony of the coach and gazed with brimming eyes and bowed shoulders into the dusk . . . The enemy was about to occupy Pretoria, and he had to be with General Louis Botha's retreating army. Kruger took his Government to Machadodorp — and never saw Pretoria again. Later when he was forced to flee once more (first to Waterval-Onder and then to Lourenço Marques, where he took a ship to Holland), the coach was left behind. In Waterval-Onder retreating Boer troops came upon the State coach and stripped it of everything.

The dining-car in one of the tourist trains in Cape Town, 1924

Special trains ran between 1924 and 1933 to convey tourists (most of them from America) throughout the Union and what was then Rhodesia. Acting Catering Inspector L.J. Koen was one of the people responsible for serving them. Interviewed by the railways' magazine before assuming his duties as Chief Steward on the White Train in 1947, he recalled that the Americans were very appreciative travellers and were especially impressed by the catering on South African trains. On one occasion, said Mr Koen, the boisterous passengers carried the chef shoulder-high through the saloon. The Chief Steward found the tourists' eating habits somewhat disconcerting in the beginning: they would call for two or three courses at once and then either mix the food into 'one glorious mess' on one plate or take mouthfuls from each plate in turn.

The visitors were very enthusiastic about the Kruger National Park — one excited youngster approached the Chief Steward with excited anticipation: 'Mr Koen, if I come back in a lion skin you'll know what has happened to me!'

Natal's railways offered luxurious travel facilities

cherry mahogany, and consists of a dressing table with stool, wardrobe, bedside fitment with built-in loudspeaker, and bed with innerspring mattress. The princesses' private bathrooms are finished in pale cream oil paint and the full-size bath and washbasin in green porcelain. A hand shower, bath stool and wall cupboard door has an electric element fitted behind to prevent the condensation of moisture on the mirror face.'

Meals on the White Train were prepared in a stainless steel kitchen from produce selected en route. Health inspectors travelled ahead to ensure that supply sources were scrupulously clean and only pasteurized milk and milk products were accepted. Of the almost 9 000 litres of milk taken aboard, only 45 litres turned sour — and that in the extreme heat at Livingstone. Water, in large glass bottles, had been taken from Albion Springs in Rondebosch.

On Royal instructions, menus aboard the train had to conform to South Africa's postwar restrictions, and when offered a menu for approval, Queen Elizabeth often ruled out what she considered superfluous or extravagant dishes. However, fresh eggs, still a rarity in England, were breakfast favourites, and the Royal family enjoyed many meals prepared from traditional South African recipes.

In May 1947, a senior SAR official wrote in the railways' magazine of the final scene in the Royal tour as the battleship HMS *Vanguard* sailed from Cape Town: 'The Duncan Dock looked curiously empty with *Vanguard* no longer there, and the White Train, untenanted, stood forlornly nearby, its splendour a mute reminder of the end of an experience which will live in history . . .'

A private lounge was provided for the Royal tourists. It was panelled in English walnut and featured a settee, easy chairs and tables. The curtains were of silk

RHAPSODY IN BLUE TRAIN

In 1946 a traveller on the Blue Train sang its praises in a letter to the System Manger, Kimberley. It was reproduced in the *South African Railways and Harbours Magazine*:

'After dining in great comfort
You stroll along to bed
To find it's been made ready
While you were being fed!
Blue pillows and blue blankets
(The sheets are blue as well),
You've never had such luxury
If you the truth would tell!
You cannot feel the motion
Nor can you hear a sound
In fact it is the "dream train"
We think at last we've found.
So travel by the Blue Train,
It's well worth the extra fare.
You'll step off clean and smiling,
There is no wear and tear.'

The Royal family leaves Cape Town in the White Train. South African Railways planned the tour with the painstaking precision of a military exercise

The Royal dining-car accommodated three long tables, with chairs upholstered in green marabout satin. The furniture was designed in period style

The pilot train, preceding the White Train by 30 minutes, carried railway officials, police officers, reporters and photographers — and a post office

Majestic reminders of the age of steam

It is dawn, and a man crouches beside a railway line in a remote part of the Karoo. Suddenly he tenses: in the distance he has seen a wisp of smoke. A moment passes, and he feels the earth tremble slightly. He puts his camera to his eye, checks the light reading for the sixth time, and waits. Then it rounds a bend — a whistling, clanking, smoke-belching monster that he has travelled hundreds of kilometres to capture on film.

The camera clicks . . . once, twice, three times and more . . . and the man grins with satisfaction. He has recognised the locomotive as a Class 25NC, one of the many dying breeds of steam locomotive in South Africa, and he has what he came for.

Enthusiasts from all over the world are drawn to South Africa for nostalgic looks at some of the increasingly rare steam locomotives still in operation. Economic expediency has led to the retirement of all but a few of these workhorses, and there are locomotive 'graveyards' of varying size in many parts of the country.

The South African Railways Museum in Johannesburg houses much of the memorabilia associated with the Steam Age, and the collection is growing continually.

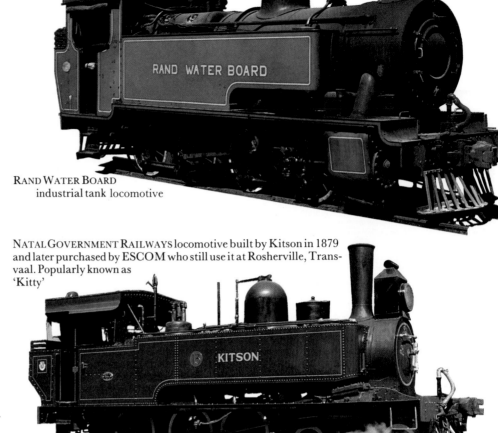

RAND WATER BOARD
industrial tank locomotive

NATAL GOVERNMENT RAILWAYS locomotive built by Kitson in 1879 and later purchased by ESCOM who still use it at Rosherville, Transvaal. Popularly known as 'Kitty'

BRASS NUMBER-PLATE on the cabside of an SAR steam locomotive. '25NC' is the class designation. Builders' plate below

NZASM (Nederlandsche Zuid-Afrikaansche Spoorweg-Maatschappij) 46-ton locomotive. Preserved in working order and used for special trains and filming

CLASS 16DA 4-6-2, an American-inspired passenger engine design dating from the 1920s, and preserved for working special trains

A GARRATT LOCOMOTIVE of the former Rhodesian Railways, used by
Landau Colliery in the Witbank area. An immensely powerful engine, having about
twice the hauling power of conventional locos designed for similar service

CLASS 25
condensing 4-8-4. Ninety
of these large locomotives
were built during the
1950s and were perhaps
the most successful
class of condensing
steam locos ever
constructed. One is
preserved in working order

FORMER SAR Class 15BR
used by Randfontein
Estates Gold Mine.
Note the whimsical
addition of a
propeller on
the front of
the smokebox,
below the two
headlights

'MILLY', a Hendrie-designed
4-8-2 Class 15A, in
original condition, and now
preserved at De Aar for
working special trains.
This mixed-traffic
locomotive is
typical of those
working on SAR
during the period
1912 to 1925

Life aboard

TRAVELLING IN STYLE

'It was a fortnight of cloudless skies and calm seas, through which the Cape liner cut her way with placid unconcern. She did not even increase her speed above the ordinary commercial rate. Absolute tranquility lapped the peaceful ship. The usual sports and games of a sea voyage occupied her passengers, civil and military alike.'

Thus did young Winston Churchill sum up the serenity of shipboard life. Although it was October 1899 and the guns had already begun to thunder across the veld, the Royal Mail steamship *Dunottar Castle* carried her cargo of reinforcements (and the new Commander-in-Chief) at the unruffled pace of the years of peace. It was one of those rare periods when Churchill, the war correspondent, had little to report.

An endless succession of fun

One gets a delightful picture of life aboard the big liners of the early 1900s from J. Salter-Whiter's *A Trip to South Africa*:

'After dinner, darkness had fairly set in, and a keen easterly wind did not invite passengers to leave the comfortable and magnificent saloon with which the ship is furnished. This is one of the chief features and attractions of the ship, and

Deck games on the Union (later Union-Castle) liners was a daily feature of shipboard life almost from the start — but often they were so highly organised and intimidating that many a non-British passenger was frightened away! The seriousness of this aspect of sea travel is illustrated by the appointment of no less a personage than Major-General Sir E.T. Brabant as head of the sports committee aboard H.M.S. Saxon *some 80 years ago*

WINING, DINING AND MUSIC IN GRAND HOTEL CLASS

Menus at the turn of the century were of the grand hotel class. An elaborate example was the dinner menu aboard *Hawarden Castle*, mentioned by Laurens van der Post in his book *Last of the Line*, on 28 June 1902, which featured caviar and olives, turbot with mousseline sauce, quenelles of veal, salmi of quails, fillet of beef with Madeira sauce, Surrey fowl, new potatoes, green peas, salad, savarin with Curaçao, nesselrode pudding, assorted pastries, cheese, dessert and coffee. The soup, of course, was Imperial Soup.

And the wine-list complemented the stylish indulgence of the cuisine.

Diners were offered Vino de Pasto, Forster Kirchenstuck 1893, Chateau la Tour Garnet 1893, Perrier Jouet 1893 and Heidsieck's dry Monopole 1895 — all consumed to the strains of a small orchestra.

Said a contemporary travel review: 'Not only did malnutrition and scurvy cease to be a problem: indigestion and dyspepsia soon took their place.'

For passengers not interested in deck games, there was ample opportunity to sleep off over-indulgence at the luncheon table

Women were always enthusiastic participants in deck games on the early liners. They cheerfully bowled in the general direction of batsmen in mixed cricket matches

The 1907 Springbok cricket team thoroughly enjoyed their sea trip. Nourse and Vogler are pictured skipping

is certainly one of the finest apartments on any vessel afloat . . .

'Above the saloon we have the ladies' saloon and music room, a beautiful compartment, with a second room for the exclusive use of ladies only, fitted with luxurious couches, a boon greatly valued by the delicate . . .

'Leaving the saloon towards the stern we find a spacious quarter-deck, well protected from the wind and spray by high bulwarks, a capital place for a promenade, cricket, quoits, and other games . . .

'Quite forward we find the first-class smoking room. A capital one it is, too, lined with white marble, which makes it one of the coolest places in the tropics . . .

'We appointed an entertainment committee, and these gentlemen provided us with an endless succession of fun. Cricket, quoits, and ball forming our out-door sports, concerts and minstrel entertainments for the saloon; whilst the captain and officers most generously decorated the quarter-deck with flags and bunting for outdoor dances, which were well patronised. Then there is the excitement of a sweepstake on the run of the ship the last 24 hours; then some very excellent music.

'I think the most successful of all our sports were the Athletics. We organised tournaments for the first-class passengers both at "bucket quoits" and "bull". The competition in these was very keen and caused great excitement.

'These games were followed by a tug of war between the first and second-class passengers, which was in every instance won by the first-class, only for them to be ignominiously thrashed by the crew, against whom the landsmen could make no headway.'

Lifts, pools, and air-conditioning

Life aboard the mailships changed slightly over the decades as the latest improvements were incorporated. Marconi radio apparatus was installed on the new *Balmoral Castle* in 1910; the first shipboard lift, greatly appreciated by the elderly, was built into *Llanstephan Castle* of 1914. *Arundel Castle* of 1921 was the first to have 'forced air ventilation' of inner cabins, doing away with fans.

She also had the first swimming pool — for first class passengers only.

Perhaps the most significant change came in 1914, when unescorted ladies on deck at 11.30 p.m., the time that the deck lights were dimmed, were no longer politely requested to go below. And in the mid-1920s they were accepted into that formerly exclusively male preserve, the smoking room.

Too lovely, too short

Madge Barker travelled on *Stirling Castle* in 1937 as private nurse to a wealthy invalid returning 'Home' to England. She recalls: 'We were given a beautifully printed list of passengers, and it seemed that the entertainment committee were all chosen from the "nobs" in first class, but they did arrange a lot of fun.

'There were some lovely dances, although sometimes the music was pretty awful, I don't know why. The children's fancy dress party was very pretty and the tape-cutting derby was great fun. There was even dog-racing, and a lot of

Warm nights and sundrenched days — a halcyon time. First to have a swimming pool was Arundel Castle

people played tennis and quoits. The number of balls they hit over the side!

'On the Sunday the Captain held the morning service, and the lounge and gallery were packed. Evensong was held on deck and was followed by a tip-top concert.

'A few days before we reached Southampton we ran into what must have been a 100 mile an hour gale. Suitcases were playing hide-and-seek all over the cabin. The boat was rolling hopelessly, and was I sick! Only 20 out of 240 passengers were on deck, and the bridge drive was cancelled. It was too awful.

'When I did manage to go up on deck it was much calmer. I saw several schools of porpoises and a lot of little black birds with white breasts. There was a haze over the sea. The sun hung like a ball of fire with a small patch on it, very peculiar. Oh, but I was sad when the trip was over. It was all too lovely — and too short.'

But not even Union-Castle could please all passengers. One disgruntled individual recorded: 'To one not utterly frivolous . . . a voyage in a Mail Steamer is a restless, noisy round of human nothingness.'

KEEPING NAUSEA AT BAY

There were also the smaller companies, operating coasters between South African ports. One such vessel was the 427 ton iron steamship *Agnar*, owned by the Thesen Company of Knysna. The experience of a young Knysna girl, returning aboard *Agnar* to boarding-school in Cape Town early this century, has been recorded:

'She [the ship] had now become the foe of many schoolgoing generations of Knysna's children and had earned the nickname of "Agony". Up the steep gangway we would have to climb, then slip down the companion-way into her suffocating bowels. The atmosphere down there . . . took possession, giving us a foretaste of doom. Gingerly we would enter our cabins and regard the narrow bunks as coffins . . . The days, we spent on deck, lying on the hard boards rolled in rugs and trying to dismiss physical distress by means of song. We would go repetitively through our whole repertoire of hymns and ditties, hoping thereby to keep nausea at bay.'

Gleaming silverware, oil paintings and ornate columns greeted diners in the first-class dining saloon of Arundel Castle *in 1937. A first-class return voyage cost £90 in that year, a tourist-class ticket only £30*

The mailships

ONE FINAL BLAST OF THE SIREN, AND A VOYAGE INTO HISTORY

On Tuesday 6 September 1977 the 16-year-old *Windsor Castle*, flagship and sole remaining passenger vessel of the Union-Castle Line, sailed from Table Bay for the last time. Said the *Argus*: 'As the Cape Field Artillery band struck up, and the crowd sang Auld Lang Syne, an elderly man summed up the feelings of all: "It's sad seeing her go. It's like the end of a way of life".'

One of the proudest fleets in the history of the British mercantile marine, Union-Castle had begun a century and a quarter before as the Southampton Steam Shipping Company, formed in 1853 to carry Welsh coal to Southampton. Shortly afterwards it changed its name to the Union Steam Collier Company. Why the word 'Union' was adopted remains a mystery, but in view of the company's future links with South Africa the choice could hardly have been more apt. In 1857 it was awarded the mail contract between England and the Cape and that same year the modest, 530-ton steamer *Dane* arrived in Table Bay.

Of twice this displacement was *Cambrian*, launched three years later, the first steamship to be designed specially for the Cape route. By then the service had become monthly; the passage time 42 days.

The rivals

Ships of the Castle Mail Packets Company entered the Cape Trade in 1872, and soon the end of the Union Line's monopoly was in sight. Donald Currie, a shrewd, publicity-conscious shipping magnate who made a fortune in the gold and diamond market as well as from the sea, named his ships after British castles, and the first *Windsor Castle* broke all speed records for the Cape passage with a time of just under 23 days.

Rivalry between Currie's Castle Line and the Union fleet was intense; at times downright ungentlemanly. After *Windsor Castle* went aground

Farewell to the flagship and sole remaining passenger ship in the Union-Castle fleet. Windsor Castle *is cheered by thousands as she edges out of Table Bay for the last time on 6 September 1977. Two years later she lay at anchor in the Saudi Arabian port of Jeddah, serving as a dormitory for dockworkers*

near Dassen Island in 1876, Currie publicly alleged that the Union ship *Nubian* had passed 'within 3 or 4 miles' of *Windsor Castle* but had offered no assistance, nor had its master reported the incident on arrival in England. The allegation didn't stand up to examination, but it did ensure headline treatment for the Castle company. From October of that year the Cape contract was shared equally between the two lines. For almost 30 years they were to vie for the Cape custom, their ships sometimes racing one another to impress passengers and clients with yet another headline-making 'fastest time'.

Negotiating through intermediaries, Currie later acquired a major shareholding in the Union Line, and the two companies amalgamated in 1900. Management of the Union Castle Line was vested in Donald Currie and Company. The newly-combined fleet, starting with a total tonnage less than that of a modern supertanker, was to carry more South Africans abroad than any other line for the next 77 years.

At the time of the merger the fastest passage from Southampton to Cape Town was 14 days, 18 hours and 57 minutes — a record which had been set by the Union liner *Scot* in 1893. It re-

mained unbroken until 1936 when *Stirling Castle* did the voyage in 13 days and 9 hours. In 1938 *Carnarvon Castle* cut this to 12 days and 14 hours, and in 1954 *Edinburgh Castle*, her departure having been delayed, completed her passage in 11 days and 23 hours by steaming at full speed. The final record to be held by Union-Castle was that of the *Windsor Castle* in 1966 — 11 days and 10 hours. The mailships, though, were not really designed for speed. During the Second World War, *Queen Mary* made the passage in nine days, which included a stop for bunkers in Freetown.

Private Gibbs remembers

When the brand new *Kildonan Castle* steamed out of Southampton in November 1899, carrying a record number of 3 000 troops for the South African front, one of the soldiers was 21-year-old Robert Ernest Gibbs, who recalled the voyage many years later: 'There must have been hundreds of us, climbed into the rigging and crowded along the rail, until one of our officers chased some of us across to the other side.

'Perhaps he was afraid the weight of us all on one side was going to make the boat tip over. The band on shore was playing "Soldiers of the

Charles Smythe, Prime Minister of Natal before Union, received the invitation pictured left to a reception marking the first crossing of the bar at Durban by a mailship. The 13 000-ton Armadale Castle *entered the harbour for the first time on 26 June 1904. For many years the mailships had had to anchor off Durban and East London, and passengers were taken aboard in wicker baskets like the one above*

A forest of masts in East London's Buffalo Harbour in 1903. The days of sailing ships were already numbered

Queen" I think, while we held on to the ropes and cheered and shouted for all we were worth. Some of us were singing "Dolly Gray".'

Private Gibbs's first impression of Table Bay was one of utter confusion: 'My, I never saw so many ships; not even at Southampton when we sailed. It was like a forest with all the masts and funnels.'

During those few years up to mid-1902, sailing ships outnumbered steamers in Table Bay, but the spars and sails of centuries were about to be engulfed and obscured forever by clouds of smoke. From puny single-cylinder affairs, intended only as alternative propulsion when lack of wind left sails slack and lifeless, the steam age had progressed to the relatively powerful and reliable quadruple-expansion engine. Sails, if fitted at all to the latest liners, were no more than stand-bys, occasionally used as stabilisers. The sailing ships were dying.

Wider and deeper

The crush of shipping during the Anglo-Boer War highlighted the shortcomings of South Africa's harbours. At Table Bay, convict labour was slowly extending the vital breakwater. Only since 1881, when the North Jetty was constructed, had Port Elizabeth's surf-boats fallen into disuse. Now, passengers came off the liners by companion-ladder and were taken by tug to the jetty. East London, with its winds and high swells, was the least popular of the Cape harbours, and until the channel was deepened and the bar removed, passengers were hoisted from the liners' decks in an iron-reinforced basket and lowered to a lighter heaving alongside. It was the same at Durban, where the notorious bar restricted access to all but fairly shallow-draught vessels.

But a post-war immigrant boom was expected, and shipping companies and harbour authorities prepared themselves with large-scale expansion programmes. Durban ordered a new floating dry-dock — though it now lies rusting on a lonely Southern Cape beach, after having broken loose from the ship which had towed it all the way from England in late 1902. Not until 1914 would ships of 8 000 tons venture in-

The Mayoress of Cape Town, Mrs J.D. Low, travelled to the Harland and Wolff shipyard in Belfast in 1937 to break a bottle of South African wine across the bows of Capetown Castle, *left. The 26 500-ton liner, with a length of nearly 224 metres and accommodation for 792 passengers, was the largest built by a British shipyard since* Queen Mary. *Above: Union Castle was well into the cruise business during the Thirties*

side the port of East London. Improvements to Table Bay included a pier that was a continuation of Adderley Street. Eventually, work begun in Cape Town before the Second World War was to result in the reclamation of over 145 hectares of level ground from the sea.

Swarming sealanes, and the last farewell

Union-Castle was not the only company to operate a regular service between Europe and South Africa: in May 1911 the magazine *South Africa* listed the movement of steamers of nine other lines, and there were more, including the Clan Line, British and Colonial, German East Africa Line, Shaw Savill and Albion, Bucknall Line and the New Zealand Shipping Company.

But Union-Castle provided the quickest and most regular service. A Mail Steamer left Southampton every Saturday, and its passengers, who had paid fares ranging from £15.15s. to £39.18s., were duly disembarked in Cape Town 17 days later. There were also the slower Intermediate and Extra Steamers.

When *Windsor Castle* edged out of Table Bay on her farewell voyage she carried, reported the *Argus*, a crew of 'subdued sentimentalists and

800 passengers who had booked months in advance to bid her bon voyage in a style to which world travellers are no longer accustomed'.

Thousands on the quayside cheered as the ship, with a thunderous blast on her whistle, steamed gracefully through the harbour entrance, dressed overall in bunting and with a 15-metre paying-off penant flying at her main masthead. Ships in the harbour hooted their last salute and two of the four escorting tugs shot feathers of spray from their hydrants. Small craft skimmed and darted across the water; the frigate *President Pretorius* kept station on the liner's port beam. Three Albatross aircraft of Maritime Command roared overhead as the naval frigate, flying the 'Jolly Roger', ordered *Windsor Castle* to heave-to.

A boatload of 'pirates' was sent across to the liner. They made straight for the bridge to present the Master, Captain Patrick Beadon, with a symbolic ornamented mailbag embroidered with the names of *President Pretorius* and *Windsor Castle*. From the shore, and from the slopes of Signal Hill, thousands of people watched as the great liner turned her bows northwards and, with a last blast of her siren, sailed into history.

Carnarvon Castle *arriving at Durban in 1945 with returning Springbok troops.* Carnarvon Castle, *left, sailed from Southampton to Cape Town in a record 12 days, 13 hours, 38 minutes in 1938*

Riding to work on tram and trolley

MONSTROUS MASSES OF ROWDY TIN

·The first electric trams — imported from the United·States — ran on 6 August 1896 between Cape Town's Adderley Street and Mowbray Hill. Commuters found a new thrill in riding in from the suburbs on what were to be called 'monstrous masses of rowdy tin'.

By 1897, the year of Queen Victoria's Diamond Jubilee, Port Elizabeth also had electric trams, and during the next 13 years the other major cities established their systems. Pietermaritzburg's was said to have been the smallest in the southern hemisphere.

Most of the early trams were open at both ends and the 'motorman', or driver (a rather underprivileged person — he was completely exposed to the elements and seldom provided with a seat), regulated the power with a tiller-like lever. To apply the brakes he screwed down a large spoked wheel, and there was a foot-operated gong to warn pedestrians and traffic of his approach.

The upper deck normally consisted of little more than a floor and a roof. In bad weather canvas blinds were rolled down to close the sides, and passengers had to peep through little flaps to establish exactly where they were.

Clanking and clattering

In 1926 a disgruntled passenger called the trams an 'unmitigated nuisance' and added: 'This noisy, uncomfortable, nerve-shattering, slow and annoying form of locomotion has already been with us too long . . . their huge, unwieldy bulk obstructs the narrow roads; their slow progress impedes all other traffic; and their

Horse-powered tramcars at the corner of Musgrove and Marriot roads, Durban, in 1895. Electric trams were introduced to the city in 1902 and enjoyed a goodly life-span of 47 years

Johannesburg's Commissioner Street in the days of the horse-drawn tram. These and the later electric trams were notorious for their overcrowded discomfort. They were also a constant source of irritation to drivers of carts, whose wheels tended to get caught in the tramlines

clanking and clattering along the straight, varied by demoniac shriekings when they are rounding curves, are torture to the least sensitive ears.'

Cape Town had one of the most scenic tram rides in the world — up the steep Kloof Street to the Nek, where the tranquil suburb of Camps Bay fell away toward the sparkling Atlantic Ocean. The track then zig-zagged down the mountain to the sea-front and back to town. The line was opened in 1902 at the instigation of property developers. These people owned most of Oranjezicht and Camps Bay and hoped to attract buyers.

The scheme was a dismal failure, but the spectacular scenery along the route made it a firm favourite with both locals and visitors for picnic parties and Sunday excursions.

For two decades the trams reigned supreme, both loved and hated. They were so swift that office workers could take the lunchtime special home to the suburbs. But they irritated motorists, whose car wheels would stick in the metal grooves and who were obstructed when the trams halted.

Victory for the buses

In the end, however, it was the petrol engine that won. In the early 1920s, unhampered by the regulations covering trams, motor-bus operators scooped the cream off popular routes. Run by one-man or man-and-wife enterprises, the

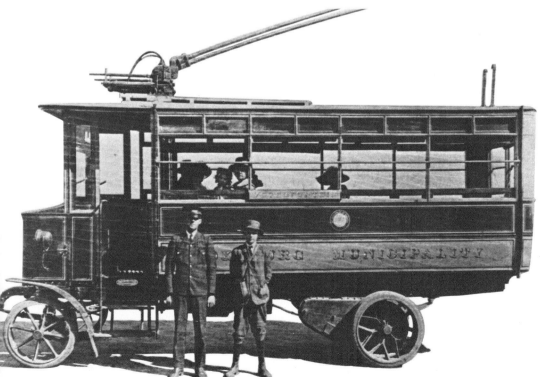

One of Boksburg's experimental trolleybuses, introduced in 1914 and abandoned in 1925. A much-improved model appeared on the South African scene five years later, and stayed

Johannesburg's last tram, given a rousing farewell in 1961 by spectators and passengers, many of them dressed in Edwardian costume

Church Square, Pretoria, when trams ruled the streets. They moved more people more quickly than their horse-drawn predecessors, but were the instruments of many a fatal accident. Passengers slipped and fell overboard in wet weather, or foolishly jumped off between scheduled stops ('Jumping was part and parcel of the express tram system' says author P.R. Coates); pedestrians were run down. For this last eventuality many trams were equipped with special scoops or fenders

buses did not have to meet safety standards and tended to carry an oversized body to pack in as many fare-payers as possible. One critic accused the Cape Town City Council of willingness 'to license every sardine tin on wheels'.

The tram operators countered by putting private detectives aboard buses to report on every deviation from time-tables and routes. The 'bus war' had, however, doomed the tram. Old-established operators took stock and most decided to phase out their trams, replacing them with buses.

Some cities, including Durban, Cape Town and Pretoria, chose trolleybuses, but retained the tram for their busier routes.

THE COMING OF THE TROLLEYBUS

How Cape Town's streets looked in the mid-1930s. The trolleybus was phased out in favour of the more manoeuvrable diesel bus — though today's energy crisis has caused some rethinking and South Africans could, just possibly, ride the trackless tram again

A new era in passenger transport began when the freighter *Halizones* docked in Table Bay on 25 August 1930. As a crane swung its cargo onto the dockside, surprised onlookers saw what appeared to be a squat, double-decker bus with the overhead booms of a tramcar. The trackless tram — or trolleybus — had arrived.

Many cities and towns were looking for an alternative to the conventional tram. Some — Bloemfontein, Germiston and Boksburg — had in fact experimented with trackless trams during the First World War, but without much success.

The trolleybus that arrived in 1930 was a much-improved model. Like the tram, its course was restricted by the overhead power lines, but it could move some five metres from the cable. More important, with its pneumatic tyres and smoothly-humming electric motor, it was almost silent. For the tortured ears of city commuters this was a blessing.

It had been built specially for demonstrations in South Africa by a British company, Guy Motors. The first run was to the Cape Town suburb of Rondebosch. The power lines carried only positive current overhead and a 'snake' of pipe and chain, attached to the bus's negative circuit, was trailed in the groove of the rails. It needed excellent driving to keep it there. On the tailboard an assistant stood ready to slot it back when it pulled clear — which it often did.

The trolleybus was later demonstrated in Durban, Johannesburg and Pretoria. Every-where, experts declared that trackless trams were the mass transport of the future. In 1934 a special law was passed to allow the introduction of trolleybus services, and a fleet of 50 came into operation in Cape Town the following year. Johannesburg bought its first buses in 1936, and Durban and Pretoria soon followed.

But, like the old rail trams, the trolleybus had a fixed route, and its dependence on electricity meant that a power failure could put a whole fleet out of action. Moreover, the Second World War intervened: enormous post-war increases in installation costs scuttled the ambitious plans of the late 1930s. Operators turned to cheaper and more flexible diesel buses.

Nevertheless the trolleybus (it was known as such everywhere in South Africa except Cape Town, where the name 'trackless tram' survived, and Johannesburg, where the *Star* still refuses to spell 'trolley' with an 'e') took a long time dying and might even be resurrected. In the late 1950s Johannesburg took delivery of 90 double-deckers. Some, capable of carrying 107 passengers, were the longest in the world. About half were built by the Italian firm of Alfa Romeo, much better known as manufacturers of high-performance cars.

And in the late 1970s, with the energy crisis escalating dangerously, the government made it known that it would support the experimental re-introduction of trolleybuses to the streets of Johannesburg.

STREAMERS AND BEADS AT THE BEACH

In the early days young couples in Durban would, almost as a matter of course, go to dances by ricksha — the light, elaborately decorated cart pulled by a Zulu resplendent in horned headdress, plumes and skins.

It was sugar pioneer Sir Marshall Campbell who introduced the ricksha to Natal in the 1890s from Japan, where it had been devised by an American missionary in 1853 for his invalid wife. The popularity of the ricksha — in 1903 there were over 1 000 in Durban — soon spread to Cape Town, Pietermaritzburg, Pretoria and even to Rhodesia. The first ones were unadorned and purely functional, but competition from motor transport led the pullers to decorate both themselves and their carts in a bid for fares. Beadwork, streamers, furs and ornaments soon became a dazzling feature of the Durban beachfront.

The race to be airborne

THE PROSPECT OF IMMORTALITY

In the year 1900, no man anywhere had left the ground in a heavier-than-air, powered machine. There had been scores of flights in balloons and airships since the first ascent by Jean-François Pilatre de Rosier in France in 1783, but they were all lighter-than-air efforts. South Africa's first ascent is credited to a Mr Coussy of Cape Town, who sent his cat aloft in a balloon in December 1816.

Nineteenth century enthusiasts also experimented with kites and gliders. Around 1875, South African John Goodman Houshold built his own glider and flew it successfully on the farm Der Magtenburg, north of Howick in Natal. Apparently his technique resembled that of modern hang-gliders: he ran down a grassy slope of the Karkloof Hills until he had enough speed for lift-off.

But the real race was for the honour to be the first to fly a steerable, powered, heavier-than-air machine.

South Africa's first powered flight took place in the year that Blériot flew the English Channel. On 28 December 1909 a visiting Frenchman, Albert Kimmerling, who did not hold an aviator's licence, lifted his Voisin into the air over Nahoon racecourse, East London, and reached a height of six metres.

From 200 eager volunteers, Kimmerling's sponsors selected Miss Ismay Nangle to 'go down to posterity as the first lady to leave South Africa's soil in an aeroplane amid the plaudits of assembled thousands'. This was to have taken place on New Year's Day 1910, but

John Weston aboard his Bristol biplane. This remarkable man was born in an ox wagon in 1873 and was at various times a sailor, whaler, diver, explorer and big-game hunter, and built and flew a glider in America in 1892. He received the British Aeronaut's Certificate No. 38 as well as the Airship Pilot's Certificate No. 23. He was even made an honorary Rear Admiral in the Greek Navy

on landing after a preliminary test flight, the Voisin damaged its undercarriage and the wooden propeller blades shattered as they struck the turf. The honour that was to have been Miss Nangle's went to Julia Hyde Stansfield, social editress of the *Rand Daily Mail* and the *Sunday Times,* later that year in Johannesburg, after a new propeller of 'aluminium-copper riveted over steel web' had been fashioned by a Johannesburg engineer and toolmaker, Silvio Marucchi.

Miss Stansfield, though, was beaten to it by a man. The very first aeroplane passenger in

South Africa was Thomas Thornton, who paid Kimmerling £100 after being taken up on 19 March 1910 from the top of Sydenham Hill, Johannesburg. Coloured flags flown from prominent buildings advised the citizens of Johannesburg if the weather was suitable for flying, 'so that the sightseers will have ample time to make arrangements for the trip to Sydenham'.

There were dozens of South African designers of flying machines, but few of their ideas ever left the drawing board, and none left the ground until the Blériot-type monoplane,

RISING ABOVE IT ALL, THE BALLOON

Early balloons were lifted aloft by hot air or hydrogen and in the beginning, ballooning was more of a life-or-death adventure or military necessity than a sport. And when it became more popular it was still very much a sport of the 'mad gentry' — primarily because of the expensive equipment and incredibly complicated operation.

Addressing the Southern African Museums Association in 1976, Hannes Oberholzer, author of the book, *Pioneers of Early Aviation in South Africa,* recalled an early flight in which George Kingswell, editor of the *Sunday Times,* joined Lionel 'Sos' Cohen and the celebrated Swiss balloonist, Captain Spelterini, for a trip — with a case of champagne on board to boost morale.

On being informed that the release valve cord had come adrift, Cohen (having consumed a large quantity of liquid courage) risked his life by climbing up the thin ropes to the release valve. The intrepid team sank back to earth without mishap.

South Africa possessed only one balloon, the *Bergwind,* until the mid-Seventies, when an international balloon race was held in South Africa for the first time. The first South African-made balloon flew for the first time in March 1977.

A modern hot-air balloon hovers in the Cape air. The heat source is a gas flame

This balloon, photographed over Durban in 1912, was used for advertising and aerial photographs

Balloons were used extensively during the Anglo-Boer War for reconnaissance, like this one at Ladysmith

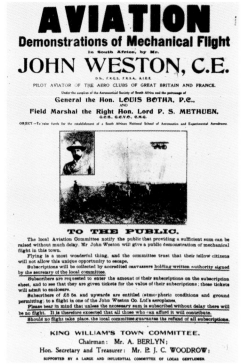

Payment of £5.5s. 'and upwards' to King William's Town Committee guaranteed a flight 'atmospheric conditions and ground permitting'. 'Flying is a most wonderful thing,' the poster encouraged

SENDING IT BY AIR

South Africa's first airmail flight took place in December 1911, when Evelyn Driver took off in his Blériot monoplane (top) from the Kenilworth racecourse carrying a bag of specially-designed and copyrighted postcards. He covered the 12,8 km to Oldham's Field, Muizenberg, in seven and a half minutes, and after the ceremonial handing over of the 'mails' he flew back, taking five minutes longer against a moderate north-westerly wind. Above: one of the first postcards airmailed in South Africa.

built by French immigrant Alfred Raison for Cecil Bredell, a prominent Johannesburg timber merchant, took to the air at Highlands North, Johannesburg, on 30 April 1911, piloted by Bredell.

With the exception of the JAP engine and the motorcycle wheels of the undercarriage, the entire aircraft had been built by Raison, working from handwritten plans of Blériot's cross-Channel model.

Just over two weeks later on 20 May, Alfred Brunett, another Frenchman, successfully flew his home-built Farman-type biplane for a short distance at Rosebank, Johannesburg.

But the first wholly South African aeroplane was that built at Brandfort in 1909 by John Weston. Although it actually flew in France before Bredell and Brunett were airborne, it made its South African début only on 18 June 1911, when Weston flew it at Kimberley.

On 6 July 1911 the *Friend* reported that 'Mr Weston . . . flew a short distance with Miss Cressie Leonard, the well-known pantomime "boy" who is appearing just now at the Standard Theatre'. Readers of the *Sunday Post* were diverted by Miss Leonard's own account of

the flight which took place on 5 July:

'I had dressed for the part in a close fitting jersey costume, with no motor scarves to vex the propeller . . . At last, as sunset waned and the photographers began to cease from troubling, I ascended to the chair of execution.' Afterwards she described her emotions: 'The biplane quivered with terrific energy; at last, bursting its bonds, it dashed forward and away. A rushing mighty wind, a feeling of entire mental detachment from everything mundane — that is what I felt. It seemed that we were the first that ever burst into this limitless ocean, cold air that for a million years had awaited its conqueror . . .'

The comments of Miss Leonard and those of other elated passengers were later published in an advertising booklet by the John Weston Aviation Co. Ltd, and sold at threepence per copy. Weston was a cautious pilot, and never flew to great heights.

A *Sunday Times* reporter described Weston as 'a wonderful man for inspiring confidence in a passenger', while another convert went into raptures over the view from aloft: 'You see a world in miniature below you; tiny men, stunted trees, hills like little wrinkles on the face of the earth, and away to the coast steamers in the river resembling the toy-boats of childhood's days. You feel like a trespasser on the Deity's preserves.'

Weston, described as 'the grandfather of South African aviation', died in 1950, having seen his 1911 prediction fulfilled: 'In the course of time . . . aviation will expand beyond all bounds, and probably before long we shall be able to carry passengers and mails by aeroplane in perfect safety.'

Albert Kimmerling's 50 hp Voisin flies over Orange Grove, Johannesburg, in February 1910. Kimmerling's 'Flying Matchbox' made the first controlled power-driven flight in South Africa on 28 December 1909 — a short flight at East London. He crashed the Voisin and damaged the propeller a few days later

A 'Flying Fortnight' was staged at the Turffontein racecourse in 1912. The programme featured aerial switchback, aerial steeplechase — and a bomb-drop

The record-breakers

THE EPIC FLIGHT OF VAN RYNEVELD AND BRAND

The London *Daily Mail* had offered a prize of £10 000 for the first flight between London and Cape Town. Little more than a year had passed since the end of the First World War, and technological progress had ushered in an era of increasingly ambitious exploits in the air. The Atlantic had been conquered; London and Sydney had been linked. But Africa was still a challenge, and two young South Africans were among those willing to pit their skill and courage against unknown flying conditions and immense distances.

Helperus Andreas (Pierre) van Ryneveld, born in the Free State town of Senekal, was a decorated war veteran of the Royal Flying Corps and a lieutenant-colonel in the Union Defence Force. His co-pilot, also a South African, was Flight Lieutenant Christopher Joseph Quintin Brand of the Royal Air Force — another wartime ace who had been credited with 13 kills in aerial combat. Van Ryneveld and Brand met for the first time shortly before the race. 'Would you like to join me?' asked Van Ryneveld. 'You bet I would,' replied Brand. 'It was always a boyhood dream of mine to fly from the Cape to London. I suppose it's the same thing if I make the trip in the other direction!'

The two airmen were joined by Vickers mechanics Burton and Sharratt, and the race was on. The route had been surveyed by the RAF during the previous year: rough landing sites had been prepared and stores deposited along the way. The South Africans were to fly a Vickers Vimy bomber, and similar machines had been entered by the RAF itself, and by *The Times* of London. Another newspaper, the *Daily Telegraph*, entered a

Top: Silver Queen *with her crew at Brooklands aerodrome, near London, before the start of the historic flight.* Right: *Quintin Brand, left, and Pierre van Ryneveld.* Far right: The Sphere *portrays Van Ryneveld greeting his mother in Bloemfontein.* Above: Voortrekker, *the second replacement aircraft supplied by General Smuts*

Handley Page 0/400, and a privately-owned De Havilland D.H.14A completed the field.

Neither South African had flown the Vimy until two weeks before the race, but they were undeterred. Their Rolls Royce-powered aircraft was painted in gleaming aluminium and christened with a name that was soon to be-

---

THRILLS AND SPILLS IN 1932

Perhaps the greatest event on the aviation calendar in 1932 was the spectacular African Air Rally, held at the Rand Airport on 17 and 18 September 1932. The *South African Motorist* reported an attendance of '45 to 50 thousand persons'. Dr Samuel Evans, first president of the Johannesburg Light Plane Club, told the magazine: 'Sunday's Rally at the Rand Airport provided conclusive evidence as to the enormous progress that has taken place in aviation since 1910.'

Features included an 'arrivals' competition, aerobatic events (during which a Mr Quinn of the Durban Light Plane Club replaced a wheel in mid-air and performed wing-walking stunts), aerial bombing, an obstacle race, 'balloon busting' and 'big-game hunting'. In another stunt the same Mr Quinn dropped over 500 metres before managing to open his parachute.

---

come a household word: she was *Silver Queen*. At 7 a.m. on 4 February 1920, *Silver Queen* took off from Brooklands airfield near London, turned into the wind, and was swallowed in the mist. Two eventful days later, Van Ryneveld and Brand landed safely at Taranto in Italy.

The Taranto-Libya stretch was to be rough. Violent turbulence tossed the large aircraft about as if it were a toy, the instrument lights failed, and lashing headwinds used up fuel so fast that tragedy seemed inevitable. Exhaustion began to take its toll. Van Ryneveld frequently shone his torch into Brand's face to ensure that he was awake, and when he took the controls at 4 a.m. he had to slap his own face to stay awake. Eleven hours after leaving the instep of Italy, *Silver Queen* skidded across the desert sand close to the Libyan coast — over 300 km from their planned landing spot. 'Fewer finer incidents than this have been known in the records of aviation,' said a British newspaper. Public interest soared in what was now definitely a race.

At Cairo, Flight Sergeant Newman replaced Burton as mechanic, and the new team took off at 7.30 p.m. on 19 February for what was planned as a non-stop flight to Khartoum. But there was a stop. After 5½ hours' flying, Brand noticed that the temperature reading for the starboard engine was dangerously high. They would have to land, and quickly. The aircraft touched down close to the shimmering Nile — and then the horrified pilots saw a pile of boulders looming out of the darkness dead ahead. There was no time for evasive action: a splintering crash, and *Silver*

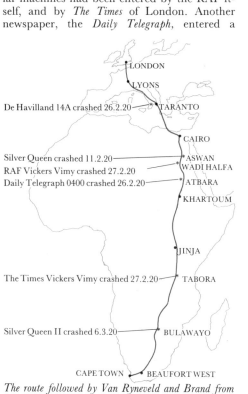

The route followed by Van Ryneveld and Brand from London to Cape Town in 1920, and crash sites

LONDON
LYONS
De Havilland 14A crashed 26.2.20 — TARANTO
CAIRO
Silver Queen crashed 11.2.20 — ASWAN
RAF Vickers Vimy crashed 27.2.20 — WADI HALFA
Daily Telegraph 0400 crashed 26.2.20 — ATBARA
KHARTOUM
JINJA
The Times Vickers Vimy crashed 27.2.20 — TABORA
Silver Queen II crashed 6.3.20 — BULAWAYO
CAPE TOWN — BEAUFORT WEST

Left: Lady Bailey was an apparently tireless flyer. In 1933 she made an unsuccessful attempt to beat the London-Cape record held by Amy Johnson, but was forced to land in the Sahara after running out of fuel. She spent four days in the desert. Above left: Lady Bailey after her arrival at Le Bourguet. Above right: posing in front of her famous aircraft before her departure for South Africa

Queen was a write-off. Luckily, nobody was injured.

Smuts to the rescue

General Smuts was not about to let the South Africans abandon the race. Within 11 days another Vimy, supplied by the RAF in Cairo and powered by the engines from the crashed aircraft, was winging its way south. *Silver Queen II* had a lot of time to make up: *The Times* aircraft was already at Jinja, 3 400 km ahead. There were more frustrating delays. Then, at the end of February, the South Africans learnt that both *The Times* Vimy and the RAF Vimy had crashed on 27 February, the D.H.14A had crashed in Italy, and the *Daily Telegraph* Handley Page had crashed near El Shereik, in the Sudan.

The race was not over yet. At dawn on 6 March, *Silver Queen II* lifted off from Bulawayo's racecourse, struggled to gain height, faltered, and plunged down into the veld. Although the full petrol tanks split open on impact, there was no fire or explosion. Four shaken and bitterly disappointed men clambered from the wreckage. Once again Smuts intervened, this time supplying the team with a De Havilland D.H. 9 — one of the 100 aircraft given by the British government to form the nucleus of the South African Air Force. Christened *Voortrekker*, the third aircraft took off (minus the two mechanics, who had continued by train to South Africa) bound for Serowe, Palapye and Pretoria. Finally, at 4 p.m. on Saturday 20 March, *Voortrekker* rolled to a stop at the Wynberg airfield, Cape Town.

Because they hadn't completed the journey in one aircraft, Van Ryneveld and Brand were not eligible for the *Daily Mail* prize, but Smuts announced that each of the pilots was to be awarded £2 500 in recognition of their feat.

A TOUSLE-HAIRED WOMAN IN RUSSIAN BOOTS

Mary Bailey, wife of the South African mining magnate Sir Abe Bailey, was old enough to know better. Or so the cynics thought. But they changed their tune when the tousle-haired, rasp-voiced aviatrix planted her Russian boots on the tarmac at the Swartkops air force base near Pretoria. It was 26 April 1928, and she had just arrived from England in a tiny De Havilland Moth. Soon afterwards this remarkable woman returned to London —and a string of honours. Lady Bailey had become the first pilot (and the first woman) to fly solo in both directions.

Lady Bailey had always been a strong-willed and adventurous woman. She received her pilot's licence in 1926 and in the following year set an altitude record for light aircraft when she climbed to a height of 5 540 metres. She also became the first woman pilot to fly across the Irish Sea. In March 1928 she took off from London, her luggage packed into two small suitcases. She was off to Cape Town for a holiday!

A sandstorm forced her down north of Khartoum, where Sudanese authorities refused to allow her to continue without the escort of an RAF officer as far as the Ugandan border. All went well until Lady Bailey reached Tanganyika. On the morning of 10 April, Lady Rossmore received a cable in London from her daughter: 'Crashed at Tabora but self alright.' It was a close shave, though. The wrecked Moth was lying upside down when she clambered from the cockpit. Despite the two-week delay caused by the wait for a replacement aircraft, Lady Bailey finally reached Cape Town 44 days after leaving London. Her husband was waiting: 'Hello, Abe, how are you?' she asked, adding: 'I am a bit late, but I got muddled up in the mountains.'

She selected the West Coast route for her return flight, arriving at London's Croydon airport in January 1929 to a tumultuous reception. For her feat, she was made a Dame Commander of the Order of the British Empire and awarded the Britannia Challenge Trophy for the most meritorious performance in the air during the year.

Lady Bailey died in Cape Town in 1960 after a life of adventure matched by few women. A veteran reporter said in tribute: '. . . she had proved . . . that women pilots with air sense and courage could share in the conquest of the air on an equality with men. Long after her personal triumph had faded, it would be remembered that Lady Bailey had flown half the length of the world alone, relying upon her own grit and the skill and workmanship of British manufacturers.'

TRIMMING THE TIME

Pioneers such as Lady Bailey and British flyer Sir Alan Cobham (who, with a mechanic and photographer, flew from London to Cape Town and back during late 1925 and early 1926 in the same aircraft) helped to inspire a host of record-breaking flights between England and South Africa. In 1930 a South African, Captain R.F. Caspareuthus, covered the distance in 8½ days. The following year saw a new record as Lieutenant-Commander Glen Kidston reduced the time to six days and ten hours, to lose it to Gordon Store and Miss Peggy Salaman (five days, six hours and 40 minutes). In March 1932 Jim Mollison trimmed the record to four days, 17 hours and 30 minutes, but was beaten the same year by his wife, Amy Johnson.

Sir Alan Cobham flew from Croydon to the Cape, 1925/26

Flying-Officer Clouston and Mrs Kirby-Green flew Croydon-Cape-Croydon in under six days in 1937

Amy Johnson with her De Havilland Gypsy Moth before her solo flight England — Australia in 1930

C.W.A. Scott climbs out of his Percival Vega Gull after winning the England-Johannesburg air race in 1936

Briton Sheila Scott flew from London to Cape Town in 1967 in three days, two hours, 29 minutes

Commercial aviation takes off

A South African Airways Boeing 747 Combi. This 242-seater 'Jumbo', introduced by SAA in 1980, has a side freight door for larger containers

FROM GYPSY MOTH TO JUNKERS

South African Airways owes its roots to one man: Major Allister Miller, the distinguished First World War pilot whose airline, South African Aerial Transports, was the first to operate in this country. In its second month, November 1919, the airline hit the headlines when the Johannesburg *Star* hired Major Miller himself to fly 1 200 copies of the newspaper to Durban. But after just a year the company was in liquidation, and Major Miller turned to politics.

'The Flying MP' finally realised his dream of a regular airmail-passenger service in 1929, when a small government subsidy enabled him to float Union Airways. Five tiny, open Gypsy Moths, each seating only one passenger, made up the initial fleet. The pilots were Major Miller, Captains R.F. Caspareuthus and G.W. Bellin, both trained by the South African Air Force, and Captain W.F. Davenport. The inaugural flight took place on 26 August 1929 when Miller took off from Maitland for Port Elizabeth with five bags of mail.

Pioneer passengers, flying in all weathers with only goggles and a flying helmet for protection, were intrepid souls. Even Port Elizabeth, then headquarters of Union Airways,

Major Allister Miller at the Johannesburg racecourse in December 1917. He launched a recruiting drive for the Royal Flying Corps during the First World War

Beaufort West, 1920, and the crashed Handley-Page. It was to have been the first commercial Cape Town/Johannesburg flight carrying mail and passengers

The first passenger-carrying machine used on regular air services: a Union Airways Fokker lands in 1930

Left: A Union Airways Junkers at the Stamford Hill Aerodrome in 1931. Union Airways, long beset by financial difficulties, signed an agreement with the Junkers Company after two disastrous crashes. Above: The interior of an SAA Junkers used on domestic services in the 1930s

possessed only a rudimentary airport. According to the publication, *South African Airways Presents: Fifty Years of Flight*, 'Mr Kenneth Dowdle . . . of Port Elizabeth . . . recalls taking a flight from Port Elizabeth to Cape Town on Christmas Day, 1931 . . . "When you arrived at the airport you saw before you a bare stretch of open veld, with nothing much more than a petrol pump to suggest that this was an aerodrome."'

In January 1930, when Union Airways introduced a faster, more luxurious aircraft, the closed six-seater Fokker Universal, a passenger on the first flight still found conditions spartan in the extreme. Dr R.D. Laurie recalled his experiences in the *Eastern Province Herald* in the mid-Fifties: 'In those days there were no paper bags, and no soft-handed hostesses to stroke a man's fevered brow, you know. I slid open a small glass side window and stuck out my head. To vomit against a

A BOAC flying boat after landing on the Vaal dam in 1948. Passengers were taken off by launch to the jetty

120-mile per hour gale was no easy matter.' Dr Laurie paid £18 for a return flight from Port Elizabeth to Cape Town.

Disaster struck on Friday, 13 November 1931, when a Union Airways Puss Moth crashed into the mountainside above Sir Lowry's Pass near Cape Town, killing Captain Davenport and both passengers. Just seven weeks later the Fokker was destroyed in a crash-landing near East London, though Major Miller and his passengers escaped injury. Bad luck continued to dog Union Airways. The Eshowe air disaster of December 1933, with a loss of five lives, was the final straw. In February 1934 the government took over the ailing airline and renamed it South African Airways.

SAA's fleet of luxurious 'giant' Junkers, each fitted with adjustable padded leather seats for 14 passengers, operated daily internal services, and regular external flights as far afield as Kisumu, in Kenya.

When civil aviation resumed (it was halted in 1940 by the Second World War), changes in the SAA fleet were rapid. Lockheed Lodestars were supplemented in 1945 by Avro Yorks and in 1946-47 by larger Skymasters. In 1950 SAA took delivery of four Constellations, replacing the Lodestars, and by 1956 was operating the fast DC7Bs on its international services. Next to follow were seven Viscounts, used until 1970 on the 'Skycoach' service.

The Boeing age began in 1960 with the Boeing 707, followed by the Boeing 727, with its distinctive tail-fin, in 1965. By 1980 SAA was transporting over four million passengers a year.

Major Miller's dream had become reality.

THE TRANS-AFRICA RUN

The Trans-Africa service was pioneered in late 1927 and early 1928 by the British airman, Sir Alan Cobham, in the first flying boat to visit South Africa. It was a courageous flight over largely uncharted air routes.

Imperial Airways began its regular service between London and Cape Town in 1932, entrusting pilots and planes to 'airports' that were little more than stretches of sand or mud (depending on the weather) marked with a white circle. Anthills and herds of wild ani-

A Lockheed Lodestar at Durban's old airport. They flew at 322 km/h and carried 12 passengers. The trip to London took 2½ days (daytime flying)

mals were not the only hazards. In *A Century of Transport*, A. van Lingen records the tale of a pilot 'much alarmed to see some natives charging across the aerodrome waving their spears ... To his astonishment and relief, however, they disappeared into a hut marked "Shell" and emerged in a much more reassuring garb' — ready to refuel his plane.

An assortment of aircraft flew the Trans-Africa route until flying boats took over the whole run in 1937, cutting the time from England to South Africa in 1932 from 10½

days (London to Cape Town) to only 6½ days (Southampton to Durban). In 1938 the fare to Durban — the trip now took 4½ days — was £125 single.

But the days of these gracious aircraft were numbered, and in 1945 they were replaced by Avro Yorks for the SAA/BOAC 'Springbok' service. Though re-introduced in 1948, flying boats were finally retired in 1950 because they were too leisurely for the new age of speed.

Comets (withdrawn after two disasters), Boeing 707s and VC10s replaced the old-style elegance with increasing size and speed: by 1971 the flying time for a BOAC VC10 between Johannesburg and London had shrunk to a mere 11 hours, 45 minutes.

A truly grand way to travel

Anyone travelling on the Trans-Africa run in its heyday would long remember the glamour and excitement of the trip. Dr Peter Hafner of Port Elizabeth recalled: 'It was a truly grand way to travel, a real Cook's tour.' Passengers on the flying boats could walk up and down the promenade saloon, watching the game below; pilots would circle obligingly over large herds for photographs.

Norah Henshilwood of Cape Town recorded her Trans-Africa flight of 1933 in a private diary. Clutching smelling salts to combat the inevitable bumps, she flew first in Atlanta monoplanes, then (from Uganda) in a Handley-Page biplane, and finally (from Cairo) in the romantic flying boats.

Dressing for dinner could present problems. A 1932 article in the *S.A. Motorist* by 'an Air-woman who has done the Trans-African trip' cautioned: 'You will find that you and your luggage, may weigh 221 lbs ... therefore wise women who intend to travel by air, will ignore the fashionable decree that curves are coming in again.' 'Air-woman' advised a light fibre suitcase, some 'diaphanous frocks and undies', including six pairs of stockings ('they cannot be procured in Central Africa'), and for daily travelling a well-cut coat with fur collar, a skirt and a silk blouse. 'You will look well turned out whether you alight from the plane in the heart of Africa, or on the busy aerodrome of Le Bourget...'

Morning sun illuminates a Boeing 727 at Jan Smuts Airport, Johannesburg. The first five aircraft arrived in 1965

Fashion Parade

Fashionable South Africans, particularly in the Cape Colony and Natal, where loyalty to the British Empire ran high, took their lead unquestioningly from London in 1900. Whatever was respectable in that cool northern climate was also here — despite the huge differences in conditions and climate.

South African women suffered layers of underwear and the vice-like grip of their corsets in ladylike silence, trailing their heavy dresses in the dust of long, hot summers with unshakeable composure. Gentlemen still wore three-piece suits of flannel, serge and tweed. Waistcoats, stiff collars and hats were considered essential for all but the most sporting of occasions.

Children, less conscious of fashion and respectability, were nevertheless obliged to endure the summer in heavy, scratchy clothes. Boys perspired in serge suits and knee-length socks; girls in frocks and underwear only a little less complicated than their mothers'. Babies protested beneath cap, robe and pelisse. Pregnant women pretended they were not. . .

The First World War broke the spell. Dress for man, woman and child alike grew more and more informal with each passing decade as concessions were made to the climate and South Africa's way of life. Frills gave way to denim jeans; moralists waxed eloquent on the subject of skimpy swimsuits and décolletage.

Styles changed with each passing decade, hemlines rising, falling and rising again until, in the late Fifties and Sixties, youth rebelled. Mary Quant, Carnaby Street and Jean Shrimpton challenged the conventions, the unwritten rules of fashion were relaxed, and South Africans, like the rest of the Western world, were soon free to wear more or less what they liked. They still are.

Johanna (left) and Elizabeth Bastiaans, daughters of a Stellenbosch chemist, in the cumbersome dresses and ornate hats worn by women in the early 1900s

Edwardian extravaganza

THE AGE OF ELEGANCE

At the turn of the century it was a woman's pride that her dress touched the ground all round — hardly a practical fashion when streets were either dustbowls or quagmires. Nor an hygienic one. 'Women cause danger to those with whom they live by bringing dirt into the house,' said a 1903 edition of the *Commercial Review and South African Storekeeper*. But, as a 1920s writer in *Outspan* recalled: 'A modest woman would rather gather up muddy filth than be so unwomanly as to show an ankle in those dark days.'

Practicalities aside, though, the first decade was very much the age of elegance — and extravagance. Materials were soft, supple and luxurious: crêpe de chine, voile, chiffon, organdie, silk muslin, worn over a frou-frou of rustling taffeta petticoats. Favourite colour of the day was mauve, preferably in pale, swooning tones of lilac but sometimes deepening to wood-violet and, reported Johannesburg's *Fashion and Music Album*, 'a purple shade called dahlia or puce'.

There was a positive mania for frills, flounces, tucks and trimmings, especially of lace. Tea gowns and the daringly décolleté evening frocks dripped with lace from collar, sleeve, bodice and petticoat. Even the more subdued street clothes — tailored suits of velvet or linen — had their share of trimmings and were worn with elaborate blouses, embroidered waistcoats, kid gloves, muffs or fluffy parasols. And, of course, with enormous hats.

Edwardian hats were a milliner's dream. Widening to accommodate the high, doughnut-

Princess Christian (centre), Queen Victoria's daughter, visited the Cape in 1904. The women in the group display all the trimmings and finery of Edwardian high fashion: lace and tucks; ornate hats (designed to accommodate high pompadour hairstyles); kid gloves; parasols to ward off the African sun, and an ostrich-feather boa

shaped pompadour hairstyle that was in vogue, they became veritable gardens of flowers, fruit, ribbons, feathers and even stuffed birds.

But fashions did become less flamboyant. Dresses became straighter in outline, at first excessively narrow (the hobble skirt) but soon looser and high-waisted. At the outbreak of war in 1914 hats became narrow-brimmed and dropped their lavish trimmings in favour of one or two feathers, a ribbon and a small hatpin. This coincided with a change in women's hairstyles: they were smaller, closer to the head and distinguished by the 'marcel wave'.

The simplicity of the new dress styles, which persisted throughout the First World War, encouraged sales of the ready-to-wear garment. Ready-made clothing had in fact long been popular in South Africa, a country far from the fashion centres of Europe, and with a small and scattered population. 'Mail order' was often combined with 'made-to-order': major department stores sent out illustrated catalogues offering everything from drawers and corsets to elaborate hats. For a frock, the buyer had to provide a dozen different measuring points to ensure a perfect fit.

Although fashionable Edwardian ladies trussed themselves up to the neck by day, necklines plunged to surprisingly sensual levels at night. This Paris model gown is typical of the trend

Mrs Joseph Chamberlain, in a 14 hp New Orleans motor car at Camps Bay. With the advent of the car and the growing popularity of motoring, monstrous Edwardian hats became an undoubted handicap, needing to be held on with enveloping veils of chiffon, while the lovely but impractical and scarcely washable gowns were protected by large, drab dust-cloaks, or 'dusters'. A writer complained in Fashion and Music Album *in 1904 that 'the motor car has not been with us long enough for the artificers of new modes to devise a substitute for the hideous motor veil'. The same writer predicted a fortune for the inventor of 'motor habiliments which shall combine beauty and utility'*

THE CADET

THE LIEUTENANT

THE CAPTAIN

THE MAJOR

THE GENERAL

The low necklines of the 1900s evening wear did not escape the comment of contemporary cartoonists

1900   1905   1910   1918   1920

A selection of dresses worn during the first two decades of the century. Clothes loosened up; the S-shape and tight waist disappeared; hemlines rose a little, and a woman's lot became much more comfortable — especially after the First World War, when fashions reflected the increasingly emancipated status of women

Formality was the order of the day at the turn of the century, even for outdoor leisure activities. This family enjoyed the pleasures of the river in their abundant and uncomfortable everyday clothes

FINE FEATHERS FOR FINE LADIES

The Edwardians may have loved lace, but for a time they loved feathers even more. Ostrich farming began, in the Oudtshoorn area of the Cape, around 1867 and the popularity of soft, billowing plumes reached a peak about 1882. The industry went through a series of slumps and peaks, which should have been admonitory. But the boom years returned with a vengeance — between 1903 and 1913 South Africa exported £19 million worth of feathers.

The bigger farms accommodated 600 or more birds; each bird brought in between £5 and £6 a year; a breeding pair sold at anything from £500 to £1 000. Fortunes were made and stone palaces were built around Oudtshoorn.

For Court Presentations, white feathers were mandatory and enormous prices were paid on the London market — up to £112 for a pound of selected prime white plumes.

Feathers had other uses: they were carried as huge, curling fans and, as swirling boas, were draped around elegant Edwardian necks. A good boa could cost ten guineas and was much prized. Norah Henshilwood, in her book *A Cape Childhood*, remembers that, in Cape Town, 'Mother kept her boa, with her best dresses and coats, in an ottoman . . . We loved to smell the sweet scents of lavender or orris root that rose whenever she opened the lid of this couch-like box to reveal the folds of tissue paper from which she withdrew her dress or feather boa'.

Hats rich in plumes also cost a great deal, but while the rage was on no South African lady would have been without one. A Johannesburg commentator described three very fashionable spring hats: the Tricorne, the Marquise and the Directoire, which was 'very wide and high in front . . . in felt and velvet . . . with a waving wide

ostrich feather on either side'. The Marquise sported an upturned brim and buckle, and like the Tricorne, or three-cornered hat, could be trimmed at home with chiffon and feathers 'placed so that they cover the crown nicely and droop over the hair'.

The boom lasted a bare decade: over-production (which relegated feathers from the special to the commonplace), fashion fickleness and the war brought about the virtual collapse of the industry, though ostrich boas and fans continued to be mildly popular during the 1920s.

Mary van Buren, leading lady of the Daniel Frawley Company, wearing the de rigueur ostrich feather boa and hat, 1904. A year earlier, the Commercial Review and South African Storekeeper, *reacting to complaints by the Society for the Protection of Birds, quoted an ostrich farmer's reassurance that removing plumes from the bird was a painless business: the feathers were cut, not plucked — unless the ostrich had died 'from accident or otherwise'*

The big squeeze

THE FASHIONABLE DISCOMFORT OF WHALEBONES AND LACES

'Physician claims that 10 000 women have been squeezed to death by corsets during the last five years.'

This extravagant report appeared in a South African newspaper in 1871. Not surprisingly, its somewhat alarmist content had absolutely no effect on ladies of fashion, who continued to cause themselves the utmost discomfort in pursuit of the 18-inch waist. Commenting on a 1903 report of a young Irish girl who died from 'cardiac syncope accelerated by tight lacing', the *Commercial Review and South African Storekeeper* said: 'It is out of the question, of course, for drapers to take upon themselves the advisory duties of medical men in the matter of attire; but we certainly think that assistants might be instructed to mention to customers, should the necessity arise, that very tight lacing is always harmful and sometimes fatal.'

The object of the corset (the term 'stays' was dropped towards the end of the 19th century) in Victorian days had been to produce a wasp waist and raise the bosom. Whalebone, laces and a strong helper, with her knee in your back, were essentials.

In 1900 standard dress was a yoked bodice with a wide gored skirt, still with a hint of a bustle at the back worn over stifling layers of underclothes: chemise, tightly-laced corset, black or brown lisle stockings, garters, camisole, long lace-edged drawers, short petticoat, a couple of muslin full-length petticoats and finally a beautifully flounced, good-quality cotton petticoat.

In 1901 the S-line took over, occasioned by what Europe insisted on calling the 'health corset'. It had been designed to avoid harmful pressure on the abdomen, but women ignored that and laced it as tightly as ever over their fashionably junoesque curves, pushing the bosom forward and the hips back into a new distorted stance. In the words of a Harvey Greenacre &

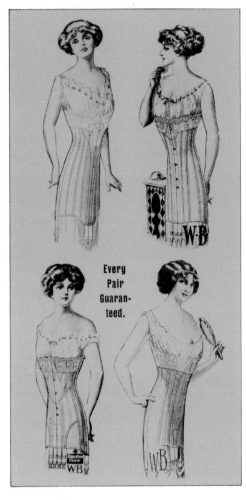

Every Pair Guaranteed.

Co advertisement for Nemo corsets, 'the flesh must be controlled'.

By 1910 the French designers had banished the elaborately corseted figure and introduced the beginnings of the natural look, which required a longer but lighter and less boned corset. European ladies let out their breath with relief.

The Empire line was soon popular every-

Norah Waugh, in her book Corsets and Crinolenes, *describes the corset as 'a miracle of cutting and shaping. It was constructed from numerous curved pieces, all expertly joined together and traversed by a quantity of whalebone and steel of varying degrees of thickness and weight'. Left: a selection of W.B. corsets advertised in a 1913 edition of* The Pictorial. *Above: John Orr's Royal Worcester model and the elegant shape it produced*

where, and a Warner's 'Daphne' rustproof corset in the longer, straighter style was advertised in *Die Brandwag* in December 1911 by Norman Anstey & Co at a cut price of 8/6. You could also buy from them their heavily boned 'Eudeline' corset, specially designed for 'stout figures', at an expensive 27/6.

But with dictates of fashion and the imminent appearance of rayon and elastic, the days of long drawers, along with all those layers of lavish white underwear, were as numbered as the days of the all-confining corset.

Handbags and face creams

The trend towards modesty, though, wasn't without the exceptions. For instance, Edwardian reticules of mesh, beads or velvet were to be replaced by larger handbags of leather and tapestry. Women were becoming more mobile, and they needed to carry a greater number and variety of personal effects than could be fitted into a sovereign purse: now it was also comb, mirror, perfume and a few discreet cosmetics. These, though, would have been no more than rouge, pale face-powder and perhaps a little lipsalve for the very daring.

Most cosmetics were prepared at home. The important exception was face powder, sold in loose or leaflet form. The 'Egyptian' brand came in three shades: pink, white and natural.

Ladies always wore hats and had not yet exposed their skins to the ravages of the southern sun. Face creams were still largely homemade

---

'AFTER I HAD TRIED PILLS, MASSAGE AND WOODEN CUPS . . .'

Quack remedies weren't confined to the world of medicine. This 1912 before-and-after advertisement, published in the *Illustrated Star*, was headlined 'How I Enlarged My Bust Six Inches In Thirty Days'. The lady in question, Margarette Merlain, vouched that she 'felt like a new being, for with no bust I realised I was really neither a man nor a woman, but just a sort of creature half way between.

'With what pity must every man look at every woman who presents to him a flat chest – a chest like his own! Can such a woman inspire in a man those feelings and emotions which can only be inspired by a real and true woman . . .?

'The very men who shunned me, and even the very women who passed me carelessly by when I was so horribly flat-chested and had no bust, became my most ardent admirers. I had been imposed upon by charlatans and frauds, who sold me all sorts of pills and appliances for enlarging my bust, but which did me no good whatever. I therefore determined my unfortunate sisters should no longer be robbed by those "fakirs" and frauds, and I wish to warn all women against them. I feel I should give my secret to all my sisters who need it. Merely enclose two penny stamps for reply, and I will send you particulars free by return post.'

Little more than a decade later Ms Merlain and her converts must have regretted their success: in the 1920s the flattest chest was considered the most 'inspiring'.

Fragrances were innocently named. Many, with such labels as Hasu-no-Hana and Shem-el-Nissin, reflected the Edwardian's fascination for the 'Mysterious Orient'

preparations of lemon, cucumber and rose water. In our climate heat must have presented problems — there were no deodorants, only dress guards of waterproof material to sew in under the arm (these were variously known as 'preservers', 'onanoffs' and 'always readys'), and the masking powers of perfume. The *South African Domestic Monthly* had a regular beauty page containing a wealth of useful hints: rub coconut oil on eyebrows; a mixture of benzine and rosewater on the ears to make them a delicate pink. An important beauty asset was a head of rich, lustrous hair, and magazines of the time were full of advertisements for treatments and dyes. Switches were also popular — a 16-inch piece of real hair cost 19/6.

Though Stuart Cloete, the South African novelist who grew up in Paris during the *belle époque*, called it 'the age . . . of heavy perfumes: patchouli, lilac, tuberose, violet, jasmine', in the hotter air of South Africa women seemed to prefer fresh English lavender water and eau de cologne. Advertisements advised no lady to be without Zenobia Eau de Cologne when 'fatigued or overcome by heat'.

The remarkable, and unnatural, S-shape appeared in 1901 with the oddly-named 'health corset'

LEGS – FROM LISLE TO A TIGHT NEW FREEDOM

1910

'A new freedom for the Sixties girl', said the 1966 advertising slogan.

The pantihose of today is a far cry from the hosiery worn by South African ladies of 1900. For them there was little choice. Lisle stockings were uniform, and the colours offered were a trendy black or brown. For evening wear those who could afford them wore black or white silk ones.

By 1911 things hadn't progressed much further – Norman Anstey & Co advertised 'Two pairs of Lisle Stockings for 1/9'. And the colours? Brown and black. Lest more colour be attempted, the *Rand Daily Mail* warned: 'Don't wear cheap bright-hued stockings; the dye may come out during wear and prove injurious.' But those ordinary lisle stockings went on forever, and stocking dyes for tired hosiery were big business, Hawley's Hygienic Black British Dye being a favourite.

By 1915 the female ankle was showing and the demand for finer stockings popularised silk. In 1920 Scotts of Cape Town advertised 'Pure Silk Stockings, English make, with Seam at Back . . . Black, white and tan, 12/6 a pair'. For the less extravagant, there were the shorter 'Silk ankle Stockings, Reinforced at all Wearing Points' in 'Black, White, Grey and Tan' at a careful 3/11 a pair. Lisle was still the best bargain, full stockings beginning at only 1/11 a pair.

The first flesh-coloured rayon stockings worn in South Africa in about 1923 were pretty unattractive and in Europe some flappers even resorted to painting their legs to look as if they had stockings on. But an im-

provement in the quality of rayon coincided with the rising hemline of the 1920s: the revealed leg positively demanded to be clothed in sheer flesh-coloured stockings. At first expensive and prone to laddering, stockings gradually became stronger and cheaper, so that by 1930 Garlicks could advertise 'American Holeproof Stockings' from 5/11 a pair, although 'good silk' were still expensive at 12/6 a pair.

By 1936 *Outspan* was carrying advertisements for 'Supersilk crêpe stockings' at 7/11 and 'sheer chiffon' at 4/11, while 'Orient clearophane shadowless chiffons' – they were 'Splash-proof too!' – were only 3/11.

It was in the Thirties that women dealt the final blow to 'intriguing the male imagination, bare legs', as writer Joy Packer noted in the *SA Lady's Pictorial* of 1936. Writing in support of stockings she said: 'When under cover of the long evening dress fashion, a band of blatant women took their crude calves into ballrooms, it was the ultimate error in good taste and good judgement. Legs, like most other things, are not at their best when completely revealed.'

Nylon stockings, first shown at the New York world fair of 1938, created a stir by being both tough and exceptionally sheer. But the Second World War intervened and South Africans were not to experience their delights until after the war.

Once nylon stockings were freely available in the shops legs began to take on many different hues. Seams were in and seams were out, and then skirts started to climb and suddenly there were tights, abandoning their heavy snug-for-winter guise and striding forth on spring, summer, autumn legs, baggy knees and all. They've stayed there ever since.

1968

Birth of the bra

INSIDE THE OUTLINE: CARESSE CROSBY'S REBELLION

Although brassières came into general use in the 1920s and were only known as 'bras' from the mid-1930s, the story properly begins in the Edwardian era. For it was then, at the turn of the century, that the low-front S-shape of the new Health corset first left the bosom free instead of supporting it or pushing it up.

It created a bow-fronted silhouette. But the bosom was still pre-eminent — women took to wearing the many kinds of bust bodices and bust improvers which had been around but had never before been quite so necessary. The bodices — for example of white cotton stiffened with whalebones — gave the well-endowed the correct rounded shape, while the improvers, ranging from pads of wool to stiffly starched frills on a camisole, added vaster dimensions to the ill-equipped.

It was in America that, in 1914, the heiress Caresse Crosby claimed to have invented the modern brassière. Slender enough to rebel against corsets and whalebone bodices, she fashioned from two handkerchiefs a short contrivance that supported, and for the first time separated, the bust. But her patent, later sold to Warner Bros, had little immediate effect on the

The bra takes over from the bust bodice — a shapelier look that developed into the 'uplift'

traditional brassière, which remained lengthy and rigidly boned for some time.

During the 1920s the slim, straight outline was carried to such extremes that the brassière worn by the fashionable flapper was designed to flatten rather than improve the bust. Made of cotton, satin or lace, these were at least lighter and boneless, but they inflicted discomfort on the well-endowed. A South African woman who was young in the 1920s remembers wearing 'straight, tight binders with hooks and eyes to flatten and elongate the bosom till it was indis-

cernible'. Slimming was all the rage. In 1925 the agents for Miracle Reducing Garments claimed that their bust squeezer, at an expensive 39/6, would 'reduce your size from three to four inches after the first fourteen days wear'. Made from 'pure gum rubber' with effectively sealed seams, it must have been sheer torture to wear.

Later in the decade the Kestos company in Britain introduced an adapted version of the Caresse Crosby handkerchief brassière — it gave added shape with darts under each 'cup' and cross-over elastic to tighten the outline. Brassières, made by companies such as Kestos, Warners and Gossard, became controllers of the figure, rather than the earlier 'improvers' or 'flatteners'. They were made of cotton or silk tricot elastic.

This shapelier look finally became the 'uplift' bra of the late 1930s, now made of satin, lace or net. In South Africa in 1938, Maidenform advertised their latest Chansonette model 'for the new "Pointed Roundness"'.

After the war the pointed bustline retained its place as part of the New Look, and by the 1950s bras were of nylon and nylon lace, with circle-stitched cups to create the full-blown 'Sweater Girl' look popularised by Hollywood stars like Jane Russell. Falsies, foam pads and wiring assisted in creating fullness — and the bra in its role of bust improver had come full circle.

In the 1950s Maidenform ran a now somewhat comic series of 'I dreamed' advertisements. The one above claimed extravagantly that 'I dreamed I was a work of art in my Maidenform bra'; and above right: 'I dreamed I went shopping in my Maidenform bra'

Belinda Lee, left, and Margo Lorenz, right, both young starlets, model the busty sweater-girl look of the mid-Fifties

'Our Underclothes Are Reduced To Vanishing Point'

'Every woman's figure is not perfect. But every woman finds, when properly corseted in a suitable garment of support, that her charms are emphasized, and her faults, minimized, pass by unnoticed.' This was the Gossard line of beauty in the 1920s. The corsets, though, would seem to have hidden rather than enhanced the lady's charms

Though underwear fashions had relaxed considerably by the 1930s, they were still restrictive compared to today's styles. These sets were worn under tennis dresses

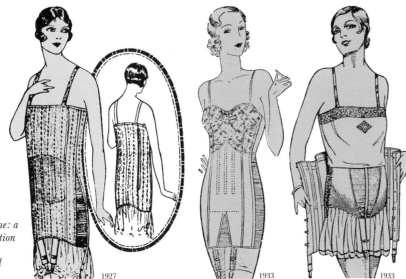

The really fashionable 1920s' woman forsook heavy nightdress for silk pyjamas. This lady, with her curious smoking instrument, appeared in a C to C cigarette advertisement

The 1920s, and the introduction of rayon (known as 'artificial silk'), ushered in the greatest changes in underwear. Bare arms; shorter, narrower skirts and lively dances like the Charleston discouraged wide petticoats and long sheath-like corsets.

For the young and slender, corsets became short and boneless, made of satin or tricot elastic and worn with a flattening bosom band to achieve the slim, straight outline of the flapper. At the height of the short-skirt era, the 'Louveen hip confiner corset', complete with suspenders for those new flesh-coloured stockings, would have cost a South African girl only 15/6. It was claimed to be eminently 'suitable for dancing and outdoor sports'. For the plumper woman, there was a wrap-around hip corset, or a corselette, which stretched from bust to thigh.

The new, lighter lingerie of the 1920s was bought in sets by everyone who could afford to do so — combinations, chemises, knickers, cami-knickers, slips and nightdresses, all embroidered with the same pattern, and generally made of pastel-coloured satin, silk or crêpe de chine.

Fashion followers carrying the boyish look as far as it would go could wear pyjamas to bed (in pure silk of course), but retained an incongruous touch of femininity by protecting their bobbed heads with boudoir caps. Indeed, the flapper was said to wear far more to bed than she did to the local dance hall.

The elastic revolution

'A petticoat — there is no such thing any more! Our underclothes are reduced to vanishing point.' So wrote an enthusiastic fashion writer in the South African Lady's Pictorial in February 1930. It was, of course, a slight exaggeration, although bulky petticoats and camisoles had certainly gone.

'Foundation garments' became an accepted term during this decade, with elasticised 'girdles', 'roll-ons' or 'step-ins' (elastic was the all-important new ingredient) teaming up with the brassière. The flat flapper was gone and the bosom had again grown shapely. Extra shapely in fact, for as Hollywood put its accent on uplift, so 'falsies' thrust their way into many wardrobes, giving hope — and sometimes acute embarrassment — to their wearers.

In A View from the Ridge John Wentzel describes a Saturday night dance at the Johannesburg Country Club where 'a well-known Frenchwoman, who was noted for her beautiful clothes and remarkably well-preserved and girlish figure, suffered an embarrassment that literally pricked the bubble reputation. Whether it was due to the ardour of her partner's embrace,

a stray pin, or just a "blowout", when she left the dance floor in a hurry it was easy to see that the secret of Madame's girlish figure was exposed, or rather deflated. Whilst her right bosom still stood proud as a pouter pigeon, the left was as flat as yesterday's champagne.'

The Second World War brought shortages of stockings — and underwear made from salvaged parachute silk. Then the New Look of 1947 refocussed fashion's attention on the waist. 'Waspie' girdles, boned and laced, made a brief comeback, worn over the roll-on corset or the new pantie-girdle.

By the 1950s foundation garments were lighter and softer than ever before, thanks to the liberating effect of nylon. 'Two-way stretch' materials finally established the all-elastic corset even for the stout older woman who had clung so long to bones.

In 1960 South African girls were still smoothing out their bulges with step-ins and holding their breath as strapless bras slipped around their shoe-string-strapped dresses. Their skirts were wide over flaring petticoats, and popping suspenders were still a problem. Gossard advertised a line of underwear 'for shapely beauty as nature intended' — it certainly was shapely, but definitely not what nature had intended.

Then everything happened at once. The Beatles, Mary Quant, the mini, pantihose, bikini panties, burnt bras, and body stockings. In South Africa prudes raged against bobbing bosoms, the T-shirt became 'disgusting' or 'delicious', and petticoats and suspenders disappeared. Although the younger South African woman was never militant enough to burn her bra, she happily discarded it — more for comfort than protest, she claimed. And comfortable, it seems, she intends to remain.

Lissom threesome: a range of foundation garments from Spracklens mail order catalogue

1927

1933

1933

The Roaring Twenties

THE NEW-LOOK WOMAN STRIDES OUT

Western women won their own victory on the home front during the First World War — a previously unthinkable liberty. They had stepped into male jobs while the men were away, and they had proved themselves. Now, after the war, they wanted to go on working, to vote, to go to university. They had emerged from their elegant purdah.

It showed in their clothes. Edwardian languor was out: the new woman was mobile, practical, hardworking. She wanted fashions that were simple but smart, frocks that were washable and easy to walk in — her ankle had been revealed for the first time during the war, and she wasn't going to relinquish this new-found freedom to stride out.

Suddenly, lightness is all

The 1920s brought fresh fashions that horrified the elderly, but delighted the young South African man. It was a look that was soon to be shorter, barer and straighter than anything ever seen before. The sheer expanse of naked flesh-coloured silk, now shamelessly visible, amply compensated for loss of curves.

It began in 1922, when hemlines slowly rose and red nail varnish made its appearance. Fashion-conscious flappers bobbed their hair and wore head-hugging cloche hats. Waistlines rose a little — and then fell to a strange new place: the hip. The tubular look was now carried to its extreme, and the ideal figure of the 1920s was flat-chested, slender and boyish. The bust had all but disappeared, and for the first time serious dieting was a must: all those ties and ruffles on the hips only accentuated any roundness that remained.

South African magazines began to carry advertisements for 'Clark's slimming bath salts' and their 'reducing paste' for slender ankles — another essential in a world of bare legs and pointed patent-leather shoes. Suddenly, light-

The leggy lady of the Twenties had to pay far more attention to shoes than her less-exposed Edwardian mother. By 1930, though, hemlines were beginning to drop again

ness was all — in clothing as much as in figure. However, the fashion writer of *SA Lady's Pictorial* was rather scathing about the fetish for slimness. She wrote: '. . . she looks, alas, what she really is — for we must call a spade a spade sometimes — skinny! Indeed, so much have they fasted, have they danced, have they been massaged and rolled, that slender women are getting rather unhappy because the reed-like figure is accompanied very often by a reed-like scraggy neck.'

For the young career girls of the day the brevity was a boon. Although in 1924 Scott Bros of Cape Town offered summer frocks in striped crêpe at 32/6 and 'French models' in georgette and marocain from 70/-, a Cape Town woman remembers meeting a friend and complimenting her on her new frock. The friend grinned and said: 'It cost me 1/7½ including the cotton.' So simple were the straight, sleeveless designs that home dressmaking had become an easy pastime for all. She herself remembers buying material with a cousin, 'doubling it over, cutting a hole for the neck, leaving holes for arms and seaming the sides — then all we had to do was hem them, make sashes for our hips and put them on'. But crêpe, she cautions, was 'chancy'. Her sisters

went to a wedding in smart new crêpe dresses. A short shower of rain during the outdoors reception 'left them looking very derelict with the fronts of their dresses all shrunk up while the backs, which had escaped the rain, were still long'.

Sportswomen welcomed the new casual separates as much as office girls. In fact, they were now so important a breed that sportswear began to have its influence on day wear, reinforcing the relaxed approach. 'Afternoon' and 'morning' ensembles, once so essential, began to give way to the 'dawn to dark' frock which could take the wearer anywhere.

But cleanliness and crisp freshness were all-important, so the materials of the 1920s were increasingly chosen for washability. Those flimsy, lacy whites of the Edwardian lady were replaced by practical tones of beige, with names ranging from 'fawn', 'stone' and 'flesh' to 'champagne' and 'Sahara desert sand'.

That tall, sinuous kind

If the 1920s girl was practical by day, by night she became a slinky vamp. The straight dress flowered into a spangled and beaded outfit often heavy and elaborate in design but always bright and glittering to match those exuberant new dances, the foxtrot and the Charleston. A woman who flirted with another's husband was described by the offended wife: 'I knew she was a vamp from the very first moment I set eyes on her. That tall sinuous kind, with red lips and black hair, green eyes and long jade earrings so often is.' Fox furs, especially the luxurious silver fox, were the ultimate in desirability. Of course, not everybody could afford the real thing. As a writer in the magazine *Eve at Home* put it, 'thousands of bunny rabbits are masquerading as Australian possum . . .' Most flamboyant of the new accessories was the long, long cigarette holder. The flapper smoked, drank cocktails and openly applied her very evident make-up. To her, enjoying her astonishing new freedom, it must have seemed as if the party would never end.

Popular, smart, modern Princess Alice, Countess of Athlone and wife of the Governor-General, exerted a strong influence on local fashions. Here she drips with diamonds and pearls — real ones. Most women, of course, had to settle for imitation jewellery

The two women on the left are dressed in the Twenties' most popular day-wear outfit: the jumper suit. Cardigans and jumpers were all the rage during the decade — a direct consequence of the wartime drive to provide knitted comforts for the troops

Right: Top-to-toe height of fashion in 1928: from cloche hat to black patent-leather Cuban-heeled shoes. The elephant is Nellie, a gift to Durban's Mitchell Park Zoo and long-time attraction to thousands of South African schoolchildren

AN AGE OF DIAMONDS AND GOLD

Jewellery in the 1920s complemented the new simplicity. Gone were the fussy Victorian favourites: the lockets, mourning rings and huge brooches of pinchbeck and paste. Bracelets of massed garnets were ousted by plain gold 'slave bangles' worn in a row on bare arms, and costing anything from £5 to £15 each in 1920. Ladies' wristwatches were a relatively new accessory, at prices ranging from 18/6 to £35.

For fingers, hoop and cluster rings were old hat; the diamond solitaire was the only thing to buy, at anything from £5 to £100. Diamonds were the fashion stone of the century and the particular toast of the Twenties. Scott Fitzgerald wrote a story called *The Diamond as Big as the Ritz;* in *Gentlemen Prefer Blondes* Anita Loos described a flapper heroine whose motto was: 'Kissing your hand may make you feel very good but a diamond bracelet lasts forever.'

Diamonds even graced such items as a lady's solid gold powder-compact, on sale in South Africa in 1924. The diamonds traced her initials on it, and the total price of this 'vanity case' was a mere £4.10s. To complete her accessories the fashionable woman needed only one more thing: an elegant cigarette case in tortoiseshell, at the eyebrow-raising cost of 9 guineas.

Women of all shapes and sizes affected the bob hairstyle, provoking much unflattering masculine comment. 'It cannot be denied,' wrote one man in Outspan, 'that the spectacle of rows of shaven necks confronting one in the theatre is a far from pleasing sight.' This is a typical contemporary cartoon

THE HATS, HEADS AND HAIR OF THE TWENTIES

The universal hat of the 1920s was the cloche. Made of anything from felt to taffeta, it was a long, usually brimless affair that came down well over the eyes and hugged the outline of the head.

Heads were small, by fashion's decree. Long tresses, even worn in a chignon or knot, were too bulky, so young girls everywhere braced themselves and bobbed their hair. Bobbing left it short but still gently wavy, covering the ears. It was often marcelled, and at night adorned by a 'headache band' or a rhinestone hairslide.

As hemlines rose, heads grew even smaller. 'Shingling' gave a shorter, straighter style. Finally, in the late 1920s came the extra-mannish 'Eton crop'. The *Outspan* warned ladies that tight hats could lead to baldness. But, the article pointed out, there was a bright side to the picture: 'Ladies might become more intelligent as in the past their brains had run to their hair.'

The liberated post-war woman: a selection of ten evening outfits of the cocktail era, bright and glittering

SCARLET AND BLONDE: THE JEAN HARLOW LOOK

The motion pictures featured vamps often dressed up as a Hollywood version of an 'Eastern Lady' whose exaggerated make-up (dictated by the rudimentary techniques of early filming) set the precedent for the more liberated South African Twenties girl. She didn't need to disguise the fact that she used make-up. It was part of her new freedom, war-paint joyfully and often publicly applied. No matter if the result was a face somewhat clown-like. She enamelled her skin with bright white face-powder and rouge. It was the claim of Poudre Tokalon face powder, which sold for 1/9 a box, that 'it clings despite perspiration from dancing in heated rooms'. Onto this startling canvas she daubed a scarlet cupid's bow of a mouth and pencilled defiantly arched brows over eyelashes laden with the new block mascara. Her nails she painted a brilliant red.

Film stars, most prominently Jean Harlow, ushered in the platinum blonde. Though hydrogen peroxide had been used to lighten hair since the turn of the century, it had scarcely been a respectable habit and its effects were often harsh and yellowing. But now bleaching was followed by a softening blue rinse. It was all the rage: the artificial blonde had come to stay.

After the ball was over

THE THIRTIES: A DECADE OF DISORDER

As the 1920s ended so skirts, suddenly, became longer — as if, according to commentator James Laver, fashion were trying to say: 'The party is over.'

It was. By contrast the 1930s were mature and gracious: femininity was back in fashion. The waist resumed its rightful place above a rapidly descending hemline. The ideal figure was still slender, but tall and shapely with no longer any hint of the boyish. For the first time in years the bust was back, softly rounded above those newly accentuated waists. The brassière became a part of every woman's wardrobe.

The Thirties was, however, a decade of fashion confusion as one style rapidly replaced another at the Paris collections. The fashion correspondent of the *South African Lady's Pictorial* in 1936 wrote: 'Praise be — Paris has decided that this year we need not all be alike, and there are three distinct trends of fashion . . . First there is the military idea [inspired by the Jubilee Pageant]; second, the Chinese note —a direct result of the Chinese exhibition; last but not least: pleats, pleats and yet more pleats . . . In fact you must pleat everything — your scarf, your jabot, your collars and cuffs —if you wish to achieve the right note.' Another writer, however, described the situation as 'bewildering'.

The one trend which could be detected was the shift of emphasis to the shoulders. First with butterfly sleeves, then by means of a slow but sure widening of the shoulders themselves, created both by cut and padding. It was most noticeable in the tailored suit and the trenchcoat, garments popularised by Hollywood stars Greta Garbo and Marlene Dietrich. Worn with a fox skin slung over the shoulder and a tilted fedora, this look led naturally to the businesslike image of the Second World War years.

Thirties' threesome. The lady on the right shows off the jauntily perched hat and draped foxskin which were high fashion items at the time

As the decade moved to its close, women's daytime ensembles became ever smarter and more tailored. Gloves and the veiled pillbox hat accompanied shorter skirts. South African magazines boasted of 'Thoroughly British tailored suits in tweed or worsted' at prices ranging from 95/- to 8 guineas. A chic day dress of 'washing Macclesfield silk' cost 39/6 in 1938.

Off-the-peg shopping

But this was the expensive end of the trade. It was in the late 1930s that off-the-peg shopping really came into its own. South African chain stores like Foschini's offered fashionable garments at prices everyone could at last afford. Women who were working girls in 1938 recall how cheap even their dance dresses were. One girl, buying her first evening dress that year in Port Elizabeth — a full-skirted, narrow-waisted frock of fine layers of chiffon and net over taffeta — paid an astonishing 7/6 for this lovingly remembered creation. Her silver pumps cost 5/-, reduced from 10/- in a sale.

But that was 1938. In 1939 war broke out and for the next six years fashions were sensible, if sometimes severe.

Every lady's ideal of elegance in 1934

THE £20 WARDROBE

Buying patterns and materials. Although off-the-peg clothing was readily available by the 1930s, women often preferred to make their own outfits. During the Depression years many had no choice

Fashion books invariably omit to mention the lot of the ordinary woman. The early 1930s in South Africa, as elsewhere, were the Depression years.

The question, 'Are our girls extravagant?' evoked an impassioned reply in a February 1930 edition of *Outspan*. A typist in an office where the girl's average monthly wage was £15 (to cover board, tram fare *and* clothing), described the working wardrobe of her colleagues. It consisted of: one or two good hats ('and the months they bought their hats they could buy nothing else'); materials from sales turned into homemade dresses, at an average cost of £1 each; a pair of good shoes to last the year; 'undies made at home'; and even homemade evening dresses and cloaks; the whole yielding a dress bill which 'rarely went beyond £20 for the year'.

Contemporary advertisements in *Outspan* reveal that dress materials were indeed cheap. Crêpe de chine was 5/11 a yard, guaranteed not to 'split, crack or perish'; Viyella varied from 4/11 to 6/6, depending on thickness. Silk georgettes cost 6/11, spun and tussore silks only 1/6.

Champions of Bloemfontein offered mail-order materials for homemade lingerie and pyjamas: celanese satin at 6/11 a yard, art silk (as artificial silk was known) at 4/6, and fine Limbric lawn at only 1/3. Cash's 'washing ribbons' were sold for shoulder straps, while home dyes promised rejuvenation for tired underwear.

Those 'good shoes to last the year' could have ranged from fancy 'Java Lizard' high-heeled court shoes at 89/6 a pair, to the more likely choice of suede or patent courts at 35/- and 32/6 respectively.

'COMING OUT' IN 1937

The apex of social achievement in the 1930s was to be presented at Court and, during the London Season, South African magazines were full of pictures of local debutantes. Dress instructions, issued by the Lord Chamberlain's Office, were minutely detailed. The 1937 notice specified:

'Ladies attending their Majesties' courts must wear long evening dresses with Court trains suspended from the shoulders, white veils with ostrich feathers will be worn on the head. The train, which should not exceed two yards in length, must not extend more than eighteen inches from the heel of the wearer when standing. Three small white feathers mounted as a Prince of Wales Plume, the centre feather a little higher than the two side ones to be worn slightly on the left side of the head, with the tulle veil of similar colour attached to the base of the feathers. The veil should not be longer than forty-five inches. Coloured feathers are inadmissible, but in cases of deep mourning Black feathers may be worn. Gloves must be worn. There are no restrictions with regard to the colour of the dresses or gloves for either debutantes or those who have already been presented. Bouquets and fans are optional.'

The long satin evening gown of the Thirties must have turned a few heads. Necklines plunged, revealing a daring expanse of skin

SILK STOCKINGS WITHDRAWN.

America has stopped the Manufacture of all Silk Stockings. The result is that we cannot offer many makes in Pure Silk. Our Stocks have been rapidly bought out. We are expecting a few limited shipments but we are not certain if we will get them

We CANNOT therefore offer our usual lines in "Kayser," "Holeproof," "Supersilk," "Butterfly" "Berkshire," etc.

We have fairly large stocks of the FAMOUS "TRUWEAR" PURE SILK STOCKINGS and one or two other makes. But we cannot supply more than 2 pairs of these to each customer. Later on perhaps even less

A notice from the 1941-42 Spracklens mail-order catalogue. Clothes were practical and hard-wearing in the war years, and there was little or no ornamentation to break up the severe lines. One exception was the exaggerated shoulders on coats and some dresses: the style enjoyed a brief popularity. These coats, fashioned in silk marocain, were typical

THE WARTIME LOOK: THEN THE NEW LOOK

Short skirts, square shoulders, functional shoes (toes were round and heels low, sometimes wedge-shaped) — these were the distinctive features of the 1940s wartime look. It was a no-nonsense age, typified by the tailored two-piece suit.

While praising the well-cut suit, a writer for *Femina* pleaded that it should be worn with plain court shoes — but complained that some wealthy women, in an excess of patriotic zeal, went as far as wearing brogues 'with huge flat clumsy heels'.

'I might add,' she went on, 'that the majority of them completely overlook the fact that they are sporting a mink coat and the family heirlooms clipped about here and there.'

It doesn't sound as if South Africans were having a very hard war. Indeed, compared with Europe, South Africa experienced few serious shortages of either food or material goods. While their sisters in Britain were running up dirndl skirts from old curtains and fashioning blouses from scarves, women here could still buy shoes, dresses and most dress materials. Only best quality imported cloths like velvet, chiffon and silk were in short supply, though even the latter was available at times in the form of parachute silk of so fine a quality that it was also in great demand for evening dresses, blouses and underwear.

Stockings were a scarce fashion item. Some women remember queueing for them when a new shipment reached Cape Town or Port Elizabeth. Many made do with flesh-coloured lisle; pure silk stockings became impossible to find, and were largely replaced by artificial silk stockings, though the supply of these was largely dependent on shipping. Nylon, to South Africans, was still only a name.

A relaxed element crept in with wartime hairstyles, which were longer and sexier — swept up in front with combs, or falling in a wave over one cheek à la Veronica Lake. But these were still solemn times, when hats and fancy trimmings could be castigated as 'frivolous' and in bad taste. Family magazines like *Outspan* were full of advertisements for practical things like knitting wools, dress materials, patterns-by-post and Singer sewing machines.

For the wartime bride it was a case of borrow, beg or be lucky. A WAAS corporal stationed on Robben Island in 1942 took shore leave for her wedding. Hearing that she was about to be married in her uniform, a horrified friend donated a white Indian sari, from which one of Cape Town's Malay dressmakers hastily fashioned a most becoming wedding gown.

Feminine fashions re-emerged after the war on the crest of a nostalgia wave. French designer Christian Dior launched his revolutionary New Look in 1947: skirts long, waists small and tightly belted, and the bust — so long over-shadowed by square shoulders — uplifted and prominent. There was a return to extravagance — a reaction against years of enforced economy. The wide ballerina skirts of the New Look reached to the lower calf. Petticoats of rustling taffeta once again gave dresses fullness. Coats were enormous tent-like affairs with high-standing collars. Heels were high, handbags fat, and only hats — now finally on their way out — were small.

Post-war winter fashion from Milady, *1948. The New Look had its critics. In 1948 the business-girls group of the National Council of Women in Durban claimed that it re-introduced the uncomfortable corset. Mrs Bertha Solomon M.P. said that the fashion was ill-timed — prices were high and material was still in short supply*

The rebirth of fashion

FROM CONFORMITY TO YOUTHFUL REBELLION

For the young of the Fifties, a revolution had begun. First there were the Teddy Boys with their elaborate Edwardian-style clothes — an overreaction perhaps to wartime austerity. And then came the 'ducktails' in their blue jeans and leather jackets, their folk-heroes Marlon Brando (tough and inarticulate star of *The Wild Ones*), James Dean *(Rebel Without a Cause)*, and of course the sideburned, swivel-hipped Elvis Presley. Their girls wore aggressive sweater-girl bras under tight tops; full skirts with metres of starched nylon net petticoats; wide belts, flat shoes and a tumble of casual Brigitte Bardot locks round faces thickly plastered with pancake make-up. Even the quieter Pat Boone fans wore the new styles — but with pony-tails and demure ankle socks.

Designers and manufacturers concentrated more and more on big-spending youth. As the 1950s progressed, styles came thick and fast. The waistline moved in bewildering fashion, bringing the A-line, the 'Trapeze, dress, the H-line, and finally the shapeless 'sack' dress. It looked as if anything would go. The scene was set for the next, startling decade.

The Swinging Sixties

The 1960s fashion world was dominated by young British designers, led by the imaginative and vocal Mary Quant. Though Paris put up a good space-age show of plastic — yellow PVC raincoats and shiny white boots from Courrèges, metal clothes by Rabanne — the centre of the fashion revolution shifted firmly to London.

London's Carnaby Street became the new fashion Mecca (later superseded by King's Road, Chelsea). Delighted South African teenagers went into Chelsea shifts, lacy stockings,

Governor-General Ernest Jansen arrives at the ball for Benoni's debutantes in 1956

sling-back shoes, long straight hair and a new, paler make-up that loaded the eyes with eyeliner, thick coatings of mascara and as many false lashes as the lid could support. Each year brought a new fad — op art, psychedelic, flower power and more. The Beatles introduced men to longer hair.

It was the era of leggy, wide-eyed models like Jean Shrimpton and Twiggy. In fact it was 'The Shrimp' who launched that sensation of the mid-Sixties, the mini-skirt. She did it at the Melbourne Races in 1965, revealing her knees to a scandalised Australia. Twiggy's childlike stick-figure carried the fashion with gamine grace, but it was ill-suited to plumpness.

Nevertheless, whatever their shapes, South

African legs were soon being revealed. The mini (known at first as the 'above the knee' skirt) enlivened every city man's day — and upset, if not alarmed, the conservative watchdogs of our society.

Hem and haw

The Rev. Arthur Sexby ordered five women out of his Johannesburg church in April 1969 — because they were wearing mini-skirts. 'This is my own private war,' he said. 'If it comes to a last resort my congregation will have to choose between me and mini-skirts.'

It was, in fact, a very public war. Reverend Sexby became joint leader of the National Association for Public Morality and Welfare, formed

Elizabeth Taylor's pale skin, red mouth and arched eyebrows typified the sweetheart face of the Fifties. The Fifties, Sixties and Seventies produced a galaxy of lively new fashion terms, including bikini, teased hair, unisex, hot-pants, body-stocking, pantihose, sack dress, tank top, T-shirt, terylene, psychedelic, beehive

Above: Norma Vorster, 1956 Miss South Africa, with fashionable clutch bag, gloves and full skirt. Left: rocking in the Fifties; right: swinging in the Sixties

Turning heads in Cape Town's Adderley Street. Fashion buyers in 1965 were predicting that a skirt 4" above the knee would be unlikely to sell but, as this 1968 picture shows, they were proved delightfully wrong

expressly to 'crush the evils of the mini'. His fellow campaigner was Mr Gert Yssel, the man who claimed that 'until the shameful parts of women are covered, I am convinced God will not fill the Vaal Dam'.

Newspapers gave wide coverage to their campaign, and the letters pages were full of comments, some serious. A few people even joined the cause — at one meeting 22 attended, but 11 turned out to be members of the Press, four of whom were wearing minis.

The two crusaders were firmly convinced that minis were 'of the world, of the flesh and of the devil', and they let the nation know it. 'Mini skirts give rise to beastly thoughts,' they warned. 'Girls don't realise the awful forces they arouse in men. Christian men have told us that miniskirts have been a grievous temptation to them.' One minister came forward to say that members of his congregation complained that they couldn't concentrate at communion when mini-skirted girls were kneeling at the rail.

Mini-skirt wearers took no notice whatever. Nor, alas for the NAPMW, did members of the Government, whose support was ardently solicited. The question did get as far as the Assembly, however, when Dr Connie Mulder, then Minister of Social Welfare, was asked if he was contemplating taking any action in the matter. He wasn't. The mini continued, astonishingly, to rise. So, too, did the water level of the Vaal Dam.

Winkle Pickers . . . up-to-the-minute fashion

Winkle-picker toes and stiletto heels — a style which caused much public controversy. Doctors claimed that the narrow-toed shoe could do irreparable harm to feet. The thin steel heel, it was reported, exerted a pressure of over 8 000 pounds a square inch when worn by a 130-pound woman. It also seriously damaged floors, and stilettos were banned from many buildings (women entered either in stockinged feet or wearing slippers provided at the doors)

Mini, midi, maxi — the Sixties scene

1903

1913

1931

WARTIME

1948

1957

EARLY SIXTIES

1965

Seven decades of shoes. The Pictorial said of the 1913 style: 'The forthcoming mode for skirts slashed up at the front, back or sides, which allows glimpses of chaussure and hosiery as the wearer walks, will necessitate a very careful choice of shoes, for only the smartest can stand the ordeal'

A man's world

FROCK COATS AND FORMAL SOLEMNITY

Men's fashions at the turn of the century were as unsuited to the South African climate as were the feminine modes of the time. In the cities, and even in platteland towns, an Edwardian South African was expected to wear full gentleman's attire at all times.

This comprised a frock coat or morning coat of worsted, vicuna or serge, always dark in hue and worn with matching or striped flannel trousers (turn-ups first made their appearance in 1902), and a waistcoat which could be fancy by day but was black by night – except in the case of full evening dress, when white was mandatory.

The Diary of Iris Vaughan delightfully, and with its somewhat original approach to spelling, records the quality of South African life and style in the small towns of the Eastern Cape. Sundays, Iris noted, occasioned much 'putting on of best clothes and hats'. Her father, the Magistrate, wore 'his tail coat and best black bouler hat', though on other days he prudently wore 'his old bouler hat'. One Good Friday in Adelaide indicated how little the clothes of the time suited semi-rural life. The family returned from church to find the pig in a potato patch. Father leapt into the fray 'with his coat tails flying and his bouler hat tight on his head in front' and 'Mom calling leave the pig you spoiling your good clothes'.

For two decades colonial gentlemen continued to suffer layer upon layer of discomfort rather than let down the side. Beneath their suits they wore vests, woollen drawers, silk or cotton shirts with high, stiff collars and loosely knotted neckties. A tweed overcoat, or the new waterproof 'mackintosh' (costing about 6/6), bowler,

and boots or woollen spats worn on top of patent leather shoes, completed the outfit. Accessories: a gentleman always wore gloves, carried an umbrella or cane, and if he were a dandy he might sport a monocle and mother-of-pearl cufflinks.

The brash digger population of bustling new Johannesburg was an appreciative market for ready-made tweed suits costing anything from 8/6 to 40/-. But stigma was still attached to ready-mades, known scornfully as 'reach-me-downs'. A gentleman preferred his suits hand-tailored (a speedy affair in those days: an outfit could be completed in a mere twelve hours) and tended to reserve his tweeds for sport and walking. For these activities his trousers would probably be kneebreeches, or 'knickerbockers' teamed with a Norfolk jacket, thick stockings and tweed cap.

Blazers, boating and the beach

But casual summer wear did gain some favour as the century progressed. White suits in drill, duck or tussore silk, or white trousers with gaily-striped blazers, became perfectly acceptable for boating, the beach and of course for cricket and tennis. During the evening a gentleman might even lounge around in a pair of light pyjamas.

One man alone seemed to stay cool and comfortable in clothes little changed for a century: the rural Afrikaner. He clung tenaciously to his slouch hat, flannel shirt, short jacket and moleskin or corduroy trousers. His shoes were *velskoene*, homemade from hide; socks he regarded as a church-going luxury.

Only the depopulation of the platteland and the urbanisation of the Afrikaner brought to an end a unique sartorial era that had been born of isolation and hard necessity.

Motion pictures introduced new fashions — the 'plus fours' and 'Oxford bags' of the 1920s;

the Clark Gable hats and wide lapels of the 1930s. Much of the very strict formality of men's wear was gone by the end of the Thirties. The lounge suit of flannel or serge had finally ousted the morning coat for everyday wear. The tweed 'sports coat' could be worn with flannel trousers, while the dinner jacket, or 'tuxedo', had long replaced the evening tail coat.

But it was also during the 1920s and 1930s that South African men began to get their reputation as bad dressers. 'A South African Tailor' observed in a 1927 issue of *Outspan* that 'Whatever part clothes may play in making the man, they do not seem to matter very much to the average South African . . . the average man knows little and cares less'.

He went on to say that to a certain extent he could understand this, since 'The heat and the dust have a lot to do with it. The heat of the body creates wrinkles and the ubiquitous dust covers shoes and trousers and gives an unavoidable appearance of general untidiness that gradually kills a man's regard for clothes, however fastidious he may have been in the beginning'.

Shoes were now more common than boots, and spats were entirely obsolete. Trouser turn-ups became increasingly fashionable from the 1920s, and trouser-legs gradually widened. In 1930, a South African could order, from a Johannesburg firm, a pair of flannels with turn-ups and 'ample fullness in legs, side and hip pocket' for 10/9 plus 1/1 postage.

But despite this steady trend towards greater informality, and the occasional introduction of a brave non-conformity — Fair Isle sweaters and suede shoes, for instance — sombre sobriety has persisted among South African city men. The suit — grey, navy, black, brown — is still one of the most common sights on our streets.

Variety was the keynote of men's headgear around 1900, as demonstrated by this group sitting around Cecil Rhodes. Early this century, though, the silk topper which, with the frock coat, had ruled supreme in Victorian days, gave way to the hard bowler, while the sportily inclined cut a dash with wide-brimmed straw boater or flat cap. The felt homburg, popularised by King Edward VII, caught on in South Africa in the second decade

THE WELL-DRESSED CLERK

Standard wear for a 1900s office clerk comprised:

Suit		Collar studs	1/2
(ready to wear)	40/-	Cufflinks	1/-
Waistcoat	5/6	Tie clip	1/-
Shirt	3/6	Shoes	22/6
Collar	9d	Handkerchief	3/9
Tie	1/6	Hat (boater)	3/6
Braces	1/-	Socks	1/-
Vest	3/-	Gloves	6/6
Underpants	3/6	Walking stick	3/-

MODEST SUCCESS OF A SENSIBLE SUIT

Remarked *Outspan* in 1928: 'No wonder we hear of men swooning in the streets of Johannesburg.' A full decade went by, however, before another magazine, *The Pictorial*, announced the arrival of the 'bush shirt', predicting that it would invade South African beaches and golf-links that summer. In 'Natural, Guardsman (Butcher's Blue), Ivory or Mocha', it was to be worn with matching beach trousers or shorts. Khaki drill had been advertised in South Africa for the first time in 1899, but as *The Pictorial* put it, 'you, at St James or Muizenberg are not expecting to bump into a lion or encounter the menaces of wait-a-bit-thorn'. The bush shirt, predictably, was made of a more comfortable material: silk hopsack.

Yet this eminently practical fashion, renamed the 'safari suit', only became generally acceptable wear for leisure and business alike in the 1960s. The colours are the same safe tones of 'sand, sea and sky'. In spite of its obvious advantages, though, most South Africans still prefer the ordinary suit for the office, and even for semi-formal occasions. The fashion writer who, in 1938, complained in *The Pictorial* that 'South African men are innately conventional, regarding clothes as a painful necessity', could still say the same in the 1980s.

Typical South African 1930s informal wear: baggy trousers, sleeveless V-neck sweaters; rolled-up shirtsleeves

At left (opposite page) is the 1930s look. Thirties fashions were much influenced by screen stars such as Clark Gable (above). Right: the well-dressed gentleman of the 1950s

'A CORRECT DRESS CHART': 1904

Full Dress Day. Before 6 o'clock and Sunday Church: Coat, black frock; Waistcoat, single-breasted, light fancy; Trousers, fancy cashmere; Shirt, white, small round corners to cuffs; Collar, wing, rounded corners; Neckwear, fancy puff; Gloves, natural suede or grey (for weddings very light grey; bridegroom may wear white suede gloves).

Full Evening Dress. After 6 o'clock: Coat, dress; Waistcoat, single-breasted, white, three buttons; Trousers, black dress; Shirt, plain front, one stud, plain cuffs, small round corners; Collar, wing, rounded corners; Tie, white evening; Gloves, pearl kid.

Informal Evening Dress. Coat, dinner jacket with step collar; Waistcoat, black or white single-breasted; Trousers, black dress; Shirt, plain front one stud, small round cuffs; Collar, wing, with sharp corners; Tie, white dress bow, rounded ends; Gloves, any.

Semi-Dress. For General Wear: Coat, black morning; Waistcoat, single-breasted, match coat; Trousers, fancy cashmere; Shirt, white, small round cuffs; Collar, wing, sharp corners; Neckwear, sailor knot or puff; Gloves, brown doe or reindeer.

Informal Dress. Business: Coat, dark grey morning; Waistcoat, single-breasted, light fancy; Trousers, fancy cashmere; Shirt and Cuffs, white, pleated front, small round corners to cuffs; Collar, white, sharp corners; Cravat, black knot or dark puff; Gloves, tan.

Reception Dress. Knickers, match jacket (no ends); Trousers, match jacket; Waistcoat, single-breasted, fancy flannel; Shirt, flannel or coloured zephyr; Shoes, calf lace Oxford; Collar, double; Tie, one coloured dark knot.

From *Fashion and Musical Album*, 1904

The right and wrong outfits. The stout party, said an Outspan *cartoonist in the 1920s, 'wouldn't know what to wear if invited to a reception'*

The vanishing swimsuit

SOUTH AFRICAN GIRLS IN SEARCH OF A SUN-TAN

The Edwardian belle who braved the South African surf wore 'bathing dresses' that well deserved the name. They were indeed complete dresses, voluminous affairs with puffed sleeves, knee-length skirts and ample bloomers made from materials such as heavy serge and black flannel. In addition, she had to wear bathing shoes, a rubber bathing cap, stockings and a bathing corset, which was guaranteed not to rust. Around the beginning of this century mixed bathing was something of a novelty, considered rather daring, and convention forbade women to reveal any more flesh than they would when wearing ordinary clothes. The *SA Lady's Pictorial*, in 1911, advised its readers to wear stockings with the bathing costume 'particularly where mixed bathing is the rule'.

By 1918 a South African magazine offering a free pattern for 'A Useful Bathing Dress' showed a model without the thick stockings, but still wearing the laced bathing shoes and little mob cap of earlier years. Some concessions were made to South African weather: 'The old-fashioned heavy serge is out of place in our warm climate,' counselled the magazine, suggesting instead twill, alpaca, heavy cotton or light woollens. Nor were black or navy the only colours possible: 'Turkey Red' and green 'look well in the water'.

But it was sun-bathing rather than swimming

Bathing was uncomfortable for both adults and children before the First World War: modesty demanded that as much as possible of the body was well covered. Women often wore stockings as well as the all-enveloping costume. As swimming became more popular, most women adopted the one-piece woollen outfit, but it was not until the 1920s that costumes started to become smaller and more sensible. The 1930s and 1940s saw the first tentative moves towards separating top and bottom, leading eventually to the two-piece swimsuit. The bikini, named after the Pacific atoll of atomic bomb test fame, was introduced in the late 1940s and has remained in fashion. Each year has seen the introduction of even briefer costumes, though the annual rumour that the topless swimsuit is about to become commonplace on some South African beaches has yet to be realised

that brought about the revolution in bathing costumes. Before the 1930s a visit to the seaside involved a swim or paddle and then possibly a visit to the pavilion, bandstand or tearoom. Exposing oneself to the sun for long periods was unheard of. However, during the Thirties, more and more South Africans became sunworshippers (the craze had started in California and Miami and was sweeping the French Riviera). Tans were suddenly the thing and costumes

shrank to meet the new acceptability of exposed skin.

Costumes, while still one-piece and woollen, were often backless, halter-necks supporting the bust, now at last accommodated by the built-in brassières.

To this new shaping, a 1936 Jantzen costume, advertised in *The Pictorial* as the 'Bra-Zip' model, added a zip front which promised 'marvellous fit and comfort'.

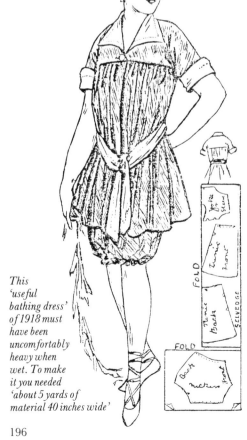

This 'useful bathing dress' of 1918 must have been uncomfortably heavy when wet. To make it you needed 'about 5 yards of material 40 inches wide'

Demure Durban in 1907, when the bathing costume was worn only for taking a dip – women wouldn't have dreamed of sun-bathing. For the stroll along the sands it was back to full dress, perhaps with parasol to shield the complexion. Sandcastles, however, appear to have changed little

Swimmers at Margate in 1910. The modest, voluminous costume on the left was considered out-of-date by the other ladies, one of whom is actually exposing her knees

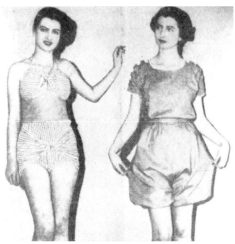

The demands of decency. An 'appropriate' bathing costume (right) approved by a special commission of the Dutch Reformed Church in 1947 contrasts with a two-piece swimsuit of the time

Taking the plunge in 1925

Birth of the bikini

In July 1946 the United States began its atomic bomb tests at Bikini atoll in the Pacific, and in that month Louis Reard, a Parisian fashion designer, made world news by introducing the first bikini swimsuit. The impact of the bikini was almost comparable to that of the bomb and Micheline Bernadini, the dancer who modelled it, received more than 50 000 fan letters when photographs were published. It made its appearance on South African beaches in the late 1940s, initially with waist-high briefs, but gradually diminishing.

It was, however, to be some years before the bikini became generally accepted in South Africa. The summer season of 1949-50 saw the introduction of the strapless swimsuit. The new lastex, self-supporting swimsuits had cunningly-placed stiffeners of bone and metal to prevent them from slipping off in even the heaviest surf.

The bikini was the subject of lively controversy, condemned by outraged traditionalists, welcomed by modern-minded sunlovers, a gift to news photographers. An added complication was the appearance of a two-piece bathing costume which was joined in the middle by a piece of net material — the so-called 'see-through bikini'. This presented the superintendent of a public swimming bath in Bloemfontein with a dilemma when he ordered a woman who was wearing a bikini from the pool and she returned wearing the 'see-through' two-piece. She was allowed to stay for that day only.

South African swimwear laws in the Sixties were hopelessly outdated. It was only in 1965 that the municipality of Cape Town revised the 1935 injunction that all swimwear should cover the body 'between the shoulder and the knee'. The amended law required ladies to 'comply with the requirements of decency'. Durban only repealed its outdated bikini ban in 1969.

Figure-fitting and decidedly brief were these knit-material costumes of the 1940s. An advertisement described the costume on the left as 'very alluring' with its 'trim lines and the contrasting shoulder straps and tie-cord of soft woolly stuff'

When the surf board was just a board: Durban in the 1940s. Although by now it was respectable for men to bare their chests, at least one preferred the striped cover-up of earlier years

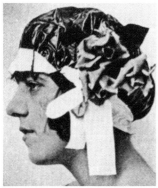

This 1921 summer hat had a dual purpose: untying the ribbon bow converted it into a 'neat little waterproof cap'

Mixed but well-covered bathing at Durban early in the century, when striped costumes, reminiscent of rugby jerseys, were the fashion for men

A two-piece bathing costume of 1962. Sunglasses, as a fashion accessory, appeared in the late 1930s and despite medical opinion that the 'human eye is perfectly able to cope with bright sunlight', their popularity grew rapidly

Sporting ladies

BREATH-DEFYING TENNIS

Said the old lady: 'Talking of tennis, we were one of the first families in Pretoria to have a tennis court. Of course it wasn't smooth like they are today but we had great fun and we never knew if the boys had come courting or to play tennis. I was quite a young thing in 1900 and I used to cheat with my corsets — not make them too tight you know, so that I could enjoy the game more. But then I had a waist that was naturally 18 inches.'

For those less fortunate, a casual game of tennis required fortitude, for tight bodices and breath-defying corsets hardly encouraged sizzling services, even when delivered underarm. But wear them they did, along with huge hats, the occasional bustle, long skirts and layers of petticoats.

Tennis was absolutely *the* social game from the 1880s onwards and, though the fashions changed and relaxed over the next 50 years or so, the ritual was very much the same until the Second World War swept aside the old formalities.

'People would ride or walk miles for the fun of tea and tennis parties,' says one Zululand farmer. 'They were always immensely social occasions. There would be 10 to 20 people, the men in long whites, the women in longish dresses, and the table would groan under the silver tea service, cakes, scones, cream and maas. Maas [thick, soured milk] was always fantastically popular in the hot weather . . .'

By 1911 men had discarded their hats and ties, but women were less fortunate.

They still wore the obligatory hats and stockings, and their high-waisted starched dresses covered long-line corsets. Although the maze of

In 1930, when the Mowbray Ladies won the Reserve Doubles Cup, stockings were being replaced by more sensible ankle socks

petticoats had gone, the hemline had only been raised enough for a peep at the instep.

None of this, however, dissuaded game girls from entering tournaments, usually in doubles matches. The English Tennis Team paid South Africa a visit in 1912 and were 'a picture in crisp white with red, white and blue neckties'. And in 1915 the inter-club championship for Ladies' Doubles was won by Turffontein after snow had played havoc with the timetable. That year racquets 'with best British gut' were advertised at 36/6.

By the end of the First World War, ladies' singles were on the map. Stockings were still worn but dresses were loose and corsets a thing of the past. In 1924 Suzanne Lenglen wore a bandeau at Wimbledon and hats disappeared from the courts.

Also in the Twenties hems went up, socks came in and stockings went out. Some lengthened their skirts again in the 1930s but others, following Alice Marbles' scandalous public appearance in shorts in 1933, were actually showing a bit of thigh by 1936! The evil influence of Europe was once again blamed for this distressing state of undress by the keepers of public morals, but the playing public skipped blithely toward frilly panties and the shortest of shorts.

Sandra Reynolds, first South African to reach the Wimbledon women's singles final (in 1960), in the style of tennis dress she favoured

Right: suntans were still unfashionable in the 1920s. Beetham's claimed that their La-rola removed 'roughness, redness, tan'

By 1915 the lady tennis player's ankles were visible. This 'Smart Turn-Out' cost £1.10s—skirt and blouse 13/4½; shoes 7/6; hat 6/11½; stockings 1/6½; buttons, hooks, etc 7½d

YOUR SKIN and COMPLEXION

can be kept in a Perfect Condition all the year round by a regular use of

BEETHAM'S La-rola

It effectually removes all Roughness, Redness, Tan, Irritation, etc., and is delightfully Soothing and Refreshing at all times.
Of all high-class Chemists and Stores.

Turn of the century, and ready for a ladies' foursome

The South African Domestic Monthly of 1914 advised that 'the correct thing to wear for tennis is always white . . . but you must not go in anything at all fussy or frilly. If you do this your hostess will feel that what she meant to be quite a simple and friendly little entertainment has been turned into a party'

No Breeches in the Sachsenwald

'The only time my father really lost his temper with me was when I borrowed a pair of breeches from a friend and went riding in the Sachsenwald.' The elderly lady gave a youthful smile. 'He said if I wanted to behave like a boy I should be punished like a boy and waved his riding crop around in an alarming way. Luckily for me his highly conservative upbringing prevented him from giving me the hiding he threatened.'

That was in Johannesburg in 1915 and, though she defied her father and continued to ride astride, the fear that chivalry might succumb to blind rage put her back into divided skirts for many years.

At the end of the 19th century most women could ride — sidesaddle of course — and were reported as 'presenting a pretty picture' while their men 'cut a dash'. Very trim and straight-backed they were as they rode out with their young men. Indeed, trim and straight-backed they had to be, for they were as tightly corsetted in their riding habits as they were in their ball gowns. And what, after all, was a bruised rib or two in the pursuit of an 18-inch waist? Brown was a favoured colour along with green and black, and top hats and bowlers were the very epitome of transplanted Englishness. In tropical Natal the solar topee was more practical, if a little less chic.

By 1911 women were allowed to bend a little, and cut quite a dash themselves riding, still sidesaddle, at gymkhanas — in ladies' competitions of course. In the Cape, mounted paperchases were wonderful fun even if the girls' big picture hats did blow off and frighten the horses, and in the Transvaal drag hunting was the vogue.

Around the middle of the second decade the first daring divided skirts began arriving from Europe, for those who were determined to ride astride. Censured as indecent and indelicate, this innovation was treated with averted glances and dire warnings that it would interfere with childbirth. Such forebodings seemed insignificant against the new freedom, and the young Amazons of the day galloped astride into the 1920s during which, with increasing emancipation on their side, they slid their legs into jodhpurs and kept them there.

Edwardian compromise – breeches and tunic

Towards more practical sportswear – South African Ladies' Golf champions Mrs Vernon, 1925, and, far right, Mrs Crosbie, 1930

Unladylike at the Tee

Said one 1902 magazine with delight: 'Women are now beginning to take up golf in large numbers.' Male golfers were not quite so cheerful. They'd had it all their own way up to then and now they had to contend with 'visions of womanhood addressing the tee in most unladylike poses'. However, women ignored these chauvinistic grumblings and marched onto the few golf courses South Africa had to offer. Once there, they learned to play a neat game, apparently undeterred by long-line corsets, ankle length skirts and wide-brimmed hats. To make doubly sure that nothing should go wrong they also wore a wide, tight corselet (belt) to prevent separation of shirt and skirt.

By 1911 the patronage of Lady Gladstone had encouraged many more of 'the weaker sex' (men being called 'the sterner sex' by flowery women reporters) onto the golf courses. Still tightly laced, long-skirted and sporting manly neckties, ladies competed hotly for coveted prizes in the Durban Championship. That year Mrs Hardy won, being six up and Lady Gladstone herself came a creditable seventh out of 25 ('a record number of entries'), and 'gracefully presented the prizes'.

Long 'golfing' cardigans with plenty of swing room ousted tailored jackets in 1914 and by 1925 the champion of the day, Mrs Vernon of Johannesburg, won the Ladies' SA Golf Tournament dressed in mid-calf skirt, floppy cardigan, neat hat and thick stockings.

In 1930, to raised eyebrows, Mrs Crosbie won the South African title in a thrilling struggle at Umkomaas with her feet firmly encased in ankle socks and her knees showing. It was the end of elegance. For though the hemline went up and down over the next decade, and stockings hung in there grimly, the sock and the 'useful' skirt had come to stay, to be joined permanently by trousers after the Second World War.

THE SPORTY LADY: GAITERS AND KNICKERBOCKERS

The one concession a 1903 woman made to a 'commonsense garb' was when she mounted a bicycle. So grumbled a superior male in 1903 in the pages of the *Illustrated Natal*. What it was that actually won this grudging approval is hard to say, for though the cycling skirt had been slightly shortened, it was still remarkably voluminous and the tantalising glimpse of ankle that could have attracted the writer was in fact discreetly encased in gaiters. Genteel progress was still ensured by the steel hand of the corset.

Bicycling was very much a must at the turn of the century, both for those who couldn't manage the equipage of horse and trap, and for those who wished to be considered sporty. It

couldn't have been much of a pleasure for the women — leg o' mutton sleeves, constricting corsets, high necklines, floor-length skirts, petticoats and the obligatory hat not being quite the outfit one would choose for a carefree pedal in the African sun.

In fact there was considerable controversy when someone suggested that South African womanhood should adopt the knickerbockers sported by France's saucy wheelwomen. Shock-waves ran through strait-laced society and a hasty compromise was reached. Knickerbockers there should be — but worn under skirts. These skirts were no more than 15 cm above the ankle and hid the knickerbockers completely.

To love, honour and obey

FROM THE CATALOGUE: EVERYTHING BAR THE FLOWERS

Weddings have always been occasions of much receiving and spending — never more so than in the early 1900s. In a colony far from the passing parade of Royalty, and before the era of cinema and mass entertainments, a wedding provided as fine a feast for curiosity as a circus or a carnival.

The bride was naturally the focus of everyone's attention: her wedding gown, even if she was a country girl and lived far from civilisation, could still be the very height of fashion. Department-store catalogues offered a comprehensive range of made-to-order wedding gowns and bridesmaids' dresses.

Stuttafords of Cape Town promised distant customers the swift translation of their own ideas or of any design 'cut from a Fashion Journal . . . We will estimate and faithfully copy it with the greatest accuracy'. Prices suggested ranged from £3.19s.6d. to 11 guineas, depending on the quality of the materials. Veils, hats for the bridesmaids, gloves and shoes were extra. Everything, bar the fresh floral bouquets, could be safely ordered by post.

Bridesmaids were in plentiful attendance, resplendent in dresses even fussier than the bride's and topped with magnificent hats. After the church ceremony, bridal party and guests streamed to the reception, preferably held out of doors in South Africa's wonderful sunshine. Middle-class gardens, then, were usually large

An illustration from the Stuttafords catalogue at the turn of the century. Even when it came to wedding dresses the store was 'no further away than your nearest letter box'

enough to accommodate the vast company of invited guests.

Juliet Marais Louw, who grew up in Sandton when Johannesburg was still young, relates in her book *Wagon Tracks and Orchards* that in her childhood it was a sign of gentility to have 'a picture of oneself being married in a high-necked blouse and a little veil, with numerous brides-

maids wearing cartwheel hats . . . and a row of little boys and girls sitting cross-legged in front, and as many relatives as possible, fore and aft, mostly ladies with shiny satin stretched over bosoms supported by spiky corsets'.

Inside the house the wedding gifts were on display: everything from silver cutlery and photograph frames to hand-embroidered tablecloths and crocheted tea-cosies. A few framed watercolours or popular prints of the day did not come amiss. Relatives and friends meandered by with admiring or critical comments.

If the bridal pair of 1900 were lucky enough to come from fairly affluent families, they would go on honeymoon. Especially fortunate couples, like the Oudtshoorn heirs and heiresses, went overseas on the traditional Grand Tour of Europe.

Remote Afrikaner farming communities clung to older rituals of courtship and marriage.

During a fairly short *opsit* period, tallow *opsitkerse*, or courting candles, governed the time the couple could spend together. When the candle had burnt out, the boy had to return to his own homestead. Often the prospective bride would prepare the candles herself — and she'd make quite sure they were top-quality and longlasting. Matters then progressed straight to the altar. The *Outspan* in 1927 described the typical country wedding: 'A regular cavalcade sets out for the village church, the bridal pair in a Cape cart, drawn by bays for preference, in red, brass-mounted harness, the horses' heads decorated with white ostrich plumes. In close order came more carts and buggies, bearing parents, relatives and friends, all in Sunday finery. Flanking the train some "jong kêrels" on skittish

FASHIONS AS FUSSY AS THE BRIDE'S

Brides early in the century rose to astonishing flights of fancy in dressing their attendants. Little girls were bedecked in satin, flounces and frills; little boys transformed into silk-clad page boys or miniature cavaliers. Trainbearing was and to an extent still is part of the bridesmaid's duties. At rural Afrikaans marriages, wrote Olive Schreiner, bridesmaids ceremoniously led the bride to the marital chamber and there undressed her.

An elaborate – but not unusually so – wedding cake advertised by the Attwell Baking Co in 1913

In the 1900s it was customary to circulate a full list of wedding gifts and the names of their donors. The gifts were prominently displayed at the reception for all to view

The wedding of Rev. Martinius Daniel and Charlotte Murray, daughter of Rev. and Mrs George Murray of Graaff-Reinet, in the grounds of the Old Pastory in Graaff-Reinet, around 1900

mounts act as escort. In some parts of the Transvaal the procession is headed by an outrider with a small, white flag, who precedes the bridal carriage.'

Afterwards, the bride's parents provided a merry, all-night dance and a feast which Olive Schreiner described, in her *Thoughts on South Africa*, as comprising 'large quantities of mutton, milk-tart, and boiled dried fruit and coffee'. She continued:

'About two o'clock the bride is taken to the bridal chamber and undressed by the bridesmaids; the bridegroom is brought to the door by the best man, who takes the key out of the door, if it have one, and gives it to the bridegroom, who retires locking the door on the inside; and the dancing is kept up till after daylight, when the guests betake themselves to their carts and wagons and return to their homes, often a day's journey distant. Then the great event of the Boer's life is ended.'

Rituals of the rich

Magazines and newspapers in the 1900s reported weddings, and especially Society weddings, in extraordinary detail. Not only were the dresses of the bride and bridesmaids described down to the last sequin, but the glittering array of gifts received meticulous coverage. In 1903 Raymond Schumacher married Hope Weigall in London and, according to the London-based periodical *South Africa*, 'all the "haute finance" of South Africa attended. The handsome wedding gown,' the magazine went on, 'was of white satin entirely trimmed with "Brussels Point de Gaze" lace (the gift of her mother) and ornamented with little silver gauze horseshoes and orange blossoms. The bride wore no ornaments and her tulle veil was caught with orange blossoms. The tulle Court train lined with silver gauze was almost entirely covered with Brussels lace, and borne by two little white-clad train-bearers. As the bride passed bearing her bouquet of orchids and lilies, many admiring murmurs were heard'.

It was customary that presents be displayed for all the guests to view. The 'crowd filled every available space, jostling amicably through tents and conservatories, or passing slowly round the billiard room where about 400 presents awaited inspection and admiration'. Among the presents were 'pianola and music, silver centrepiece, painted china bowl, crystal and silver spirit decanters and diamond and pearl brooch, silver candlesticks, enamelled buckle, bronzes, silver tea tray, clock, silver and cut-glass scent bottles, silver paper knife, inlaid and silver Japanese tray, silver cake basket, silver seal, sugar sifters, silver card case, gold fountain pen, silver-mounted coffee cups, silver coffee set'.

Of the guests with South African connections, Mr and Mrs Otto Beit gave a silver bowl, Sir J. Percy and Lady FitzPatrick a work of art, Mr and Mrs Lionel Phillips a Parisian toilet set.

Mother and child

FOR THE YOUNG: DISCOMFORT AND INDIGNITY

Edwardian women may have suffered for fashion in South Africa's climate, but if prizes are to be awarded for endurance perhaps they should go to their children, who had little choice in the matter of clothes.

Babies appeared in public swathed in long dresses and elaborate pelisses or capes of cashmere or silk. Their heads were usually protected by a bonnet (for a girl) or a cap (for a boy), perhaps of ruched silk.

Initially it was the little boy who endured the greatest indignity. He was kept in skirts until he was 'breeched' at the age of four or later. Stuart Cloete, the South African author born in Paris of a British mother and a South African father, vividly recalled his long golden curls (washed in egg-yolk and twisted in paper every night to make ringlets) and his frocks made of 'broderie anglaise with ribbons through them and a wide blue sash . . . and a sort of floppy Ascot hat'. He was so pretty that people stopped in the street to ask his mother about her 'lovely little girl'.

Then he had to undergo a 'little Lord Fauntleroy' period, a lace-and-velvet look vastly unsuited to little boys' activities. This is borne out in Pauline Smith's *Platkops Children*, which describes a child's life in hot and dusty Oudtshoorn at the turn of the century. There she and her friends joyfully watched a snooty, lisping young visitor named Arthur Perceval Gordon-Gordon get his fancy 'welwet suit' thoroughly wet in the dam.

More fortunate boys were dressed for play in the popular sailor suit of navy serge, but once they went to school discomfort caught up with them again — this time in the guise of thick woollen knickerbockers fastening below the knee and worn with a Norfolk jacket, stout stockings and boots. Norah Henshilwood's *A Cape Childhood* records that 'piles of stockings waited every week for mothers to darn large holes in them'. She also remembers how her brothers continually lost or broke the small bone studs that held their stiff Eton collars in place.

What smart boys wore at the turn of the century

A cute 1900s twosome with their mother. Knickerbockers and smocks were de rigueur *for young boys*

But if it seems that girls had a better time of it, the reason is possibly that they were less complaining. Because girls certainly did suffer. A lady born in a strict, well-off Grahamstown home in 1902 described one of her earliest memories, which occurred when she was only three years old:

'I was coming down stairs dressed in a rather voluminous blue velveteen frock; on my head a sailor straw hat with daisies round it; pulling on white silk gloves that put my teeth on edge every time they caught on a rough place on my hands. At the bottom of the stairs stood Janet (who was then 17) and she said very severely to me, "Maud, a lady is always known by her gloves and her boots and just *look* at your boots".'

'I looked and considering my age it was hardly surprising to see they were wrongly laced. They started off all right where the laces began in holes, but above the ankle where they laced diagonally on to metal hooks, I had missed out some here and there. So Janet marched me back to my bedroom (no dressing in the hall!) and re-did my laces so I should at least "look like a lady".'

Although in the 1900s little girls were no longer laced into corsets straightaway — that came with puberty — they nevertheless shared with their Edwardian mothers the burden of excessive underwear. Their frocks were loose-waisted, more practical than their parents', but beneath each simple smock lurked a vest; a flat 'stay bodice' ending in buttons, on which fastened the drawers; a petticoat, and black stockings held up by uncomfortable elastic garters like Mother's.

The Grahamstown lady who was a little girl of three in 1905 wore drawers that were 'slit down the side, so that one undid two buttons and a back flap for obvious purposes'. In winter her stay bodice and drawers were changed for 'a ghastly thing called combinations — a very

Two of the daughters of Reverend George Murray of Graaff-Reinet, their dresses protected by the customary pinafore

muddling, all-in-one thing with either a back that let down or, worse still, a slit in the bottom'. Not surprisingly she comments: 'I hated them.'

In all ways girls were at the mercy of the strict female conventions of the day. They never appeared on the streets without hat and gloves; and though their dresses stopped just below the knee, they might never reveal a hint of underclothing apart from their stockings — and even these had to be girded carefully in case of a letdown.

We would scarcely credit such little paragons with being allowed to move, yet Norah Henshilwood mentions that she and her sister wore shoes with 'metal toecaps to withstand our strenuous play'. She was also fortunate enough only to be put into stockings at six. She must have had an understanding mother.

It was the First World War which swept away the straitjacket of convention, finally releasing children from their thrall. Family photo albums and fashion magazines show a marked change from about 1918, with South African children allowed increasing freedom to run about in short frocks (with vest, slip and brief bloomers) for girls; vest, shirt and unrestricting shorts (they reached to the knee but were unfastened) for boys. Hats and gloves were out except for best wear; hair was short; and stockings had given way to socks. Shoes were simple and tough. The general trend towards looser, more practical clothing was reinforced by the introduction of organised games and gymnastics into the school curriculum.

In 1918 fancy 'button boots' were only advertised for babies; they came in 'Black Glace' at 10/9 a pair. Children were offered instead a 'Tan Glace One Bar Shoe with Veldschoen sole' at 6/11 — very sturdy and practical. Note too the *'veldschoen'* sole: at last fashion and the indigenous style had achieved a union, even if it was only in the realm of children's wear.

THE EMBARRASSMENT OF HAVING CHILDREN

Pregnancy in Edwardian South Africa was a subject shrouded in euphemism. Women were *enceinte*, not pregnant. When they gave birth, they were 'lying in' — and the new baby's brothers and sisters believed firmly that the infant had arrived in the doctor's bag, or perhaps that it had been found under a gooseberry bush.

The carefully-protected ignorance of well-brought-up children was, however, not enough to shield a lady-in-waiting from the eyes of the world. To hide the whole embarrassing business, she wore — as a woman then young remembers — 'special corsets, a skirt with plackets or pleats that could be let out as needed, and over it a loose large jacket'. Thus dressed, the expectant mother would remain at home as much as possible, particularly towards her 'lying in' time.

By 1915 the new Empire line, followed for a long time by loosely waisted tunic and 'barrel' styles, brought relief to South African women. Even the look of the 1920s, ultra-slim though it was, could be stretched to suit pregnancy, since it was waistless and easily adapted.

It was in the 1930s, with the return of the waistline and the slow erosion of the conversational taboos of pregnancy, sex and birth control, that maternity wear really began to improve. By the late 1930s and early 1940s some South African women were buying made-to-order maternity frocks at shops like Cape Town's 'Babyland', while the rest felt free to make their own home-sewn adaptations.

Commonest style was the wrap-over dress, which could be let out gradually; but as this did little to hide the bulge, many dresses were given the addition of a free-floating front panel that artfully concealed what lay beneath. Home dressmakers usually contented themselves with wrap-around skirts and loose smock tops, but one sophisticated Pretoria lady remembers creating for herself, in 1941, a full-sleeved smock dress in navy-blue satin. Gathered in front but tying at the back, it was finished off at the neck by a flamboyant emerald-coloured artist's bow.

A Swiss woman who came to Cape Town in the late 1950s was so disgusted by the dowdiness of our pregnant ladies that she vowed to start a shop selling her own maternity designs. 'I saw them all walking about in navy wrap-around skirts with holes for the stomach, grey tops and Peter Pan collars,' she says. 'They looked hideous.'

Her designs, which started selling in 1960, have since become a well-established part of the fashionable woman's pregnancy, specialising in areas previously neglected — graceful cocktail dresses, for instance, and comfortable but still elegant slacks. Bold colours — red, apple green, yellow — are also a fairly recent innovation.

From time to time, fashions of the day have unwittingly helped expectant women by introducing the sack, or the tent, dress: waistless styles with a looseness which helps to conceal the bulge. But today the aim of maternity fashions is less to avoid embarrassment than to help a woman feel as elegant and comfortable as her condition will allow.

NAPPY DAYS

One could buy the following layette at Stuttafords in 1900 for £5.10s. In 1980, the equivalent would cost about R100.

	s	d
3 woollen shirts, 2/6	7	6
3 night flannels, 3/11½	11	10½
1 each day flannels, 4/11, 5/11	10	10
3 night gowns, 3/6	10	6
2 day gowns, 4/11	9	10
2 day gowns, 5/11	11	10
1 doz. Turkish napkins	8	11
1 flannel pilche	2	6
1 waterproof pilche	1	11½
1 head flannel	5	11
1 each wool bootees, 9½d, 1/0½	1	10
2 cotton bibs, 9½d	1	7
2 silk bibs, 1/6½	3	1
1 robe	12	11
1 shawl	8	11
	£5 10	0

Johan Rissik (after whom Johannesburg's Rissik Street was named) in 1903 with his four sons, each wearing the enduring sailor suit. The popularity of these outfits — for both boys and girls — lasted a full five decades. Costume-historian Elizabeth Ewing has traced their first appearance to 1882, and Spracklens of Cape Town were still advertising them in the 1930s. They were most widely worn in the first years of this century, when royalty and the navy had their closest associations

The suffering of South Africa's youngest daughters: an overdressed and constricted Lilian Mavis Smith at Val in 1911

Not all children were fussily dressed. This solemn group, photographed in a Johannesburg street, was outfitted in a motley assortment of hats and clothes

Princesses Elizabeth and Margaret Rose, far left, pictured in a 1947 edition of South Africa's Milady *magazine. Usually dressed in comfortable, practical outfits, they set the post-war fashion trend in children's clothing*

A 1957 South African girl in a dress made of 'Tootoile — double tested for crease-resistance and smooth drying . . . no pressing'

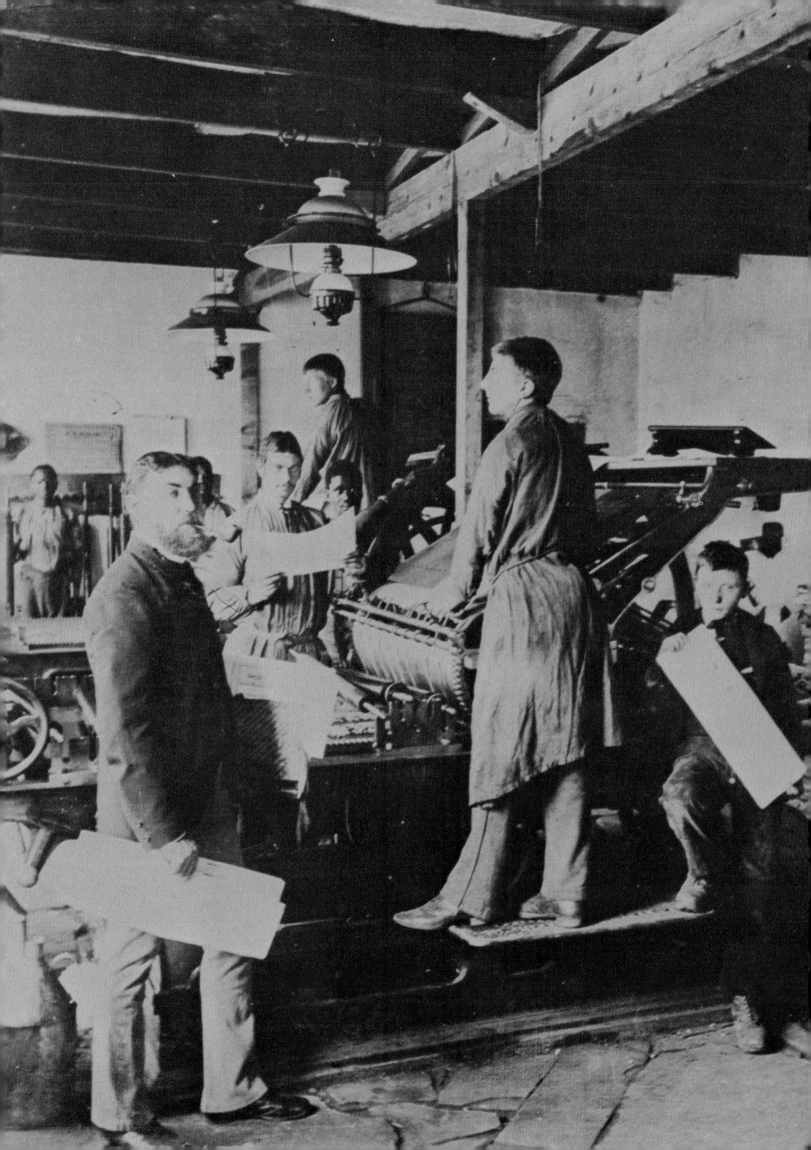

The Printed Page

Before television arrived in South Africa in 1976 the printed page was the chief medium for the communication of news, ideas and trends. Newspapers and periodicals flourished, providing jobs and reputations for talented writers and artists. Winston Churchill came here to report on the Anglo-Boer War, as did Arthur Conan Doyle, creator of the immortal Sherlock Holmes.

Rudyard Kipling made friends with Cecil Rhodes (himself convinced of the might inherent in the pen) and spent several summers in a Cape Dutch house provided by the magnate, working on his famous children's books. The Reverend D.F. Malan, destined to be Prime Minister of South Africa, was first editor of *Die Burger*. Years later, another future prime minister took the helm of *Die Transvaler* to ride the crest of the Nationalist wave — 100 years after the Great Trek. He was Hendrik Verwoerd.

Early cartoonists and writers mocked such venerable figures as 'Oom Paul' Kruger (the uncompromising *Star* was banned for its pains) and small critical journals ignited public interest in displays of literary pyrotechnics that doomed them to brief lives. Some produced only a single issue.

South African authors wrote of Karoo mornings and Cape sunsets, ebony-skinned tribesmen and wild animals. Among the better writers was a convicted murderer, a drug-addict, the wife of a British admiral and a future Governor-General of Canada. Some of their books were praised; others were reviled or banned outright.

In advertising, too, there was a vigour that alternately beguiled and infuriated. One entrepreneur boasted of a device which could make hats fit '. . . even the Most Deformed Heads', while another described a cigarette which was certain to prevent plague! The illustrations of panaceas and mysterious electric machines were bold and all-too-convincing.

Comic-strips, once invariably jolly and wholesome, evolved into printed soap operas and satirical cameos. Little Orphan Annie and Tiger Tim were overtaken by Brick Bradford, Juliet Jones, and the apparently immortal Blondie and Dagwood. Then came the super-sophisticated adventures of Modesty Blaise, and finally, the semi-naked sultriness of Axa.

Van der Merwe, that stereotyped butt of scores of jokes, appeared in all his safari-suited glory — and South Africans laughed, sometimes not realising they were laughing at themselves.

There was constant change. Steam-powered presses, Linotype machines and hot lead gradually gave way to lithographic reproduction, and computer keyboards and electronic typesetting came to South Africa in the Seventies. The printed page was being prepared for the 21st century.

The printing works at De Volksstem *in Pretoria in the late 19th century. The newspaper was established in 1873*

All the news

CONTINUING SAGAS AND JOLLY GYMKHANAS

There was nothing flamboyant or vulgar about the newspaper of 1900. Banner headlines and dramatic, six-column photographs were far in the future, and one had to look carefully for the real news.

'Sporting Intelligence' and theatre announcements featured on page four and only then, in a mass of grey type and diminutive headlines, came the 'Latest News'. In the *Cape Argus* of 2 January 1900, this began with British news (such as the New Year Honours List) and the departures of steamers, and then progressed to the dominant topic of the day: 'The War'. But even this cataclysmic event was handled in a curiously undramatic way: numerous small items detailed troop movements, war casualties, Boer prisoners, the Queen's New Year greeting, Lady Buller's present of Christmas puddings and cigarettes to a regiment in Natal, and a jolly gymkhana at Modder River.

But while these newspapers might have been amateurish operations by today's standards, the industry was well-established and healthy. George Greig's independent newspaper, the *South African Commercial Advertiser*, had appeared as early as 1824, *De Zuid-Afrikaan* (a bilingual paper which was published for over 100 years) came six years later, and by the mid-19th century, South African newspapers had really taken root. The *Eastern Province Herald* appeared in 1845, followed by the *Natal Witness* (both published weekly) in 1846, *The Friend of the Sovereignty and Bloemfontein Gazette* (it became *The Friend* in 1902), the *Cape Argus* in 1857 and the *Cape Times* — the oldest surviving daily newspaper — in 1876. The Transvaal papers were established some time later.

The rise of the Afrikaans press

The story of the early Afrikaans press in South Africa is also the story of the struggle to gain recognition for the emerging language.

Di Afrikaanse Patriot, the first newspaper dedicated to the acceptance and preservation of Afrikaans, was launched in 1876 by the Genootskap van Regte Afrikaners — ardent and

Mastheads from some early issues of South African newspapers. The country has enjoyed a wide variety of newspapers for well over a century

vociferous campaigners for the language.

But it was in 1915 that the Afrikaans press really came into its own, the year when Nasionale Pers was founded in Cape Town. The voice of the newly-established National Party was to be Nasionale Pers's *Die Burger*, at first largely Dutch (and called *De Burger*), but by the 1920s fully Afrikaans. Its editor was Dr D.F. Malan, leader of the party in the Cape and the man who, in 1948, became the first Nationalist Prime Minister. The paper's strongly-expressed political policy and its

In 1902 a new newspaper, the *Rand Daily Mail*, rose from the ashes of the old *Standard and Diggers' News*. A young Anglo-Boer War correspondent became its first editor, operating from cramped premises in Johannesburg. He was Edgar Wallace, later to become a world-famous author. The man who once sold newspapers in the streets of London had made a name for himself by sending daring reports to the London *Daily Mail* under the noses of the military censors. It was his account of alleged Boer atrocities at Vlakfontein, followed by his reporting of the supposedly secret peace negotiations at Pretoria in 1902, that put him firmly in the limelight. He sent cables disguised as stock exchange deals, gathering information from a helpful sentry at the peace camp. When the *Daily Mail* finally spilt the beans, Wallace became an instant hero.

healthy financial association with a new and popular magazine (*Die Huisgenoot*) gave it the muscle to survive and flourish.

Other Afrikaans newspapers — *Die Vaderland, Die Volksblad* — soon followed, but it was *Die Transvaler*, founded in 1937 with future Prime Minister Hendrik Verwoerd as its first editor, that was the paper which best expressed the intense Afrikaner nationalist emotion of 1938, the centenary of the Great Trek.

By 1948, when Verwoerd resigned to stand for election to Parliament after his long repub-

Men at work. Staffers on the Braamfontein Baton *sit before an intriguing array of machines. Early newspapermen were generally a hardy breed, working long hours for a pittance in buildings which were often very shabby*

lican crusade, the Afrikaans press was established as the powerful voice of politically triumphant Afrikanerdom.

Black journalism in South Africa has a long, honourable and imaginative history.

The most respected black editor of the 19th century was the founder of the weekly newspaper, *Imvo Zabantsundu* (1884) — John Tengo Jabavu. Sir James Rose-Innes, who became Chief Justice of the Union of South Africa, wrote of the man who was his close friend: '. . . Mr Jabavu never looked back. He proved to be a born editor, with a facile trenchant pen in both Kafir [sic] and English. Subscribers came in shoals and the demand for *Imvo* increased rapidly — as did the printer's bill!'

This small King William's Town newspaper and its vigorous editor campaigned and cajoled, and issues of profound importance to the people were debated in its columns.

The black Johannesburg daily paper, *The World* (published as *Bantu World* until 1956), was established in 1932. By 1962 it had a daily sale of over 80 000 copies — the fourth largest of all South African dailies. It was published in English, Afrikaans, Sotho, Tswana, Xhosa and Zulu, so leaping the tribal language barrier, and this contributed to its impressively large circulation. But the paper's outspokenness on racial matters finally led to its banning in 1977.

MAGAZINES:
GENTLE, FUNNY, ACID

A host of South African magazines have flowered and died since the turn of the century. The lives of some were brief; others caught on and stayed. Publishers discovered the fickleness of the reading public in courageous but doomed efforts that even such dynamic talents as Stephen Black, Herman Charles Bosman, Roy Campbell and William Plomer could not save.

In the early days of the 1900s, readers could peruse genteel magazines such as *The Veld*, one of the first glossies. Stronger medicine was administered by Cape Town's robust *South African Review*, which claimed to be 'the smartest and most up-to-date Weekly Journal in South Africa'. At 2d a copy it was a bargain, and it bristled with lively satirical cartoons, acid political snippets and humorous anecdotes.

Calling all women
Women's magazines came into their own when the *South African Lady's Pictorial and Home Journal* appeared in 1912. It presented a winning medley of the latest society gossip, fashion news, recipes, beauty and gardening hints until 1936, when it became the *Pictorial*, and brimmed over with sepia-toned photographs of weddings, garden parties and sporting celebrities in South Africa.

For Afrikaners, *Die Boerevrou en Ons Kleintjie* (1919 to 1931) provided not only their first women's magazine, but also a forum for excellent Pierneef drawings and the new Afrikaans poetry of Leipoldt and Eugene Marais. But the first South African magazine to appeal to

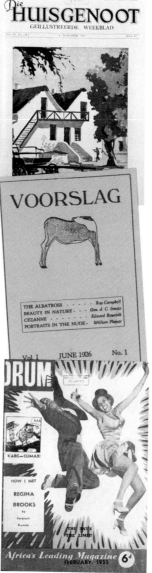

A selection of South African magazine covers spanning the first six decades of this century. Sjambok *(April/May 1929 — March 1931) and the even more critical* Voorslag *(June 1926 — May/June 1927) had brief and stormy lives, while others such as* Huisgenoot *(launched in 1916) and* Drum *still flourish*

AN ADVENTUROUS EDITOR

When the country's first Sunday newspaper was born in Johannesburg in 1906 (President Kruger was no longer there to oppose this 'work of the devil'), its first editor was George Herbert Kingswell, known as both a rolling stone and a near-genius.

Kingswell's bohemian lifestyle carried him to places most people only dream about. He covered the Boxer uprising, the Klondike gold rush, went on a camel ride across the Gobi desert and reported on minor wars in almost every corner of the globe. He returned to South Africa to establish the *Sunday Times*.

Using the presses of the *Rand Daily Mail*, the new paper hit the streets on 4 February 1906. It was an immediate success, and the initial run quickly sold out.

both men and women with equal force was *Outspan*. Born in 1927, it survived for 30 splendid years, and although outshone in longevity by the Afrikaans magazine, *Huisgenoot* (launched as early as 1916), *Outspan* enjoyed a resounding popularity matched by no other South African magazine of its time.

The secret of *Outspan's* unique success lay in its strong South African flavour. Circulation rose by thousands each week after the initial cautious print of 40 000, until at over 100 000, the magazine reached the biggest circulation of any magazine in Africa. But in the 1950s, fighting rising costs (the price was now 6d) and a change in editorship, *Outspan* gradually lost both its unique local flavour and its extreme popularity.

Finally, in 1957, *Outspan* died — and though a phoenix called *Personality* rose in its place, this new magazine never quite made the grade. South Africa still enjoys a wealth of magazines aimed at all sections of the community. Among the top-selling monthlies are the *Reader's Digest* magazine, *Living and Loving*, *Your Family* and the black periodical, *Bona* (the last had an average monthly circulation of over 350 000 for the second half of 1980).

Fair Lady and the two Afrikaans magazines, *Sarie Marais* and *Rooi Rose*, had the highest circulations among the fortnightly magazines towards the end of 1980, while *Huisgenoot* dominated the weekly market with a circulation of over 287 000 copies.

Stories of the century

TELLING IT LIKE IT IS

South Africa's chequered and turbulent history has provided newspapers with a steady source of dramatic, frightening and sometimes poignant stories. Its growth to nationhood, its rebellions, riots, weddings and wars have been recorded faithfully by journalists in widely varying styles designed to inform, entertain and sometimes shock the reading public.

One of the first stories to receive five-star treatment by our early 20th century newspapers was the dramatic roundup that ended the criminal career of the notorious Foster Gang in 1914. It was a field day for photographers.

Foster and his accomplices — two bandits known as Maxim and Mezar — were cornered in a cave on a Kensington farm after a police roundup which had tragic consequences — a doctor and the Anglo-Boer War General De la Rey were shot when they drove through the police cordon ringing Johannesburg.

Foster's family were allowed to enter the cave, but they emerged later without Peggy, his wife. Three shots rang out (Mezar had died a while before — he had either shot himself or been shot by his companions), and detectives entered the cave to find four bodies. They had taken their own lives rather than surrender.

Arsenic and old photographs

Murder trials have never failed to attract the public's attention, and newspapers were

Armed police and curious onlookers surround the cave in Kensington, Johannesburg, where the notorious Foster Gang took refuge in 1914. The siege, which ended with the death of the entire gang, captured the public's imagination and drew a large crowd. The manhunt also led indirectly to the deaths of two innocent people

well aware that a photograph could make considerable impact. Elegantly-dressed Maria Lee, hanged in 1948 for poisoning her lover with arsenic, actually complained about the poor quality of her photographs in the press. And she was not the first murderess to wish that her portraits were more flattering.

Daisy de Melker, arrested in 1932 on charges of poisoning two husbands with strychnine and killing her own son with arsenic, made the same complaint. In *Genius for the Defence*, veteran crime and court reporter Benjamin Bennett tells how an old photograph of her — she scorned it, saying she was

'much better looking than that' — provided the vital evidence leading to her conviction.

Mrs de Melker had been evading newspaper photographers outside the court, but someone handed the Johannesburg *Star* an old picture of her. For Johannesburg chemist Abraham Spilkin it was a revelation: he recognised the woman as the 'Mrs Sproat' who had bought arsenic from him several months before 'to get rid of a cat'. Daisy's second husband had been Robert Sproat, but she had been re-married for 13 months.

Without Spilkin's vital evidence, Daisy de Melker might have stood a chance of escaping

---

A twisted mass of metal is all that remains of one of the dynamite trucks which blew up at Braamfontein, in Johannesburg, on 19 February 1896. The explosion left a huge crater and killed scores of people

COLLISION, EXPLOSION — AND DEATH

Although rare, South Africa has experienced some horrific rail smashes. Probably the first major disaster occurred in February 1896, when ten trucks loaded with dynamite were shunted into the Braamfontein goods yard. On 19 February a goods train crashed into the dynamite train, and the resulting explosion shook the whole of Johannesburg. A huge hole was blasted into the ground, and at least 80 people perished. About 500 others were taken to hospital.

On 22 April 1911, a train from Port Alfred, consisting of six trucks, three carriages and a guard's van, was passing over the Blaauwkrantz bridge when one truck — laden with stone for the Grahamstown Cathedral — was derailed. Within seconds almost the entire train toppled from the line and plunged to the rocks nearly 50 metres below. A relief train carrying doctors and nurses steamed for the bridge — and met a horrifying sight. From the twisted girders hung parts of carriages and clothes of the victims. Far below lay the shattered remains of the rest of the train, and from the splintered carriages came the wails of the injured and dying. Twenty-eight people died.

Fifteen years later, on 9 June 1926, an evening express from Cape Town to Simonstown crashed at Salt River when a coupling broke between the fourth and fifth carriages. The second half of the train was jerked off the rails, and one coach smashed into a bridge. The toll was 17 dead and 30 injured.

The red dot shows where seven-year-old Hazel Smith clung to Blaauwkrantz bridge after the derailment in 1911. She was rescued unharmed. Below: Headlines describe the Salt River rail smash

CAPE TIMES, THURSDAY, JUNE 10, 1926.

SUBURBAN EXPRESS WRECKED.

FIFTEEN KILLED, MANY INJURED.	AT CAPE TOWN STATION.	CASUALTY LIST.	SIR M. SEARLE KILLED.	EXTRICATING THE DEAD AND INJURED.
	Rush Hour Crowds Held Up.	Official: 15 Killed, 26 Injured.	Judge-President Among the Victims.	Harrowing Work For Willing Helpers.
Passengers Dashed To Death in Uncoupled Coaches.	DRIVER SAVED BY HIS TENDER.	DEAD.		GENERAL IMPRESSIONS OF THE SMASH.
TERRIBLE CRASH AT SALT RIVER.		IN POLICE MORGUE, WOODSTOCK. MRS. ROLINE FOSTER, aged 33, Ilaya, Sandhurst road, Wynberg. MRS. LEAH WALT, aged 42, Plumstead MISS FREDA WALT, aged 19, Plumstead. MISS JANE WALT, aged 17, Plumstead. TWO LADIES UNIDENTIFIED.		

notoriety as the first woman poisoner to be hanged in South Africa. A newspaper photograph had brought her to the death cell.

Left: Maria Lee was hanged in 1948 for poisoning her lover. Above: 'Bubbles' Schroeder, photographed shortly before her death. Her body was found in a plantation in 1949, and the unsuccessful hunt for her killer caused a sensation

The Rivonia sensation

The trial was one of the longest and most sensational in South Africa's legal history. Rivonia was the name on everyone's lips for the first half of 1964 as the seven-month sabotage trial ground through accusation, argument and sometimes high drama.

It ended on 12 June 1964 when Mr Justice Quartus de Wet sentenced eight men to life imprisonment after telling them that their crime was essentially one of treason. They were Nelson Mandela, a lawyer and former secretary-general of the banned African National Congress; Walter Sisulu, also a former ANC secretary-general; Dennis Goldberg, a civil engineer from Cape Town; Ahmed Kathrada, a former secretary-general of the Transvaal Indian Congress; Govan Mbeki, a Port Elizabeth journalist; Raymond Mhlaba, Andrew Mlangeni and Elias Matsoaledi. A ninth man, Lionel 'Rusty' Bernstein, was acquitted.

They had been charged under the General Law Amendment Act (the 'Sabotage Act') and the Suppression of Communism Act and were accused of conspiring to commit nearly 200 acts of sabotage in preparation for guerilla warfare and an armed invasion of South Africa.

Over 1 000 people waited outside the Palace of Justice to hear the sentences, and police used dogs to disperse them. The Rivonia trial was over.

The assassination of Dr Verwoerd

On 6 September 1966 the Prime Minister, Dr Hendrik Verwoerd, awoke early. He was due to address the House of Assembly in the first session of Parliament since the general election. At 2.11 p.m. he entered the lobby of the Houses of Parliament with his wife, Betsy, and two minutes later took his seat in the Chamber.

A swarthy man in the distinctive blue uniform of a parliamentary messenger suddenly lurched towards the Prime Minister. His right hand was raised high in the air — clasping a sheath knife. The gleaming blade plunged into the Prime Minister, once, twice, three times, four times . . .

Dr Verwoerd appeared to be unaware of what was happening. He sat, motionless, then sagged, head back, glazed eyes looking straight up at the press gallery, a crimson stain spreading over his white shirt.

At two minutes to four the *Cape Argus* ran a banner headline:

VERWOERD STABBED TO DEATH IN THE HOUSE OF ASSEMBLY

'The Prime Minister (Dr H.F. Verwoerd) died of stab wounds inflicted on him in the Houses of Parliament this afternoon by a man wearing the uniform of a parliamentary messenger. The SABC, announcing the death of Dr Verwoerd, gave the name of his assailant as Dimitri Tsafendas.'

South Africa was plunged into mourning.

The end of the Rivonia trial — one of the longest and most dramatic in South Africa's history. Security precautions were strict, the homes of the presiding judge and State prosecutor being placed under police guard

In September 1966 the country was shocked by the assassination of Dr Hendrik Verwoerd. There had been a previous attempt on his life: in April 1960 he was wounded by two bullets fired by David Pratt, an epileptic

In 1975 an Israeli Consulate security guard named David Protter took over the building in Fox Street, Johannesburg, and held its occupants hostage while police and army units massed outside. Protter killed the consulate's chief security officer and then sprayed the street with fire, wounding 34 people. He gave himself up after a siege lasting 21 hours

Dr Eschel Rhoodie in 1978. The former Secretary for Information was a key figure in the controversial 'Information Affair', in which newspapers revealed clandestine propaganda operations, including Government funding of the Citizen newspaper

Making South Africa laugh

LAUGHING AT THE POMPOUS AND POWERFUL

Cartoonists at the turn of the century took their politics seriously, yet were always ready to laugh at the pompous and powerful in pictorial satire. The result was a steady flow of comic relief in newspapers and periodicals and a lasting record of political and social life ranging from the gentle to the vitriolic. No-one was safe; victims included prime ministers, racetrack beauties, authority in general, and the little bundle of prejudice that makes up the man in the street.

But cartoons were not always satirical. Before the advent of photographs in print, they were the only means of illustrating local life and events.

Personalities there were aplenty during the first years of the 20th century. The gold rush and the Anglo-Boer War had thrown tycoons, generals and politicians into sharp relief — and Daniël Boonzaier, the Cape-born cartoonist with a true gift for caricature, was there to record them for posterity. The young Boonzaier began drawing in Carnarvon and later moved to Cape Town, where he studied the work of W.H. Schröder, cartoonist on *The Knobkerrie*. The paper published one of Boonzaier's sketches in October 1884.

He was the official cartoonist on *Die Burger* from 1915 to 1940, during which time he earned widespread praise for his ability to tell a tale in his drawings without spite or vulgarity. General Smuts and General Louis Botha were among his favourite targets.

In the 1920s a cartoonist named 'Quip' (E.A. Packer) continued the game of poking

German artist Heinrich Egersdörfer arrived at the Cape in the early 1880s. Left: His portrayal of a group of cyclists was printed by the South African Illustrated News in 1885. Right: An Anglo-Boer War cartoon

Caricatures by cartoonist Daniël Boonzaier. From the left: Dr D.F. Malan (1930); Ben Pienaar with Mussolini (1929); Rand magnate Solly Joel (1929). All were published in The Sjambok and signed Nemo

President Kruger, in ermine robe and full regalia, prepares to crown himself in an 1897 cartoon by Kidger Tucker, a popular figure on the diamond fields

Need a fourth? A 1927 drawing by Major E.G. Ridley illustrates a humorous Outspan article

This cartoon by Victor Ivanoff in 1940 shows Mussolini being wooed by Hitler and Neville Chamberlain

gentle fun at politicians. Tielman Roos, one of the era's best-known cabinet ministers, was one of his favourite subjects. Though Roos was portrayed in ridiculous situations, he was depicted as a fat, jolly man; this was seen by some as a sign that the really painful sting was going out of satire. The focus of cartoonists was moving away from the acute personal barb towards wider-ranging social comment. Political cartoons were by no means dead — but the jokes about ordinary South Africans, a recognisable breed since Union, were gaining ground.

Fresh blood was introduced to the body of South African cartooning when tycoon I.W.

Schlesinger brought American Bob Connolly to Johannesburg in 1937 to work for his *Daily Express*. When the paper folded a year later, Connolly moved to the *Rand Daily Mail*, where his cartoon figure, the 'Little Man', remains a familiar and well-loved character.

The 'Little Man' and Van der Merwe

Connolly wrote in his autobiography, *The Bob Connolly Story*: '. . . if you want to know, he represents the man in the street, the taxpayer and the S.A. public.' The pot-bellied, bespectacled figure ('Apart from a curl on top and a few hairs around his ears, he is as bald as a golf ball') was the focus of a £1 000 compe-

Dagwood Bumstead introduces fiancée Blondie Boopadoop to his wealthy parents. One of the world's most popular comic strips, it was launched in 1930 by American cartoonist Chic Young

A 1957 cartoon by Connolly of the Rand Daily Mail. *Dr Dönges tries to balance a stack of identity cards*

Jakkals en Wolf, *created by cartoonist Thomas Honiball, was published in* Die Jongspan *from 1942. Honiball was principal cartoonist on* Die Burger *for many years, becoming widely respected*

tition to name him. The winning name was 'Johnny Elkeman', but he remains the 'Little Man'.

But the 'Little Man' was an individual cartoonist's creation. It was only in the early 1960s that South Africa finally produced its own folk figure of fun: Van der Merwe. This thick-set, slow-thinking and unashamedly bigoted person quickly climbed to top place in the South African joke book — and has remained there ever since.

Attempts to chart his ascent have been only partly successful. The authors of *Van der Merwe* and *Not Again, Van der Merwe* attributed the cult to Fanus Rautenbach, an announcer with the SABC, who used to crack early morning Van der Merwe jokes during the early 1960s.

But a look at the work of two highly popular cartoonists, David Marais of the *Cape Times* and John Jackson of the *Argus*, reveals that in the late 1950s they frequently used the name Van der Merwe to personify the comic common man, a South African 'Everyman' who could be laughed at by both his English- and Afrikaans-speaking compatriots.

Van der Merwe (it is, after all, one of the commonest names in South Africa) could be a policeman, smart-aleck schoolboy, soldier, a dumb ox of a man, a con-artist's dream — or even a female version, Lettie van der Merwe.

An exaggeration of the worst faults, failings and prejudices of the nation, Van der Merwe was a sure sign that South Africans had learned to laugh not only at their politicians but also at themselves.

John Jackson, cartoonist on the Argus *in Cape Town since the 1950s, portrays South Africa's 'Everyman'*

Launched by American cartoonist Harold Foster in 1937, Prince Valiant *recounts the adventures of one of King Arthur's knights of the Round Table*

A typical scene from The Katzenjammer Kids, *the oldest comic strip still in existence. The infernal twins were created by Rudolph Dirks in 1897*

OUR REGULAR SATURDAY TREAT

South Africans have always enjoyed comics and cartoon-strips. In the late Thirties, Forties and Fifties children would gather religiously at the local cinema for their regular Saturday treat — swapping comics. Cowboys and Indians were a favourite subject, and the adventures of Felix the Cat, Hot Stuff the Little Devil and Casper the Friendly Ghost never failed to appeal.

The first 'superheroes' made their appearance, and Superman comics became a valuable commodity; they could probably be swapped for up to three of the tamer offerings. War comics were also collected zealously. These, usually in a smaller format, portrayed the adventures of such patriotic giants as Battler Britten, the scourge of the Axis in the Second World War. His German foes were usually depicted as snarling troops whose morale quickly crumbled at his onslaught, at which they would shout '*Himmel!*', '*Donner und blitzen!*' and the ever-popular '*Achtung!*'.

Although Mickey Mouse, Donald Duck and other Walt Disney characters enjoyed enduring appeal, they lost ground in later years to a new breed of hero. The chiselled features of heroes were retained, but the costumes became outlandish. It seemed everyone wanted

to wear a cape or mask, and soon Batman and Robin began to look almost conventional. There was one inviolate rule, though: no matter what the setbacks, no matter how evil the villains, Good always triumphed over Evil.

It was inevitable that the Americans should spot the commercial possibilities of cartoon strips and develop them into the form we know today. Early this century there was keen rivalry among New York newspapers to attempt to convert the public to the new art form, and it was then that someone came up with the idea of 'balloons' to contain the characters' dialogue. Previously the text was placed below the strips — generally in doggerel form.

The first series with a constant set of characters and a complete incident in each strip was the Kaztenjammer Kids. A.E. Hayward's Cam O'Flage, the scatterbrained typist with office problems, was another of the early cartoon-strips featured in South African newspapers. We met folk hero Robin Hood in 1934, spaceman Brick Bradford three years later, and finally the evergreen Blondie and husband Dagwood.

Charles W. Schultz created Charlie Brown, the awful Lucy — and Snoopy, the long-suffering First World War fighter ace, author, philosopher and part-time beagle who is probably one of the best-loved cartoon characters in the world.

Advertising with style

IMPOSSIBLE CLAIMS AND OUTRAGEOUS PROMISES

Advertisements in the closing years of the 19th century were naively exaggerated, pompous and desperately polite. Shopkeepers 'begged to inform' their customers that the latest shipment of frocks, button boots and hats had arrived in Table Bay.

By today's stringent standards, many advertisements were also downright unethical. Quack remedies abounded, and merchants made extravagant claims for impossible cure-alls. One advised people to try his ingenious mechanical device for making hats fit 'all Regular and even the Most Deformed Heads'.

Techniques were markedly different, too: most firms relied almost entirely on the printed word. A typical advertisement of the 1890s would combine several typographical tricks — from bold black capitals to italics and highly ornate lettering, embellished for emphasis with double lines, dots, stars and a liberal scattering of exclamation marks. Pointing hands, complete with neat Edwardian cuffs, drew attention to wordy notices and, where imagination failed, an advertiser might fall back on the simple device of repetition, filling line after line with the proud name of his product.

The power of the picture

Others, though, were not content to let the name speak for itself. A 1904 advertisement for Doan's Backache Kidney Pills insisted: 'Every Picture Tells a Story.' In this case the picture was intentionally comic (a portly Edwardian gentleman clutching his back with an expression of pained indignation). Other illustrations were simpler: three large bottles of beer set boldly across the page for Castle Ale; a single startling eye for an optician; before-and-after drawings of a face dramatically cleared of pimples by Cuticura soap — a still-popular technique.

One of several wagons fitted with large 'teapots' and used as mobile advertisements for Nectar Tea

Don't despair—things are never really so bad as a despondent mind sees them. There is hope for you if you will but adopt the "Ajax" way—Nature's way of restoring lost Vitality and Vigour. From the very day you start wearing the "Ajax" body Battery will dawn a new era for you of vigorous Health which will enable you to once more participate in the joys of living.

OGDEN'S 'GUINEA-GOLD' ARE HIS ONLY SOLACE.

OOM PAUL WANTS SOMETHING SOOTHING NOW. WE SUGGEST AN OGDEN'S 'GUINEA GOLD' CIGARETTE. They have great Soothing CAPE-abilities.

Advertisers made much use of the personal testimonial, genuine and invented. In 1904 a certain Dr Sanden could quote one grateful buyer of his magical Herculex, a kind of electrified belt:

'My Dear Dr Sanden,
I deem it a duty I owe to you and to mankind in general, to let you know the results obtained from the use of your Herculex. For over 25 years I have suffered from the most severe Rheumatic pains. . .
A year ago a friend persuaded me to try your Herculex, with the result that the pains were eased at once, and within 30 days from the first application I considered myself completely cured, and have had no recurrence of the pain since.

BARTOLOMI CONSI,
Buenos Ayres.'

Advertisers have never hesitated to use the most outrageous gimmicks to promote their products. The long-suffering man with the unique 'sandwich board' (top right) was one early example (the significance of the roller skates is not known). Ogden's 'Guinea Gold' cigarette advertisements introduced South African personalities (left and far left), and men who had exhausted 'life's vital forces' were advised to write to the Electropathic Institute of South Africa and inquire about their Dry Cell Body Battery (top left)

The Art Nouveau influence could sometimes be seen in grandiose designs with fancy lettering and elaborate scrolls. Not for them the wry sophistication of the 1960s Volkswagen advertisement which conceded that the 'Beetle' might be considered ugly.

Most of those early names, scattered so confidently over the pages of newspapers and magazines, have disappeared for good. The militant 'Warrior Soap' of Anglo-Boer War fame has gone; Ayer's Sarsparilla is no more, and Mrs Spendlove no longer supplies corsets to Cape Town's fashion-conscious ladies.

The image and the slogan

By the 1920s, advertising styles had changed dramatically. Black-and-white photographs were beginning to oust line drawings in magazines which could offer a high quality of reproduction. Soon famous

Reserve Squadron, 12th Royal Lancers, Colchester, September 21st, 1900.

GENTLEMEN,—I have great pleasure in forwarding you the facts of a little incident which occurred to me personally during the recent operations in South Africa.

On the 13th February last, while under Lord Roberts and General French, we surprised and captured the Boer laager at Klip Drift. I was one of the first to cross the Drift, and I noticed a portmanteau in the laager which the Boers had left behind in their flight. It was open, and on my examining the contents, I found six small packages, which I opened and found to be bottles of your Dr. William's Pink Pills for Pale People.

I distributed them amongst my chums, and all informed me that they derived great

Left: An Anglo-Boer War soldier acclaims Dr William's Pink Pills. Right: An early Sanatogen advertisement featured endorsements by some well-known personalities

Olive Schreiner:
The gifted Authoress writes from De Aar, Cape of Good Hope, as follows : "Sanatogen's effect upon me has been most remarkable. Nothing that I have taken for years has given me the same sense of vigour and restored circulation."

beauties were plugging toilet soap and wide-eyed children, all too good to be true, were being used to prove the health-giving properties of baby foods.

But advertisements remained wordy, and testimonials continued to thrive. There were a few bold exceptions to the standard format: a bright picture, a catchy slogan, a clever pun. Amami Shampoos stated that 'Friday Night is Amami Night!' which became a catch-phrase of the 1920s; 'Did you Maclean your teeth to-day?' of the 1930s.

Those whose products became between-war household words — names such as Brasso, Silvo and Bisto — proved the power of advertising so effectively that is was not long before merchants and manufacturers became aware that they had to advertise or go under. Campaigns became hectic and imaginative: cigarette makers turned to cash prizes as well as their ever-popular cigarette cards; Moir's offered a 22½-inch pearl necklace to anyone who collected 72 empty jelly packets.

Competition and control

Competition became even fiercer after the Second World War with the advent of natural colour printing in magazines, and an exciting advertising era was launched in 1949 when commercial radio was introduced to South Africa. Printed advertisements became vividly pictorial; Hollywood stars and a new breed of model exhibited their ideal proportions in a

MR CARROLL'S BIG IDEA

In 1891 one of William Lever's 'young men', a certain Mr Carroll, was sent to the Cape Colony to spread news of Britain's first branded and packaged soap. Forced to abandon his scheme to write the words Sunlight Soap in huge letters on the slopes of Table Mountain, he moved to Port Elizabeth, where he settled for a more modest approach. He had the brand name painted at intervals along the pavements in the main street. Confronted by the city's irate Mayor, the enterprising salesman asked: 'Would you really like to have the signs removed?'
The Mayor: 'Of course.'
Mr Carroll: 'Do you know what is the best way to get the paint off?'
The Mayor: 'No.'
Mr Carroll: 'Buy a case of Sunlight Soap and . . . set your men scrubbing.'

This appealed hugely to the Mayor: he roared with laughter and the two men became good friends. Sunlight Soap had arrived in South Africa, and stayed.

Motor car manufacturers employed unusual methods and settings to draw attention to their products. A Ford was pictured atop Table Mountain (left) and a Dodge was up-ended on another to create what must have been one of Durban's most unusual vehicles

technicoloured parade of legs, bosoms and vacuous smiles. Sex — unsubtle, perhaps, but effective — had arrived on the advertising scene.

Growing concern over the ethics of advertising led, in the late 1940s, to publishers of newspapers and magazines accepting a strict code of standards designed to protect the public from misleading or untrue statements. Were he in business now, the 1902 advertiser of Jones' Rheumaticuro would no longer be able to say that his 'Great South African Remedy (for rheumatism, neuralgia, lumbago, sciatica *and* gout) cures when everything else fails'.

Attractive women, including stage and film stars, have often featured in South African advertisements

213

ADVERTISING: THE WAY IT WAS

South Africa's advertising industry — worth R500 million a year at the close of the 1970s — has come a long way this century. And not only in terms of the money invested in it. Today it is a highly refined science, enjoying almost limitless use of full colour photography — a rare medium before the Second World War, when colourful advertising was confined largely to posters, cards and labels, a selection of which are shown here.

Advertising cards came in many sizes, some as small as a calling card and others large and elaborate. Manufacturers and merchants were aware that their cards, especially those bearing illustrations in colour, were likely to find their way into collections. It was an excellent medium for the promotion of products.

The demand eventually became so great that virtually every household item, from soap powder to corn remover, was promoted on a card. Local shopkeepers handed them to customers or wrapped them with purchases while others were given away by salesmen. Some manufacturers packed their cards with products such as cigarettes and confectionery. By the standards of the 1980s the message of yesteryear's advertising was direct, the selling point quite unmistakable, the humour obvious (laboured puns were much favoured). Wholesomeness was the keynote throughout.

Many products became household names, largely through the impact of colourful advertising. Some of these — Sunlight, Lux, Vinolia — still are.

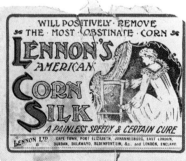

Romance of Africa

KIPLING, POET LAUREATE OF THE EMPIRE

Gold, diamonds and the sheer space of Southern Africa before the turn of the century attracted great men, and men who were destined to be great, like bees to an exotic bloom. Among them was the writer regarded as the Poet Laureate of the British Empire: Rudyard Kipling.

The creator of *Kim* and the immortal Mowgli of the *Jungle Books* was born in India in 1865 and educated in England. In 1882 he returned to India, where he eventually became editor of the *Pioneer Weekly* in Allahabad. Here he wrote *Plain Tales from the Hills*, the first of the short stories upon which his massive reputation still rests securely. By the 1890s his rousing verse was as popular as the hit songs of today — though it popularised not love but the dream of Empire, and struck a responsive chord in every good British heart.

A trip around the world with his American wife in 1891 brought Kipling to the Cape, where he spent the months of September and October. He was to return again in 1898, when he met Cecil Rhodes, the man who personified the Imperial dream in Southern Africa. The two men became firm friends, and soon the entire Kipling family, complete with nurse and governess for the children, was spending every summer in The Woolsack, a Cape Dutch house lent to them by Rhodes and extensively altered by architect Herbert Baker to Mrs Caroline Kipling's taste.

It was here that Kipling began writing *Puck of Pook's Hill* and his famous *Just So Stories* (published in 1902; two of the tales were inspired by a trip to Rhodesia, arranged for him by Rhodes).

How the Leopard Got its Spots begins in the 'bare, hot, shiny High Veldt' where Baviaan, the 'barking Baboon', described by Kipling as 'Quite the Wisest Animal in All South Africa', advises the leopard to acquire his spots for camouflage. Perhaps the best of the *Just So Stories*, *The Elephant's Child*, relates how the elephant went north to get his trunk:

'He went from Graham's Town to Kimberley, and from Kimberley to Khama's Country, and from Khama's Country he went east by north, eating melons all the time, till at last he came to the banks of the great, grey-green, greasy Limpopo River, all set about with fever-trees . . .'

Writing was not Kipling's only concern on these South African visits. As he wrote to a friend, 'my half year at the Cape is always my "political" time, and I enjoy it'. He was deeply stirred by the Anglo-Boer War, and when his friend Rhodes was caught up in the siege of Kimberley, he threw himself into the war effort with *The Absent-Minded Beggar*, a poem published by the *Daily Mail* and recited in British music halls and drawing rooms until it had raised over a quarter of a million pounds towards his fund for soldiers' dependants.

A few Anglo-Boer War stories (including *A Sahib's War)* and poems such as *South Africa*, *Two Kopjes* and *Piet*, the poem described by

Above: Kipling's lavishly-illustrated poem, The Absent-Minded Beggar, *earned threepence for soldiers' dependants for every copy sold. Top: It dwelt on the poignancy of the soldier's farewell and (left) reminded those who stayed behind of their roles, too*

Angus Wilson in his biography, *The Strange Ride of Rudyard Kipling,* as 'his curious backhanded olive branch to the defeated Afrikaners' were the only other fruits of those turbulent years. In the end the South African experience proved a disappointing one for Kipling. He arrived as court poet to Rhodes and Milner, but stayed to watch with dismay as the Boer republics were handed back.

Rhodes had died in 1902 and the Union of South Africa was on the horizon. It was the funeral of Kipling's Imperial dream, and in 1907 he wrote to a friend: 'I will go to the Cape in December to see the burial, but I must then hunt for another country to love.'

He was a contradictory man with streaks of both pride and self-effacement. He refused the poet-laureateship on the death of Tennyson in 1895, turned down a knighthood and declined the Order of Merit on three occasions, believing that public honours could interfere with a writer's freedom. In 1907, though, he accepted the Nobel Prize. Kipling's 1907-08 summer was his last in South Africa.

Rudyard Kipling. The University of Cape Town's Jagger Library houses a fine collection of his works

YEARS OF ZEAL AND HOPE

One of Kipling's neighbours in England was Arthur Conan Doyle, creator of Sherlock Holmes, the fictional detective in whose name tourists haunt Baker Street, London. He, too, came to South Africa with his butler in tow — as a voluntary field doctor during the Anglo-Boer War. His experience did not result in any South African fiction, but he wrote a forthright record of *The Great Boer War,* published in 1900 and today a piece of valuable Africana.

Another writer on whom South Africa made its mark was John Buchan, later 1st Baron Tweedsmuir. As one of Milner's private secretaries from 1901-03, and then as Acting Commissioner of Lands in the Transvaal, he took an active part in the re-organisation of the concentration camps. Author J.A. Smith describes in *John Buchan: a biography* how the young Englishman became deeply involved in the problems of repatriating many thousands of Boers at the end of the war.

The time he spent in South Africa gave him

Conan Doyle at the front during the Anglo-Boer War. He accompanied the British forces as surgeon in a field hospital, and was knighted in 1902, the year he published The War in South Africa

the background for his novel *Prester John* (1910); the character of Pieter Pienaar, a Boer hunter appearing in several of his books; and the birthplace of his hero Richard Hannay in *The Thirty-Nine Steps* (1915), the novel that established Buchan's fame. He wrote *The African Colony: Studies in Reconstruction* (1903) and was commissioned by the South African Government to write *The History of the South African Forces in France* (1920).

In his posthumous autobiography, *Memory Hold-the-Door* (1940), Buchan recalled: 'Those were wonderful years for me, years of bodily and mental activity, of zeal and hope not yet dashed by failure . . . I trust that my work was of some benefit to the country; it was beyond doubt of enormous benefit to myself. For I came to know and value a great variety of human beings, and to know and love one of the most fascinating lands on earth.'

The Refugee Camps have made my hair grey. When we took them over they were terrible—partly owing to the preoccupation of the military with other things, partly to causes inherent in any concentration of people accustomed to live in the sparsely peopled veld. I shall never forget going through the hospitals three months ago, when the children were dying like flies. We have now revolutionised the whole system, and the death rate is down to something nearly normal now. I have visited most camps, and have had to decide in emergencies all kinds of complicated questions of rations, water supply, sanitation and hospital management. I was very much struck by the heroism of some of the nurses, I got Lord M. to write his name in their albums, which pleased them. It has been a hideous grind for everybody, but I think we are all better for having gone through it. I say nothing about the original policy of forming camps: it was certainly not wise: but everyone who knows the country admits that it was humane.

A letter from John Buchan to his friend, Lady Mary Murray, in January 1902. Buchan, though shocked by the conditions in the concentration camps (he preferred refugee camps), considered them a 'humane' solution

Left: Author John Buchan with his horse. He was born in Perth, Scotland, in 1875 — the son of a clergyman. He was a member of the British House of Commons for the Scottish Universities, and in 1935 became Governor-General of Canada. He was created 1st Baron Tweedsmuir of Elsfield. Above: The frontispiece of Buchan's book, The History of the South African Forces in France *(1920), vividly illustrated the ferocity of the battle for Delville Wood*

Lure of the Karoo

OLIVE SCHREINER: REBEL WITH MANY CAUSES

In 1883 the English-speaking world was startled by the appearance of a brilliant new literary star. A young South African woman had produced a first novel that made her famous almost overnight. It was *The Story of an African Farm*.

The book told the story of two girls, Lyndall and Em, and a boy, Waldo, growing up in the Karoo. Lyndall, at the age of 17, conceives a child in an attempt to assert her independence. G.S. Findlay, in *English and South Africa*, describes the story in the following terms: 'This was a *tour de force*. The Victorian world oscillated between strict conventional priority on one hand and lewd and secret self-indulgence on the other. Olive Schreiner tolerated neither of these insincerities.'

Olive Emilie Albertina Schreiner was born in the Cape of German parents in 1855. She was employed as a governess to farm children in the Karoo when she began her novel in 1876. After each day's work she would retreat to her bedroom to write. Much of *African Farm* was written by moonlight — Olive wanted to avoid arguments with her employers over the use of candles.

The Story of an African Farm was published under the pen-name of Ralph Iron: in those days women authors were still fighting for acceptance. The book was a protest against society's hypocrisy and its attitude to women —but it was also about the Karoo, its people and its natural beauty which she had learned to love.

A doomed love affair

The Story of an African Farm was acclaimed by English critics and drew letters from numerous celebrities — among them Havelock Ellis, the British medical student who was later to revolutionise Victorian attitudes to the psychology of sex. Friendship blossomed swiftly.

Olive Schreiner was undoubtedly looking for a man who was both sexually dominant and intellectually capable when she began corresponding with Ellis.

Ellis later wrote of the impossibility of marriage between himself and the woman whose 'elementary, primitive nature' he found too demanding: 'We were not what can be technically, or even ordinarily, be called lovers. But the relationship of affectionate friendship . . . meant more for both of us, and was really even more intimate, than is often the relationship between those who technically and ordinarily are lovers.'

Yet in 1891, when he married Edith Lees, Ellis wrote: 'Tell Olive Schreiner that I am to be married tomorrow. Five years ago she chose to murder our friendship, and with it what was best and noblest in life . . .'

It was Olive's old enemy, asthma, coupled with a fierce longing for creative solitude, that finally drove her from London back to South Africa in 1889. She took with her the fruits of her years in Europe: feminist writings which were to form the basis of her influential *Woman*

Left: Olive Schreiner as a young woman. In London the little governess was lionised by literary hostesses and befriended by the leading writers of the day — including such greats as George Bernard Shaw, Oscar Wilde and Rider Haggard. Her correspondence with Havelock Ellis, above, blossomed into a close relationship which ended painfully, leaving Ellis bitter and convinced she had 'murdered' their friendship

and Labour (1911), numerous allegories published as *Dreams* (1891) and much in vogue at the time, and the bulky manuscript of the unfinished novel, *From Man to Man*, that she was to carry about with her until her death.

The Karoo years

From Matjiesfontein, the tiny settlement beside the trans-Karoo railway line, Olive Schreiner wrote to Havelock Ellis: 'Now I am going to put my hat on and go out for a walk over the Karoo. Such a sense of wild exhilaration and freedom comes to me when I walk over the Karoo . . .'

She attacked Rhodes and his Chartered Company's dealings with the Matabele in his new territory north of the Limpopo in a book entitled *Trooper Peter Halket of Mashonaland*. Its frontispiece was a shocking photograph of a group of black men strung up on a tree with

---

WOMAN AND LABOUR: A PARASITE?

Woman and Labour (1911), published 28 years after *The Story of an African Farm*, is still regarded as an exciting and relevant work today. Olive Schreiner was 56 when it appeared, and she regarded the book as only a tiny part of a major work on the subject of Woman. She believed it was unnecessary for a baby to be produced every year, and in a developing industrial society, there was no need for a woman to remain at home. Instead of becoming a parasite, the woman should be absorbed, as an equal, into the labour market. Olive Schreiner was equally critical of male and female attitudes. Some extracts from the book:

'And the woman who to-day merely produces twelve children and suckles them, and then turns them loose on her society and family, is regarded, and rightly so, as a curse and down draught, and not a productive labourer, of her community.'

'Even for these of us, child-bearing and suckling, instead of filling the entire circle of female life . . . becomes an episodal occupa-

tion, employing from three or four to ten or twenty of the three-score-and-ten-years which are allotted to human life. In such societies the statement that the main and continuous occupation of all women from puberty to middle-age is the bearing and suckling of children, and that this occupation must fully satisfy all her needs for social labour and activity, becomes an antiquated and unmitigated misstatement.'

'Repeatedly throughout history, when among human creatures a certain stage of material civilisation has been reached, a curious tendency has manifested itself in the human female to become more or less parasitic.'

'If the ideal of the modern woman becomes increasingly inconsistent with the passive existence of woman on the remuneration which her sexual attributes may win from man, and marriage becomes for her increasingly a fellowship of comrades, rather than the relationship of the owner and the bought, the keeper and the kept; the ideal of the typically modern man departs quite as strongly from that of his forefathers in the direction of finding in woman active companionship and co-operation rather than passive submission.'

Olive Schreiner and her husband, Samuel Cronwright. He read of her death in a newspaper report

self-satisfied whites standing by. It was a courageous work which had immediate appeal for humanitarians, but it also lost the author many English-speaking admirers in South Africa.

Even marriage to Karoo farmer Samuel Cronwright in 1894 — he took the name Cronwright-Schreiner in deference to her views — brought Olive no lasting happiness. Increasing asthma attacks forced them to leave the Karoo and settle in Kimberley, where a baby daughter was born in 1895. The baby lived only a few hours.

A wicked, wicked war

The Anglo-Boer War years, 1899-1902, were traumatic for Olive. Her sympathy for the Boer cause earned her the antagonism of English-speaking South Africans. She was also an ardent pacifist. 'Oh, this is a wicked wicked war.' she wrote to a friend. 'When I see our bonny English boys falling and know how many hundreds have yet to fall, and our own brave South African lads dying . . . a bitterness rises in my heart that I never thought could.'

Confined to the Karoo village of Hanover in 1901 by Martial Law and a barbed wire fence, she wrote the book which was hailed by Vera Brittain in her *Testament of Youth* as the 'Bible of the Women's Movement'. *Woman and Labour* appeared in 1911, long after peace, but it had succeeded a little in distracting her from what she described as the horror of the world around her — the wounded and the dying, the rebels executed in the market-place.

In 1913 Olive Schreiner returned to Europe alone — and lonely. The First World War found her in lodgings so shabby that her friends were appalled. Worse still, she was socially ostracised by people who misunderstood her pacifist beliefs. Her German name added to her difficulties.

When Cronwright was finally able to join her in 1920, he was shocked by the change in his wife: 'She had aged greatly, her hair was grey, her glorious eyes were almost closed, and but little remained in that sick woman of that bursting, elemental force . . .'

Unable to face another English winter, Olive returned to South Africa ahead of her husband. On 11 December 1920 she died alone in a Wynberg boarding house. In *Olive Schreiner. Portrait of a South African Woman*, Johannes Meintjes tells how Olive sensed her death was at hand: 'A week before, she dined at the Scotts and told her niece Ursula that she would like to have a post-mortem to be held after her death'. He describes how she was found: 'She lay just as if she had gone to sleep, a hot water bottle under her shoulder, her glasses on; the book she had been reading *(The Memoirs of Ismail Kemel Bey)* lay open on her chest, and beside her the candle had burnt out. Olive Schreiner had come home to die, and she had done so, as she would have wished, alone and in her sleep.'

MY DAUGHTER WRITES A LITTLE

The Karoo — this time the Little Karoo surrounding Oudtshoorn — was also the setting beloved by the second South African woman to achieve literary fame both in this country and abroad.

Pauline Smith's collection of short stories appeared as *The Little Karoo* in 1925. The tales, marked by an almost biblical simplicity of language and concept, might have caused less of a stir had they not been introduced by the noted British novelist, Arnold Bennett.

She had met Bennett while staying in a Swiss hotel with her mother in 1908. Her mother confided that her 26-year-old daughter 'wrote a little'. Bennett demanded to see her work — and was interested enough to become both her friend and her untiring mentor.

While revisiting the scenes of her early Oudtshoorn childhood in 1913-14, Pauline gathered the material for the stories which were to establish her as a major South African writer. She portrayed the simple farming communities of the Little Karoo as a society struggling against the hardships of poverty and isolation and sustained only by their stoical capacity to endure.

But despite the deceptive simplicity of her style, Pauline did not find writing easy. She claimed: 'Every short story I wrote was written not in the joy of creation but in the pain of it, through a misery of diffidence and despair and in indifferent health which only his [Arnold

> Built into the wall between the living-room and the bedroom were three small shelves, and here Deltje kept their few treasures: her Bible, two cups and saucers, thick and heavy, with roses like red cabbages around them, a little pink mug, with 'A Present for a Good Girl' in letters of gold on one side of the handle and a golden Crystal Palace on the other, a green-and-red crocheted wool mat, a black-bordered funeral card in memory of Mijnheer van der Wenter's mother, an ostrich egg, and a small box lined with blue satin and covered with rows of little shells round an inch-square mirror. This was the pride of their simple hearts, and these, after fifty years of life together, were their treasures.

This extract from one of Pauline Smith's best-known stories, The Pain, *displays her gentle style*

Pauline Smith in her Dorset home in 1957

Bennett's] dogged persistence and belief in me enabled me to find the courage to overcome.' Yet her only novel, *The Beadle*, which appeared in 1926 and described the same desolate Karoo world and its isolated people, is considered a classic: one of the best novels produced on South Africa.

Continually fighting the torment of a painful neuralgia, Pauline Smith was still to produce stories for the *Cape Argus* and *Outspan* and *A.B. . . . a Minor Marginal Note* (1933), a slim volume on her patron Arnold Bennett. A new edition of *The Little Karoo*, with two additional stories, was published in 1930, and a volume of charming children's stories, *Platkops Children*, actually written in 1912, was published in 1933.

Pauline died in England in 1959, some 30 years after the death of Arnold Bennett, who had once described her talent as 'strong, austere, tender and ruthless'.

PAULINE SMITH, BY HER PEERS

Just before her death, William Plomer and Roy Macnab presented Pauline Smith with an illuminated scroll signed by South African writers including Guy Butler, Nadine Gordimer, Dan Jacobson, Uys Krige, S. Gertrude Millin, Alan Paton and Laurens van der Post. It read: 'We South African writers in English and Afrikaans have felt moved to join our names together in offering you a tribute of our admiration. We wish to assure you of the respect and affection in which your name and work are held by us and by other South African readers. We feel that by the delicacy, tenderness and precision with which you have written of South African ways of life you have transcended the barriers of race and language and made essential humanity real.'

Fellow author Alan Paton reviewed *The Little Karoo* in the *Herald Tribune Book Review* of 18 October 1959: 'She never avoided the harsh and the ugly, nor the fiercest of passions . . . When she writes of love and fortitude and self-sacrifice and mercy, she does not do it to compensate us for the harshness and bitterness of life, but because she sees them too. She weaves them altogether into a tragic and beautiful cloth of life.'

One man and his dog

THE UGLIEST PUPPY

James Peter FitzPatrick was born in King William's Town in the Eastern Cape in 1862, the son of an Irish judge who had been appointed to the Bench of the Cape Supreme Court. FitzPatrick — he re-christened himself Percy, and was known by his family and friends as 'Fitz' — was thoroughly Irish, yet remained fiercely loyal to the country of his birth and declared himself a South African at a time when the country was divided into Englishmen, Free Staters, Transvalers, Natalians, Cape colonials and numerous African peoples.

He is remembered best for a story about a dog. FitzPatrick's account of the runt's courage and his adventures in *Jock of the Bushveld* became a worldwide best-seller, being translated into French, Dutch, Afrikaans, Xhosa, Zulu and several other languages.

FitzPatrick had a varied and exciting career which began with a job as a bank clerk in Cape Town and took him to the Transvaal goldfields as digger, storekeeper, transport rider, editor of the *Gold Fields News*, partner in the vast Wernher-Beit gold mining concern, and storyteller.

As an active 'Reformer' campaigning for the rights of uitlanders in Kruger's republic, he was imprisoned for his part in the planning of the Jameson Raid of 1895. After his release in May 1896, he was true to his promise not to take part in politics for three years. Then, only

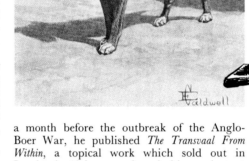

The frontispiece of FitzPatrick's famous book. Jock was the odd puppy of a litter of six, 'a poor little rat of a thing about half the size of the others'

a month before the outbreak of the Anglo-Boer War, he published *The Transvaal From Within*, a topical work which sold out in London in 48 hours and made him an instant celebrity.

After the war he settled with his family in Johannesburg, and according to his daughter, Cecily Niven, in the *Standard Encyclopaedia of Southern Africa*, it was during this period that he was advised by his friend, Rudyard Kipling, to write about the plucky dog with whom he had shared his days as a transport rider. Kipling sat in on the bedtime story sessions with Fitz's children, and insisted: 'You must *write* these. They must not be lost to future generations.'

FitzPatrick did write his stories. He had been introduced to Jock when a fellow transport rider, Ted Sievwright, gave him the sixth and ugliest puppy of the litter rather than see it drowned. The affection between man and dog grew until they were inseparable and they went through countless experiences together.

FitzPatrick described how Jock, still half-blind, fell from his perch on the wagon and

struggled through long grass in a desperate attempt to catch up. 'He was not big enough or strong enough to push his way — even the stems of the down-trodden grass tripped him — and he stumbled and floundered at every step, but he got up again each time with his little tail standing straight up, his head erect and his ears cocked. He looked such a ridiculous sight that his little tragedy of "lost in the veld" was forgotten — one could only laugh.'

Jock soon became renowned for his fearlessness and devotion — and then tragedy struck. One day he was kicked by a kudu and his ear drums were so badly damaged that he became deaf. FitzPatrick gave a moving account of the effect of deafness on a dog who could no longer hear his master's voice and could not understand why.

FitzPatrick feared that Jock would be run over while sleeping in the shade of a wagon, as nothing would rid the dog of his habit of taking a nap on a patch of warm sand anywhere in the road. He later found that Jock could detect the vibrations of oncoming wagons, and would move out of the way. But a near miss in

FitzPatrick badly needed an illustrator for *Jock of the Bushveld*. After an extensive search he finally stumbled across a masterly painting of a kudu in a Bond Street gallery in London. He traced the artist to his home in Primrose Hill and discovered that the myopic little man had never been to Africa, and had sketched the kudu at the zoo in London.

Edmund Caldwell was whisked to Hohenheim and then by mule-wagon to the bushveld where Jock had once followed his master. The illustrations were a triumph, and the book quickly sold out.

There was a tiny error in the first edition. Naturalists all over the world spotted a decidedly unconventional dung beetle which Caldwell had depicted using his forelegs instead of its back legs, standing head downwards, to roll home its ball of dung. FitzPatrick had already seen the mistake, but wrote to the publishers too late to change the first edition — which subsequently became extremely valuable.

Left: 'Fighting Fitz' grew a ginger beard in his transport riding days, but later shaved it off, leaving only an impressive moustache. Middle and right: Formal portraits of Sir Percy and Lady FitzPatrick

the busy mining town of Barberton, where FitzPatrick now lived, forced him to a painful decision: he could no longer keep Jock.

First he tried to 'board' his friend with a man who lived about 22 km from Barberton. Jock chewed through the rope that held him and was back in Barberton by the time his master arrived home. FitzPatrick then sent him to live with his friend, the trader Tom Barnett, in Moçambique. There, defending Tom's chickens against marauding wild dogs one night, the courageous terrier was accidentally shot dead.

'It gives me much gratification . . .'

In November 1902, FitzPatrick received a letter from Balfour, the British Prime Minister: 'I have had the pleasure of making a submission to the King that the honour of a knighthood should be conferred on you in recognition of your work in connection with the South African War and it gives me much gratification to inform you that His Majesty has been graciously pleased to approve the recommendation.'

Cecily Niven relates that during the Anglo-Boer War, Sir Percy FitzPatrick had been employed in Britain in an unofficial capacity as adviser to the British Government. He became a friend and confidant of Lord Milner and gave valuable advice on repatriation at the end of the war, when there were 200 000 troops to be shipped home to Britain, 24 000 Boer prisoners of war to bring back from exile, and some 100 000 women and children and others still in the concentration camps.

Whatever his Imperial loyalties, FitzPatrick was first and foremost a South African — and he was here to stay. He defeated General Louis Botha at the Union polls in the Pretoria East constituency in 1910, and spent a large part of his personal fortune in promoting Cecil Rhodes' plan for British settlers by developing citrus farming for immigrants in the Sundays River Valley in the Eastern Cape. Here, on a hill called The Outlook, Sir Percy FitzPatrick lies buried.

He had concluded at a banquet for Chamberlain in 1903: 'I believe, sir, in this our people. I believe in this, my native land.' For this dedication FitzPatrick was dubbed, by author A.P. Cartwright 'the first South African'.

Sir Percy FitzPatrick at the Johannesburg Stock Exchange after his victory in the 1910 election

AFRICAN ADVENTURE

The romance of Africa was a powerful force in the literature of the late 1800s. Novelist Anthony Trollope, author of *Barchester Towers*, toured South Africa in 1877, publishing his two-volume *South Africa* the following year.

French novelist Jules Verne did not consider it necessary to visit South Africa to write his 26th novel, *L'Etoile du Sud* (The Star of the South) published in 1884. Kimberley was a byword of the day and Verne had only to read his newspapers to concoct a parable round a black diamond and man's insatiable greed — with a Rhodes-like villain.

A deeper knowledge of Southern Africa lay behind the works of Sir Henry Rider Haggard, the sixth son of an English barrister, who had come to South Africa in 1875 as secretary to the Governor of Natal and was involved in the first annexation of the Transvaal in 1877. Haggard's plan to breed ostriches in Natal was abandoned and he returned to London to become a barrister and produce a stream of romantic novels with African settings. Most famous of these was *King Solomon's Mines* (1885), set against the backdrop of the Zimbabwe Ruins — the novel even stole the best-seller crown from R.L. Stevenson's *Treasure Island*.

This cartoon, published in 1877, reflected the colonists' opinion that author Anthony Trollope could not do justice to his study of South Africa in the few months at his disposal. 'A Novel Trick,' reads the caption, and it continues: 'There is no deception. I place the cover over these materials. On its removal you will find them transformed into my second colonial success.' The Saturday, *in a flippant review, praised the author in that 'on so dull a subject as South Africa, there is scarcely a dull page'*

Left and centre: The cover and frontispiece of Jules Verne's book on South Africa, L'Étoile du Sud. *Right: Verne's earlier work on South Africa,* Meridiana: The Adventures of Three Englishmen and Three Russians in South Africa *(1872), was an imaginative account of an expedition to measure an arc of meridian in South Africa. In the book Verne tells how the group kill four lions outside their den, battle an angry hippo intent on eating their boat, and tread carefully to avoid '10 to 12 ft mambas' during their adventures along a distinctly unfamiliar Orange River. In fact Jules Verne never visited South Africa*

Left: Sir Henry Rider Haggard first came to South Africa in 1875, when he was appointed secretary to Sir Henry Bulwer, Governor of Natal. Haggard at first planned to breed ostriches in Northern Natal, but later gave up the idea and returned to London, where he was called to the bar in 1884. Africa's ruggedness and vitality gripped the imagination of the young colonial official, and he began to write the adventure stories that were to make him famous. King Solomon's Mines *came out in 1885 (with the Zimbabwe Ruins as a setting), followed by* Jess *(1887),* She *(1887),* Allan Quatermain *(1887),* Nada the Lily *(1892), and many others. Right: In 1878 Haggard and his friend Arthur Cochrane built this 'funny little house' in Berea, near Pretoria's present railway station. Haggard's novel,* Jess, *was set mainly in this cottage, and for a long time it was believed that he wrote his books there (he did not). With the 1880 siege of Pretoria as a background, the novel describes the cottage's beautiful setting: 'The garden of the cottage sloped down towards a valley, on the farther side of which rose a wooded hill. To the right, too, was a hill clothed in deep green bush'*

The great book robbery

TERMITES AND A NOBEL PRIZEWINNER STIR UP A STORM

In 1923 a South African lawyer, poet and naturalist began publishing a series of articles in Afrikaans newspapers and in the popular magazine *Die Huisgenoot*. Four years later an uproar broke out in the press when the author accused a Nobel prizewinner of stealing his ideas. The unlikely subject of controversy was — termites.

The writer making the accusation was Eugene Nielen Marais, a multi-gifted man in his fifties who, in 1905, had published what is agreed to be the first successful lyric poem in Afrikaans, *Winternag*, and who had become the owner of a newspaper, *Land en Volk*, at the age of 21. In a biographical note to *The Soul of the White Ant*, his son, also named Eugene, relates that Marais received his early schooling in Pretoria, where he was awarded 'a prize for divinity' because he could recite the entire Catechism of the Church of England. Marais adopted journalism as his profession, and his son recalled:

'At first he was a parliamentary reporter of the Volksraad and because of his caustic comments on the proceedings he had the distinction of being expressly excluded from the press gallery by a resolution of the Volksraad. He became editor of various papers, both English and Dutch, and his wholehearted support of General Joubert against Kruger resulted in his being tried for high treason, on which charge he was acquitted by the Supreme Court in Pretoria.'

Marais now claimed that the Belgian dramatist and Nobel laureate Maurice Maeterlinck had stolen his *Huisgenoot* pieces (collected in 1934 in a book called *Die Siel van die Mier* and translated into English as *The Soul of the White Ant* in 1937). In these Marais had set out his extraordinary and exciting theory that a colony of termites, or white ants, was in fact a composite organism . . . with the soldiers, workers and flying termites performing the vital functions of the 'body' and the queen, in her secret chamber at the heart of the community, providing the unifying power and

Eugene Marais. He was a brilliant, complicated man who must have felt at times that fate was against him. In 1894, when he was only 23 years old, he married Aletta Beyers — only to see his young wife die the following year, shortly after the birth of their son

mysterious motivation. They had a group soul.

'How can one compare this soul with that of a human being?' asks Marais. 'When one sees a tiny worker hastily placing a single grain of sand on the wall of a building which eventually will become a massive tower twelve or fifteen feet high, millions upon millions times larger than itself, can one assume for one moment that the worker knows, in the human sense, what the final result of its work is going to be? If this were so its intelligence would be that of a god, compared with our own.'

The South African press took up the cudgels on Marais' behalf and printed excerpts from his work, comparing them with passages from the Belgian's book, *The Life of the White Ant*. In 1935 Marais wrote to Dr Winifred de Kok, who was translating *The Soul of the White Ant*: 'The publishers in South Africa started crying to high heaven and endeavoured to induce me to take legal action in Europe, a step for which

Maurice Maeterlinck and his wife in 1932. He was the celebrated author of The Life of the Bee, *a mixture of philosophy and natural history, and* The Bluebird. *He was awarded the Nobel Prize for Literature in 1911*

I possessed neither the means nor inclination . . . The Afrikaans publishers of the original articles communicated the facts to one of our ambassadorial representatives in Europe and suggested that Maeterlinck be approached. Whether or not this was done, I never ascertained. In any case, Maeterlinck, like other great ones on Olympus, maintained a mighty and dignified silence.'

A new dream — and the final tragedy

Maeterlinck's book, originally published in French, was translated into English and many other languages. Marais, by this time an alcoholic and drug-addict, spent the next few years brooding, writing only fitfully.

Then in 1935 Marais excitedly wrote to Dr De Kok about a book in which he was recording his observations of baboons — a scientific sequel to a lighthearted series of sketches for *Die Vaderland* and *Die Huisgenoot*, published in 1938 as *Die Burgers van die Berge* and in an English translation in 1939 as *My Friends the Baboons*. In the early years of the century, Marais had retreated to a farm in the Transvaal's Waterberg district, where he had studied the behaviour of termites — and of baboons. The termite studies had led to *The Soul of the White Ant*. Now he was working on a book about the apes.

But the following year, on 29 March 1936, aged 64, Eugene Marais died on a farm near Johannesburg. He had been addicted to morphine for years, and he was physically and mentally shattered. He had shot himself.

Genius or charlatan?

Marais' study of baboons also created a controversy: his conclusions were disputed by one of the most eminent scientists of the century, South African-born Lord (formerly Sir Solly) Zuckerman.

In a work entitled *The Social Life of Apes and*

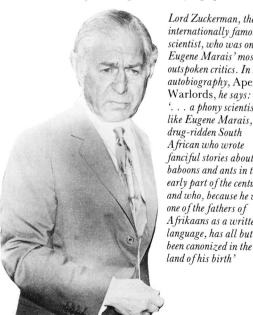

Lord Zuckerman, the internationally famous scientist, who was one of Eugene Marais' most outspoken critics. In his autobiography, Apes to Warlords, *he says: '. . . a phony scientist like Eugene Marais, a drug-ridden South African who wrote fanciful stories about baboons and ants in the early part of the century, and who, because he was one of the fathers of Afrikaans as a written language, has all but been canonized in the land of his birth'*

Athol Fugard's haunted face peers from a farmhouse window in a scene from The Guest, *in which the actor and playright portrayed Marais' unhappy visit (he was addicted to morphine) to an isolated farm*

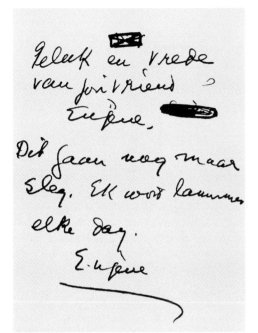

This note from Marais illustrates his growing depression. He shot himself on a farm near Pelindaba

Dr Lyall Watson, the Johannesburg-born author of such best-sellers as *Supernature* (1973), *The Romeo Error* (1974) and *Lifetide* (1978), has been described as a 'scientific nomad'. His career has taken him all over the world, and his findings have aroused both widespread interest and heated controversy.

Watson was educated in South Africa and abroad (he was awarded a Ph.D. at the University of London in 1963) and was director of the Johannesburg zoo during 1964-65. He has researched and led expeditions to Antarctica, Indonesia, the Amazon River area and other remote spots.

In *Contemporary Authors* he is recorded as saying of himself: 'Since 1967 I have travel-led constantly, looking and listening, collecting bits and pieces of apparently useless information, stopping every two years to put the fragments together into some sort of meaningful pattern.' He never planned ahead, said Watson, but simply followed 'whichever strange god calls the loudest'.

Among Watson's many interests is the exploration of the paranormal. He has delved into physical and psychic phenomena, and investigated strange people and even stranger events. In *Supernature* he describes how a pyramid constructed to certain proportions can keep a razor blade sharp if the blade is placed at a specific spot in the interior.

Monkeys, published in 1932, Zuckerman had described his observations of apes in captivity at London zoo, drawing a sharp distinction between the basic impulses of apes and humans. Marais, however, blurred these differences, anticipating the science of 'ethology' (study of animal behaviour) that was later developed by animal-watchers like Konrad Lorenz, and popularised by Desmond Morris in his books *The Human Zoo* (1969) and *The Naked Ape* (1969).

Zuckerman had first criticised Marais in the Thirties, but the real headlines came in 1975. The former chief scientific adviser to the British Government, whose influence and wide knowledge earned him the epithet 'Czar of the sciences', charged at a public lecture at the University of Cape Town that Marais' work was 'science fiction', that he had claimed authorship of scientific papers that did not exist, that the poet's alleged years among baboons had in fact amounted to three at the most (and then from a farmhouse or hotel) and that he had observed baboons in 'Baboon Valley' for only three months.

Zuckerman declared that Marais was 'not averse to deceiving others', and in a review of *My Friends the Baboons* in *The Times Literary Supplement* in 1976, he described the book as a 'tissue of zoological nonsense', accusing Marais of having no understanding of science. Added Zuckerman: 'Marais lived on the borders of fantasy. . .'

However the American writer Robert Ardrey, in dedicating his book *African Genesis* to Marais, described him as 'the purest genius that the natural sciences have seen this century'. Wrote Ardrey: 'As no gallery of modern art can fail to be haunted by the burning eyes of Vincent van Gogh, so the pages of no future science can fail to be haunted by the brooding, solitary, less definable presence of Eugene Marais.'

THE WEDDING GUEST WHO TURNED OUT TO BE THE MISSING LINK

An Australian anatomist called Raymond Dart took up a professorship at the University of the Witwatersrand School of Medicine in 1923. Like Eugene Marais, his name was destined to echo around the world, for he was the man who found the missing link. Or rather, it found him.

It began one day in 1924 while the Darts were preparing for the wedding of a friend at their home. Two boxes arrived from a place called Taungs (earlier, Dart had received an interesting baboon skull from the area, and had asked for more). In one of the boxes he found a chunk of lime and sand bearing the impression of a child's face, with a brain too big for an ape's but too small to be human.

Convinced that this was the 'missing link' between ape and man, in 1925 Dart published a paper in the British scientific journal, *Nature*, naming his find *Australopithecus africanus* — the Southern Ape of Africa.

A long quest crowned by triumph

A scientific outcry erupted. Experts proclaimed Dart's find to be merely the skull of an ape, and he was held up to ridicule. Popular songs came out about 'the young horror from Taungs'. But Dart's paper impressed the famous fossil hunter, Dr Robert Broom, who set out to find the skull of an adult *Australopithecine*. His expeditions into the bush, over hills and valleys, always clad in a sober black suit, were legendary.

And he did find the skull — at the Sterkfontein Caves, near Krugersdorp, in 1936. This, and later finds over a long period, proved that *Australopithecus* was indeed an intermediate stage between ape and man.

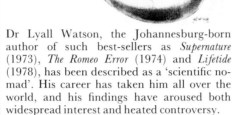

Left: Archaeologist Dr Robert Broom on the site where Australopithecus transvaalensis *was found. This photograph, taken in 1936, shows him in his invariably formal attire. Broom wore a stiff wing collar and black tie — even in the blazing sun of the Karoo. Right: Professor Raymond Dart holds the skull of the famous Taungs child*

The Herman Charles Bosman story

THE LITERARY GENIUS WHO WAS SENTENCED TO DEATH

Few people reading the headline in Johannesburg's *Star* on 15 November 1926 would have guessed that the young man sentenced to hang for shooting his stepbrother would live to become one of South Africa's greatest short story writers.

Herman Charles Bosman was a schoolteacher when the event occurred which was to change his life. While on a visit to his mother's house during the school vacation in July 1926, he heard an altercation in his stepbrother's bedroom (it later transpired that Bosman's younger brother, Pierre, had stumbled against a washstand in the darkness and wakened David Russell, the stepbrother).

Picking up a heavy rifle, Bosman hurried to the bedroom. Seconds later a shot rang out and David slumped on the bed, mortally wounded. The bullet had pierced his arm, passed through his heart and shattered a window pane. Hysterically, Bosman pleaded with Pierre and David's father to shoot him, and in desperation seized a kitchen knife in an attempt to slit his own throat. He inflicted a wound before the knife was taken from him, and he fainted. Bosman later claimed that the shooting was an accident, and when questioned at his trial on his request to his brother to shoot him, he explained: 'Everything was black then and misfortune seemed to be following me.' The judge found the case a 'sad

Left: Bosman at 21. Although best known for his Oom Schalk Lourens stories, he was also a poet. He published The Blue Princess *in 1932 and a collection of his poetry was published in 1974 under the title* The Earth is Waiting. *Right: Vera Sawyer at the time of her marriage to Bosman in 1926*

and pathetic one' and noted that relations between the families had been strained to the point that they hardly spoke to each other. He passed the sentence of death.

The tragic affair was dramatically symptomatic of the confused and contradictory life led by this brilliant man. His friend, artist Gordon Vorster, described Bosman to Valerie Rosenberg for her biography, *Sunflower to the Sun:* 'Bosman was a man, a woman, an angel, a devil, a tenderness, a cruelty, a brave man and a coward, an emasculated satyr, a womaniser, a racist and a liberal. He searched for purity in filth, and, like Wilde, found stars in the gutter.'

The shadow of the gallows

In *Cold Stone Jug*, an account of prison life based on his experiences in the shadow of the gallows, Bosman told how, on hearing of a hard-labour prisoner being beaten for a misdemeanour, he felt that the man was infinitely privileged because he was regarded by the warder as a living person: 'For no warder

would dream of hitting a condemned man with a baton. To a warder a condemned man was something already dead.'

But Bosman's morbid observations did not deter him and his cell-mate 'Stoffels' from poking fun at the prison staff. Their teasing of a particular night warder once reached such extremes of hilarity that they were reprimanded by the head night warder: '"You condemned men mustn't laugh so loud," he said. "The hard-labour convicts got to sleep. They got to work all day. You two don't do nothing but smoke cigarettes all day long and crack jokes. You'll get yourselves in serious trouble if the Governor finds out you keep the whole prison awake night after night, romping about and laughing in the condemned cells."'

'I wondered vaguely,' wrote Bosman, 'what more serious trouble we could get into than we were already in.' They came for Stoffels and hanged him, but Bosman's sentence was commuted after nine days in the death cell to ten years' imprisonment. He was released on parole after serving three years and nine months — and his real career began with an astonishing outburst of creativity.

Editing an outspoken new literary magazine, *The Touleier*, with Jean Blignaut, Bosman was so impressed by his colleague's 'Ruiter' stories that he wrote one of his own in a similar vein. It was *Makapan's Caves*, narrated by his creation Oom Schalk and displaying the skilful blend of ironic humour and pathos which was to become Bosman's trademark and make this character one of the best-loved in South African fiction.

The language of Oom Schalk was striking and curiously appealing. It conveyed, in English, the authentic flavour of rural Afrikaans — an outstanding accomplishment.

The berries of the karee-boom

Mampoer, a famous Bosman story, effectively illustrates his unique style: 'The berries

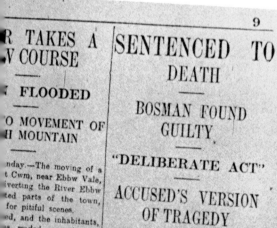

Left: Bosman's trial caused a sensation, and the court was packed. Above: Bosman, second from left, leaves the New Law Courts in Johannesburg after being sentenced to death

PATRICK MYNHARDT

Veteran South African actor Patrick Mynhardt opened in *A Sip of Jerepigo* at Johannesburg's Civic Theatre in 1969 with an endearing protrayal of Bosman's character, Oom Schalk Lourens. His characterisation of the grey-bearded old storyteller was so good that the show ran for over 1 000 performances in theatres throughout South Africa, Rhodesia and South West Africa. The programme included material from Bosman's account of prison life, *Cold Stone Jug*, and excerpts from *Mafeking Road* and *Bosman at his Best*.

Nearly four years later, the actor opened in Pretoria with *More Jerepigo* — and again the Oom Schalk Lourens stories stole the show. A third Bosman show, *Just Jerepigo*, was staged for the first time in the H.B. Thom Theatre at Stellenbosch in 1977.

Herman Bosman with two of the three women he married. On his right is Ella, who sometimes danced naked at the couple's wild parties in Pietersburg. Helena, on his left, was his third wife

THE ANGLO-BOER WAR JOURNAL THAT BECAME A BEST-SELLER

Deneys Reitz, son of the President of the Orange Free State, had spent a pleasant and what he described in *Commando* as a Tom Sawyer-like childhood engrossed in hunting, fishing and swimming. He was 17 when the Anglo-Boer War broke out — too young to join up, until President Kruger heard of his willingness and insisted: '". . . the boy must go — I started fighting earlier than that."' General Piet Joubert in person handed the young recruit his new Mauser and bandolier.

At the end of the war, when the former president and two of his sons (two others were prisoners of war) refused to sign the undertaking to abide by the peace terms, they were forced to leave South Africa. It was during a precarious year of transport-riding in fever-stricken Madagascar that Deneys Reitz wrote down the story still so fresh in his memory. His experiences on commando — he fought at Spionkop and later as a bitter-ender in Smuts's guerilla bands — provided the rich material for *Commando*, written in English, published in 1929 and soon a best-seller for its unique inside view of 'the other side'. The war had produced a flood of English books, but few memorable versions of the Boers' struggle.

Commando has since become an Anglo-Boer War classic, noted especially for its vivid account of the daring raid Smuts led into the Cape Colony, stronghold of the English. His band of intrepid burghers came within 80 km of Port Elizabeth before swinging west for Calvinia and Malmesbury; some of them even came within sight of Table Mountain. The hardships of this epic ride were legion: sickness, hunger, exposure to nights of drenching rain, and always the danger of capture by British troops or the local loyalist militia.

In 1904 Mrs Smuts persuaded Reitz to return to South Africa, where he studied law, saw active service in the First World War, and entered politics under Smuts's government. In 1942 he became South African High Commissioner in London — a long journey from the wasteland of the Anglo-Boer War.

Colonel Deneys Reitz in 1944. He had recently completed his last book, No Outspan

of the karee-boom (Oom Schalk Lourens said, nodding his head in the direction of the tall tree whose shadows were creeping towards the edge of the stoep) may not make the best kind of mampoer that there is. What I mean is that karee-brandy is not as potent as the brandy you distil from moepels or maroelas. Even peach-brandy, they say, can make you forget the rust in the corn quicker than the mampoer you make from karee-berries.

'But karee-mampoer is white and soft to look at, and the smoke that comes from it when you pull the cork out of the bottle is pale and rises up in slow curves.' Bosman drew on his life prior to the shooting tragedy for his Oom Schalk stories. For a brief but significant period he had been a schoolteacher in the Groot Marico district of the Western Transvaal — a tough stretch of bushveld peopled by a hardy breed of farmer who struggled against drought, cattle disease and isolation. Surprisingly, Bosman had spent only six months in the Marico.

Marital rows and outlandish parties

Bosman's marital life was characteristically unorthodox. His first wife, Vera Sawyer, kept her job as an insurance clerk and remained at home with her mother while Bosman went to the Marico — and then to prison. The marriage stood little chance of survival, and they did not live together even after his release from prison.

Bosman's first volume of poetry, *The Blue Princess*, was inspired by Ellie Beemer, a talented *Touleier* contributor and secretary. Then the writer met Ella Manson, whom he married in 1932 after Vera agreed to a divorce. Together Bosman and Ella led a bohemian life — six years of it in London, where Bosman continued to write. He produced a steady stream of Oom Schalk stories for *South African Opinion* while struggling to establish a Fleet Street career. It did not work, and the couple

returned to South Africa, penniless, in 1940.

By 1943 Bosman was on his feet again, this time as editor of the *Zoutpansberg Review and Mining Journal* in Pietersburg, the Transvaal town he re-christened Kalwyn in his story, *Jacaranda in the Night* (1947), and Willemsdorp in the novel of the same name, which he was still re-writing when he died in 1951.

The staid community of Pietersburg was shocked by the distinctly unconventional behaviour of the Bosmans. In *Sunflower to the Sun*, Valerie Rosenberg has described their marital rows and outlandish parties which sometimes ended with Ella dancing naked for the edification of the guests. But soon that marriage also broke down. Bosman fell in love with Helena Stegmann, a Pietersburg schoolteacher. She became the third and last of his wives.

Philosophy and black humour

In 1947 *Mafeking Road*, the first volume of the Oom Schalk Stories, was published to critical acclaim, rewarding Bosman with the recognition he had sought for so long. *Cold Stone Jug* followed in 1949, bringing a mixed reception from critics — though it was a commercial success with its mixture of home-grown philosophy, anecdote and black humour. By 1950 he was writing more Marico tales — his 'Voorkamer' series, later published as *Jurie Steyn's Post Office* and *A Bekkersdal Marathon*, were printed in the weekly *Forum* while he worked as a proofreader for a Johannesburg newspaper.

On 14 October 1951 Herman Charles Bosman died. Obituaries recalled his jaunty shrug, romantic streak, eccentricities and unique talent. In the decades that followed, his stories gathered popularity and acclaim and won a place in the hearts of many thousands of South Africans.

Bosman the man remains an enigma; Bosman the writer is an acknowledged master of the printed word.

Writers who cared

A CRY TO THE WORLD

In 1948 the world was moved by a powerful and tragic novel from South Africa: *Cry, the Beloved Country*. The author: 45-year-old reformatory principal Alan Paton. Written in grave and rhythmic, almost biblical prose, the novel tells the story of a humble Zulu country parson searching for his missing son, Absalom, in the warrens of Alexandra, one of Johannesburg's black townships — only to find that Absalom is to be hanged for his part in the robbery and murder of a white man.

Though it laid bare the clash of cultures in South Africa, this is a novel of faith: subtitled *A Story of Comfort in Desolation*, it ends on a note of reconciliation between black and white.

Cry, the Beloved Country rapidly became a best-seller. One of the first works to focus world attention on South Africa's problems of race and colour, the film version was released in 1952.

Paton's only other novel, *Too Late the Phalarope* (1953), did not match the success of his first, but he has written well-received biographies of Jan Hofmeyr and Geoffrey Clayton, Archbishop of Cape Town. Paton also wrote some fine short stories, including *Sponono*, *Ha'penny* and *Death of a Tsotsi* — which, with the collaboration of Krishna Shah, he adapted into the play *Sponono* — and the first volume of his autobiography, *Towards the Mountain*.

Cool, sharp, analytical prose

A story by a girl of 15, published in *Forum* in 1939, heralded a major new literary talent. This early promise was fulfilled in the 1950s, when Nadine Gordimer emerged as South Africa's foremost modern writer of short stories and novels.

Childhood in a Reef mining town and politically conscious student days at Witwatersrand University were reflected in an impressive first novel, *The Lying Days* (1953). But it was her second novel, *A World of Strangers* (1958), that established her as a writer of distinction.

Fine passages in *A World of Strangers* contrasted white suburban Johannesburg with the bleakness of black townships, a prominent theme in her work. Gordimer's relentlessly honest powers of observation are also evident in this book. Of wealthy Rand tycoons she

Left: The cover of Alan Paton's first book, published when he was 45 years old. Right: Lionel Ngakane, Tom Enigboken and Barry Johnson in a scene from the film version, directed by Hungarian-born Zoltá Korda

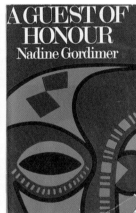

Nadine Gordimer (centre) won the Booker Prize for Fiction in 1974 for the The Conservationist. *Her first two books were* Face to Face *(1949) and* The Soft Voice of the Serpent and Other Stories *(1952)*

wrote: 'The men wore the clothes of whatever sport they had just left off playing, or, pasty and wattled, sat, stranded, in a well-pressed get-up of flannels, silk shirts and scarves that covered the ruin of the hardened arteries, the damaged liver or the enlarged heart that lay heavily in the breast.'

In 1966 her fourth novel of conscience, *The Late Bourgeois World*, was banned in South Africa. In a talk at the University of the Witwatersrand entitled *South Africa: Towards a Desk-Drawer Literature*, she described it as 'an attempt to look into the specific character of the social climate that produced the wave of young white saboteurs in 1963-64'. The ban on *The Late Bourgeois World* was lifted in the 1970s — the decade in which Nadine Gordimer received international acclaim as winner of the Booker Prize for Fiction.

EARLY AFRIKAANS WRITERS

The pioneers of Afrikaans literature were men of outstanding versatility — but few were more so than C.J. Langenhoven, who gave the language its first truly popular novels.

Brought up in the Little Karoo dorp of

Hoeko by an uncle he called 'Pappie' — his own widowed father he called 'Anderpa' (Other Daddy) — Cornelis Jacob Langenhoven revealed an early flair for languages.

Although he proved to be an eloquent debater during his legal studies at Victoria College (Stellenbosch University), and was called to the Bar in 1901, Langenhoven chose not to remain an advocate. Instead, he set up practice as an attorney in the small town of Oudtshoorn, surrounded by the well-loved Swartberg mountains of his Hoeko childhood.

As a provincial councillor for the district, he was directly responsible in 1914 for replacing Dutch with Afrikaans as the medium of instruction for Afrikaans children in Cape schools up to Standard IV, a move vital to the language struggle. He had been championing the cause of the Afrikaans language in *Het Zuid-Westen*, a bi-weekly newspaper of which he had become editor in 1912. In 1920 he was elected to Parliament as the Nationalist MP for Oudtshoorn, and in 1921 he became a senator. All through this busy career he remained one of the most prolific and influential of Afrikaans writers.

A steady stream of novels, articles and a weekly column for *Die Burger*, 'Aan Stille Waters', boosted his reputation, but he is prob-

Alan Paton. The writer has long been a spokesman for the cause of humanitarianism in South Africa

Langenhoven's children's stories, Brolloks en Bittergal. *Langenhoven (right), in* U Dienswillige Dienaar *(1932) wrote: 'Two things have made life worth living for me — the love I gave and the love I received'*

Writer Breyten Breytenbach with his wife, Yolande. He was among the most outspoken of the 'Sestigers'

Left: C. Louis Leipoldt with his Congolese manservant, Tito (who had a diploma in cooking). They conversed in French. Right: The cover of Leipoldt's 1932 collection of short stories about the supernatural

Etienne Leroux flanked by the covers of two of his books. Magersfontein, O Magersfontein, *which won the Hertzog Prize for Literature, was initially declared undesirable. The embargo was lifted in March 1980*

ably best remembered for his 1918 poem, *Die Stem van Suid-Afrika,* which, set to music composed by M.L. de Villiers, was to become South Africa's national anthem. Langenhoven was still writing at the diningroom table of his Oudtshoorn home, Arbeidsgenot, when he died in July 1932. He left an unfinished book *(Die Mantel van Elias),* a house preserved today exactly as it was when he died, and the abiding memory of a writer and patriot who had dedicated his life to the Afrikaans language.

A handful of grit from the Hantam

The rugged slopes of the Cedarberg mountains near Clanwilliam — a part of the Western Cape known as the Hantam — set the scene for the formative years of Christian Frederik Louis Leipoldt, the young man destined to be one of the most celebrated poets in Afrikaans literature.

Leipoldt's early career in journalism on the *South African News* had ended in 1901 when martial law closed down the paper for its pro-Boer sentiments.

Travel as far afield as America and Russia did not deter him from writing in the new language of his distant homeland. *Oom Gert Vertel en Ander Gedigte* appeared in 1911, a volume of

poetry inspired by a strong sense of injustice at the suffering he had witnessed both as an Anglo-Boer War correspondent and as a reporter in the Circuit Court which had tried Cape rebels.

Leipoldt stirred Afrikaners to national pride; he also celebrated with a fresh exuberance the natural beauties of the land:

> *'A handful of grit from the Hantam —*
> *The Hantam district I adore!*
> *A handful of grit and bone-dry leaves,*
> *Wagonwood leaves, ghnarrabush leaves!*
> *Rich am I now who was yesterday poor.*

This extract is from *'n Handvol Gruis,* translated by Guy Butler.

Leipoldt returned to South Africa in 1914, a nationally-acclaimed writer who nevertheless continued to work both in medicine and journalism. He recounted his experiences as a medical inspector in *Bushveld Doctor* (1937). In his later years he increasingly turned his attention to South African food and wines. *Kos vir die Kenner* (1933) has long been a classic among Afrikaans cookbooks; before his death in 1947, Leipoldt had also prepared (in English) the manuscript published in 1976 as *Leipoldt's Cape Cookery,* noted both for its easy, confident style and the wealth of historical and culinary information it provides.

LIGHT ON A DARK HORSE

Ignatius Royston (Roy) Dunnachie Campbell was born in Natal in 1901. He loved horses, guns, adventure and wildlife — and he was determined to become a poet. He went to England in 1919, reading voraciously and discovering the work of T.S. Eliot and the French Symbolist poets.

Visiting Europe the following year, he fell in love with Provence and Spain — and the people who lived there. He was living in Wales (by this time he was married) when he wrote *The Flaming Terrapin.* Recalls the *Lantern* of June 1965: 'Its publication in 1924 brought him enthusiastic critical notices and established his early reputation as a poet of brilliant, if uneven, ability.' Campbell served as a private with the British forces during the Second World War until he was disabled and discharged. Later he settled on a small farm near Lisbon. He was killed in a motor accident in 1957, and his legacy was a wealth of poetry, some of it good, some of it great, and some of it just a little barbed:

ON SOME SOUTH AFRICAN NOVELISTS

'You praise the firm restraint with which they write —
I'm with you there, of course:
They use the snaffle and the curb all right,
But where's the bloody horse?'

South African best-sellers

THE THUNDER OF WHEELS

Stuart Cloete was a provocative author. His most famous work, *Turning Wheels*, so infuriated some South Africans with its vigorous account of adventure and sex-across-the-colour-line that he was threatened with horse-whipping and his novel was banned.

Born of South African parents into the glamorous milieu of late 19th century Paris, Cloete was to become one of South Africa's most popular and prolific writers. He answered the call of Africa with an enthusiasm that remained with him until his death in Cape Town at the age of 79. 'South Africa was in my blood,' he wrote in the second volume of his autobiography, *The Gambler*. 'I had been brought up on stories of hunting lion and elephant, of kaffir wars.' And of the Great Trek.

These were the tales that generated his first and most controversial novel in 1937. He discovered that Francis Brett Young, author of a book on South Africa called *Pilgrim's Rest*, was writing a Great Trek novel. So was Cloete. It was the eve of the Voortrekker centenary, and as he recalled in *The Gambler*, Cloete's response was immediate: 'I worked day and night. I hardly stopped to eat. *Turning Wheels* had been accepted by two great publishers, but there was still the race. I must win it. I must finish before Brett Young. At the end I had no idea how to finish the book, so I killed the lot.'

The result was a photo-finish. The novels appeared at the same time and were reviewed together. Despite Young's careful research for *They Seek a Country* — in 1936 he had personally travelled the ox wagon route of the Voortrekkers — the rumbustious style and characterisation of *Turning Wheels* secured an overwhelming victory for Stuart Cloete. His book became a runaway best-seller.

Anger in Afrikanerdom

An unprecedented wave of indignation swept across the country at Cloete's larger-than-life portrayal of the Afrikaners' pioneering ancestors: a Voortrekker hero who slayed his own son and took a coloured woman as his mistress proved too much to swallow.

Cloete was accused of inflicting a 'terrible injustice' and of 'incredible slandering'; students met in Stellenbosch and resolved to ask the Government to ban the book, and Dr Eric Louw, Minister of External Affairs at the time, swore that if Metro Goldwyn Mayer went ahead with plans to make a film, they would never screen an MGM production in South Africa again.

More than two thousand copies of *Turning Wheels* were sold before the novel was banned in South Africa. Asked by the *Cape Times* to comment on the ban, Cloete said: 'What they should have done was to have publicly thrown the banned copies into Table Bay. Think of the publicity. The book would have sold in millions.' Abroad, it did in fact sell millions and was translated into 14 languages. The book remained forbidden fruit for South Africans until 1974, when the ban was finally lifted.

Left: The cover of Cloete's controversial book. Centre: The author. Right: A Boonzaier cartoon reproduced in Die Burger *in 1937. It portrays the 'Spirit of the Voortrekker' with Jan Hofmeyr, then Minister of Education*

Left: Joy Packer. Her first book was published in 1947. Right: Joy Packer and film star Belinda Lee visit Suzie the lioness during a break in the filming of her best-selling book, Nor the Moon by Night

Although he never again matched the spectacular success of his first novel, Cloete made a very profitable living as a writer of countless short stories and a string of novels — several more of which were banned in the 1950s and 1960s. These include *Mamba* (1957), *Gazella* (1958) and *The Abductors* (1965), the last dealing with the evils of prostitution in Victorian England.

In 1974 Cloete stopped sending his manuscripts to Boston University in the United States. Instead he donated them to the newly-established National English Literary Museum and Documentation Centre in Grahamstown. The Centre now has a large collection of his works.

When Cloete died in 1976 he had 25 books to his name and an international reputation that is unlikely to fade. Critics and writers all over the world paid tribute to a true professional.

THE ENTERTAINER

As the wife of Admiral Sir Herbert Packer, Commander-in-Chief of the Royal Navy in the South Atlantic, Cape Town-born and bred Joy Packer was an unlikely candidate for authorship of best-sellers. But she quickly established herself as, and remained, one of the world's most successful writers.

Between 1947 and 1953 she produced her three popular non-fiction works, *Pack and Follow*, *Grey Mistress* and *Apes and Ivory*. Then came the swing to fiction.

'I'd run out of facts,' she told Alan Scholefield of the *Cape Times* in 1959. 'And I went to London and saw the fiction editor of Eyre and Spottiswoode and said: "Look, what do I do now, I've run out of facts," and she said why didn't I write fiction. So I wrote two books of fiction — and tore them up. I've got no feeling about that sort of thing, you know. Doesn't hurt a bit. I keep on throwing away all the time. My typist has some heartaches.'

Her first published novel was *Valley of the Vines*, followed by *Nor the Moon by Night* (filmed by Rank) and *The High Roof*. *Valley of the Vines*, wrote Scholefield, 'blasted off like a rocket with a nose cone full of £ signs. In America it sold more than 400 000 copies, was selected by the Literary Guild (which guarantees £10 000), sold in serial form in England for "between £1 000 and £2 000", and then went on to sell about 80 000 copies in the Commonwealth, 30 000 in England alone. It has been translated into 11 languages. In other words, it went along nicely.'

Other best-sellers followed, including *The Glass Barrier* (1961), *Home from Sea* (1963), *The Blind Spot* (1967) and *Veronica* (1970).

'Even Bertie avoids me . . .'

Joy Packer found it difficult to start a book. She worked long hours, displayed a ferocious concentration: she refused to answer the telephone, go visiting, or do any entertaining. 'I'm pretty hard to live with,' she admitted.

'Even Bertie [her husband] avoids me . . .'

'But then, usually when I've written 20 000 words or so, something happens. Till that time, you know, it's rather as though I were in charge of the characters and the story. Then something seems to click over and the characters begin to dominate me.'

She wrote to entertain her millions of readers but, she qualified, 'If there is one thing that does run through my books it is tolerance. All my books deal in some way with apartheid in South Africa — I don't see how one could write a book set here and ignore it.'

LIFE, DEATH AND ADVENTURE IN AFRICA

Few South African writers have gained more affection and respect in their own country than Lawrence Green, that dedicated, solitary traveller with a keen nose for the sort of stories that missed the history books.

According to John Yates-Benyon in *Lawrence Green — Memories of a Friendship*, the man who claimed at one time to have 'the finest collection of politely worded rejection slips and foreign postage stamps in South Africa' was determined to break loose from his early career in journalism and become a successful writer. He did — and lived to see his books become valued Africana.

An introvert with a reputation as a social enigma, Green worked every weekday morning for precisely 3½ hours, producing a flow of works with evocative titles like *Where Men Still Dream* (1945), *Lords of the Last Frontier* (1953), *Something Rich and Strange* (1962) and *On Wings of Fire* (1967). The romantic ring of the titles proved as appealing as the easy, informal style in which he conveyed his delight in such varied subjects as ghosts, shipwreck dramas and the pleasures of traditional Cape cookery.

In fact he had strong feelings on the subject of cookery books. 'Most modern cookery books,' he told Yates-Benyon, 'are invariably disappointing, merely trumped-up forms of old and hackneyed cooking principles dressed up in newer clothes, and are simply not worth the space in kitchens.'

Schooldays spent haunting Cape Town's colourful streets and harbour before the First World War bred a deep love of the Mother

Wilbur Smith signs copies of his first book

Lawrence Green in the 'forbidden territory' of South West Africa. From his book, To the River's End

City that is reflected in two of his most endearing books, *A Taste of South-Easter* (1971) and *Tavern of the Seas* (1947) — an early bestseller of which Yates-Benyon recalled Green saying: 'It was the easiest book I've ever had to write, a paste and scissors job which was at once an all-out best-seller . . . It needed hardly any effort, yet the book has gone into edition after edition, and it looks as if readers will never tire of it.'

There is still no sign that they have.

In search of a lost world

'I was born near the Great River, in the heart of what for thousands of years had been great Bushman country. The Bushman himself as a coherent entity had already gone, but I was surrounded from birth by so many moving fragments of his race and culture that he felt extraordinarily near.' The words of Laurens van der Post in *The Lost World of the Kalahari*.

Born in 1906 into a family with strong South African ties (his grandmother had survived a massacre of the Voortrekkers in the 1830s), Van der Post served during the Second World War in Africa and the Far East, where, for a few grim years, he was a prisoner of the Japanese.

Though he later settled in England, Van der Post always kept one foot firmly in Africa, never forgetting the attraction he had experienced as a boy for the Bushman, whom he described in *The Lost World of the Kalahari* as 'gay, gallant, mischievous, unpredictable. . .'

He goes on to describe how, as a boy of eight in 1914, he wrote in his secret diary: 'I have decided to-day that when I am grown-up I am going into the Kalahari Desert to seek out the Bushman.' The grown man was true to that youthful vow: *The Lost World of the Kalahari* (1958) and its sequel, *The Heart of the Hunter* (1961) became two of his best-known and most moving books, celebrating the culture and folklore of the tiny people. In *The Lost World of the Kalahari*, he said the Bushman 'appeared to belong to my native land as no other human being has ever belonged'.

The censors roar

In 1964 anyone caught with a copy of Wilbur Smith's first novel faced a stiff fine. Dogeared copies were passed from friend to friend with discretion because there were only

Sir Laurens van der Post. He was knighted in 1981 for his services to Britain

10 000 in circulation and each one was precious. The ban was to last eleven years.

When the Lion Feeds had immediate appeal because of its lively blend of fact, adventure, and occasional sex — the latter explicit enough to attract the attention of the South African censors. By the time it was banned, 25 000 copies had been sold abroad and the novel was about to be translated into ten languages.

Judgements handed down in court, on appeals against the ban, labelled the book variously as 'exciting', 'poor' and 'packed with action and dangerous living'. Its language was described as 'robust'. Objections to the novel were mostly based on a number of sexual passages, defended in court by fellow author W.A. de Klerk as 'mild' in comparison with Bocaccio's *Decameron* — a work which was freely available in South Africa.

During the eleven-year period of the ban, not even the author was allowed to receive copies of his book. Though Smith protested that his own writing was hardly likely to 'deprave or corrupt' his mind, copies sent by his British publishers for his private collection were confiscated and destroyed by customs officials.

By the time the ban was lifted in 1976, the book had sold nearly three million copies abroad and been translated into 18 languages.

Wilbur Smith has since become one of South Africa's most successful writers, and each new thriller is assured of international best-seller status.

Best-selling authors Geoffrey Jenkins and Desmond Bagley have close South African ties

Sporting Life

'The colonial youth, having a goodly share of pride and conceit, had not the kindliest feelings towards the newcomer when the latter took the field on even terms and beat them.' So wrote G.A. Parker in *South African Sport* in 1897. The newcomers were immigrant sportsmen who were to introduce to South Africa most of the major games played in Britain.

They found the colonials eager to learn and willing to work hard for the victories their fierce pride always sought. It was not long before the vanquished were conquerors, and South Africans were competing on equal terms with the best the Mother Country had to offer. Commented Parker: 'Skill, or what is known as science, wrought through long months of patient training, solved the problem.'

In 1893 the Johannesburg cyclist, Lourens Meintjes, became South Africa's first world champion when he triumphed at the Chicago World's Fair. In 1906 Paul Roos's rugby team became the first to wear the Springbok emblem when they played in Britain, and two years later the Durban sprinter, Reggie Walker, was wearing the badge when he became his country's first Olympic gold medallist by winning the 100 yards event in London. A galaxy of individual talent emerged over the succeeding decades, and sportsmen and sportswomen from South Africa were respected throughout the world as formidable and tenacious competitors.

South African rugby players dominated the international game for a long time, and the cricketers of the 1970s, had they been allowed to compete as a national team, would almost certainly have proved themselves world champions. In other sports, too, South Africans proved themselves among the world's best. To select just a few names: in tennis, Eric Sturgess, Sheila Summers, Bob Hewitt and Frew Macmillan; in swimming, Joan Harrison and Karen Muir; in golf, Bobby Locke and Gary Player; in soccer, Bill Perry and Kaizer Motaung; in motor racing, Jody Scheckter and Kork Ballington; on the track, Gert Potgieter, Kenneth McArthur and Paul Nash; in boxing, Vic Toweel, Arnold Taylor, Gerrie Coetzee and Peter Mathebula.

Today more than 90 varieties of sport are played on a national basis by millions of South Africans of all races. For some it began as, and remained, a form of recreation; for others it was a driving need, reflecting their determination to keep South Africa in the forefront of sporting nations. More would have made it to the very top but for the intrusion of politics and, in recent years, the exclusion of South African sportsmen from the world arena.

Three cheerful members of the South African International Hockey Team, photographed in Johannesburg in 1925. They played against a touring British team, losing all three tests

Here at the Wanderers

FROM MANAGERS TO MINERS

The Wanderers, at the turn of the century, was the lively focus of sporting and social life on the Reef. Each Saturday, when the mine headgear shut down at noon, just about everyone who was sportingly inclined, from managers and office clerks to the white miners who dug for gold, headed for the club. Founded by public-spirited men in 1888 as a recreation park for the mining community, it had become the largest sporting centre in the southern hemisphere, with a membership running to almost 1 500.

Wanderers' chairman Harold Strange reported in 1902 that of the club's six active sections, gymnastics was the biggest with 132 members. Tennis came a close second with 121 players (including 18 ladies) and support for rugby, cricket, athletics and football was equally enthusiastic. By recognising baseball as an official club sport, the Wanderers made sure that the game would survive and grow in South Africa — though not without some teething troubles. In 1904 the Sunday matches became so rowdy that the players were banished from the Wanderers to Driehoek, where they continued to attract crowds of up to 1 500 each Sunday.

Cricket had long been established at the Wanderers, and when Sir Pelham ('Plum') Warner brought his M.C.C. side out in 1906, he described the wicket as 'the fastest run-getting ground I know. There is not a blade of grass anywhere, the colour of the soil being reddish brown. The wicket is exceptionally fast and the ball simply fizzes to the boundary when hit.'

The area occupied by the Wanderers is now a network of railway lines (it was expropriated despite a legal tussle that went to the Supreme Court), but the memories linger on: Dudley Nourse's majestic 231 runs; the time when the boss of Charlie Frank's office allowed his staff to watch the match, provided they returned to work when Charlie was out. They went back a day and a half later.

It was from that matting wicket that another Wanderers player, the test cricketer and rugby Springbok Jimmy Sinclair, supposedly hit a ball to Cape Town. He was a renowned big hitter and one of his sixes landed in a railway truck passing on the line to the south of the ground. Presumably the ball was found when the train reached its destination, 1 300 km away.

Over the red soil (the ground was not turfed until 1935) trod the hallowed feet of Hobbs, Barnes, Hammond, Taylor, Faulkner, Macartney, Woolley and many more of the most famous cricketers of their day.

Boxing, wrestling — and a fighting preacher

It was on the same ground one night in 1934 that Laurie Stevens, knocked down for the first time in his career, recovered marvellously from the hammer blows of the Italian Aldo Spaldi to gain a points decision. It was also there that he scored a thrilling win over Kid Berg, the Whitechapel Whirlwind, to become Empire lightweight champion, and there too

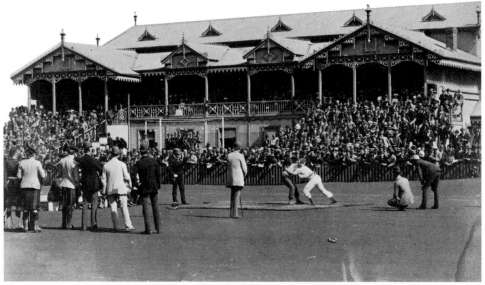

Wrestling in front of the Wanderers Pavilion in the early 1900s. It was highly popular with spectators

Spectators in the members' stand at the Wanderers during an early test match between England and South Africa

THE ALL SOUTH AFRICAN SPORT

Though it has been likened to the American game of horseshoe pitching — itself a pioneers' game — jukskei is the only sport that originated in South Africa. Born on the Great Trek, the game's name derives from the pin (*skei*) of the ox-yoke. At dusk, as the wagons gathered in laager, the trekkers would draw the long *skeie*. One *skei* would be planted in the soft earth, the throwing distance marked in the soil, and each player would have his own *skei* to throw at the

stake. The winner would be the player who toppled the stake most times.

The disappearance of the ox wagon brought a decline in the popularity of the sport, but the symbolic Centenary Great Trek in 1938 gave many Afrikaners their first opportunity to see the game played by their forebears. *Laers* (clubs) were formed, joined together in *wyksbond* (sub-unions) which collectively formed the *bond*. At the head of each *laer* was a commandant (the head of a Boer commando).

The language of jukskei is still very much the language of the trekker. *Die wiele moet rol* ('let the wheels turn') is the signal for every member of a team to score falls with his or her two *skeie*. *Neef* (boy cousin) and *niggie* (girl cousin) are regular players, while a *penkop* is a novice — who gets an advantage in the throwing distance. The elders of the game are *tannie* and *oom* (auntie and uncle).

Every year hundreds of jukskei enthusiasts gather at Jukskei Park in Kroonstad in the Free State for the South African championships — one of the biggest sporting rallies in the country.

Lining up for the start of the One Mile (Visitors) Cycle Race at the Wanderers in the 1890s

The Wanderers A.F.C. won the Transvaal Challenge Cup in 1889 — the year of the football club's inauguration. C. Aubrey Smith (holding the ball) later became a Hollywood film star

that he fell to the hard-hitting world featherweight champion, Petey Sarron.

Over the road the 'B' ground was the headquarters of Transvaal rugby. There was ethnic rivalry: 'Cousin Jacks' (immigrant Cornishmen) vied with Afrikaner and Briton, and this gave colour and character to the highly popular matches. Cove-Smith's team of 1924 was the last to play an international there: the final game provided an incident both rare and unseemly for those gentlemanly days when the Reverend A.F. Blakiston and Mervyn Ellis took a swipe at each other before bending into the scrum. Four years later, big rugby moved to Ellis Park.

Credit to the country

The 'C' ground was used mostly by athletes and cyclists, and there were many exhilarating contests. Some of the best would later go on to the Olympic Games. It was also a site for baseball, bowls, tennis, dirt-track racing, women's hockey internationals and big soccer matches: when South Africa played the English F.A. team in 1920, Joe Smith of Bolton Wanderers was ordered off the field — a very unusual procedure in those days. He appeared to take a deliberate kick at Joe Green. Referee Arthur Ruffels at once told him to go off, but before he could leave the South African captain, Alf Lowe, hurried up to the referee and said: 'It was accidental. Surely, old man, you don't want us to beat ten men. That won't be much credit to the country.' Smith stayed on: the F.A. team won 3-1.

Despite a 99-year lease, the Railways Administration gradually expropriated pieces of the ground for extensions to the station, and in October 1946 the old club was closed and the new premises opened 8 km away in the northern suburbs. The new area was called Kent Park after the president, Victor Kent, who in 1936 had had the foresight to acquire property as a site for the club's future home when the lease expired in 1989.

The new Wanderers could not hope to attain the unique atmosphere of the old club, but in the summer of 1956-57 it started to build its own traditions: that season the Wanderers was the venue of one of the most thrilling cricket matches yet seen in South Africa. South Africa was already 2-0 down in the

series against Peter May's M.C.C. team. Then Hugh Tayfield took nine wickets in England's second innings, and 13 in the match, to bring victory by 17 runs. South Africa went on to share the rubber.

THE SOCIABLE ENGLISH

Most 19th century Afrikaners were men of the veld, their sporting activities confined largely to riding and shooting (skills that made them such formidable enemies against the British). English-speaking South Africans, on the other hand, tended to organise themselves in clubs: a habit given impetus by the gregarious redcoats who came to fight Victoria's wars in South Africa. Some of the clubs were formed for a single sport: cricket, rugby, soccer, tennis, cycling. Others, like the Wanderers, and Collegians in Pietermaritzburg, were multi-

purpose, with vastly superior facilities.

Durban had its Lord's — named after cricket's Mecca — which offered its members rugby, soccer, athletics and cricket. The name was dropped when the club moved to Kingsmead in 1922. The Crusaders Club in Port Elizabeth is still host for international and provincial matches at St George's Park, a cricketing venue since 1843.

At first, the Western Province cricket and rugby clubs shared the same ground. In 1888 they leased part of Mariendal farm in Newlands, Cape Town, and then bought it for £3 000 in 1894. Later the two sections split, rugby settling on its own ground across the railway line. Cricketing Newlands became what *The Cricketer* called a paradise: '. . . the stately oaks on one side and the towering mountains on the other, like a majestic sentinel guarding a greensward in a setting unparalleled for beauty in any cricket ground in the world.'

Twenty-eight thousand cricket fans jammed the Wanderers for the test against Bill Lawry's touring Australian team in 1970. South Africa won by an impressive 307 runs — thanks to all-rounders such as Goddard and Barlow

Rugby fever in South Africa

MAULIANA! AND THE GAME KICKS OFF

South Africans took their rugby seriously in the early 1900s. Friendships, and sometimes personal enmity, grew from discussions on matches and the various merits and demerits of the players. For some the game was becoming almost a way of life.

Love of the sport overcame language, geographical and (more recently) racial barriers, and on at least one occasion the Anglo-Boer War was politely set aside in the interests of rugby:

> The Honourable Major Edwards,
> O'Kiep.
>
> Dear Sir,
> I wish to inform you that I have agreed to a rugby match taking place between you and us. I from my side will agree to order a cease-fire tomorrow afternoon from 12 o'clock until sunset, the time and venue of the match to be arranged by you in consultation with Messrs Roberts and Van Rooyen who I am sending in to you.
>
> I have the honour etc.
> pp S.G. Maritz
> Concordia   Field General
> 28 April 1902   Transvaal Scouting Corps

The crest shone first

Adriaan van der Byl launched the country's most popular sport with a kick-off on Cape Town's Green Point Common at 3 p.m. on 23 August 1862. An anonymous poet recorded that historic moment with the words:

> Van der Byl started the football,
> Mauliana!
> His crest shone first among us all.

His Excellency the Governor and Mrs Wodehouse; the Colonial Secretary, Lieutenant-Colonel and Mrs Jenner, and a large crowd watched the challenge match between the military and a civilian side that day. A newspaper described the game: 'Over and over again did the combatants roll in their brave

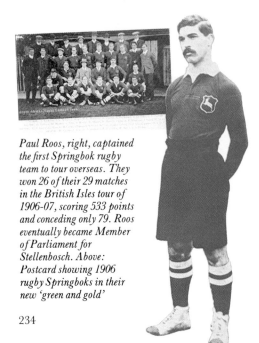

Paul Roos, right, captained the first Springbok rugby team to tour overseas. They won 26 of their 29 matches in the British Isles tour of 1906-07, scoring 533 points and conceding only 79. Roos eventually became Member of Parliament for Stellenbosch. Above: Postcard showing 1906 rugby Springboks in their new 'green and gold'

Otto Landsberg's view of a match between Pretoria College and the Diocesan College (Bishops) in Cape Town in 1888. The Winchester code game was already out of fashion by this time and most clubs were playing the style of rugby made popular by the famous English public school of that name

charges; over and over again did the unerring drop kick of the goal keepers save the game as those terrible rushing outsiders swept past the crowd; frequently the tallest leaders of the fray worked the ball from amongst the contending rivals, but no ungenerous hurt was received, and no advantage beyond that of superior weight was taken.'

In the same year the Diocesan College (Bishops) challenged a combined military and civilian team and defeated them by three goals to one.

A healthy and manly exercise

Bishops was the first school to introduce rugby. Canon George Ogilvie, who became principal in 1861, immediately set about introducing the Winchester Code game of rugby because he believed his boys needed 'a

> ### WHAT'S IN A NAME?
>
> The British Press treated them like colonials from darkest Africa. Readers were told of the sinister-sounding battle cry of the South Africans — *Igamalio!* It was, newspapers informed their appalled readers, the shout of a warrior as he thrust an assegai into his enemy's heart.
>
> Back in South Africa, Paul Roos, the former schoolmaster turned captain of the first rugby team to visit Britain, knew that the London press would invent a name for the visitors if they didn't produce one of their own first. 'The team thought of mimosas,' Roos said later, 'but did not like the idea of being called after a thorn bush.' Proteas were also suggested, but neither did that name really fit footballers.
>
> Finally Roos decided his men would be known as *De Springbokken* — later Anglicised and shortened to Springboks.

healthy and manly winter exercise'. South African College Schools (SACS), the forerunner of the University of Cape Town, followed suit a year later.

'Gog's Football', as it became known, remained the prevalent style of rugby until 1878, when William Henry Milton, a lively and forceful former English Rugby Union international, persuaded local sportsmen they were old-fashioned and playing the wrong game.

Five years later, students at the mainly Afrikaans-speaking Victoria College (later the University of Stellenbosch) adopted the game. Rugby and rugby rivalry spread rapidly into rural areas and soon the talents and deficiencies of players were being dissected in pubs and parlours all over South Africa. Stellenbosch has produced over 100 Springbok players and exerted a powerful influence on the development of the sport.

The Western Province Rugby Union was created in 1883 after a formal proposal was adopted at the annual meeting of the Hamilton Football Club — said to be the oldest in the country, although it is thought that a club might have existed in Swellendam as early as 1868. F.L. Aitcheson, the honorary secretary of Hamiltons, told other clubs: 'Matters such as uniformity of rules, purchase of a challenge cup, selection of teams, such as the Mother Country and Colonial born etc, would be attended to.'

Rugby quickly caught on in the Eastern Province, had spread to Kimberley by 1886, and finally took root on the Rand during the gold rush. The South African Rugby Board was formed in 1889 with Mr Percy Ross Frames of Kimberley as its first president. It was stated at the meeting that the Board's credit balance was £24.19s., and it was further resolved that the Board would adopt the rules of the English Rugby Football Union. The first union to become a member of the Board

A Somerset West family distinguished itself between 1903 and 1928 by fielding ten of its sons under the Springbok colours. In that period the 'Sporting Morkels' notched up 48 appearances for South Africa. This view of Douglas Morkel shows the concentration that won him acclaim as the father of place-kicking in this country

was Western Province, in 1883. Eastern Transvaal became a member only in 1947.

For the first 56 years of the 20th century the Springboks were near-invincible; undisputed rugby kings of the world. They lost the occasional test but never a series — until their defeat by the All Blacks in New Zealand in 1956.

The best in the world

South Africa's entrance into international rugby was not long in coming. It was inauspicious, but within a few years the colonials were to stagger the sporting world. Their debut was in 1891, only 13 years after the Rugby Union style of play was introduced, with the first of the two 'educational' tours undertaken by British teams in the 19th century.

The South African Rugby Board hosted W.E. Maclagan and his team for a 19-match series in which the visitors conceded only one try. Five years later, J. Hammond's team proved equally devastating, losing only their final match.

But these defeats were very soon forgotten as tutor became pupil and South Africa, its pride and fighting spirit aroused, rampaged to some glorious victories. In 1903 'Fairy' Heatlie led the South Africans to their first-ever win in a series — against Mark Morrison's British touring team. The next half-century produced some of the world's greatest players: Phillip Nel's 1937 team in New Zealand and Basil Kenyon's magnificent 1951-52 Springboks, on tour in Britain, were almost certainly the best South African sides.

Although the post-1956 period was not as successful, the Springboks nevertheless won their fair share of games both at home and abroad. They lost series to France (1958), Australia (1965), New Zealand (1965) and the British Isles (1974), and also lost single tests against France, Scotland, England and Ireland. But between 1960 and 1980 South Africa beat the British Lions in three series (1962, 1968 and 1980), Australia in two (1961 and 1969), France in five (1967, 1968, 1971, 1974 and 1975) and New Zealand in three (1960, 1970 and 1976).

Rugby fever has never abated in South Africa. It has long been the major sport at schools and universities; its players are heroes. In 1955 a crowd of 95 000 fans pushed into Ellis Park in Johannesburg for the first test between South Africa and the British Isles — a world record for Rugby Union which was still standing in 1980.

THE SPORTING MORKELS

If the First World War had not intervened, a unique rugby team would have toured England — all the players would have been named Morkel. The sporting Morkels of Somerset West were a legend, and when mining magnate Sir Abe Bailey had the idea of sending a Morkel team to England, 22 of them were playing first team rugby in the Union. Between 1903 and 1928 rugby's most famous family gained ten Springbok colours — a record that is unlikely to be beaten.

Philip Morkel arrived at the Cape in 1691 as a gunner on board the *Oosterstyn*. He and his brother Wilhelm settled at what was still a primitive half-way station for ships of the Dutch East India Company, and Philip produced the four sons from whom rugby's most famous clan is descended.

Their interest in the game is thought to have started on the family farm, Rome, where the bare-footed youngsters laid out their own field and challenged all comers. The Somerset West Rugby Club is believed to have evolved from this core of enthusiasts. Between 1903 and 1928, Morkels were to notch up 48 appearances for South Africa as well as many games for provinces. It was not unusual for half the Western Province team to consist of Morkels!

Writing in the *Cape Argus*, Weldon Broughton recalled the last test against the All Blacks in Wellington in 1921, when Morkels were still very much in evidence. 'Each side had scored a victory,' he wrote. 'This was the match which the New Zealand papers called the world battle for rugby supremacy. It rained throughout the match and the players' vision was obscured. The Springboks could hardly see their full-back, Gerhard Morkel. But they heard the smack, smack of the ball in his hands as he caught it, and they knew they were safe.'

The game ended without a score.

Douglas Morkel is widely accepted as the father of place-kicking in South Africa. During a test at Bordeaux in 1913, the Springbok captain Billy Millar handed him the ball for a penalty and suggested he boot it straight at the French full-back.

'Billy,' replied Morkel, 'I'm going to take a pot shot at goal.' And he did. The ball soared between the posts from well inside the Springbok half, the crowd went wild, and a Frenchman dashed from the crowd to kiss Douglas Morkel.

Japie Krige's rugby career was at its height in the decade after 1896. This small, blond player was rated the best centre three-quarter of his era and was one of the first players to stir the public's imagination

Barry 'Fairy' Heatlie was recalled to lead the South Africans to their first-ever win in a rugby series in 1903, when they beat Mark Morrison's British touring team by 11 matches to eight

H.H. Castens led South Africa in its first rugby international — and then went on to become this country's first touring cricket captain as well when he led the 1894 side that visited England

Above: South Africa plays the British Isles at Cape Town in the third and final match of the 1891 tour. W.E. Maclagan, right, led the British tourists in the 19-match series

Magic moments: magnificent men

RUGBY CHAMPIONS OF THE WORLD

When Philip Nel's 1937 Springboks left Durban for their tour of Australia and New Zealand they knew it wouldn't be easy. In more than half a century the All Blacks hadn't lost a rubber to a touring side.

The tour began with two wins against Australia and a 17-6 loss to New South Wales — a defeat given exaggerated significance by the New Zealand rugby writers, who predicted a string of losses for the visitors. The 'boks were left in no doubt that the New Zealanders considered the series to be the rugby championship of the world.

Auckland fell to the Springboks in the first match, and was quickly followed by Waikato, Taranaki, Manawatu (39-3) and Wellington (29-0) before the first test — also in Wellington.

The 'boks outplayed

It had rained steadily for days before the match, and the field was a muddy mess. But the 'boks, clearly given confidence by their successive victories over the provincial sides, sang and joked in their dressing room. Older Springboks believe even today that singing or facetiousness before a big game can mean losing it. Danie Craven was so worried by the attitude of the team that he told Nel they would lose.

There was never really any doubt. The All Blacks played like men inspired, the mud and rain obviously hampered the South Africans, and by half-time it was probably all over — and the crowd knew it. New Zealand won the first test 13-7.

It had been a major triumph for the All Blacks forwards, but many critics felt that selection blunders by the South Africans had greatly contributed to their downfall.

Revenge was not long in coming, though: the second — and psychologically decisive — test was played at Christchurch before a crowd of 45 000 wildly cheering spectators. The 'boks pushed the All Blacks into their own half and kept them there while they launched attack after attack. Then came the setback which challenged their spirit — two unconverted tries which took the New Zealanders to a 6-0 lead at half-time.

It was the second half of this game that rugby writer Chris Greyvenstein described as a 'fight back which must rank with the most glorious in our rugby history'.

We are not amused

It was early in the second half that the mighty Boy Louw received a head injury, transforming him from a magnificent player into a confused, giggling clown.

Louw ran around the field, demanding to know from everyone just what was going on, and chuckling throughout. 'It may be funny now, but it wasn't funny then,' Craven said years later. 'The seconds were ticking away and we just could not break through the All Blacks' defence, and with a stalwart like Boy incapacitated, our future looked grim indeed.'

But slowly the Springbok machine began to

Danie Craven's bullet-like dive pass proved a nightmare to the All Blacks during the 'bok tour of Australasia in 1937. Their exaggerated respect for it allowed the Springboks to use it as a tactical ploy

Five members of the Springbok team which toured New Zealand and Australia in 1937. From the left: Danie Craven, Gerry Brand, Lucas Strachan, Boy Louw and captain Philip Nel. The powerful Louw was knocked on the head in the first test at Wellington, and dissolved in giggles

move into gear. Freddie Turner sped across the line for a try and Gerry Brand converted to bring the 'boks within one point of the All Blacks' score. Then scrum-half Craven was tackled illegally and a penalty awarded on the halfway line, at a sharp angle. Gerry Brand placed the ball with care as the crowd quietened. Seconds later it was soaring over the cross-bar to put the 'boks in the lead by two points. There were only a few minutes left in the game, but they were not about to relax.

Ebbo Bastard, still half-dazed from a bruising tackle, sailed over the line for another try and Brand converted with yet another unerring kick. It was over, and the Springboks had won the second test 13-6.

A crowd of 55 000 watched Nel and All Blacks captain Ron King lead their teams onto the field at Auckland for the third and final test. If the All Blacks were determined to win, their supporters were no less enthusiastic: one even offered to bet his farm on the result! It was a hard, magnificent game, and the Springboks were in control for most of it. The final score was 17-6, and the 1937 Springboks were rugby's world champions. They were to hold the title for two glorious decades. Noted one sportswriter: 'On the boat returning home, Philip Nel formally announced his retirement from rugby by throwing his boots into the sea. He had no further need for them because like Alexander the Great, he had no more worlds left to conquer!'

THE MAN WHO MADE PLACE-KICKING LOOK EASY

April 20, 1944. It was Hitler's birthday, and everyone in the huge prisoner of war camp at Thorn, in Poland, was allowed an extra hour in bed.

It was also the first day on which the first rugby trials matches were to be played —in preparation for a 'test series' between South African and New Zealand prisoners. One of the stars of the game that followed was a thick-set man from Johannesburg who was later to earn international respect for his devastating kicking — Okey Geffin.

Though he made place-kicking look easy, success lay in the intense concentration 'Ox' Geffin applied to his art. His greatest performance was at Newlands against the 1949 All Blacks. He made sure of his first three points after a penalty was awarded ten metres from touch. But the visitors were ahead at halftime with the score 11-3, and the crowd was gloomily silent. Felix du Plessis told Geffin to take the next penalty (Jack van der Schyff was the usual kicker) and he collected another three points, this time from 30 metres. Then came another, and suddenly, after a 50-metre kick from near the touch-line, South Africa was in the lead.

Geffin capped a magnificent game with a sitter in front of the posts just before the whistle to make the final tally 15-11. He had won the match with his boot.

THE LONELIEST SPORTSMAN
IN THE WORLD

The crowd at Ellis Park on 6 August 1955 was almost frighteningly large. Nearly 100 000 excited fans had crowded into the stadium to see Stephen Fry lead his Springboks onto the field for the first test against the 1955 British Lions.

It was a day and a match that has been called the most thrilling of all time. The rugby was splendid and the result was in the balance until the last few seconds of the match, when a hush swept across the arena and Jack van der Schyff took four steps back in preparation for his kick. The angle wasn't difficult, but the tension in that moment was shattering.

Story-book finish

Never before in rugby history had there been such a build-up of excitement and tension. The Lions had already endeared themselves to South Africans with their friendliness and good humour, but the selectors were aware that the visitors were also intelligent and powerful opponents who played a disciplined game. The Springbok team contained no less than nine new caps.

The Lions were in a determined mood but, say some rugby men, the Springboks were not properly motivated. After watching the casual behaviour of the home team, Danie Craven commented: 'Some of the younger ones were far too concerned with other matters and also ate too much.'

The score see-sawed throughout the game, with the Lions dominating after the interval: three tries, converted by Angus Cameron, gave them a seemingly unbeatable lead. But the South Africans shortened the odds with a lucky try; and then Chris Koch weaved his way through a swarming defence to make it 19-23.

With just 30 seconds of injury time left, Western Province wing Theunis Briers took a pass, beat two opponents and crashed over midway between posts and corner flag.

It was a story-book finish. One point behind; a conversion to come — from a very kickable position.

Chris Greyvenstein describes that last and most dramatic moment: 'Tommy Gentles placed the ball for Van der Schyff with the referee, Ralph Burmeister, resting on his haunches a few paces behind and to the left of the kicker so that he would have a clear view to the centre of the crossbar.

'The tall full-back, then playing for Western Transvaal, took four steps back and then ran up for the kick that would decide the result. It was a moment that I and probably 90 000 others will always be able to recall at will.

'The instant his boot struck the ball we knew that it was going to swing outside the left-hand post and that the Springboks had lost. His head down in utter dejection, Van der Schyff turned away as the Lions, standing behind the goalline, jumped for joy. If ever a man was desperately lonely in spite of the thousands of people around him it must have been Jack Henry van der Schyff on the afternoon of August 6, 1955.'

Jack van der Schyff was the world's unhappiest full-back on 6 August 1955. His head slumps dejectedly after missing the conversion that would have given the Springboks victory over the British Lions at Ellis Park in a game watched by nearly 100 000 people. This one failure banished him to rugby's wilderness

OSLER — THE
DON BRADMAN OF RUGBY

Whenever and wherever rugby enthusiasts gather, the conversation usually gets around to 'the greatest'. If the Ellis Park clash of 1955 was the greatest test, which was the finest team, and who were the best players? Are Basil Kenyon's 1951-52 'boks in Britain at the top of the list?

Dr Danie Craven, president of the South African Rugby Board, is in no doubt on one point: 'There has been no greater rugby name or genius than Bennie Osler.' Osler himself cited Phil Mostert, who won 14 caps between 1921 and 1931; Frank Mellish, who played for both England (1920) and South Africa (1921 to 1924); Theuns Kruger; Mervyn Ellis; Boy and Fanie Louw; Ferdie Bergh; Phil Nel; George Daneel; S.P. van Wyk and, of course, his brother Stanley Osler.

But there's small doubt that most South Africans agree with Dr Craven. Osler, the tough, often dictatorial player has been called the Don Bradman of rugby — an autocrat on the field and an aristocrat off it. He created a brand of rugby that dominated Springbok play — and determined how other international teams would challenge it — for almost four decades.

It was a game that was termed 'modern rugby', but which the spectators called 'ten-man rugby' and found boring. It also won matches and, for Osler, that was what it was all about. His diagonal kicks were planned to bring the 'boks within striking distance.

Osler brought his ten-man rugby style to perfection when he led the Springboks on a tour of the British Isles in 1931-32. The relentless routine of kicking and movement of the pack upfield was relieved only when Osler judged his backs to be in an attacking position. Once again his formula worked. The British hated it; O.L. Owen wrote in *The Times* of London: 'Many people felt, and always will feel, that a really great side can be attractive as well as invincible.'

Bennie Osler, right, and his brother Stanley are among the greatest names in South African rugby history. Although Bennie's devastating boot won him a worldwide reputation, he always maintained that his brother was the better player

Hennie Muller leads the Springboks onto Murrayfield for the test against Scotland during their tour of the British Isles and France in 1951-52. Muller replaced captain Basil Kenyon, who had to adopt a spectator's role after receiving an eye injury early in the tour

Smokebombs and tintacks

...PLUS 1 017 POLICEMEN

It had to be one of the strangest rugby series ever. A Springbok team led by a future Ambassador to the Court of St James versus the British Isles, regiments of demonstrators, smokebombs, tintacks — and a jinx.

As captain of the 1969-70 Springbok touring side, Dawie de Villiers was placed in probably the most demanding position he would ever experience. The pressure on the team was intense throughout the tour. Wallace Reyburn, a veteran New Zealand journalist and former war correspondent, wrote later: 'The genuine anti-apartheid demonstrators were surrounded by as fine a rabble as you could wish to see, representing every breed of political and religious trouble-maker, trade union agitators, SinnFein, Young Socialists, communists, Britain-haters, Maoists, anarchists...'

As if this was not enough, the 'boks were hampered by injury, bereavement and poor form on the part of such key players as Piet Visagie and Mannetjies Roux, who was flown over from his Victoria West farm to replace the injured Johann van der Schyff.

Springboks versus demos

Judged against the background of harassment both on and off the field, the team's record of 15 wins out of 24 matches, with four draws and five defeats, is remarkably good, though it cannot, of course, compare with the achievements of previous all-conquering South African teams. For the first time the Springboks failed to win any of the tests against the Home Countries.

It went down in history as the demo tour. Extraordinary security measures were taken to protect the Springboks from well-organised demonstrators memorable for their viciousness. Smokebombs were thrown onto the field at some matches and even tintacks were scattered in the grass.

Typical was the game against Midlands East in Leicester, where 1 017 policemen were turned out to hold back the demonstrators, who kept up a constant chant of anti-apartheid slogans throughout the match. Dawie de Villiers and his team, obviously unsettled after being incarcerated in the grounds for two

hours before the match, nevertheless won with a score of 11-9 to earn a standing ovation from the 'real' spectators.

British rugby transformed

Traditionally known for robust play, these Springboks were strangely gentle in most of their matches. There was also evidence that British rugby had undergone a transformation that put zip into their game. For the first time the England team had a professional coach. Even at club level it was apparent that they were putting more effort into their training.

It was only in the final match of the tour that the 'boks discovered they had a solid kicker in their captain, who scored nine points against the Barbarians. In this game, rated the best of the tour, the Springboks emerged victors with a score of 21-12 and Dawie de Villiers was chaired off the field by Barbarians Gareth Edwards and Mike Gibson. It was a fitting tribute to a plucky captain.

Above: Demonstrators interrupted matches throughout the United Kingdom tour of 1969-70. Left: The South Africans were captained by Dawie de Villiers (seen here in action against the All Blacks), an internationally respected player and tactician. The former theologian was named South Africa's Ambassador to the Court of St James in 1979, and joined the Cabinet in 1980

Ever since Bennie Osler invented 'modern rugby', South Africa had relied on power, possession and a kicking game for territorial advantage.

But by the early 1970s, there were signs that the Springboks were losing the discipline and motivation that this type of play demanded.

Syd Millar, who was to manage the 1974 British Lions tour of the Republic, recognised the signs. He spotted a lack of dedication on the part of the South Africans, and dedication was something he was determined to instil in his own team. As a result, says former Springbok John Gainsford, 'they were mentally tougher, physically harder, superbly drilled and coached and disciplined and united. They were dedicated fellows who were trained to peak fitness...'

And there was an abundance of talent, too. Willie-John McBride, a tough, good-humoured Irishman, was a leader to respect;

Dr Danie Craven, president of the South African Rugby Board and the country's most powerful rugby administrator. He introduced South Africa to racially mixed rugby and in frequent trips abroad acted as a roving diplomat. Few people were able to intimidate him, but one of the few was the volatile A.F. Markötter (Mr Mark), the Springbok selector of his youth. Markötter's quick temper was legendary

'Is there an Englishman, Scotsman, Irishman or Welshman in the house?'

An Argus *cartoon recalls the injury-plagued British Lions tour of South Africa in 1980*

A MAN FOR ALL SEASONS

Morné du Plessis — 'a relentless competitor with iron in his soul'

For Morné du Plessis the road to rugby's top spot was a rough one. He braved disappointment, unfair criticism and worse to emerge as one of the country's greatest-ever players.

Du Plessis was born in Vereeniging on 21 October 1949, only a few months after his father, Felix, had taken the Springboks to three successive victories over the All Blacks. At Grey College he featured prominently in the South African Schools cricket XI in 1967 and, while serving in the SA Navy, won the Admiral's Award for cricket, rugby and golf. As a Stellenbosch University student, he captained the Western Province Under-20 rugby team and a year later was a member of Hannes Marais' triumphant side in Australia. His was a proud record, but it was not enough to prevent his confidence from crumbling after the 'boks' devastating defeat by the Lions in 1974. He was dropped from the team. A year later, though, he came back to lead South Africa against France.

When the All Blacks came to South Africa in 1976, Morné du Plessis was once again the clear choice to captain South Africa. He led Western Province to an unforgettable victory over the visitors at Newlands, and the Springboks eventually won the series 3-1.

The Lions' 1980 tour of South Africa eliminated any doubt that Du Plessis had become one of South Africa's great rugby captains.

of a Springbok skin, once so highly valued, is of very little value at this time . . . who wants a goat's head above his mantelpiece?'

But then came the Lions tour of 1980. South Africa was still smarting after the 1974 thrashing at the hands of McBride's team, despite a series win over the All Blacks in 1976, and the Springboks were determined on revenge. The visitors won the first six matches of what was to become known as the 'injury tour': nine players went home because of illness or injury, and the Lions called for eight replacements — the highest number in rugby history.

Saturday, 31 May 1980 dawned bright and clear. Newlands began to fill with excited fans from all over South Africa while harassed traffic officers fought to control their thousands of cars. Skipper Morné du Plessis led the Springboks onto the field to the roar of 43 500 spectators.

The match was on. Rob Louw scored the first try for the Springboks and from then on it was a see-saw game as both sides put their all into the scrums and lineouts. Victory was clinched for South Africa by Divan Serfontein in the first minute of injury time after a display of attacking rugby that left the fans breathless. The 'boks took the first test with a score of 26-22. Two weeks later they triumphed in Bloemfontein with a tally of 26 points to 19, and on 28 June they beat the Lions 12-10 at Port Elizabeth. The final test, in Pretoria on 12 July, deservedly went to the Lions (17-13).

Lions skipper Billy Beaumont and Springbok captain Morné du Plessis paid moving tributes to each other after the final test. It had been a hard-fought, incident-free tour. It had also signified South Africa's second entry into the international rugby world it had once ruled.

Ian 'Mighty Mouse' McLauchlan, a scrummaging tactician; and the great Gareth Edwards worked wonders behind the scrum. Phil Bennett was a brilliant fly-half and a dropkicking wizard; J. P. R. Williams, the tall, long-maned Welshman, an uncompromisingly tough fullback and a danger to the 'boks whenever he touched the ball.

The first test at Newlands showed up the differences. The home side were clearly not the co-ordinated team they should have been.

The Lions won 12-3 after three penalties by Bennett and a drop-goal by Edwards.

The South African selectors panicked. Altogether 33 different players were fielded in the four tests; the Springboks were demoralised and lacked cohesion. They lost 28-9 in Pretoria and 26-9 at Port Elizabeth. There was, though, some consolation in their controversial 13-13 draw at Ellis Park.

Writing in the French sports paper, *L'Equipe*, Georges Mazzocut said: 'The price

Three rugby greats of recent times. Left: The mighty Frik du Preez trots onto the field for his final big match in 1971. He was one of the most powerful and effective forwards in the history of Springbok rugby. Below: Piet Visagie's ice-cool temperament and deadly boot won him a record for the most points scored in test matches. Between 1967 and 1971 he notched up a spectacular 130 points in 25 tests. Right: Jan Ellis earned a reputation as an attacking flanker with a remarkable ball sense. He shares the record with Frik du Preez for the most appearances in test matches — 38 in all — and was one of South Africa's leading try scorers

Golden days

FULL TOSS INTO THE WORLD ARENA

It was the series that put South African cricket firmly on the map. In 1905 'Plum' Warner — later Sir Pelham and doyen of the game for two decades — sailed for Cape Town with the first official M.C.C. team to tour the subcontinent. The side, though not fully representative of English talent, was a strong one. Nevertheless, in the words of one-time M.C.C. president Harry Altham, they were to be 'routed horse, foot and guns'.

The South Africans had not won a match since their first tentative, unofficial entry into the international arena in 1889 (in that year C. Aubrey Smith, later of Hollywood fame, brought an English team over), but the game had matured quickly under the hot African sun. Warner in fact had toured with Lord Hawke's English side in 1898-99 and recorded in *Cricket in Many Climes* that 'cricket is played quite as enthusiastically as at home. Step by step we have forced our way up north and the cricket-pavilions that have sprung up along our track may almost be called the milestones on the road of the nation's progress'.

Now, on 2 January 1906, he led his side onto the Wanderers ground for the first test match.

Looking the losers

The home side, which included fine players in captain Percy Sherwell, Dave Nourse, Aubrey Faulkner, Reginald Schwarz, Albert Vogler and Gordon White, started badly. Unable to scramble even half England's modest first innings total of 184, the M.C.C. looked fair set for victory. Consistent bowling by Faulkner (4 for 26) kept the lead down to 283 when South Africa went out to bat for the second time, but their chances of reaching the target were not, on the run of play, highly rated, and indeed, when six wickets had tumbled for 104, defeat seemed certain.

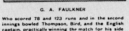

THE LION CUB LICKS THE LION
Outstanding Personalities of the Magnificent South African Team who Won the First Test Match.

G. A. FAULKNER — Who scored 78 and 123 runs and in the second innings bowled Thompson, Bird, and the English captain, practically winning the match for his side against England

S. J. SNOOKE — The popular captain of the South African team and as fine a batsman as he is resourceful a captain. Snooke showed by his play in the first test match that he is a vastly-improved batsman

R. O. SCHWARZ — The googlie fiend, who seems never to have done himself full justice with the bat for the South African side. In the first test match his score was not a big one

Three of the South Africans who distinguished themselves when the M.C.C. toured South Africa in 1909-10

A stunning seventh wicket stand of 121 between White and Nourse propelled South Africa back into the game, but then came further disaster as White, Vogler and Schwarz were shot out with the addition of just 13 runs. The last man in, Percy Sherwell, rose to begin his long walk to the matting. If ever a captain's innings was needed, this was it.

'How many runs do we need?' he asked.

'Forty-five.'

'We'll get them,' he promised, and joined the imperturbable Nourse at the wicket.

A streaky boundary off the first ball Sherwell faced had the crowd screaming 'Leave it to Nourse,' but thereafter both South Africans kept their heads down and the score inching up. Plum Warner varied his field and his bowlers (he used seven as against three in the first innings) in desperate attempts to break the stubborn partnership; late-afternoon storm-clouds and rolling thunder added to the tension around the ground.

Eight needed. Four runs through the slips. A scamper between the wickets for three more to level the scores and bring, as Percy Sherwell recalled, an 'outburst of cheering which never has been equalled before or since on the Wanderers ground'. One to make and a deathless hush as he faced Sussex spinner Alfred Relf. The ball was a full toss, a dolly that deserved to be banged to the boundary — and was. Plum Warner recalled in *The M.C.C. in South Africa:* '"Relf, Relf!" his captain later lamented. "What were you about that at the crisis you should have presented Sherwell with a four . . . the one blot on a superb day's cricket."'

The two South African batsmen were car-

South African captain Percy Sherwell, left, and M.C.C. captain Pelham ('Plum') Warner in January 1906. The closely-fought test matches produced some of the most exciting cricket ever seen in South Africa

ALL SMILES—MR. J. SINCLAIR, THE CAPTAIN OF THE TRANSVAAL TEAM, LEADING HIS MEN INTO THE FIELD

J. Sinclair, captain of the Transvaal team, leads his men onto the field at the start of their match against the touring M.C.C. in 1909-10. He is followed by G.A. Faulkner, hero of the first test match, E.A. Vogler, J.W. Zulch, G.C. White, T. Campbell, C.E. Floquet and J.H. Mareden (behind whom are hiding two others)

Silk memento of the Australians' visit in 1902-03. Australia won two tests; the third was drawn

Mrs Dale Lace wields the willow during a ladies' cricket match in Johannesburg early this century

sure to thousands during the austere post-war era. In the M.C.C. team were Len Hutton, Paul Gibb, Wally Hammond (who eventually settled in South Africa), Les Ames, Bill Edrich, Hedley Verity and Doug Wright. Among the South Africans were Alan Melville, Eric Rowan, Bruce Mitchell, Dudley Nourse and Ken Viljoen.

The big lead

The clock, for the first time in modern cricketing history, could be ignored, and the batsmen dug themselves in. South African opener, Pieter van der Byl, took 45 minutes to get off the mark and crawled on to 125; Nourse scored 103, his first 50 coming in $3\frac{1}{2}$ hours. The Springboks closed their innings at 530. In reply the tourists managed to scrape together a modest 316, and newspapers predicted that 'only a miracle can save the M.C.C.'.

In their second innings, the South Africans put on 191 for the first wicket and were eventually, on the sixth day, all out for 481, giving them what seemed to be an unassailable lead of 695 runs.

Against all predictions, the visitors almost made it. On the seventh day they knocked up 253 for the loss of one wicket; rain washed out the eighth; out came the heavy roller to restore to featherbed condition what would normally have been a wearing pitch.

At the close of the ninth day, England were just 200 runs short with seven wickets still standing. On the South Africans the heat, the humidity, the sheer physical strain of what was now almost a test of endurance, were taking their toll. Runs came slowly on the tenth and last day, too slowly — the morning's sunshine gave way to heavy clouds after lunch.

In the race against the weather, the rain won. England were just 42 runs short of victory, with five wickets in hand, when the umbrellas went up and the players scampered for their dressing rooms. Within a couple of hours Wally Hammond and his men were on the train bound for Cape Town and the mailship.

The South African team in Australia for the 1910-11 tour. Standing (from left): Vogler, Pegler, Zulch, Stricker, Reid (chairman), Campbell, Llewellyn, Pearse. Seated: Hathorn, Faulkner, Schwarz, Nourse, Snooke. Australia won four of the five tests

ried jubilantly off the field. For his magnificent 93 runs, the crowd collected and presented Nourse with £111. It was a game Warner said he would 'remember to my dying days . . . a classic contest'.

An unchanged South African side played itself into Springbok history by going on to win three of the remaining four close-fought tests.

Twisting to victory

'It was the "googly" that undid us,' said English cricketer and writer Harry Altham after the 1905-06 M.C.C. team had been beaten at Newlands and, twice more after that first great match, at the Wanderers. Wrote Altham in his book, *A History of Cricket:* 'Men who have played Schwarz, Vogler, Faulkner and White on the fast matting wicket of the Wanderers' ground were almost unanimous in describing it as the severest test they have ever known.'

Englishman B.J.T. Bosanquet invented the googly — an off-break from an exaggerated, deceptive leg-break action — but it was the South Africans who adopted, developed and used it with lethal effect on matting wickets.

Bosanquet, originally a fast-medium bowler, discovered the 'leg-break reversed' while playing a game of Twisty-Grab in the pavilion on a rain-soaked day in 1900. After months of net practice he introduced it to first class cricket when playing for Lord Hawke's tourists in Australia, shattering Victor Trumper's wicket with his first delivery.

Though Wisden, the cricketers' almanac, dismissed the googly (it was not then named) in seven lines, Bosanquet's Middlesex teammate Reginald Schwarz, an Englishman who made his home in South Africa, saw its possibilities. On the 1904 Springbok tour of England his colleagues, sceptical to begin with, were dazzled by his first effort: five Oxford wickets for 27 runs. By the end of the tour he had taken an impressive 96 wickets at an average of 14 runs.

The 1929 Springbok team drew with England in three of the five tests, but lost at Leeds and Manchester

ON WITH THE GAME . . .

The date: March 1939; the place: Durban's Kingsmead; the event: the Timeless Test, that extraordinary, no-limits final game at the end of a series during which the M.C.C. had won one test and three had been drawn. In 12 days ($9\frac{1}{2}$ of actual play) on the heat-scorched pitch, 5 070 balls were bowled, 1 981 runs scored, including five single centuries and one double, and 19 records shattered. And, after all that, nobody had won — the marathon was abandoned to allow the Englishmen to take passage home on *Athlone Castle*. It was the longest cricket international ever played.

There were famous names in the line-up, some of whom would return to the scene six years later, their talents matured, to give plea-

Scenes from the 'Timeless Test' — South Africa versus the M.C.C. in the final match of the series at Durban in 1939

Tension tests

THE LAST BALL

For both England and South Africa it was a time for taking old skills out of mothballs. It was 1948, and first-class cricket was only beginning to limber up after the end of the Second World War. England's tour of South Africa was a feast for the many thousands of hungry fans at Newlands, Kingsmead, the Wanderers and St George's Park. Years of war had not dulled the passion aroused by names like Len Hutton, Cyril Washbrook, Bobby Simpson, Denis Compton, Alec Bedser or captain F.G. Mann. Against them were Dudley Nourse's Springboks, with names that were soon to fill record books and scrapbooks alike: Eric Rowan, Bruce Mitchell, Athol Rowan, Tufty Mann, Cuan McCarthy.

The first test opened at Kingsmead. Nourse won the toss with his lucky gold sovereign, choosing to bat on a wicket that looked full of runs. But it began badly: the South Africans were all out for 161 just after tea on the first day. England openers Hutton and Washbrook held their wickets to go in for the evening after a successful appeal against the light, and gloom descended upon the South Africa fans.

On the third day, spin bowlers Mann and Rowan demolished the English batsmen with tallies of six wickets for 59 runs and four for 109 respectively. But England were still 92 runs ahead when South Africa went in to bat. Once again the Springbok opening pair were in trouble. Denis Compton flung himself at a flashing ball just five metres from the wicket to catch Rowan for 22. Still two behind, with all four leading batsmen in the pavilion. In his book, *Out of the Magic Boks*, Bruce Heilbuth tells how, years later, Nourse said: 'I felt that if we could get a lead of about 120 runs we'd still have a sporting chance on that wicket . . .'

The final day

The third day's play was again curtailed by rain, and it was Wade and Begbie, not highly rated as test batsmen, who walked out for the final day — a day that would become known as the most exciting in South African cricket. And the large crowd sensed it.

The fifth wicket pair built up a lead with sparkling cricket. A six off Bedser put them level at 46 and then Wade made the boundary to be greeted by a standing ovation. Heilbuth recalled how, only two runs short of his well-earned half-century, Begbie handed Mann a dolly of a catch to make it 174 for five. Another wicket down and only the tailenders were left, with Compton bowling 65 balls before conceding a run.

England needed 128 runs in 135 minutes, and Hutton and Washbrook were in no doubt: they were going for the runs. Washbrook slammed a high one which Owen Wynne dropped on the boundary, but Hutton was held by Dawson for five. Washbrook was on his way (l.b.w.) for 25 then captain George Mann, having pushed himself up in the batting, was dropped after a wild swing.

The man who had dropped him was a lad of 19 — Cuan McCarthy. He looked so dejected that Nourse called him on to bowl. It was

Springbok Dudley Nourse, one of the best batsmen ever produced by South Africa, displays his vigorous style. Nourse scored 2 960 runs in a test career of 34 matches (including nine centuries), at an average of 53,82

quite a tonic. As Nourse himself recalls: 'I wish I could have bowled him from both ends.' McCarthy tore into the England attack taking six wickets for only 43 in a brilliant test début. England refused to appeal against the light — it would probably have been granted — and sought victory instead. Their trump card was Denis Compton. He scored only 28, but the runs were worth a century under such conditions. His stint ended after a thunderbolt from McCarthy that he did not even see.

'When the hour cometh . . .'

Two wickets to go. Cliff Gladwin, a good paceman from Derbyshire, came out with a wry smile on his face. Years later he was to tell of a little exchange between him and Dudley Nourse as he crossed to the crease: 'What the hell are YOU laughing about?' asked the 'bok captain. 'When the hour cometh,' quipped Gladwin, 'so doth the man!' And the hour had come.

Finally there were only eight balls to go. The last over and eight runs to win (in those days they played eight balls to an over). Lindsay Tuckett to bowl. Gladwin launched the batting with a single that thudded off Bedser's pad. Gladwin slammed the next ball towards the midwicket boundary and saw Eric Rowan standing right underneath it. 'Happily,' said Gladwin, 'he was too foxed by the terrible light and misjudged its flight completely. It went over his head and I'd notched the luckiest and most valuable boundary of my career.'

A single came off the third ball, the fourth Bedser missed, the fifth he stone-walled and the sixth went wide of Bruce Mitchell and the England pair charged through for another single. The scores were tied!

In the middle of the pitch, the two batsmen pow-wowed. 'Run like hell if you miss the ball,' Bedser told Gladwin. 'I'll be running, so for heaven's sake don't hesitate.' The advice

nearly cost him his wicket and the match. In the excitement, Gladwin did miss but forgot to run. Bedser, no lightweight, scampered back. 'So. The last ball, one to win and Mrs Gladwin's little lad carrying the can for England,' the Derbyshire player said later.

'Lindsay Tuckett put everything he had into the last ball. I saw it all right, but couldn't hit it and it smashed into my thigh . . . I heard Alec yelling at me "Run!" This time I did just that, as if my shirt-tail was on fire.'

Gladwin made the crease and turned to see Bedser under a pile of South Africans . . . but safe. 'We'd won off the last ruddy ball!'

Athol Rowan, who helped to demolish the English batsmen in the first test at Kingsmead in 1948

The Springboks at Manchester's Old Trafford in 1947. Bruce Mitchell is at the crease and Edrich is bowling

Left: Bruce Mitchell and Dennis Dyer opened the batting in the first match of the 1947 tour of England. Centre: Johnny Waite, Jackie McGlew and Paul Winslow all scored centuries in the third test at Manchester during the 'bok tour of 1955. Right: Trevor Goddard goes out to bat in the fourth test at Leeds in 1955

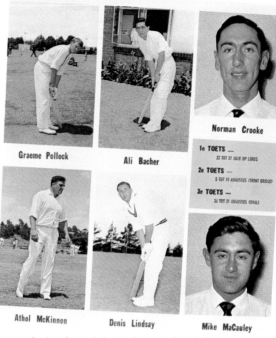

Graeme Pollock   Ali Bacher   Norman Crooke

Athol McKinnon   Denis Lindsay   Mike MaCauley

Some of the Springbok cricketers who defeated England in the 1965 series. They were captained by Peter van der Merwe

A MEMORABLE CLIMAX

The date: 7 July 1955. Two down and three to play in the last 135 minutes of the third England versus South Africa test at Manchester's Old Trafford. It would be the turning point of the tour — and one of international cricket's most memorable climaxes. The Springboks were without their captain, too: Cheetham had taken a knock from Freddie Truman that chipped his left elbow. It was left to Jackie McGlew to lead the South Africans — a captain who had collected a 'pair' in the previous test. Into the spare berth came Rhodesian Paul Winslow to make his début in test cricket.

England went in to bat first, Peter May having won the toss. A mistaken choice, as the green wicket favoured the pace of Neil Adcock and Peter Heine. In his second over, Adcock had Tom Graveney caught at short leg with only two runs on the board, and then Heine saw an outswinger snicked into the hands of Johnny Waite by Don Kenyon. At last the Springboks had broken through the psychological barrier of defeat. With a steadying innings by May and a handsome 158 from Denis Compton, England were fortunate to close the innings at 284.

In their first innings, South Africa took complete charge. McGlew and Trevor Goddard built up an opening partnership of 147, with the captain reaching his century in four hours and forty minutes.

The six they still talk about

But memories centre on the newcomer Paul Winslow. Dropped early in his knock, Winslow became reassured as he topped 90. He was facing Tony Lock's spinners and had reached 94. 'I looked at the scoreboard,' Winslow recalled, 'and saw there were only a couple of overs more before the new ball. That meant Tyson and Bedser, both of whom would be dangerous with the new ball. So I decided to try for my hundred before they returned to the attack.' Then came the six they still talk about. 'Lock just happened to pitch one where I liked it,' explained Winslow, 'and I had a full go at him.' The crowd roared its appreciation. A six and a maiden century for Paul Winslow.

The third test century of the innings was hit by Johnny Waite, and South Africa declared at a magnificent 521 for eight wickets. Amazingly, England were able to claw their way back into the match. Godfrey Evans was the courageous last man who ignored the pain of two fractures in a little finger to score 36 runs in just 35 minutes. His last-wicket partnership with Trevor Bailey produced 48 runs — putting England 144 ahead and leaving South Africa only 135 minutes to match their score.

Tyson's devastating bowling took a heavy toll. Jackie McGlew was one of those who had painful souvenirs of those lifting deliveries: 'They were big, angry welts. One, just under the heart, looked like a big ... green and yellow apple.'

Later, with South Africa needing 16 runs in 33 minutes to win, 5 000 tense spectators watched Frank Tyson trap Percy Mansell l.b.w. With the score at 129 for five, Johnny Waite walked to the wicket, but only three runs were added when Jackie McGlew was bowled after trying to turn a full toss from Tyson to leg. Russell Endean came in, was caught in the slips, and then there were only 18 minutes to go, with ten runs needed.

Tayfield hurries to the wicket and misses with two cow-shots. Waite cuts a superb four, a few more runs are scrambled, and there are a bare three minutes left, with four runs for victory and the last over to come. Some South African spectators, unable to bear the tension, leave the ground. An over-pitched, very fast ball from Tyson. Waite drives it through the covers. It is high and safe, but so slow that it seems doubtful the stroke will carry to the boundary. The batsmen turn for the fourth run when the ball crosses the line ... and the match is over. 'In a glorious exhilarating moment for South African cricket South Africa beat England by three wickets yesterday with a nerve-wracking margin of 3 minutes,' reported Duffus in the *Star*. '... thus a match in which 1 331 had been scored, was decided with the richest touch of drama in the last gripping moments of 30 hours of memorable cricket.'

Lindsay Tuckett bowling against England at Trent Bridge in 1947. He took five wickets for 68 runs

The curtain falls

THE D'OLIVEIRA AFFAIR

In the late 1960s a coloured cricketer from Cape Town's Malay quarter found himself the centre of a controversy that rocked international cricket and banished South Africa to the sporting wilderness. He was Basil D'Oliveira. This resilient all-rounder was the innocent cause of one of cricket's most dramatic and painful crises simply because he played cricket — and played it well.

D'Oliveira developed his game in the grimy streets on the slopes of Signal Hill; his devastating hook shot was practised on the steps of tenement buildings. Tin cans, lamp-posts or bricks improvised as wickets; his bat was a piece of wood he had shaped and smoothed himself. He recalled later: 'The big fun in those days was trying to hit the ball over the top of the telephone wires.' Often the youngster would thump it through a window.

At the age of 17 he was chosen to play in a non-white inter-provincial game; at 19 he was captain of a local club, and a few years later he was chosen to captain a black South African side against Kenya's national cricket team on a tour of that country. The cricketing world was beginning to notice D'Oliveira. In January 1960 an offer from the Central Lancashire League's Middleton club launched his cricketing career in Britain.

First the Lancashire League, then Worcestershire, then the England selectors pushed Basil D'Oliveira along the road to fame. In 1967 he played in five test matches, coached in South Africa, and played for the M.C.C. in the West Indies. He appeared to have achieved everything a cricketer could hope to achieve.

Only a dream

But not quite. What he wanted more than anything else was the chance to play cricket with his peers at Newlands: a match on a major South African cricket pitch was something he had long dreamed about.

Then, on 23 August 1968, D'Oliveira was recalled to play for England against Australia at The Oval. He turned a ball from Gleeson for a single to complete his century, and went on to score a brilliant 158 runs — which made him a likely candidate for the 1968-69 M.C.C. side to tour South Africa.

Until South African politics intervened. 'M.C.C. have documentary evidence that Basil D'Oliveira will not be admitted to South Africa as a member of England's cricket team,' wrote Ian Wooldridge in the London *Daily Mail*. The *Daily Express* reported: 'Jan de Klerk, South Africa's Minister of the Interior, has sent this directive to sport organisations: "Teams comprising whites and non-whites from abroad cannot be allowed to enter."' In Britain's House of Commons, members of all parties signed a motion calling for the removal of colour discrimination in South African sport.

Waiting for one name

The crisis developed rapidly. Louis Duffus, the South African sports commentator, maintained: 'As far as the SACA [South African

Basil D'Oliveira. He batted his way from the back streets of Cape Town to international stardom

Cricket Association] is concerned, the tour is on as planned.' Wrote political columnist Stanley Uys: 'There is no chance of the South African Government relenting on its attitudes to the coloured cricketer, Basil D'Oliveira.'

On 27 August, eight English selectors — including chairman Doug Insole, Alec Bedser, Don Kenyon, Peter May and Colin Cowdrey — chose the M.C.C. team for South Africa. Their line-up was approved by the full M.C.C. committee.

Basil D'Oliveira, playing in a test at The Oval, listened in as BBC cricket commentator Brian Johnson read the list of names. 'I do not remember being aware of any of the names as he was reading them. I was waiting for only one. My own. And it wasn't there.'

The shattered cricketer broke down and cried. He could derive little comfort from his wife's philosophical opinion that inclusion in the team might have made him vulnerable to incidents which could be exploited to the detriment of other coloured South Africans.

British MPs protested. Some M.C.C. members resigned. But Cowdrey announced: 'Sport is still one of the most effective bridges in linking people and I am convinced that it is right that I should lead the M.C.C. to South Africa.'

In September D'Oliveira agreed to accompany the M.C.C. on their South African tour as a correspondent for *News of the World*. But Prime Minister John Vorster, who had declared earlier that the player would not be acceptable, was adamant: He told the *Cape Times* on 12 September: ' . . . we cannot allow those organisations, individuals and newspapers to make political capital out of such relations or to use certain people or sportsmen as pawns in their game to bedevil relations, to create incidents and to undermine our way of life . . .'

A few days later, the M.C.C. pronounced Tom Cartwright unfit, and D'Oliveira was invited to join the team in his place. But Mr Vorster, describing the player as a political cricket ball, said he was not prepared to accept any M.C.C. team which had been forced upon South Africa by people with certain political aims. A week later the M.C.C. stated that the tour would not take place.

The cancellation led to the abandonment of at least three Springbok overseas tours. 'South Africa plunged into worst sports crisis,' lamented the *Cape Argus* on 18 September. 'All ties with the outside world affected.' Trevor Bisseker wrote in the *Star* a week later: 'There hardly seems a chance of another team replacing the M.C.C. this season and future tours by the Springboks have been thrown into doubt.'

South Africa was on its way out of the international arena.

Star batsman Graeme Pollock. In 1970 he scored a phenomenal 274 runs in an innings against Australia at Kingsmead — the highest score by a South African in test cricket. His brother, Peter, was also a fine player

THE ALL-CONQUERING 'GHOST' TEAM

Mike Procter, the Natal-born fast bowler and attacking batsman rated by experts as one of the world's greatest all-rounders. He has been playing first-class cricket in England and South Africa since 1968

At Newlands, the Wanderers and hundreds of little clubhouses all over South Africa, conversation inevitably gets round to the country's 'ghost' test team — the side that would have conquered the world had they been given the chance. No-one could deny the loss to the international game when South Africa became the pariah of the cricketing world in the late 1960s.

Before the veil dropped, a few players were able to grasp fleeting glory in the series against Bill Lawry's touring Australians in 1970. One was Lee Irvine. With the Wanderers crowd firmly behind him, his bat flashed time and again to crack Johnny Gleeson's spin bowling all over the ground. But that was the final series. Fans at home had to be satisfied with Currie Cup games. More and more local players joined English county sides for the northern summer and treated crowds to fine displays of first-class cricket.

Mike Procter, a master with both bat and ball, in the book, *Cricket in Isolation*, picked his own side to take on the world. This was in 1977, almost a decade after the D'Oliveira affair. That South African cricket had declined somewhat was not doubted, but Procter felt there was still enough talent to beat an England side, have a fair chance against the Australians, and only slightly less than an even chance against the West Indians.

His team: Eddie Barlow, Barry Richards, Stuart Robertson, Graeme Pollock, Peter Kirsten, Henry Fotheringham, Clive Rice, Mike Procter, Tich Smith, Vintcent van der Byl, Garth le Roux, Denys Hobson, Alan Lamb, John Traicos, Gavin Pfuhl and Paddy Clift.

Inter-provincial matches, such as this clash between Western Province and Transvaal at Newlands, always draw enthusiastic crowds. One-day limited-over cricket came to South Africa in the 1969-70 season

Springbok cricketers remembered the internationals of the 1960s with delight. 'But,' Eddie Barlow recalled, 'we were naive to have ignored all the factors leading up to our isolation. The government, cricket administrators and players believed people overseas could not do without us; that their teams would always come here.'

It was a vain hope. Although South African cricketers were popular competitors, they could not hope to counter international criticism.

Said Jim Swanton, doyen of cricket writers: 'It was one of the ironies and frustrations of the '60s that as the quality and character of their play rose to new heights — Barry Richards and Mike Procter, two cricketers of world class by any estimation, were due to emerge on the Test scene in a year or two —so the policies of the South African Government forced them into isolation.'

Starved of competition and recognition, South African cricketers pondered the reasons for their exclusion from world participation. Some 1971 newspaper opinion polls indicated that white players were a hundred per cent in favour of multiracial cricket in South Africa. And during a match between Currie Cup champions Transvaal and the Rest of South Africa — part of the 1971 Republic Festival celebrations — all the players walked off the field for two minutes to deliver a statement supporting SACA's intention to include two non-white players in the side to tour Australia '. . . and, furthermore, to subscribe to merit being the only criterion on the cricket field'.

In 1978 Kerry Packer's World Series Cricket gave South Africans a brief chance to play at top level. Barry Richards — one of the greatest of all batsmen — Mike Procter and Eddie Barlow formed the nucleus of a strong WSC combination. Their team won the series.

Eddie Barlow — one of South Africa's cricketing greats. This veteran batsman, named Sportsman of the Year in 1964, has thrilled many thousands

Tony Greig was one of the top South African cricketers who had to go abroad in the 1970s to further his career. He played for Sussex and captained England

Alan Lamb made his début for Western Province in the 1972-73 cricket season and in the ensuing years built up an enviable reputation as an attacking batsman. He, too had to go to England to counter South Africa's cricketing isolation. In 1978 he played for Northamptonshire, heading that county's averages and, in 1980, scored more first-class runs than any other batsman in England

Call of the sea

Tess, *the Durban-built yacht which won the first Lipton Cup races in Table Bay in 1911*

YACHTING: A SPORT FOR GENTLEMEN

Sailing ships remained purely functional for the first two hundred years of the Cape Colony's existence. Although modern South Africa owes its origins to the Dutch East Indiamen, the early settlers seldom ventured out to sea unless they had to. But by the 1850s attitudes had changed, and gentlemen in Port Natal and elsewhere were discovering the pleasures of yachting. The Royal Natal Yacht Club was constituted in 1858 (it received its charter 33 years later), and by the early 1900s there were regular races between the ports.

In the Cape, too, enthusiasts began to take to the sea. The Southern Cross Yacht Club, formed in 1888, gave way to the Table Bay Yacht Club in 1905, by which time there were fifteen little boats tethered at Cape Town's Rogge Bay. The clubhouse was a simple boatshed, later to be replaced by an iron shack. In 1911 Cape sailors raced around the point, from Table Bay to Simonstown. There were four starters. A small crowd watched from the foreshore — at that time a spray-lashed embankment at the bottom of Adderley Street. The winner was a cunning fisherman, owner of *Patricia*, who knew everything there was to know about the Peninsula coastline.

South African yachting had, in fact, taken a formal step forward three years before, in 1908, when tea-baron and ocean-racing enthusiast Sir Thomas Lipton presented a trophy to the Table Bay (subsequently re-named the Royal Cape) Yacht Club. The club's vice-president, Sir Pieter van Blommenstein Stewart-Bam, had told members that he was 'determined to get the largest I could'. He did: a splendid metre-high affair decorated with the five South African colonial coats of arms (Southern Rhodesia was thought a possible inclusion in the Union).

Competition for the cup was confined to ocean-going yachts, and 'no race was to be sailed on Sunday'. In 1911 only two craft could meet Lipton's condition: the Durban-built eight-metre *Tess* and Table Bay-Simonstown winner *Patricia*. The races were sailed between 25 and 28 August, *Tess* taking the honours on all three legs.

From the Cape to Guanabara Bay

In June 1968, South African yachtsman Bruce Dalling and his *Voortrekker* came second in the first Singlehanded Transatlantic Race. Geoffrey Williams's *Sir Thomas Lipton*, the winner by just 24 hours, had in fact been helped by a computer, which some sailing men thought wasn't quite playing the game.

The event caught the public's interest, enthusiasm mounted, and a run to Rio was proposed. Sponsors came forward, and the entries flowed in — not only from South Africa's ports, but also from inland centres, and from overseas. And, unexpectedly, they were not limited to the rich and the active. As veteran sailor Frank Robb noted in the *Cape Times*: 'The youngest was six years of age. There were several over seventy [including Cornelius Bruynzeel, who had a heart condition]. There were grandfathers and grandmothers. Some wore spectacles, some toted hearing aids. Some were physically handicapped. There were professors, students, directors, office boys, matrons, typists, mechanics,

Yachting in Durban. The Royal Natal Yacht Club and the Point Yacht Club (Durban's longest-surviving yacht club) held their first joint regatta in 1898

Johannesburg's first yacht. She was built by N.W.L. Scruse in 1896 and sailed on Rosherville Dam

The Thesen family's yacht, Albatros II, during the Cape to Rio race in 1971. She came first on handicap

Above: Yachts lined up at the Royal Cape Yacht Club before the 1971 Rio race. Left: The Mayor of Cape Town fired a gun to start the colourful array

school-girls, millionaires and paupers.' The excitement brought a festival atmosphere to Cape Town harbour, where the entrants gathered before the Royal Cape Yacht Club.

At 4.30 p.m. on 16 January 1971, in a picture-postcard setting of brightly coloured sails against the backdrop of Table Mountain, a cannon signalled the start of the first Cape to Rio yacht race. The waterfront from the harbour round to Sea Point and Camps Bay was crowded with spectators, as were the slopes of Signal Hill and the penthouse gardens and roofs of seafront flats and offices.

In the days ahead, South Africans were kept closely informed of the race's progress by radio and newspaper reports. Charts plotted the progress of each yacht; experts translated winds and speeds into handicap positions, and tension mounted as first one and then another boat swept across the finishing line in Rio. Line honours were taken by *Ocean Spirit* which glided into Guanabara Bay after covering the 5 900 km in 23 days and 42 minutes. Overall winner on handicap was the Knysna yacht *Albatros II*, skippered by John Goodwin.

Hardly were the celebrations over than the committee got together in the shadow of Table Mountain to plan the next race.

HANGING TEN AND HITTING THE LIP

Early South African surfers on their large, heavy boards

In 1938, a visiting South African swimming coach was intrigued by the novelty of a sport he saw off Sydney's famous Bondi Beach. He sketched the apparatus used, and from this, Fred Crocker of Durban was able to fashion his own craft for riding the waves. Crocker's 'surfboard' was just that — a plank of meranti 4 m long, 750 mm wide and 165 mm deep. It had no fin and was covered with canvas stuck down with aircraft 'dope' and copper nails. For his initiation into surfing as sport, Crocker needed helpers — the ski was much too heavy for one man to carry.

The first South African surfers were members of the Surf Lifesaving Club — already established on the Australian pattern.

After the war, surfers parted company from lifesavers and developed their own spe-

cial sport. Boards became slightly lighter (though still over 20 kg), and had thick blocks in front to prevent them digging into the sand when they dived.

Surfers developed their own language, too: 'All the way!' signalled the big ride to the beach; 'Hang ten' meant that all toes were splayed over the end of the board; the much sought-after 'Hitting the lip' — flying up the face of a wave to its crest.

By the 1960s, sportsmen were riding the waves on sleek, ultra-light boards. In that decade, too, the number of active participants rose into the thousands. The first official surfing Springbok competed in Australia in 1964, and in the 1970s Shaun Thomson won an enviable reputation at international surfing events.

The ever-popular Dabchick, a boon for junior sailors

BOATS AND BUILDERS: IN CLASSES OF THEIR OWN

Before the Second World War, the Sharpies and Goodrickes — dinghies up to six metres long — were the most popular craft among South Africa's small boat racers. Then, in 1938, Herbert McWilliams was inspired by the design of an American sailing boat and conceived a light plywood-hulled craft without decking. War interrupted his plans, but in 1946 a plywood '14-footer' called *Stroppy* was launched at Zwartkops, Port Elizabeth. This was the forerunner of the famous Sprog. In its first regatta, *Stroppy* overhauled the tested Goodricke of experienced sailor Colin Mogg, and the new class had established itself.

Jack Koper had a different quest: to find the boat best suited to his schoolboy son. The Flying Dutchman class was too large for a youngster to handle, and the pram-dinghy runabouts were too unexciting. He set to work on his own design, producing a light, cheap boat that looked like a blunt-ended, oversized surfboard with a solitary mainsail. Sixteen-year-old Gerhard Koper persuaded his friends to build them too, and the Dabchick was born.

The lure of speed

Jody Scheckter leads the field in his Tyrrell Ford at Leeukop Corner during the 1975 South African Grand Prix at Kyalami — South Africa's premier motor racing circuit

BOYS' OWN HERO

Like some schoolboy dream coming true, Jody Scheckter, the lad from East London whose early taste for speed had been weaned on go-karts, buzz bikes and a home-made racer, flashed by the chequered flag to win the South African Grand Prix before a home crowd in 1975. For a young driver who only a season or two before had been labelled on the international motor racing scene as 'Sideways Scheckter' because of his ability to skid through corners, it was a thrill that was to confirm his potential as a world class driver.

In the 1977 World Championship, the up-and-coming Scheckter surprised his colleagues by switching from Tyrrell to the new Wolf Ford of Walter Wolf, an Austro-Canadian millionaire. In the first race of the series in Buenos Aires, the car and Scheckter looked unimpressive in practice, lining up on the sixth row of the grid. But the uncertainties disappeared as Jody pushed his way through the field to snatch the lead in the last six laps for victory. That year he was to gain three Grand Prix wins — Argentina, Monaco and Canada — to finish second in the championship.

In 1979 Jody Scheckter became world champion, driving a Ferrari — the first South African to win the title.

A pensive Jody Scheckter, South Africa's first Formula One world champion. Scheckter took the Formula One championship in 1979, driving a Ferrari. He announced his retirement from motor racing in 1980, and returned to his home in Monaco

Preparing for the start on the 'Brooklands' track at Halfway House, near Pretoria, in the early 1930s

BRUD BISHOP'S BORDER HUNDRED

A scenic drive on a warm summer's day in the early 1930s was the watershed of motor racing in South Africa. 'Brud' Bishop, motoring editor of the *East London Daily Dispatch*, was taking his girlfriend along a new coastal road in his open car when he suddenly thought to himself what a fabulous motor racing circuit this would make.

He gunned the engine and took the banked corners along the 25 km route at an exhilarating speed. That day, Edward Farmer Garrett Bishop lost his girlfriend, but he also gained for South Africa a world-recognised motor racing event.

Motor sport was still in its infancy then, but there had always been enthusiasts. The introduction of the motor car to South Africa in the late 1890s was soon followed by speed events, and by 1912, hill-climbs were being held regularly at Muldersdrift, outside Johannesburg. A race called a 'Grand Prix replica' was held between Potchefstroom and Johannesburg in 1912, with a Sunbeam coming in first on handicap, and many other casually-arranged contests were staged on roads outside the city.

Brud Bishop's vision and pioneering spirit brought the first real international race to the Union — an event that came to be called the Border Hundred. It was scheduled for the Christmas holidays of 1934 — a time when thousands of holiday-makers headed for East London. Then, just two months before the race, Bishop's efforts were rewarded in a way that he had never dared hope.

The European independent driver, Whitney Straight, and the famous Richard Seaman offered to participate. There was one snag, though. Straight wanted a starting fee of £700, and the organisers had less than £70 in the kitty. The wily Bishop was unfazed, and quickly raised more than enough money by approaching East London businessmen for sponsorship.

Motoring fever built up as the day neared — and it was mostly engineered by Bishop in a series of newspaper stories that aroused interest all over the country. There was another problem: spectators would have to make a long detour to see the race unless a newly-completed railway bridge was opened to traffic. But this was solved after a personal interview with the Minister of Railways, Os-

An enthusiast takes to the road in the Twenties. South Africans succumbed readily to the lure of speed

A.S. du Toit in his Maserati at the second Rand Grand Prix, Lord Howe circuit, Johannesburg 1937

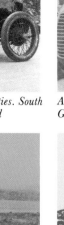

Taking a curve during the 1937 Silver Springbok Trophy event at Johannesburg's Lord Howe circuit

Lord Howe, in an E.R.A., wins the second Grosvenor Grand Prix in Cape Town on 14 January 1938

Verneukpan is aptly named. Its name (*verneuk* — cheat) is derived from its deceptive mirages and the scant layer of water on its surface which sometimes gives the false impression of a massive lake. In early 1929 the pan became a hive of activity. Malcolm Campbell was to make an attempt on the world land speed record with his Napier-powered *Bluebird*.

There were problems from the start. Black pebbles embedded in the baked surface and outcrops of shale would rip *Bluebird's* tyres. Then it rained — for the first time in five years!

With the camp finally ready for the record attempt (Campbell had meanwhile been injured in *two* air crashes), the worst news of all came through — Henry Segrave had raised the land speed record to 231,8 m.p.h. (373,2 km/h). At this altitude, *Bluebird* could not hope to match that. Campbell determined to go for the five mile and five kilometre records, despite the fact that Dunlop had told him the tyres were only designed for the mile.

Would the tyres last? At the end of the first run, they were so badly cut that no tread remained. On the return run, *Bluebird* travelled on the canvas of the tyres. The tyres *did* last, and Campbell broke Segrave's records in the five mile and five kilometre categories, averaging 211 m.p.h. (339,6 km/h) and 216,03 m.p.h. (347,6 km/h) respectively. But the world land speed record had eluded him. Verneukpan had, indeed, cheated.

wald Pirow. The Minister even agreed to present the trophies.

On race day, 42 000 spectators flocked to the course, and farmers made money by dropping their fences at good viewing spots along the route. It was a spectacular circuit, winding beneath craggy cliffs perched above thundering surf. It was also very fast.

In the 1930s, when massive sponsorship was far in the future and most of the competition came from local drivers and works teams, races were run on a handicap basis.

Straight was the scratch man, with Seaman's MG Magnet 6 minutes 54 seconds ahead and Whitney's younger brother, Michael Straight, in a 4 ℓ tourer, another 12 minutes in front. A little 750 cm³ Austin '65' was flagged away with 22 minutes and 24 seconds in hand.

Despite the hazards of a course that combined houses and hotels, and included hair-raising curves beside the sea, there was only one casualty.

Taking the bridge at Leach's Bay, English driver L.G. Williamson shot off the track into the valley below. The car careered through the lush vegetation of the bank and when first aid men found it ten metres below the track, Williamson was embedded in prickly pear bushes. 'For the next two days,' Bishop wrote in *South African Grand Prix,* 'it took two pretty nurses all their time with tweezers to extract the needles from various parts of Williamson's anatomy. But no bones were broken. He just laughed.' Whitney Straight won the race at an average speed of 152 km/h. J.H. Case of Queenstown was the first South African home.

East London was to become the centre of grand prix racing in South Africa, and one of the diamonds to be gained in the world championship crown. The success of Bishop's first international race was to be the spur that moved motor racing fans to build the Lord Howe circuit on the Reef, and eventually Kyalami, current centre for the South African Grand Prix.

Motorcycle enthusiasts with their machines (note the belt drive) in Heidelberg, Transvaal, early this century

Moto-cross, a fast-growing sport. On the asphalt racetrack, Kork Ballington took the 250 cc and 350 cc world championships in 1978 and 1979 and Jon Ekerold won the 350 cc championship in 1980

Racing fever

THE FASHIONABLE SPORT OF KINGS

Horse-racing is one of the oldest established sports in South Africa. The first meeting was held in Cape Town in the late 18th century, and since then the 'sport of kings' has become a multi-million-rand business employing thousands of people. Betting has entered the electronic age: computers and other sophisticated equipment are now the norm for many race-courses.

Yet the going was not easy. Early racing was often chaotic and there was little or no collaboration between the turf clubs. The result — rules varied considerably, penalties imposed by one club were not heeded by others, and races would often be held on the same day in different parts of one town. A governing body was finally set up in 1882 with the formation of the Jockey Club of South Africa. Its headquarters moved from Port Elizabeth to Johannesburg 22 years later.

Aristocrats, actresses and accidents

The races have always been a glorious excuse to dress up and be seen. The *London Morning Chronicle* described a milestone in the social season of 1798: '. . . a ball and a supper was given by the club and the Hon. Mrs Campbell, patroness, appeared in an elegant dress with a bandeau on which was marked "African Turf Club".' But the person who attracted the most attention, said the *Chronicle*, was Lady Anne Barnard in a splendid vehicle drawn by eight Spanish stallions. 'The gay scene was disturbed by only two mishaps,' reported the paper. 'Lord Macartney's groom broke his leg when the horse fell during one of the events, and Mr Maxwell, his lordship's secretary, narrowly escaped drowning when he tumbled into a pond coming from the ball.'

And the big races have attracted the famous as well as the fashionable.

Like Lily Langtry, known as the Jersey Lily and mistress of King Edward VII. In February 1906 she appeared at Cape Town's Opera House in *The Degenerates*, a play specially written for her by Sydney Grundy. Noted the critic of the *Cape Argus:* 'Mrs Langtry's breezy manner soon won the favour of the audience. But there was a lack of subtlety in her presentation, a tendency to monotony in voice and action to a too constant adherence to the same key. Her personality won the day.'

Later that year Lily Langtry played at Durban's Theatre Royal in *The Degenerates*, *Mrs Dering's Divorce* and Shakespeare's *As You Like It.* She was met on her arrival with flags, bunting and a noisy band. The President and Stewards of the Natal Jockey Club were also there to greet her, since she was a well-known racehorse owner. Huge crowds cheered as she drove to her hotel (the Marine). Ernest Dudley, in his book, *The Gilded Lily,* records that for transportation during her stay she was given a ricksha and a puller called Jim, who trotted her to and from the theatre. Her wardrobe mistress made a turquoise-and-fawn loin cloth for Jim — the racing colours carried by her horse, Mr Jersey.

The Metropolitan Handicap, the Cape's most popular race, draws thousands of spectators every year

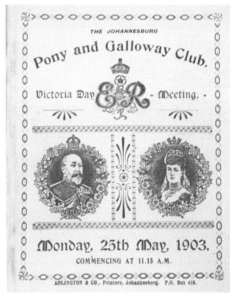

Above: The Johannesburg tote was always crowded on race day in the early 1900s. There were frequent efforts to 'keep the sport clean', and some social reformers even called for an outright ban on horse-racing. Provincial authorities and turf clubs, on the other hand, were concerned about the money they were losing through 'bucket shops' and other illegal operations. Right: Prince Arthur of Connaught, British Governor-General and High Commissioner in South Africa, marks his race card at the Johannesburg Turf Club's summer meeting in January 1921. Above right: One of the special race programmes issued to Johannesburg racegoers

SEA COTTAGE'S GREAT COMEBACK

RED SANDS

KING WILLOW

SEA COTTAGE

JOLLIFY

On a chilly winter's morning in June 1966 the sharp crack of a pistol began the greatest sensation in the history of South African horse-racing. The favourite for the following month's race was being exercised on Durban's Blue Lagoon beach when a gunman, concealed in a concrete shelter at the southern end of the Rupert Ellis Brown viaduct, opened fire. Sea Cottage limped back to trainer Laird's stables. He was soon lame.

Laird was in tears. He loved the horse and had said before the shooting: 'I don't believe I've ever had a certainty for the July like Sea Cottage. The only way they'll stop him is to get at him.' Prophetic words?

The bullet could not be located, even by X-rays, and it remained in him for the rest of his racing career. But there was hope — a veterinarian announced that with regular exercise there was no reason why Sea Cottage shouldn't race again. Race day dawned, and the name of one horse was on everyone's lips. Money kept pouring in on Sea Cottage and he started the race as favourite. Minutes later the crowd erupted into applause as the country's most popular thoroughbred finished a gallant fourth. Two weeks later, Sea Cottage won the Clairwood Winter Handicap at 7-4 on.

The next year he passed the post with the second favourite, Jollify, in the 'July's' first-ever dead-heat. The photo-finish picture revealed not a whisker between the two. It was fitting triumph for a remarkable horse.

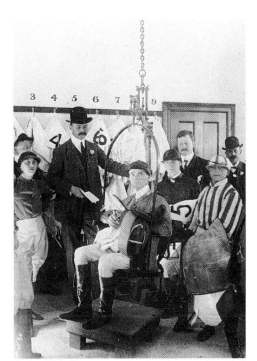

Jockey Ted Shaw poses for the photographer while being weighed in at the Kimberley racecourse in 1910

THE JULY: 'A SUB-TROPICAL DISEASE'

South Africa's most glamorous horse-race was launched as the Durban Turf Club Handicap at the end of the last century with a purse of 500 sovereigns. Apart from being the country's richest handicap race in terms of prize money, the Rothmans July Handicap has since become a winner in the popularity stakes. Racing editor Peter Atkins has described the enthusiasm as 'a strange sub-tropical disease which makes its annual appearance in Durban around the middle of May and reaches epidemic proportions throughout the country within the next month'.

The Durban July, as it became known, grew in popularity through the years. By the 1920s it had become *the* race to win. The mining tycoon, Sir Abe Bailey, spent lavishly in attempts to produce a winner: he had to wait until 1925 to see his Bird of Prey take the honours. By the end of the 1970s, sponsorship by big companies had boosted the 'July' stake to R50 000 (the Johannesburg Summer Handicap carried a stake of R40 000 and the Metropolitan Handicap, run over ten furlongs at Kenilworth in Cape Town, was worth R35 000).

Veteran trainer Sydney Laird produced seven 'July' winners in three decades. His first victory came in 1961, when Kerason romped home ahead of the field. In 1963 Colorado King, one of the most famous racehorses in South Africa, won him yet another laurel. Java Head won in 1966 (setting a record time), Sea Cottage dead-heated with Jollify the following year, Mazarin took the honours in 1971, Yataghan in 1973 and Politician, South Africa's record stake-earner, in 1978.

Percy Cayeux, left, rode Left Wing, Harold 'Tiger' Wright, centre, rode Thunder Sky and T. Lange rode Tokio in the 1960 Durban July Handicap. Tiger Wright won four 'July' races in a career of 1 200 victories

'July Day' in Durban, 1961. Part of the race's appeal to the public is the parade of ladies in costumes varying from the tasteful to the bizarre. In recent years male racegoers, too, have adopted more flamboyant outfits

A nation of sports

MUSCLE, TALENT AND A DRIVE TO WIN

South Africans have always been addicted to sport. In decades of competition on track, field and lawn, the country has produced some of the best sportsmen and women in the world, and their drive to excel has become a byword. Sometimes, though, they have had to go abroad to earn the recognition they deserved.

Eddie Firmani was one of the top soccer players who left to join a professional team in England after the Second World War (he once fetched a record transfer fee of £35 000). Kimberley schoolgirl Karen Muir won the country's hearts in the 1960s when she broke the world backstroke record at Blackpool with apparent ease. South African bowlers have challenged and conquered the world, and local karate and judo experts have fought their way to the top ranks. Our cyclists have taken world and Olympic records; our motorcyclists have beaten the best. We have even produced world boxing champions.

South Africa's withdrawal from the Olympics was a heavy blow — but not a fatal one.

Croquet has been played in South Africa since the 1870s. The first national championships, held in Durban in 1935, were won by Captain R.G. Belcher. Two years later the South African Croquet Association was established by A.C. Oakeshott, and this body still controls the sport. The country's best-ever player was probably Edward L. Ward-Petley of Bellville, in the Cape, who won the English men's open doubles (1935), mixed doubles (1939 and 1947) and men's championship (1947). In 1946 he tied for first place in the President's Cup in England — generally regarded as the world croquet championship

The Port Elizabeth Football Club's 'Colonial-Born' team in 1863. They played a 'Mother Country' team, and each side had 16 players! The South African Football Association was founded in 1892, and the first international contact came in 1897 when the touring English club, Corinthians, won all of their 23 matches

A bang and a puff of smoke signal the start of the second heat in a cycle race held in the late 1890s. Bicycle races have been staged in South Africa for over a century. The first cycling club was founded in Port Elizabeth in October 1881, and 12 years later the first South African championships were held in Johannesburg. Lourens Meintjes, who used the first racing bicycle fitted with pneumatic tyres, won some spectacular victories in Europe and America in 1893. He won five world titles and established 16 world records over distances ranging from 4,8 to 80,5 km

The polo team of Sergeant-Major Kenyon of the Cape Mounted Rifles sometime in the early 1890s. Women's polo was introduced after the First World War. The game has been played in South Africa since the 1870s, and it still flourishes

The start of the 120-yard race at the Caledonian Sports Club in 1899. The first recorded athletic contests took place in Natal, where local runners competed against British soldiers. The first national championships were held in 1894

The Mayor of Johannesburg, J.W. O'Hara, throwing the first bowl at the opening of the Turffontein Bowling Green in December 1916. South Africa's first bowling club was established at Port Elizabeth in 1882, and the first inter-club match was played between Port Elizabeth and Kimberley two years later. At the start of the Second World War there were an estimated 13 000 bowlers (including 3 200 women) in nearly 400 clubs across the country. By 1947 the number of players had grown to over 24 000 (365 men's clubs and 200 women's clubs). 'Snowy' Walker of Pretoria was arguably the best bowler ever produced in South Africa. His team won the South African championship in 1935, 1948, 1955 and 1960, and he won the singles championship four times. He also played in the Empire Games — twice as skip — and captained the Springbok pair against Australia in 1964, when the South Africans won 2-1. In 1972, South African women became the world bowls champions at the first championships held in Australia. South Africa again emerged triumphant when the third world bowls championships were staged in Johannesburg in 1976

In 1965 a shy schoolgirl from Kimberley galvanised the swimming world and won a place in the hearts of thousands of South Africans when she climbed out of a swimming pool in Blackpool, England, with a new world record for the 110-yard backstroke. She was Karen Muir, and she was only 12 years old. In 1966 the Johannesburg swimmer Ann Fairlie trimmed a tenth of a second off this record, but five days later Karen reduced the time to 68,3 seconds, and three days after that cut it to a spectacular 68 seconds. In 1969 Karen set a record of 65,6 seconds for the distance

The country's first hockey matches are believed to have been played at Newlands in 1899. (The game was introduced by British units who had remained in South Africa after the Anglo-Boer War.) The first hockey club for women was founded in 1901, the first provincial union (Western Province) was established six years later

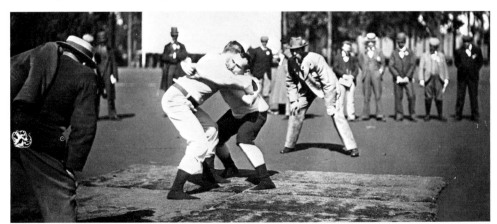

Two wrestlers in action at the Caledonian Sports Club. Wrestling is still one of the most popular spectator sports in the country, the participants drawing large crowds with their blend of skill and ham acting. They appear to derive great satisfaction from the simple process of tossing their opponents out of the ring

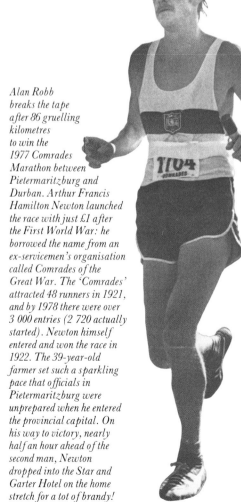

Alan Robb breaks the tape after 86 gruelling kilometres to win the 1977 Comrades Marathon between Pietermaritzburg and Durban. Arthur Francis Hamilton Newton launched the race with just £1 after the First World War: he borrowed the name from an ex-servicemen's organisation called Comrades of the Great War. The 'Comrades' attracted 48 runners in 1921, and by 1978 there were over 3 000 entries (2 720 actually started). Newton himself entered and won the race in 1922. The 39-year-old farmer set such a sparkling pace that officials in Pietermaritzburg were unprepared when he entered the provincial capital. On his way to victory, nearly half an hour ahead of the second man, Newton dropped into the Star and Garter Hotel on the home stretch for a tot of brandy!

Fighters to the finish

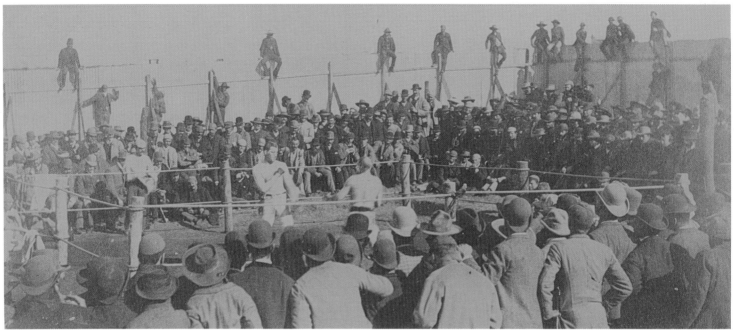

Woolf Bendoff, left, comes out for the last round of his fight against James Couper, who finished the fight with a contemptuous, jaw-breaking right in the 26th round

JAMES COUPER, THE TWO-FISTED 'PROFESSOR'

South African boxing was born in the rough, uncompromising shanty settlements that mushroomed in the Kimberley diamond diggings and the gold-mining communities of the Witwatersrand.

At night, the miners would gather in dimly lit saloons to celebrate success or drink themselves into a stupor after a bad day. They would bid raucously for the favours of a barmaid, lose their cash at poker — or fight. When women began to get on their nerves, gambling, drinking and fighting were their remaining forms of relaxation. And there weren't too many women, either.

Wealthy and powerful 'barons' like Barney Barnato and Abe Bailey, both handy men with their fists, were deeply interested in organised boxing — and they were also prepared to spend money. Then James Robertson Couper arrived.

This quiet, well-educated Scot had learned his art under the famous 'Professor' Ned Donnelly in London, and by the time he met Barnato, had already made a name and a reputation in South Africa.

One day at his boxing establishment in Cape Town, Couper — who also styled himself 'Professor' — received a letter signed by some of his former pupils. It appeared that a giant of a man named John Coverwell was terrorising Kimberley, and becoming more and more of a bully every day. Nicknamed 'the ladies' pet' by his hangers-on, Coverwell proclaimed himself the champion boxer of South Africa.

The letter concluded: 'Would Professor Couper please come to Kimberley to teach this man his manners?' It was just the sort of thing that appealed to Couper's romantic nature. He travelled to the diamond-mining town, battered the much heavier Coverwell to pulp within minutes, and was promptly declared the champion.

Barnato, for all his wealth, was a somewhat rough and ready Cockney, and he was irritated by Couper's quiet personality and cultured manner. Woolf Bendoff, a London bruiser with considerable experience, was imported with Barnato's backing to give the 'Professor' a thrashing. South Africa's first major fight was scheduled for 26 July 1889, at Eagle's Nest, just south of the centre of Johannesburg.

The two pugilists met for a stake of £4 500, the biggest anywhere in the world during the

RAGS TO RICHES TO RAGS

Arthur Douglas grew up in the dirt-littered streets of Cape Town's District Six — and died in the same squalid surroundings 64 years later. This tough, sturdy coloured fighter developed the ability to hit with deadly effect and soon his fame began to spread. Boxing fan Harry Brophy recalled the power in Douglas's fists at the height of his career in the early part of this century: 'Friendly as he was, he was a demon in action.'

Although Douglas earned an estimated R20 000 in the professional ring, he retained very little of it: he was happy as long as he had a pocket full of sovereigns to treat his friends and hangers-on. It was not to last. A succession of 'managers' matched him against far heavier opponents in a punishing series of fights that reduced his once springy step to a pathetic shuffle. He was abandoned in Australia by his exploiters, and sportsmen and friends in South Africa collected enough money to bring him home. He returned a physical and mental wreck, and never recovered. He died alone in a small room in District Six.

James Couper was a parson's son from the Scottish highlands whose fists made him the toast of Johannesburg in the late 1800s. He shot himself in July 1897 after losing heavily in several business speculations

era of skin-tight gloves and prize ring rules.

Couper won in the 26th round, becoming the first generally-recognised champion of South Africa, and a national hero to boot. He retired after this notable victory, but his pupils carried on the 'Professor's' tradition of winning in style.

One of them, Barney Malone, had shown his mettle in the early 1880s, when he fought William Bushell in the Theatre Royal, Johannesburg. Both boxers damaged their two-ounce gloves early in the contest . . . and fought on in the old style, with bare knuckles. Bushell finally collapsed in the 60th round.

Even that 60-round marathon was eclipsed by an epic battle that Malone was to fight later, against the massive Jake Silberbauer. It was a brutal affair, fought with skin-tight gloves, and lasting an awesome 212 rounds. It nearly caused the deaths of both boxers. Malone emerged bloody but victorious, and that night he had cause to remember the man who taught him his ringcraft, the man whose coaching, promoting and gentlemanly conduct laid the solid foundations on which South African boxing is built — 'Professor' James Robertson Couper.

THE RISE AND FALL OF ANDREW JEPTHA

A brown face was something of a rarity in South African boxing rings 80 years ago. And certainly Andrew Jeptha never dreamed that a coloured man such as himself would ever hit the big time.

His training was involuntary in the beginning. His schoolmates at Marist Brothers College in Cape Town used to thump him regularly, and it was only at the age of 15 that Jeptha discovered his fists. He then began to return the beatings with gusto.

He learned the rudiments of boxing at a rough-and-ready academy in Buitengracht Street, a few blocks from his school, where for fourpence a youth could 'don the mitts'. His training programme was simple, to say the least. It often consisted only of walking and cycling — and stopping for a few drinks along the way.

In 1902 the optimistic boxer boarded the *Briton* to seek his fortune in England. He soon recognised that British boxers took their training more seriously, so he started jogging, in heavy boots and a sweater, and, for the first time in his life, hammering a punchball.

Jeptha's comment on his new training schedule: 'Well, if this is boxing, I'll go back home and chuck it, for the work seems to be killing me.' He met lightweight boxer Jimmy Green, then rated the best in his class on the Merseyside, in Liverpool, for a prize of £25. Jeptha lost over 13 rounds, but the fight was to teach him a more professional style. He began to train in earnest, determined to become a champion.

Then, in 1907, came Jeptha's big chance. He had gradually worked his way to the top and was finally matched with the British welterweight champion, Curly Watson, at the

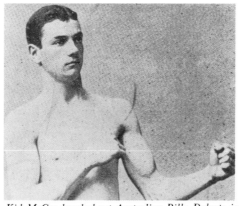

Kid McCoy knocked out Australian Billy Doherty in Johannesburg's Amphitheatre in December 1896

Good-looking Ben Foord was a brave fighter, but lacked the necessary dedication to his craft

Wonderland in London. Watson had already beaten the South African in two previous bouts; this was probably his last chance.

It happened in the fourth round. Jeptha leapt from his corner, snapped a straight left to Watson's stomach and, as his opponent's head dropped, 'I stepped in and upper-cut as hard as ever I could on his chin; poor Watson fell as though he had been shot. I stepped away from him and distinctly heard one of my supporters say: "That's done it; he's put."'

And he was. Andrew Jeptha had become the first coloured man to hold a British title.

But his career was to end in tragedy. Fighting had ruined his eyes, and he went blind. Returning to Cape Town, he wrote his life story and for years he used to take up his position near the Adderley Street flower-sellers and offer the flimsy pamphlets for a shilling each. When he died, in his early fifties, he was totally blind.

BARE FISTS AND HOBNAILED BOOTS

South Africa's diamond and gold fields were violent places in the late 19th century. Arguments were normally settled with bare fists and hobnailed boots — and sometimes with guns and knives. Fighting in the streets was a form of free entertainment, and newspapers solemnly reported the better of these scraps.

One of the best must have been the clash described in a Johannesburg newspaper under the headline 'Another Merry Mill'. It involved a bookmaker and a broker, who resorted to blows after a dispute over money. Hundreds of people watched as the broker was given a thrashing, suffering 'two beautiful black eyes and a nasty cut on the cheek, to say nothing of minor injuries'.

With rough-and-ready adventurers from all parts of the world swarming into South Africa's booming mining towns, violence knew no frontiers. Even the sober and dignified atmosphere of the council chamber could be enliv-

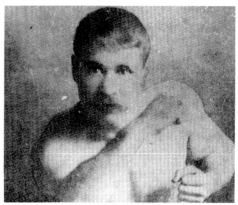

Barney Malone, a tough and colourful boxer. In his time fights often continued for dozens of rounds

Bantamweight Willie Smith, winner of an Olympic gold medal in 1924, was rated among the world's best

ened by a stand-up fight.

At a town council meeting in Beaconsfield, now a suburb of Kimberley, Councillor Cowie called Councillor Schaumann a liar. Councillor Schaumann returned the insult, whereupon, reported the local newspaper, Cowie launched 'a crushing blow to the face'.

A reporter described how the Mayor walked out of the chamber, leaving a third councillor as the only witness to the combat. This man was an undertaker 'who no doubt thought that if he had the patience to wait, a coffin would be wanted, and so stood by to contemplate the results'.

Cowie was making a sad mess of his opponent's face when Schaumann grabbed two handfuls of his fleecy beard and began tugging it in opposite directions. The pain was so excruciating that Cowie shrieked for help and the undertaker, possibly disappointed, separated the two fighters.

South Africa's Don McCorkindale was matched against one of America's best heavyweights at Ellis Park in 1932. Stribling won in 12 dreary rounds

The ring masters

A Hero with Cold Feet

Victor Anthony Toweel had dark, mournful eyes, and they showed no expression as he heard the fateful words: 'Ortiz has signed, Vic. You're fighting for the world title in six weeks!'

It was April 1950, and the diminutive bantamweight with a professional boxing career going back only 16 months was to become the first South African to fight for a world title. His opponent was the formidable Manuel Ortiz, a 33-year-old veteran of 12 years in the prize ring. Ortiz had first won the title eight years before and had defended it successfully 15 times before losing it briefly to Harold Dade (he regained it three months later).

Vic Toweel launched himself into a punishing training programme, running several kilometres every morning while dressed in a special tracksuit made from thick Basuto blankets with layers of inner tubing wrapped around his hips and torso to melt away the excess mass. The little woodcarver from Benoni demolished whole teams of sparring partners and honed his reflexes until his punchbag blurred with the rapidity of his blows.

And then, two weeks before the fight, Toweel began to suffer from cold feet. Literally. Sometimes it became so bad that several blankets had to be stacked over his feet before he felt comfortable enough to sleep. If this phenomenon was due to pre-fight nerves, though, it was certainly the only way they affected him.

Suddenly it was 31 May. Toweel rose early to celebrate Mass at St Patrick's Church in Benoni, and returned home to find his house surrounded by groups of fans eager for a sight of the challenger. A drunk insisted on presenting the boxer with a squawking chicken.

That night, Vic kept repeating 'Don't worry, don't worry' as members of his family beseeched him to be careful. He appeared to be the calmest person in his dressing room.

At 9.15 p.m. excitement mounted in Johannesburg's Wembley Stadium as nearly 30 000 people watched Toweel climb through the ropes to the strains of *Sarie Marais*. In his

Manuel Ortiz staggers and nearly goes down under the relentless attack of little Vic Toweel in their 1950 world title bout. Toweel kept up the pressure for 15 rounds to win the bantamweight championship for South Africa

book, *This Brutal Glory*, Chris Greyvenstein tells how the boxer acknowledged their cheers with a slight wave of his right hand. His face was pale. He later described his feelings: 'You often hear people talking about mixed emotions. That night I knew what they meant. I was proud to be the first South African to fight for a world title, but at the same time I was very nervous . . . the bell rang and, taking a deep breath, I walked towards Ortiz and the roaring of the crowd faded as it always did. And all that's left then is you and the other guy.'

For two or three rounds Toweel boxed well within himself, getting the feel of his opponent. He realised he was dealing with a strong man who could hit a crunching blow, and decided that his speed was his only trump card.

'I'm chucking this fight

Greyvenstein recalls Toweel's description of the fight: 'For a couple of rounds everything

went fine and then in the eighth all hell broke loose. Ortiz started catching me with his right and the punches felt like bricks in my face. One of those whistling rights landed full on my damaged ear . . . my nose was knocked completely out of shape, my head was singing and I was certainly kept conscious only by the sharp pain in my ear. My only thought was: "I'm chucking this fight." I admit it — I wanted to give up because the pain was just too much. Somehow I saw out the round, but when I got to my corner I was a beaten fighter.'

The punishment continued as Ortiz kept pounding away with his chopping right, but the plucky South African kept going. 'When the bell ended the ninth round I was numb with pain, but my head cleared, and for the first time I knew that I was going to win. I thought: "Mr Ortiz, if you couldn't knock me out now you'll never do it." What's more, I could feel Ortiz weakening ever so slightly

Johnny Ralph became the country's most popular boxer overnight when he defeated Nick Wolmarans for the South African heavyweight championship in 1947. Boxing fans loved Ralph's diffidence and courtesy out of the ring, but they liked his tigerish ringcraft even more, and there was pandemonium when he knocked out Wolmarans

---

FOR THE RECORD

Golden gloves Six South African boxers have won gold medals at the Olympic Games: bantamweight Clarence Walker (Antwerp, 1920), bantamweight Willie Smith (Paris, 1924), light-heavyweight Dave Garstens and lightweight Laurie Stevens (both at Los Angeles in 1932), and light-heavyweight George Hunter and welterweight Gerald Dreyer (both at London in 1948).

The champions Bantamweights Vic Toweel and Arnold Taylor and flyweight Peter Mathebula are the only South Africans ever to have won world titles. Toweel was champion from 1950 to 1952, and Taylor from November 1973 to July 1974. Ben Foord (heavyweight), Laurie Stevens (lightweight), Vic Toweel (bantamweight), Gerald Dreyer (welterweight), Willie

Toweel (lightweight), Jake Tuli (flyweight) and Dennis Adams (flyweight) are South Africans who won Empire titles prior to South Africa's departure from the Commonwealth.

Trailblazing Tuli Jake Tuli, a quietly-spoken Zulu from Johannesburg, was South Africa's most successful black fighter during the period when boxing was segregated. He took the Empire flyweight title in 1954 when he defeated England's Terry Gardiner.

End of an era Boxing is now a totally integrated sport in South Africa. The colour bar was first broken in a South African ring on 1 December 1973, when the American negro Bob Foster successfully defended his world lightweight title against South Africa's Pierre Fourie.

BANTAMWEIGHT KNOCK-OUT

When bantamweight Arnie Taylor knocked out Mexican fighter Romeo Anaya at Johannesburg's Rand Stadium in November 1973, he became South Africa's second world champion in one of the most dramatic turnabouts in boxing history. Anaya had dropped Taylor in the eighth, but Taylor earned a 'long' count when the Mexican refused to go to a neutral corner.

Calling on all his courage and skill, Taylor boxed his way back into the fight. Then in the 14th round, he found the strength to produce a crashing overhead right that stopped Anaya in his tracks. But the blaze of glory for Arnie Taylor was short-lived. In the first defence of his title, he lost the fight on points over 15 rounds to South Korean Suan Huan. A year later, newpapers reported that Arnie Taylor, the ex-champion, was back at work as a pastry cook, with nothing left of the thousands of rands he had earned during his brief reign.

In late 1954 a young panelbeater stepped into a boxing ring with South African middleweight champion Eddie Thomas. Twelve gruelling, bloody rounds later, the referee held up the hand of the new champion: he was Mike Holt, and he had entered the fight as a last-minute substitute! For nearly ten years Holt was the name on everyone's lips. Right: Holt is about to throw his vaunted left hook at the jaw of Canadian champion Yvon Durelle. He tried hard, but could not match the tough Durelle and had to withdraw from the fight at the end of the eighth round — one of the few occasions in his long career when Holt called it quits. Above: Light-heavyweight Pierre Fourie was a tenacious boxer with more than his fair share of courage. His clash with M.B.A. champion Victor Galindez in September 1975 was one of the most exciting bouts ever seen at Johannesburg's Rand Stadium. Galindez retained his title on a split decision. American champion Bob Foster had already defeated South Africa's hope twice within a year, winning a points decision against Fourie in New Mexico in August 1973 and a second victory in Johannesburg four months later

near the end of that round.' The last few minutes of that fight will never be forgotten by those who saw it. Toweel was a clear winner on points. Bedlam broke loose as photographers crowded into the ring to get a picture of the new world champion. Papa Toweel fell flat on his face and half-crawled to his victorious son through a crowd that seemed to have gone mad.

In the middle of it all was a badly battered but happy young champion. All he wanted to do was go home and sleep.

Vic Toweel went on to defend his title successfully against Danny O'Sullivan, Peter Keenan and Luis Romero, but lost it on 15 November 1952 in Johannesburg when Australia's Jimmy Carruthers knocked him out in the first round.

The Toweels were a fighting family. Four other brothers, Jimmy, Willie, Alan and Frazer, were professionals. The sixth, Maurice (crippled by polio), became one of South Africa's leading fight promoters.

In 1980 flyweight Peter 'The Terror' Mathebula beat Korean Tae-Shik Kim at Los Angeles to become South Africa's third world champion in three decades. His children, Patrick and Ellen, express their satisfaction at his victory

Gerrie Coetzee became the first South African to fight for the world heavyweight championship when he met John Tate of the United States at Pretoria's Loftus Versveld (above) in October 1979. Coetzee shook the American with his powerful left jab on several occasions, but was outclassed in a fight that went the full 15 rounds. Earlier the same year, Coetzee demolished former world champion Leon Spinks in one round at Monte Carlo. In October 1980 he lost to Mike Weaver at the Sun City stadium in Bophuthatswana

The centre court

PLAYERS, PLACES AND 95 000 SPECTATORS

South Africans are believed to have first played tennis in the 1870s, when it was introduced to a rapidly growing fraternity by E. Nevill and other English players. In 1884 E.L. Williams became the first South African to appear in a final at Wimbledon when he partnered E. Lewis of England in the men's doubles. The winners were the famous Renshaw brothers. Two years later Williams defeated H.F. Lawford (later to become Wimbledon champion) in the covered courts championship.

Port Elizabeth became the hub of South African tennis in the early years — and the town hosted the first national championships in 1891. Thereafter the championships were held in six different towns before Ellis Park, Johannesburg, was established as the permanent venue in 1931.

The popularity of tennis as a spectator sport grew and, as prize money became more attractive, an increasing number of professionals were drawn to the local circuit. By 1973 the South African Open Tennis Championships ranked fourth in the world in paid attendance. That year saw the participation of players from 15 countries — and 95 000 spectators paid over R170 000 to watch them in action.

Abe Segal and Dozing Dorothy

As a lad, Abe Segal was uninterested in tennis. But one day he climbed a fence at Johannesburg's Ellis Park and learned a game that eventually became an obsession.

He worked his passage to Europe, and hitch-hiked to London, where he was nabbed by a policeman after scaling a wall at Wimbledon. But a few days later he made his way to the Centre Court — this time after a legal entry — and watched the final between Jaroslov Drobny and Ted Schroeder. Segal recalled later, in an *Outspan* article, that he crouched on a step and 'As I watched, a funny feeling came over me. It's the feeling when you want something really badly'.

The young player dreamed that one day the Wimbledon crowd would be cheering him. Five years later they were. He went down in four sets to the incomparable Ken Rosewall — to an ovation from the crowd.

In a career packed with incidents both dramatic and funny, Segal remembered one in particular. He was playing the final point against Clark Graebner on a back court at Wimbledon when Graebner drove the South African's service out of court. Segal ran to the net to shake hands with his vanquished opponent but, surprisingly, the American withdrew his hand. 'You haven't won the match till the linesman calls,' he announced.

Sure enough, there had been no call — because the woman line-judge was fast asleep. 'I thought she was unconscious,' laughed Segal later. A combination of cocktails and hot sun won for the official the title of 'Dozing Dorothy' in the next day's papers. Segal did, in fact, win the match.

A young Abe Segal (left) and Meyer Schneider take a break during their first tour overseas in 1949

PAGEANTRY AND TENSION AT WIMBLEDON

It was the year of Gorgeous Gussie and Eric Sturgess. The Wimbledon of 1949. Britain had succeeded in shrugging off the scars of war, and the pageantry surpassed everything that had gone before. That year's lawn tennis championships were graced by Queen Mary and other Royalty — and for once the clouds had given way to the sunshine of a glorious English summer.

Now, as the day drew to a close, Sturgess stood on the hallowed turf of the Centre Court with his fellow South African, Sheila Summers. Facing them were the formidable John Bromwich and Louise Brough, winners of the mixed doubles title for the previous two years. The South Africans took the first set 9-7; the

The maestro in action. Eric Sturgess winning the South African singles title in 1957 — his 11th victory

Americans triumphed in the second 11-9.

'There was never more than one game between us over 48 games,' recalled Sturgess.

And finally the moment the crowd had been waiting for: match point. The atmosphere was electric. Thousands of kilometres away, South Africans were glued to their radios. Sturgess glanced backwards at his partner as she rose on her toes like a ballerina. The ball rocketed across the net. It was in.

'Louise hit her return service into the net,' remembered Sturgess. 'We both spontaneously jumped high into the air and ran to shake hands. The crowd went mad.'

It was a quarter to ten when the victorious couple finally emerged from their dressing rooms. Sturgess described his amazement on finding a mass of people outside: 'They had waited to give us a rousing cheer. It was an exhilarating experience.' For Sturgess, 1949

Ilana Kloss won the Wimbledon Junior Invitation in 1972 and the U.S. Open doubles title in 1976

Ray Moore. He won the South African Junior title in 1965 and reached the Wimbledon quarter-finals in 1968

was his finest Wimbledon. He had reached the semi-finals of both the men's singles and men's doubles: his singles' tussle with Ted Schroeder of the United States was described as a classic.

Making allowances for the South African's tiredness and his defeat in the fourth set, *The Times* correspondent averred that 'this match could rank among one of the best that has ever been seen here'.

It was a fine tribute to a tennis player who was widely regarded as having the most perfect court manners in the world.

The Prime Minister was proud

The Sturgess-Summers win, electrifying though it was, did not signal the start of a golden age in South African tennis.

The lean times made victories all that more memorable. When the Federation Cup came to Ellis Park in 1972, the local girls were seeded only sixth and rated very low among the 31 participating nations. Pat Pretorius, Brenda Kirk and Greta Delport were admired for their gritty determination, but considered to be of only modest talent. South Africa had a bad start in its first-ever Federation final when British player Virginia Wade scored a runaway victory over Pat Pretorius. But then came Brenda Kirk's match against Winnie Shaw. Shaw started badly, and her game developed into a display of nerves. Commented sportswriter Frank Rostron: 'Brenda steadily improved until she made Winnie look like a frustrated second-rater in an embarrassing 6-0 final set.' That left it evens for a nail-biting doubles.

The South Africans took the first set, and with the score at 6-5 in the second set, Brenda Kirk served. Then it was 40-15, and the volleys became desperate: all four players were frequently at the net. Pat Pretorius to Joyce Williams, a return . . . out of court. The match, the Federation Cup and the glory had been won.

Rostron watched in amazement as the crowd erupted into 'the most emotional fervour of national rejoicing I have ever known in this sports crazy country'. The winners leapt high into the air, their arms flung aloft. Prime Minister John Vorster said: 'I am proud that our girls held our country's flag high today.'

A do-it-yourself champion

When colour dominates tennis conversation, there is usually a reference to Arthur Ashe and Althea Gibson, who made the breakthrough for minority groups in the United States and in world tournaments. Yet in the early 1950s, a young coloured music teacher from Cape Town was steadily making his mark in tournaments across Britain. His collection of trophies was impressive.

David Samaai dominated the South African Tennis Association's championships from 1946 until his retirement in 1958. He was self-taught — simply because no coach was available — and was barred from the major South African championships because of his colour. By the start of the 1950s he had had enough: he had to go abroad to face top-class oppo-

Frew McMillan, one of the world's best. He partnered Hewitt to win three Wimbledon championships

Bob Hewitt, who shared the Wimbledon men's doubles title in 1962, 1964, 1967, 1972 and 1978

Left: Greer Stevens partnered Bob Hewitt in two mixed doubles victories at Wimbledon. Centre: Sheila Summers at Wimbledon. In the early 1960s, Sandra Reynolds and Renée Schuurman were to revive hopes of a doubles win. Right: Brenda Kirk. She helped to win the Federation Cup for South Africa in 1972

nents. In 1951, living on £300 raised by friends in the Association, he gained six titles on the British circuit. His agility and lightning reactions were often too much for his better-groomed, more experienced opponents. A few years later he became the first coloured person to play at Wimbledon.

An unforgettable final

One of the country's greatest tennis triumphs was soured by political protests from countries on the other side of the world. It came in 1974 when South Africa played Italy in the zone final of the Davis Cup at Ellis Park. Argentina had decided not to contest the third round, and the Indian government had ordered its team to withdraw from that year's cup, so the Ellis Park clash on 3 October became the final.

An estimated 27 000 South Africans crammed themselves into the stadium, hoping the Springboks would capture the game's most coveted team trophy. The contest was

over in two days. South African Bob Hewitt beat Antonio Zugarelli 4-6, 6-0, 9-7, 4-6, 6-1 in the opening singles, and Ray Moore, the colourful and agile player with characteristic long hair and sweatband, boosted the lead to 2-0 with a 4-6, 6-0, 6-3, 6-4 victory over Adriano Panatta.

Then came the doubles, and such was the record and reputation of Hewitt and his partner, Frew McMillan, that most people thought the result a foregone conclusion. Their optimism was justified. Panatta and fellow Italian, Paolo Bertolucci were beaten in straight sets.

They fought back ferociously in the first and third sets, but in the end Hewitt and McMillan won the cup with a 7-5, 6-4, 10-8 tally that made the result of the reverse singles of only academic interest. But Moore, as if to underline the fact that this was South Africa's greatest moment, beat Zugarelli 6-3, 7-5, 6-3 (Hewitt, playing the anticlimatic final singles, was beaten 8-6, 6-3, 6-2 by Panatta).

The fair way to victory

'TEMPER NEVER GOT ANYONE ANYWHERE!'

In 1938 a clerk in a Rand mining finance house was faced with a difficult decision. He was 20 years old, had good prospects — and he wanted to become a professional golfer.

In an era when lavish sponsorship was unheard of, and existing professionals jealously guarded the purses on the golfing circuit, young Arthur D'Arcy 'Bobby' Locke might have been forgiven if he opted for security rather than hefty travelling expenses and doubtful pay cheques. He chose the riskier course, and within two decades his name had been inscribed on just about every major golf trophy in America and Europe, as well as his native South Africa.

Bobby Locke learned his skills on the golf courses that sprang up as the Reef mines evolved into settled and civilised communities. His tutor was his father, an Irishman with an outfitter's business, who was careful to instruct his son on the bearing of the gentleman golfer. In his book, *Bobby Locke on Golf*, he recalls a lecture by his father after he was found taking out his frustration on his clubs. 'The very next club you throw will be the end of golf for you,' he warned. 'Now remember this: if you think you are going to lose your temper, start to count three, and by the time you have counted one you will have control of yourself.'

It was a lesson that Bobby Locke never forgot, and he was to say later: 'Temper never got anyone anywhere in golf.'

His career in the game was promising from the start. In the mid-1930s he took both the South African Amateur and Open golfing championships; was top scorer among the amateurs at the British Open in 1936, and repeated the performance at Carnoustie the following year.

Rusty but determined

Locke's decision to turn professional was made easy by the patronage of financier Norbert Erleigh, and he went on to capture the Irish, New Zealand and Dutch open

Bobby Locke — the gentle veteran of the world's fairways. He won the first 'Sportsman of the Year' award in 1950

championships in his first two professional years. Then suddenly he was in uniform, flying for the South African Air Force in the Second World War.

Demobilisation saw a determined, if slightly rusty, golfer pick up his clubs for another assault that was to be long remembered. In 1946 he triumphed in South Africa's two major events, and won the British Dunlop Masters. It was the tuning up he needed for his entry into the lucrative but notoriously tough American circuit.

The American professionals probably saw this 30-year-old ex-pilot as something of an upstart, and certainly not as a serious challenge. The year 1947 was to prove them wrong. Locke blazed his way across the country, winning five major tournaments and featuring near the top in four others. Television — still three decades away in his home country — brought him into the homes of millions. Golfing writers praised his play and a top tournament supervisor discribed Locke as the most accurate golfer in the world.

Two years later, at Troon in Scotland, Locke and Harry Bradshaw went to a 36-hole play-off after turning in equal scores of 283 for the 72 holes. Coolly, Locke shot birdie after

South Africans have taken to golf with gusto for nearly a century. Their first golf balls were the very hard old 'gutties', made of solid gutta-percha

birdie to notch 135 against Bradshaw's 147 — and he had won his first British Open. The following year he was to return to defend his title with a stunning 279 — breaking the magic 280 barrier that golfers rated equivalent to the four-minute mile.

The Maestro's touch

It was not just Locke's unshakeable determination that earned him the title of the Maestro. It was rather his style of golf, his courtesy and complete lack of temperament. Yet Locke himself would have admitted to the same fears and failings experienced by other golfers.

Fellow golfer Peter Thomson, who played more than 150 matches against Locke, said of him: 'It is doubtful whether the world will ever again see such a natural player who was able to pile up a majestic record with such apparent ease.'

The Royal and Ancient at St Andrews honoured Bobby Locke by making him an honorary member — a distinction shared with admirals and generals, American Bobby Jones

Putting Green, (8th Hole) Keiskama Hoek, C. P.

South African golfing was first recorded in 1885 at Wynberg, when the Cape Golf Club (later the Royal Cape Golf Club) was founded. Its first chairman was Lieutenant-General H. d'Oyley Torrens, commander of the British troops in South Africa

Gary Player — superbly fit and totally dedicated

and the French amateur, Quimet. In America his name was inscribed in the Hall of Fame, and in South Africa he is remembered as one of this country's sporting greats.

The winner who thought he had lost

Muirfield, July 1959. The eve of the final day in the British Open Golf Championship. Gary Player, yet to make his mark on the international scene, and trailing eight strokes behind the leader, turns to a companion and makes a prediction that, coming from any other 23-year-old, would sound brash. But Player, recalling the occasion in his book, *Grand Slam Golf*, speaks with an assurance beyond his years: '. . . tomorrow you're going to see a large miracle. I'm going to win the British Open.' However his self-assurance was soon to be dented.

Player's final round the following day will be talked about as long as the game of golf is played. Everything he did went gloriously right . . . until he came to the last fairway, and drove his tee shot into a bunker. Even worse

agony was to follow, for once on the green, he missed a 'sitter' of a putt, and finished with a disastrous six for the hole.

'It was reported that I cried,' said Gary later. 'I didn't, but I certainly felt like it. To have botched a great round, to have squandered a championship in that way, was criminal.'

Sunk in dejection, Player left the course — despite the fact that the overnight leaders still had nine holes left to play. Normally he was teetotal, but his friend Harold Henning insisted that, once back at the Marine Hotel, he should have a cold bath, followed by a stiff drink.

Henning stayed on the course and kept calling the hotel with the latest scores. And gradually Player realised that something remarkable was happening: his rivals were in trouble, too. It was going to be a close finish after all. In the final seconds of the game, the Belgian player, Flory van Donck, drove into a bunker and was left with a 12-metre putt to tie. He did not make it: Gary Player had won.

It was the first important skittle in the line-up that Gary Player was to topple within the space of seven years. He won the South African Open in 1960 and took the U.S. Masters title the following year. By then he was top earner on the American circuit. In recent times, only four men have won the 'Grand Slam' of golf — the British Open, U.S. Masters, U.S.P.G.A. tournament and U.S. Open. They are Gene Sarazen, Ben Hogan, Jack Nicklaus — and Gary Player.

The little wizard of golf has won laurels at just about every major tournament in the world and has been named 'Sportsman of the Year' — for the first time in 1956 — more often than any other South African sportsman. He travels widely and often, and after more than 20 years at the top, he is still a fanatic for fitness and shows no sign of retiring. 'I'll always be playing golf,' he says, 'even if it is with a bunch of fellows from the local pub, twice a week, for the price of a glass of lemonade.'

THE COURSE WAS ONE BIG HAZARD

Black golfers — most of whom worked as caddies at exclusive white clubs — had a rough time of it in post-war South Africa.

A typical course was an eight-hole affair hacked out of the bundu; the 'greens' were unpretentious patches of levelled Transvaal soil. As golfer Simon Malaza pointed out in 1947, a hazard was unknown because the course itself was one big hazard. Golf clubs were usually hand-me-downs with battered and shattered shafts, or made at home with bits of wire and piping (these were known as 'pipesticks').

Vincent Tshabalala was a black caddie at the old Virginia Park course, earning a living from the 'bobs' and florins flicked to him by the white golfers.

One of his regulars was Gary Player, and during the five years from 1953 to 1958 that he carried Player's clubs, a firm friendship developed. 'I told him my ambitions as a golfer,' said Tshabalala, 'and he took the time to watch me play and give me advice.'

The free lessons from one of South Africa's greatest golfers paid dividends. In 1974 Tshabalala became the first black South African to enter the United States professional circuit. In 1976 he was drawn to play with his own mentor, Gary Player, in the South African Masters. He came in fifth to claim a prize of R1 000.

'When they handed me my prize,' he said, 'I was so excited I nearly dropped it.'

Bobby Cole, consistently good locally and overseas

Dale Hayes. World junior golf champion in 1969

Sally Little, South Africa's best woman golfer

Going for gold

Reggie Walker wins the 100 metres event at the 1908 Olympic Games in London's White City stadium

Left: Gitsham and McArthur are chaired by their supporters after their stunning victory in the 1912 Olympic Marathon at Stockholm. Right: Charlie Winslow, who won the men's singles championship the same year

A HALF-CENTURY OF COMPETITION

When the Olympic Games were held in London in 1908, South Africa sent only 14 athletes. Reggie Walker, a Natal sprinter, was not included in the Springbok team, but the people of the colony were so sure of his ability that they raised the cash for his fare.

Ironically, Walker became the first South African to win an Olympic gold medal when he streaked 100 metres in a record 10,8 seconds. It was the only gold medal the Springboks won that year, though marathon runner Charles Hefferon took the silver.

In all, 17 gold, 28 silver and 27 bronze

Louis Raymond took the gold medal in the men's singles in Antwerp at the 1920 Olympic Games

medals were won by South Africans between 1908 and their last appearance at the Games in 1960. Though invited to Tokyo in 1964 and Mexico City four years later, the Springboks had to withdraw for political reasons.

The marathon men

On a scorchingly hot day in 1912, Kenneth McArthur and Christopher Gitsham stirred the patriotism of their fellow South Africans when they scored a magnificent one-two in the most gruelling contest of the Olympics — the Marathon.

The course was set over 40,2 km on a high country road north of Stockholm.

The trainer of the South African team, H.B. Keartland, described this moment of South African glory nearly half a century later: 'A still silence made it known that the first runner had left the road and entered the long passage leading to the track . . . A distant lone figure emerged from the black tunnel, shambled into the blazing sunlight, hesitated . . . then shuffled his weary way to the finish. Through the discoloration of sweat and dust we could discern the green and gold of South Africa and recognise the figure of Kenneth McArthur, the Potchefstroom policeman, realising the highest hopes of the small band of South Africans present.'

As McArthur staggered towards the line, an official threw a laurel wreath over his shoulders. Close behind him came Springbok Christopher Gitsham.

'Incredible!' said Keartland. 'As the little group of South Africans made their way home from the stadium along the tramless streets they were recognised by hero-worshipping Swedes, who encircled them with joined hands and escorted them to their pensions. Police cheerfully cleared the way and women threw flowers and blew kisses from windows.'

Gitsham nearly didn't make the Olympic

squad after failures in the five and ten mile events in the home championships. Only at Keartland's insistence was he tried out for the marathon — a distance he had never run before. Gitsham might well have been the gold medallist, too. He had run with McArthur for some 15 kilometres, but the sight of a trickle of water from a fountain along the route was too much to bear. He stopped to quench his thirst, and in so doing cramped his leg muscles. Even so, he made up a lot of ground to come in second.

Before South Africa became a republic, she participated in six British Empire and Commonwealth Games (later known officially as the Commonwealth Games) from 1930, winning a total of 190 medals (72 gold, 60 silver

---

OUR OLYMPIC GOLD-MEDALLISTS

Track and field

1908 R. Walker	100 metres
1912 K. McArthur	Marathon
1920 B. Rudd	400 metres
1928 S.J.M. Atkinson	110 metres hurdles
1952 E. Brand	High jump

Tennis

1912 C. Winslow and H.A. Kitson	Men's doubles
1912 C. Winslow	Men's singles
1920 L. Raymond	Men's singles

Cycling

1912 R. Lewis	320 km road race

Boxing

1920 C. Walker	Bantamweight
1924 W. Smith	Bantamweight
1932 L. Stevens	Lightweight
1932 D. Carstens	Light-heavyweight
1948 G. Dreyer	Lightweight
1948 G. Hunter	Light-heavyweight

Swimming

1952 J. Harrison	Women's 100 m backstroke

A jubilant Marjorie Clarke after her victory in the 80 metres hurdles race at the 1934 Empire Games in London

and 58 bronze) — a proud record indeed.

Harry Hart won both the shot-put and discus events in the first Games in 1930, and repeated his golden performance four years later. No other competitor has matched his achievement. In addition, Hart won a silver medal in the 1930 javelin event and a bronze for this in 1934.

But it was the wrestlers who really walked away with the awards. Between 1930 and 1958, 20 South African wrestlers won 12 gold, four silver and seven bronze medals. At Vancouver in 1954, the six wrestlers in the Springbok team all took gold medals!

Sliding to a medal

Hurdler Jacob Swart is the only man to have won a Commonwealth Games medal on his backside.

He was considered the strongest challenger to K. Gardener of Jamaica, holder of the 120-yard hurdles title at the 1958 Games in Cardiff. Swart had come through the semi-finals just 0,2 seconds outside the Games record, and at the start of the final was out in front with Gardener.

Barbara Burke wins the 80 metres hurdles at the Empire Games in 1938 — equalling the world record

Tom Lavery wins a gold medal (and sets a new world record) in the 220 metres hurdles in Sydney in 1938

They took the last hurdle together — and either could win the race. Then, just short of the tape, disaster struck the South African. He stumbled and fell, crossing the line on his back.

Initially, the judges put Swart last in the final, but the picture taken by the photo-finish camera showed that the Springbok had slithered to a silver medal less than a metre behind the winner.

It was at the 1958 Commonwealth Games that Gert Potgieter established himself as one of the world's greatest hurdlers. In the heats he broke the Games record, and in the final fought off the challenge of D.F. Lean of Australia to come down the back straight in the 440-yard hurdles in a world record shattering time of 49,7 seconds.

Potgieter, a thick-set athlete, was perfectly built for the gruelling event. But ill-luck was to wreck his Olympic hopes. In the 1956 Games, he was lying third, 50 metres from the finish, when he hit the last hurdle and fell heavily, finishing last. Before the 1960 Olympics in Rome, he had lowered his record to 49,3 seconds, although this was never ratified. Then, driving through West Germany before the Games, the South African was involved in a car crash.

He was badly injured and lost an eye. Yet he was to return to the track a couple of years later, covering the 400 metres in 52,1 seconds — an almost unbelievable feat for a man in his condition.

Left: South Africans Johannes Colman, right, and Syd Luyt lead Korean Yun Bok in the 1948 Olympic marathon in London. Colman and Luyt finished in the first six. Above: High-jumper Esther Brand, left, and swimmer Joan Harrison with the Mitchell-Hedges Trophy after their victories in the 1952 Olympics at Helsinki

Earning and Spending

South Africa entered the 20th century in the middle of a conflict so bitter and so expensive that it tore the country apart. Then, on 31 May 1910, the *Friend* greeted Union as 'one of the greatest revolutions ever effected in South Africa'. Warned the newspaper: 'From today the mere parochial view of South African affairs often distorted by the petty squabbles of individual States must cease, to be exchanged for the greater and nobler outlook upon a young nation struggling into life.' With the wealth of the gold mines and the long-awaited stability of a unified nation there was reason for optimism. By 1910 the miners were the country's best-paid skilled workers, earning an average weekly wage of £5.18s.

Yet for those outside the industry, the ever-rising prices were making life intolerable: the benefits of progress did not reach everyone. Shop assistants still rose before dawn to walk the long road to work, and thought twice before buying a loaf of bread. Trade unionists were denounced as 'Reds' (some of them *were* Reds), pickets clashed with police and scabs at factory gates, and angry garment workers armed themselves with tomatoes and rotten eggs in last-ditch stands against uncaring industrialists.

But the clashes which followed the general strike of 1922, with its terrible cost in lives and property, galvanised the country into concerted action. The Industrial Conciliation Act of 1924 established the machinery for negotiation between employers and trade unions through a system of collective bargaining. (The Wage Act was introduced the following year.) In 1928 the South African Iron and Steel Industrial Corporation (ISCOR) was established by Act of Parliament (it first produced steel in 1934), the SASOL oil-from-coal complex was established in 1950, and South Africa was on its way to becoming one of the continent's industrial giants. Between 1933 and 1965 the real national product grew at an average rate of about 5 per cent, and between 1932 and 1937 the gross national product jumped from £217 million to £370 million.

The Depression came and went; another world war took its toll. These were stirring times, and often unkind, but the standard of living was rising all the time and fewer people were going hungry. South Africa had found its feet.

A worker tends a steam hammer in a blacksmith's shop in the 1930s. Factory workers sweated through long shifts for meagre wages; black employees survived on even less

A fair and reasonable wage

THE HAVES AND HAVE-NOTS

The Act of Union in May 1910 heralded an era of swiftly rising prices, and a clamour for wage increases that was largely ignored.

The first Governor-General was Lord Gladstone, son of the famous Liberal Prime Minister. His salary was £10 000 a year plus an additional £8 000 to cover travelling expenses and entertainment. During the period 1910-11, however, he managed to spend £25 409 — £15 409 on salaries and wages (for himself and his staff of 11), £8 191 on travel and entertainment (including what must have been a costly visit by the Duke of Connaught to open the first Union Parliament), and £1 877 on 'incidentals'. During the same period, the Prime Minister, Louis Botha, came out on the relatively modest sum of £6 960. This was made up of salaries for himself and five members of staff (his own salary was about £3 500), £838 for transport and £271 for incidentals.

Astronomical though these figures seemed to a clerk struggling along on less than £100 a year, the phenomenal boom in gold mining had in fact created a new class of *nouveau riche*. By comparison with their Empire cousins in New Zealand and Australia, miners on the Witwatersrand were living high on £45 a month. The average miner would earn £1.2s. a shift, and shift bosses considerably more. Other skilled workers were also cashing in on the demand for labour — carpenters and fitters could command £1 a day, sometimes more.

Contrasting sharply with these relatively generous rewards was the abysmal pay earned by black workers — as little as £4 a month. And the cost of living on the Rand was high.

Tough life for the unskilled

For most white workers outside the mining industry, too, life was hard. Even before Union, Alexander Aiken, former president of the Transvaal Society of Accountants, reported in his Witwatersrand survey that average family budgets ran from £16.17s.1d. to £36.19s.1d. (however, this did not include money spent on liquor and tobacco — to have asked about these 'might have seemed inquisitorial'). Aiken believed that a man earning £25 or £26 a month

Shorthand typists being trained in the 'New Shorthand' studio in Cape Town. In 1910 employers regarded this system of rapid writing as a godsend. At that time shorthand typists earned an average of £132 a year

Johannesburg's Crown Mines Ltd. broke a world record in 1925 by sinking a 97 m shaft in 31 days. In those days machine stoppers were paid at the rate of £1.1s.6d. per shift; fitters slightly more at £1.1s.8d.

'can do no more than subsist if he has a family to support'.

Skilled artisans were well-to-do compared with the large body of clerical workers and salesmen. Aiken found that the average pay of a male shop assistant was £22.13s.4d. a month. Some clerks and bookkeepers came out on £21.11s.4d. a month, though the majority were paid around £20.

His survey focussed attention on the vast number of family men on the Witwatersrand drawing less than the minimum living wage, and, in the private commercial concerns he investigated, more than three-quarters of the clerks, excluding the managers and juniors, were earning 'too little upon which to risk matrimony and the comfort of another fellowbeing'.

SWEATED LABOUR ON THE FACTORY FLOOR

'In the sweet industry there has been a considerable amount of sweating that is not equalled in England today, and could not be surpassed there in the old sweating days.'

Thus were factory conditions described in 1926, when the Wage Board was looking closely into the whole question of workers' pay.

The truth was that secondary industry and the urban working class were relatively new ingredients of South African society. The country did not have Britain's industrial traditions. Unions were still something of a novelty and often powerless to combat the merciless exploitation of men, women and children in factories and workshops across the country.

Many of the young factory girls were raw recruits from the rural areas. Katie Viljoen

left school at the age of 15 to help her parents. She moved from her Orange Free State farm to Johannesburg in 1932 and found work in a dressmaking factory.

Her day began at seven in the morning and ended 11 hours later. On her first day she 'walked home from work with my friend Lena, who, though she lived in an entirely different suburb, acted as my guide. To make sure that I would not lose my way I took a piece of white chalk with me and made various marks on the route from the factory to my lodgings. Next morning I left the house at five-thirty, as I had to walk a distance of about four miles . . .' Katie was paid £1 a week.

The meagre wages usually supplemented a small family income and very often the girls had no money at all for themselves. A 1923 report revealed that many turned up at their factory without cash and were unable to buy even a cup of canteen soup.

Said the report: 'In one instance some undernourished and anaemic workers who frequently fainted at work were given a free meal daily for a fortnight in order to show their parents how they improved by having a hot well-balanced midday meal. They were still refused the necessary money and soon relapsed into their old state of weakness and inefficiency.'

Other industrialists were less enlightened. One was asked by a board of enquiry sitting in the mid-1920s how much he would suggest as an apprentice's wage. He replied, reported the South African Press Association, that he 'did not believe in apprentices, as they never learnt anything'. The man who had to teach his apprentice really taught him nothing owing to the fear of being ousted . . . by the apprentice! He also denounced tea-breaks (because they interrupted production) and canteens, explaining: 'It seems to me that the Board wants to turn the business

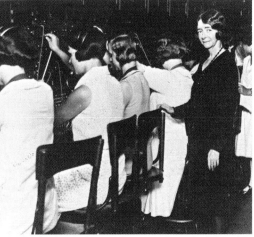

Durban's telephone exchange in the early 1930s. The operators earned about £14 a month and their supervisors more than twice that amount. The operators would have paid an average of 15/- for their shoes, 13/11 for their frocks and 4/11 for silk stockings

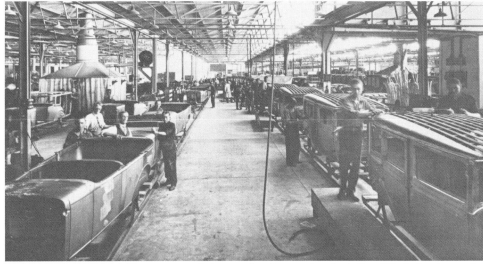

By 1929 Ford and General Motors were producing cars from fine new factories in Port Elizabeth, where craftsmen and engineers such as these at GM's body line took pride in their creations of pressed steel and wood. The bodymakers earned about 2/6 an hour in 1930, and the cars sold for between £250 and £350. General Motors maintained a palatial showroom for the display of their latest models, which by then included Opel, Oakland, Marquette, La Salle, Vauxhall and Bedford

into a hotel, or a tea-party. I might as well import than manufacture.'

The rag trade, said the chairman of the Board, was another area that needed 'very considerable clearing up'. A journeyman tailor could expect to take up to 12 hours to make a coat, for which he received £1. Four shillings of this was spent on workshop expenses and sewing materials. To make ends meet, the Board was told, the man had to work a 16-17 hour day.

Katie sees stars

Garment workers were among the first to voice their protest. When employers tried to cut their wages in 1932 — for the second time — the union called a general strike. Katie Viljoen described the clash between pickets and police outside the Germiston factories: 'The pickets had to be outside the factories early in the morning, even before 5 a.m., as the employers were doing their utmost to bring in scabs. The pickets did not use violence against them, but resorted to booing and singing uncomplimentary songs or pelting them with tomatoes and eggs.' When a policeman arrested one of the girl strikers, Katie tried to pull her from his grasp, and 'suddenly I saw stars. The policeman had slapped me violently across the face and, for a whole week, I proudly bore my badge of honour — a black eye'.

CINDERELLA BEHIND THE COUNTER

While the shelves of South Africa's larger stores reflected the well-being of middle class whites, those who served in them often lived in abject poverty.

In 1905, an apprenticed counter hand would start on £1.10s. to £2.10s. a month. A man with seven years' service could only expect £12 or £15 — if his employer was generous. A sales girl would earn around £10.

In his book on the shop trade, Norman Herd tells the story of little Gertrude:

'When Gertrude's father went on pension — it was £6 a month — schooling became a luxury. So they hiked her out midway through Standard VI and put her in a shop. It was 1915 . . . she was a tiny cog in a stuttering economy. She manned a shop counter from eight to five for a wage of 30s a month . . . There was no staff room; facilities for personal comfort were primitive, embarrassing.

'Four years went by: her pay had inched up to £10 a month. She was due for another rise . . . the senior notch.

'So they said sorry, not our fault, this absurd system of prescribed wages — the profits won't stand it. Somewhere at school, and marking time — another Gertrude.' Her plight was typical of the times.

Minimum wages had been prescribed, but in some respects they were punitive. Employees, like Gertrude, would often be sacked when they reached the senior level, and replaced by a junior. Shop assistants would cheat about their length of service in order to remain just below the senior notch.

In 1937, the National Union of Distributive Workers called for a cut in the working week, from 52 to 44 hours. They also called for Saturday afternoon closing throughout the Union. The demand fell on deaf ears. At that time a senior male assistant received £18 a month. But Act 41 of 1939 introduced new provisions covering the entire spectrum of working hours, establishing a 46-hour week of 5½ days. Stocktaking on Sundays and public holidays was forbidden and overtime was restricted to two hours on any one day; 12 hours a week and 30 hours in a year. No assistant was permitted to spend more than one hour a week completing sales after the shop doors were closed.

ABOVE AND BELOW THE BREADLINE

This table compares the annual income of South Africans in 1924. For the humble factory worker, an empty stomach was a fact of life: fainting spells were commonplace for people living below the breadline. Although wages were generally higher on the Witwatersrand, the cost of living there had soared. It was an era of depression; many were earning just about what their fathers had earned 20 years before.

Governor-General	£10 000
Prime Minister	£ 3 500
Administrator of the Cape	£ 2 500
Administrator of Natal	£ 2 000
Commissioner of Police	£ 2 000
Secretary for Education	£ 1 520
Headmaster	£ 520
Cabinet maker	£ 260
Teacher	£ 255
Male shop assistant	£ 240
Baker	£ 195
Postman	£ 180
Cinema usherette	£ 44
Clothing factory worker (1st year)	£ 26

Bon Marché claimed to be Durban's most popular store in 1941. Shop assistants earned about £11 a month

The typewriter: 'A blessing. . . especially to womenkind'

The typewriter inspired a revolution in offices around the world. South Africans were among the hundreds, thousands and finally millions who succumbed to the appeal of a mechanical marvel that could reproduce the boss's memoranda, directives and final demands in clear, neat type. It was a boon to the longest-suffering of office workers — the women.

In The Enormous File, *Alan Delgado refers to the Sholes-Gidden machine, possibly the first commercially-produced typewriter, which appeared on the market in the 1870s. Maintained Sholes: 'I do feel that I have done something for the women who have always had to work so hard. This (typewriter) will enable them more easily to earn a living. Whatever I may have felt in the early days of the value of the typewriter, it is obviously a blessing to mankind, and especially to womenkind'.*

By July 1887 The Phonetic Journal *could quote an expert from America who stated that 'typewriting has become quite fashionable even among the upper classes here, and the schools devoted to its instruction find among their number many sons and daughters of wealthy citizens, who regard a knowledge of the manipulation of the machine as a sort of safeguard against possible future need . . '*

But for some years the employment of 'typewriting women' was a novelty. The Enormous File *relates a case in 1890, when Britain's Board of Agriculture 'placed one woman typist in a dingy room in the basement and the Chief Clerk issued a firm order that no male member of the staff over the age of fifteen was to visit her'.*

THE AMERICAN-DESIGNED HAMMOND 2 of 1893 is one of the outstanding machines in typewriter history. The two rows of keys, arranged in a semicircular pattern, provide up to four characters per key and the type is quickly and easily interchangeable

AN 1891 OLIVER 3, manufactured in the United States, was one of the strongest and most elegant of the early typewriters. Its 'mouse ear' banks of keys moved sideways and down, providing partly visible type (at that time most typists could not see what they were typing)

GERMANY'S 1904 MIGNON was one of the most unusual typewriters to enjoy commercial success. Its pointer-index system enabled operators to type at speeds of over 250 characters a minute. The Mignon was produced until 1940

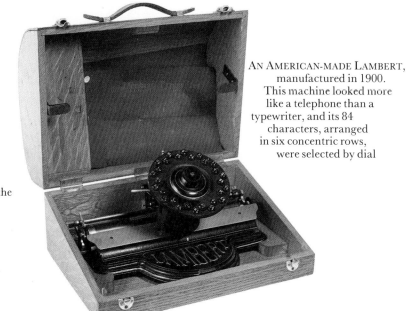

AN AMERICAN-MADE LAMBERT, manufactured in 1900. This machine looked more like a telephone than a typewriter, and its 84 characters, arranged in six concentric rows, were selected by dial

THE BLICKENSDERFER 8, made in America in 1907. Despite the overwhelming trend towards the 'QWERTY' keyboard, Blickensderfer clung to the 'Ideal' keyboard until 1917. (QWERTY is derived from the top row of keys)

THE UNDERWOOD 3 was one of the earliest machines to offer long carriages (lengths ranged from 11 in. to 26 in.). It was produced with the Underwood 5 from 1900 to 1931

1919 IMPERIAL MODEL D. This was the first straight three-row keyboard to be introduced by the British manufacturer (the earlier Imperial typewriters all had curved keyboards) and was considered old fashioned at the time. It was overtaken in 1927 by a conventional front-strike machine

1930 UNDERWOOD. This American-made portable four-bank typewriter sold more than 1,5 million models between 1926 and 1947

ANOTHER OF AMERICA'S successful typewriters was this IBM Electric Model 01, produced from 1933. This machine was imported by a Somerset West woman in 1947, and is thought to have been the first electric typewriter in Cape Town

BY 1957 typewriters such as this Italian Olivetti Graphika were assuming a more streamlined shape — and were even being offered in pastel colours. This was the only manual standard typewriter with proportional spacing

The poor whites

HELPLESS AND HOPELESS

The Great Trek had shown how ruggedly independent the Afrikaner was; when he settled on the land his greatest strength was that he was master of himself and nodded to no-one. But poor agricultural conditions over the decades — drought, rinderpest and locust —and failure to adapt to new farming methods, reduced many of these hardy individuals to little more than squatters on small plots of land. Often their holdings were mortgaged and, as debts increased, the farmer became less inclined to till his soil or graze his sheep 'because my work only benefits the mortgage holder'.

Unable to cope with the hardship and hopelessness, the spirit of many impoverished South Africans broke. The will to rise above their wretchedness simply was not there. This was to compound what was to become a national problem and frustrate early efforts to solve it.

The 'poor white problem' in South Africa was first identified in 1890, and the Transvaal Indigency Commission of 1906-08 revealed how poor farmers had migrated to the urban areas with little idea of what work they could do and were living 'in wretched shanties on the outskirts of the towns'. There they faced serious competition from the black labour being drawn into the industrial system at low rates of pay.

It was an unfair match. Unskilled work usually went to the blacks because as a rule they were paid less. In addition many poor whites had an ingrown prejudice against the kind of job usually reserved for blacks.

But finally something was done about it. In 1927 the Carnegie Corporation of New York agreed to fund an investigation, whereupon the Union government and the Dutch Reformed Church each matched the Carnegie's generous grant. The Commission calculated that of a white population of just over 1,800 000 in 1931, more than 300 000 could be classed as 'very poor'. The Commission added that these figures were obtained before the effects of the depression became so noticeable, and pointed out that according to the 1926 census, nearly 58 000 white males of 15 years and older fell into the 'lowliest' occupation groups such as shepherds, foresters, diggers, unskilled industrial workers and *bywoners*. And it recognised that the problem was getting worse.

Among the commissioners who visited the humble homes and shanties was Maria Rothmann, the Afrikaans authoress who wrote under the pseudonym 'M.E.R.'. She and her fellow commissioners found the issue went a lot further than the 'laziness' often ascribed to the poor white by townsfolk.

More than anything, it was the *bywoner* who personified the poor white problem. Some lived permanently on farms, tilling a little soil, tending an emaciated cow or two. They paid rent to the farmer with the crops they grew and in times of drought or disease simply left the land to swell the ranks of the unemployed.

Many came from once-prosperous landowning families. Drought had been their fier-

The Carnegie Commission reported: '. . . the living conditions of this family are very wretched. They occupy a two-roomed dwelling made of packing-cases with an iron roof. Eleven people sleep in two small rooms, only 8 by 10 feet each. The father has, however, bought a plot of ground, and intends building a suitable house later on.' Below: Some of the dwellings in which poor whites eked out their precarious existence

cest enemy: it reduced them to poverty and forced them off their farms. One told of living in a wagon for 20 years after being wiped out in the 1913 drought. Others were forced to trek, only to find the promise of greener fields an empty one indeed. If a farmer did grant them grazing rights, it would, most likely, be in return for 'some service'. But generally, the *bywoner* became nothing more than a hired hand, receiving a pittance in cash and free board and lodging.

But drought was not the only hazard. On the death of the owner, a farm was often divided equally between the sons of a family. 'None of my descendants need ever be landless,' declared one farmer in his will. 'Every one of them must possess fixed property.' The result, in that family, was strife — £1 900 worth of legal costs and a good farm split into unproductive 28-hectare plots.

Home is a hovel

Of more than 600 houses visited by Carnegie commissioner J. R. Albertyn, secretary of the Dutch Reformed Church's education commission, only a quarter were fit to be lived in. In a railway town, a hovel 2 m by 1,5 m was home for a mother and her five children. Two

sides of a corrugated iron fence formed part of the walls and an old bedstead covered with bags was the roof.

The Carnegie Commission's report quoted some tragic case histories:

'I was born in Middelburg, Transvaal. My father was a pioneer. He went to the Transvaal in 1838 and acquired land in the above district. From the proceeds of my inheritance and the fruits of my own toil I bought a farm in Vryheid and became quite prosperous. Then came the war. All my farm buildings were burnt, and I lost all my stock. . . I lost everything and had to trek around, looking for employment. At last I heard that work was plentiful on the Rand, so I came here. I worked for the city council for six months, but was retrenched; since then I have been doing odd jobs. My wife and I now live on the old-age pension.'

Evils of relief work

When the Carnegie Commission reported in December 1932, many cherished misconceptions of the poor white question were shattered. Charity was seen as short-sighted; hand-outs and relief work to cause 'loss of independence and may imbue them with a sense

Diggers run to peg their claims at the Grasfontein diamond diggings in 1927. It was among the last great 'rushes' — virtually a short cross-country race to peg the most likely diamond-bearing ground

'Mrs. B. (a widow) lives with an unmarried son in a one-roomed cottage, near the dwellings of a married child, and of a grandchild. The three houses are built on the same pattern — wooden boards with an iron roof. . . Everything is untidy and dirty. There is a small patch of mealies and sweet potatoes near the door. The chief item of diet is sweet potatoes; also bread or mealiemeal, and coffee. The rent for each cottage is 2/6 per month. Parents and children look anaemic and pale . . . The men work so far away that they can come home only for the week-end. All complain bitterly of their lot, but remain where they are.'

'S.S., from Willowmore, now living in Port Elizabeth, states: *'I was a "bywoner" at Willowmore. Th.ough the kindness of friends my daughter of 18 got work in a boot factory here. Seeing how well she got on — she gets 20/- a week — we decided to move to Port Elizabeth, as existence at Willowmore was impossible owing to the droughts. I am now a railway labourer earning 6/- per day. Two of my children work in boot factories, and one is a bottle-maker. Our combined income enables us to live and to look after the six smaller children. Our prospects are much rosier now than in the old days.'*

Even so the living conditions of this family are very wretched. They occupy a two-roomed dwelling made of packing-cases with an iron roof. Eleven people sleep in two small rooms, only 8 by 10 feet each. The father has, however, bought a plot of ground, and intends building a suitable house later on.'

Elephant power. A wagon carrying water is pulled by an elephant at the Lichtenberg diggings

A cheerful group pose beside washing equipment at the Grasfontein diggings in December 1926

ONCE A DIGGER, ALWAYS A DIGGER

The one great hope of thousands of poor whites was to find an Eldorado — a quick rags-to-riches fortune. Like so many other South Africans, they were drawn to the diggings 'to try their luck'. Ironically, the diggings were often the cause of further impoverishment. The Commission pointed out that some people sold all their belongings in an effort to sustain themselves until they struck it lucky. Many did not.

Farmers, tired of subsistence living, set out for the promised land. Their farms were neglected, they were unable to meet mortgage debts, and so lost all they owned.

More then 25 000 men had taken part in the Grasfontein 'rush' of 1926 and 1927. When the Commissioners visited the area the 12 000 or so whites who were left lived in squalor — but still in hope.

In fact, if these people had one thing in common it was unbounded optimism. The thought of that one massive diamond lying there for the finding held a singular fascination for all. Each twist of the sieve could reveal it. When a man did make a discovery valuable enough, perhaps, to enable him to leave the diggings, he would tell his wife he wanted to 'try just once more'. And anyway, he could still convince himself that it was a good life, better than he could live anywhere else: he was 'his own master here and not the rich man's dog'.

of inferiority, impair their industry, weaken their sense of personal responsibility and help to make them dishonest'.

In the following year, at a conference to discuss the Commission's report, ideas germinated that would eventually alleviate the poor white problem.

The Government steps in

The Union Government tackled the issue by setting up vocational schools, establishing a separate social welfare department of state and encouraging the training of professional social workers, and launching schemes to bring rural workers into the burgeoning industrial economy.

But one factor more than any other led to the solution of the poor white problem — increased government support for manufacturing industries (ISCOR was founded by Act of Parliament in 1928) which, as they grew, absorbed an increasing number of workers. Wilson and Thomson in their book *Oxford History of South Africa* note that in 1924-25 about 115 000 people were employed in manufacturing. Within a few years the figure had climbed to 141 000, and by the late 1930s the poor white problem had virtually ceased to exist.

Finds such as this one sustained diggers' hopes and kept most in a state of abject poverty. Jacobus Jonker holds a 726-carat diamond found at Elandsfontein, north of Pretoria, in 1934. The stone was sold to Sir Ernest Oppenheimer for £63 000. Right: A woman digger at the Bakerville Diggings has two parrots for company. Note the veil and high-heeled shoes

Workers unite: revolt on the Rand

THE 'RED' REVOLUTION

Faced by a mob of strikers in front of Boksburg jail on 28 February 1922, Police Captain Jock Fulford instructed his men to kneel down in the road and, on the order being given, to fire one round each. This was for 'moral effect'. He then shouted 'Present! Fire!' Three of the strikers were killed.

Despite the opinion of a magistrate who witnessed the incident that 'a little tact and patience would have saved the situation', Captain Fulford and his men were exonerated at the inquest. The miners of Boksburg were stunned at what they were convinced was an injustice.

At the Union Grounds in Johannesburg, a workers' commando and sympathisers numbering 5 000 gathered as the Last Post was trumpeted. In Pretoria, work stopped at noon: churches held services of mourning. Parliament debated the crisis. Red flags hung at half mast; a women's commando banner was inscribed with the words: 'Our comrades, murdered in cold blood by the police.'

5/- cut in pay

The seeds of the Rand Revolt were sown in

Rounding up prisoners at Fordsburg. Among the dead were fiery rebel leader Percy Fisher and his lieutenant, Spendiff — they preferred suicide to capture. Their final announcement was written in blood

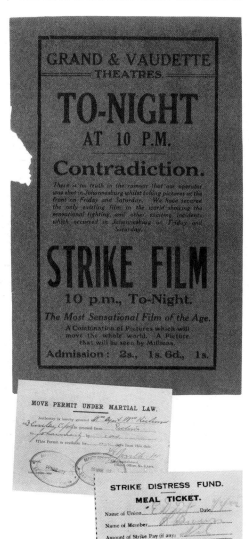

Members of a loyal burgher commando — the graffiti indicates that some were veterans of the Flanders trenches — relax outside their sandbagged headquarters. Sympathy for the 'White South Africa' cause evaporated when strikers overplayed their hand and went on a rampage of violence. Final toll: 153 killed, 534 wounded. Left: The drama was recorded on film and enthralled cinema-goers

December 1921 when coal miners were told they would have to take a five shilling cut per shift. Then the gold miners were informed that some 2 000 semi-skilled jobs held by whites were to be taken over by blacks. Black labour was very cheap, and the President of the Institute of Engineers noted in July 1921 that if 50 per cent of the whites could be replaced by blacks, the gold mines would save £1 million a year. The temptation to employ black miners at a rate of only 2/2 a day was irresistible, and the white miners knew it. Their union immediately raised the spectre of *swart gevaar* (black peril).

Early in January 1922, 22 000 miners, power station and engineering workers — under the auspices of the Augmented Executive of the South African Industrial Federation — declared themselves in favour of a strike. Fewer than 1 500 voted against. Strikers formed commandos to stop 'scab labour' (strike-breaking workers) and to thwart police action.

All this represented tough but essentially non-violent action. The real threat was hidden: among the strikers' leadership there were rabid red activists intent on a workers' revolution and the creation of a wholly 'white South Africa'. How these men managed to reconcile anti-black sentiment with Marxism remains a mystery.

The 'scab' worker was one of the prime targets of the strikers and their commandos. A shift boss at Geduld was kidnapped and badly thrashed for refusing to stop work. Three Springs miners were taken from their homes and beaten. If strikers were unable to break through police cordons to get at their victims, they turned on the homes, wrecking them and intimidating the women. A worker returned to his mine house to find it in ruins despite the valiant defence of his 16-year-old son.

At first, Johannesburg businessmen took the call for a general strike with cynical good humour. But the situation rapidly became ugly. On the morning of Tuesday, 7 March, the Vrededorp commando, led by a 'general' mounted on a white horse and shouting 'No-one is working today', marched into the city centre.

A women's commando attacked the telephone exchange and began dragging out the occupants. Wrote an observer: 'A little hello-girl first knew of something having gone amiss by a frowsy amazon biting her arm. She retaliated by hitting her over the head with a receiver.'

Other clashes were more serious. In Jeppe Street, the 300-strong Fordsburg commando, armed with sticks and revolvers, assaulted the police lines after hearing that a young striker had been bayoneted. They stoned and rushed the police and fired into the 'blue line'.

Black Friday

General Barry Hertzog, then in opposition to Smuts's South African Party government, believed that fully 90 per cent of the country was behind the strikers. Platteland commandos had been formed under the 'white South Africa' banner and were ready to join their city brethren if called upon.

But within 24 hours the strikers lost public sympathy. The leaders overplayed their hand.

Smuts's policy was one of restraint: the police, reservists and Citizen Force troops, he believed, needed no special powers to bring the 'Reds' (as they were known) to heel. Others demanded such powers. 'Without martial law to back the forces,' declared the commander of the Civic Guard, 'the strikers and hooligans have full uncontrolled liberty to intimidate and terrorise.'

Friday, 10 March 1922, proved Smuts wrong. Percy Fisher and his rebels had set up their headquarters at Market Buildings in Fordsburg. Fisher had called in the strikers the day before and pointedly asked them whether they had brought their 'music'. Rifles and pick-handles were produced. A cache of arms was opened and distributed. The scene was set.

At first light on Friday Fisher's mobs attacked mines, railway property and police stations. Butchers' shops and grocery stores were looted for supplies. Other traders in Johannesburg closed down. Almost the whole of the Reef was in the hands of the 'Reds'.

At Brakpan Mine, the manager and his officials prepared to repel invaders. Women and children were sent to safety. Lieutenant Vincent Brodigan assured his brother, the manager, that reinforcements of police would soon be along — little realising that hour by hour police posts were falling to the rebels. At 8.30 a.m., having refused to surrender, mine officials and police specials started the defence of the mine. It was an uneven struggle.

William Urquart in his book, *The Outbreak on the Witwatersrand*, described the frenzy as the revolutionaries surged into various buildings: 'Shouting and yelling, slogging with the butts of their rifles, wielding clubs and whirling lengths of chain, the Reds fell on the men at the mine with the utmost ferocity and barbarity.' The wounded were shot at point blank range: those who nursed them were clubbed or bayoneted. The survivors were those who feigned death or those who, beaten senseless, had been left for dead. The defence of Brakpan Mine cost nine lives, including that of Lieutenant Brodigan.

At 10 a.m. that Black Friday, martial law was declared.

The Battle of Fordsburg

In reality the Rand Revolt was no Bolshevik uprising — the true 'Reds' were very much in the minority. Nor could it have succeeded. Once violence was unleashed the rebels lost any support they enjoyed within the National Party and among the people. Even the platteland burghers answered the government's call.

The battle, though, was hard while it lasted. During the weekend following Black Friday the rebels managed to seize large areas of Johannesburg. Only in isolated places like Newlands, where the barracks survived a three-day siege before being relieved, did the police hold out. Citizen Force troops were badly mauled in a number of engagements. Amateurs who flocked to the government colours came ill-prepared — and paid for it. A commentator noted that it was perfectly possible for a young man to enlist as a

Strike meetings in 1907. The 9th Lancers and the Cameron Highlanders were called out to keep order. There was serious labour unrest on the Rand before the 1922 revolt — notably in 1907, 1913 and 1914

soldier and be killed within an hour.

But the forces of law and order steadily gained the upper hand. Suspected strike leaders, including some of the most respected trade unionists, were rounded up. Benoni, a rebel stronghold, was bombed by Sir Pierre van Ryneveld's fledgling South African Air Force. Finally, troops and police moved against Percy Fisher in Fordsburg.

The rebels held strong positions opposite Sacks Hotel in Central Road. Trenches had been dug, and Main Road between Mayfair and the Fordsburg Dip barricaded. A plan to bombard the Market Buildings with artillery had to be abandoned because the police garrison was being held hostage. But government units were sweeping in, clearing the trouble spots along the West Rand, and the Brixton Ridge, a strategic target, was retaken. Police and troops were now ready to strike at Fisher himself.

Leaflets were dropped by air warning women and children to evacuate Fordsburg and make for Milner Park. The Market Buildings were kept under fire, a pincer movement trapped the rebels, and a party of men made their way through backyards to a bottle-store, where they had a clear view of the rebels in the trenches.

At 2 p.m. on 14 March, the rebel headquarters surrendered. Troops found the bodies of Percy Fisher and his chief lieutenant, Spendiff. Each had apparently shot himself. The story goes that a note was found, written in blood, reading: 'March 14, 1922. I died for what I believed to be right. The Cause.'

Of the 687 people killed or wounded in the clashes, most were State forces. The final toll was 72 State forces killed and 219 wounded; 39 strikers killed and 118 wounded; 42 civilians killed and 197 wounded. Many revolutionaries were put on trial and 18 were sentenced to death. Of these only four were actually hanged; the rest had their sentences commuted. All the prisoners were released on 17 May 1924, prior to the General Election.

With time came a healing of the wounds and, among trade unionists, a more mature attitude to black labour.

The Revolt had political consequences, too. Before the first shot was fired, Tielman Roos had told the miners that their strength lay in the ballot box. In 1924 Smuts called a general election, and his South African Party lost to the Nationalists (52 to 63, with the Labour Party holding the balance). Smuts lost his seat.

THE RED FLAG — AND A CALL TO SURRENDER

South Africa was particularly strike-conscious when railway workers downed tools in January 1914. The previous year had seen arson and bloodshed in clashes between mineworkers and the authorities, and the leaders of those strikes were once again calling for a general strike. Although only one small labour union was recognised by mine owners at the time, the movement was making rapid progress among the 20 000 white and 200 000 black workers. Radical leaders from abroad inspired them with ideas of a syndicalist revolution, and *The Red Flag* was sung everywhere.

But this time the Government moved quickly. Burgher commandos under General De la Rey surrounded the Trades Hall in Johannesburg and guns were trained on the building while two officers went to the front door to demand surrender. The strike leaders complied, and nine were deported under martial law regulations. They were rushed under strong police escort to Durban, where they were quietly sneaked aboard the *Umgeni*, bound for Britain.

They were photographed by the *Illustrated London News* at Las Palmas. From the left: Mason, Livingstone, Watson, Bain, Morgan, Crawford, Waterston (he was later elected to Parliament as the Member for Brakpan), McKerrill and Poutsma (who became organising secretary for Smuts's South African Party). After the outbreak of the First World War they were all brought back to South Africa at government expense.

Years of the locust

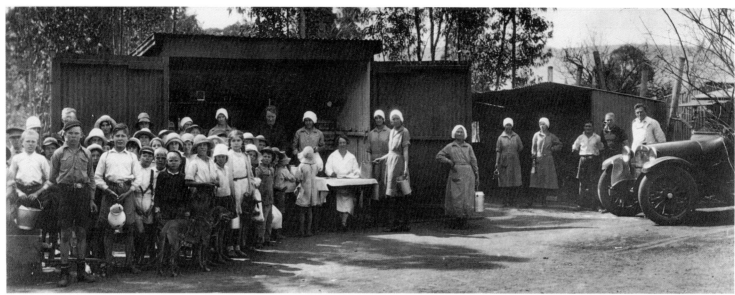

Soup kitchens fed the hungry and the desperate throughout the country as the Depression tightened its grip. People arrived with mugs, pitchers and even buckets

THE GREATEST DEPRESSION

At first, most South Africans were complacent enough. During the first months of 1929 they had read of America's booming stock-market, of crazily-rising share prices and speculation madness. They shrugged.

Came 'Black Thursday' — 24 October — and Wall Street's sensational crash: few on the southern tip of Africa were more than mildly concerned. South Africa's major newspapers pointed out that few industrialists in South Africa had investments in America, and the crash was more or less dismissed as a sad but entirely trans-Atlantic affair. On 6 December 1929, *South Africa* quoted the Prime Minister as saying that there was 'no reason to anticipate a slump'.

But the country's optimism crumbled over the next two years as the recessionary trends of the 1920s culminated in the Great Depression. There were many contributing factors to the country's economic collapse — one being the over-concentration of South Africa's economic resources in mining and agriculture. And there was yet another drought. The unemployed made their pathetic appearance on the street corners of Johannesburg and other cities. Almost unbelievably, hitherto stable families faced starvation: men openly begged for food.

Nearly every industry felt the effects, and many gave in under the strain. Maize exports earned only £523 000 in 1931, compared to £3,520 000 in 1925. Wages also dropped rapidly. In 1920 a typesetter earned £8.8s. a week: in 1933 he earned only £6.3s. Carpenters and plumbers were paid 3/7½ an hour in 1920, but in 1933 this had fallen to 2/8 an hour. Yet for those who remained in employment, the worst year of the Depression saw a rise in *real* wages: although a worker's income dropped, prices dropped even more.

Officialdom stayed cool, though. Indeed, the Minister of Labour, Colonel Frederic Creswell, assured Parliament in 1932 that in South Africa the unemployment rate was lower than in other nations. Like most of his countrymen, he ignored the vast pool of black jobless. It was assumed by white politicians of all parties that blacks displaced from the labour market could be absorbed into peasant agriculture in the reserves with very little hardship.

As the number of unemployed rose, volunteers opened soup kitchens and distributed food parcels. At labour bureaux there were complaints that some men registered only to get food handouts. Cape Town sent a plea to the nation's jobseekers to keep away from the city as it had enough workless of its own, and soup kitchens were closed to those living beyond city limits. There was no choice.

Life on the dole

In June 1931, a newspaperman joined soup queues in Cape Town and visited unemployed at home. His report spoke of horror and degradation. 'In many cases as many as 30 people were herded together in one small house,' he wrote. Children with running sores on faces and hands were a common sight.

'In hovels where one would hesitate to keep a pet animal, whole families carried on the business of living under conditions of absolute misery. These holes in the wall consist of one or two rooms, and a so-called kitchen. In many cases the kitchen is a corner of the room in which a paraffin stove, mounted on a soap box, smothers the wall behind with a coating

In 1932 everyone needed a job — any job. Wives, mothers and grandmothers knitted and sewed for a few extra pennies

HOW TO LIVE ON A SHILLING A DAY

In July 1932 a South African housewife described to *Outspan* readers how she went about feeding her family during the harsh years of the Depression. 'Having had a husband without a regular billet for eighteen months, and having a large family to feed and bring up under these conditions, I am much interested in an article in a daily paper on "How to Live on a Shilling a Day".'

The writer said she had been faced with having to provide meals from the contents of her pantry for two or three weeks at a time, with no money coming in and little likelihood of opening accounts with tradespeople. 'I have always tried to keep up my little stock of such things as beans, rice, flour, tea, potatoes, onions etc, the usual things used in any house, and fortunately we always have milk, so I had a little stock to go on.'

When faced with 'rockbottom living' one had to make one's own bread, she said, and if one could afford it the best plan was to send to a mill for a hundred pound bag of boer-meal, which would cost about 12/6. 'While that lasts, and it lasts for some time, you will always at least have your bread, and mealie-meal porridge is a very satisfying stand-by for the times when the larder is otherwise empty.'

The writer recommended dried beans as a valuable food and as a substitute for meat.

	Sunday	Monday	Tuesday	Wednesday	Thursday	Friday	Saturday
LUNCH	Beans and bacon, or fried fish, bread pudding	Bean soup, bread, fruit and custard	Macaroni cheese or vegetables and cheese, bread and butter, tea	Curried beans with rice (unpolished), sweet potatoes	Panaggelty and simmered vegetable or fish and potatoes	Pea-soup and toasted bread, boiled rice pudding	Fish cakes or bean soup
SUPPER	Bread and butter, scone, tea, salad	Simmered vegetable with bread and butter or toast, tea	Vegetable soup with bread or whole-meal scones, fruit and custard	Tomatoes on toast or simmered vegetable and toast, tea	Fish soup, scone and tea, or porridge	Savoury porridge, fruit and custard	Bean soup or simmered vegetables

A sample week's menu provided by an Outspan *reader. Her 'meatless menu' did not make allowance for breakfast, she wrote, 'as we always have rusks'. Vegetables were included for most days' menus*

Men worked on roads, dug ditches and did just about anything to keep their families alive

of greasy soot. On heaps of sacks, old clothing and piles of other people's washing, three or four children are put to sleep.'

Another reporter wrote: 'After midnight is the time to see them. When the streets are deserted except for the cleaning gangs, these pariahs prowl the gutters in search of offal that the very dogs disdain.'

Sentenced to work

Government — national, provincial and local — did what little it could to help, or at least to control, the situation. Under the Work Colonies Act anyone who habitually begged or made his children beg to support the family could, if physically able to work, be sent to a colony for at least a year. His wife would not be forced to join him, but if she elected to do so, she and her children could then leave only by permission of the Minister of Labour. These 'forced labour camps' barely got off the ground. One pleasant work colony, boasting 200 asbestos huts, was built amid the pines of Nuweberg near Elgin in the Cape, but only 17 families were sent there in the year before the Minister of Labour closed it down. It had cost £26 000. The *Cape Times* called it a 'Won't-work colony'.

Jobs were specially created: there were roads to be dug, railway lines to be relaid, buildings and sites to be watched by night. One of the greatest projects, which was to bear fruit only 40 years later, was the reclamation of land on Cape Town's foreshore. The South African Railways did what it could by absorbing thousands of unemployed. In 1924 the Railways employed 4 760 white labourers, and by 1929 this figure had climbed to 16 248.

The Depression in South Africa reached its depth in 1932, when 188 000 whites alone registered for work at labour bureaux. Some registrations were duplicated, but the staggering toll the crisis had taken could not be disguised despite the soothing noises that emanated from Parliament. Of 45 000 handymen and unskilled workers who had registered, a mere 500 were given jobs.

As late as 1937, when drought had devastated large areas of South Africa, 25 000 men were still on poor relief or subsidised work.

Off gold

South Africa weathered the Depression better than most other Western countries. Even so, with no money coming in, both the diamond and wool industries were threatened, and Sir Ernest Oppenheimer warned that many diamond mines would collapse. The shining hope was gold.

In September 1931, Britain came off the gold standard, and Leader of the Opposition, Jan Smuts, wired South Africa's Parliament to follow suit. Nicolaas Havenga, Minister of Finance, refused. So did Prime Minister Barry Hertzog. Then Tielman Roos, a veteran politician and Judge of Appeal, resigned in order to campaign against Hertzog's refusal. In less than a week Hertzog capitulated. Gold that had been worth £4 an ounce went to £7; mines about to close now worked the ore they had thought useless. South Africa slowly returned, if not to prosperity, then to normality.

Year of the Great Thirst Trek

AND THE WHEELS CLANKED ON IN VAIN

On 20 September 1933, South Africans prayed. Government offices and businesses closed, shops put up their shutters, court cases were suspended and churches of every denomination were filled to 'beseech Almighty God with the greatest possible unanimity to give relief from distress'.

The distress was the Great Drought. There had been other 'great droughts' — in 1864, 1903, 1916. But this year it had become not merely a drought; it was *the* drought. In parts of the north-western Cape and the Orange Free State there had been no rain for five years. Vleis and dams held only sun-baked clay, and borehole waterwheels clanked on in vain. The *Cape Times* reported in October 1933: 'The Orange Free State is a barren sandy desert. It is impossible to plough. The blade turns over a sliding sandy mass which is blown away and levelled out in the first wind.'

Driven by fear — and hope

Farmers, using their families as drovers, took to the roads with their herds, seeking more fertile pastures. Trek farming had been part of the pastoral scene for over a hundred years, but this was something tragically new. The railways offered preferential rates for the carrying of stock to what were hopefully better grazing areas, and farmers were obliged to keep a servitude of up to 400 metres either side of the road for herds to roam along. Unlike their forebears, these Boers came in cars, Cape carts, even bicycles.

The cars, like the ox wagons of yesteryear, became their homes, and when their luck finally ran out, their vehicles were sold — usually for a few pounds.

These latter-day trekkers were at first scorned by the more established farmers. 'Trekking,' complained one old-timer, 'is caused through fear . . . and the hope of finding grazing on overstocked farms. So the farmers trek, and become a menace and positive nuisance to prudent and under-stocked farmers. The end is that the wise farmer goes down as well as the maniac and so all become poor whites. They all have to die, be rehabilitated or become spoon-fed babies, living upon the government.'

In the countryside, animals without water, without food, abandoned by farmers who had lost all hope and faith, stood waiting to die. Around them lay carcasses, swollen and decaying in the harsh sunlight. Some landowners stayed, sustained by slowly dwindling boreholes, sitting on their stoeps, counting their losses, knowing the next day would bring more. A government official declared that one farm he had visited some months earlier had once accommodated 2 500 sheep; now it had only 1 000 and the numbers were rapidly decreasing.

A glance at the sky would occasionally bring a sight of clouds. 'They look promising,' said one farmer, 'but the wind will change and nothing will happen. I've watched it for years, and I know.'

Over-grazing and other poor farming habits frequently ruined large tracts of otherwise valuable land. Flash floods carved deep dongas in clumsily-ploughed soil before scientific methods succeeded in halting the erosion. Although much of the damage has since been put right, some of the land will probably be lost to farmers forever

Skins for cold shoulders

Typical were the great stock-farming areas of Gordonia and Kenhardt in the north-western Cape where, during the three years of drought, losses were put at 40 per cent. Slaughter animals were in too poor a condition to find a ready market and, because of the Depression, there were few buyers. Promising pastures at Kakamas and Upington were beyond reach. Most farms were hundreds of kilometres from railheads and the animals were too weak to move.

For those hardy enough to trek there was the almost certain prospect of finding new grazing lands already overstocked. By the end of June 1933, sheep by the truckload were arriving at the station in Matjiesfontein. In one fortnight 55 000 animals were offloaded and another 161 truckloads were due within three days. Police were called in to sort out the chaos and some 5 000 sheep were pulled dead from the rolling-stock. Luckless farmers sold sheepskins for 1/3 apiece. Others bartered them for food — or draped them over their shoulders against the bitter cold.

The Free State, once the finest grazing country in the Union, had become a sandy, wind-swept wilderness. The abundance of game had disappeared. Barely a blade of grass could be seen anywhere. Gaunt cattle wandered in search of the scrubby bush which was all they could find to eat. One farmer graphically illustrated his plight by holding up the stem of a dessert spoon. 'There's not that much water in the Orange River,' he said.

Many animals were too thin to be worth slaughtering; farmers and their families were reduced to living on mealiepap and government handouts. Cows produced no milk, vegetable gardens burned up. People faced starvation.

Newcastle, which had long been a host to trek farmers, hesitated to ask the authorities to declare the area drought-stricken in case it injured the town's credit. Johannesburg faced water restrictions after the Vaal stopped flowing at Engelbrechtdrift. Ladysmith, Natal, was put on a week's notice of disaster on 9 October. The Natal Steam Collieries faced a shut-down for lack of water.

Prayer — and rain

In 1933 wool brokers put losses of merino sheep at between eight and ten million. A fifth

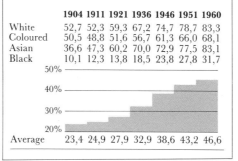

THE MOVE TO THE CITY

A drift from rural areas to cities and towns began to speed up in the last decade of the 19th century. By 1904 the white urban population was 590 926 — 53 per cent of the total. By 1931 the figure had climbed to 61 per cent. Blacks were also leaving farms in increasing numbers for better wages on the gold and diamond mines. This table shows the growing migration of all race groups to urban areas since 1904.

	1904	1911	1921	1936	1946	1951	1960
White	52,7	52,3	59,3	67,2	74,7	78,7	83,3
Coloured	50,5	48,8	51,6	56,7	61,3	66,0	68,1
Asian	36,6	47,3	60,2	70,0	72,9	77,5	83,1
Black	10,1	12,3	13,8	18,5	23,8	27,8	31,7
Average	23,4	24,9	27,9	32,9	38,6	43,2	46,6

---

of the sheep population was lost; 7 500 000 more in the Free State alone seemed doomed.

So at the end of September that year, Prime Minister Barry Hertzog summoned the people of the Union to turn to God, confess their sins and humbly pray for His help. 'The chastening hand of the Lord' was on South Africa.

Some reverend gentlemen thundered that drought was not an Act of God; others produced Biblical evidence that it was. They saw the drought as divine retribution for the exploitation of the land by man.

The prayers over, the nation waited.

Before the end of October, weathermen were reporting an expected change. A few days later news of 'welcome showers' came from the Free State. Throughout October and the following month, in that terminology used only in a country that measures its rainfall with gratitude, 'good', 'splendid' and 'beautiful' rains were reported. Home-going office workers in Pretoria stared in wonder at a downpour. Gutters, bone-dry for months, gushed and waves washed through shop doorways.

In the country, families ran laughing into the veld. Some fell to their knees praying that this wasn't just a freak thunderstorm. As rivers burst their banks, people gathered along them, watching in fascination as the water came down in three-metre-high torrents. The sight of Hartebeespoort Dam brought holiday-like hordes of motorists. Farmers who had quit their land, and were on relief work, deserted their jobs to return to homesteads they had left two or more years before.

Happy New Year

What the Great Drought proved to thousands of farmers was that trekking could no longer sustain their flocks. Vast areas of the Transvaal and Free State were turned over to crops. Sheep disappeared from areas once rich in wool production. It was reckoned that 10 million sheep were lost in the Great Drought; they were never to be replaced.

Rinderpest, the highly contagious and usually fatal disease of cattle, invaded South Africa in 1896. It spread over the entire country and killed an estimated 2½ million head of cattle before being halted through the use of an immunising agent produced from the bile of animals which had died of the disease. Strict controls were instituted in an attempt to prevent the spread of rinderpest and huge areas were quarantined

Boers on trek in the Transvaal. Destitute families abandoned their drought-stricken farms and packed their few remaining possessions into wagons

A sheep and ostrich farm in the Karoo at the turn of the century. Farmers were hard put to keep their stock alive in the dry wastes they called their lands, and sometimes they abandoned the uneven fight

LIFE ON THE LAND IN THE 1930s

In 1936, 33% of the whites of South Africa lived in rural areas; most of them were Afrikaners. Following the Depression and the Great Drought, thousands of them were reduced to poverty, and once-prosperous farms lay barren, desert-like, their cattle slaughtered.

Yet, says writer W.A. de Klerk, the Afrikaner people had an amazing resilience: many farmers started all over again.

Though as a boy De Klerk was one of the first Afrikaners to have his education at an Afrikaans school in the city, he remembers the longed-for visits to the farms of his relatives.

His step-mother had a large farm at Fort Beaufort in the Eastern Cape. 'The pattern of life,' he says, 'had not changed for centuries.' The farm was prosperous, bringing in an income of some £2 000 a year. Even so, housekeeping was economical. Like most farmers' wives, step-mother made most of her own clothes. On visits to town she would look over the stocks of material the general trader kept for her and other farming families. Even the men's trousers and jackets would be handmade.

The servants and labourers were part of the family. Often they would join the farmer, his wife and children at tea time to talk over the day's problems, how the work had gone, what new stock and seeds to buy.

On Sundays, the farmer would make sure his labourers and servants attended church.

Specially-designed trapbalies *were still being used to crush grapes in the 1930s. J.P. Duminy recalled in his autobiography: '. . . I often wondered how hygienic this old-fashioned, even bible-blessed operation really was, although I had seen them giving their feet a good scrubbing before they climbed into the tub! But any wavering doubts were soon forgotten when the precious product of their labours appeared a few days later as the delicious* mos' *(must, or unfermented grape juice)*

He took the same paternal interest in their children: on many of the farms De Klerk visited during his youth, schools had been built and a teacher imported. This is still the case today.

The farm of De Klerk's step-mother was considered wealthy; others he visited were a lot less so. The average income of a landowner in the district would be about £300 a year. Still, even that was munificent when compared with the £25 or so eked out by many *bywoners*, or the trek boers.

THE END OF A LONG, LONG ROAD

Drought, soil erosion, rinderpest, locusts and abject poverty were adversaries many early farmers found impossible to resist. In 1933, two farmers trekked 225 kilometres from Kenhardt to Carnarvon, hoping the stories of fertile grazing were true. Of the 3 000 sheep they had started with some months before, there were only 60 left when they reached Carnarvon. At nightfall, they drew up at a homestead and asked if they might water the remains of their flock. In the even voice of those who live in great desolation, the homesteaders explained their water was finished. All they had left were a few litres for their own needs. 'The two farmers went out,' reported a newspaper, 'and stood looking for a moment at the heaving flanks of their parched sheep. One went and with his hunting knife scientifically slit the throats of the sheep before taking his own life.' The other farmer poisoned himself.

The money-makers

CONJURING UP A FORTUNE

In September 1872, a Signor Barnato (his real name was Harry Isaacs) burst upon New Rush (later to evolve into Kimberley), billed as 'The Greatest Wizard'. He performed conjuring tricks at the iron hut grandly known as the Mutual Hall, and in the next year was joined by his brother Barney (Barnett Isaacs). Barney had arrived in Cape Town with about £30 in cash and 40 boxes of extremely bad cigars with which he intended to start a business at the diggings. Harry had started diamond buying as a sideline, and the junior Barnato followed in his footsteps, going into partnership with one Lou Cohen. Their office consisted of a tin shack, in which they worked by day and slept by night — on the bare floor.

Barney later broke off with Cohen to join Harry, and the two brothers soon became claim owners. By 1878 their holdings were raising £1 800 a week. Barney, too, was exploiting his doubtful Thespian talents (though now in legitimate theatre) with some enthusiasm, but the boisterous audiences were too much for his volatile temperament. In *The Diamond Magnates*, Brian Roberts describes one of his most memorable performances at a special benefit — when, as Othello, he made a dramatic entrace looking, as one observer put it, 'more like an Ethiopian minstrel on the Margate Sands than Shakespeare's Heroic Moor', and convulsed the crowd. The line 'Unhappy that I am black' was greeted with a shout of 'Then go and wash your face'. Incensed, Barney forged over to the footlights and berated the audience. Later, he lay in wait for the man whom he imagined to be the ringleader, and beat him up.

Digger's tools . . . and a Greek lexicon

Cecil Rhodes, the fifth son of a Hertfordshire parson, sailed for South Africa in mid-1870 to join his brother, Herbert, who was growing cotton on an 80-hectare estate near Pietermaritzburg. Herbert Rhodes, a keen explorer, made frequent trips into the interior. One of these took him north to the Vaal river diggings, and with the news of the finds at New Rush, Cecil decided to join him. His

Cecil John Rhodes, the vicar's son who had a country named after him. He was only 49 when he died

'Sammy' Marks arrived in 1868. He created an industrial empire, and was a friend of President Kruger

Beit was an unassuming man — and clever. He amassed a larger fortune than any of the other early magnates

Newspaper readers were introduced to the rotund Hoggenheimer, a figure symbolising Rand capitalism and its influence in politics. Cartoonist Daniël Boonzaier borrowed the name from an operetta, The Girl from Kay's

Barney Barnato with his wife and children in 1897, the year he leapt overboard and drowned during a voyage to Britain

J.B. (later Sir Joseph) Robinson arrived at the Witwatersrand goldfields in the 1880s

Sir Abe Bailey and Lady Bailey. He was reputed to have won and lost three fortunes in his lifetime

Colourful Solly Joel (Barney Barnato's nephew) was imprisoned for his role in the Jameson Raid

Harry Openheimer, left, and Anton Rupert: two of South Africa's richest, most influential industrialists

Jan Marais revolutionised South African banking when he founded the Trust Bank of Africa in 1954

luggage comprised digger's tools, volumes of the classics and a Greek lexicon — he was determined to complete his education by going to Oxford. Herbert was soon disenchanted and sold his properties to Cecil, moving on to the Transvaal. In 1879 he was burnt to death in Nyasaland (now Malawi) when a keg of rum exploded and caught fire in his hut.

The young Cecil Rhodes worked the claims energetically — wielding a pick himself when necessary — and studied in every spare minute. By the time Rhodes was 28, he and his partner, Charles Rudd, had formed the De Beers Mining Company, with an authorised capital of £200 000. By now the Barnatos had also leapt upon the corporate bandwagon. The *Independent* reported on 10 March 1881 that 'Messrs Barnato Brothers have started four Mining Companies within the last fortnight. The total capital subscribed was considerably over half-a-million and covered the amount asked for many times over. The shares for all four companies are at a premium . . .'

The brilliance of Beit

Alfred Beit had arrived in South Africa in 1875, sent by the Lipperts, a firm of gem importers who had employed him in Amsterdam. Quiet, shrewd, watchful, he soon perceived the pickings to be made in Kimberley.

Beit's expertise stood him in sterling stead. He offered high prices for diamonds where appropriate, and swiftly built up a healthy clientele. Before long he had severed his connection with the Lipperts and was branching out on his own. He also ventured into real estate — one property which he bought very cheaply and upon which he erected a dozen shanty offices, sold a few years later for £260 000. Once his diamond business was well under way, he set about acquiring interests in Kimberley Mine. Rhodes, always quick to spot potential, began to cultivate Beit, realising that his brilliant business acumen and integrity would make him an invaluable ally.

The big fight

The last 20 years of the 19th century were turbulent for the diamond barons. Fluctuations on the market, flooded claims, landfalls, erratic machinery, riots and strikes were problem enough, but all these paled beside the red-hot question of amalgamation of the big mining interests (which everyone in his heart knew was inevitable and desirable) and the consequent ferocious in-fighting which took place between Barnato, Rhodes and, to a lesser degree, Robinson, for control of the industry.

Barney put up a spectacular fight and might have emerged as victor had it not been for Beit's recruitment of the largest financial house in Europe, Rothschilds, to Rhodes's cause. Despite the fact that Rhodes (or so the story goes) none too tactfully told Lord Rothschild that the only man he feared in South Africa was 'a cunning little Jew called Barnato', Rothschild came to his aid.

In the main, though, Rhodes and Barnato sustained a somewhat uneasy camaraderie. Roberts relates how Rhodes invited Barnato

to the exclusive Kimberley Club, saying: 'I propose to make a gentleman of you.' (Later, with Rhodes's backing, he was accepted as a member.) Rhodes won the battle for control: the resultant amalgamated concern, called De Beers Consolidated Mines, was incorporated in March 1888 with a capital of £100 000 in £5 shares, and Barnato was made one of the four life governors.

South Africa's mineral treasure-house provided rich pickings for anyone with a capacity for hard work and a fair share of luck. When Joseph Benjamin (J.B.) Robinson reached the Witwatersrand in 1886, he toured the diggings and, as Roberts relates, placed a few samples in his pith helmet. '"I . . . panned it in a stream of water," he was to say later. "The moment I saw the gold in the dish and could see the reef running in the way it did, I decided that a grand discovery had been made."'

He bought his first property, which transpired to be the very core of the goldfields, for £6 000, and his investments on the Rand were to make him a multi-millionaire.

Portrait of a magnate. Artist Terence Cuneo paints Sir Ernest Oppenheimer at work. Oppenheimer was 16 when he joined a London diamond firm at a wage of £1 a week. He went to Kimberley, centre of the diamond industry, and began to work — hard. He founded the Anglo American Corporation in 1917, and was instrumental in saving the diamond industry in 1929 when the market was flooded and falling prices threatened to shut down many mines

Before the supermarkets

DOOR-TO-DOOR DELIVERY IN TOWN AND VELD

In the days before supermarkets, shopping was a pleasant, leisurely and personal affair. Cities like Cape Town and Johannesburg boasted the huge emporiums of Stuttafords, Ansteys, Garlicks and John Orrs, but until the advent of the first supermarkets in the 1950s most housewives did their daily shopping at the numerous small suburban shops.

In 1905 grocers started their own journal, the *South African Grocers' Record and General Dealers' Gazette*. This magazine, and others which followed, offered the small dealer advice on the various aspects of their business. 'Greet every customer as soon as she or he enters the shop,' it cautioned. 'If you cannot wait on her or him at once, at least find out if possible (in a diplomatic way) what they want, so as not to keep them waiting needlessly. This is always appreciated.' The habits of travelling salesmen also came under scrutiny: 'A Hamburg commercial traveller was arrested on the charge of assault, because when they declined to give him orders for his goods, he soundly boxed the ears of seven different shopkeepers upon whom he had called with his samples.'

For at least the first quarter of this century much of South Africa's food and most other consumer goods were imported, so journals such as the *Commercial Review and South African Storekeeper* kept traders informed on the latest trends overseas and also listed the ships (and their cargoes) which had docked at South African ports.

Traders in the veld

Albert Jackson, describing his years as a country trader, tells how Paris fashion plates gave way to 'Dutch' and 'German' *blaudruck* print, check gingham, *kapje sis* (a light cotton material) for the traditional bonnet, brown and white linen (Horrockses preferred), nainsook (for underwear), *swart merino* or sateen (black dress material), silk ribbons and woollen stockings.

Black crêpe was always in stock for the occasions of mourning which, with large families the norm, tended to be frequent. Men wore it around their large felt hats and on the sleeves of their shirts.

In town, or on *plaas*, the question of the proper dress following the death of relatives and friends was taken very seriously, bringing profit to the drapery trade. 'Widow's costumes,' Stuttafords noted, 'range in price from 3½ to 4 guineas' and they could be trimmed with light to heavy crêpe from 4½ to 5 guineas. The customary mourning materials were nun's veiling, cashmere and crêpe cloths. Children's mourning costumes were a speciality.

The highlight of the week for many country folk was the visit to their local store. Among other things the rural shop catered for the farmer's sweet tooth with *lekkergoed*. Colonial Mixture came in cheapest at 3d to 4d a pound, Dutch Mottoes (peppermint) were 5d a pound, sugarsticks 6d. These sugarsticks were the original 'penny openers' with which car drivers bribed 'piccanins' to open the many gates across the roads. Much favoured was English Mixture, including Callard & Bowser's butterscotch at 6d a pound. Chocolate was not as popular as it is today.

'It was quite permissible,' recalled Albert Jackson, 'for our customers to step behind the counter and dip into the boxes of sweets — free, gratis and for nothing.'

Dealers on wheels

Competing with the traders were the *smouse* — hawkers or travelling salesmen, many of whom were Jewish immigrants. The *vrugte-smouse* would load up at the last main town before heading into the veld.

They were virtually travelling general dealers, carrying a huge range of items, including a variety of fruit: dried peaches, apricots, pears, apple rings, raisins, sultanas, mebos, buchu (a herb), and even dagga, which farmers would dispense to their servants and labourers.

And, of course, rooibos tea, which was gaining great popularity in the years before the First World War. It was bought both for drinking pleasure and as a health cure. A 75 lb bag sold for between 2d and 4d a pound.

Describing the working life of a *smous*,

R.M. Masters' store in East London in 1904. In those days carrying the shopping home was considered beneath the dignity of most white women. Before the advent of the motor truck, weekly groceries were delivered in a horse-drawn cart, and for the smaller orders the grocers used delivery boys on bicycles. Below: an early delivery van — slow but reliable

THE ROMANCE OF BUYING BY MAIL

Early South African catalogues displayed an incredibly wide range of goods. The artwork was superb and the text cleverly worded. They tended to stress the elegant rather than the practical, and customers were often disillusioned on discovering that the lavishly-illustrated items in the booklets were available from local merchants at a low price. But the romance of mail-order purchase could not be denied, and for many years this form of marketing was the most exciting and, for many, the most convenient way of buying what one needed.

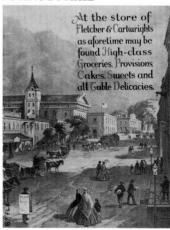

Above: Fletcher and Cartwrights' catalogue stressed elegance and good taste; left: turn-of-the-century head-wear from Stuttafords; below: Spracklens was a leading South African mail-order firm for decades

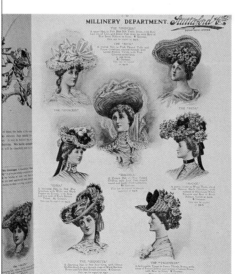

Laver's Store in Middelburg: the kind of friendly, personalised service that the supermarkets eroded in the 1950s. But for many people, self-service was long overdue

Jackson wrote of these nomadic tradesmen:

'At each farm he unpacked, displayed his wares in front of the homestead — usually on the stoep — did his business, collected his sheep, which travelled with him until he reached his destination, where he disposed of the livestock and in due course started *de novo.*'

Smous living expenses were practically nothing because they slept in their carts and were usually entertained generously by farmers. Some would sell their ox wagons to farmers once they had disposed of their products and produce, buy a little donkey cart and drive back home, herding along the goats and sheep given in payment for their wares.

Buying by catalogue

Early in the century, rural stores tended to stock a narrow range, so many platteland folk did their shopping by post. Stuttafords' catalogue brought to the veld 'a complete Kodak on a small scale. Not a plaything. For pictures 2″ x 1½″. Size of camera 2⅜″ by 3⅞″. Weight loaded with 12 pictures, 7 ounces.' The price, with a film, was £2.

Spectacles were a popular mail-order line. Country customers were able to have their orders made up from prescriptions: 'Persons residing at distance are requested, in order to facilitate the despatch of orders, to send a pair previously used with instructions as to requirements and to state age, or if wanted convex for reading or distance, with any other information they possess.'

Other favourites were bicycles, including the Premier Cycle 'as ridden by His Royal Highness, the Prince of Wales', and the primus stove: 'You can fry, cook or boil three dishes at a time quicker than on a coal fire, on a Primus cooking range,' the catalogue declared.

A Doornfontein butcher's shop in 1906. There was no separate cold room — the carcasses were hung around the walls and customers selected their meat from a wide range. The average price of beef then was 9d for 0,4 kg

Cash-and-carry revolution

EVERYTHING AT THE O.K. IS OK

'The greatest event in shopping history' happened, if the claims of the advertisers could be believed, on Saturday, 25 June 1927 when, at 9 a.m., the doors of Sam Cohen and Michael Miller's store in Johannesburg's Eloff Street were opened for the first time. The razzmatazz and the accompanying tea-room jazz set the celebratory mood — a mood not shared by traditional shopkeepers who thought the partners had broken the rules by opening up on the wrong side of Eloff Street and south of Pritchard Street, the lower limits of the fashionable shopping district.

But it was these very trading conventions that Cohen and Miller challenged when they set up the O.K.

Goods fell into three price categories — 3d, 6d and 1/-. Threepenny lines included large glass tumblers, records and large jelly moulds. At sixpence you could get white and gold china cups and saucers, Eau de Cologne and violet toilet soap in boxes of three, enamel soup ladles and fish slices, ribbed ladies' vests. A shilling would buy white damask tablecloths, glass decanters, Wedgwood cups and saucers, electro-plated butter dishes, children's nursery overalls, coloured rubber aprons, liberty bodices, ladies' and children's handbags, leather motor gloves, galvanised buckets and cork bath mats.

From the outset, the O.K. policy was not, like the other bazaars that had sprung up in twentieth century South African cities, to sell cheap goods, but to sell goods cheaply. Eye-catching window and floor displays and a well thought-out advertising campaign lifted the O.K. from the plate glass and mahogany image of their more conservative rivals. The aim was cash and a quick turnover.

The first day lived up to expectation. With police patrolling the crowd that overflowed from pavement into street, bringing traffic to a standstill, shoppers cleared the counters of £1 250 worth of goods. By the first Wednes-

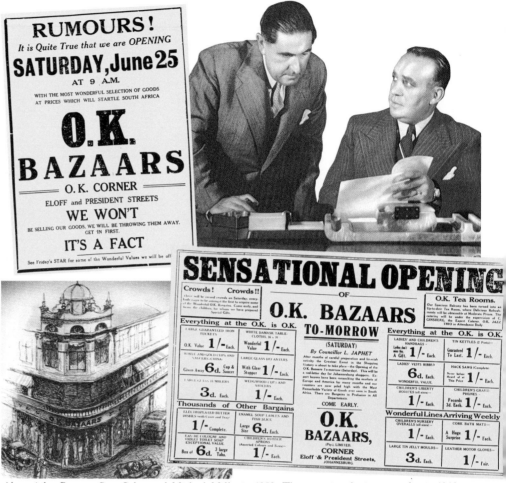

Above right: Partners Sam Cohen and Michael Miller in 1952. They went into business together in 1918, combining their talents in a first venture called United Commercial Enterprises. Bottom left: This first O.K. Bazaars occupied part of the old Store Brothers building in central Johannesburg

day, £4 000 had been topped. Cohen sent his partner, Miller, who was buying in Europe on a cautious £10 000 budget, a cable that simply stated: 'Buy like hell'.

Miller and Cohen had become partners in 1918 as wholesale agents feeding the burgeoning platteland trade, their grandly-named United Commercial Agencies operating from a £10-a-month showroom. Having expanded into importing, the partners could see the advantages of owning a store as well as a wholesaling business: they could be their own profit-taking middle-men and they could cut prices. They could also eliminate the expensive, time-consuming process of billing and debt-collecting.

THE STARS PREDICT

Charles and Samuel Chudleigh opened their first shop in Queenstown in 1881 and nine years later moved to Johannesburg. In 1913, their famous store opened. Two decades later, after Charles' death, Samuel decided to sell. In *The Johannesburg Saga* J.R. Shorten describes how Michael Miller and Sam Cohen met him in his glass-cage office in the store. Chudleigh's first questions were curious: 'Where and when were you born, and how many children have you?'

Then, excusing himself, he departed to work out their horoscopes. Returning, he told Miller: 'You are a good and honest businessman because you are a January man and so am I.' Then in a stage whisper: 'But be careful of Smulian [the O.K.'s lawyer]. He is an August man. Watch out!'

The O.K. Bazaars bought Chudleigh's but Smulian proved a worthy lawyer.

Fichardt Ltd, a well-known deparment store in Bloemfontein. It now belongs to the Greatermans group

MARKET, SUPERMARKET, HYPERMARKET...

In 1967 a man named Raymond Ackerman spent about R500 000 on four shops in Cape Town's southern suburbs. He was determined to build a retail giant. A year later he applied to the Johannesburg Stock Exchange for a public listing, and by 1969 he had expanded the group by another five stores.

Drastic price-cutting and revolutionary trading methods were paying dividends, and by 1980 the Pick 'n Pay group's 56 stores were producing an annual turnover of R750 million. Not content with supermarkets, Ackerman went to France to study the hypermarket, with its greater variety of merchandise. Manufacturers and developers were initially reluctant backers, believing that people were unlikely to patronise a shopping complex outside a town.

In March 1975 the first Hypermarket opened at Boksburg, in the Transvaal. Within a few days the turnover was approaching the one million rand mark. Several of these huge stores were built, and it was only then that the other large chains, O.K. Bazaars and Checkers, followed Ackerman's lead with their Hyperamas and Multimarkets.

The growth of Pick 'n Pay:

	1967	1980
Selling area	8 000 m²	108 000 m²
Number of stores	4	56
People employed	130	11 000
Annual turnover	R5 million	R750 million
Wages and welfare	R240 000	R31,8 million
Number of trolleys	300	28 000 approx.
Number of tills	36	1 500 approx.

Above: One of the first Pick 'n Pay shops bought by Raymond Ackerman in 1967. Left: A special report in June 1980. Bottom: The Durban Hypermarket, opened in 1978

The opportunity came when the well-known retailers, Store Brothers, closed down. Many shops which had boomed during the diamond and gold rush days had failed to keep pace with commercial trends, and Cohen and Miller took over premises on the corner of Eloff and President streets. The striking novelty of the store was the island counter on which goods would be displayed.

Advertising was both bountiful and brash, but the O.K. had a far more powerful pusher of their products and sales methods — the women of Johannesburg. What was happening in Eloff Street was passed by word of mouth, and the tills jingled with tickeys, sixpences and shillings.

The original trio of price tags were quickly dropped when Cohen and Miller realised they could carry virtually every article the thrifty housewife demanded — at a bargain price.

The O.K. had opened just as the world was heading for the greatest financial crash in history. In his book, *The Johannesburg Saga*, J.R. Shorten tells how their competitors complained that 'Cohen and Miller don't seem to know that we're having a depression ...' Having launched the company in 1927 with a capital of £10 000, they managed to sail through with an annual salary bill of £57 000 in 1931, the height of the Depression, without faltering.

By 1931 there were stores in eight South African centres. Expanding in Johannesburg itself, the O.K. bought out Chudleigh's store, a sober emporium in the Victorian style. Miller and Cohen paid £400 000 for it and immediately transformed the mahogany counters into the now-familiar glass compartments filled with price-tagged merchandise.

NOT A SINGLE BILL

In 1902 a Lithuanian immigrant named Harry Herber arrived in South Africa to begin work in his uncle's store at Pretoria West. His younger brother, Somah, joined him 17 years later, and the two opened a small shop in Jeppe.

Then, in September 1927, they opened the first Greatermans store in Brakpan. They had a capital of R570 and a staff of six.

Herber had one boast: 'Never have we sent out one single bill. NEVER have any of our customers split the air with loud BILL-ious bellows. Families who trade with Greatermans speak in civil, affable tones to each other on the first day of any month as on a holiday and the good reason is: NO ONE IS IN DEBT AT GREATERMANS. They are happy from sheer debtlessness.'

Herber had originally called the business Cheapermans. Then he tried Supermans; then Biggermans; then Brightermans, until Greatermans stuck. When the group opened their prestige branch in Cape Town's Cavendish Square in 1974, early advertisements that had asked shoppers 'to consider our strictly cash record' were long forgotten. Sales staff and placards urged shoppers to open six-month accounts.

Above: Greatermans' first store opens in Brakpan in 1927. Right: The store featured 5/-bargains (shirts, jerseys, blankets and tablecloths were among the special offers). Far right: An intriguing stockings promotion

Running the household

GIVING A MAN CREDIT

In a small store in the platteland in the 1950s, a young couple negotiated the purchase of a stove. New government legislation insisted the shopkeeper display his terms — the deposit to be paid 'and only 37s.6d. a week'. The couple agreed to the salesman's terms, paid the deposit and said they would pay each month. The agreement was waved at them to sign. 'Sign?' queried the customer. 'Whatever for? I've said I will pay and when I will pay and that is sufficient.' Credit, to many South Africans, involved merely trust between seller and buyer.

This was one of the reasons why the hire purchase revolution arrived in the Union at least a quarter of a century after it had swept Europe and America. No one would dare ask a farmer to sign a hire purchase agreement because this would be a clear and insulting gesture of distrust.

But whether under written or unwritten

A between-wars shop advertises its hire purchase service. Formal hire purchase (as opposed to credit-on-trust) came late to South Africa. Legally controlled in 1942, it really caught on in the 1950s

agreement, South Africans have always enjoyed easy credit — and it has enabled them to live well beyond their means over the decades.

Eighty per cent of cars were sold on terms before the Second World War. In post-war South Africa there was virtually unrestrained credit buying.

A Johannesburg *Star* reporter found, in March 1959, that in one day he could buy a holiday in Europe for £40 down, £10 fitted him out handsomely, a new piano was delivered for £7 to his new flat which had already been furnished with a radiogram, carpets and washing machine for a £50 deposit. Though he had to give two references at each shop or travel agency, and though an assistant might check his credit rating, he was able to run up £2 000 of debt in a day on purely luxury items. In keeping up with the Joneses, he noted, there was just one snag — his inability to pay the monthly instalments. 'But there,' he remarked, 'I will be in company of thousands of my fellow citizens who overbuy and live precariously from summons to summons.'

The snatchers

Hire purchase, in the correct sense of the term, had in fact arrived in South Africa in the 1890s, when the Singer Sewing Machine Company sold the bulk of their machines to lowly-paid families for ten guineas over a period of 28 months. The buyer did indeed 'hire' the sewing machine, which became his property when payment was complete. However, should he fail to make his payments, the machine would be taken back.

George Plunkett Morris, Singer's agent in South Africa, told an inquiry into the Insolvency Act in 1926 that the beauty of his company's system was that a lawsuit was not needed to recover a machine. About 15 per cent of the machines sold in the 12 years Morris had been in the business were taken back. Three quarters of these had been voluntary surrenders by buyers who could not afford to keep up the payments. It was possible to repossess a machine on which only £2 was owing.

It was the 'snatch back' system used by so

many traders that brought calls for legal controls.

But despite the Hire Purchase Act of 1942 —which, among other things, regulated deposits, payments and repossessions — buy-now-pay-later, or the never-never, became a way of life for South Africans.

In March 1980, consumer credit was running at R1 783 million a year.

FEEDING THE FAMILY ON 32/- A WEEK

In 1937, with the Great Depression still a painful memory for most South African families, the National Council of Women organised a series of lectures and demonstrations for the housewives of the East Rand town of Benoni. The aim: to teach them how to feed their husbands and children properly. A Benoni housewife, whose miner husband earned a basic wage of £7.11s. a week, could feed him and their two children, aged 8 and 9, on £1.12s. a week.

'Save 6d a day by thrift marketing,' lecturer Mary Higham told her audience, 'and you will save more than £9 a year.' In budgeting for her family's food, Mrs Average Benoni was advised to spend a quarter on vegetables and fruit, a quarter on milk and cheese, the third quarter on meat, fish and eggs, and the remainder on bread, cereal, fats, sugar and other groceries. She should keep a strict record of her buying for a few months, adjusting according to the family's needs.

Mrs Benoni bought all the food herself and paid cash. 'You will see,' said Miss Higham, 'that her budget contains all the constituents of a healthy diet in reasonably well-balanced proportions.' The housewife saved by buying only what could be stored in her pantry (electric refrigerators were not yet common): 'Cleanliness and coolness in pantry and kitchen are the two prime requirements to prevent spoilage, and so prevent waste.'

STOCKING THE LINEN CUPBOARD: THEN AND NOW

These are the comparative prices of 24 items of linen sold by Stuttafords in 1900 and 1980. The turn-of-the-century costs included 'all linen hemmed and marked free of charge'.

		1900 £ s d	1980 Rand
3	Superior damask table cloths	1 17 6	270,00
1	Dozen superior damask dinner napkins	15 9	54,00
3	Tray cloths or carving napkins	11 8	7,50
2	Side board cloths (embroidered)	9 -	25,00
2	Kitchen table cloths	9 10	15,00
2	Pairs double-bed cotton sheets	2 10 -	40,00
2	Pairs single-bed cotton sheets	15 10	21,00
12	Hemstitched frill pillow cases	1 1 -	66,00
2	Pairs cotton sheets (servants)	11 10	21,00
4	Cotton pillow cases	5 -	8,60
1	Doz. Linen huckaback towels	1 1 -	30,00
1	Doz. bedroom towels	12 6	90,00
6	Bath towels	15 -	60,00
6	Glass cloths	5 -	8,94
6	Tea or china cloths	5 -	5,34
6	Housemaid's cloths	6 -	2,16
1	Doz. dusters	3 11	2,88
6	Knife cloths	3 6	1,68
6	Sponge cloths for lamps etc	1 3	3,60
2	Pairs double-bed wool blankets	3 15 -	107,50
2	Under blankets	9 -	25,00
1	Pair single-bed wool blankets	19 11	50,00
1	Under blanket	2 11	10,00
1	Pair blankets for servants	12 11	37,00
	Totals:	£19 0 4	R962,20

THE COST OF EATING

Prices of basic foodstuffs steadily rose during the six decades since the year of Union, as this table shows. Incomes also climbed, though many South Africans would argue that they haven't kept pace with the increasing cost of food.

	1910 (pence)	1930 (pence)	1950 (pence)	1970 (cents)
Beef av. per lb	7,2	7,2	13,2	54,5
Mutton av. per lb	6,8	9,1	14,6	38,8
Milk per pt	3,2	3,4	5,1	7,1
Condensed milk (14 oz tin)	6,4	9,1	11,2	15,8
Eggs per dozen	17,0	21,9	35,0	31,5
Butter per lb	18,0	21,2	31,8	39,5
Potatoes per lb	0,9	1,4	3,7	6,3
Tea per lb	22,0	32,2	81,9	72,0
Sugar per lb	3,0	3,8	4,1	8,0
Jam per lb	6,0	7,0	19,9	17,0
Rice per lb	3,0	4,1	9,4	15,9
Flour per 25 lb	48,0	80,6	93,2	114,0
Bacon per lb	16,0	22,1	32,6	56,0
Coffee per lb	15,0	20,5	51,8	88,3

That family ate less meat and drank more milk than most working class South Africans. Yet the menus were far from dull, and varied from day to day. At the Portuguese market garden, Mrs Benoni bought 13 lb of greens, carrots, turnips and other root vegetables, 12 lb of potatoes, ½ lb of tomatoes, 4 lb of fresh fruit, 8 lb of bananas, 21 oranges and 2 lb of dried fruit.

Bread and milk

She allowed at least a pint of milk a day for each of the children and another pint for herself and her husband.

She bought two white loaves each week, but the children took sandwiches of wholemeal bread to school.

Each day started with mealie meal, and she saved by buying the brown government sugar, 3 lb of which cost only 7½d. She never bought dripping, but suet, and rendered it down. She kept the stock from meat and vegetables to enrich soups and stews.

Housewives who followed the thrifty habits of Mrs Average Benoni were advised that, should the family income fall, they could maintain a balanced nutritional diet by cutting out fats and sugar and substituting eggs for meat. 'The most expensive food,' they were cautioned, 'is not always the most nutritious.'

There was also advice on good eating habits: 'Give your stomach time to do its work, let meal times be a pleasure, and after each meal rest a while. A quarter of an hour of real rest, with your feet up, after lunch each day will give you an extra year on your life.'

It was suggested that children should eat at their own table and that they should not be allowed to leave it for at least twenty minutes: 'They don't find it fun to rush during the first five minutes of the meal if they have to remain at table for a definite length of time. If they dawdle over the meal, plan some attractive activity to follow the meal.'

Stretching the pennies

Some of Miss Higham's money-saving recipes included using the green leaves of carrots, beets and celery normally discarded in the Portuguese market garden as useless. These simple ingredients made some tasty dishes.

Two soup recipes:
Potato soup: 1 lb unpeeled potatoes; ½ lb peeled onions; 1 stick celery with leaves; a little of any other vegetable if liked; 1 oz butter or other fat; 1 qt vegetable stock; ½ oz sago; ½ pt milk; salt and pepper; 1 tbs chopped parsley.

Vegetables cut up roughly and sautéd in fat. Add to the stock and simmer till just tender. Rub through a sieve. Return to pan, add milk and sago and boil till latter is clear. Add chopped parsley, season to taste. Serve with fried croutes. (Serves six)

Milk soup: 1 lb chopped vegetables with stems and leaves; 1 oz fat; 1 pt vegetable stock; 1 oz cornflour; salt and pepper; 1 tbs chopped parsley; 1 pt milk.

Sauté the vegetables in the fat. Add stock and simmer till just tender. Blend the flour with the milk. Add to the stock. Bring to boil, boil for three minutes. Season to taste, add parsley and serve with fried croutes. (Serves four to six.)

HOW MRS BENONI FILLED HER SHOPPING BASKET IN 1937

The food items in these four pictures cost the 1937 housewife £1.12s. Total 1980 cost: R43,72

Bread, suet, jam, sugar, tea, coffee, gelatine, rice, mealie meal. Cost in 1937 — 5/5½; cost in 1980 — R5,51

Nine hundred grams dried fruit, 11½ kg mixed vegetables and 6,8 kg mixed fresh fruit cost 8/8 in 1937. Cost in 1980 was R8,50

Six hundred grams fish, 15 eggs, 3,6 kg meat. Cost in 1937 — 6/11; cost in 1980 — R12,19

Twenty-seven litres milk, 400 g cheese, 1 kg butter. Cost in 1937 — 10/11½; cost in 1980 — R17,52

South Africans at War

Still recovering from the ravages of the Anglo-Boer conflict, and just four years after the Act of Union forged them into a single nation, South Africans found themselves being drawn into what the optimistic predicted would be the war to end all wars — against the Kaiser's Germany.

The country's entry into the lists in 1914 was not a formality — memories of Kitchener's concentration camps were fresh, and Britain, in the minds of many people, was still 'the enemy'. But for all that, tens of thousands of South Africa's sons volunteered to endure the heat, disease and privation of campaigns in South West and East Africa, and to fight and die in the mud of Flanders. Their most glorious moment in an inglorious war — one most notable for the blunders of generals and the heroism of the ordinary soldier — was at Delville Wood. There, for five days in July 1916, troops of the newly-arrived South African Brigade held their positions against wave after wave of advancing German infantry and hellish artillery barrages that reduced the wood to a devastation of stumps and splinters. When the guns of that battle fell silent, only 755 of the Brigade's 3 153 officers and men were still unwounded.

There were parallels during the Second World War. In 1939 the country was again divided. And again, South African soldiers distinguished themselves in the theatres of Africa and Europe. They spearheaded the conquest of Benito Mussolini's East African empire, helped fight Rommel in the Western Desert, suffered disaster at Tobruk, shared the triumph of Alamein, slogged their way up the spine of Italy and into the soft underbelly of the Nazi fortress.

South Africans were luckier than most of the other Allied peoples in the two wars. Far from the major battle lines, life carried on very much as usual: there was no threat of invasion; no bombs devastated the cities; shortages were few; many businesses actually profited from the free world's appetite for raw materials, food and equipment.

But drama there was — a full-scale rebellion in 1914; the sinister activities of the Ossewa-brandwag in the 1940s. And, of course, plenty of war-inspired emotion. Some of its expression is best forgotten — especially, during the first war, the senseless persecution of South Africans of German origin, the white feathers, the cruel propaganda. But much of it is memorable – and remembered. The ordinary people of the Union, most of them, rallied magnificently to the cause in each of these epic struggles. Fund-raising associations worked tirelessly; women knitted; the much-loved Isie Smuts and her legions produced their glory-bags; the people of Cape Town and Durban opened their homes and hearts to Allied troops in transit; and the Lady in White sang — and sang.

To many of today's South Africans, Perla Gibson's *Wish Me Luck As You Wave Me Goodbye* gave voice to the deepest, most immediately recollected sentiments of those years — the poignant heartache of leave-taking, and the joy of home-coming.

The post office was never far from the front line during the Second World War. This field post office was established and distributing mail to troops only a day after the Allies recaptured Tobruk in November 1942

Patriotic songs and armed protest

REFUSING TO BOW THE KNEE TO BAAL

South Africans, it appeared, were rallying to the Imperial flag almost to a man. Large crowds gathered outside newspaper offices and, it was reported, 'on reading the announcements they immediately sang "God Save the King", followed by "Rule Britannia" and three cheers for the King and Sir Edward Gray. Tremendous enthusiasm prevailed'. South Africa's declaration of war on 8 September 1914 was welcomed by everyone, said the *Star*: 'On every hand, irrespective of party and whether British-born, Colonial or Dutch, there is intense relief that . . . the British Government has maintained British prestige and refused to "bow the knee to Baal".'

In fact, even before the outbreak of hostilities in Europe, preparations were under way in South Africa. Naval volunteers were mobilised; the government prohibited maize exports, censored cables, forbade the transmission of messages in code or in languages other than English, Dutch and French; merchants hiked food prices 'to cover war risks'; Minister of Defence Jan Smuts announced harbour traffic controls and warned that vessels infringing them would be fired on; British troops garrisoned in the Union began gathering at ports for the voyage home. There were rousing ex-servicemen's rallies; petitions for volunteers; patriotic concerts and shows throughout the country.

Rebels with a cause. Many Afrikaners were bitterly opposed to helping a nation they still considered to be their enemy. But the rebellion was easily crushed, allowing Prime Minister Louis Botha to concentrate on the invasion of German South West Africa. Above: a rebel commando in Harrismith. Left: a rebel burgher leader — the image of traditional Afrikaner defiance

But it wasn't as simple as that. Spionkop, Paardeberg and the concentration camps were fresh in men's memories, and many Afrikaners resented what they considered 'the enemy's' call to arms.

'If Britain suffers,' said *De Volksstem*, 'South Africa must suffer with her.' Added the *Star*: 'One of the most gratifying features of the position locally is the excellent feeling displayed by ardent Hertzogites, who now give place to no one in their professions of readiness to as-

sist the Crown . . .' All of which was very far from the truth. General Barry Hertzog, Leader of the Opposition, and his followers vehemently opposed South Africa's entry into the war.

On 9 September the Cabinet agreed to Britain's request for an invasion of German South West Africa. Prime Minister Louis Botha then convened a special session of Parliament to approve this aggressive policy, which it did by 92 votes to 12, but not before a

The surrender of a great soldier. Christiaan de Wet, scourge of Kitchener's regiments in the Anglo-Boer War, opposed violence in the beginning, formed a 'peace commando' and ordered his Free Staters not to fire the first shot, but the inevitable clash occurred on 8 November at Doornberg. Very soon afterwards the back of the rebellion in the Free State was broken and De Wet was captured at the end of the month

Two troopers pose with their rebel prisoner. The armed protest lasted into 1915, but at no time were the rebels a match for disciplined Government forces

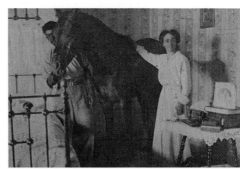

Mrs F.F. Moore, of the farm Jamaica in the Heilbron district, hides the farm's one remaining horse from the rebels — in her bedroom!

Rallying to the Imperial flag. This picture, published in the magazine South Africa *on 15 August 1914, was captioned 'How Cape Town can mobilise her manhood'. The recruits were plentiful and eager*

great deal of angry debate during which, reported *Round Table*, there had been 'bitter personal attacks on the Prime Minister, and references to the South African War which could only have the effect of reviving racial hatred . . .' Revising its previous opinion, the *Star* said: 'Substantially, the Hertzog policy amounts to one of benevolent neutrality, to a plea that the Government and people of the Union should sit still till such time as they happen to be attacked within their own borders . . .'

As it turned out, such an 'attack' had already occurred: after a brief skirmish, the border post of Nakop was occupied by a 'Free Corps' of South West African Boers, supported by armed Germans and led by Andries de Wet. This minor incident gave Botha valuable ammunition.

Afrikaner ranks were split on the issue. Many, including war heroes Christiaan de Wet; Christiaan Beyers (then Commandant-General of the Defence Force); Koos de la Rey, the 'Lion of the Western Transvaal'; and senior UDF army officers Lieutenant-Colonel Manie Maritz and Major J.C.G. Kemp, were set firmly against the proposed South West campaign; some saw in the war situation a golden opportunity to reassert Afrikaner independence. English-speaking South Africans looked on in some bewilderment.

Beyers formally resigned his command. Replying to his letter, Smuts said that 'for the Dutch-speaking section in particular I cannot conceive anything more fatal and humiliating than a policy of lip-loyalty in fair weather and a policy of neutrality and pro-German sentiment in days of storm and stress'.

Both letters were published in *De Volksstem* and became the manifestos of the opposing factions within Afrikanerdom. The stage was set for open rebellion.

Tragedy at Langlaagte

De la Rey, the most powerful of the anti-war leaders, certainly planned some kind of protest, but probably not armed revolt. He felt strong personal loyalty to Louis Botha, and he

had been persuaded that Holy Scripture condemned rebellion.

But what his exact intentions were may never be known. On the night of 15 September 1914 he and Beyers set out from Pretoria for the Defence Force camp at Potchefstroom. Rand police patrols, on the look-out for the notorious Foster gang of robbers, were under orders to open fire on cars that failed to stop at checkpoints. At Langlaagte railway station Beyers instructed his driver to ignore a con-

stable's summons; shots were fired and De la Rey, probably the only dissident influential enough to keep the peace, was killed.

The situation deteriorated rapidly after Manie Maritz and 500 of his men, stationed near the South West border, defected to the Germans on 9 October. The unrest spread; some 10 000 to 11 000 burghers took up arms against the government; commandos were formed under Beyers, De Wet, Kemp, Chris Muller, Jacques Pienaar, Jopie Fourie and others. This was the traditional Boer 'armed protest', the almost customary Afrikaner response to unwelcome British pressure.

But this time the Boers did not enjoy enough active public support. *De Volksstem* accused De Wet of 'plunging the country into civil war so as to turn it into a German vassal republic'. *Ons Land* reported a minor but significant incident: Afrikaners in Bredasdorp had taken De Wet's portrait down from its place of honour and thrown it on the fire. 'The portrait of Beyers,' added the paper, 'is not common here or it would have shared the same fate.'

Predictably, the rebellion was short-lived. The commandos, ill-armed, too few in number, too uncoordinated, were soon scattered by disciplined Government troops. The last of the burghers surrendered early in 1915. By then, De Wet was in prison, Maritz in exile, Beyers had drowned while trying to cross the Vaal. Jopie Fourie was captured, tried, convicted and shot.

Louis Botha could now set about the invasion of German South West Africa.

COMMANDO AND REGULAR: THE UNION'S FIRST ARMY

At the time of Union in 1910, South Africa had no defence force of her own: the country was protected by a garrison of some 30 000 British troops.

The following year General Smuts, Botha's Defence Minister, was charged with the task of establishing the Union's first unified command, which he succeeded in doing by marrying the traditional Boer commando system with the more formal British military structure. He told Parliament: 'We want an organisation that shall be neither Boer nor English, but a South African army.'

The Union Defence Force was created by the South African Defence Act No. 13 of 1912. The popular Anglo-Boer War leader Christiaan Beyers was appointed its first Commandant-General. The Act made provision for a small permanent force of 2 500 men and a Citizen Force of 25 000.

In January 1914, when labour unrest erupted into a general strike, Smuts was able to call on 6 000 SA Mounted Riflemen and Police, and 27 000 Citizen Force and Commando troops. This was the UDF's first 'engagement'.

Officers of the Transvaal Scottish, one of South Africa's most famed regiments, relax at their temporary camp in early 1914. Together with other units of the recently-formed Union Defence Force, they were called out during the general strike on the Witwatersrand

First blood

LINGERING ON THE MARCH FOR ROME

It was to be 'volunteers only' — Boer-Briton sensitivities and the delicate political balance dictated as much.

At the declaration of war in Europe there was the predictable rush of young men enthusiastic for the cannon's mouth. Typical of these was the Transvaal field cornet who told the *Star* that members of rifle clubs throughout the Union had volunteered to fight anywhere in or out of South Africa. 'My rifle is clean,' he said, 'and an hour's notice is sufficient.' The *Standard* reported the story of a diminutive shop assistant who volunteered for the Irish Regiment. The recruiting officer had looked dubiously at him and asked his height. 'Five-foot-five, sir,' said the little man. 'The same as Napoleon.'

At the end of September 1914 Botha appealed for recruits for his imminent campaign in German South West Africa. The *Cape Times* seemed confident that the 2 000-man quota from the Western Cape would be met within a few days and, borrowing from Macaulay, added:

> Shame on the false Etruscan
> Who lingers in his home,
> When Porsena of Clusium
> Is on the march for Rome.

Regiments began placing their own advertisements (the South African Mounted Rifles needed under-45s 'who can shoot and ride'). Universities arranged that students could volunteer without prejudice to the resumption of their academic careers. Large department stores were soon offering uniforms, tailored at 12 hours' notice 'with true military precision and exactness'. Newspapers did a brisk trade in 2/- war maps and cheap infantry and musketry drill books and signalling manuals.

Holding back

But towards the middle of 1915 the numbers of those coming forward began to decline and continued to do so as people learnt of the grim realities of war.

In July 1915 the minimum height for a recruit was 5 ft 8 in; two weeks later it was lowered to 5 ft 6 in. Even so, the medical rejection rate remained high, reaching 50 per cent on occasion (one of the major reasons: poor teeth), provoking the *Standard* to complain that the country had a 'Governor-General, the recruiting officers and mayors doing their utmost and here we find the medical examiners industriously rejecting men as if their whole object was to find defects, real or imaginary'.

Though medicals became less stringent as the need grew for more fighting men (and, let it be said, after a rash of suicides by rejected volunteers), recruiting continued to be a slow business. South Africa's overseas contingent rarely received its required 600 men a month, and the *Standard* lamented that 'many men whose plain duty it is to be in the fighting line won't go. Neither the spirit of adventure, nor the call to their manhood from their brave fellow countrymen in Flanders, moves them

... perhaps the lamest excuse of them all is the one advanced by many young men that their employers won't let them go ... Has such a one realised that he is a perfectly free agent — a free-born Britisher, and that he is at liberty to hand in his resignation and quit?'

Botha rejected demands for compulsory conscription. Should there be any such attempt, he said, then he would have to recall the entire South African Brigade from France to quell the consequent rebellion. The Anglo-Boer War was too recent in men's memories.

There was less of a problem in raising men for the Cape Coloured Corps and for the

The funeral of eight East London soldiers killed in a troop train derailment at Hex River in 1914

The Union Government refused to introduce conscription — South Africa's was to be a volunteers-only contribution to the Allied war effort. After an initial stampede to join the ranks, the recruiting rate declined.

Newspaper editors were among those who sustained a vigorous campaign to encourage enlistment. Johannesburg's Star *ran these two posed and rather unsubtle pictures in August 1916. The civilians were invariably portrayed as layabouts*

Native Labour Corps, who filled largely noncombatant roles. At one stage the Government had to halt coloured recruitment — too many preferred going off to war to working in the Union. In January 1918 the *Rand Daily Mail* interviewed 'Charlie', a black soldier on three months' home leave from France: 'Charlie had just cashed his big cheque and was busy refilling a huge Gladstone bag with a new rig-out. He said that the Native contingent were happy in their work and proud to be of service to the Empire.' There were others like 'Charlie'. Enlistment for the Native Labour Corps totalled 82 769, of whom 25 090 served in France.

The final, dangerous German offensive in March 1918 — a push that threatened Paris itself — provoked a flurry of last-ditch exhortation. Newspapers excelled themselves in somewhat bloodthirsty recruitment campaigns. Some samples from the *Observer:* 'The finest sport in the world is hunting the Hun. Join up and have a cut at the beggar'; '. . . Come on! Fix them!' And: 'Are you downhearted? Then why not go and pay your compliments with a 303 bullet to the square-head?'

At war's end the tally showed that a total of 231 000 South Africans had enlisted during these four grim years: 146 000 white troops, 2 000 coloured and 83 000 black.

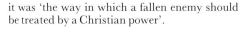

Contemporary cartoons by W.H. Kirby enabled Cape Argus *readers to see the campaign through the eyes of the ordinary soldier. Left: the discomforts of the march. One writer of the time, H.C. O'Neill, described a few of them: 'Dense masses of intractable brush formed a barrier that could only be passed at the cost of clothes torn from the back and wounds which refused to heal in the scorching sun. Terrible sand-storms raged almost continuously. Tents were torn to shreds. Railway tracks disappeared in a day, and horses sank to their girths in the soft heaps. The sand invaded the food, and the men could not eat or breathe without consuming it. In some places flies swarmed in such numbers as to cover completely the whole inside surface of the tents.' Right: 'Mounted men,' wrote Kirby, 'generally appeared to have brought* all *their belongings with them'*

THE ROAD TO WINDHUK

'First stop, Windhuk Brewery' was the optimistic sign chalked on the carriages of troop trains leaving Bloemfontein soon after General Louis Botha announced the invasion of German South West Africa. And it was indeed a highly successful campaign, though not without its problems.

Although the Union Jack was flying over Lüderitzbucht (Luderitz Bay) as early as September 1914, it was not until February 1915 that Smuts and Botha took the field in force to occupy German South West Africa.

Botha landed at Swakopmund with 12 000 men and Smuts at Lüderitzbucht with 6 000. Other columns marched in from the Orange River to swell the invasion force to nearly 50 000. Opposing them were some 5 000 Germans and a hostile terrain nearly three-quarters the size of the Union itself.

Many of the burghers in the volunteer force had never left the platteland before, never seen the sea. At Cape Town, troopers of one Transvaal commando could not understand why their horses refused to drink sea water, and an irate soldier claimed he had been swindled when his soap would not lather in it.

The Germans fought a skirmishing war of retreat, and in their wake left 'millions of empty beer bottles', poisoned wells, and what Deneys Reitz describes, in *Trekking On*, as 'infernal machines'. These were buried mines and booby traps. One of Botha's staff officers later recalled that the Germans had planted 6 000 mines and 'used more dip for poisoning wells than would be required for all the sheep in the Union'.

As they pursued the enemy, South African troops found time to rename the streets of captured towns. One soldier wrote from Lüderitzbucht: 'You will now see King George Street taking the place of Wilhelm Street, while our Premier has given Von Kluck a nasty knock by having his name given to Von Kluck Street.'

Troopers bore blistering days and bitter nights on the campaign (but there were, for some, glittering compensations — the *Friend* reported in March that during one off-saddle period troopers picked up 200 surface diamonds!) and eventually the Union forces won through. On 9 July 1915 the Germans surrendered unconditionally. Said *The Times* of London: 'To the youngest of the sister nations belongs the glory of the first complete triumph of our arms and the disappearance of Germany from the map of South Africa.' Referring to Botha's generous peace terms, the *South African Weekly Standard* reflected that

The German camel corps: ideal transport for the South West African dunes. They faced a daunting enemy, though — in one five-day hike South African and Rhodesian soldiers marched 290 km. 'The Germans,' according to a contemporary account, 'were beaten as much by the superb endurance of the Union troops as by the skill of their leader'

it was 'the way in which a fallen enemy should be treated by a Christian power'.

Writing home

South Africans at home received surprisingly incomplete news of the desert war being fought, and fought well, by their own boys: the media seemed more interested in what was going on in Europe. One mother complained in the *Standard*: 'You see the English papers full of pictures of what the British army and the Canadians and Australians are doing, but not a word about our own poor fellows, who have been footslogging for the past eight months through a sand desert in temperatures anything above 120 . . . Do you call this fair?'

But there were reports, and news did filter in from the field. Typical extract from a soldier's letter home: 'Today General Botha addressed us. The General said he had written to Mrs Botha telling her that he would be in Windhuk [Windhoek] on her birthday. A thousand voices inquired when this day would be? General Botha humorously replied: "The day we get to Windhuk." '

On the whole, though, the public remained largely in ignorance of the hardships of the campaign and the nature of the enemy. On leave in Johannesburg, one of Botha's troopers was told that the Germans in South West Africa did not seem so bad as the ones in Europe. 'No,' he replied, 'they have had the advantage of several years' contact with the superior civilisation of the Hereroes.'

The Mayor of Windhoek surrenders his town to Louis Botha on 12 May 1915. Windhoek had beamed information about Allied shipping to Berlin

General Botha and his escort ride towards Windhoek. Reported the Pictorial *in 1915: 'So tired did the horses become after the long daily trek that they were quite ready to sit down and feed with their masters'*

Prime Minister Botha poses for the camera in Pretoria just after his return from the successful campaign

Business as usual

THE ANCIENT FERVOUR OF FISHWIVES

'After three years of cataclysm, disruption and appalling death by every form of furious and scientific violence,' said the *South African Weekly Standard* in November 1917, 'there is no disruption of the human spirit, no deep changes in thought and living such as were foretold by thinkers in the year 1914. In South Africa, we have been haggling over the price of wool with the ancient fervour of fishwives bartering for herring.' An irritable British letter-writer agreed: 'We sometimes wonder whether South Africa really appreciates the fact that there is a very big war waging.'

In short, it was very much business as usual on the home front. At war's outbreak Prime Minister Botha had warned of the impending 'cyclone', but in practical terms the carnage on Flanders' fields affected the stay-at-home South African's life very little.

The public, of course, did get its share of fashionable jingoism: men of honour were expected to join up; the appeal to patriotic sentiment through Press, poster and from platform was constant and powerful. Throughout the four years both Bench and pulpit were called on to help boost the recruitment figures. Magistrates were prone to denounce 'shirkers', and the Bishop of Pretoria said, when opening a bazaar in Johannesburg in April 1917, that there were eligible young men in the city who ought to be 'cut' by every decent girl. Until their lives were made miserable, they would go on 'slacking'.

A clever South African versifier, one of many, asked:

> *How will you fare, sonny,*
> *How will you fare*
> *In the far-off winter night*
> *When you sit by the fire in an old armchair*
> *And your neighbours talk of the fight?*
> *Will you slink away, as it were from a blow,*
> *Your old head shamed and bent?*
> *Or say — I was not with the first to go,*
> *But I went, thank God, I went?*

South African society was not kind to those men who stayed. Inevitably, the white feather, traditional badge of cowardice, made its appearance. Reported the *Standard* in 1917: 'The other day a young fellow who was severely wounded in Delville Wood, has an aluminium shoulder and is bursting with joy because he can now move the little finger on his left hand, was presented by a pert young miss with one of these emblems while standing in Adderley Street, Cape Town, and told he ought to be in khaki. His reply is unprintable.'

Life, for most South Africans, remained relatively undisturbed throughout the war years, though the nation was of course very conscious of its active and important contribution to the Imperial effort. In October 1914, *South Africa* reported a meeting of 'leading South Africans' in London at which Sir David Graaff announced a grant of £40 000 to the Governor-General's Fund, a relief fund established at the start of the war '. . . raised by South Africans for a South African purpose — the relief of distress in the Union'.

Fund-raising was a prominent feature of life on the home front during the First World War. Concerts, fêtes and raffles bought comforts for the troops. Above: a selection of campaign stickers

Newspapers gave their readers daily war intelligence, weekly recruitment figures, and kept them well informed of the amount of money being raised for the dozens of war funds organised by enthusiastic campaigners. This was mostly women's work — as so much else became during these years. They organised patriotic concerts, street produce sales, bazaars, fêtes.

Women took over many of the jobs left vacant by the South African serving soldier: in factory, shop, even in the police force. An advertisement in the March 1917 issue of *Women's Outlook* gave the opinion that 'Every woman can be proud of . . . war work, particularly in the field of traction, driving motor buses, ambulances and cars . . .'

The carnage in Flanders brought deep grief to many families — but also much sentimentality. The Natal Mercury *published this picture of a girl reading 'News from her three soldier brothers at the front'*

The jaunty styles of war

In due course the distant guns of war were heard by the followers of South African fashion. Readers of the *Domestic Monthly* were told in March 1915 that 'Since the war began the world has learnt two things — how smart soldiers' headgear is, and how well it may be adapted for women's wear'. Hats modelled on the forage cap were 'a most jaunty and becoming headdress for a smart tailored woman'.

The *South African Shopkeeper and Commercial Gazette* noted in mid-1916 that the military uniform — and a shortage of starch — had given fashionable respectability to the gentleman's soft collar. Cloth-topped footwear made its appearance later in the same year: all

'Biffing the Kaiser' was the most popular attraction at a fund-raising fête held at Johannesburg's Zoo Lake towards the end of 1914. Balls were thrown at effigies of the German Emperor

GOOD-BYE, DOLLY GRAY! (2).

Good-bye, Dolly, I must leave you, though it breaks my heart to go,
Something tells me I am needed at the front to fight the foe:
See, the soldier-boys are marching, and I can no longer stay.
Hark! I hear the bugle calling! Good-bye, Dolly Gray!

The Vogue Velours

THE growing popularity of Velours Hats is evinced in the special Display we are now making of these Hats in many new and charming styles.

You will find here hundreds of Velours, all very exclusive Shapes in such beautiful tones as Jade-Green, Copper, new Blue Fuchsia, and Cherry, besides hosts of other shades equally fascinating and full of colour. The very best choice, of course, is to the first comers.

Cartter-Holwills
SHRINE OF FASHION.

The war — and its uniforms — had its effect on fashion. Cartter-Holwills of Durban ('Shrine of Fashion') advertised this hat modelled on that worn by the Canadian Mounties

Sentimental and patriotic postcards were common during the war. Left: King George V inspects a captured dug-out at the front, and right, the song so well-known from the Anglo-Boer War — and sung again in 1914

available leather supplies were being used in the manufacture of army boots. Dresses, too, became less voluminous; one writer succinctly observed that 'As the war gets longer the skirts get shorter'. Wool prices rose and other fabrics — silk, taffeta, flannel and cotton — became increasingly popular.

Keep it in the country

Government and press urged the public to conserve food, but few took the appeals seriously. A typical response: the Cape Town Club's committee notified its members that 'in consequence of the European war and the desirability that all consumers should assist to conserve the supply of foodstuffs, the committee has instructed that . . . the menu for the club dining room be slightly curtailed'.

Not only was the average South African's standard of living comfortably maintained, but world conflict actually brought prosperity to a lot of people.

'A shortage of tea and sugar,' said the *Standard*, 'would stimulate the Natal output and condensed milk, if cut off, could be made locally. The effect of the war, as the British Navy commands the seas, should be to stimulate production in South Africa. It would also do much to cement relations between English and Dutch.'

By November 1917 trade returns were showing a marked decline in the value of imported goods, and the *Standard* observed that 'The war has given the farmers who produce mealies, butter, eggs, meat and other foodstuffs an export price of £2 600 000 for the past nine months compared to £256 000 in 1913.'

Until 1918, when petrol coupons were introduced, South Africans experienced no critical shortages. There were some annoying gaps on the shelf — for instance, men could no longer buy their briar pipes (Germany had been a supplier) — but these simply served to stimulate inventiveness: one periodical suggested that the millions of mealie cobs thrown away every year could replace the briar.

Price increases were relatively modest during the four years of war. By 1918 food costs were, on average, about 25 per cent higher than in 1914 and, although the buying power of the gold sovereign was assessed at a low 9/2½d, a spokesman for the Johannesburg Town Council could say, in 1918, that the city had 'never been so prosperous'.

AND SUDDENLY THEY WERE ENEMIES

Predictably, German residents of South Africa were subjected to ostracism and outright antagonism. At the outbreak of hostilities they were obliged to register themselves, and to surrender firearms and ammunition to their nearest magistrate.

As the war progressed, so anti-German feeling grew stronger, fanned by newspaper reports with brutal headlines such as 'Germans Claim to be Human'. Eventually, those not naturalised were interned by the Government.

In parts of the Union, German-sounding streets and roads were given new names. The town of Berlin in the Cape became Brabant, and a reader of the *Cape Times* suggested that German South West Africa be renamed 'Bothaland'.

Public antagonism turned to public violence after the sinking of *Lusitania* in May 1915. There were reports that South African Germans had 'gleefully celebrated' the disaster. Mobs went on the rampage, destroying German (and often non-German) property. The riots in Johannesburg caused between £200 000 and £250 000 in fire damage alone.

Germans were asked not to enter the Johannesburg Stock Exchange; restaurant patrons refused to be served by German waiters; newspapers came out in a rash of advertisements placed by people disclaiming German nationality.

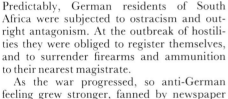

A mob burns the contents of a Johannesburg beer hall after the sinking of Lusitania *in May 1915*

The burnt-out shell of Baumann & Co, the biscuit manufacturers, in Durban's West Street

Johannesburg demonstrators overturn and burn a German-owned carriage and car

The long march

BRASS BAND BUZZERS ON THE ROAD TO VICTORY

'Manufacturers and merchants are already anticipating General Jan Smuts's conquest of German East Africa and are investigating the products of the territory,' the *Weekly Standard* informed its readers on 2 March 1916. Commerce's confidence in General Smuts was eventually to be justified.

Smuts was appointed Commander-in-Chief of the Imperial Army in East Africa in February 1916, the first South Africans having arrived at Nairobi on New Year's Day. Smuts himself reached Mombasa on 19 February. His task: to break the stalemate between the British in Kenya and the Germans, commanded by Paul von Lettow-Vorbeck, positioned across the border.

Within a month Smuts had driven the enemy out of their strongholds in the Kilimanjaro and Arusha districts and was pushing them steadily southwards. South of the Rufiji River, though, a stalemate developed, enlivened by sporadic attack and counterattack in which the forces of Von Lettow-Vorbeck (later promoted to General) acquitted themselves as well as the South Africans. Eventually, desperately short of supplies and ammunition, the wily German commander led his forces across the Robuma River into Moçambique. This was in November 1917, some months after Smuts had been called to England for the Imperial War Conference, where he was hailed, somewhat prematurely, as the 'Conqueror of East Africa'.

From Moçambique, Von Lettow-Vorbeck raided into Northern Rhodesia as far as Abercorn, where he formally surrendered on 25 November 1918 — two weeks after the Armistice in Europe. His troops, still undefeated in the field, were the last of the 'enemy' to lay down their arms. Between Smuts and Von Lettow-Vorbeck there existed a mutual admiration that extended to the forces under their respective commands — a collective respect that was to recur in North Africa, albeit under different commanders, in the Second World War.

Flea-bite for the blighters

Wrote a South African medical officer shortly after the start of the East African campaign: 'The climate here is perfect. It seems difficult to believe that we are in equatorial Africa. I have not seen a mosquito since we landed and we have had no cases of malaria. With reasonable care, fellows should keep fit.'

He spoke too soon: it was not to be a comfortable war. Troops had to contend with extremes of heat and cold, drenching rains, dysentery, jigger fleas, tsetse fly, and a host of enervating tropical diseases, including malaria. Sickness wiped out 30 000 horses and 28 000 oxen. Among the men, mosquitoes took a heavier toll than German bullets: nearly a third of the army went down with malaria — as did Smuts himself.

'When we see some of these poor blighters come in I feel all we can do for them is a flea-bite,' said another doctor, towards the end of

The rugged East African terrain and mosquitoes inflicted more casualties on the Union forces than did the enemy. A third of Smuts's men, and Smuts himself, went down with malaria; sickness killed 30 000 horses and 28 000 oxen. An officer wrote that: '. . . if anything wins this war, it will be the Transport and Veterinary Corps'. It was a long campaign: the elusive German commander, Von Lettow-Vorbeck, far left, surrendered two weeks after the Armistice in Europe. Above and below: crossing two of the numerous rivers: in one 29 km stretch there were 17. Left: officers share a joke

the year. 'I tell you, I am just waiting for a chance to take my hat off to many a man I had no time for before . . . I am proud of them, and I am proud of South Africa. I am proud of this army.' Fred Tossel of Krugersdorp put it more succinctly: 'This country as a producer of the brass-band-buzzer devouring mosquito comes in an easy first.'

The troops, weakened by reduced rations, slogged their weary way southwards. The terrain and inadequate transport and equipment made it hard going. 'In German South West our trouble was drought,' said an officer. 'Here we have 17 rivers in 18 miles [29 km] with mud and black turf in between. A motor lorry goes at the rate of three miles [4,8 km] a day in such country. Then, after that, you get a stretch of desert where there is no water at all. If anything wins this war, it will be the Transport and Veterinary Corps.'

In fact it was the ordinary infantryman who bore the brunt of this particular little war. He saw little of the retreating Germans and their Askaris. His real enemies were exhaustion and hunger. 'We have just completed a 200 mile [322 km] journey away from the railway in less than 20 days in full kit,' recorded Private Salisbury of the 8th South African Infantry. 'Some out us were very much exhausted when we reached here, more particularly when I tell you that for days our rations were three-quarters of a cup of flour which we had to cook ourselves.' Their oxen, he wrote, were eaten by lions on the second night.

In September a Reuter's correspondent reported the closing stages of the campaign. 'Scarcity of transport combined with fever, dysentery, fly and horse sickness, fought for the Boche,' he wrote, 'but our columns over berg, river, forest and jungle pushed onwards and today the knell of the German Overseas Empire tolls insistently . . .'

Said Smuts: 'To me the real hero of the East African campaign is the South African citizen soldier. Disease and hunger sapped them on long marches . . . they kept marching on.'

The big welcome. Ladies at Germiston station, Transvaal, meet troops returning from East Africa

BOOTLACES, BORACIC AND OLD-STYLE DRAWERS

South African women knitted, sewed and collected for victory throughout the war. Union soldiers in German South West Africa were the first to benefit — they received balaclava hats for freezing nights and face veils for the dusty desert days.

At first, not all the gifts were so welcome. An officer writing from Lüderitzbucht compained that 'If only the public would spend their energies in collecting fruit, instead of making flannel shirts and pyjamas, I am sure their efforts would be far more appreciated by the troops.' Other acceptable articles were 'toothbrushes, bootlaces, towels, boracic powder and short stockinette drawers (old style pattern — opening down the front) to prevent chafing'.

By October 1915 the Post Office was helping the effort by accepting parcels up to 5 kg free of charge for mailing to men in the South African Overseas Contingent.

In the first three months of 1917 South African women shipped 18 000 pairs of socks and 20 000 scarves, mittens, caps and waistcoats to troops in the frozen trenches of northern Europe. There were grimmer, though no less useful, items: a newspaper reported that African chiefs in Natal and Zululand had sent, through the Secretary of Native Affairs, 8 770 sticks and crutches for wounded Union soldiers. The *Standard* announced that the South African Gifts and Comforts Organisation had also provided 'some fine logs of South African wood, red pear, stinkwood and witels for use by convalescents in English hospitals to make furniture and other articles'. By 1918 the organisation had collected and delivered 82 105 pairs of socks, 22 345 gloves and mittens, 67 361 bags, 10 696 scarves and caps, 13 030 shirts and vests, 2 005 sweaters and waistcoats, 42 600 handkerchiefs, 5 502 shorts and pants, 5 327 towels, 81 tons of South African tobacco, 15 000 000 South African cigarettes, 8 390 pipes, 324 747 tins of sweets, 94 245 cartons of dried fruit, 59 433 pieces of soap and 109 718 private parcels were sent free of charge.

Coloured troops received quarterly parcels from the Cape Corps Gifts and Comforts Fund. Money was raised by local committees — in 1917 the Oudtshoorn branch collected £68.2s.1d., an effort which showed, said the *Observer*, that the coloured people had 'really given till it hurt'.

SWEEPING THE MINES IN TABLE BAY

Call of the sea. This recruiting poster enticed South Africans with promises of the good life. The reality was somewhat harsher

South Africa had no navy of her own during the First World War, although a South African division of the Royal Naval Volunteer Reserve was formed and saw service in most of the theatres. Simonstown's trawlers and whalers were mobilised under the White Ensign, and after the disguised German raider *Moewe* laid mines in Table Bay and off Cape Agulhas (sinking several ships), some of the trawlers were equipped for mine-sweeping. Britain paid homage to South Africa's role in the sea war by giving local names to some of the Royal Navy's new ships — the destroyers *Botha* in 1915 and *Springbok* the following year, and at the end of the war the light cruisers *Capetown* and *Durban*.

THE MEN WHO SANG, SAID THEIR PRAYERS AND CAPTURED A HILL

Coloured, black and Indian citizens served South Africa well in both world wars, putting nearly 100 000 men in khaki during the first and more than 123 000 in the second. They filled vital, largely non-combatant roles in nearly every operational theatre.

Two infantry battalions of Cape coloured men were raised to form the Cape Corps in late 1915. Recruiting centres were swamped with volunteers, and those chosen were so enthusiastic — 'keen as mustard' said an officer — that they practised drill in their spare time. The Cape Corps saw service in Nyasaland and German East Africa, and then helped Allenby defeat the Turks in Palestine.

The capture of Square Hill

Their most notable achievement during this campaign was the capture of Square Hill on 19 September 1918. An officer's diary records, of the battle, that 'between rests the men sang, made their wills, said their prayers and washed their teeth. At the immediate prospect of a scrap at close quarters they were high-spirited and full of vim'. John X. Merriman, former Prime Minister of the Cape Colony, also expressed his admiration: 'No collection of men ever showed more zeal, devotion to duty, or discipline.'

The Corps was disbanded after the Armistice but came together again during the Second World War under command of a former officer, Colonel C.N. Hoy. Another of its earlier battalion commanders, Colonel G.A. Morris, established the Indian and Malay Corps which, in July 1940, and in company with the Native Military Corps, became known as the Non-European Army Services. This umbrella unit provided auxiliaries for the Union forces in the East African and Mediterranean theatres. Later on, however, the NMC merged with the Cape Corps.

In 1917 a Native Labour Corps was formed and attracted nearly 83 000 blacks from the Union and the High Commission Territories, of whom 25 000 served in Europe. The NLC suffered its greatest single disaster when the troopship *Mendi* collided with a heavier vessel and sank in the English Channel. Seven hundred men were lost.

Its successor in the Second World War, the Native Military Corps, trained recruits as stretcher-bearers, batmen, cooks, guards, medical orderlies and drivers, and for services in field and coastal gun detachments in the Union. By the end of the war 77 239 volunteers had served in the NMC, of whom 182 had been killed in action. The Cape Corps' contribution was 45 015 men and its losses 246.

Towards the end of 1945, at an investiture in Johannesburg, 34 men from the Cape Corps and the Native Military Corps were decorated for gallantry in action.

Black stretcher-bearers display their skill. Almost 83 000 blacks joined up; 25 000 served in Europe

In Flanders' fields

THE BATTLE FOR DELVILLE WOOD

On Monday 17 July 1916, newspapers throughout the Union reported that South African forces taking part in the great Somme offensive on the Western Front were heavily engaged in a wood near the French village of Longueval.

This was the battle for Delville Wood.

The *Cape Times* said that day: 'It has . . . been ascertained from the wounded that the men acquitted themselves in a manner of which South Africa may indeed be proud. When the moment arrived to leap over the parapets and enter the zone swept by machine guns, none faltered. There were just some preliminary handshakes before the leap, and then the South African war cry rang out.

'A few minutes later they were at death grips with the Huns, bayonetting, clubbing and stabbing, but they went on over the German corpses, broken entanglements and man-traps.'

It was months before the full story was known of what, in John Buchan's words, was 'an epic of terror and glory scarcely equalled in the entire campaign'.

At all costs

Early in July, after the German lines had been heavily bombarded, the South Africans began their advance. Two weeks later they had captured Longueval and were on the fringe of Delville Wood. Brigadier-General Lukin was ordered to take the wood, a key position, and hold it at all costs.

On Saturday 15 July, 121 officers and 3 032 men stormed the wood and carried it, despite obstinate resistance from the Germans who, Reuter reported, 'fought to the death . . . Duels were fought in which both combatants were pierced and thus fell dead. Every other tree bore machine gun men. The latter when shot fell to the ground or their bodies were caught and suspended in the branches'.

The Brigade entrenched itself, and for almost a week withstood a constant bombardment of shell and mustard gas, repulsing determined and seemingly endless attacks.

By 17 July the troops were exhausted; none had been in battle for less than 48 hours. Lukin protested to headquarters that his men faced certain death unless relief came immediately, but the orders stood. Later that night the Germans mounted a shattering barrage, denuding the wood of its trees. The death toll climbed alarmingly.

Two eye-witness reports paint a graphic picture of the battle: 'The enemy now launched an attack in overwhelming numbers amid the continued roar of artillery,' recalled Private S.A. Lawson of the 3rd Regiment. 'Once more they found us ready, a small party of utterly worn-out men, shaking off their sleep to stand up in the shallow trench. As the Huns came on they were mowed down — every shot must have told. Our rifles smoked and became unbearably hot; but though the end was near it was not yet. When the Huns wavered and

Soldiers return for a rest after several days of bitter fighting in the appalling conditions of the Flanders front

For month after horrific month troops lived, fought and died in seas of mud

Soldiers hacked out trenches like these in attempts to survive the hell that was Delville Wood

Delville Wood — graveyard of so many heroic South Africans — after the battle in July 1916

SAD, SWEET REMINDER

The Flanders Poppy, symbol of remembrance. Legend has it that wherever battles were fought, the fields which had been bare of flowers before the carnage became carpeted by poppies after the guns fell silent. In 1920 the British Legion, of which the South African Legion is a constituent member, adopted the emblem, and its poignant brightness is a feature of every anniversary of the Armistice signed on 11 November 1918. On that day each year the Legion collects money, which it uses to help those who served, and the dependants of those who died, in the two world wars.

---

broke they were reinforced and came on again. We again prevailed and drove them back. Only one Hun crossed our trench to fall shot in the heart, a few yards behind it. The lip of our trench told more plainly than words can how near they were to succeeding . . .'

Ivan McClusker wrote to his parents in Victoria West before he died of the wounds ('a bit of shell in my left side') he received in Delville Wood. 'As you know,' he said, 'I am No 1 on the gun and so am in charge of it, and of course do the actual firing. My No 2 was Charles Hugo from Beaufort West. He was as game as a fighting cock.

'Well, I managed to fire over 2 500 rounds into the Germans in massed formations at ranges varying from 300 to 800 yards. So I guess I put over 300 Germans out of action with my little Lewis before I was hit. The targets were too good to miss, and the Lewis is very accurate. It is a fine gun . . .

'Well, the shelling was getting heavier and heavier; shells were bursting all around us

and very, very near. I said to Hugo, "Charles, our number is up". He just grinned. Not long after (about) 4 p.m. a 5.9-inch shell plunged right amongst us and put my whole gun team out of action. What happened to the Brigade after this I don't know much . . . but we have made a glorious piece of history for South Africa.

'By Jove! I am proud of our boys. They were simply IT! None wavered or faltered, though we entered that day and the next into the very inferno of hell.'

At sunset on Thursday 20 July, the Brigade was relieved. Unwounded survivors of the battle numbered five officers and 750 men. They marched out of their hell-hole and into the military hall of fame.

Much later, the German Kaiser asked a group of captured British officers whether any was from the 9th Division. 'I want to see a man from that Division,' he said, 'for if all divisions had fought like the 9th I would not have any troops left . . .'

A dressing station on the Flanders front is concealed behind a bridge and protected by sandbags

Taking ammunition to the guns. British light railways played an important part in the advance

Shells and bullets were not the only hazards. Both sides developed new weapons: the Germans used poison gas early in the war; the British introduced the tank in 1917

These Delville Wood survivors were driven around Johannesburg as part of a recruiting drive

NO SUPERIOR AND NOT MANY EQUALS

'A less boastful body of men never appeared in arms. They had a horror of any kind of advertisement. No war correspondent attended them to chronicle their doings; no picturesque articles in the Press enlightened the public at home.'

So English author John Buchan remembered the South Africans who fought through the mud and horror of the Western Front from April 1916 until the Armistice in November 1918. And he added: 'The South African Infantry Brigade may be said, without boasting, to have had no superior and not many equals.'

Some 7 500 South Africans were already serving in various Imperial units before the Brigade of four battalions, under the command of Brigadier-General Henry Timson Lukin, arrived from Egypt to join the 9th Division in Flanders. All along the front, from the sea to the Alps, it was a bitter war of attrition. Colossal infantry assaults were mounted for 'limited objectives'; men died by the thousand for a few hundred metres of pitted wasteland.

The South Africans went 'over the top' for the first time on 1 July, during the great Battle of the Somme. By 20 July the Brigade's casualties were 2 815, most of them incurred at Delville Wood.

'No wild animals except rats'

So heavy were its casualties that twice in the two following years the South African Brigade effectively ceased to exist as a brigade — during the Somme retreat in March 1918 when, at Marrières Wood, it stemmed the German advance and held the British front, and again at the Battle of Lys 45 days later. Although it remained a brigade in name, the remnants of the SA Brigade then fought to the end of the war in a composite battalion. By 23 January 1918 the brigade had been whittled down to 1 740 men.

Its casualties in France were almost 15 000, a third of them killed in action. Most of these died in the long, harsh months of trench warfare. The trenches, said poet Robert Graves, 'were our homes, our prisons, our graveyards' and the land the men fought over had 'no trees; no birds; no crops; no flowers except an occasional rash of wild poppies; no wild animals except rats'.

South African raiding and wire-cutting parties wormed across no-man's-land at night with blackened faces. To confuse the enemy, orders were often given in Zulu. Their fighting spirit was renowned. Demonstrations of individual courage were legion. Typical incidents: in the Ypres Salient, according to Buchan, 'One NCO and two men of the 2nd Regiment took 70 prisoners. Another man of the 2nd Regiment engaged a German in a bayonet duel and killed him; then a second, whom he also killed; then a third, when each killed the other'. Recalled a divisional officer: 'One saw a large party of South Africans at full stretch with bayonets at the charge — all dead; but even in death they seemed to have the battle ardour stamped on their faces.'

Coming home

FLAGS, BUNTING AND THE BUGLES OF CHRISTENDOM

The news had been expected but there was anything but a sense of anti-climax when it actually came. 'End of World War,' shouted the *Star* and a host of other newspapers on 11 November 1918. 'Armistice signed at five this morning. Hostilities ceased at 11 o'clock,' and the country indulged in an orgy of jubilation.

In Cape Town thousands gathered to hear the Prime Minister, General Louis Botha, move a resolution congratulating the King, the Fleet and the armies of the Allies on their victory. 'Were it not for the valour and strength they have displayed this day might have been a very different one for us,' he said. 'Let God be thanked that our faith and prayers have been heard.' He then asked his private secretary to read from Rudyard Kipling's *Recessional*:

> *The tumult and the shouting dies:*
> *The Captains and the Kings depart:*
> *Still stands thine ancient sacrifice,*
> *An humble and a contrite heart,*
> *Lord God of hosts, be with us yet,*
> *Lest we forget, lest we forget.*

Thanksgiving services, fireworks displays and patriotic concerts followed in Cape Town and throughout the Union, and the next day was declared a public holiday.

The 'bugles of Christendom' had sounded victory; the 'forces of diabolism' defeated. Johannesburg's Mayor appeared on the steps of the Town Hall to be greeted by the roars of a huge, flag-waving crowd. All over the country church bells pealed, bunting and streamers festooned the streets, crackers exploded, ships hooted, fog-horns blared, guns boomed, loco-

BACK FROM THE WARS

A soldier is re-united with his family in South Africa at the end of the First World War. Right: A programme for a civic reception held in Boksburg in 1917 to honour the returned soldiers

motives and trams whistled, and men sang. 'The happiness,' reported one newspaper, 'amounted to delirium. People who had never spoken to one another, stopped, shook hands and exchanged congratulations as if they had known each other for years.'

Taking stock, the *Star* said in an editorial: 'The signing of the armistice yesterday was fully expected, and yet when the great news arrived everyone realised, almost for the first time, how tense had been the strain during the period of suspense and uncertainty. Never again in our day or generation will men and women experience the thrill with which they learned yesterday that fighting had ceased, and that the Great War was over.'

ONE CARTOON, AND A BROTHERHOOD IS BORN

Most soldiers brought back fond memories from the war. Not, of course, of death, mutilation and destruction on the grandest scale ever — these were best forgotten — but of the human warmth of comradeship in bush, desert and trench.

In 1927 a film called *Roses of Picardy* was screened at a Durban picture house. The British-born cartoonist of the *Natal Mercury*, Charles Evenden ('Evo'), had served in Europe and he came away from the war film wondering what had become of all the men he had known. He drew a cartoon depicting 'forgetfulness'.

In his autobiography Evo writes: 'The tin hat was the most symbolic item of the war and into my mind's eye came a capsized tin hat like a capsized lifeboat. Improving on that I thought of a waterlogged tin hat sinking away into a sea of forgetfulness. Comradeship fading out — and in the background the lonesome figure of a Fallen Soldier, whose thoughts one might safely leave to the reader.'

From this symbolism Evo conceived the idea of a brotherhood of old soldiers. Its name: Memorable Order of Tin Hats, a society within which former comrades-in-arms

FORGETFULNESS

could meet and remember together, and to offer their collective help to families fallen on hard times. They wore tin hat badges; their club branches were 'shellholes'; their chairmen were called 'Old Bill'; their song was *Old Soldiers Never Die*.

A network of Shellholes soon spread across South Africa, into adjoining territories, and then into Britain and the Commonwealth. In 1977 the MOTHs celebrated their 50th anniversary, and they still hold to their creed: 'We will remember them.'

THE SLOW AND SLUGGISH BLOOD

But while the ladies of the South African Gifts and Comforts Organisation Committee were still handing out free refreshments to soldiers and sailors in uniform, and the producers of Ellis Brown coffee were offering a prize to the first person guessing the correct date of the signing of the Peace Treaty, South Africa's returned soldiers were looking uneasily to the future.

Wounded and disabled had been drifting back to the Union since the German East African campaign; the battles on the Western Front had added thousands to the flow.

In November 1917 the *Standard* reported that men wounded at Delville Wood were met by the Mayor of Cape Town and half a dozen councillors 'but there were no crowds of enthusiastic friends, no stir in the city, no flags, no movement of the slow and sluggish blood . . .'

The lot of the returning South African veterans was that of warriors throughout history: as soldiers they had been heroes, now many, and especially the disabled, were an embarrassment. One man reported that he was refused a job on the mines because of his inju-

PAUSE FOR REMEMBRANCE

Dedication of the Delville Wood Memorial, France, in 1926. The cemetery where South Africans who died in the action are buried is next to the monument — the cemetery and memorial were designed as a unified scheme by Sir Herbert Baker, noted architect, and sometime resident of South Africa. The weeping cross in the Garden of Remembrance, Pietermaritzburg, is made of timber brought from Delville Wood, and almost every year, on the anniversary of the battle, the cross has 'wept' droplets of resin

Each day towards the end of the war the noonday gun that fired on Signal Hill was the sign for Cape Town citizens to be silent and bow their heads in prayer for two minutes. The noon pause was initiated on 14 May 1918 by the Mayor, Councillor H. Hands, who explained: 'In some places in the Union it has been the practice during the last few weeks to call a halt at midday in order to direct the minds of the people to the tremendous issues which are being fought out on the Western Front, and to afford a minute or two for silent prayer for the forces of the Allies engaged there.

'This seems to be an excellent example to copy, and I now appeal to all citizens to observe the same practice in Cape Town as from to-morrow (Tuesday). Upon the sound of the midday gun, all tramway cars will become stationary for three minutes and other traffic should halt wherever it may be for the same period.'

The Mayor asked pedestrians to remain standing wherever they might be when the gun sounded, and everyone, however engaged, to desist from their occupation and observe silence for the short spell. Employers could greatly assist by advising their staff to this effect, he added.

The *Cape Argus* reported the following day: 'This morning the citizens of Cape Town and residents in the suburbs responded to the Mayor's appeal to observe a few moments' silence at midday in sympathy with the gallant fellows fighting at the front, and as a token of respect to those who have fallen, or been wounded. As the midday gun sounded traffic was brought to a standstill. A soldier on Cartwright's balcony sounded *The Last Post*. Pedestrians came to a halt and the majority of males removed their hats.'

However, one person wrote to the *Cape Argus* to complain of 'a lamentable lack of adherence to the three minute halt requested'. Taxi-cab drivers, said the writer, were flagrant offenders in Adderley Street traffic, and by two minutes past twelve, 'the length of Adderley Street was in a state of ordinary animation again'.

On the second day the pause was more effective, and the *Cape Argus* stated that 'never has there been a more impressive three minutes in the heart of the Mother City of South Africa'. The Mayor subsequently decided that the pause would 'retain its hold on the people if it is altered to two minutes instead of three'.

The noonday pause continued until 17 January 1919, and was revived during the Second World War. No longer a pause, the boom of the gun is nowadays a signal for thousands of Capetonians to check their watches.

ries and couldn't get work on the land because farmers considered him 'a Government man'. Another said that his old job had been filled by a woman, and he could have it back only if he accepted the very much lower wage. There were thousands of similar cases.

Many associations were formed, but it fell largely to 'Comrades of the Great War' to lobby on behalf of neglected ex-servicemen. On the day after Armistice, its Cape Town branch promised 'perpetual remembrance' and vowed to 'take such steps as are necessary to protect them now, during and after demobilisation'. Between them, the Comrades and other bodies raised funds, found work for the men, reminded the public of its moral debt and pressured the government into action.

Tens of thousands of Capetonians gathered in the streets to celebrate the peace in 1918. These two photographs, taken from roughly the same viewpoint, show only a part of the tightly-packed crowd gathered in Adderley Street

In the face of the enemy

FOR VALOUR

RAF Captain Andrew Weatherby Beauchamp Proctor, V.C., D.S.O., M.C. and bar, D.F.C. was only 1,58 m tall but, said his commanding officer, 'That little man had the guts of a lion'. A somewhat modest lion, too. South Africa's most decorated serviceman, he could smile gently when telling of the time when a London policeman apprehended him for 'masquerading' behind a row of medals 'to which he was not entitled'. On his release, the apologies were predictably profuse and the faces red.

Serving in France with the Royal Flying Corps (it became the Royal Air Force in April 1918), Proctor shot down 22 enemy aircraft, forced 16 others, out of control, to the ground and destroyed 16 kite balloons. Moreover, his reconnaisance work and attacks on German ground troops were officially described as 'almost unsurpassed . . . in brilliancy'. His was the fifth highest battle score of the British aces and, astonishingly, he chalked up all his victories between 2 January and 8 October 1918.

On 20 September 1917 Lance-Corporal William Hewitt was awarded the Victoria Cross for bravery in the Third Battle of Ypres, during which he led his section in an attack on a German strongpoint. He later described the action: 'I make for the "pill-box" which has a sort of doorway low down on the right-hand side. I heave a grenade down it and shout "Come out, you so-and-so's." They do, two of them and fire with rifles at me at about 10 yards range and miss. Then some stinkpot throws a jampot on a stick bomb, which hits me on the chest and explodes. But the mutt who made it forgot to fill it with the odd bolts and nuts; so apart from blowing off my gas-mask and half my clothes, knocking out four teeth, breaking my nose, giving me a couple of black eyes with a lot of little cuts here and there, and knocking me backwards into a convenient shellhole, it didn't really do any damage — only made me damn mad.

'You see, I had become engaged to be married, and when I felt my teeth and face I thought, that's spoilt my beauty. She won't fall for me anymore.'

Moments later, however, Hewitt was severely wounded in the throat. Persisting with the attack, he was hit in the arm but still managed to dislodge the defenders of the strongpoint by tossing a bomb through the hole.

For the record

Private William Faulds of Cradock gained the Victoria Cross during the epic battle for Delville Wood. Braving intense machine-gun fire he rescued a wounded officer lying between the South African and German trenches at Delville Wood. Lieutenant Craig, the rescued man, said afterwards: 'No words of mine can portray my delight at hearing that Faulds gained the V.C. Faulds was my only chance in a million and Faulds pulled it off.'

Captain Oswald Austin Reid, the first Johannesburg man to win the award, told a civic reception in the city: 'It's all a matter of luck.' He won his Cross in Mesopotamia in

A.W.B. PROCTOR

W.H. HEWITT

W.F. FAULDS

March 1917, when his 'dauntless courage and gallant leadership' held a small post for 30 hours against repeated assault by bomb, machine-gun and shell.

Posthumous V.C.s were awarded to Captain Arthur Moore Lascelles and Colonel Richard Annesley West. Lascelles died of his wounds after routing an attacking German force of 60, with just 12 men. Colonel West strode up and down the front line under heavy enemy fire encouraging his troops to withstand a German attack. While he was shouting, 'Stick it, men! Show them fight! . . . For God's sake put up a good fight!' he fell, riddled by machine-gun bullets.

Other South Africans performed as impressively. Among those who won the Empire's highest award for gallantry during the First World War were:

Major (Acting Lieutenant-Colonel) John Sherwood-Kelly. In action near Cambrai in 1917, he personally led his battalion through 30 metres of barbed wire and murderous machine-gun fire to capture a German strongpoint, and shortly afterwards 'led a charge against some pits from which a heavy fire was being directed against his men, captured the pits, together with five machine-guns and 46 prisoners, and killed a large number of the enemy'.

Captain William Bloomfield was a Scotsman who had fought for Kruger against the British in the Anglo-Boer War and now fought for the British. During an action in the

campaign against Von Lettow-Vorbeck in East Africa, Bloomfield 'found that one wounded, Corporal D.M.P. Bowker, had been left behind. At considerable personal risk he went back across [about 370 metres of open ground] . . . The area was in full view of the enemy and swept by heavy machine-gun fire. Despite the hail of bullets, he managed to reach the wounded man and carry him back to safety'.

Lieutenant Reginald F.J. Hayward displayed 'almost super-human powers of endurance and consistent courage of the rarest nature' in March 1918, in France, when he successfully defended his entrenched position against wave after wave of attacking infantry. Although seriously wounded three times he 'continued to move across the open from one trench to another with absolute disregard for his own safety'. The position was held.

The Second World War produced its heroes too. Among the South Africans who won the Victoria Cross were:

Sergeant Quentin Smythe, in action in the Western Desert in June 1942. Although weak from loss of blood from a head wound he led his platoon against a strongpoint, captured it and then 'came under enfilade fire from an enemy machine-gun nest. Realising the threat to his position, Sergeant Smythe himself stalked and destroyed the nest with hand grenades, capturing the crew'. He continued the advance, encountered and destroyed an enemy anti-tank position.

O.A. REID

J.S. KELLY

W.A. BLOOMFIELD

Lieutenant Gerard Norton's courage was of a similar brand. Leading his platoon during the assault on Monte Gridolfo, a key point on Kesselring's massive Gothic Line defence of Italy, he 'attacked the first machine-gun emplacement with hand grenades, killing the crew of three. Still alone, he then worked his way to the second position containing two machine-guns and 15 riflemen. After a fight lasting ten minutes, he wiped out both machine-gun nests with a tommy-gun . . .' Norton went on to clear the cellar and upper rooms of a strongly defended house and, although wounded, 'continued calmly and resolutely up the valley to capture the remaining enemy positions'.

Squadron-Leader Edwin Swales, a 'Master Bomber' of the RAF's famed Pathfinders, won the D.F.C. on a daylight raid on Cologne's railway marshalling yards in 1944 and, the next day led a second raid on Pforzheim, setting off some minutes before the squadron in a Lancaster bomber equipped with special navigational aids. He lost two engines and his rear gun turret area but continued to manoeuvre the 'near crippled and defenceless aircraft', directing the other raiders on their run-ins. Swales didn't make it home. He kept the doomed Lancaster steady enough to allow his crew to bale out, and remained behind the controls until the aircraft crashed. He was awarded a posthumous V.C.

AND PRAISED BE WAR

Lieutenant William St Leger M.C., the son of a George doctor, was 23 when he was killed during the Battle of Lys in April 1918. He had been in France for 18 months, and he kept a detailed diary.

There is a poignantly schoolboyish charm about many of the entries. 'Huns' were 'bagged'; 'coalboxes' (high-explosive, large-calibre mortar shells) whistled overhead and leg wounds were equated with 'a hard hack at football'.

St Leger noted that ginger ale froze as it was poured into the glass and 'two oranges this morning were as hard as cricket balls'. His favourite poem was *A Plea for War*, written by his friend Denis Buxton, only son of the Governor-General of South Africa. Buxton was killed in Flanders in October 1917. His verse, published in the *Westminster Gazette*, concluded with gentle humility:

'And praised be war,
If only that it brings,
Rest from the weary strife
With little things.'

For St Leger the brutality of war was all too real. From his front-line trench, 300 metres from the Germans, he looked out on a ghastly no-man's-land. 'The ground,' he wrote, 'is simply pitted with shell holes, dead men lie here and there, heads towards the enemy, and nearly every one is lying on his face.' Snow fell and 'all the bodies in front of our trench turned white . . . One had been torn in half by artillery fire. One body lay on its back with its face facing the enemy, as if the poor fellow,

THE VICTORIA CROSS

The Victoria Cross is the highest British military decoration for valour in the face of the enemy. Instituted in January 1856, the bronze Maltese Cross may be awarded to any member of the Commonwealth forces (South Africans were eligible until the coming of the Republic in 1961).

South Africans who were awarded the Victoria Cross while serving with South African Forces:

W.F. Faulds	France	1916
W.A. Bloomfield	East Africa	1916
W.H. Hewitt	France	1917
F.C. Booth (Rhodesia)	East Africa	1917
Q.G.M. Smythe	North Africa	1942
G.R. Norton	Italy	1944
E. Swales	Stuttgart	1945

South Africans by birth or domicile who received the Victoria Cross while serving with other Commonwealth Forces:

T.E. Rendle	Belgium	1914
P.H. Hansen	Gallipoli	1915
W. Dartnell	East Africa	1915
F.A. de Pass	Flanders	1915
G.R.D. Moor	Dardanelles	1915
G.R. O'Sullivan	Dardanelles	1915
O.A. Reid	Mesopotamia	1917
J. Kelly	France	1917
A.M. Lascelles	France	1917
R.F.J. Hayward	France	1918
R.V. Gorle	Belgium	1918
A.W.B. Proctor	France	1918
H. Greenwood	France	1918
R.A. West	France	1918
J.D. Nettleton	South Germany	1942
C.G.W. Anderson	Malaya	1942

mortally wounded, had propped his head against something to watch how the others fared'.

One writer thought trench warfare the equivalent of 'ten Waterloos a week' but added that even 'a dozen Napoleons rolled into one could not move heavy artillery and launch infantry attacks over ground in which men sink down over their knees in the mud with every step they take'. In many trenches the men stood in a metre of mud; wounded had to be dug out quickly, before they sank and drowned. John Buchan wrote: 'So awful was the mud that each stretcher required eight bearers . . . battalion runners, though carrying no arms or equipment, took from four to six hours to cover the thousand odd yards between the front line and battalion headquarters.'

Chats and golf

There was mud, with its attendant 'trench foot'. There were also 'chats' — lice. In winter two men would share a bed, taking turns to hang out blankets and clothing. It needed two nights of hard frost to kill the lice. In summer, a soldier would run a lighted candle over seams to burn the eggs.

The troops were nearly always cold, nearly always hungry. But they seemed to have an almost limitless capacity to endure misery cheerfully. They sang songs both bawdy and sentimental, re-told old jokes and quipped in the sort of macabre vein that could only be appreciated by men who knew that they might die at any time. When they weren't killing or being killed they played golf, using the shell-holes for bunkers. And football: sometimes a ball would be passed from man to man during an infantry assault on the German lines.

Some soldiers were initiated into the horrors of war by mustard gas. A not unpleasant initiation for the first few moments — it smelt vaguely of pineapple — but the agony followed swiftly. Wrote a South African survivor: 'It seemed as if my lungs were gradually shutting up and my heart pounded away in my ears like the beat of a drum. On looking at the chap next to me I felt sick, for green stuff was oozing from the side of his mouth.'

After the war, one veteran summed up life in the trenches: 'We lived like rats, fed like rats, and died like rats.'

Q.G.M. Smythe

G.R. Norton

E. Swales

The second round

PARLIAMENT VOTES, AND THE CROWD ROARS

To fight or not to fight — in August 1939, as in August 1914, South Africans were divided on the question. 'Every Afrikaner,' said *Die Transvaler*, 'will agree with [Prime Minister] General Hertzog that it is unnecessary for any Afrikaner to be shot for the unjust stipulations of the [Versailles] Treaty. If the Britons and French made a mess of things that is their own affair.' The *Rand Daily Mail* took the opposite view: 'The path of duty which South Africa chose in 1914 is the only course of true patriotism.'

The issue was quickly resolved. Britain declared war on Germany on 3 September 1939. Next day Hertzog told Parliament that there was disunity within his cabinet and asked the House to endorse his policy of neutrality. Deputy Prime Minister Smuts proposed that the Union should sever relations with Nazi Germany and, reported one newspaper, after anxious argument and 'excited scenes in the precincts of Parliament . . . the House seemed overjoyed when at 8.40 p.m. the debate on the war question finally lapsed and the divisions began.

'General Hertzog, who found himself on the Opposition side of the House when the last division was over, did not recross to the Treasury benches. Looking aged and drawn he moved the adjournment of the House from the centre of what has hitherto been the Nationalist preserve.' Smuts had carried the vote by 80 to 67. Roared the tense crowd outside the building: 'We're in!'

Hertzog resigned, and Governor-General Sir Patrick Duncan asked Smuts to form a new government. Along with the premiership (his second tenure of the office, which Hertzog had held for the past 15 years) he assumed the portfolios of Defence and External Affairs. A state of war between South Africa and Hitler's Third Reich was proclaimed on 6 September.

Jan Smuts, said one periodical at the time, was an Afrikaner with 'prescience and a sufficiently broad spirit of inter-nationalism to lead the nation at the outbreak of what may well prove to be the world's most disastrous war'. In the course of the next five years, tens of thousands of fellow-Afrikaners, together with their English-speaking countrymen, would lend support to that leadership.

September fever

Nervousness, anticipation and busy preparation were features of the first few days.

Many stores immediately imposed self-conceived rationing systems to discourage hoarding, even though, as one journal pointed out, 'the population of the Union is roughly 60 per cent greater than it was in 1914 but food production has far outstripped the growth . . .' The *Cape Times* reported some 'panic buying' in the city; the price of a pound of best fillet went up by 2d; oil companies limited deliveries to the June-August average and demanded cash-on-the-nail payment from traders. One woman bought a gross of candles although she had electricity in her home: 'In case of air raids,' she told the storekeeper. And so it went on.

Key personnel — reservists, nurses, artisans — were forbidden movement out of the country. Simonstown dockyard job advertisements stipulated that applicants 'must be natural-born British subjects whose parents are also British subjects. Birth certificates must be produced'. The Mayor of Johannesburg launched a £1 million national fund for the Allied cause — and also to encourage 'our factories and primary producers, from whom we will buy all our products'.

Thousands of young women enrolled with the Red Cross or the St John Ambulance Association to learn basic first aid. Everyone wanted to help.

On 8 September the German freighter *Hagen* was seized at Durban's Maydon Wharf to become the 'Union's First War Prize'.

One columnist noted a sudden rush to the altar or, rather, to the Magistrate's Court: 'Nearly all the men . . . remarked that they were marrying in haste since they expected to be called up for service.' It transpired, though, that it was to be 'volunteers only' again — Smuts, for the same reasons that had prevailed 25 years earlier, felt unable to introduce conscription. Nevertheless, as the *Star* put it, there were immediate and countless 'enthusiastic offers of service by men and women of all classes, and creeds, English and Afrikaans-speaking . . .'

South Africans were at war.

The bitter fruits of Versailles and Munich. On 3 September 1939 European armies were on the march for the second time in the century. South Africa entered the lists three days later under the command of Smuts

POSTERS, BADGES, MEN AND GUNS: THE NATION RALLIES

The drive for recruits proved very effective. 'You Can't Appease Your Conscience,' posters told the people: 'Join In — Join Up'; 'Ons Springbokke Is Vegters. Komaan — Sluit Aan'; 'Who ME? Yes, YOU! We've Got To Win . . .'

Dozens of private and semi-official bodies gave moral and practical support to the recruiting effort. Two examples: the SA Corps of Ex-Servicemen called on all available members to enlist; the Women's Aviation Association, whose membership leapt to 3 000 within days of the outbreak of war, placed itself at Smuts's disposal.

In August the Defence Department had started issuing National Reservist badges at the rate of 1 000 a day (the most the Post Office in Pretoria could cope with). By 9 September 13 000 had been processed.

Four months later the *Rand Daily Mail* was able to say that 'the young manhood of South Africa has rallied magnificently to the defence of the country, which faces the future today with a steady confidence in its national preparedness'.

Of the Union's 570 000 white males between the ages of 20 and 60, nearly 190 000 — one out of three — volunteered for full-time military duties between 1939 and 1945, along with nearly 80 000 blacks and 45 000 coloureds, Indians and Malays. For a country with divided loyalties it was, in Smuts's words, 'an incredible feat'.

South Africans rallied to the Allied cause with gratifying alacrity. Within weeks of the declaration of war, many thousands of volunteers had turned up at makeshift recruiting offices (above) all around the country. The recruiting drive was enthusiastic and highly successful. Buildings, motor cars and fences were plastered with a variety of posters calling on all able-bodied men and women to join the Union Defence Force. 'Join to-day, Save tomorrow,' exhorted one poster. Another, in both official languages, asked: 'Are YOU helping to win the war?' Even teenagers could play a role — the Youth Training Brigade served as a military preparatory school

A NATION UNPREPARED

Troops on manoeuvres near Barberton, Transvaal, before their departure for the front. South Africa was ill-prepared for war. In September 1939 the country's tiny Defence Force boasted just two home-made armoured cars; two First World War tanks; 63 obsolete Hawker Hartbees aircraft (most of them unserviceable), two modern bombers; six Hawker Hurricane fighter aircraft, and SAA's Junkers airliners; the training ship HMSAS *General Botha* (an engine-less vessel moored at Simonstown); 70 decrepit field guns with enough ammunition for one day's good shooting, and a small-arms factory at Pretoria. An old six-inch howitzer, part of Cape Town's war memorial, was removed to serve as a training piece for artillery recruits.

The nation, in fact, had been ill-prepared for war. While Polish cavalry units were charging German tanks on the plains of their invaded homeland, Smuts pondered the even more woefully inadequate ranks, arms and equipment of his Defence Force.

In September 1939 the Permanent Force comprised 3 350 officers and men. There were 14 600 part-time soldiers in the Active Citizen Force; the Seaward Defence Force had a meagre 70 officers and 900 men. The country was even shorter on military hardware.

Smuts and his staff, military and civilian, set to work. By the end of the year there were 137 000 men under arms, and the volunteers were still pouring in. Trawlers and whalers had been converted into minesweepers and patrol-boats. The Seaward Defence Force, responsible for the security of 6 500 km of coastline, had been equipped with Junkers Ju-86s for reconnaissance and anti-submarine work.

Adolf Hitler was reported to have laughed derisively when he learnt of South Africa's entry into the lists — perhaps with justification at the time — but in May 1940, when his *blitzkrieg* columns were powering their way over northern Europe, the Union was re-arming heavily, slipping smoothly into high-gear war production.

From Iscor came steel for armoured cars, shells and bombs, guns and tanks; South African Railways' workshops turned out munitions and heavy armament; mine workshops produced shells, howitzers and mortars.

The initial trickle became a flood and by the time the war ended, South Africa had produced 768,3 million rounds of .303 ammunition, five million hand grenades, 2,6 million mortar bombs, 3,6 million shell bodies, 4,4 million shell cases, two million steel helmets, 5 770 armoured cars, ten million pairs of army boots and five million army blankets.

The 'happy warriors'

A SWIFT STRIKE FOR FREEDOM

Six weeks after Italy entered the war, threatening British East Africa and the vital Red Sea route through the Suez Canal, Smuts had a fighting brigade group in Kenya. Four months later he had a whole division there.

His plan to send South African troops north had drawn heavy fire from the Nationalist Opposition, who argued that the Union Defence Force had been established for the sole purpose of defending the country's borders. In answer, Smuts promised that only volunteers would serve outside the Union. Thousands took the oath to fight 'anywhere in Africa'. In the army and air force they were distinguished by an orange flash or 'red tab' on the shoulder strap, while naval volunteers wore an orange diamond on the sleeve.

Major-General Brink's 1st Division in Kenya comprised the 1st Brigade of the Duke of Edinburgh's Own Rifles, the 1st Transvaal Scottish and the Royal Natal Carbineers — better known as the Dukes, the Jocks and the Carbs; the 2nd Brigade of the 1st Natal Mounted Rifles and the 1st and 2nd Field Force Battalions; and the 5th Brigade of the 1st South African Irish, the 2nd Regiment Botha and the 3rd Transvaal Scottish. The Italian dictator's East African Empire was their first target.

When the 1st Brigade sailed for Mombasa and the battlefields of Abyssinia and Italian Somaliland, their Commander-in-Chief told them:

'We have fought for our freedom in the

Gleeful members of the 1st Transvaal Scottish (Lieutenant-Colonel E.P. Hartshorn is in the centre) after the capture of Addis Ababa in 1941. It was the first major prize to be taken in the war

South African troops arrive in Kenya, starting point for the hard-fought and highly successful campaign to oust Mussolini's troops from East Africa

Roads became quagmires after the first rains fell during the battle for Mega. Lieutenant-Colonel Harry Klein (centre) was one of those bogged down

---

'IT WASN'T VERY COMFORTABLE'

In January 1942 a new 1½d postage stamp was added to South Africa's 'War Effort' series. It depicted an adaptation of Neville Lewis's painting of an airman in tunic and flying helmet.

The airman was Lieutenant R.H.C. (Bob) Kershaw, a SAAF fighter pilot who won South Africa's first Distinguished Service Order of the East African campaign when he landed his Hurricane under heavy enemy fire during an attack on Diredawn airfield in March 1941 to rescue his flight commander, Captain J.E. Frost.

Captain Frost, who had been trying to set his aircraft alight after a forced landing, clambered into Lieutenant Kershaw's cockpit and, with enemy guns still bombarding the airfield, they took off. Said Lieutenant Kershaw afterwards: 'It wasn't very comfortable with two of us in the cockpit.'

The first wedding of a 'Mossie' in Kenya. Private A.M. Colbourne of the S.A. Women's Auxiliary Army Service married Private T. Kirkland

Springbok humour. This 'advertisement' by a heavy anti-aircraft unit was spotted in Kenya. Other signs proclaimed 'Grand Hotel' and 'Musso's Tomb'

past. We now go forth as crusaders, as children of the Cross to fight for freedom itself, the freedom of the human spirit, the free choice of the human individual to shape his own life according to the light that God has given him. The world cause of freedom is also our cause and we shall wage this war for human freedom until God's victory crowns the end.' After visiting his men in the field in East Africa, Smuts took to calling them his 'happy warriors'.

Hammer blows from the air

The South African Air force had been hammering the Italians in the air and on the ground from the very beginning. Four hours

before South Africa formally declared war on Italy on 11 June 1940, SAAF bombers raided an Italian outpost. By the end of the year, air force units were attacking Italian positions to clear the way for the advance of Brink's 1st South African Division into Southern Abyssinia and the 11th and 12th African divisions into Italian Somaliland.

On 10 January 1941 the Italian losses were estimated at 139 aircraft, 98 officers, 186 pilots and 67 non-commissioned officers. Sir Archibald Sinclair, Britain's Secretary of State for Air, later said: 'When the Italians come to draw up a list of factors which caused them to lose their East African Empire, they will place

South African soldiers after the capture of the fortress at Mega in February 1941. Inset: Two colour postcards, dropped by the retreating Italians, depict Abyssinians who fought on the Italian side in East Africa

The commanding officer of a medical unit in the front line hands out boxes of chocolates at Christmas

Abyssinia, 1941. Members of the 1st South African Infantry Brigade rest on the high slopes before preparing for the final assault on Amba Alagi

the SAAF bombers somewhere near the top of the list.'

The first 'cutting out' operation of the East African campaign was the raid on El Wak on 16 October 1940, when the South Africans, complete with air and artillery support, over-ran the garrison.

One corporal of the Dukes recalls this action and subsequent triumphs on the road to Addis Ababa and Amba Alagi — more with amusement than with pride. 'When we went into action on Dingaan's Day the Italians were flying six miles up, dropping bombs on us that didn't go off. They would have killed you only if they'd hit you smack on the head.

'It was the same throughout the campaign; the Italians would throw hand-grenades at us but forget to take out the pin. We used to collect them and go fishing with them.'

'Retreating in good order'

After El Wak, the next objective for the 11th and 12th African divisions, which included the 1st Brigade, was to drive out the Italian forces occupying the eastern boundaries of Kenya. Stifling dust in the Abyssinian lowlands turned to driving sleet and grey mist of the highlands as the South Africans advanced. Brigadier Dan Pienaar's brigade, with British Colonial troops, swept into Italian Somaliland and Abyssinia with a vigour that had the Italians reeling. Italian army documents picked up by South African forces in their drive against Mussolini's East African Empire reported the rout with an almost whimsical

logic: 'The Italian troops are retreating in good order. The South African troops are advancing in the wildest confusion.'

Scorpions and snakebites

Operations by the 2nd and 5th Brigades to seize Southern Abyssinia plunged South African troops into some of the most desolate and inhospitable battlefronts of the war. They faced not only the enemy forces, but also sand and lava deserts, dense bush and rocky outcrops that made travel a nightmare. Battles were fought in blistering heat, torrential rain and biting cold.

Many soldiers carried gramophone-needle tins filled with permanganate of potash for scorpion and snake bites. And the heat, at times, was almost unbearable. 'If you sit in the shadow of an acacia tree the sun will turn you the colour of a nicely baked tomato,' wrote one correspondent. 'Goodhouse or Komatipoort or the California Desert would seem arctic compared to this.' On the Southern Abyssinian Front opened by Major-General Brink's two South African brigades, Mega fell on 18 February 1941. The capture of this strongly-defended garrison, manned by blackshirt troops and defended by heavy artillery, was an important victory.

Italian-held positions in Somaliland and Abyssinia were soon falling like skittles, and at Amba Alagi, hundreds of kilometres to the north, the Duke of Aosta, Italian viceroy and commander-in-chief, was forced to surrender on 19 May (the Duke was held captive in Kenya, where he died on 3 March 1942). But the war in East Africa was not yet over, and there was more bitter fighting before General Pietro Gazzera surrendered at Dembidollo on 4 July and General Nasi's 22 000 Italian troops in their almost impregnable fortress at Gondar capitulated on 27 November.

Within less than a year the East Africa Force and Sudan Force had rolled up Mussolini's empire like a tattered carpet. In its 100 days of campaigning, the 1st Brigade had covered a remarkable 4 220 kilometre advance, and the South African land forces lost only 73 men killed in a total of 270 casualties suffered during the defeat of more than 350 000 enemy troops.

General Smuts in good humour during a visit to a forward operational airfield. He promised Air Mechanic A. McEwan (left) that in future 'Ouma' (Mrs Smuts) would see to it that he was kept supplied with razor blades

The home front

THE GREATEST ADVENTURE OF ALL TIME

'If South Africa's worth living in it's worth fighting for . . . on the home front, too,' proclaimed *Arthur Barlow's Weekly* in 1941. It was a time of posters and slogans, patriotism and mild austerity. War was shamelessly glamorized in the recruiting drive: 'Don't be left out of the greatest adventure of all time,' cried one poster. Another made a brazen appeal to vanity: 'Was there ever a girl who didn't prefer a man in uniform?'

There were warnings, too: 'Careless talk costs lives' and 'Don't talk about ships and shipping'. Factory workers ('The man in overalls wears a fighter's uniform') were exhorted: 'If you make a mistake do not cover it up . . . a hidden fault may cost a man's life.' Under the War Measures Act the destruction of old motor car tyres became a punishable offence. Old car batteries had to be handed in whenever new ones were bought, and even light bulbs were sold on the same basis.

Newspapers could not be used for lighting fires, but had to be stored for collection by municipal officials. The shortage of many types of containers was so acute that the breakage of a bottle was often more serious than the loss of its contents. The humble razor blade assumed new significance and people wrote to newspapers to boast of the long service given by blades.

Forswear Gorgonzola cheese?

If the war brought much confusion and unhappiness, it also created some ridiculous situations. Shortly after Italy entered the lists, the Cape Town Municipal Orchestra was prohibited from playing Verdi's *Requiem* — because Verdi was an Italian! The South African Broadcasting Corporation had refused to relay the concert anyway on the grounds of 'national feeling'. A member of the South African College of Music was moved to wonder whether people

Defences on the home front changed the whole face of South Africa. Barbed-wire entanglements, such as this complex erected on Durban's South Beach, became a familiar sight

would now 'burn Botticelli's pictures and forswear Gorgonzola cheese'.

Parliament debated State control of the SABC, alleged by one newspaper to be 'a hotbed of Nazi intrigue', but decided against it. The SABC's Afrikaans service was having enough trouble of its own with some of the war jargon. Thus, 'dreadnought' came over the air as *bang vir niks* and 'sea shanties' became *see pondokkies*.

Vera Lynn became the forces' sweetheart with such songs as *The White Cliffs of Dover* and *We'll meet again*, and classics like *Tipperary* and *Pack Up Your Troubles In Your Old Kitbag* were revived and sung with gusto by departing soldiers. Songs were both sentimental and patriotic, reflecting the need for companionship in an ugly war from which many never returned.

Sometimes the soldiers didn't sing. *Arthur Barlow's Weekly* explained: 'Unlike the last war, this is not a singing war, the men leaving the railway stations are sombre and serious. This probably means our soldiers realise that war is a horrible thing . . .'

A million and more stitches

Exhorted to 'Save for Peace', the public contributed the massive sum of £11,2 million to the National War Fund. The Post Office saved paper by printing small stamps; newspapers carried daily hints on saving money and materials. Men's suits appeared without pocket flaps or turn-ups, and frills, pleats and buttons disappeared from women's dresses.

The Mayor of Johannesburg announced that

Too many South African soldiers were fighting and dying for anyone to forget the war. In Durban this huge map of the European war zone, erected outside the City Hall, kept residents informed of its progress

Metals, and especially aluminium, were needed for the war effort. Dumps like the one pictured left, sprang up all over the country, with housewives donating tea kettles, frying pans and other utensils to 'Keep 'em flying'

Below left: a selection of South African petrol coupons, issued from 1942 onwards

Fund-raising tickets and posters — and a sombre warning

he would attend fewer functions, and walk to those nearby. Bicycle manufacturers enjoyed a boom in sales, and a Colonel Gordon rode to work in a hansom cab — 'patriotically declining lifts in any petrol-consuming vehicle'.

'Penny Plane' boxes were placed in factories and offices and workers were each expected to contribute one penny a day for every Axis aircraft reported shot down. As enemy air losses soared the poorer contributors asked to have Italian aircraft devalued to a halfpenny.

Women's magazines printed patterns for pullovers, mittens, balaclavas and socks, and some champion knitters emerged — each trying to beat the output of a mythical 'Mrs Ceaseless'. Wrote one woman: 'There must be many of us who have knitted a million and more stitches for the troops in the present war.'

Everyone wanted to be involved. The Union Unity Fund (motto: Win the Battle on the Home Front) swept the platteland with a blizzard of pamphlets to counter the supposed activities of 'Fifth Columnists', and a 'Truth Legion' was formed to counter Nazi propaganda.

Increased German naval activity and the fear of Japanese air raids prompted the Government to order nightly black-outs of ports and coastal towns. Wardens of the Civilian Protective Services made sure that citizens complied with the rules. Motorists drove with masked headlamps which emitted only a narrow beam of light. Weekend petrol sales ceased in November 1941, the month before Pearl Harbour was attacked. Japan's threat to the tanker lanes prompted petrol rationing in February the following year. Coupons allowed motorists to buy enough fuel — calculated according to the weight of the vehicle — to travel a basic maximum of 400 miles (640 km) a month.

And ever present was the sadness experienced by so many thousands as trains and troopships pulled away to the deceptively light-hearted strains of *Wish Me Luck As You Wave Me Goodbye . . .*

Recording (above) and collecting (left) for victory. Women threw themselves into fundraising projects with enthusiasm, organising fêtes, jumble sales and concerts for the war effort. Altogether, the South African public — and the country was not very wealthy at the time — contributed an impressive £11,2 million to the National War Fund

A production line turning out army boots by the thousand. Women also handled letters and parcels for the troops, helped in hospitals, ran recruiting campaigns, arranged hospitality for visiting troops from many nations — and, of course, knitted

Although not a thing of beauty, this was one of the attempts to run a car without petrol. The device mounted at the rear produced enough gas from charcoal to power the engine. Motorists were allowed enough petrol to travel 640 km a month

HAND GRENADES AND COLD-BLOODED MURDERS

General Jan Smuts spelt it out early on: 'We are fighting this war not only at the front, but internally as well.' He was referring to that sharp focus of anti-British (and pro-German) sentiment which was the Ossewa-brandwag — the 'Ox-wagon Sentinels'.

Founded in the Orange Free State during the centenary celebrations of the Great Trek in 1938, the organisation soon attracted members from all the provinces. Although launched with the aim of preserving and protecting Afrikaner culture and traditions, it quickly assumed a military character, arranging itself into 'commandos' and proclaiming its own brand of national socialism. The *Rand Daily Mail* described its goals as 'a republic and the breaking down of money power'.

The first leader of the Ossewa-brandwag was Colonel J.C. Laas, an officer in the permanent force. He was succeeded in 1941 by Dr H.J.H. (Hansie) van Rensburg, a brilliant attorney who had been appointed Secretary for Justice at the age of 30 and six years later, in 1936, became Administrator of the Orange Free State. That year he attended the Olympic Games in Berlin and met Adolf Hitler, whom he admired enormously.

Fervently hoping and working for the defeat of the Allies, the Ossewa-brandwag believed that a victorious Germany would assist in the establishment of an Afrikaner republic, and on many occasions its members clashed viciously with servicemen in the streets of the larger towns. Hand grenades were manufactured from water pipes, arms and ammunition were accumulated, and acts of sabotage and arson were committed

in the name of 'National Socialist South Africa'.

The Ossewa-brandwag was responsible for at least two cold-blooded murders of 'treacherous comrades', and on one occasion four of its *Stormjaers* (Storm Troops) abducted a National Party Member of Parliament and used a sjambok to thrash him 'to within an inch of his life', according to the doctor who attended him. The *Stormjaers* were the organisation's strong-arm squads. Although they all belonged to the Ossewa-brandwag, the organisation denied responsibility for their actions.

In a country-wide swoop in 1942, hundreds of its members were arrested and interned at Koffiefontein. Most were released in 1944, when an Allied victory seemed assured. One of those interned was B.J. Vorster, later to become Prime Minister and then State President of South Africa. Although the anti-war National Party shared certain of the Ossewa-brandwag's aims, the party leader, Dr D.F. Malan, time and again denounced the organisation.

As Germany's fortunes declined, so did the activities of the Ossewa-brandwag. There were fewer demonstrations, fewer radio messages to Berlin via the German Consul at Lourenço Marques. By 1947 the movement had virtually ceased to exist.

In May 1948 the National Party came to power, and the following month the new Minister of Justice (later to become South Africa's first State President), Mr. C.R. Swart, announced the release of Ossewa-brandwag members who had been convicted for crimes against the State. There were protests at this leniency — some members had been sentenced to life imprisonment — but these were ignored. It was the final chapter in the history of a movement which had been more of a nuisance than a threat to South Africa's war effort.

The big welcome

OASES OF THE OCEANS

When the war ended there were hundreds of thousands of men and women in all parts of the British Empire who had cause to remember South African hospitality. In Cape Town alone some 1 200 naval men and imperial troops were guests in private homes in and around the city each month of the war years. Members of one departing convoy wrote to the *Cape Times* in 1941: 'You showed us the true spirit of the Empire. We go on to fight against evil powers that would destroy this. When this is done you can prepare for a peaceful invasion of Cape Town by the British.'

Some of the visitors did in fact 'invade' South Africa after the war. Many had spent just a few days in Cape Town or Durban — but it was enough to draw them back for good.

Reporting on the success of the South African Women's Auxiliary Service canteen in the Mayor's Garden, the *Cape Times* said: 'Many thousands of visiting and South African soldiers, airmen, sailors and mercantile marines have been given entertainment there, with meals, snacks and teas prepared by expert home cooks and supplied at very small cost. Three thousand eggs have been served to guests in a single day. During May, June and July 65 544 eggs, nearly a ton of bacon and three and a half tons of sausages were served to hungry soldiers and sailors.'

The 'guest' children

Among those who responded to another kind of South African hospitality were the evacuees who trickled in from Britain, the Middle East and the Far East.

In August 1940 the chairman of the National Advisory Council, set up to administer the 'guest children' scheme with the Department of Social Welfare, announced that a deluge of offers of homes, farms and land had been received. Would-be hosts were carefully

Looking after sailors and soldiers on leave in South Africa was one of the tasks undertaken by SAWAS. The men and women were put up in hostels such as this or taken in by private families

The child guests at Cape Town Harbour. This group was taken to Westbrooke in Rondebosch, one of the many centres set up in South Africa to take in children from Britain, the Middle East and Far East

THE LADY IN WHITE — REMEMBERED BY THOUSANDS

Allied servicemen were packed off to war with little ceremony, leaving families and familiar sights for crowded troopships, foreign climes — and death. But there was one smiling, matronly personality whose voice and unselfish good humour endeared her to many thousands leaving Durban harbour, making the business of war just a little easier. She was the 'Lady in White'.

It was April 1940, and Perla Siedle Gibson was a comforting sight to the shipload of troops alongside the Durban dockside canteen. The young soldiers chanted encouragement: 'Hey Ma . . . sing us a song, Ma . . . come on, be a sport, Ma . . . give us Land of Hope and Glory, Ma . . .'

She hesitated for a moment, then cupped her hands to her mouth and sang the first notes of the stirring song. The troops fell silent, and then thousands of voices joined in, turning the harbour into a vast concert hall. For the 50-year-old mother of three, the response to that first song had the impact of a vision. She vowed to sing to every ship entering and leaving Durban harbour on the business of war — a promise she kept by meeting more than 1 000 troopships, over 350 hospital ships and many other vessels. She sang her way into the hearts of millions of Allied servicemen.

Always dressed in white and wearing a wide-brimmed hat, Perla Gibson, a trained opera performer, sang up to 250 songs a day — a feat which astounded professionals. She often sang through a megaphone salvaged from a torpedoed liner by a British sailor. *Time* magazine described her as 'a smiling, stocky, Wagnerian soprano' and *Life* christened her the 'Dockside Diva' in describing a typical parting scene:

'At first when the ship is untied the men join in so heartily that when an offshore breeze is blowing the song can be heard in central Durban a mile away. But by the time the ship is over the bar Perla is singing alone. Farewells are always charged by misty-eyed emotion on both sides . . .' On one occasion Perla's rendition of *Waltzing Matilda* brought so many Australians to the wharf side of their ship that the vessel listed, and her masts crashed into a grain elevator.

Perhaps the most poignant moment of her career was in 1963, when the 51st Highland Division invited her to be guest of honour at its reunion in Perth, Scotland. A Highlander who had heard her sing *Will Ye No Come Back Again* told her in front of the packed City Hall: 'To us you were the mother of all men as you sang us on our way.'

The Lady in White died in Durban in 1971, a few weeks before her 83rd birthday. Today a stone cairn with a brass plaque, erected by the Royal Navy, marks the spot where, in all weathers, she once stood and sang.

SAWAS — the South African Women's Auxiliary Services — were largely responsible for the magnificent hospitality extended to the visitors. Known as the 'Universal Aunts of South Africa', they ran clubs and canteens, organised dances, parties, film shows, outings — and performed a hundred other useful functions. The women of Cape Town and Durban welcomed convoys carrying anything up to 40 000 men, usually at little more than two hours' notice. Top: the 'Stand Easy Club', situated in the Old Beach Pavilion, Snell Parade, Durban. A three-course meal, bed, bath and morning coffee would cost a soldier about 1/6. Left: looking after the Royal Navy. Many of the Allied servicemen who called at South Africa's seaports, or trained as aircrew in the Transvaal, settled in South Africa after the war. Right: a dance at the Free French canteen in Durban

screened. Among other things, an applicant had to be 'of good standing in the community and earn not less than £250 a year when he has no dependant, and £300 a year when he has. The home must have proper and sufficient sleeping accommodation. One bedroom should not accommodate more than three people'.

The first evacuees arrived while Goering's Luftwaffe was pounding England by night and day, and as the war continued still more poured in from other trouble spots. When Japan entered the war in December 1941, women and children began to arrive from Malaya and India, more than 2 000 passing

through Durban in February 1942 after the fall of Singapore. Evacuees from Cyprus, Malta and Alexandria were landed at East London, and in mid-1942 the Administrator of Natal asked holidaymakers to return home from coastal towns to make room for 4 000 evacuees expected from Egypt.

From Abadan, in the Middle East, Mr S. Taylor wrote to the *Cape Times*: 'To the people of South Africa I, along with thousands of others, owe a debt of gratitude for the refuge they gave to our wives and children during those dark days of 1940 and 1941 when we were being hounded from all quarters of the globe . . .'

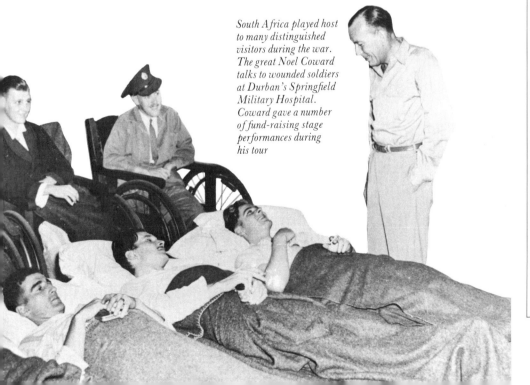

South Africa played host to many distinguished visitors during the war. The great Noel Coward talks to wounded soldiers at Durban's Springfield Military Hospital. Coward gave a number of fund-raising stage performances during his tour

ABLE SEAMAN JUST NUISANCE

Nuisance, the dog who joined the Royal Navy

In April 1944 an able seaman of the Royal Navy was buried with full honours on Red Hill, overlooking Simonstown. Around the draped White Ensign, 200 officers and men stood with heads bared as the strains of the Last Post and the crash of the firing party's volley died into echo. Just Nuisance, the Navy's most famous dog, had gone to his rest.

Just Nuisance had become a legend long before his death. He was known to thousands of British seamen as faithful shoremate, resolute other-ranker who kept his distance from officers and as spurner of civilians.

Once a perfectly ordinary Great Dane belonging to the manager of the United Services Institute in Simonstown, Nuisance had 'adopted' the Royal Navy. He went for walks with groups of visiting sailors, and was soon accompanying them on the train to Cape Town where they went on liberty leave.

The Railways authorities objected, and Nuisance's owner was preparing to sell him when the Navy stepped in, and the big dog was formally accepted into the Senior Service. His enlistment papers give his trade as 'bonecrusher' and his religion as 'scrounger', later changed to 'Canine Divinity League: Anti-Vivisectional'. His conduct sheet lists his character as 'very good', efficiency as 'moderate'; and among his seven recorded offences are travelling on trains without a ticket, sleeping in a bed at the Sailors' and Soldiers' Home, and resisting ejection from the Home.

He became a regular at the sailors' pubs, and was not above downing a beer with the best. He enjoyed the devotion of his mates and repaid it in the most practical way. Many a sailor, unsteady on his feet, felt a firm grip on his sleeve as Nuisance led him gently to Cape Town station. And on arrival at Simonstown, the dog always made sure that none of his charges remained sleeping in the train.

In January 1944 Nuisance was hurt while jumping from a bus, and was admitted to the Royal Navy Hospital, Simonstown. His official 'bed ticket' records 'paralysis of the sciatic nerve' and among the X-ray and laboratory reports is a sick-voucher signed by Surgeon Captain H.E.Y. White, later an admiral and personal physician to the King and Queen during the Royal tour in 1947.

The verdict was stunning: Nuisance would never walk again. He was put to sleep, and the Royal Navy went into mourning.

The Western Desert

BULLY BEEF, BREW-UPS AND BOREDOM

The Desert War, in which South Africans played a major part, was waged across a terrain regarded as perfect for 'war by the manual' — 'miles and miles of nothing'.

But at the eastern end of the nothingness was the prize of the Suez Canal, and until the surrender of the Axis forces in Africa in May 1943 the battle rolled backwards and forwards along the coastal strip of North Africa, with towns and vital ports being taken, lost and retaken.

Among the total of 160 000 South Africans who served in the Middle East Theatre was Corporal Bill Brierly, then with the Royal Corps of Signals. He has vivid memories of the food — or rather, the lack of it. 'We didn't see potatoes for years,' he recalls. 'If we were lucky we got a bit of goat or camel with onions. The main fare was army biscuits, which we boiled up with condensed milk. This was breakfast. For dinner we had biscuits boiled up with bully beef.

'Sometimes you couldn't eat for the flies. The bread looked like a currant loaf with them. Brew-up was the big thing. We filled up an empty petrol tin with sand, poured petrol in and set it alight. It made a perfect stove.

'Bugs and lice were terrible. Where they came from in the wasteland nobody could figure out. Desert hawks were also a menace sometimes. You'd be walking out of the mess tent with your plate of bully stew and there'd be a flash and a splash and your food would be gone. Those birds were better dive-bombers than the Stukas.'

A ration of 100 cigarettes a week brought some cheer, as did the irregular issue of brandy, known as 'ish', and the rum which was variously called 'Ouma's Blood', and 'Stuka Juice', 'Doodgooi' and 'Anti-Blitz'.

Shortage of water was another problem. Says Corporal Ted Artman, who served with

Surrounded by sandbags, soldiers take time off for a game of cards at Mersa Matruh, in the Western Desert

Members of the 1st South African Infantry Brigade dig in at Charing Cross, west of Mersa Matruh

Water was a crucial factor in the desert war: a soldier draws his section's ration for the day

Bathing was hardly a treat in the Western Desert. Half an oil drum was often all they had

ERWIN ROMMEL: EVERYONE'S HERO

In the desert, waiting to fight became a way of life for the Springboks. Searingly hot days were followed by freezing nights; there were the miseries of flies, sand-storms, hunger and thirst, slow-to-heal wounds, de-sert-sores, and the wracking agony of 'Gyppo guts' — the dysentery that few escaped. Small wonder that many men went 'sand happy'.

The tedium was occasionally relieved by a spell of leave in Cairo, where the bands in some of the clubs used to play behind wire netting to avoid the flying bottles and glasses. There were also, of course, the less savoury 'houses of a thousand delights'. Ex-servicemen remember that there seemed to be more fighting in Cairo than anywhere else in North Africa. Says one: 'It was a great place to let off steam.'

Then it was back to the sandy wasteland, perhaps to the enlivening news that Rommel was rumoured to be ready to start a new offensive. The admiration of the troops for the skilful and chivalrous General Erwin Rommel, nicknamed the 'Desert Fox', became a source of some concern to Allied commanders. General Auchinleck instructed that 'The important thing now is to see to it that we do not always talk about Rommel when we mean the enemy in Libya. We must refer to "the Germans" or "the Axis powers" or "the enemy" and not always keep harping on Rommel.' The instruction had little effect, and it remained high praise indeed to say a commander had 'done a Rommel'.

It was largely due to Rommel's integrity and professionalism that the North African war never sank to the savage levels of other theatres.

These Durban soldiers took their own piano to war (they even hired it out to concert organisers)

Egypt's Sphinx and pyramids were a favourite subject for picture postcards sent to the folks back home

'Corps de ballet' took on a new meaning when desert troops undertook to entertain their comrades

the Duke of Edinburgh's Own Rifles: 'At one stage in 1941 we didn't bath or wash for six weeks because the water was rationed. When I took my socks off they stood up on their own. We had to bath in our tin helmets, and a sponge was a great thing in the desert. We all wrote home for them. To save water we washed our uniforms in petrol. This also helped to kill the lice.'

To pass the time, the troops played cards and other games provided from the Gifts and Comforts Fund; cricket, rugby and football; ran Desert Derby Donkey Stakes, wrote letters home — and listened to the radio. There was 'Sarie Marais Calling', broadcast from Cairo,

South African officers enjoy a good meal after returning from their heroic stand at Sidi Rezeg

and also 'Marlene', who sang every night, at midnight, on Zeesen Radio, for the Germans of Rommel's Afrika Korps.

It was not long before *Lili Marlene* and other German songs became as popular with the Allied Eighth Army as with their enemies. Perturbed, the Union Defence Force organised a competition among South African troops to compose two 'suitable' marching songs: one in English and one in Afrikaans. The winning numbers, announced in *Springbok*, the force's weekly newspaper published in Cairo, were *Seuns van Suid-Afrika* and *Marching Song*.

Undeterred, the South African troops carried on singing *Lili Marlene*.

THE TRAGEDY OF TOBRUK

On 21 June 1942, fortress commander General H.B. Klopper surrendered Tobruk, and numbed South Africans heard Zeesen Radio gloat that Rommel had done the Union's Afrikaners a good turn by removing so many South African 'jingoes'.

News of the fall of Tobruk stunned the entire British Empire — 35 000 prisoners, of whom 10 722 were South Africans, went 'into the bag'.

An earlier garrison, proudly calling themselves 'The Rats of Tobruk' — the original 'Desert Rats' — had held out against everything the Axis could throw at them. But in the interim, many of the town's defences had been removed: anti-tank and anti-aircraft artillery, as well as mines, had been sent elsewhere. The Allied command had virtually abandoned the fastness. The panzers of the crack Afrika Korps and two Italian armoured divisions roared through the inadequately-

protected perimeter after a 'softening up' attack by Stuka dive-bombers.

Escape to a minefield

Flight-Sergeant Eduard Ladan of Kalk Bay was with 40 Squadron, SAAF, at Tobruk when it fell. He remembers: 'Tobruk was supposed to be impregnable, but after it had been flattened by Stukas and the remaining minefields blown up, the German tanks came rumbling in by the score. A lot of people blame Klopper for surrendering but he had no option. It would have been a massacre if he hadn't.

'The Germans came so quickly there was no time to get out. The next thing, a German officer came up and said, just like in the movies: "For you the war is over. You are now prisoners of the German Reich." And that was it.'

Ladan was one of the many who escaped. He had been put to work clearing wreckage in Tobruk harbour when a British bombing raid began. 'The Germans dived for cover. This was my chance. I jumped into a German truck with a couple of friends, jammed a German steel helmet on my head and put my foot down.'

They were waved through a German checkpoint and headed for the desert, picking up other stragglers as they went. After spending part of the night in the open they went on, and eventually saw movement ahead. Someone was signalling them with a lamp. A shot was fired over their heads but they kept moving, came to a halt among British troops, and 'A major of the Green Howards came up and said, "You must have come through on the wings of Jesus — this is a minefield".'

Just a year later the war in North Africa ended. Tobruk was avenged.

THE PAINTER'S VISION: SOUTH AFRICANS AT WAR

South Africa produced many fine war artists. They ranged from soldiers who made sketches in the field to professionals who were especially appointed by the Department of Defence to create a visual chronicle of the conflict. These artists accompanied South African forces to the battlefronts of the world, and returned with paintings that revealed all the drama, discomfort, pathos and occasional humour of war.

One of the best collections of war paintings is that of the South African National Museum of Military History in Johannesburg. It includes work by such artists as Francois Krige, Philip Bawcombe, Leslie 'Ben' Burrage, Terence McCaw and Gordon Taylor. Neville Lewis, the first official war artist, produced many portraits of the prominent military commanders as well as men and women decorated for bravery. Geoffrey Long, one of the best-known artists, was actually dropped by parachute behind enemy lines in Italy.

TERENCE McCAW *In billets*

ROSA HOPE *Hospital blues*

NILS ANDERSEN *Surrender of the 'Ammiraglio Cagni'*

LESLIE THOMAS BURRAGE *Shell burst*

GORDON TAYLOR *Arab grave diggers, Alamein cemetery*

NEVILLE LEWIS *Lt. Kershaw D.S.O.*

DOROTHY KAY *Parachute room*

NATALIE FIELD *Convoy time at the Playhouse, Durban*

GORDON TAYLOR *Royal Navy and S.A.N.F. Section Liberty Cavalcade*

NEVILLE LEWIS *Sailor*

Women at war

WAAFS, WAASIES AND SWANS

South Africa's women were more than ready to serve. They were unselfish, brave, went just about everywhere the male troops went, and without them the war effort could have faltered.

As early as 1938, farsighted women were compiling the names of those willing to help in any capacity in the event of war. The South African Women's Auxiliary Service (SAWAS) was established by the Department of Defence and was soon forming such volunteer units as the Women's Auxiliary Air Force, Women's Auxiliary Army Service, South African Women's Naval Service and South African Women's Military Nursing Service. Other volunteers served in munitions factories, in coastal defence units and as secretaries and clerks in various Allied agencies in the Middle East. At top strength the SAWAS numbered 65 000 women. General Smuts said of their contribution in early 1942: 'One of the most gratifying features of our war effort since the fateful days of 1939 has been the efficient and selfless response made by women from all walks of life. Without them we could not have done half of what we have done.'

Writing in *Outspan* in 1940, Jean McIntyre captured the spirit of women's involvement: 'After arriving at Pretoria station our transport arrived to take us to the barracks, and for the first time in our lives we were all bundled into a troop carrier; needless to say, this has been almost a daily occurrence since then. We rolled along merrily, all singing *Tipperary* and *Pack Up Your Troubles* in true military style.'

Women in uniform created a few problems of etiquette, though. As one observer recorded: 'What fiendish joy the friends of Private Jones derive from the sight of Private Jones meeting his wife, Captain Mary Jones, in the street, and coming smartly up to the salute.' To avoid these embarrassments at military social functions, the onus appears to have been on the women to change into mufti 'unless both partners are officers or of the same rank ...'

'Up North', the women faced different problems. One of the most taxing was the constant battle to protect their army-issue stockings from the voracious mandibles of the cockroaches. A report from Cairo reveals that the 'Mossies' of the WAAS (they were nicknamed by General Smuts) found that storing their stockings in bottles was the best solution.

Pink slippers and pom-poms

Air-Corporal Gladys Thompson enlisted as an ack-ack (anti-aircraft) gunner at a Cape Town battery in 1942. She described how she was trained as a specialist instructor: 'We sat around and learned how, since we were to be put in charge of instruments, including the identification telescope, the responsibility for deciding in a split second whether 'planes thousands of feet above us were friend or foe would rest almost entirely on our shoulders.'

While in training Gladys and her fellow pupils had to answer alarms in the middle of the night and rush out to 'man' the guns. She

South African WAAFs on board a tank in North Africa during the Second World War. The barracks at their Cairo headquarters were often the scene of parties and pranks, but the war was too close to forget

The 'Waasies' hold a sing-song in their headquarters in Egypt. Although discipline was strict, there was plenty of relaxation and entertainment

Wartime service in Italy was no picnic! Private Joan Dobie of Rustenburg and Private 'Steve' Neergard of Middelburg go to it with oil can and grease-gun

Many servicewomen returned home with photographs such as this. To stand in the shadow of the Sphinx and the Pyramids was an experience few forgot

OUMA SMUTS AND GLORY BAGS

For the entire Union Defence Force in the Second World War, one tiny old lady with curly grey hair and bright blue eyes symbolised home. Isie Smuts, wife of the Prime Minister, General Jan Smuts, was 'Ouma' (Granny) to all servicemen. And she called them all 'my boys'.

Ouma Smuts threw herself wholeheartedly into her war work. As president of the Gifts and Comforts Fund, she was responsible for the distribution of about three million cigarettes, one-and-a-half million pairs of socks, a million handkerchiefs, and tons of sweets, toiletries, tinned foods and sports equipment to South Africa's fighting men. Her 'glory bags' — made of khaki drill — brightened the lives of the whole Defence Force.

At both Groote Schuur and Libertas (the Premier's official residences in Cape Town and Pretoria), rooms were set aside for working parties. Ouma herself put in hours at her sewing machine making glory bags.

She had always hated social appearances, but now she lost no opportunity to speak in public if doing so would encourage her team, recruit new helpers, or raise funds. In all, some R2 million was found to pay for the contents of the glory bags and recreational equipment sent to the troops.

She accompanied General Smuts on a visit to the forces in Kenya and Egypt, and thereafter, wherever the general spoke, he had first to answer the soldiers' cries of: 'How's Ouma?' But there was a limit to the frail old lady's endurance, and in late 1942 she collapsed while visiting canteens and hostels in Muizenberg in the Cape. After that she made few public appearances, but her enthusiasm was undimmed. Not only did she continue making comforts and spurring on her helpers, but she exchanged an enormous number of letters with servicemen and their families.

Suitcases of correspondence accompanied her at all times. Her daughters and friends helped her to reply to the thank-you letters, but the special letters — those asking for advice or understanding — Ouma dealt with herself.

Her intense involvement and her deep concern for the troops may seem remarkable when her early life is recalled. She had known desolation and anxiety when Smuts was a commando during the Anglo-Boer War, and, during that hard time, she was implacably anti-British. Perhaps it was this personal experience of the loneliness of war that created her intense compassion for the fighting men and their families.

South Africa can have produced few women more universally loved and respected than Ouma Smuts.

went on: 'We snatched coats and tin-hats, somehow got our feet into slippers or shoes, and ran for all we were worth towards the gun-emplacements . . . some of us had our hair in curlers, and as we ran they clanged most comically against our tin-hats beneath which tangled curls struggled incongruously. We looked at each other and laughed. Pretty fringes of lace belonging to pyjamas or nightdresses showed beneath our heavy army greatcoats. Some girls wore pink slippers with fluffy pom-poms. One, in the darkness, had put on gold evening shoes by mistake. But she said she didn't care. The main thing was she had not been left behind.'

Women were equally active in the South African Navy. The Swans (the official title was Women's Auxiliary Naval Service) was inaugurated in October 1943 with a nucleus of 50 women who were attached to the service for clerical duties. Soon they were referring to floors as 'decks' and undergoing extensive training at SAS *Unitie* in Cape Town.

Miss Labuschagne gives it the works

It was shortly before midnight when Leading Swan Sue Labuschagne took control of the instruments connected to the mines guarding the entrance to Saldanha Bay harbour. Something was entering the harbour, yet nothing was in sight on the surface. It could have been an enemy submarine.

'Sir, please tell me when to fire,' said Swan Labuschagne to the officer in charge. The officer was aware that they couldn't afford to take chances. 'Give her the works,' he replied. Miss Labuschagne pulled the firing lever, and there was a terrific explosion as a group of mines was detonated. Out in the bay, the sea heaved up and spray was blasted hundreds of feet into the air. 'I was in a daze for at least forty-eight hours after the event,' she said afterwards.

Most women at war were stoic — and most managed to retain their femininity. Eve Norton, who was attached to the Union Bureau of Information in Cairo, told of her visit to a casualty clearing station at Mersa Matruh, in the Western Desert, in 1942: '. . . somehow I expected the conversation to consist entirely of the size of the bombs which fell the night before, or the noise of the ack-ack guns, or even the latest war developments. Instead no-one mentioned air-raids; no-one talked of the war. One girl was busily sewing in a corner, and the others were giving helpful advice about the best way to embroider the nightgown she was making out of a piece of parachute silk.'

Air-Corporal Gladys Thompson, left, was a WAAF 'Ack-Ack' instructor and found her job 'strenuous but interesting'. Far left: Leading Swan Sue Labuschagne missed a party to stand duty at Saldanha Bay harbour. That night there was an alarm, and she pulled a lever to cause an explosion that shook the area for kilometres around

Making up before the show. Entertainment Unit No 4 ('The Ballyhoos') provided much-needed diversion for South African troops in Europe

As part of her duties in Egypt, Sergeant-Major C.E. du Toit of Johannesburg had to visit scattered WAAS units. So she pedalled there

The Italian campaign

CHASING THE ENEMY

After a short but bloody campaign had reduced the island of Sicily, prompting the overthrow of Mussolini and the surrender of Italy, the way was open for the invasion of the Italian mainland and the defeat of the Germans in the final stage of the war. Troops of Montgomery's Eighth Army and General Mark Clark's American Fifth Army landed in Italy in September 1943. They were pushing the Germans northwards when the Sixth South African Armoured Division landed at Taranto in April 1944 to join battle for the first time.

The Division, formed on 1 February 1943 under the command of Major-General W.H. Evered Poole, was in action within a month of landing in Italy. From then on until news of the cessation of hostilities reached the Springbok troops outside Milan a year later, the South Africans helped pursue and plague the Germans who were retreating through the formidable Adolf Hitler and Gustav lines into Rome, Florence and through the Gothic Line to Bologna, Treviso and Milan. While the Division's forces — the 11th Armoured Brigade, the 12th Motorised Infantry Brigade and the 24th Guards Brigade — were rolling northwards, non-Divisional units of engineers and signallers as well as seconded South African officers were serving with other Allied forces. Meanwhile, squadrons of the South African Air Force were helping provide close support and raiding far into Europe and the Balkans from bases in occupied Italy.

The German forces in Italy surrendered unconditionally on Sunday 2 May 1945 and, with the end of the campaign, the Sixth South African Armoured Division settled down to garrison north-west Italy and guard the alpine frontiers with France and Switzerland.

Private Just goes to war

At the end of 1942, 17-year-old Bruce Just of Paarl joined the army to have a crack at the Germans who had killed his brother at Alamein in July that year. 'While I was doing infantry training, the Colonel called for volunteers for the 1st Royal Natal Carbineers,' Just recalls. 'He told us: "We're going into this fight to kill Jerries and wipe out this character

Cassino, in ruins, a month after its capture by the Allies. South African troops had their baptism of fire in Italy during the battle, one of the war's toughest

Units of the 6th South African Armoured Division fording the River Arno. The lighter vehicles were hauled through the shallow water by tanks

South African engineers distinguished themselves in Italy. The Ponte Jukskei bridge over the Arno, for instance, was a triumph of engineering skill: it took just over six days to build. It was 94,5m long and 12 m above the water. Divisional commander Major-General Poole, riding on a scout car, makes the first crossing

Two peoples, one victory. Axis propaganda tried to cement a shaky alliance between Germans and Italians

called Hitler and all I can guarantee is that a lot of you won't come back."

'One pace forward and I was in the "Carbs". Six months later I was boarding the *Stratheden* for Egypt. As we sailed, the Lady in White was singing *Wish Me Luck As You Wave Me Goodbye* and Zeesen Radio was announcing from Berlin that they knew we were sailing and that the German U-boats were waiting for us outside the harbour. "It is very sad that all of you are going to drown," Zeesen said. We didn't. After training in Egypt we sailed with the rest of the Division to Taranto and then on to Gravina. From there we went into the line for the first time, at Aquafondata, near Cassino.'

One of the key German defence points was at Cassino, where the Allies tried four times to

clear the road to Rome. Some of the most desperate battles of the Second World War were fought there when the Allies began to push the Germans out of Italy. In January, February and March of 1944, various Allied forces tried to fight their way past the determined Nazi forces, but each time they failed, and each time they suffered heavy casualties. By March more than 1 000 tons of bombs had been dropped and nearly 200 000 rounds of artillery fire poured into the village.

On 11 May, with back-up South African forces, the Allies tried to break through again. That night 2 000 Allied guns opened fire in what must have been one of the greatest bombardments of all time. Crossing the river, the soldiers encountered a maze of mines and barbed wire — and fanatical Germans. As

The rugged Italian terrain. This barely passable road was the only one from Florence to the South African positions. The going was muddy and slow

Cape Corps stretcher-bearers lift a wounded soldier on to their jeep-ambulance at the battle for Monte Sole, the last major attack by the South Africans

'The Modernairs', a UDF concert group, attract amused glances as they parade down a street in a northern Italian village. All four girls are sergeants

The unpretentious but welcome 'Outspan Club' in the freezing Apennines, which served up to 4 000 cups of tea and coffee a day to Springbok troops

Allied prisoners of war showed remarkable ingenuity. These newspapers — written, edited and printed behind barbed wire — exemplified their determination to live as civilised a life as possible. Writing styles and formats varied, but humour appeared to be a common denominator

Just's brigade group held the enemy north of Cassino, they were subjected to a continuous bombardment by mortars. For the South Africans, who had trained in the vast spaces of the African desert, getting used to fighting an enemy perched on a steep hill above was anything but easy. 'Mortars are terrifying,' recalls Just. 'You can hear them whistling as they come but you don't know where they are going to land. They come straight down on top of you.'

The young private was in the thick of fighting near Cassino. Although the first brutal assault shook the Germans, it took a week for the Allied forces to clear the debris of the fight.

Allied soldiers died for every metre of territory at Cassino. Roads had been mined and the rubble of war provided cover for the enemy soldiers and machine-gun emplacements. It was only on 19 May that the Germans were pushed back from their defence frontier and South African engineers could begin clearing the old highway — and converting the railway into a second road — leading to Rome.

The 'Carbs' pushed on to Frosinone. Recalled Just: 'The Germans were always ahead of us, perched on the heights, watching us. As we came up they would pick us off with their 88s and they'd have machine gun nests on the bends of the little walled lanes so that they could rake us as we came around.'

On 4 June the Allies were greeted by throngs of jubilant Italians in Rome. The South Africans passed through two days later. 'We didn't see much of this great city,' says Just, 'as we pushed on to Civita Castellana and Celleno, where there was one of the few real tank battles of the Italian campaign. I was riding on the back of a tank and it put the fear of death into me . . .

'At Chiusi, where the Jerries were again above us, we were shelled all night and mortared by *Nebelwerfers* — six-barrelled mortars. I went with our company sniper to the top of a building and he was a marvel to watch. It was 900 yards across the valley and we could see Jerry's steel helmets moving in the trenches. Ken would take a shot and a steel helmet would go flying. I was terribly impressed.

'When we got to Greve, I was given a supply jeep to drive to deliver rations to the troops. I thought it would be marvellous: nothing would be shooting at us. On the first breakfast run we had gone about 500 yards when the first shells hit us. Every time the shells came down we threw ourselves in the ditch . . . On the way back, I drove round a bend just as a huge Sherman tank came crashing down. The tracks caught me on the side of my chest and broke all my ribs.

'When we took Florence, I was in hospital in Rome.' Florence had to be taken before the Allied armies could stage their final assault on the underbelly of Europe. Just rejoined his regiment at Prato after convalescing in Naples. The next task was to get through the Germans to Bologna.

'Just south of Bologna we came up against the most fanatical of the Germans. All these blond young soldiers came in extended order, wave after wave, singing *Deutschland Über Alles* and being mown down. For a youngster like me, it was more than I could take. When we went to war we thought it would be like our schoolboy heroes Tom Mix and Buck Jones coming unscathed through a hail of bullets. It was nothing like that at all.'

For the South Africans, the worst part of the campaign was the winter of 1944. The troops had to battle through a narrow front and mountainous country up to their necks in snow and later sludgy ice. They were on their way past Bologna and then northward.

'The spring breakthrough was the hardest fighting we had to do. After Bologna, the war was a piece of cake. Even the food improved. We couldn't eat any more bully beef and the Yanks couldn't face Spam. So we swopped, and life was rosy.'

The 6th South African Division cemetery near Castiglione. Italian women frequently visited the cemetery to put flowers on the graves. Union troops were involved in fierce fighting just north of the area

Peace and goodwill

THE MAD, MERRY AND UNFORGETTABLE MOMENT

On the morning of 8 May 1945 the Union seethed with suppressed excitement. Johannesburg, said the *Star,* was 'like a bride dressed for the wedding who has been informed at the last moment that the ceremony would be unavoidably postponed for several hours at least'.

The city was ready and eager to take part in the rejoicing at the end of the war in Europe, but nobody knew quite when to begin. Some jumped the gun, but most waited for the formal announcement contained in Winston Churchill's broadcast speech from the British House of Commons at three in the afternoon. Finally it crackled from countless wireless sets: 'The German war is at an end,' and for South Africa, VE (Victory in Europe) Day celebrations officially began.

In Johannesburg, the boom of guns from Berea, the scream of sirens and the blast of mine hooters greeted the announcement. Offices and shops had closed at noon and the streets of the flag-bedecked city filled with jubilant crowds.

Reported the *Star:* 'Soon after noon a snow-drift of white ticker-tape and scraps of office paper swirled down from the skyscrapers in Commissioner Street. Caught in a westerly breeze, the papers fluttered like a swarm of white butterflies and skimmed over the highest buildings. The air, the pavements and the roadway were white with paper, which alighted on stockbrokers and mining magnates with bright nosegays in their lapels and on city typists with colourful favours pinned to their frocks.

'By 3 p.m. the City Square was packed with more than 10 000 people among whom were many soldiers, sailors and airmen. All listened

Coming home. South African veterans return from the theatres of war, and pose a serious resettlement problem. The Government acted swiftly, efficiently and generously, promising that 'No volunteer will be discharged from the force unless he or she has a suitable job'. No other Allied government gave the same undertaking. Altogether, 155 000 ex-volunteers were placed in employment. There were also substantial gratuities, interest-free loans and outright grants to help them build homes, start farms, resume college careers

VE — Victory in Europe — Day in Cape Town. Thousands throng Adderley Street on 8 May 1945. Three months later Japan surrendered after the cities of Hiroshima and Nagasaki were obliterated by the atom bomb

to Mr Churchill's speech and at the closing words ". . . saved the freedom of the world: God save the King", the trumpets rang out and the crowd took up the anthem with full hearts, and roared out the words "Send him victorious, happy and glorious". As the last notes died away the sirens blared again. Motorists sounded their hooters. Tram-drivers rang their gongs. People cheered, shouted and sang.

'A young man on the City Hall steps called out "Three cheers for our Springboks". The gathering responded with a will and answering shouts echoed from crowds gathered outside the Supreme Court.

'Young men started dancing like Dervishes on the lawns and threw fire-crackers into the air. Others ran like monkeys along the ledges of the City Hall. It was a mad, merry, unforgettable moment into which the people tried to compress all the relief they felt from the suspense, anxiety and strain of five years of terrible war.'

On the gold mines, work was halted as the hooters blared at three in the afternoon, and the 'natives were given extra beer'. There was joy even in the gaols. With the exception of the 'lifers', each convict was granted a three month remission of sentence.

Within 15 minutes of Churchill's broadcast,

Repatriated South African prisoners of war — many of them bewildered defenders of Tobruk — on their way to dispersal at Snell Parade, Durban

CHRISTMAS 1945: HALFWAY BETWEEN AUSTERITY AND PLENTY

Two weeks before South Africa was due to celebrate its first post-war Christmas, a Government notice made the hoarding of butter, sugar, condensed milk, tea and rice an offence punishable by heavy sentence.

Not that there was much to hoard. These and most other foodstuffs, as well as beer, spirits and petrol, were in short supply. Despite all this, observed one newspaper, shortages would not be allowed to kill the planned celebrations and reunions which, for many families, would be the first such carefree occasions since September 1939.

The *Cape Argus* reported that 'the choice of novel or luxury gifts of good quality and reasonable price is limited. The shadow of war still hangs heavily over the first peacetime Christmas'. But in fact, many goods unobtainable since the outbreak of the war were back on the shelves, including lingerie sets, hand hair-dryers, prams and silverware. Toys, though, were scarce, expensive and for the most part crudely made. Jewellers, lacking supplies from abroad, offered a wide variety of locally manufactured wooden novelties.

As Christmas approached, the meat queues grew longer. In Johannesburg, one began forming at seven in the evening outside a butchery in Loveday Street. By midnight 50 people were waiting, and when the staff arrived at three there was no parking space to be found near the shop. The doors opened at six and, when stocks ran out three hours later, 412 people had each bought a maximum of 10/- worth of meat, and a further 300 would-be customers went away empty-handed.

A newspaper predicted that the average family's Christmas dinner would be midway between the war-time 'austerity level' and the pre-war level of plenty, adding that there was 'at all events an abundance of goodwill . . .' The shortage of beer, particularly, was described as 'acute'; a long period of drought limited the supplies of fruit and vegetables.

The Christmas Day issue of the *Cape Times* reported that, scarcities notwithstanding, there had been a record shopping and spending spree: 'Bottle stores were swamped with orders and in many cases these could not be fulfilled . . . The spirit of good fellowship found its way even to the staid and stern precincts of the magistrate's court, where "drunks" were let off with a caution.'

To cheer its readers, the newspaper pointed out that things were not as bad as they might be, and published a comparison of consumables available in Cape Town and London. This showed that while South Africans had 'abundant' candied fruits, nuts and raisins, these were unobtainable in London, where the price of turkey, on the black market, was 15/- a pound — more than seven times the cost in Cape Town. In Cape Town there were 'ample' eggs at 2/6 a dozen, while Londoners, with the end of rationing not yet in sight, were each limited to a single egg.

---

a notice announcing the birth of a baby boy, Victor, was placed in the Pretoria office of the *Star*. 'There will be many Victors born during these historical days, but this was probably the first in South Africa,' said the newspaper's columnist. Pretoria, too, outdid itself in decoration: the city was a riot of red, white and blue. Children were dressed from head to foot in Allied flags, and even the dogs wore red, white and blue ribbons.

In a message to the Union, Churchill said: 'History will record the heroic achievements of South Africa's fighting men who once again on land and now in the air and at sea have proved themselves second to none.'

Perhaps the most moving sights were the troopships at Durban and Cape Town, with South Africa's warrior sons, who had been through the battles of North Africa and Europe, streaming down the gangways. The boys were coming home.

Part of a volunteer's scrapbook. War had given thousands of South Africans the chance to sample the sights, smells and sounds — and the food and drink — of exotic places. This serviceman spent half the war years in East Africa, went on to the Western Desert, then joined the navy, which took him to many countries in the east, including Hong Kong, Australia, New Guinea and the Solomon Islands

---

SOUTH AFRICA — A PRISON WITHOUT BARS FOR 90 000 ITALIANS

Of the 93 000 prisoners of war interned in South Africa, all but 4 000 were Italians. Many were employed by the Government — in the Forestry, Lands and Agriculture Departments, and by the National Roads Board. Others worked on farms.

Some elected to settle in South Africa after the war. Raffale D'Amato was one.

D'Amato had been a member of the gun-crew of the last heavy howitzer to fire on the Australians who took Tobruk in January 1941. For him the war was over, and at the other end of the continent lay a new life.

After spending two months 'in the cage' in Alexandria, he boarded a ship for an unknown destination. 'We're in America,' he shouted weeks later as the ship berthed against a background of skyscrapers. It took a long time to convince the 25-year-old Italian that this was Durban — he had supposed South Africa to be a place of no more than 'grass huts'. He spent 18 months in the camp at Sonderwater, of which former sergeant Ugo Spettu, now of Cape Town, wrote: '. . . for the first few months life was very pleasant. It changed when the Italian Blackshirt POWs arrived and started to cause political friction . . . Eventually they were put into another section and separated from us by barbed wire . . .'

D'Amato had been apprenticed to a watch-maker, and he soon made contact with a former Russian refugee of the First World War who had established himself as a jeweller in George. He began taking home work which he would return on the following Friday, until in 1945 he was sent back to Italy. But it was an Italy he no longer recognised.

Three years later he was back in George, where his old friend the jeweller took him to the holiday resort of the Wilderness. D'Amato promised himself then that he would one day have a home there.

Today, a large home, distinguished by Doric columns and other features of classical Mediterranean architecture, catches the eye of passers-by. The former gunner in Mussolini's army had become a successful South African jeweller and watch-maker, and had built the holiday home of his dreams.

Italian prisoners of war on arrival at Durban in 1941

The era of 'Slim Jannie'

'I HAVE PROFOUND FAITH IN THIS COUNTRY'

Throughout the first half of this century, in war and in peace, one figure stood tall at the epicentre of the country's turbulent affairs. Soldier, statesman, scholar, sage — to many, Jan Christiaan Smuts personified the nation's best qualities.

Smuts was something of a political prodigy: before he reached 30 he had been appointed State Attorney of Paul Kruger's Transvaal Republic. In *The Thoughts of General Smuts*, P.B. Blanckenberg, Smuts's private secretary from 1933 to 1939, recounts Smuts's own description: 'I did not look a day more than twenty. I entered the Raadzaal to looks of surprise on the faces of many members, and I distinctly heard Commandant Koos Malan, a brother-in-law of the President say to a neighbour *sotto voce:* "My Gods, man, het Paul heeltemal mal geword? Die nuwe Staatsprokureur is 'n pure seun." (My God, has Paul [Paul Kruger] gone stark mad? The new State Attorney is a mere boy).'

Known to his people as 'Slim (clever) Jannie', and later as 'Oubaas', Smuts went on to become Kruger's chief adviser in the negotiations with Britain before the Anglo-Boer War. He later conducted some of the outstanding guerilla campaigns of the war.

The record of his achievements during the following 45 years, and the honours that went with them, is long and impressive. He was the leading architect of Union in the first decade of the century; appointed commander of the British forces in East Africa in 1916; South African representative at the 1917 Imperial Conference in London, and a member of the British War Cabinet. In the latter capacity he

General Smuts on a First World War recruiting poster

Three faces of Jan Smuts — the academic, the soldier and the apparently tireless old man of the mountain

was instrumental in creating the Royal Air Force as a separate fighting service.

Working for peace

At a banquet held in his honour in the Royal Gallery of the House of Lords in 1917, Smuts outlined his scheme for a new kind of Empire — ideas which eventually, in 1931, were translated into reality by the Statute of Westminster. This proclaimed the British Commonwealth of Nations, the concept first defined by Smuts. Before returning to South Africa in 1919, he helped with a temporary settlement of the Anglo-Irish nationalist confrontation (three years later, back in England, his advice helped to bring about the Anglo-Irish settlement), and published a paper which suggested the framework of the future League of Nations. Ironically it was Smuts, a South African, who helped give the world a new hope for unity in the 1940s by drafting the preamble to the constitution of the League's successor, the United Nations.

Sarah Gertrude Millin, in her biography, *General Smuts*, reports his description of those hectic and rewarding early years in London: 'I had no time for anything but work. There was no end to the work they wanted me to do. I have never worked so hard in my life. My hair became white. My brother, at sixty, has hardly a white hair. My brother is a happy man. My hair was nearly white at fifty.'

Smuts served twice as South Africa's Prime Minister (1919-24 and 1939-48), his last terms of office encompassing the dramatic years of the Second World War. As Winston Churchill's close friend and confidant, his was a powerful behind-the-scenes influence on the conduct and course of that global conflict.

The private Oubaas

Complementing this remarkable range of achievement was a commanding presence. Sarah Gertrude Millin reported T.P. O'Connor's description of his 'strange eyes . . . a cold clear blue, steely to hardness, brilliant, almost dazzling, almost affrighting'. The result was that most people tended to be in awe of the Oubaas, not realising that he was at heart a very human man who never lost the common touch.

And a compassionate man. After the Second World War, he sought out General Paul

von Lettow-Vorbeck, the German commander who had opposed him in East Africa three decades earlier. In an ironic twist of history, he came upon the Von Lettow-Vorbeck family penniless — and did what he could to help them.

One of the greatest tributes to Smuts as a man is the esteem in which he was held by that great judge of men, Mahatma Gandhi. Although the two were antagonists during the latter's campaign of resistance against South Africa's Indian laws, Gandhi came to respect the Oubaas so much that he made him a pair of sandals while in prison. Smuts cherished them for the rest of his life.

This picture of Smuts was written in 1942 by Lord Harlech, then British High Commissioner to the Union, in a private letter to Clement Attlee, Secretary of State for the Dominions: 'He is 72 years of age, still erect, spare of body, dapper in his clothing, and intensely full of vitality. He keeps himself physically fit by eating little, and taking long walks over his 2,000 acre country estate at Irene, some ten miles from Pretoria. He is a non-smoker and almost a teetotaler. He takes a great personal interest in his two farms ... At Irene he leads a patriarchal Afrikaner life surrounded by his wife, daughters and many grandchildren. This ramshackle house was bought by him over thirty years ago and is completely "unmodernised" and always gloriously untidy ...

'He intensely dislikes having to sleep in or occupy the rather "grand" new official residence of the Prime Ministers of the Union in Pretoria. When he is compelled to spend a night there to entertain guests he refuses to occupy any of the principal bedrooms but has had an iron bedstead and severely plain furniture put in the box room, which he declares is the only tolerable room in the house!'

At Doornkloof, the Smuts home, Smuts's inner sanctum was his study, a large library crammed with books that ranged from contemporary volumes on philosophy, history and science, to 16th- and 17th-century works in Latin and Dutch. He was a brilliant man of wide learning. In the Anglo-Boer War he led his guerilla raiders with a copy of the German philosopher Kant's *Critique of Pure Reason* in his saddlebag.

In 1932 he delivered a paper to the South

Jan and Isie Smuts with their family in 1921. They were married at Stellenbosch in April 1897

African Association for the Advancement of Science, setting out his theory about the relationship of geology and climatology to human history. It was hailed as a landmark in the science of anthropology.

But the pinnacle of Smuts's intellectual life was the book that he wrote between September 1924 and September 1925, *Holism and Evolution*. This 140 000-word volume sets out the Oubaas's conception of the universe, embracing the nature of space, time, life and the mind itself. Winston Churchill confessed that he was awed by the book. Alfred Adler, the psychoanalyst who created the system of Individual Psychology, said Smuts had supplied the scientific and philosophical basis for an advance in psychology.

Silence and solitude

'When I want a rest,' Smuts told his private secretary, 'I turn my face to Nature and the Mountains for silence and solitude.' He loved, especially, to climb Table Mountain, though he was fascinated by all of the natural world. According to Dr John Hutchinson of London's Kew Gardens, the Oubaas had so mastered the study of botany that no more than six experts could match him in identifying, at sight, the grasses of South Africa.

Smuts had known much suffering and tragedy in his decades of public life, yet he remained an optimist. He believed in humanity, and in his land.

'I have profound faith in this country and its people,' he said in a speech at Komga in 1935. 'I have seen them beaten and hammered and on every occasion they have run true. I have seen them in the Boer War and in the Great War, pitting their strength against the greatest and bravest in the world. I have seen them do their duty without flinching. I have faith in the human material of which our nation is made.' He had faith in them all, said Smuts, black and white, and he was proud to be a South African.

Jan Smuts died in September 1950. Isie Smuts, whom he had met while a young man at Stellenbosch and who had shared his long life, did not go to his funeral. But two nights later a teacher from a black school came to Doornkloof with a children's choir. The funeral train had sped through the railway station too fast for them to sing for the Oubaas, and they wanted to know if they could sing for Ouma now.

Yes, Isie replied. She wanted them to sing.

The Big House on the Smuts family farm, Doornkloof. It became a national monument in 1969

Smuts's library, of about 6 000 volumes, is preserved at the University of the Witwatersrand

Prince George and General Smuts (then well into his sixties) at the summit of Table Mountain in 1934

At No. 10 Downing Street with Britain's wartime Prime Minister, Winston Churchill, and Mrs Churchill

A cartoon by Packer (Quip), reproduced by the Star *in 1924. General Hertzog looks on*

Smuts's 80th birthday celebrations (note the huge 'birthday cake') drew large crowds in Johannesburg

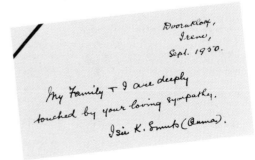

Isie Smuts acknowledges an expression of sympathy after her husband's death in September 1950

Chronology

This chronology provides a selective summary of South African and world events, some of major importance and others of nostalgic interest, from 1880 to 1980. It is not intended to be exhaustive, but instead serves as a many-spanned bridge linking 100 tumultuous years.

1880
- The Cape Parliament rejects a scheme for a South African federation.
- Transvaal claims independence from Britain and declares itself a republic. The start of the first Anglo-Boer War.
- In France Louis Pasteur identifies Streptococcus bacteria.
- In the U.S.A., T.A. Edison and J.W. Swan independently make the first practical electric light.
- In Britain W.S. Gilbert and Arthur Sullivan write 'The Pirates of Penzance'.
- William Ewart Gladstone (Liberal) becomes Prime Minister of Britain.
- Major-General H.H. Clifford replaces Sir Bartle Frere, becoming Acting High Commissioner and Acting Governor of the Cape, and after two weeks is succeeded by Sir G.C. Strahan.
- G.P. Colley succeeds H.E. Bulwer as Lieutenant-Governor of Natal.
- The Afrikaner Bond, with 'Onze Jan' Hofmeyr as its leader, is founded in the Cape Colony.

1881
- The Boers defeat the British at Laing's Nek and Majuba Hill. Britain concludes the Pretoria Convention, recognising the independence of the South African Republic (Transvaal).
- Pablo Picasso is born in Spain.
- Western outlaw Billy the Kid is killed in New Mexico by Sheriff Patrick Garret.
- James Abram Garfield (Republican) succeeds Rutherford Birchard Hayes as U.S. President, is assassinated, and is in turn succeeded by Chester Alan Arthur (Republican).
- T.C. Scanlen succeeds J.G. Sprigg as Prime Minister of the Cape Colony.
- Sir Hercules Robinson becomes High Commissioner and Governor of the Cape.
- Germany, Austria and Russia form Three Emperors' Alliance.

1882
- Italy joins the Austro-German alliance, which becomes the Triple Alliance.
- Franco-British dual control of Egypt is established.
- Tuberculosis bacillus is identified by Dr Robert Koch in Germany.
- Married Woman's Property Act in Britain gives married women the right of separate ownership of property of all kinds.
- Gottlieb Daimler builds the first petrol engine, in Germany.
- Psychoanalysis is pioneered by Viennese physician Josef Breuer, who uses hypnosis in treating hysteria.
- Republics of Stellaland and Goshen proclaimed on the western border of the Transvaal.
- London's Savoy Theatre, built by Richard D'Oyley Carte, opens with the first electric illumination in any British public building.
- St Gothard Tunnel, first railway tunnel through the Alps, opens.
- H.E. Bulwer becomes Lieutenant-Governor of Natal.

1883
- Paul Kruger becomes President of the South African Republic.
- Germany begins settlement of South West Africa and Angra Pequena.
- Secret Austro-Rumanian alliance formed, prompted by Rumanian fear of Russia.
- Portuguese government grants a concession to a U.S. promoter for a railway from Delagoa Bay to the Transvaal.
- Orient Express first runs between Paris and Constantinople — Europe's first transcontinental train.
- Ferdinand de Lesseps starts work on the Panama Canal.
- Robert Louis Stevenson writes 'Treasure Island'.

1884
- Germany occupies South West Africa.
- The London Convention removes most of the Transvaal's grievances stemming from the Pretoria Convention.
- Charles Parsons in England invents the first practical steam turbine engine.
- Divorce re-established in France after abolition in 1816.
- Cetshwayo dies and is succeeded as king of the Zulus by his son, Dinuzulu.
- A number of Transvaal burghers under Lucas Meyer establish the New Republic, with Vryheid as capital.
- Thomas Upington becomes Prime Minister of the Cape Colony.
- Cocaine is used as an anaesthetic by New York surgeon William Halsted, who becomes addicted to the drug.
- John Tengo Jabavu founds the weekly newspaper 'Imvo Zabantsundu' in King William's Town.
- E.C. Williams becomes the first South African to play in a final at Wimbledon.

1885
- Khartoum falls to the Mahdi Mohammed Ahmed (it is later re-taken by Kitchener).
- Congo State is established as a personal possession of Leopold II of Belgium.
- Italy occupies Massawa, Eritrea.
- German East Africa Company is chartered; Germany annexes Tanganyika and Zanzibar.
- Gladstone (Liberal) resigns as British Prime Minister and is succeeded by Lord Salisbury (Conservative).
- First anti-rabies vaccine is administered by Louis Pasteur in France.
- The Rover Company of England introduces the 'Safety' bicycle, designed by J.K. Starley.
- William Gilbert and Arthur Sullivan write 'The Mikado'.
- Grover Cleveland (Democrat) becomes U.S. President.

1886
- Gold is discovered on the Witwatersrand and Johannesburg is born.
- Lord Salisbury resigns and Gladstone, re-elected British Prime Minister, introduces the Home Rule Bill for Ireland. The Conservatives contest the Bill and after the ensuing general election form a new ministry under Lord Salisbury.
- Last major Indian war ends in the U.S.A. with the capture of Apache chief Geronimo.
- J.G. Sprigg becomes Prime Minister of the Cape Colony for the second time.
- Coca-Cola goes on sale in Atlanta, Georgia, formulated by local pharmacist John Pemberton.
- Television is pioneered by German inventor Paul Gottlieb Nipkov, who devises a rotating scanning device.
- Haymarket massacre in Chicago: on 1 May, Chicago police fire into a crowd of strikers, killing four and wounding many. At a peaceful rally held by the Knights of Labour Organisation to protest against the shootings, a small bomb is thrown, killing one policeman and mortally wounding another six. Police fire into the crowd and workers sustain three times as many casualties as the police. This marks the beginning of May Day as a worldwide revolutionary day.
- Statue of Liberty is dedicated in New York harbour.
- South Africa's first electric trams, imported from the U.S.A., run between Adderley Street and Mowbray Hill, Cape Town.
- A.E. Havelock becomes Lieutenant-Governor of Natal.

1887
- In a public speech Otto von Bismarck advocates a larger German army.
- First Colonial Conference in London opens.
- British East Africa Company is chartered.
- Russo-German Reinsurance Treaty replaces expiring Three Emperors' Treaty Alliance, which Russia had refused to renew.
- Britain annexes Zululand, blocking the Transvaal's attempt to gain communication with the coast.
- Golden Jubilee of Queen Victoria celebrating her 50 years on the British throne.
- 'Bloody Sunday' with casualties and arrests in Trafalgar Square at Socialist meeting attended by Irish agitators.
- Britain, Austria and Italy sign the Triple Alliance 'to maintain status quo' in the near East.
- Lazarus Zamenhof, a Warsaw oculist, invents 'Esperanto', the international language.
- Aluminium produced electrolytically for the first time, in Switzerland.
- Electricity introduced to Japan by Tokyo Electric Light Company.
- In the U.S.A. Thomas Edison invents the first motor-driven phonograph playing cylindrical wax records.
- Kruger grants a concession to a Dutch group for a railway from Komatipoort to Pretoria and Johannesburg. The Nederlandsche Zuid-Afrikaansche Spoorwegmaatschappij is created.

1888
- The New Republic unites with the Transvaal to become the district of Vryheid.
- Lobengula, King of the Ndebele, accepts British protection.
- Through the Rudd Concession, Cecil Rhodes obtains mining rights in Matabeleland and Mashonaland.
- Cecil Rhodes forms De Beers Consolidated Mines.
- The President of the O.F.S., J.H. Brand, dies and is succeeded by F.W. Reitz.
- George Eastman in the U.S.A. perfects his 'Kodak' box camera which makes it possible for any amateur to take satisfactory snapshots.
- 'Jack the Ripper' makes headlines in London by feeding streetwalkers with poisoned grapes and then disembowelling them.
- Norwegian Fridtjof Nansen successfully leads an exploring party across Greenland's ice-cap.
- First patent for a pneumatic bicycle tyre is awarded to Scottish veterinary surgeon John Boyd Dunlop in Belfast, Ireland.
- Benz motor-carriages are advertised for the first time at Mannheim, Germany, by Karl-Friedrich Benz.
- The Burroughs adding-machine is patented by inventor William Burroughs of St Louis (Mississippi). It is the first successful key-set recording and adding machine.
- Johannesburg's first theatre, the Globe, opens.
- The Wanderers Club is founded in Johannesburg.

1889
- Rhodes forms the British South Africa Company (Chartered Company).
- King Leopold bequeaths the Congo Free State to Belgium in his will.
- Austria's Crown Prince Archduke Rudolph is found dead with his 17-year-old mistress, Baroness Marie Vetser, at his hunting lodge, Mayerling. His nephew, Franz Ferdinand, becomes heir apparent.
- Adolf Hitler born at Braunau, Austria-Hungary.
- Sir Henry Loch becomes High Commissioner and Governor of the Cape Colony, succeeding Lieutenant-General H.A. Smyth.
- Benjamin Harrison (Republican) becomes U.S. President.
- Cordite is patented by English chemist Frederick Abel and Scottish chemist James Dewar.
- World's first lifts are installed by the Otis Company in New York's Demarest building on 5th Avenue.
- The Eiffel Tower, designed by French engineer Alexandre-Gustav Eiffel, is completed in Paris.
- London's Savoy Hotel opens.
- In the U.S.A. George Eastman produces the first roll-film for cameras.
- The South African Rugby Board is formed.
- James Couper defeats Woolf Bendoff in South Africa's first major boxing match at Eagle's Nest, Johannesburg.
- C.B.H. Mitchell becomes Lieutenant-Governor of Natal.

1890
- Cecil Rhodes becomes Prime Minister of the Cape Colony.
- The Chartered Company's Pioneer Column reaches the site of Salisbury and the town is founded.
- The O.F.S. and the Transvaal conclude a treaty of commerce and friendship, and a political alliance guaranteeing mutual aid.
- German East Africa Company cedes its territorial rights to the German government.
- The first commercial dry cell battery is introduced under the name 'Ever Ready' by the National Carbon Company in the U.S.A.
- London's first electric underground railway goes into service, passing beneath the River Thames.
- First tetanus antitoxin is produced by Berlin bacteriologist Emil von Behring and Shibasaburo Kitazato.
- Vincent van Gogh shoots himself at Auvers, France and dies there 2 days later at the age of 37.
- The 'Gibson Girl' created by New York

illustrator Charles Dana Gibson makes her first appearance in the weekly magazine, 'Life'.
• Tchaikovsky's 'The Sleeping Beauty' is produced for the first time at St Petersburg's Maryinsky Theatre.
• Kaiser Wilhelm of Germany forces Prince von Bismarck to resign as Prime Minister.
• Peanut butter is invented by a St Louis, Mississippi, physician who developed it as a health food.
• First aluminium saucepan is produced at Cleveland, Ohio, by Henry Avery, whose wife will use it until 1933.
• Herman Hollerith's new tabulating machine is used to process U.S. census data. His Computing Tabulating Recording Company, together with two other companies, is to become IBM.

1891
• Triple Alliance of Germany, Austria and Italy is renewed for 12 years.
• Leander Starr Jameson becomes Administrator of the British South Africa Company's territories.
• Work on Trans-Siberian Railway begins at Vladivostok. It will link Moscow with the Pacific coast.
• Arthur Conan Doyle's 'Adventures of Sherlock Holmes' first published in the 'Strand' magazine.
• Nyasaland becomes a British protectorate.
• Henri de Toulouse-Lautrec produces his first Montmartre music-hall posters.
• Basketball invented at Springfield, Massachusetts, by Canadian-American physical education director James Naismith.

1892
• William Gladstone (Liberal) becomes British Prime Minister for the fourth time.
• The uitlanders on the Witwatersrand form the Transvaal National Union.
• The railway from the Cape coast reaches the Vaal River, and the railway from Komatipoort to Johannesburg is opened.
• In Germany Rudolf Diesel patents the diesel internal-combustion engine.
• Haile Selassie, future Ethiopian emperor is born.
• In England, C.F. Cross and E.J. Bevan discover viscose, making possible the production of rayon.

1893
• Natal is granted self-government, with Sir Walter Hely-Hutchinson as Governor and Sir John Robinson as first Prime Minister.
• Ndebele revolt against the rule of the British South Africa Company. Leander Starr Jameson crushes the revolt and occupies Bulawayo.
• Paul Kruger is re-elected President of the Transvaal for the third time.
• Grover Cleveland (Democrat) is inaugurated as U.S. President.
• The railway linking Pretoria to Cape Town is completed.
• World's first open-heart surgery performed by Chicago surgeon Daniel Williams.
• Women's suffrage is adopted in New Zealand, the first country in the world to give women the right to vote.
• Wall Street stock prices take a sudden plunge, the market collapses, 100 banks close their doors, and more than 15 000 businesses fail. This depression is to last 4 years.
• Johannesburg cyclist Lourens Meintjes triumphs at the Chicago World's Fair to become South Africa's first world champion.
• Norwegian Fridtjof Nansen leads an expedition to the North Pole.
• Karl Benz constructs his four-wheel car in Germany.
• Mohandas Gandhi arrives in South Africa.

• Johannesburg's Parktown suburb is laid out by the Braamfontein Estate Company.

1894
• Uganda becomes a British protectorate.
• Japan declares war on China.
• Fourth Gladstone ministry ends after Gladstone has shattered the Liberal party with his fight for Irish Home Rule. Liberals retain power with Lord Rosebery as Prime Minister.
• Leander Starr Jameson completes the occupation of Matabeleland.
• In England, Rudyard Kipling publishes 'The Jungle Book'.
• Tsar Alexander III of Russia dies and is succeeded by his son Nicholas II.
• Oil is discovered in Texas as a well being bored for water starts spouting oil.
• Opening of London's Tower Bridge, spanning the Thames.
• Death duties (inheritance tax) are introduced in Britain.
• Pêche Melba is created by chef Auguste Escoffier at London's Savoy Hotel to honour Australian Nellie Melba, who is singing at Covent Garden.

1895
• British South Africa Company territory south of the Zambezi is consolidated as Rhodesia.
• Italian troops march into Ethiopia.
• Britain annexes Tongaland.
• East African Protectorate (later Kenya) is created on dissolution of the British East Africa Company.
• Lord Salisbury (Conservative) begins 3rd term as British Prime Minister.
• First public motion picture is shown in Paris by Louis and Auguste Lumière.
• The railway between Pretoria and Delagoa Bay is completed.
• London School of Economics and Political Science is founded.
• Oscar Wilde brings an unsuccessful libel action against Marquess of Queensbury and in a sensational trial is found guilty of homosexual offences.
• Bavarian physicist Wilhelm Röntgen discovers X-rays.
• In Italy Guglielmo Marconi invents wireless telegraphy transmission.
• Sir Hercules Robinson (later Lord Rosmead) becomes High Commissioner and Governor of the Cape Colony.
• Dr L.S. Jameson raises a force of Bechuanaland police and volunteers and invades the Transvaal.

1896
• Dr L.S. Jameson is captured by the Boers and handed to the British for trial.
• J.G. Sprigg becomes Prime Minister of the Cape Colony after indignation at the Jameson Raid leads to the fall of the Rhodes government.
• Rinderpest, the highly contagious and usually fatal disease of cattle, invades South Africa.
• Goods train crashes into dynamite train in the Braamfontein goods yard. Eighty die in the resulting explosion, which rocks Johannesburg.
• The railway linking Pretoria to Durban is completed.
• Edward Alfred Jennings, a Briton living in South Africa, invents the wireless independently of Marconi.
• The Ndebele and Mashona rebel against the British South Africa Company.
• Mark Twain arrives in Durban for a two-month tour of South Africa.
• French physicist Antoine Henri Becquerel discovers radioactivity in uranium.
• M.T. Steyn becomes President of the O.F.S.

1897
• President Kruger visits Bloemfontein and a new agreement is concluded

between the Transvaal and O.F.S.
• Sir Alfred Milner (later Lord Milner) becomes High Commissioner and Governor of the Cape Colony.
• William McKinley (Republican) becomes U.S. President.
• Harry Escombe becomes Prime Minister of Natal, and is succeeded in the same year by Sir Henry Binns.
• British scientist Joseph John Thomson discovers the electron, the first sub-atomic particle to be identified.
• The first car arrives in South Africa.

1898
• W.P. Schreiner becomes Prime Minister of the Cape Colony.
• Sir William Butler becomes commander-in-chief of British forces in South Africa.
• U.S.A. goes to war with Spain; peace is reached in the same year.

1899
• Lord Milner, Governor of the Cape, obtains the recall of Sir William Butler.
• Kruger issues an ultimatum demanding the withdrawal of British troops from the Transvaal border and from 11 October a state of war exists between the two countries. The O.F.S. is automatically drawn into the conflict.
• Sir Redvers Buller assumes command of British troops in South Africa. The Boers take the initiative, invade the Cape Colony and Natal, and inflict a number of defeats on the British forces, culminating in 'Black Week' in November.
• A.H. Hime becomes Prime Minister of Natal.
• Enoch Santonga writes 'Nkosi Sikelel' iAfrika' (God Bless Africa).
• The Mount Nelson Hotel opens in Cape Town.
• The new 'Kildonan Castle' steams out of Southampton, carrying 3 000 troops to the S.A. front.

1900
• Field Marshall Lord Roberts arrives in South Africa as commander-in-chief. Kimberley is relieved and Roberts enters Bloemfontein.
• The Orange Free State is annexed by Britain and becomes the Orange River Colony.
• Pretoria is occupied.
• Roberts returns to England, and Kitchener launches his 'scorched earth' strategy.
• The British establish refugee camps which later become concentration camps.
• President Kruger goes into exile in Europe.
• The Labour Party is founded in Britain.
• The Boxer Rebellion begins in China.
• J.G. Sprigg becomes Prime Minister of the Cape Colony for the 4th time.

1901
• The positions of British High Commissioner for South Africa and Governor of the Cape Colony are separated. Lord Milner continues as High Commissioner, undertaking the administration of the former Boer republics, and Sir Walter Hely-Hutchinson becomes Governor of the Cape Colony.
• Queen Victoria dies after a 63-year reign, the longest in British history. She is succeeded by Edward VII.
• U.S. President William McKinley is assassinated, and is succeeded by Theodore Roosevelt (Republican).
• Boer commandos invade the Cape Colony.
• Boxing becomes a legal sport in England.
• Hemlines creep up to the ankle.
• Japanese-American chemist Satori Kato of Chicago invents the first soluble 'instant' coffee.
• H.E. McCallum becomes Governor of Natal.
• Plague kills hundreds in S.A.

• Emily Hobhouse visits the concentration camps, and returns to stir the British conscience.

1902
• The Anglo-Boer War ends with the Treaty of Vereeniging.
• Financially unsuccessful visit to Europe by the three Boer generals, Christiaan de Wet, Jacobus de la Rey and Louis Botha, who seek assistance for citizens of the former republics who lost everything in the war.
• Cecil John Rhodes dies at the age of 49.
• The Triple Alliance between Germany, Austria and Italy is renewed for another six years.
• Arthur James Balfour (Conservative) becomes British Prime Minister.
• Charles Mambretti of Cape Town imports the country's 1st motor-cycle.
• Turn-ups on men's trousers make their first appearance.
• The 'Rand Daily Mail' rises from the ashes of the old 'Standard and Digger's News'. The editor is Anglo-Boer War correspondent Edgar Wallace.
• Kipling publishes his 'Just So Stories'.

1903
• Lord Milner creates his own Legislative Assembly in the Transvaal.
• The Wright brothers, Orville and Wilbur, make the first manned flight in a petrol-engined aircraft at Kitty Hawk, North Carolina, U.S.A.
• Activists of the Women's Social and Political Union smash windows and throw firebombs in London. The Suffragists are jailed and go on hunger strikes.
• The first motion picture to tell a story — 'The Great Train Robbery' directed by Edwin Porter in New Jersey, U.S.A., is shown. It runs for 12 minutes.
• Pius X (St Pius) becomes Pope, succeeding Leo XIII.
• Britain sets a 20 mph speed limit for motor cars.
• G.M. Sutton becomes Prime Minister of Natal.
• The Tivoli theatre opens in Cape Town.
• Inter-Colonial Council of four (later 12) nominees and 14 officials comes into being.
• S.A.'s first serious motor accident — the Johannesburg express hits a car at Maitland level crossing, near Cape Town.
• There are over 1 000 rickshas in Durban.

1904
• President Kruger dies in Switzerland. His body is brought to South Africa and lies in state in Cape Town and Pretoria before burial in the Heroes' Acre.
• Chinese labour is imported for the Transvaal mines. Mass meetings are held in England in protest.
• Dr L.S. Jameson becomes Prime Minister of the Cape Colony.
• The Trans-Siberian railway links Moscow and Vladivostok, and is the longest in the world.
• A woman is arrested in New York for smoking in public.
• Massive floods damage Cape Town and Bloemfontein.
• Deneys Reitz returns to South Africa.
• The 13 000 ton Union Castle mailship 'Armadale Castle' enters Durban harbour, the first Royal Mail Steamer to cross the bar.
• Rhodes University evolves from senior classes of St Andrew's College, and admits 50 undergraduates.

1905
• 'Bloody Sunday' launches a Russian revolution when Czar's troops fire on demonstrating workers. Seventy killed and 240 wounded. Order restored the following year.
• Lord Milner leaves South Africa and is succeeded by the Earl of Selborne as High

Commissioner and Governor of the Transvaal and Orange River Colony.

• The Cullinan diamond — at more than 3 000 carats the largest yet found — is discovered at the Premier Mine, Transvaal.

• Sir Henry Campbell-Bannerman (Liberal) becomes British Prime Minister.

• Japan defeats Russia in the naval battle of Tsushima Strait.

• Einstein produces history's most famous equation (energy = mass x speed of light squared, or $E = mc^2$).

• The Second Language Movement is re-born in South Africa.

• Count de Revertera drives from Johannesburg to Cape Town in 11 days.

• C.J. Smythe becomes Prime Minister of Natal.

• Het Volk formally established.

1906

• The British Government grants responsible government to the Transvaal.

• World's first radio broadcast of music and voice. Signal picked up by ships several hundred kilometres away from transmitter at Brant Rock, Massachusetts.

• Earthquake and resulting fires kill more than 450 people in San Francisco.

• Paul Roos's rugby team become the first to wear the Springbok emblem when they play in Britain.

• Electric trams replace horse-drawn trams in Johannesburg.

• The first issue of the 'Sunday Times' appears.

• The Carlton opens in Johannesburg.

• Sydney Grundy's 'The Degenerates' opens in Cape Town with Lily Langtry in the lead.

• A London hairdresser introduces the permanent wave. It takes 8-12 hours to be done.

• F.R. Moor becomes Prime Minister of Natal.

1907

• The Orange River Colony receives responsible government.

• In the Transvaal an elective Legislative Assembly of 69 members is constituted.

• In the Transvaal the coalition between Het Volk and the English Nationalists is victorious, and Louis Botha becomes Prime Minister. In the Orange River Colony Abraham Fischer becomes Prime Minister.

• The Transvaal government sends almost 50 000 Chinese back to China.

• Baden-Powell founds the Boy Scouts movement in Britain.

• M. Nathan becomes Governor of Natal.

• Percy FitzPatrick's 'Jock of the Bushveld' is published and becomes a best-seller.

• Andrew Jeptha of South Africa becomes the first coloured man to hold a British boxing title.

• Colonial Conference is held in London.

1908

• John X. Merriman becomes Prime Minister of the Cape Colony.

• First sitting of National Convention, in Durban, to create basis for unification of colonies in South Africa.

• British explorer Ernest Shackleton gets to within 160 km of the South Pole.

• Henry Ford produces the Model T.

• South Africa's first motor show is held at the Wanderers, Johannesburg.

• South Africa competes in the Olympic Games, in London, and Durban sprinter Reggie Walker wins a gold medal.

• Herbert Henry Asquith (Liberal) becomes British Prime Minister.

1909

• William Howard Taft (Republican) becomes U.S. President.

• Bakelite is invented by Belgian-American chemist L.H. Baekeland. It is the world's first polymer.

• American zoologist T.H. Morgan begins research into genetics at Columbia University.

• American explorer R.E. Peary reaches the North Pole.

• First crossing of the English Channel in a monoplane is made by French engineer Louis Bleriot in 37 minutes from Calais to Dover.

• The Royal Hotel in Durban is re-built.

• Visiting Frenchman Albert Kimmerling makes South Africa's first powered flight over Nahoon racecourse, East London.

1910

• Lord Methuen becomes Governor of Natal.

• The Union of South Africa is established. Herbert Gladstone becomes High Commissioner and Governor-General. In the first general election, Louis Botha's National Party wins 67 seats against 59 of L.S. Jameson's Unionist Party of South Africa.

• Louis Botha becomes Prime Minister of the Union of South Africa.

• King Edward VII dies and is succeeded by his son, George V.

• Halley's Comet appears.

• South Africa's car population numbers 2 000.

• The South African Railways and Harbours Administration is established.

• John Buchan's 'Prester John' is published.

1911

• South African National Party (in later years S.A.P.) formally established, comprising Het Volk, the Orangia-Unie, the South African Party of the Cape (formerly the Afrikaner Bond), Transvaal English-speaking Nationalists formerly absorbed by Het Volk, and some Natalians. Ranged against this Government party is the Unionist Party, comprising former Progressive Parties of the various provinces and the rest of the Natalians.

• Norwegian explorer Roald Amundsen reaches the South Pole.

• Winston Churchill is appointed First Lord of the Admiralty in Britain.

• Italy declares war on Turkey.

• Russian Prime Minister Petr Stolypin is assassinated.

• First wholly South African-built aircraft is flown by John Weston at Kimberley.

1912

• The first Balkan War begins as Bulgaria, Serbia, Greece and Montenegro join forces against Turkey. An armistice ends the war.

• Treaty of Lausanne is signed between Italy and France.

• The South African Defence Force Act is passed and the Union gets its own defence force, commanded by General Christiaan Beyers.

• General Hertzog delivers a speech which causes a South African cabinet split the following year. This leads to the founding of the National Party.

• R.F. Scott reaches the South Pole but dies on his return journey.

• The SS 'Titanic' sinks on her maiden voyage, drowning 1 513.

• The South African Native National Congress (forerunner of the A.N.C.) is formed.

• South African runners Kenneth McArthur and Christopher Gitsham win gold and silver medals at the Olympics in Stockholm, Sweden.

• First successful parachute jump from an aircraft is made by U.S. Army Captain Albert Berry.

1913

• Mohandas Gandhi launches a passive resistance movement.

• Imperial troops mobilised against workers in second Rand Strike. Trade unions are recognised after a judicial inquiry.

• The Natives Land Act is passed to deal with black ownership and occupation of land on the basis of reserving areas for blacks only.

• London Peace Treaty ends the second Balkan War.

• British suffragist Emily Davison is killed when she runs in front of the King's horse at the Epsom Derby.

• 'African Mirror', an actuality newsreel, is launched.

• First definitive issue Union stamps, showing a profile of George V, are printed in London.

• I.W. Schlesinger creates the conglomerate which later becomes African Consolidated Theatres.

• Woodrow Wilson (Democrat) becomes U.S. President.

1914

• The assassination of Austrian Archduke, Franz Ferdinand, and his wife by Serbian dissidents triggers the outbreak of the First World War.

• Austria-Hungary declares war on Serbia.

• Germany declares war on Russia and France. Occupies Luxembourg and invades Belgium.

• Great Britain declares war on Germany and Austria-Hungary.

• Austria-Hungary declares war on Russia.

• France declares war on Austria-Hungary.

• The Russians are defeated at Tannenberg in Prussia, but they force the Germans out of Poland.

• Turkey joins the war on Germany's side and closes the Dardenelles Strait.

• The first Battle of the Marne stops the German advance to Paris, leading to a four year war of attrition.

• Russia declares war on Turkey.

• England and France declare war on Turkey.

• Zeppelins carry out the first air-raids on Britain.

• At the request of the British government, South African troops under Louis Botha invade German South West Africa. A rebellion against this by pro-German Boers takes place in the Transvaal and the Orange Free State.

• General de la Rey dies in a shooting incident on the Rand.

• Foster Gang commit suicide in cave after being trapped by police.

• Rebel leader Christiaan de Wet is captured.

• Strikes in the coal mines of Natal and among railway workers culminate in a major strike on the Rand. The Minister of Defence, J.C. Smuts, calls out commandos and the strike collapses. He banishes 9 of the leaders. Jopie Fourie is executed.

• The Kimberley Mine, or 'Big Hole', is closed to further digging.

• The Indian Relief Act and a Smuts-Gandhi agreement ends the S.A. passive resistance campaign. Gandhi returns to India.

• Benedict XV becomes Pope.

• Sydney Charles Buxton becomes High Commissioner and Governor-General of the Union of South Africa.

• First Charlie Chaplin films appear.

• U.S.A. officially opens the Panama Canal to traffic.

1915

• The Germans sink a British ocean liner, 'Lusitania', which brings Germany and the U.S.A. to the brink of war because of the loss of American passengers on board.

• The German army drives the Russians 290 km beyond Warsaw. Some 2 million Russians are killed, wounded or taken prisoner.

• Turks defeat the British on the Gallipoli Peninsula.

• Italy turns on her former ally, Austria.

• Germans surrender unconditionally to Union forces in South West Africa.

• Prof. Hugo Junkers in Germany designs the first fighter aeroplane.

• The Cape Coloured Corps is formed.

• Nasionale Pers founded in Cape Town. Its newspaper, 'De Burger', is to be the voice of the new National Party.

• Henry Herbert Asquith heads a British Coalition Government.

1916

• First South African troops reach Nairobi. General Smuts is appointed Commander-in-Chief of the Imperial Army in East Africa.

• Battle of Verdun, between Germans and French.

• 140-day Battle of the Somme involves 3 million men on a 33 km front. Allied armies lose 794 000 men and the Central Powers lose 539 000.

• The South African Brigade loses thousands at Delville Wood.

• Liberal leader David Lloyd George heads a Coalition Government in Britain.

• The Easter rebellion in Dublin by the Irish Republican Brotherhood is suppressed by the British.

• The first woman member of the U.S. Congress is elected — Miss Jeanette Rankin of Montana.

• Einstein's general theory of relativity is published.

• 'Huisgenoot' magazine is launched.

• Margaret Sanger, author of 'Family Limitation', is jailed after opening a birth control clinic in Brooklyn, New York — convicted for creating a 'public nuisance'.

1917

• The United States declares war on Germany.

• German civilians starve after Britain's blockade prevents food and supplies from entering Germany by sea.

• China declares war on Germany and Austria.

• In the Middle East, Jerusalem is captured from the Turks when the Allies win the Battle of Gaza.

• In Russia, Czar Nicholas II abdicates.

• Russia is declared a republic by Prime Minister Alexander Kerensky.

• The Kerensky government is overthrown in the October Revolution. Lenin becomes Chairman, Trotsky becomes Commissar of Foreign Affairs, and Stalin is Commissar of Nationalities.

• Russia signs an armistice with Germany and withdraws from the war.

• Finland declares its independence from Russia and a Finnish Republic is proclaimed.

• Freud writes the book 'Introduction to Psychoanalysis'.

1918

• U.S. President Wilson proposes the Fourteen Points, precursor of the League of Nations.

• The German armies advance in France, but are halted and then defeated after massive counter-offensive by British, French and American forces.

• Kaiser Wilhelm II abdicates.

• Austro-Hungarian Emperor Karl abdicates, and Austria becomes a republic.

• Poland becomes a republic.

• Czar Nicholas II and his family are executed by order of new Russian regime. Some evidence suggests that Anastasia may have survived.

• Yugoslavia and Czechoslovakia gain their independence.

• An armistice is signed, formally ending the First World War.

• Von Lettow-Vorbeck surrenders at Abercorn, Northern Rhodesia (Zambia),

two weeks after Armistice in Europe.
• Statistics of war casualties are published: 8,5 million killed; 19,5 million wounded; 6,5 million prisoners and missing. South African losses total 12 000. Total shipping losses are 15 million tons, 9 million of which are British.
• Cornelis Langenhoven writes 'Die Stem van Suid-Afrika'. (It is accepted as the official national anthem 40 years later.)
• Spanish Influenza sweeps the world.
• The U.S. Post Office burns issues of an American newspaper, 'Little Review', containing instalments of James Joyce's 'Ulysses'.

1919
• A conference of 32 nations (including 5 British Dominions) convenes in Paris to draft the treaty ending the First World War.
• The Treaty of Versailles is signed. Key figures in its drafting are Georges Clemenceau of France (Chairman of the conference), David Lloyd George of Britain and Woodrow Wilson of the United States. As a result, Germany is told to surrender most of her wartime equipment, her army is limited to 100 000 men and much of her territory is relinquished. A harsh programme of reparation is instituted.
• Louis Botha dies and is succeeded as Prime Minister of the Union by General J.C. Smuts.
• Race riots in Chicago leave 15 whites and 236 blacks dead.
• The German Workers' Party is formed in Germany. It becomes the National Socialist (Nazi) Party in the following year.
• The first non-stop Atlantic flight (Newfoundland to Ireland) is made by British air officers J. Alcock and A. Whitten-Brown in 16 hours 27 minutes.
• South African Aerial Transports, run by Major Allister Miller, is the first 'airline' to operate in South Africa.
• An 18th amendment is made to the U.S. Constitution, forbidding the sale and manufacture of alcohol. Prohibition becomes effective the following year.

1920
• The League of Nations is formally constituted, and the venue changes from Paris to Geneva. It consists of 42 members. Mesopotamia and Palestine become British mandates.
• The British Parliament passes the Government of Ireland Act, and Northern and Southern Ireland each have their own parliament.
• Gandhi emerges as India's leader in its struggle for independence.
• The Russian civil war ends.
• The 19th Amendment gives American women the right to vote.
• Rent control is introduced in the Union.
• World's first broadcasting station begins operating in East Pittsburgh, U.S.A.
• Pierre van Ryneveld and Quintin Brand make the first flight from England to South Africa, and are knighted.
• Olive Schreiner dies in Wynberg, Cape.
• Scott Fitzgerald publishes his first novel, 'This Side of Paradise'.
• Irish Republican Army is formed to oppose British rule.
• Prince Arthur of Connaught becomes High Commissioner and Governor-General of the Union of South Africa.

1921
• At Bulhoek near Cradock, 163 members of the 'Israelites' religious sect die when police action to evict them from their illegal settlement turns into a massacre.
• Hitler's storm troops begin to terrorise opponents.
• South West Africa is granted a nominated advisory council, with Germans and South Africans represented equally.

• Winston Churchill becomes British Colonial Secretary.
• Washington Naval Conference: the U.S.A., Britain, France, Japan and Italy decide to limit arms expansion.
• Warren Gamaliel Harding (Republican) becomes U.S. President.

1922
• Mussolini's 'blackshirts' march to and occupy Rome. Fascist government is formed in Italy. Mussolini is appointed Prime Minister and is known as Il Duce.
• Egypt gains independence from British rule. Kingdom of Egypt is proclaimed; Sultan Ahmed Fuad assumes the title of King.
• Ireland is torn by civil war. Irish Free State is constituted.
• Gandhi is sentenced to 6 years' imprisonment after his first civil disobedience campaign against British rule in India.
• Labour troubles on the Rand escalate into a full-scale revolt. Smuts takes personal control: 230 people die before order is restored.
• Southern Rhodesia chooses responsible government under British rule rather than join the Union of South Africa.
• Insulin is first used in the treatment of diabetes.
• Pharoah Tutankhamen's tomb is discovered at Luxor, Egypt, by English Egyptologists George Molyneux, Earl of Carnarvon, and Howard Carter.
• Pope Benedict XV dies and is succeeded by Pius XI.
• Andrew Bonar Law (Conservative) becomes British Prime Minister.
• British Broadcasting Corporation is established.
• First Reader's Digest appears in the U.S.A. with articles of 'lasting interest condensed from books and other magazines' into a pocket-sized monthly. It is published by De Witt Wallace and Lila Acheson Wallace.

1923
• Russia becomes the Union of Soviet Socialist Republics (U.S.S.R.) consisting of Russian Soviet Federative Socialist Republic, the Ukraine, White Russia and Transcaucasia. The U.S.A. refuses recognition.
• Nazi leader Adolf Hitler attempts to overthrow the Bavarian government in Munich but fails. He is sentenced to 5 years' imprisonment, but serves only one year, during which time he writes 'Mein Kampf'.
• Mussolini establishes a one-party Fascist dictatorship in Italy.
• The centres of Tokyo and Yokohama are destroyed by an earthquake which kills 120 000 people. Two million are left homeless.
• The first English F.A. Cup final is played at Wembley Stadium in London. The match is won by Bolton Wanderers.
• French and Belgian troops occupy the Ruhr Valley in Germany following German default on coal deliveries promised at Versailles in 1919. The occupation lasts till 1925 and will add to economic disruption in Germany.
• The Ottoman Empire ends as Turkey becomes a republic under the leadership of General Mustafa Kemal 'Atatürk', who has destroyed the political power of the Muslim leaders of the old Empire.
• Calvin Coolidge (Republican) becomes U.S. President.
• Stanley Baldwin (Conservative) becomes British Prime Minister.
• Southern Rhodesia is formerly annexed by Britain as a self-governing colony.
• Union Parliament passes the Natives (Urban Areas) Act.
• German nationals in South West Africa become British subjects. German remains an official language.

1924
• James Ramsay MacDonald (Labour) becomes British Prime Minister in January, to be replaced in November by Stanley Baldwin (Conservative).
• Smuts's government falls and is replaced by a Nationalist-Labour coalition. General J.B.M. Hertzog becomes Prime Minister.
• The Industrial Conciliation Act establishes machinery in South Africa for negotiation between employers and trade unions.
• Regular radio broadcasts begin in Johannesburg, Cape Town and Durban.
• Lenin dies, aged 53, and Petrograd is renamed Leningrad in his honour.
• French poet André Breton publishes his 'Surrealist Manifesto'.
• In this year more than half the cars in the world are Model T Fords.
• The Earl of Athlone becomes High Commissioner and Governor-General of the Union.

1925
• Afrikaans replaces Dutch as an official language of the Union.
• Paul von Hindenburg is elected President of Germany.
• The Prince of Wales tours South Africa.
• South Africa's first radio sports commentary is broadcast from Newlands rugby ground.
• Cosmic radiation is identified by American R.A. Millikin.
• A French team of motorists reaches Cape Town from Algiers — the first to cross Africa by car.
• The Locarno Pact is signed in Switzerland by the principal Western nations, including Germany. It provides guarantees against violation of European frontiers.
• Contract bridge is invented by U.S. railway heir Harold Van der Bilt while on a Caribbean cruise.
• Charlie Chaplin's 'The Gold Rush' is released in the U.S.A.
• The massive Empire Exhibition is held at Wembley, London.
• The teaching of Darwin's theory of human evolution is banned in Tennessee, U.S.A.

1926
• Josef Stalin begins his 27-year leadership of the Soviet Union.
• The South African government formally announces the need for a new national flag.
• More than 25 000 men take part in the Grasfontein diamond rush.
• First liquid fuel rocket is launched by U.S. physicist Robert Goddard in Massachusetts.
• English writer A.A. Milne's first juvenile book, 'Winnie the Pooh', is published.
• Italian-born Rudolf Valentino, silent screen heart-throb, dies of peritonitis in a New York hospital. His death causes worldwide hysteria, several suicides, and riots at his lying-in-state, which attracts an 11-block-long queue.
• Olympic champion from New York, Gertrude Ederle, becomes the first woman to swim the English Channel.
• First blue jeans are introduced by the H.D. Lee Company in the U.S.A. They have slide fasteners.
• Herman Charles Bosman is condemned to death for shooting his step-brother.

1927
• American Charles Lindbergh accomplishes the first non-stop transatlantic flight in his monoplane, 'Spirit of St. Louis', in 37 hours.
• The last Model T Ford is manufactured.
• First tourist cars enter the Kruger National Park. Tourists may carry firearms and sleep out in the bush.
• The Carnegie Corporation of New York

agrees to fund an investigation into the 'Poor White' problem in South Africa.
• Oil is discovered in northern Iraq by prospectors.
• Harry and Somah Herber open their shop, Greatermans, in Brakpan.
• 'Talkies' — shorts shown after the silent feature film — are shown in Cape Town by Kinemas S.A.
• The Schlesinger Organisation forms African Broadcasting Corporation in Johannesburg.
• Sam Cohen and Michael Miller open the first O.K. Bazaars in Eloff Street, Johannesburg.

1928
• Scottish bacteriologist Alexander Fleming discovers (at St Mary's Hospital, London) antibacterial properties of penicillin, thus launching the 'antibiotic' revolution in medicine.
• Nationalist leader Chiang Kai-shek is elected President of China after conquering Peking.
• Kellog-Brand Pact, denouncing war and providing for peaceful settlements of disputes, is signed in Paris by 65 countries.
• The South African Iron and Steel Industrial Corporation is established.
• South Africa's new flag is flown for the first time, alongside with the Union Jack.
• Amelia Earhart, of the U.S.A., becomes first woman to cross the Atlantic when she flies solo from Newfoundland to Wales.
• German dirigible Graf Zeppelin arrives in New York from Germany thus completing its first commercial flight.
• D.H. Lawrence (U.K.) publishes his 'Lady Chatterley's Lover' privately in Florence, Italy. The book is banned in Britain.
• The Oxford English Dictionary is published in 12 volumes after 44 years of research, mostly by Scottish editor-in-chief James A.H. Murray and his family.
• Mickey Mouse is born.
• Rugby test matches are broadcast for the first time in South Africa.

1929
• The Wall Street stock market crashes, heralding the Great Depression.
• British Labour leader Ramsay MacDonald begins his second term of office.
• Graf Zeppelin airship makes its first round-the-world flight in 21 days.
• Herbert Clark Hoover (Republican) becomes U.S. President.
• Deneys Reitz's journal 'Commando' is published and becomes a best-seller.
• Hypertension (high blood pressure) and heart disease are linked for the first time by Harvard physician Samuel Levine.
• German film producer Louis Blattner designs the world's first tape recorder, the Blattnerphone.
• German novelist Erich Maria Remarque publishes 'All Quiet on the Western Front'.
• First crease-resistant cotton fabric is introduced by Tootals of St Helen's, England.
• A small Government subsidy allows Major Allister Miller to float Union Airways, a regular airmail-passenger service.

1930
• A general world depression sets in. International trade declines, production drops, unemployment rises.
• Statesman Ras Tafari succeeds Empress Zanditu as Emperor of Ethiopia. He adopts the name Haile Selassie 1.
• Constantinople is renamed Istanbul by Turkish president Mustafa Kemal 'Atatürk'.
• In India, Mahatma Gandhi leads a civil disobedience campaign, seeking independence from British rule.
• South Africa's white women are given the vote.

• The planet Pluto is discovered by astronomer C.W. Tombaugh at the Lowell Observatory in Arizona, U.S.A.
• British aviatrix Amy Johnson becomes the first woman to fly solo from London to Australia.
• British airship R101 crashes and burns at Beauvais in France, killing 54.
• African Film Productions produces its first 'talkies'.

1931

• Spain's Alfonso XIII is forced into exile after Republican forces win an election. A Spanish Republic is constituted.
• Britain's financial crisis forces the resignation of Ramsay MacDonald's Labour government. Ramsay MacDonald forms the coalition National Goverment.
• Atomic energy production is pioneered by Columbia University physicist Harold Urey. He and his associates announce their discovery of heavy water.
• First photographic exposure meter is invented by William Nelson Goodwin, jr. of the Weston Electrical Instrument Corporation at Newark, New Jersey.
• New York's Empire State Building opens: the tallest building in the world.
• Vitamin A is isolated by Swiss chemist Paul Karrer.
• Japan invades Manchuria, so launching the Sino-Japanese war.
• Britain comes off the gold standard and Jan Smuts wires S.A. Parliament to follow suit. After initial opposition from Hertzog, S.A. follows suit.
• Sound-recording engineer John Hecht produces the first records for the Singer Gramophone Company in Johannesburg.
• Ellis Park becomes venue of S.A.'s tennis championship.
• Maize exports earn only £523 000 for S.A., against £3,520 000 in 1925.
• The Earl of Clarendon becomes Governor-General of the Union.

1932

• English physicist John Cockroft and his associate Ernest Walton split the atom for the first time.
• English physicist James Chadwick discovers the neutron.
• Kingdom of Saudi Arabia is established by Bedouin king of Hejaz, Abdul-Aziz ibn-Saud.
• Former Labour Party MP, Sir Oswald Mosley, founds British Union of Fascists.
• Sydney, Australia, completes its Harbour Bridge to connect the city with its suburban areas. It is the world's largest single span bridge.
• Sixty countries attend the Disarmament Conference at Geneva. U.S.A. and U.S.S.R. are both present.
• 'The Bantu World', a black Johannesburg daily paper, is established.
• The Depression reaches its depth in South Africa — 188 000 whites register for work at labour bureaus. Black unemployment is also critical.
• Imperial Airways begins its regular service between London and Cape Town.
• Amy Johnson sets a new London-Cape Town-London air record.
• Gerry Bouwer in his Terraplane car sets the final record for beating the Union express train on the Cape Town-Johannesburg run.
• The old Tivoli in Cape Town is demolished.

1933

• The National Party and the South African Party form a coalition. Dr D.F. Malan refuses to join the coalition.
• U.S. pioneer radio inventor, Edwin H. Armstrong, perfects frequency modulation (FM), providing static-free radio reception.
• Nazi leader Adolf Hitler becomes Chancellor of Germany, and his regime assumes dictatorial powers.

• Franklin D. Roosevelt (Democrat) begins the first of his three terms as U.S. President, and launches his 'New Deal'.
• Japan withdraws from the League of Nations.
• 21st Amendment to the U.S. Constitution repeals prohibition.
• The Great Drought: South Africa prays for rain.

1934

• Germany's Von Hindenburg dies and Chancellor Adolf Hitler assumes the presidency. He now has complete dictatorial powers.
• Austrian Nazis shoot Austrian Chancellor Engelbert Dollfuss.
• Gandhi suspends civil disobedience campaign in India.
• First practical radar tests are conducted at Kiel Harbour by German Navy signals chief Rudolf Kuhnold.
• Hertzog and Smuts form the United Party.
• The first steel rolls off ISCOR's production line.
• U.S. men's underwear sales slump after filmgoers see Clark Gable remove his shirt in the film 'It Happened One Night' to reveal his vestless torso.
• Gangsters Clyde Barrow and Bonnie Parker die in gun battle after a 2-year career in which they killed 12 people in Texas, Oklahoma, Missouri and Iowa.
• Famed architect Norman Musgrove Eaton's first house is completed for Miss L. Boyes in Brooklyn, Pretoria.

1935

• Germany repudiates the disarmament clauses of the Versailles Treaty.
• Britain signs naval treaty with Germany, in which Germany undertakes not to expand her navy to a size larger than 35% of the Royal Navy.
• German Jews are deprived of citizen's rights. Intercourse between 'Aryans' and Jews becomes a capital offence.
• Italian troops invade Abyssinia.
• Stanley Baldwin becomes Prime Minister in Britain's coalition government.
• English physicist Robert Watt devises radar equipment to detect aircraft.
• Persia changes its name to Iran by order of Reza Shah Pahlavi, ruler since 1925.
• Sir Malcolm Campbell drives his 'Bluebird' at a speed of 484,6 km per hour at Daytona Beach, Florida.
• Nylon is developed by U.S. chemist Wallace Carothers.

1936

• King George V of Britain dies after nearly 26 years of rule, and is succeeded by his eldest son, Edward VIII, who abdicates in December to marry American divorcee Wallis Simpson. His brother, the Duke of York, succeeds him as George VI.
• Germany re-occupies the Rhineland, violating the conditions of the Treaty of Versailles.
• Italians occupy Abyssinian capital of Addis Ababa.
• Civil war erupts in Spain when right-wing army led by Francisco Franco and Emilio Mola revolts against the left-wing populist government under Manuel Azaña.
• Hitler and Mussolini sign the Berlin-Rome Axis.
• The United Party under Hertzog places black people on a separate voters' roll.
• Sir Patrick Duncan becomes the first South African to be appointed Governor-General of the Union.
• The South African Broadcasting Corporation is established.
• World's first television service inaugurated by the British Broadcasting Corporation.
• England's Penguin Books Ltd begin a publishing revolution by selling paperback

editions of literary works at 6d a copy.
• Beginning of the modern computer age: English mathematician Alan Turing publishes a paper 'On Computable Numbers'. In Germany designer-engineer Konrad Zuse begins to build a programmable calculator.
• Eugene Marais shoots himself.
• In America Dale Carnegie publishes his 'How to Win Friends and Influence People'.
• Dr Robert Broom finds fossil remains of Australopithecine creatures, among the most primitive of early human beings, at Sterkfontein, near Krugersdorp.

1937

• Irish Free State adopts a new constitution and becomes the Republic of Eire.
• San Francisco's Golden Gate Bridge is completed, linking the city with Marin County.
• German airship, 'Hindenburg', is destroyed by fire at Lakehurst, New Jersey.
• Japanese forces invade China. World opinion is roused against Japan when millions of Chinese civilians die in the conflict.
• George Gershwin, American composer, dies.
• U.S. aviatrix Amelia Earhart disappears while flying over the Pacific Ocean.
• Xerography is pioneered by New York law student Chester Carlson, whose dry-copying process will revolutionize mass duplication of documents.
• Neville Chamberlain (Conservative) becomes British Prime Minister, leading a coalition government.
• The song 'Sarie Marais' first appears in print.
• The SABC begins presenting programmes in Afrikaans.
• The Johannesburg stock market booms, but 25 000 men are still on poor relief or subscribed work.
• 'Die Transvaler' is founded, with Hendrik Verwoerd as editor.
• A contract is awarded for reclamation of land on Cape Town's foreshore.
• Philip Nel's Springboks return from their tour of Australia and New Zealand as world rugby champions.
• In England, Frank Whittle develops the jet (gas turbine) aircraft engine.

1938

• Adolf Hitler assumes command of Germany's armed forces and occupies Austria.
• British Prime Minister Neville Chamberlain says 'I believe it is peace for our time — peace with honour' in a speech on his return to England after signing the Munich agreement, by which Italy, Britain and France agree to German occupation of the Sudetenland.
• The Ossewa-brandwag is founded in the O.F.S. during centenary celebrations of the Great Trek.
• 'Die Stem' is sung together with 'God Save The King' at the opening of Parliament.
• Hungarian chemist George Biro and his brother Ladislao design the first ball point pen.
• First nuclear fusion of uranium is accomplished by German physicists Otto Hahn and Fritz Stassman.
• American Howard Hughes sets a new round-the-world record, flying a twin-engine Lockheed from California to California in 3 days, 19 hours, 14½ minutes.
• The Volkswagen (people's car), with an air-cooled rear engine, is assembled for the first time in Germany. Austrian automotive engineer Ferdinand Porsche had been commissioned to design the car by Adolf Hitler.
• Walt Disney's 'Snow White and the

Seven Dwarfs' is the first full-length animated cartoon feature film to be shown on the American circuits.
• Prof. J.L.B. Smith of Rhodes University identifies a recently-caught coelacanth, a fish thought to have been extinct for many millions of years.

1939

• Spanish Civil War ends with victory for right-wing forces led by Francisco Franco. Spain leaves the League of Nations.
• Germany and Russia invade Poland, which is divided between the two powers.
• Britain and France declare war on Germany.
• The Union of South Africa declares war on Germany after a vote in Parliament. General J.C. Smuts becomes Prime Minister in place of General Hertzog.
• Pius XII becomes Pope.
• Swiss chemist Paul Müller develops the insecticide DDT.
• First commercial transatlantic passenger air service begins as 22 passengers and 12 crew members take off from Port Washington, New York, for Marseilles, via the Azores and Lisbon, aboard the Pan American Airways 'Yankee Clipper', a Boeing aircraft.
• 'Gone with the Wind' with Clark Gable and Vivien Leigh has its world première at Atlanta.
• Germany flies the first jet aircraft, a Heinkel HE178.

1940

• German armies overrun Belgium, the Netherlands, Luxembourg, Denmark, Norway and Rumania, and invade France. British forces are evacuated from Dunkirk.
• Neville Chamberlain is succeeded by Winston Churchill as head of an all-party coalition government in England. He tells the House of Commons, 'I have nothing to offer but blood, toil, tears and sweat.'
• French Prime Minister Paul Reynaud resigns, and is succeeded by First World War hero Marshal Petain, who concludes an armistice with Germany after German troops occupy Paris. Petain sets up a government at Vichy, the southern part of France remaining technically independent while Germany occupies the rest.
• Italy enters the war.
• The Battle of Britain — German attempts to bomb England into submission are successfully resisted by the Royal Air Force.
• Japan joins the Axis, signing a 10-year military and economic agreement. Hungary and Rumania join the Axis later the same year.
• The world's largest passenger liner is completed in Britain and goes into service as a troop ship. It will go into commercial service for the Cunard Line after the war as SS 'Queen Elizabeth'.
• World's first electron microscope is demonstrated at the R.C.A. Laboratories at Camden, New Jersey.
• The Lascaux Caves, containing wall drawings showing how man lived nearly 16 000 years ago, are discovered by schoolboys near Perigueux, France.
• The Rh factor in blood (named after the Rhesus monkeys used in research) is discovered by haematology pioneer Karl Landsteiner and his colleague Alexander Wiener at the Rockefeller Institute, New York.
• The first nylon stockings go on sale in the U.S.A.

1941

• German army invades Russia, overrunning Russian-occupied Poland, the Ukraine and the Baltic states.
• The Duke of Aosta, Viceroy of Ethiopia and Commander-in-Chief of the Italian forces in East Africa, surrenders at Amba Alagi, where his force is surrounded by the

5th Indian Division and the 1st S.A. Infantry Brigade.
• National Service Bill in England lowers age of call-up to 18½ years and single women aged 20-30 years become liable for military service.
• Japanese planes bomb Pearl Harbour on the island of Oahu, Hawaii. Five U.S.A. battleships are sunk, 9 other ships are damaged and over 2 300 men are killed.
• Britain and U.S.A. declare war on Japan. The U.S.A. declares war on Germany and Italy.

1942
• Fortress Commander H.B. Klopper surrenders Tobruk.
• Germans besiege Stalingrad, and Russian armies trap them in a counter-offensive. Russians lose 750 000 troops, the Germans 400 000, the Rumanians, Italians and Hungarians 450 000 in the fighting on the Stalingrad front.
• Ossewa-brandwag members are arrested and interned at Koffiefontein.
• Battle of Alamein in Egypt. British defeat the Germans.
• World's first controlled, self-sustaining nuclear chain reaction is achieved at the University of Chicago's Stagg Field by a small team of physicists calling themselves the Manhattan Engineering District.
• The 26 Allied countries pledge themselves not to make separate peace treaties with the enemy.
• Deneys Reitz becomes South African High Commissioner in London.
• The first 'golden record' is presented to U.S. musician Glen Miller, whose 1941 hit 'Chattanooga Choo Choo' has been sprayed with gold by U.S. company RCA-Victor after the record had sold more than 1 million copies.
• Oxfam is founded by an Oxford University classical scholar, Gilbert Murray, to combat world famine.

1943
• German and Italian forces are defeated in North Africa.
• Fascist leader Benito Mussolini is deposed.
• Italy surrenders and joins the war against Germany under new leader Marshal Pietro Badoglio.
• U.S. microbiologists Selman Waksman and A. Schatz discover streptomycin.
• United Nations Relief and Rehabilitation Administration (U.N.R.R.A.) is established by an agreement signed in Washington.
• Battle of the Warsaw Ghetto: 5 000 Jews are killed and 20 000 are deported to death camps such as Auschwitz and Belsen.
• Hallucinogenic effects of LSD (lysergic acid diethylamide) are discovered accidentally by Swiss chemist Albert Hofman.
• In the U.S.A. mathematician Howard Aiken's computer (The Harvard Mark I) is switched on at IBM headquarters. It is later re-assembled at Harvard University.
• The Rt Hon. N.J. de Wet becomes Officer Administering the Government, declining the title of Governor-General of the Union.

1944
• During April, Allies drop 81 400 tons of bombs on Germany and occupied Europe.
• First V-1 and V-2 rockets are launched on Britain by the Germans.
• American and British forces capture Rome.
• D-Day — U.S., British and Allied forces land in Normandy with 76 000 troops, over 700 ships and 4 000 landing craft, and they liberate Antwerp, Brussels and Paris.
• French leader Charles de Gaulle sets up a provisional government in Paris.
• Franklin D. Roosevelt is re-elected for the 4th time as U.S. President.

1945
• Harry S. Truman (Democrat) becomes U.S. President.
• Benito Mussolini is executed by Italian partisans.
• Adolf Hitler commits suicide in the ruins of Berlin and Germany surrenders.
• VE (Victory in Europe) Day is celebrated on 8 May.
• At the Potsdam Conference, Truman (U.S.A.), Stalin (U.S.S.R.) and Churchill and Attlee (U.K.) meet to settle Europe's future.
• U.S. bombers drop atomic bombs on Hiroshima and Nagasaki. Japan surrenders and VJ (Victory over Japan) Day is celebrated on 14 August.
• It is revealed that Nazi genocide has killed an estimated 14 million 'racial inferiors' including Poles, Slavs, gypsies and nearly 6 million Jews.
• In Britain, the Labour Party headed by Clement Attlee defeats Churchill's Conservative Party in the general election.
• United Nations Organization is formally constituted.
• Vietnam (part of French Indo-China) becomes independent.
• In the U.K., George Orwell publishes his anti-communist fable 'Animal Farm'.
• The Scientific Research Council is created in South Africa.
• Major G.B. van Zyl becomes Governor-General of the Union.

1946
• United Nations General Assembly holds its first session in London. Trygve Lie (Norwegian) is elected Secretary-General. New York becomes the U.N.'s permanent headquarters.
• Peace conference of 21 nations is held in Paris.
• Verdict of Nuremburg Tribunal. Von Ribbentrop, Goering and 10 other Nazis are sentenced to death. Hess and Funk are sentenced to life imprisonment. Goering commits suicide the evening before his execution.
• Communist regimes govern Albania, Bulgaria, Yugoslavia and Czechoslovakia.
• Winston Churchill first uses the phrase 'Iron Curtain' in a speech at Fulton, Montana.
• King Vittorio Emanuele III of Italy abdicates in favour of his son, Umberto II, who leaves Italy after a referendum favours a republic.
• A National Health Service Bill is enacted, making medical services free to all Britons.
• New York psychiatrist Benjamin Spock publishes his 'The Common-sense Book of Baby and Child Care'.
• The two-piece bikini swimsuit is designed by French couturier Louis Read. It is modelled 4 days after the U.S. atomic bomb test on the island of Bikini.

1947
• United Nations Organization approves a plan for the partition of Palestine.
• India becomes independent, and divides into the two dominions of India (Hindu) and Pakistan (Muslim). Millions die in faction fighting.
• Ceylon (Sri Lanka) becomes independent from Britain within the Commonwealth.
• A shepherd boy discovers the Dead Sea scrolls in an earthenware jar in a cave north-west of the Dead Sea at Qumran, Jordan.
• King George VI and Queen Elizabeth tour South Africa with Princesses Elizabeth and Margaret.
• South Africa annexes Marion Island.
• Princess Elizabeth of England marries Philip Mountbatten, Duke of Edinburgh.
• The Mau Mau terrorist movement begins its activities in Kenya.
• 'The New Look', designed by Paris couturier Christian Dior, lowers skirt

lengths to 30 cm from the floor and unpads shoulders.
• Norwegian anthropologist Thor Heyerdahl crosses 7 170 km of open Pacific in 101 days on a balsa raft named 'Kon-Tiki'.
• The State-subsidised National Theatre Organisation, is formed.
• Lourenço Marques radio is taken over by John Davenport and Colonel R.L. Meyer. This successful commercial service is beamed into South Africa until 1972.
• First commercial microwave oven is introduced by Raytheon Company, of Waltham, Massachusetts.

1948
• Indian leader Mahatma Gandhi, aged 78, is assassinated by a Hindu fanatic in India.
• British mandate in Palestine expires and Jews proclaim the State of Israel. Arab-Israeli war begins.
• D.F. Malan's National Party triumphs at the polls, and he becomes South Africa's first Nationalist Prime Minister.
• Harry S. Truman (Democrat) is re-elected U.S. President.
• The transistor is developed at Bell Telephone Laboratory. It replaces the glass vacuum tube pioneered by Bell Laboratory's physicist H.D. Arnold in 1912.
• Honda motorcycle is introduced by Japanese entrepreneur Soichiro Honda.
• United Nations establishes the World Health Organization with headquarters at Geneva, Switzerland.
• Alan Paton's 'Cry, The Beloved Country' is published.
• First long-playing record, turning at a rate of 33 1/3 revolutions a minute instead of 78 rpm, is introduced by CBS engineer Peter Goldmark in New York.
• Prince Edward Island is annexed by South Africa.
• Olympic Games held for the first time since 1936, in London.
• Crisis in Bechuanaland (Botswana) when Seretse Khama marries an English girl.

1949
• Communist forces under Mao Tse-tung seize power in China. President Chiang Kai-shek withdraws to Formosa (Taiwan). Mao Tse-tung proclaims the People's Republic of China.
• North Atlantic Treaty signed. Belgium, Britain, Canada, Denmark, France, Iceland, Italy, Luxembourg, the Netherlands, Norway, Portugal and the U.S.A. pledge mutual assistance against aggression within the North Atlantic area, and co-operation in military training, strategic planning and arms production.
• West Germany becomes the German Federal Republic with Konrad Adenauer as its Chancellor and Bonn as its capital.
• Eire becomes a republic and leaves the Commonwealth.
• The South African Atomic Energy Board is constituted.
• The Voortrekker Monument is inaugurated.
• Antibiotic chloramphenicol is introduced by U.S. firm Parke, Davis under the trade name Chloromycetin and is hailed as the first major breakthrough in the fight against typhoid fever.
• U.S. chemical engineer Robert Boyer introduces the first edible vegetable protein fibre made from spun soy isolate.
• Dancers Alicia Markova and Anton Dolin tour South Africa.

1950
• U.S.S.R. announces it has the atomic bomb.
• U.S. Atomic Commission begins development of the hydrogen bomb.
• Korean War begins when North Korea invades South Korea.

• South Africa sends her 2nd Air Force Squadron — the 'Flying Cheetahs' — to Korea.
• J.C. Smuts dies at his home in Irene, aged 80. He is succeeded as Leader of the Opposition by J.G.N. Strauss.
• There are race riots in Johannesburg as black people oppose the new government's apartheid programme.
• George Bernard Shaw, British playwright, dies in England, aged 94.
• Bilingual and commercial Springbok Radio goes on the air.
• Jamie Uys produces the first Afrikaans film in colour — 'Daar doer in die Bosveld'.
• South Africa's Victor Toweel defeats Manuel Ortiz for the world bantamweight title.

1951
• Britain's Labour Party, under Clement Attlee, is defeated at the polls, and Winston Churchill returns as Prime Minister at age 77.
• In Iran, nationalist leader Muhammad Mosadeq becomes premier and nationalizes Iran's oil industry.
• The Bantu Authorities Act is passed, largely on the initiative of H.F. Verwoerd, Malan's Minister of Native Affairs.
• British diplomats Guy Burgess and Donald Maclean, recruited as spies for the Russians in the 1930s, flee to the U.S.S.R.
• Electricity is produced by atomic energy in the U.S.A. (Arcon, Idaho).
• Dr E.G. Jansen becomes Governor-General of the Union.
• Herman Charles Bosman dies in Pietersburg, Transvaal.
• The first commercial television transmission in colour begins in New York.
• 'The Catcher in the Rye' by U.S. novelist J.D. Salinger is published.

1952
• King George VI of England dies of lung cancer and is succeeded by his daughter, Queen Elizabeth II.
• During August 16 000 people escape from East to West Berlin.
• In Egypt, army officers led by General Mohammed Neguib and Colonel Gamal Abdul Nasser seize power. King Farouk is forced to abdicate.
• A state of emergency is declared in Kenya as the Mau Mau crisis escalates.
• In a speech at Boksburg, Verwoerd for the first time mentions complete independence for the black homelands: 'If they want it, they can have it.'
• The High Court of Parliament Act is passed. It sets aside the entrenchment of the coloured vote in the Act of Union. The High Court Act is later declared invalid by the Appeal Court.
• The English translation of 'Die Stem' is formally approved.
• Mycenean texts of 1450 B.C. are deciphered by English archaeologist Michael Ventris.
• John Cobb is killed establishing water-speed record of 244,8 km per hour at Loch Ness, Scotland.
• In the U.S.A., Ernest Hemingway publishes his 'The Old Man and the Sea'
• In London, Agatha Christie's play, 'The Mousetrap' is performed for the first time. It will still be playing when Miss Christie dies in 1976.
• U.S.A. explodes its first hydrogen bomb at Eniwetok Atoll in the Pacific Ocean.
• Tercentenary Festival marks the founding of the European settlement in South Africa.

1953
• The Korean War ends with the signing of a peace treaty at Panmunjan.
• The Federation of Rhodesia and Nyasaland is created.
• Dwight D. Eisenhower (Republican) becomes U.S. President.

• Iran's Shah Mohammed Reza Pahlavi regains power through a coup engineered and financed by the U.S.A. to prevent a Soviet takeover.
• Former resistance leader Josip Tito becomes the first president of Yugoslavia.
• Queen Elizabeth II is crowned.
• Edmund Hillary of New Zealand and Sherpa Tenzing Norgay of Nepal reach the summit of Mount Everest.
• Dag Hammarskjöld (Swedish) becomes 2nd Secretary-General of the United Nations Organization.
• Egypt becomes a republic under the leadership of General Mohammed Neguib.
• U.S. genetic researcher James Watson and English geneticist Frances Crick produce a model for the structure of DNA (Deoxyribose nucleic acid), the key to gene replication.
• British novelist Ian Fleming writes his first James Bond novel, 'Casino Royale'.
• Joseph Stalin dies, and is succeeded by G. Malenkov as Chairman of the Council of Ministers in the U.S.S.R. N. Kruschev is appointed First Secretary of the Central Committee.
• The strong possibility that excessive cigarette smoking contributes to lung cancer is expressed in several U.S. medical journal reports.
• Bertha Solomon steers the Matrimonial Affairs Bill through Parliament.

1954
• D.F. Malan retires and is succeeded as South African Prime Minister by J.G. Strijdom.
• The Natives' Resettlement Act launches the process leading to Soweto and other large black townships being established outside the 'Bantu' areas.
• World's first nuclear power station begins producing electricity for Soviet agriculture and industry at Obninsk, 90 km from Moscow.
• Colonel Gamal Abdul Nasser overthrows the regime of General Mohammed Neguib and becomes premier and head of state of Egypt.
• Communist forces in Indo-China capture the towns of Hanoi and Dien Bien Phu from the French. Under an armistice, the French recognise the independence of Laos, Cambodia and North Vietnam.
• South-East Asian Defence Treaty signed by Australia, Britain, France, New Zealand, Pakistan, the Philippines, Thailand and the U.S.A.
• Dr Kwame Nkrumah becomes the first Prime Minister of Ghana.
• The solar battery is developed by Bell Telephone Laboratories, making it possible to convert sunlight directly into electric power.
• Bloemfontein-born J.R.R. Tolkien publishes his 'The Lord of the Rings'.
• U.K. medical student Roger Bannister runs the mile in 3 mins 59.4 secs. to break the 4-minute barrier.

1955
• British Prime Minister Winston Churchill resigns at the age of 80 and is succeeded by Foreign Secretary Anthony Eden (Conservative).
• West Germany becomes a member of the North Atlantic Treaty Organization.
• U.S.S.R. creates the Warsaw Pact as a counter to NATO.
• Nikolai Bulganin succeeds Malenkov as premier of Russia.
• First British fluoridation of community drinking water begins at Anglesey, Wales.
• U.S. physician Jonas Salk develops an anti-poliomyelitis vaccine at Pittsburgh University.
• Sasol (South African Coal, Oil & Gas Corporation) starts production.
• Disneyland opens at Anaheim, 40 km south of Los Angeles, California.

1956
• The Suez Canal is seized by Egypt. British, French and Israeli forces invade Egyptian territory. Egypt blocks the canal. Invading forces halt operations under world pressure (especially from the United States).
• Britain imposes petrol rationing as a result of the Suez crisis.
• Soviet troops march into Hungary after an anti-communist revolution has flared up. Martial law is set up and 150 000 refugees flee to the West.
• Alan Jay Lerner and Frederick Loewe (U.S.) present their musical 'My Fair Lady' in New York. It is based on the play 'Pygmalion' by George Bernard Shaw.
• Anglo-American chairman Sir Ernest Oppenheimer arranges a R6-million loan for black township development.
• Bob van Niekerk, Willie Meissner and Verster de Wit build the prototype of the first S.A. car — the Dart.
• Prince Rainier of Monaco marries U.S. film star Grace Kelly.
• Margot Fonteyn and Michael Somes visit South Africa.
• Riotous Assemblies Act is passed in South Africa.
• Separate Representation of Voters Act removes coloured voters from the common roll.

1957
• Russia launches 'Sputnik I', the world's first unmanned orbiting spacecraft.
• The Treaty of Rome establishes the European Economic Community. Members are Belgium, France, West Germany, Italy, Luxembourg and the Netherlands.
• Langenhoven's poem 'Die Stem van Suid-Afrika', set to the music of M.L. de Villiers, is officially accepted as the South African national anthem.
• Ghana becomes the first African state south of the Sahara to attain independence. Kwame Nkrumah begins his 15-year rule.
• British Prime Minister Anthony Eden resigns owing to ill health and is succeeded by Harold Macmillan (Conservative).
• Israeli forces withdraw from the Sinai Peninsula and Egypt re-opens the Suez Canal.
• J.G.N. Strauss retires from politics and is succeeded as leader of the Opposition by Sir De Villiers Graaff.
• Major John Glenn (later an astronaut) sets the speed record from California to New York in a jet. The journey is completed in less than 3½ hours.
• European Atomic Energy Community (Euratom) created by a treaty signed in Rome.
• U.S.A.'s Leonard Bernstein presents his musical 'West Side Story' in New York. Music by Leonard Bernstein and lyrics by Stephen Sondheim.
• South African poet Roy Campbell dies in a motor accident.

1958
• J.G. Strijdom dies and is succeeded as Prime Minister by Dr. H.F. Verwoerd.
• General Charles de Gaulle becomes President of France and forms a 'government of national safety' following the escalation of hostilities in Algeria.
• In U.S.S.R., Nikita Kruschev succeeds Nikolai Bulganin as Chairman of the Council of Ministers. Bulganin is dismissed from the Communist Party.
• Boris Pasternak publishes his novel 'Dr. Zhivago'.
• U.S.A. launches Earth Satellite 'Explorer I' at Cape Canaveral.
• The U.S. nuclear submarine 'Nautilus' completes the first undersea crossing of the North Pole.
• Pope Pius XII dies and is succeeded by Pope John XXIII.
• South Africa's Gert Potgieter sets a world

record of 49,7 seconds for the 440 yards hurdles at the Commonwealth Games, Cardiff.
• The first parking meters are erected in London.

1959
• The President of Cuba, Fulgencio Battista, flees to Florida, U.S.A., as rebel leader Fidel Castro captures Santiago and Havana. Castro assumes premiership of Cuba.
• The hovercraft is pioneered by English engineer Christopher Cockerell. His SRN-1 crosses the English Channel on a cushion of air.
• Russian spacecraft 'Lunik II' reaches the moon, and 'Lunik III' photographs the back of the moon.
• British palaeontologist Louis Leakey discovers skull fragments and crude stone tools in Tanganyika's Olduvai Gorge. He suggests that this man-ape lived at least 1,78 million years ago.
• India gets her first TV and villagers travel for hundreds of miles to visit 6 community TV centres at New Delhi.
• Gary Player wins the British Open.

1960
• Anti-pass law demonstrations at Sharpeville lead to the deaths of 67 blacks.
• Unsuccessful attempt on Dr Verwoerd's life.
• Leonid Brezhnev becomes President of the U.S.S.R.
• British Prime Minister Harold Macmillan delivers his 'wind of change' speech.
• South Africans vote for republican status.
• American scientist Theodore Maiman perfects the laser beam in Malibu, California.
• The Belgian Congo becomes independent; Moise Tshombe declares the secession of Katanga.
• The world's first woman Prime Minister is Mrs Bandaranaike of Ceylon who succeeds her husband as Prime Minister.
• Pan-Africanist and African National Congress activities prompt the introduction of the Unlawful Organisations Bill.
• The Springboks make their last appearance at the Olympic games.
• 435 men die when a mine shaft collapses at the Clydesdale Colliery near Sasolburg.
• Princess Margaret of England marries Anthony Armstrong-Jones.
• France explodes its first atomic bomb over the Sahara Desert in South-West Algeria.
• The U.S.A. launches 'Echo I', the world's first communications satellite.
• The blue crane is adopted as South Africa's national bird.
• Lionel Bart writes the musical 'Oliver', which is produced at London's New Theatre.
• C.R. Swart becomes Governor-General of the Union, the last to hold this office.
• Albert Luthuli is awarded the Nobel Peace Prize.

1961
• South Africa becomes a republic outside the Commonwealth. C.R. Swart is the first State President.
• J.F. Kennedy (Democrat) is inaugurated as 35th President of the U.S.A.
• East Germans build the Berlin Wall, sealing off East from West Berlin.
• United Nations troops occupy key points in Katanga.
• U.N. Secretary-General Dag Hammarskjöld dies in an aircraft accident and is succeeded by U. Thant.
• U.S.S.R. sends the first man into space. Yuri Gagarin pilots the space capsule 'Vostok' and circles the earth in 89,1 minutes at an altitude of 313 km.

• U.S.A. follows suit when Alan B. Shepard accomplishes the first U.S. manned space flight.
• South Africa adopts decimal coinage.
• The population of Tristan da Cunha island is evacuated after a volcanic eruption.
• FM radio transmissions begin from Johannesburg.
• German Nazi Adolf Eichmann, kidnapped by Israelis in South America, is tried in Israel for war crimes and sentenced to death.
• Phocomelia deforms 302 newborn infants in West Germany after the expectant mothers take the thalidomide drug.
• The Orient Express between Paris and Bucharest runs for the last time.
• The MPLA, the FNLA and Unita start rising in Angola.

1962
• U.S.S.R. and Cuba sign a trade agreement and the Russians establish a fishing fleet base on the island.
• Algeria becomes independent of France.
• Uganda becomes independent under Milton Obote as premier and Tanganyika becomes a republic within the Commonwealth with Julius Nyerere as president.
• American sex symbol, film star and comedienne, Marilyn Monroe, dies of an overdose of barbiturates at the age of 36.
• Cuban rebel force, with backing of U.S. government, invades southern Cuba and establishes beachhead at Bay of Pigs. Driven off 'with heavy losses' by Fidel Castro's forces.
• J.F. Kennedy announces the presence of Russian missile bases in Cuba. U.S. warships blockade Cuba. U.S.S.R. agrees to dismantle the bases and the blockade ends.
• The secession of Katanga is brought to an end.
• First successful measles vaccine is produced by U.S. bacteriologist John F. Enders.

1963
• U.S. President J.F. Kennedy is assassinated in Dallas, Texas. Lee Harvey Oswald is accused of the murder, but is himself shot by nightclub owner Jack Ruby before he can be brought to trial. Kennedy is succeeded by vice-president Lyndon B. Johnson.
• The Federation of Rhodesia and Nyasaland is dissolved.
• Kenya becomes independent. Jomo Kenyatta is the country's first President.
• Organization of African Unity is established.
• Britain's War Secretary, John Profumo, resigns after admitting involvement with call-girl Christine Keeler, who has also been having an affair with Soviet naval attaché Evgeny 'Honeybear' Ivanov.
• British Prime Minister Harold Macmillan resigns due to health problems, and is succeeded by Sir Alec Douglas-Home (Conservative).
• 'Nkosi Sikelel' iAfrika' becomes the Transkei's national anthem. Zambia adopts the music, with a local version of the words, as its official anthem.
• Pope John XXIII dies and is succeeded by Pope Paul VI.
• In the U.K. £2,500 000 is stolen in the Great Train Robbery.
• An artificial heart to take over the functions of blood circulation during heart surgery is used for the first time by Houston (Texas) surgeon Michael De Bakey.
• Police raid a house in Rivonia, Johannesburg, which serves as the headquarters of the 'high command' of an underground revolutionary movement.
• The anti-anxiety drug Valium is developed by U.S. chemist Leo Sternbach.
• 'Hot Line' emergency communication link between Washington and Moscow, to

reduce the risk of accidental war, comes into service.
• British rock group The Beatles score their first big success with a recording of 'I Want to Hold Your Hand'.

1964
• Ian Smith succeeds Winston Field as Prime Minister of Southern Rhodesia.
• Harold Wilson (Labour) becomes British Prime Minister.
• Northern Rhodesia becomes independent Zambia, and Nyasaland becomes independent Malawi.
• Guerilla activity by the communist Vietcong in South Vietnam intensifies. The U.S.A. becomes involved when warships patrolling the Gulf of Tonkin are allegedly attacked by North Vietnamese torpedo-boats.
• The Coloured Persons Representative Council Act is passed.
• Tanganyika and Zanzibar unite to become Tanzania.
• Moise Tshombe becomes Prime Minister of the Congo. Rebels proclaiming the 'People's Republic of the Congo' in Stanleyville (Mbandaka) are suppressed with the aid of mercenaries.
• Guerilla warfare begins in northern Mozambique.
• At the end of the Rivonia Trial, which lasts seven months, Mr Justice Quartus de Wet sentences eight men to life imprisonment.
• Cassius Clay, 22, knocks out world heavyweight champion Sonny Liston at Miami, Florida.
• In the U.S.S.R., Nikita Kruschev is succeeded by Leonid Brezhnev as First Secretary of the Communist Party, and by Alexei Kosygin as premier.
• Jerry Bock's musical, 'Fiddler on the Roof', begins its Broadway run.
• Three regional radio services are inaugurated: Radio Highveld, Radio Good Hope and Radio Port Natal.
• Johannesburg's old Carlton Hotel is demolished.
• The Springboks are invited to the Tokyo Olympics, but withdraw for political reasons.
• An earthquake in Alaska measures 8,4 on the Richter Scale and creates a seismic 'tidal' wave in the south-west part of the state. The 67 metre wave is the highest ever recorded.

1965
• U.S. involvement in the Vietnam war increases. North Vietnamese forces step up their attacks on South Vietnam. American planes attack North Vietnam. L.B. Johnson says 'The people of South Vietnam have chosen to resist [North Vietnamese aggression]. At their request the United States has taken its place beside them in the struggle.'
• Rhodesian premier Ian Smith issues a Unilateral Declaration of Independence (UDI).
• Cyclone and floods kill more than 12 000 people in East Pakistan.
• Soviet Alexei Leonov and American Edward White float and walk in space (in separate missions).
• Sir Winston Churchill dies at the age of 90.
• The miniskirt appears in 'swinging' London. Designed by Mary Quant, the new skirt is 15 cm above the knee.
• The greatest power failure in the history of the U.S.A. blacks out most of north eastern U.S.A. and parts of Canada when a relay switch in Ontario malfunctions. Thirty million people in 207 200 km^2 are affected.
• Photographs of Mars are transmitted from the U.S. satellite 'Mariner IV'.
• South Africa's Karen Muir, aged 12, sets a world swimming record for the women's 100 metre backstroke.
• Soekor (Southern Oil Exploration Corporation) is established.
• Schoolteacher Frederick John Harris hides time bomb at Johannesburg Station. Explosion injures 23 people, one woman later dying from her injuries. Harris is executed.

1966
• S.A. Prime Minister Dr. H.F. Verwoerd is assassinated and is succeeded by Minister of Justice Balthazar John Vorster.
• Bechuanaland becomes the independent Republic of Botswana.
• Mrs. Indira Gandhi becomes the Prime Minister of India.
• Basutoland becomes independent Lesotho.
• Chinese leader Mao Tse-tung launches the Red Guard movement to implement a 'cultural revolution'.
• British novelist Graham Greene publishes his 'The Comedians'.
• England wins her first World Cup by defeating West Germany 4 - 2 at Wembley.
• Floods damage art treasures in Venice and Florence, Italy.
• The electric guitar gains prominence in England when American rock musician Jimi Hendrix begins to exploit the full potential of the relatively new instrument.
• Australia adopts decimal coinage.
• At the Welsh village of Aberfan, a coal-tip landslide kills 116 schoolchildren and 28 adults when it plows into the junior school and 16 homes.
• The 'Windsor Castle' sets the Union Castle Line's final record, completing its voyage in 11 days, 10 hours.

1967
• The 'Six-Day War': an Arab invasion (by Egyptian and Syrian forces equipped with Russian weapons) is foiled by Israeli jets. The Israelis take Arab Jerusalem and incorporate it with the rest of the city. The fighting ends with a U.N. ceasefire order. The Suez Canal is closed by the Egyptians because of the scuttled ships and mines.
• S.A. surgeon Christiaan Barnard performs the world's first human heart transplant operation at Groote Schuur Hospital in Cape Town.
• The U.S. spacecraft 'Apollo III' is destroyed on its launching pad by fire. Three astronauts die.
• British yachtsman Francis Chichester sails single-handed around the world in 226 days and is knighted.
• The new British ocean liner, 'Queen Elizabeth II', is launched.
• Britain's first colour television broadcasts begin as BBC-2 transmits 7 hours of programming.
• The People's Republic of China explodes its first hydrogen bomb.
• Briton Donald Campbell is killed on Coniston Water while attempting to break his own water speed record in his 'Bluebird'.
• Louis Leakey discovers fossil remains of man-like creature in Kenya, 'Kenyapithecus africanus', claimed to be 20 million years old.

1968
• America, Russia, Britain and 58 other countries sign a nuclear non-proliferation treaty.
• Czechoslovakia is invaded by Russian troops after the leader of the Czech Communist Party, Alexander Dubček, introduces reforms. Soviet tanks patrol the streets of Prague; Dubček is arrested.
• Black American preacher and civil rights leader Martin Luther King, is shot in Memphis, Tennessee, by ex-convict James Earl Ray.
• Senator Robert L. Kennedy is killed in Los Angeles, California, by Jordanian Sirhan Sirhan.
• Swaziland becomes fully independent.
• Five million American servicemen are now involved in Vietnam. The U.S.A. loses its 10 000th aircraft over Vietnam.
• J.J. Fouche becomes South African State President.
• Floods kill eight people in Port Elizabeth.
• Jacqueline Kennedy, widow of John F. Kennedy, former U.S. president, marries Greek tycoon Aristotle Onassis.
• Britain legalizes abortion.
• British astronomers Anthony Hewish and Jocelyn Bell discover pulsars (radio stars emitting regular pulses of energy).
• An earthquake in Iran kills 12 000 people.
• The first manned orbit of the moon is made by 3 American astronauts in 'Apollo 8'.
• General Motors launches South Africa's 'own car' — the Ranger.

1969
• American astronaut Neil Armstrong becomes the first man to walk on the moon.
• Richard Milhous Nixon (Republican) is inaugurated as 37th President of the U.S.A.
• Civil disturbances rage in Northern Ireland over the rights of Roman Catholic minority groups. IRA (Irish Republican Army) terrorist activities intensify. British troops move in to restore order.
• Mrs Golda Meir becomes Israel's 4th Prime Minister.
• First Anglo-French 'Concorde' supersonic aircraft takes flight from Toulon, France.
• Queen Elizabeth invests Prince Charles as Prince of Wales at Caernarvon Castle.
• The Woodstock Music and Art Fair in the Catskill Mountains at Bethel, New York, draws 300 000 young people from all over America for 4 days to hear artists including Jimi Hendrix and Joan Baez.

1970
• Civil war in Nigeria, raging since the province of Biafra broke away from the Nigerian Federation in 1967, ends with Biafra's collapse.
• Edward Heath (Conservative) becomes British Prime Minister.
• President Salazar, dictator of Portugal, dies at the age of 81 after ruling for nearly 36 years.
• President Nasser of Egypt dies and is succeeded by Anwar Sadat.
• East Pakistan is battered by a cyclone and tidal wave. At least 250 000 die and 1,000 000 are left homeless.
• The 'most destructive earthquake in the history of the Western Hemisphere' occurs in Peru. Two towns are destroyed and more than 70 000 people are killed. 800 000 are rendered homeless.
• The U.S.A. starts withdrawing troops from Vietnam as U.S. involvement in the war is provoking widespread protest, especially among American youth.
• Charles de Gaulle dies at the age of 79.
• The Italian Senate votes to legalise divorce.
• In the U.S.A., sociologist Alvin Toffler publishes his 'Future Shock'.
• Yale classics professor Erich Segal publishes 'Love Story'.

1971
• East Pakistan breaks away from West Pakistan and declares itself the independent republic of Bangladesh.
• In a coup d'état in Uganda, General Idi Amin ousts President Milton Obote.
• U Thant resigns as U.N. Secretary-General, and is succeeded by Kurt Waldheim.
• The unmanned Soviet spaceship 'Mars III' makes a 'soft' landing on Mars.
• Two U.S. astronauts land on the moon and drive a lunar vehicle on the moon's surface.
• A financial crisis causes European currency markets to close. Austria and Switzerland revalue their currencies, West Germany and the Netherlands float theirs, and the U.S.A suspends the conversion of dollars into gold.
• Britain adopts decimal coinage.
• Sixty-six people are crushed to death at a football match in Glasgow, Scotland, when a barrier collapses.
• Cigarette advertisements are banned from U.S. television.
• First Cape to Rio yacht race starts in Table Bay.
• Newspaper opinion polls indicate white players are 100 per cent in favour of multi-racial cricket in South Africa.

1972
• 'Bloody Sunday' in Northern Ireland. Troops open fire on rioters in Londonderry, killing 13. The British government takes over direct rule of the province. The British Embassy at Dublin is destroyed as about 25 000 demonstrators rally in protest against the killings.
• The 'Watergate Affair' has its beginnings when Washington police arrest 5 men inside Democratic Party national headquarters in Washington's new Watergate apartment complex. They have with them cameras and electronic surveillance equipment.
• President Nixon is re-elected as U.S. president with a landslide majority.
• 'Washington Post' reporters Carl Bernstein and Bob Woodward investigate the Watergate affair and reveal 'FBI agents have established that the Watergate bugging incident stemmed from a massive campaign of political spying and sabotage conducted on behalf of President Nixon's re-election and directed by officials of the White House and the Committee for the Re-election of the President'. White House spokesmen deny the story.
• Arab terrorists kidnap Israeli competitors at the Olympic Village in Munich, Germany. Two are killed and 9 of the athletes are captured as hostages against the release of 200 Arab prisoners in Israel. All 9 hostages, 5 of the Arabs and 1 West German policeman are killed when police rescue attempts fail.
• Ceylon is renamed Sri Lanka, becoming a republic.
• Ex-president Juan Péron returns to Argentina after 17 years' exile.
• South African women become world bowls champions at the first championships, held in Australia.
• Bobby Fischer becomes the first American to win the world chess title. He defeats Soviet Boris Spassky 12½ games to 8½ in Iceland.
• A skull found in northern Kenya is said to date the first humans to 2,5 million B.C.

1973
• The last U.S. troops leave South Vietnam, but U.S. bombing of Cambodia continues. Nearly 46 000 Americans killed in combat between 1965 and 1973. Another 10 000 non-combat deaths and 304 000 wounded. War cost America $109,5 billion.
• Republican party officials are implicated in the Watergate break-in. Nixon aides Haldeman and Erlichman resign under pressure from Nixon. The White House releases tapes of the President's conversations with his aides in response to a subpoena, but the tapes have gaps and some are missing.
• Egypt and Syria attack Israel on the holy day, Yom Kippur. The Arabs are eventually pushed back , and an uneasy ceasefire reigns. Arab countries increase the price of oil and an energy crisis grips the world.
• The energy crisis precipitates a world monetary crisis.
• Pablo Picasso dies at the age of 91.
• The British government orders a 3-day work week on 'non-essential industries' following coal-workers' overtime ban.
• The colour bar in South African boxing

is broken when black American Bob Foster successfully defends his world lightweight title against South Africa's Pierre Fourie.
• Noël Coward (actor, composer, playwright) dies.

1974
• President Nixon resigns after being implicated in a plot to cover up a White House-inspired burglary of the Watergate building in Washington. He is succeeded by Vice-President Gerald Ford.
• Following a series of riots, army officers in Ethiopia depose Emperor Haile Selassie.
• British Prime Minister Edward Heath is succeeded by Harold Wilson (Labour).
• West German Chancellor Willy Brandt resigns when a personal aide is unmasked as a Communist spy. Finance minister Helmut Schmidt becomes Chancellor.
• A hurricane hits Honduras, leaving 8 000 dead and 300 000 homeless
• U.S. 'Mariner 10' satellite transmits detailed pictures of both Venus and Mercury. Venus has a thick, cloudy atmosphere which keeps the planet surface hidden from view.
• Charles Lindbergh, the U.S. aviation pioneer, dies aged 72.
• A smallpox epidemic kills about 15 000 in India.
• Patricia Hearst, 19-year-old granddaughter of newspaper publisher William Hearst, is kidnapped by a group connected with the radical-terrorist Symbionese Liberation Army.
• Princess Anne of England marries Captain Mark Phillips.
• Rosenkowitz sextuplets are delivered by Caesarian section at Groote Schuur Hospital, Cape Town.

1975
• South Vietnam is occupied by North Vietnamese forces.
• The Suez Canal is re-opened, by Egypt's President Anwar Sadat, to international shipping for the first time since the 1967 Arab-Israeli War.
• The Portuguese colonies of Mozambique and Angola become independent.
• Security guard David Protter takes hostages at Israeli consulate in Johannesburg.
• British humorist and novelist P.G. Wodehouse receives a knighthood a few weeks before his death.
• Work begins on the 1 315 km Alaskan oil pipeline, the largest private construction project in the history of the U.S.A.
• N. Diederichs becomes State President of South Africa.
• Chiang Kai-shek, president of the Republic of China, dies in Taiwan at the age of 87.
• The Simonstown agreement between Britain and South Africa is terminated.
• The SABC starts hour-long TV test transmissions.
• The first oil from Britain's North Sea fields is pumped from the Argyll field, off the coast of Scotland.
• In St Peter's Square, Rome, Pope Paul VI declares U.S.-born Mother Elizabeth Ann Bayley Seton a saint. She is the first U.S. woman to be canonised.
• The yellowwood is adopted as South Africa's national tree.

1976
• An Air France Airbus under way from Tel Aviv to Paris carrying 247 passengers and 12 crew is hijacked and flown to Entebbe airport in Uganda. Three Israeli aircraft make a surprise landing at Entebbe, attack the hijackers, seize the hostages and fly them back to Israel after refuelling in Nairobi, Kenya.
• Mao Tse-tung, Chinese revolutionary leader, dies in Peking at the age of 82.
• An earthquake in Guatemala kills 23 000 people and injures more than 75 000. Over half a million are rendered homeless in the worst disaster in the history of Central America
• Outbreak of Soweto riots. Unrest spreads throughout the country after black schoolchildren take to the streets, protesting the use of Afrikaans as a teaching medium and demonstrating against discrimination. Many are shot dead in clashes with police.
• Trial of Patricia Hearst. She is found guilty and is sentenced to 7 years' imprisonment. (She is released three years later.)
• James Callaghan (Labour) becomes British Prime Minister.
• Nadia Comaneci, a 14-year-old Rumanian gymnast, makes Olympic history when she wins 3 gold medals and one silver.
• Television comes to South Africa.
• South African-born comedian Sid James of 'Carry On' fame, dies in England at the age of 62.
• South African author Stuart Cloete dies.
• The Giant Protea is officially selected as South Africa's national flower.
• Soviet MiG-25 jet is flown to Japan by a pilot seeking U.S. refuge.
• Transkei becomes independent.

1977
• Worst disaster in civil aviation history occurs when 2 jumbo jets belonging to KLM and Pan Am airlines collide at the airport of Santa Cruz on Tenerife: 577 people die.
• Jimmy Carter (Democrat) is inaugurated as 39th President of the U.S.A.
• The Italian Chamber of Deputies passes one of the most liberal abortion laws in Europe.
• 'Rock 'n Roll' king Elvis Presley dies in Memphis, Tennessee aged 42.
• Comedian Charlie Chaplin dies in Switzerland, aged 87.
• Opera singer Maria Callas dies in Paris of a heart attack at the age of 53.
• The 'Windsor Castle', flagship and last remaining passenger vessel of the Union-Castle Line, sails from Table Bay for the last time.
• In Holland, South Moluccan terrorists hijack a train with 55 passengers on board near the town of Assen and at the same time a separate group takes 120 schoolchildren and 5 teachers hostage at Bovensmilde. The children are released. Six terrorists and 2 hostages are killed in the train rescue operation, while at the school, the terrorists are overcome without resistance.
• American singer and actor Bing Crosby dies, aged 73.
• 'The World', a Johannesburg newspaper for blacks, is banned.
• Arab terrorists hijack a Lufthansa Boeing 737 taking off from Palma, Majorca. At Mogadishu, in Somalia, a German combat unit fires shots to distract the terrorists, explodes flashing grenades to blind them temporarily, and penetrates the aircraft to put the hijackers out of action.
• Mass murderer David Berkowitz, who has killed 8 people and injured 7 others in New York in the space of one year, is caught when he is arrested for a minor traffic offence and confesses that he is the 'Son of Sam'.
• In Utah, U.S.A., double murderer Gary Gilmore is executed by firing squad at his own request after spending 18 years behind bars. His last words are, 'Let's do it'.
• Queen Elizabeth II celebrates her 25th year on the throne.
• Bophuthatswana becomes independent.

1978
• Former Italian premier Aldo Moro, president of the ruling Christian Democrat Party, is kidnapped in Rome by left-wing terrorists calling themselves the Red Brigade. He is held captive for 54 days and is then murdered.
• The first 'test-tube' baby is born in Lancashire, England.
• Pope Paul VI, spiritual leader of the world's 600 million Roman Catholics for nearly 16 years, dies at the age of 81. He is succeeded by Pope John Paul I who dies of a heart attack after only 34 days in office. Pope John Paul II, the first non-Italian Pontiff in more than 4 centuries, is installed.
• Three Americans, Ben Abruzzo, Maxie Anderson and Larry Newman, complete the first transatlantic balloon crossing.
• B.J. Vorster resigns as Prime Minister of South Africa and is succeeded by P.W. Botha. Vorster becomes State President.
• The worst U.S. aviation disaster: a Boeing 727 carrying 135 people collides with a private aircraft piloted by a student pilot and crashes into a San Diego residential area. In addition to the 137 casualties aboard the 2 aeroplanes, at least 10 people were killed on the ground.
• In Spain, a road tanker carrying propylene explodes in a coastal campsite. About 200 people are killed, over 100 severely burnt.
• Golda Meir, politician and Prime Minister of Israel for 6 years, dies at the age of 80.

1979
• Persistent opposition to the Iranian regime leads to the downfall of the government appointed by the Shah, Mohammad Reza Pahlavi Aryamehr, who then leaves Iran. The 'Islamic Revolution' under the leadership of Ayatollah Khomeini assumes power.
• Iranian militants seize the U.S. embassy in Teheran and take some 90 hostages.
• A major nuclear accident occurs near Harrisburg, Pennsylvania, when the cooling system of the number 2 reactor at the Three Mile Island nuclear power plant malfunctions. It takes 2 weeks for the crisis to be overcome.
• Ugandan dictator Idi Amin is overthrown after the capital, Kampala, is captured by troops consisting of some 5 000 Tanzanians and 3 000 Ugandans.
• Derelict U.S. space station 'Skylab', weighing 69 750 kg crashes to Earth in Australia and the Indian Ocean while orbiting for the 34 981st time.
• Margaret Thatcher (Conservative) becomes the first woman Prime Minister in the history of Great Britain.
• Bishop Abel Muzorewa heads the new government of Zimbabwe-Rhodesia after winning one-man one-vote election.
• Venda becomes independent.
• South African ambassador to San Salvador, Archibald Dunn, is kidnapped.
• Earl Mountbatten of Burma is killed by a bomb planted by IRA terrorists in his fishing boat.
• Jody Scheckter becomes the first South African racing driver to win the world Formula One championship.
• The State President, B.J. Vorster, resigns from his post in June and is succeeded by M. Viljoen.
• South African-born Prof. Allen Macleod Cormack is joint winner of Nobel Prize for physiology and medicine with Dr Godfrey Newbold Housefield.
• U.S. actor and film star, John Wayne, Hollywood's Western hero, dies of cancer at the age of 72.

1980
• Rhodesia becomes the Republic of Zimbabwe. ZANU/PF party leader, Robert Mugabe, becomes Prime Minister.
• Soviet invasion in Afghanistan: a new Soviet-backed regime is established under Babrak Karmal, who replaces President Haffizullah Amin. The U.S.S.R. maintains that the Afghan government has invited it to send troops in the face of provocation from Afghanistan's external enemies.
• Serious unrest among the coloured population in South Africa, arising in particular from grievances over education standards, leads to a school boycott in April-June, which is joined by coloured university and college students. The boycott is accompanied by widespread demonstrating and over 30 people are killed during the rioting, the most serious incidents occurring in the Cape Peninsula.
• The Olympic Games are held in Moscow. 81 countries are represented, including Britain (unofficially) and Australia. The U.S.A., West Germany, Japan and 59 others, boycott the games in protest against the Soviet invasion of Afghanistan.
• In China, the 'Gang of Four', including Jiang Qing, widow of Mao Tse-tung, tries to usurp supreme power in China. They allegedly bring China to the brink of economic disaster, and are arrested by the police.
• A coup d'état takes place in Turkey. Turkish armed forces led by General Kenan Evren, chief of the general staff, take control of the country.
• An earthquake rocks southern Italy, and is followed by several after-shocks in the next 10 days. Thousands of people are buried beneath the rubble in nearly 200 towns and villages. Within 10 days nearly 4 500 bodies have been recovered, 8 000 are declared injured and 350 000 are left homeless.
• Mount St Helens volcano in Washington State, U.S.A., erupts three times, killing approximately 44 people. Forty-two others are declared missing.
• Sir Alfred Hitchcock, film director-producer, dies at the age of 80.
• Joy Adamson, wildlife conservationist and author of books about Elsa the lioness, is killed near her camp in the Shaba Game Reserve 416,6 km north of Nairobi.
• 82 people are killed and more than 200 are injured when a bomb explodes at Bologna railway station in northern Italy. A right-wing terrorist group the Armed Revolutionary Nuclei (NAR), claims responsibility.
• Mrs Indira Gandhi wins a landslide victory in India's general election.
• Peter Sellers, British comedian, dies at the age of 54.
• Josip Broz Tito, the premier of Yugoslavia for nearly 35 years, dies at the age of 87.
• The former Shah of Iran dies aged 60 in the Maadi Military hospital in Egypt.
• America's voluptuous blonde sex symbol, Mae West, dies at the age of 87. 'When I'm good, I'm very good, but when I'm bad, I'm better.'
• John Lennon, British musician and former member of The Beatles pop group, dies at the hands of gunman Mark Chapman at the age of 40.
• Republican Ronald Reagan wins the U.S. presidential election.
• South African Peter 'Terror' Mathebula wins the world flyweight boxing title.

Index

Page numbers appear in bold type where subjects feature only in illustrations or captions. Main entries are in Roman type.

Scores of organisations and individuals have helped to make this book possible. However there are certain to be some whose names have been omitted from these acknowledgments. To them, and to everyone associated with the compilation of *South Africa's Yesterdays*, the editors express their sincere appreciation.

Acknowledgments

Dr C. Adler and Mrs R. Melzer, Adler Museum of the History of Medicine; Mr S. Dent, AECI Ltd; City Librarian, Johannesburg Public Library and staff of the Africana Museum, with special thanks to Annamaria Cosgrove, Riana Joubert and Charles Pienaar; Theunis van Niekerk of the Africana Toy Collection and Bernberg Costume Museum; Vic Alhadeff; Mrs W. Loudon, Photographic Section, Public Relations Dept., Anglo American Corporation; The Argus; The Argus Printing and Publishing Co. Ltd, Johannesburg; Ted Artman; Mrs Joy Bell; Mr Benjamin Bennett; Mr Nathan Cowan, Custodian, Bensusan Museum of Photography; Mr L. Biebuyck; the late Mrs Maud Blain; Capt. A. Blake; Gregoire Boonzaier; Bill Brierley; Mr and Mrs D.A. Cairns; Linda Louw, Organiser, CAPAB; Cape Archives; Editor and management of the Cape Times, with special thanks to Peter Ibbotson and Gerald Shaw; Mr J.E. Linden, Mayor's Office, Cape Town; Mr David Pollock of Car magazine; Cayzer Irvine SA (Pty) Ltd; Mr and Mrs R. Cipriani; Mrs Haidee Reef of the Civic Theatre, Johannesburg; Mr and Mrs George Coetzee; Mr A. Geragotelis, Collectors Cars UMS (Pty) Ltd.; James Cowie-Shaw; Mrs Barbara Kiddie, Mr G. Louw and Mr B. Myburgh of De Beers; Mr Verster de Wit; Johan du Plessis and Lyn Watkins; Elaine Durbach; Mr Sandy Johnston, Secretary to the Mayor, East London; Eoan Group; Mr Walter Fobian; Mrs L. Phillips, Press Relations Officer, Ford Motor Company; Chris Forsyth; Mr H. Steyn, Director of Philately, G.P.O.; Garlicks; Dane Gerneke; Miss L. Theunissen, Photographic Dept., Government Archives; Government Printing Works; Mr G.N.H. Clark, Director of Publicity, Grahamstown; Mr J. Arensburg, Public Relations Manager, Greatermans; Chris Greyvenstein; Mrs Vivia Ferreira, Public Relations Unit, Groote Schuur Hospital; Dr T. Gutsche; Dr Peter Hefner; Paddy Hartdegen; Bruce Heilbuth Snr.; Miss Norah Henshilwood; Hirt and Carter; Dulcie Howes; Human Sciences Research Council, with special thanks to Joey Fourie and Astrid Schüler of the Centre for South African Theatre Studies; Imperial Underwood College of Commerce; Mrs Inez; Mrs P. Frame, Director of Publicity, Johannesburg; Jill Johnson; Mr R.H. Johnston; Allen A. Jorgensen; Bruce Just; Marilyn Keegan; Christine Kenyon; Killie Campbell Africana Library; John Kramer; Mr I. Krynauw; Taubie Kushlick; Mr C. Swanepoel, Public Relations Manager, KWV; Mr and Mrs B. Landman; Mr Jimmie Lawrence; Mike Ledingham; Kate Lee; Mr Robert Lewis; Library of Parliament; Mrs D.H. Strutt, Curator, Local History Museum, Durban; Mr Toby Louw; Mrs C. Magid; Miss Fiona Barbour, Duggan-Cronin Bantu Gallery, McGregor Museum; Juliet Meadowcroft; Mimosa Films; Dr F.K. Mitchell; Mrs Stephney Mitchell; Lorna Aas, Sales and Marketing Manager, Mount Nelson Hotel; Patrick Mynhardt; Natal Mercury; Prof. A. de Villiers, Director, and the staff of the National English Literary Museum and Documentation Centre; National Monuments Council; Mr J.J. Oberholzer, Director, National Museum; Mr D.F. Niven; Terry O'Grady; Mr C. Holmes and Mr N. Neethling, Advertising Dept., O.K. Bazaars; Col. N.D. Orpen; Ou Pastorie Museum; Mr M. Owen-Smith; Emmarentia Hutton, Public Relations Officer, PACT; Mr Raymond Ackerman, Pick 'n Pay; the late Mr Bernie Pitman; Port Elizabeth Municipal Library, with special thanks to Mrs M. Harradine; Mr Mervyn Emms, Curator, and Mr A.J. Visser, Post Office Museum; Mr C.B. Scholtz, Publicity Director, Pretoria; Mr Daan Esterhuysen, Photographic Dept., Pretoria Municipal Archives; Pretoria News, with special thanks to Peter Ferraz; Pyott (Pty) Ltd.; Mr M.E.G.E. von Dürckheim and Miss M.M.S. Marais, Rand Afrikaans University Library; Rapp and Maister Real Estate Co. (Pty) Ltd.; Mr J.N. Raubenheimer; Dr and Mrs Percy Rosen; Eric Rosenthal; the late Mrs Rhoda Bowe; Royal Hotel, Durban; Marie-Hélène Maguire, Assistant Public Relations Officer, SAA; Ben Groenewald and Albert de Villiers, SABC; Mrs Lillian Faul, Bruce Starke and Alex Watson, SA Breweries; South African Christmas Stamp Fund; SA Cultural History Museum, with special thanks to Mrs E.M.S. du Plessis and Miss P. Warne; Ted Partridge, Editor, SA Golf; South African Legion; Chief Librarian and staff of the South African Library; Joanne Friedlander, SA Marine Corporation; South African Museum; the Director and staff of the SA National Military History Museum, with special thanks to Major Doug Tidy and Col. Viv Torlage; Sappi Ltd.; SA Railways, with special thanks to Mr R.G. Payne, Photographic Section, SAR Museum; Mr A. Shacknofsky, SATBEL; Mr B. Lello, Editor, SA Yachting; Geoffrey Seeff; Dave Shaw; Graham Shields; Simon van der Stel Foundation; Mrs Joy Smit; Mrs Joyce Winter, Secretary, Smutshuis, Doornkloof, Irene; the Editor and management of the Star, with special thanks to Mr James Clarke and Mr Harry Zeederberg; W.J. Spracklen; Gavin Stapleton; Mr Willem Steenkamp; Die Stellenbosse Heemkring; Stellenbosch Museum; Ster-Kinekor; Mr J. Stodel; Mrs Lucie Stofberg; Stuttafords Ltd; John Tabraham; Winifred Tapson; Mr and Mrs D.D. Thomson; Mrs G.J. Niewoudt, Transvaal Education Department; TWS Public Relations; Mr Ken Jacques, United Tobacco Co.; Prof. A.M. Davey, Dept. of History, and Prof. B. Helm, Dept. of Applied Sociology in Social Work, University of Cape Town; Prof. C. Harrop-Allin, University of South Africa; Prof. A.D. Guedes and Dr D.J.C. Radford, Dept. of Architecture, and Miss J.P. Biddles, Archivist, University of the Witwatersrand; Ian S. Uys; Jamie Uys; Pat van Schoor; Dirk Visser; Wanderers Club, Johannesburg; Mr J.C. Knoetze, Chairman, and Mrs S. Marais, Public Relations Officer, West Rand Administration Board; Beverley Whyte; Terry Wilks; Roger Williams; Mrs A.J. Woolley; Worcester Museum.

Bibliography: books

A.B. . . . A Minor Marginal Note by Pauline Smith (Jonathan Cape); *The Abductors* by Stuart Cloete (Constantia); *The Absent Minded Beggar* by Rudyard Kipling (Daily Mail); *Abyssinian Adventure* by J.F. Macdonald (Cassell); brochure from the Adler Museum of the History of Medicine (Wits University); *African Genesis* by Robert Ardrey (Delta); *Africa's Place in the Emergence of Civilisation* by R.S. Dart (SABC); *Afrikaans Poems with English Translations* Ed. A.P. Grové (OUP); *Ah Big Yaws?* by Robin Malan (David Philip); *Airmen Lost in Africa* by C. Birkby (Muller); *The Airposts of South Africa* by L.A. Wyndham (Cape Times); *Alan Paton* by E. Callan (Wayne); *Alfred Adler: The Man and His Work* by Hertha Orgler (Sidgwick & Jackson); *Alfred Beit: A Study of the Man and His Work* by G. Seymour Fort (Nicholson & Watson); *Allan Quatermain* by H. Rider Haggard (Macmillan); *All these Under a Summer Sun* by N.G. Henshilwood (Koston); *Along Cape Roads* by Dorothea Fairbridge (Maskew Miller); *Amy Johnson* by Constance Bebington Smith (Collins); *And Having Writ . . . Memories & Impressions* by C. Don (CNA); *Apes and Ivory* by Joy Packer (Eyre & Spottiswoode); *Architecture and Personalities* by Sir Herbert Baker (Country Life); *As We Were: South Africa 1939-1941* by Margot Bryant (Keartland); *The Audience is Waiting* by Jack Stodel (Timmins); *The Australian Journal of Politics and History* (University of Queensland Press); *Australia's Yesterdays* (Reader's Digest); *Autobiography of William Plomer* (Jonathan Cape); *Background in Sunshine* by Jan Juta (Scribner); *Ballet in South Africa* Ed. John Worrall (Timmins); *Bantu Journalism in South Africa* by Eric Rosenthal (Society Of The Friends Of Africa); *Barney Barnato: From Whitechapel Clown to Diamond King*, translated from the French by G. Saintsbury (Routledge); *Battles of the Boer War* by W. Baring Pemberton (Batsford); *The Beadle* by Pauline Smith (Jonathan Cape); *The Best of Lawrence Green* Ed. Scott Haigh (Timmins); *Better Than They Knew* Ed. R.M. de Villiers (Purnell); *B.I. Barnato: A Memoir* by Harry Raymond (Juta); *Bickel's Coin & Medal News* (Bickels); *Biographical and memorial sketch of Francis Algernon Disney Roebuck, late captain of the 23rd Royal Welsh Fusiliers* by Vane Bennett (Solomon); *The Blind Spot* by Joy Packer (Eyre & Spottiswoode); *Bloemfontein: A Short Illustrated History* (Town Clerk's Dept.); *Bloemfontein the Centre City* (Bloemfontein Municipality/SAR & H); *Bloomie: Memoirs of the Twenties* by May O'Shea (Nelson); *The Blue Princess* by Herman Malan (pseudonym for H.C. Bosman); *The Blue Train Route Guide* (SAR & H); *Bobby Locke on Golf* by Bobby Locke (Country Life); *The Bob Connolly Story* by Bob Connolly (Timmins); *The Boer War* by Thomas Packenham (Ball); *The Boer War Diary of Sol T. Plaatjie* Ed. John L. Comaroff (Macmillan); *The Book of Key Facts* (Paddington); *Born to Act: The Story of Freda Godfrey* by Margot Bryant (Donker); *Botha, Smuts and South Africa* by Basil Williams (Hodder & Stoughton); *Braai and Barbecue in Southern Africa* by Lesley Faull (Books of Africa); *British Domestic Design Through the Ages* by Brian Keogh and Melvyn Gill (Barker); *The British in South Africa* by Roy Lewis and Yvonne Fry (Weidenfeld & Nicholson); *British Passenger Liners of the Five Ocenas* by C.R.V. Gibbs (Putnam); *Brolloks en Bittergal* by C.J. Langenhoven (Nasionale Pers); *Brosjure Uitgereik ter Herdenking van die Slag van Delvillebos* by Jan Ploeger and H.F. Botha (Army Headquarters Printing & Survey Squadron Printers); *The Burning Man* by Sarah Gertrude Millin (Heinemann); *Bushveld Doctor* by C. Louis Leipoldt (Jonathan Cape); *The Campaign in German South West Africa 1914-1915* by Brig-Gen. J.J. Collyer (Government Printers); *A Canadian Girl in South Africa* by E. Maud Graham (Briggs); *Capab Ballet-Kruik Ballet: the past nine years/die afgelope nege jaar 1971-1980* by Alec Beukes (Collectors Press); *The Cape Argus: How it is Produced* (Cape Argus); *A Cape Childhood* by Norah Henshilwood (David Philip); *Cape Colony Today* by A.R.E. Burton (Townshend, Taylor & Snashall); *The Cape Coloured Franchise* by L.M. Thompson; *Cape Cookery: Simple Yet Distinctive* by A.G. Hewitt (Darter Bros. & Walton); *Cape Hills in Sunlight* by K. Heywood (Human & Rousseau); *Cape Theatre in the 1940s* by D. Hatfield (Purnell); *Cape to Cairo* by Mark Strage (Jonathan Cape); *Cape Town: A Record of the Mother City from the Earliest to the Present* by J.R. Shorten (Shorten/Shorten & Smith); *Cape Town City of Good Hope* Ed. A.H. Honikman (Timmins); *Cape Town Directory; The Cape Town Foreshore Plan. Final Report 1947* by Cape Town Foreshore Joint Technical Committee (Government Printer); *Cape Trams: From Horse to Diesel* by Fraser Gill (Gill); *Cardiac Transplantation — The Anaesthetist's View: A Case Report* by J. Ozinsky; *Carnegie Commission Reports* (Pro Ecclesia Drukkery); *Catalogue of Pictures in the Africana Museum* Comp. R.F. Kennedy (Africana Museum); *Catalogue of South African Paper Money Since 1900* by Harold Levius (Levius); *Cecil John Rhodes 1853-1902* by Ian D. Colvin (Jack); *Cecil Rhodes* by John Flint (Hutchinson); *Censorship and Press Control in South Africa* by A. Hepple; *Census of the Union of South Africa 1911* (Government Printer); *The Child in Fashion* by D.L. Moore (Batsford); *Chronology of Johannesburg* Comp. Anna M. Smith (Africana Museum); *Chronology of the Modern World: 1763 — The Present Time* by Neville Williams (Barrie & Rockcliff); *Cinema: A Critical Dictionary* Ed. Richard Roud (Secker & Warburg); *The City of Bloemfontein Official Guide* (1960); *City of Gold* by Chamber of Commerce 1967 (Felstar); *The City of Port Elizabeth* by R.D. Leigh (Felstar); *The City of Pretoria: Official Guide* by R. Beerman (Beerman); *C.L. Leipoldt* by Pieter W. Grobbelaar (Tafelberg); *The Clues Condemn* by Benjamin Bennett (Timmins for Hodder & Stoughton); *The Coinage and Counterfeits of the Zuid-Afrikaansche Republiek* by E. Levine (Purnell); *Coins* by H.W.A. Linecar (Ernest Benn); *Coins for Pleasure and Investment* by Anthony Dowle and Patrick Finn (Gifford); *Cold Stone Jug* by Herman Charles Bosman (Human & Rousseau); *Collectible Advertising* by Dorothy Hammond (Wallace-Homestead); *A Collector's Guide to Paper Money* by Yasha Beresiner (Deutsch); *The Coloured People of South Africa* (Dept. of Information/Dept. of Coloured Affairs); *The Coloured Vote and the Constitution* (Civil Rights League); *Commando* by Deneys Reitz (Faber); *A Companion to the Movies: From 1903 — The Present Day* by Roy Pickard (Lutterworth); *Compendium of Motor Laws* (Automobile Association of SA); *The Complete Encyclopaedia of Motorcars 1885-1968* Ed. G.N. Georgano (Ebury); *The Concentration Camps: 1900-1902* by A.C. Martin (Timmins); *The Conservationist* by Nadine Gordimer (Jonathan Cape); *Conservation of our Heritage* (Caltex Oil/J. Walter Thompson); *Cookery in South Africa* by Vida Heard (Books of Africa); *Corsets and Crinolines* by Norah Waugh (Batsford); *The Cost of Living in South Africa: The British and South African Association Report Vol IV* by Alexander Aiken; *Costumes Through the Ages* by James Laver (Hudson); *Counter Attack: The Story of the South African Shopworkers* by Norman Heard (Union of Distributive Workers); *Cricket in Isolation* by Mike Procter; *Cricket in Many Climes* by P.F. Warner (Heinemann); *Cry, the Beloved Country* by Alan Paton (Longmans Green); *Dancing* by Edward Scott (Bell & Sons); *Daughter of Yesterday: A Pioneer Child Looks Back at Early Johannesburg* by Alice M. Ralls and Ruth E. Gordon (Timmins); *Days of Crisis in South Africa: Events up to 15th May, 1960* by Muriel Horrell (SA Institute of Race Relations); *The Days of My Life* by Sir H. Rider Haggard (Longmans); *Dear Dr Bolus: Letters from Clanwilliam, London, New York and Europe* by C.H.L. Leipoldt (Balkema for UCT); *The Definitive Edition of Rudyard Kipling's Verse* (Hodder & Stoughton); *The Diamond Magnates* by Brian Roberts (Hamilton); *Diary of Iris Vaughan* by Iris Vaughan-Niland (CNA); *Dictionary of South African English* by Jean Branford (Oxford Univ. Press); *Disaster Struck South Africa* by José Burman (Struik); *District Six* by George Manuel and Denis Hatfield (Longmans); *Down Africa's Skyways* by Benjamin Bennett (Hutchinson); *Dreams* by Olive Schreiner (Unwin); *Durban Calling: The Formative Years, and Beyond* by Herbert Edmund Dawes (Durban Municipality); *Durban: 50 Years' Municipal History* by W.P.M. Henderson (Robinson); *Durban: (From its Beginnings to its Silver Jubilee of City Status)* Ed. Felix Stark (Felstar); *Durban Past and Present* Ed. A. Macmillan (Brown & Davis); *Early Aviation at Farnborough* by Percy B. Walker (Macdonald); *Early Motoring in South Africa* by R.H. Johnston (Struik); *The Earth is Waiting* by Herman Charles Bosman (Human & Rousseau); *East London* (East London Municipality); *Eat and Be Merry* by V.M. Fitzroy (Timmins/Allan & Unwin); *Edgar Wallace: The Biography of a Phenomenon* by Margaret Lane (Hamilton); *An Editor Looks Back: South African and Other Memories* by George Green (Juta); *Education in South Africa* by A.L. Behr & R.G. Macmillan (Van Schaik); *Education in South Africa: Vols. I & II* by E.G. Malherbe (Juta); *Education of the South African Native* by C.T. Loram (Negro Universities Press); *1820 Settlers National Monument* (pamphlet) by 1820 Settlers National Monument Foundation (The Foundation); *1820 Settlers National Monument Foundation: Grahamstown Festival 1977; Elegant Extracts: A Duobiography* by E. Malone & G. Hawes (Laurat, Dickson & Thompson); *Elthorne's London Programme of Amusements; Eminent Victorians in South Africa* by V.C. Malherbe (Juta); *Encyclopaedia Britannica; Encyclopaedia Britannica Book of the Year* (1975-1980 editions); *Encyclopaedia of Southern Africa* Comp./Ed. Eric Rosenthal (Juta); *Encyclopaedia of the Modern World* Ed. R.B. Morris & G.W. Irwin (Weidenfeld & Nicholson); *Encyclopaedia of World History* Comp./Ed. William L. Langer (George G. Harrap); *English and South Africa* Ed. A. Lennox-Short (NASOU); *English Costume From the Second Century B.C. - 1950* by Doreen Yarwood (Batsford); *The English Home* by Doreen Yarwood (Batsford); *English Women's Clothing in the Present Century* by C. Willet Cunningham (Faber); *The Enormous File: A Social History of the Office* by Alan Delgado (Murray); *Ethiopia: The Country That Cut Off Its Head* by Blair Thomson (Robson); *L'Etoile du Sud* by Jules Verne (Hetzel); *Every Man Must Play a Part* by Isadore Frack (Purnell); *Everyman's Dictionary of Dates* by Audrey Butler (Dent); *Face to Face* by Nadine Gordimer (Silver Leaf Books); *Fashion in South Africa 1652-1900* by D. Strutt (Balkema); *Fashion in Underwear* by E. Ewing (Batsford); *Fifty Years of Flight South African Airways* (Da Gama); *Fifty Years of Furnishing: The Story of Bradlows* by Eric Rosenthal (Bradlows); *Fifty Years of Progress 1922-1972: The Golden Jubilee of the University of the Witwatersrand* (Jubilee Committee, The University); *The First Forty Years: Being the Memoirs of H.H. Morris, K.C.* by H.H. Morris (Juta); *The First Hundred Years of the Standard Bank* by J.A. Henry (O.U.P.); *The First South African* by A.P. Cartwright (Purnell); *Fishermen of the Cape* by Frank T. Robb (Longman); *Fish Horns and Hansom Cabs: Life in Victorian Cape Town* by Eric Rosenthal (Donker); *Fitz: The story of Sir Percy FitzPatrick* by J.P.R. Wallis (Macmillan); *The Flaming Terrapin* by Roy Campbell (Jonathan Cape); *Fodor's Railways of the World* (Hodder & Stoughton); *Food Facts and Daily Diets* by Mary Higham and Dr C.C.P. Anning (Benoni Health Dept.); *The Ford: Yesterday, Today and Tomorrow* by J.F. Schnetler (Makro Books); *For Remembrance and in Honour of Those Who Lost Their Lives in the South African War 1899-1902* by Colonel Sir James Gildea (Eyre & Spottiswoode); *Forty Little Years* by D. Inskip (Timmins); *For Valour: The History of South Africa's Victoria Cross Heroes* by I.S. Uys; *Fotobeeld van 300 Monumente, Standbeelde en Gedenktekens Langs die Pad van Suid-Afrika* by J.J. van Tonder; *From Apes to Warlords* by Solly Zuckerman (Hamilton); *From Barter to Barclays* by Eric Rosenthal (Barclays Bank); *From Man to Man; Or, Perhaps only . . .* by Olive Schreiner (Unwin); *Frontier Family: A Chronicle of a South African Farm, Its Homestead and Its People* by Johannes Meintjes (CNA); *Full Many a Glorious Morning* by Lawrence Green (Timmins); *Further Evidence of the Structures of the Sterkfontein Ape-man Plesianthropus* by R. Broom (Tvl. Museum); *The Gambler* by Stuart Cloete (Collins); *The Gateway to South Africa* (SA Railways & Harbours); *Gazella* by Stuart Cloete (Collins); *Geïllustreerde Geskiedenis vir Senior Sertifikaat Sts. IX & X* by F.A. van Jaarsveld, Theo van Wyk, Dr Jan Ploeger, Dr J.P. Bruwer, Dr J.I. Rademeyer (Voortrekkerpers); *General de Wet* by Eric Rosenthal (CNA); *General Smuts* by Sarah Gertrude Millin (Faber); *Genius for the Defence* by Benjamin Bennett (Timmins); *Gentlemen Prefer Blondes* by Anita Loos (Hamilton); *The Gilded Lily* by T. McLaughlin (Cassell); *The Glass Barrier* by Joy Packer (Eyre & Spottiswoode); *The Golden Keel* by Desmond Bagley (Collins); *The Gothic Line* by D. Orgill (Heinemann); *Grahamstown: Cape Province: South Africa* (Grahamstown Pub. Assoc.); *Grahamstown, the University of the Eastern Province* (Gtn. Municipality & SAR Publicity & Travel Dept.); *Grahamstown: What to see in the Settler City* Comp. C.M. Sprigg Ed. Norman Clark (Grahamstown Publicity Assoc.); *Grand Slam Golf* by Gary Player (Cassell); *The Great Barnato* by S. Jackson (Heinemann); *The Greatermans Organisation Looks to the Future* (Greatermans); *Great Events of the Twentieth Century* (Reader's Digest); *Great Movie Stars — The Golden Years* by D. Shipman (Angus & Robertson); *Great Shipwrecks off the Coast of Southern Africa* by José Lionel Burman (Struik); *The Great Steam Trek* by A.A. Jorgensen & C.P. Lewis (Struik); *Grey Mistress* by Joy Packer (Corgi); *Grey Steel: J.C. Smuts, a Study in Arrogance* by H.C. Armstong (Barker); *Die Groot Verlange* by Leon Rousseau (Human & Rousseau); *Grow Lovely, Growing Old* by L.G. Green (Timmins); *The Growth & Government of Cape Town* by P.W. Laidler (Unie-Volkpers); *The Guest: An Episode in the Life of Eugene Marais* by Athol Fugard & Ross Devenish (Donker); *A Guest of Honour* by Nadine Gordimer (Jonathan Cape); *A Guide to Architecture in South Africa* by Doreen Greig (Timmins); *Guide to Bloemfontein, with a Short History and Description of the Orange River Colony* by E.L. Calverley (Argus); *A Guide to South African Wines* by Graham Etherington (Nelson); *Guide to the Museums of Southern Africa* Comp. Hans Fransen (Galvin & Sales); *Gunners of the Cape* by Neil Orpen (CFA Regimental History Committee); *Halliwell's Film Guide* by Leslie Halliwell (Granada); *The Hamlyn Dictionary of Dates & Anniversaries* Ed. J.M. Bailie (Hamlyn); *Handbook on Race Relations in South Africa* by Ellen Hellman (SA Institute of Race Relations); *Havelock Ellis* by A. Calder-Marshall (Hart Davis); *Head of Steel* by L. van Onselen (Timmins); *The Heart of the Hunter* by Laurens van der Post (Hogarth); *Heart Transplant. The Story of Barnard and 'The Ultimate in Cardiac Surgery'* by Marais Malan (Voortrekkerpers); *Heinrich Egersdörfer* by Eric Rosenthal (Nasionale Boekhandel); *Herbert Baker in South Africa* by Doreen Greig (Purnell); *Herman Charles Bosman as I knew him* by Bernard Sachs (Dial); *'Hey! Van der Merwe'* by D.D. Marais (Juta); *The High Roof* by Joy Packer (Corgi); *Hilda's Diary of a Cape Housekeeper* by Hildagonda Duckitt (Macmillan); *Hire Purchase Credit in South Africa: An Economic Survey* by T. van Waasdyk (Wits. Univ. Press); *The Historical Monuments of South Africa* by J.J. Oberholster (Nat. Mon. Council); *Historic Costume for the Stage* by L. Baston (Black); *Historic Events 1839-1939* by Helmut & Alison Gernstein (Longman, Green); *Historic Tables 58 B.C. - 1963* by S.H. Steinberg (Macmillan); *The History and Social Significance of Motion Pictures in South Africa 1895-1940* by Thelma Gutsche (Timmins); *History of Children's Costume* by E. Ewing (Batsford); *A History of Cricket* by Harry S. Altham (Allen & Unwin); *A History of Natal* by Edgar H. Brookes & Colin de B. Webb (Univ. of Natal Press); *History of South Africa, Social and Economic* by C.W. de Kiewiet (OUP); *A History of the Press in South Africa* by T.E.G. Cutten (NUSAS); *History of the Second World War* (Purnell); *The History of the South African Forces in France* by John Buchan (Nelson & Sons); *History of Southern Africa* by E.A. Walker (Longmans); *History of Twentieth Century Fashion* by E. Ewing (Batsford); *Holism and Evolution* by General Smuts (Macmillan); *Home From Sea* by Joy Packer (Eyre Methuen); *Homes of the Golden City* by A. Macmillan (Hortors); *Housecraft: Principles and Practice* by Ruth Binnie & Julia E. Boxall (Pitman); *Household Guide* by A.R. Barnes (Darter & Walton); *How it Feels to Fly. Passenger's Impressions* (J. Weston Aviation Co.); *How to Evaluate your Proof Krugerrand* (SA Gold Coin Exchange); *Hoyle's Games: Improved: Being Practical Treatises on the Following Fashionable Games* by James Beaufort (Osborne & Griffin); *Human Heart Transplantation — the Preoperative Assessment — a Case Report* by Dr V. Schrire; *The Human Zoo* by Desmond Morris (Cape);*The Illustrated Guide to Southern Africa* (Reader's Digest); *An Illustrated Social History of South Africa* by A.F. Hattersley (Balkema); *Imperial Underwood College 'Century of Typewriters' Exhibition* press release (MER Promotions); *In Search of South Africa* by H.V. Morton (Methuen); *In South African Waters* by D. Hughes & P. Humphries (OUP); *Infantiele Mortaliteitstendense en Oorsake van Dood by Blankes, Kleurige en Asiërs in Suid-Afrika: 'n Orientasie* by J.M. Lötter and J.L. van Tonder (Institute of Sociological, Demographical and Criminological Research, H.S.R.C.); *The International Aspects of the South African Indian Question 1860-1971* by B. Pachai (Struik); *International Encyclopaedia of Film* Ed. Dr R. Manvell (Joseph); *In the Shadow of Table Mountain* by J.H. Louw (Struik); *I Remember Cape Town* by George Manuel (Nelson); *It's a Long Way to Addis* by Carel Birkby (Muller); *Jacaranda in the Night* by Herman Charles Bosman (Afrikaans Press); *Jan Christian Smuts* by J.C. Smuts (Cassell); *Jan Smuts: a Biography* by F.S. Crafford (Doubleday & Doran); *Jess* by Sir H. Rider Haggard (Smith, Elder); *Jewish Trails in Southern Africa: a Documentary with Photographs & Illustrations* by Nathan Berger (Kayor); *Joanie Galant-hulle* by Adam Small (Perskor); *Jock and Fitz* by Cecily Niven (Longmans); *Jock of the Bushveld* by Sir James Percy FitzPatrick (Longmans, Green); *The Johannesburg Saga* by J.R. Shorten (Shorten); *The Johannesburg Story* by F. Addington Symonds (Muller); *Johan Buchan: a Biography* by J.A. Smith (Granada); *The July Handicap* by Molly Reinhardt (Nelson); *Just So Stories* by Rudyard Kipling (Macmillan); *Juta's Directory of Cape Town and Suburbs* (Juta); *Karoo* by Lawrence G. Green (Timmins); *Kimberley City of Diamonds & Sunshine* (SAR&H/Kimberley Pub. Assoc.); *Kimberley: Turbulent City* by Brian Roberts (David Philip/Hist. Soc. of Kimberley); *King Kong — an African Jazz Opera* by Harry Bloom (Lyrics: Pat Williams) (Collins); *King Kong — a Venture in the Theatre* by Mona Glasser (Howell); *King Solomon's Mines* by Sir Henry Rider Haggard (Penguin); *Kitchen Antiques* by Mary Norwark (Ward Lock); *Kitchenware* by Jo Marshall (Pitman); *Kos vir die Kenner* by C. Louis Leipoldt (Tafelberg); *Kruger's Pretoria* by Vivian Allen (Balkema); *Labour in the South African Goldmines, 1911-1969* by F. Wilson (Cambridge, the Univ. Press); *The Lady in White* by Mrs P.S. Gibson (Purnell); *Land of the Thirst King* by Willem P. Steenkamp (Timmins); *The Last of the Line* by Laurens van der Post (Hogarth); *The Late Bourgeois World* by Nadine Gordimer (Gollancz); *Lawrence Green — Memories of a Friendship* by J.W. Yates-Benyon (Timmins); *Lecture on Plague* by W.J. Simpson (Cape Times); *Leipoldt's Cape Cookery* by C. Louis Leipoldt (Flesch); *Life of I.W. Schlesinger* by E. Rosenthal; *The Life of the White Ant* by M. Maeterlinck; *Lifetide* by Lyall Watson (Hodder & Stoughton); *Light on a Dark Horse* by Roy Campbell (Hollis & Carter); *The Lion of Judah hath Prevailed: being the biography of His Imperial Highness Haile Selassie* by Christine Sandford (Dent); *The Little Karoo* by Pauline Smith (Jonathan Cape); *London to Ladysmith via Pretoria* by Winston Spencer Churchill (Longmans & Green); *Long Cecil* by Col. D.E. Peddle (SA Nat. Museum of Military History); *Lost Johannesburg* by Arnold Benjamin (Macmillan); *The Lost World of the Kalahari* by Laurens van der Post (Hogarth); *The Lying Days* by Nadine Gordimer (Gollancz); *Mafeking: a Victorian Legend* by Brian Gardner (Cassell); *Mafeking Road* by Herman Charles Bosman (Human & Rousseau); *Magersfontein O Magersfontein* by Etienne Leroux (Human & Rousseau); *Mamba* by Stuart Cloete (Collins); *Die Mantel van Elia* by C.J. Langenhoven (Nasionale Pers); *Mark Twain — Himself* by M. Meltzer (Crown); *Maurice Maeterlinck: a study of his life and thought* by W.D. Halls (Oxford, at the Clarendon Press); *The M.C.C. in South Africa* by P.F. Warner (Chapman & Hall); *Meet the South African Railways* (SAR&H); *Memories of Four Continents: recollections grave and gay, of events in social and diplomatic life* by Lady E.R. Glover (Seeley, Service & Co.); *Memory-Hold-the-Door* by John Buchan (Hodder & Stoughton); *Men and Dinosaurs* by E.H. Colbert (Evans); *Die Mens Langenhoven* by M.P.O. Burgers (Nasionale Pers); *Men of the Times: Pioneers of the Transvaal, and Glimpses of South Africa* (Eyre & Spottiswoode); *Meridiana: the Adventures of Three Englishmen and Three Russians in South Africa* by Jules Verne (Sampson Low); *Minutes of Evidence Taken Before the Royal Commission on the War in South Africa, Vol. I & II* (Royal Commission of Enquiry); *Minutes of Evidence Taken Before the Select Committee on the Insolvency Act, 1916 Amendment Bill; The Monuments of South Africa* Ed. C. van Riet Louw (Gov. Printer); *More Tramps Abroad* by Mark Twain (Chatto & Windus); *The Motor Car. An Illustrated History* by Gianni Marin (Blond); *Mud, Blood and Laughter* by Maurice Broll (CT War Fund); *Die Mugu* by Etienne Leroux (HAUM); *My Caricatures* by D.C. Boonzaier; *My Early Life* by Sir W.L.S. Churchill (Macmillan); *My Fifty-Odd Years in Johannesburg: 1906-1960* by Flora Behrmann; *My Flight to the Cape and Back* by A. Cobham (Black); *My Friends the Baboons* by Eugene Marais (Methuen); *My Reminiscences of East Africa* by General von Lettow-Vorbeck (Hurst & Blackett); *Nada the Lily* by H. Rider Haggard (Hodder & Stoughton); *Nadine Gordimer* by Michael Wade (Evans); *The Naked Ape* by Desmond Morris (Cape); *Natal Homes, how to furnish them; The Native Laws Amendment Bill* (SA Institute of Race Relations); *The New Era in South Africa* by Violet Markham (Smith, Elder); *New Perspectives in South African Education* by A.L. Behr (Butterworths); *A Newspaper History of South Africa* by V. Alhadeff (Nelson); *The Newspaperman's Guide to the Law* by K.W. Stuart (Butterworth); *1980 Yearbook* (Dept. of Statistics); *1922: The Revolt on the Rand* by Norman Herd (Blue Crane); *No Outspan* by Deneys Reitz (Faber); *Norman Eaton: Architect* by Clinton Harrop-Allin (Struik); *Nor the Moon by Night* by Joy Packer (Corgi); *Not Again, Van der Merwe! Vol II* Comp. A.A. Koenderman, Jan Langen & André Viljoen (Lorton); *Not Without Honour* by Vera Buchanan-Gould (Hutchinson); *OB: Traitors or Patriots?* by George Cloete Visser (Macmillan); *Official South African Municipal Yearbook 1980* (SAAME); *Official Yearbooks of the Union of South Africa* (Bureau of Stats.); *O.K. Bazaars — a Review of History & Progress in the Company's First Quarter Century; Old Fourlegs: the Story of the Coelacanth* by J.L.B. Smith (Longmans, Green); *Old Gold: the History of the Wanderers Club* by Thelma Gutsche (Timmins); *Olive Schreiner — Memories of a Friendship* by Mary Brown (Olive Schreiner Scholarship Fund Committee); *Olive Schreiner: Portrait of a South African Woman* by Johannes Meintjes (Keartland); *One Life* by Dr Christiaan Neethling Barnard & Curtis Bill Pepper (Bantam); *One Man in his Time* by Phyllis Scarnell Lean (Gen. Smuts War Veterans Foundation); *On Safari* by Ada Forrest (Hale); *On Wings of Fire* by Lawrence Green (Timmins); *Oom Gert Vertel en Ander Gedigte* by C. Louis Leipoldt (HAUM); *Oom Kootjie Emmer* by André P. Brink (Buren); *'n Oorsig van Wynbou in Suid-Afrika 1973-1974* (KWV); *Oos, Wes, Tuis Bes: Distrik Ses: Poesie* by Adam Small & Chris Jansen (Human & Rousseau); *Ostrich Country* by Fay Goldie (Books of Africa); *Other Men's Millions* by Eric Rosenthal (Timmins); *Ouma Smuts* by Tom MacDonald (Hurst & Blackett); *The Outlanders: the Men who made Johannesburg* by Robert Crisp (Davies); *Out of the Crucible* by H.A. Chilvers (Cassell); *Out of the Magic Boks* by Bruce Heilbuth (Galvin & Sales); *Out of the Stable: S.A. and its Indian Question for the Last 25 Years 1910-1935* by Dhanee Bramdaw (Natal Witness), *Owlographs* by D. Boonzaier (Cape Times); *The Oxford Companion to Film* Ed. Liz-Anne Bawden (OUP); *The Oxford History of South Africa* Ed. Monica Wilson & Leonard Thompson (Clarendon); *The Oxford Social History of South Africa* Ed. M. Wilson & L. Thompson (Clarendon); *Pack and Follow* by Joy Packer (Corgi); *The Pagel Story* by C. Birkby (Timmins for Hodder & Stoughton); *Parktown 1892-1972: a Social and Pictorial History* by A. Benjamin (Studio Thirty-Five); *Panorama of Port Elizabeth* by E.K. Lorimer (Balkema); *The Patients* by Jürgen Thornwald (Harcourt, Brace Janovich); *Pauline Smith* by G. Haresnape (Twayne); *Paul Kruger, his Life and Times* by John Fisher (Secker & Warburg); *The Peace Celebrations, Cape Town, 1919* (official programme & souvenir booklet); *The People's Chronology* Ed. James Trager (Heinemann); *Personalities in Southern African Motoring and Aviation* (Knox); *Philately of the Anglo-Boer War* by S.J. Rich (Chambers); *Pictorial History of Johannesburg* Ed. A.H. Smith (Juta, for the Africana Museum); *Pienaar of Alamein* by A.M. Pollock (Cape Times); *Pietermaritzburg Panorama: a Survey of 100 Years of an African City* by A.F. Hattersley (Shuter & Shooter); *Pilgrim's Rest* by Francis Brett Young (Collins); *Pilgrim's Rest, the First Hundred Years* by A.P. Cartwright (Wharton); *Pioneer Port* by J. Denfield (Timmins); *Pioneers of Early Aviation in South Africa* by Hannes Oberholzer (Bloem. Nat. Museum); *The Plague of the Spanish Lady* by Richard Collier (Macmillan); *Platkops Children* by Pauline Smith (Cape); *Pleasure and Problem in South Africa* by C. Harmsworth (Lane); *Politieke Prente uit die Burger* by D.C. Boonzaier (Nasionale Pers); *The Poor White Problem in South Africa* (Report of the Carnegie Commission); *The Population of Natal* by M.H. Alsop (Oxford Univ. Press for Univ. of Natal); *Port Natal: a Pioneer Story* by Janie Antonia Malherbe (Timmins); *Portrait of an Artist — Conan Doyle* by Julian Symons (Whizzard); *The Press as Opposition: the Political Role of Southern African Newspapers* by Elaine Potter (Chatto & Windus); *Prester John* by John Buchan (Nelson); *Pretoria 1855-1955* by S.P. Engelbrecht (Pretoria City Council); *The Pretoria Press Story* by H.P.H. Behrens (Pretoria City Council); *Public Service Lists; Publikasiebeheer in Suid-Afrika* by J.C.W. van Rooyen (Juta); *The Purple and the Gold* by Joy Collier (Longmans); *Railway and Customs Policies in South Africa 1885-1910* by Jean van der Poel (Longmans, Green); *Railways of Southern Africa* by O.S. Nock (Black); *Randlords* by Paul H. Emden (Hodder & Stoughton); *A Record of Achievement of the Ministry of Transport of the Union of South Africa: A Century of Transport* by A. van Lingen (Da Gama); *Regimental History: the Royal Hampshire Regiment* by C.T. Atkinson (Glasgow, Univ. Press for the Regiment); *Reminiscences of a Rand Pioneer* by Renault Courtney Acutt (Ravan); *Reminiscences of Georgina Lister* (Africana Museum); *Report from South Africa: July 1966: Commemorative Issue: Battle of Delville Wood, July 15-20 1916* (Dept. of Information/SA Embassy); *Report on the Concentration Camps in South Africa* by the Committee of Ladies appointed by the Secretary of State for War, 1902 (Eyre & Spottiswoode); *Rhodes University 1904-1970* by R.F. Curry (Grahamstown, the University); *Rivonia, Operation Mayibuye: a Review of the Rivonia Trial* by H.H.W. de Villiers (Afrikaanse Pers); *Rondebosch and Roundabout* by Adèle Naudé (David Philip); *Die Rooi Rotte* by C. Louis Leipoldt (Nasionale Pers); *Royal Ambassadors* by Theo Aronson (David Philip); *Rudyard Kipling: his Life and Work* by Charles Carrington (Macmillan); *Rudyard Kipling: the Man, his Work and World* Ed. J. Gross (Weidenfeld & Nicolson); *Rudyard Kipling's Verse: Definitive Edition* (Hodder & Stoughton); *Rudyard Kipling to Rider Haggard. The Record of a Friendship* Ed. M.N. Cohen (Hutchinson); *Rumours of Rain* by André P. Brink (Allen); *Runner and Mailcoach* by Eric Rosenthal & Eliezer Blum (Purnell); *SAA Comes of Age (1934-55)*; *SAA Presents — Fifty Years of Flight*; *SAA —Thirty years of Progress*; *Saga of the South African Horse* by Daphne Child (Timmins); *Saint Theodore and the Crocodile: the Reminiscences of Vere Bosman di Ravelli* by V.B. di Ravelli (Tafelberg); *Schooners and Skyscrapers* by Eric Rosenthal (Timmins); *1769 and Thereafter – A South African Memoir* by H.J. Raubenheimer (ms.); *Seventy Golden Years* by Felix Stark (Felstar); *Shaw in his Time* by Ivor J.C. Brown (Nelson); *She* by H. Rider Haggard (Hodder & Stoughton); *Ships and South Africa: a Maritime Chronicle of the Cape* by Marischal Murray (OUP); *Short History of the Newspaper Press in South Africa 1652-1952* by D.H. Varley (Nasionale Pers); *Silver Images* by A.D. Bensusan (Timmins); *Smuts: The Fields of Force 1919-1950 (Vol. I)* by W.K. Hancock (Cambridge Univ. Press); *Smuts of South Africa: biographical summary* (SA Govt. Info. Office, New York); *Social Life of Monkeys and Apes* by Solly Zuckerman (Kegan); *The Soft Voice of the Serpent and other stories* by Nadine Gordimer (Gollancz); *Some Beginnings: the Cape Times 1876-1910* by Gerald Shaw (Oxford Univ. Press); *Something Rich and Strange* by Lawrence Green (Timmins); *Some South African Politicians* by L.E. Neame (Maskew Miller); *Soul of the Ape* by Eugene Marais (Penguin); *Soul of the White Ant* by Eugene Marais (Penguin); *South Africa* by Anthony Trollope (Chapman & Hall); *South Africa — a Modern History* by T.R.H. Davenport (Macmillan); *South Africa and the Boer-British War* by J.C. Hopkins & M. Halstead (War Book Pub.); *South Africa Fights* by J.S.M. Simpson (Hodder & Stoughton); *South African Grand Prix* by Brud Bishop (Blue Crane); *SA Handbook, 1893* Ed. J. Noble; *SA Handbook (1905) 'Diamond Fields'; South African Handbook No. 1: Advice to Immigrants; The South African Household Guide* by A.R. Barnes (Darter); *South African Municipal Yearbook 1911* (SAAME); *South African Railways and Harbours Handbook; South African Review: Book of 50 Famous Cartoons: a unique souvenir of the Anglo-Boer War; South African Sports* by G.A. Parker (Low, Marston); *South African Statesman: Jan Christiaan Smuts* by Joan Joseph (Messner); *South African Statistics 1980* (Dept. of Stats.); *South African Traits* by Rev. James MacKinnon (Gemmell); *South African Union. Historical Souvenir of Natal* by J.W. Howard (CNA); *The South African War: Anglo-Boer War 1899-1902* Ed. Peter Warwick; *South African Yearbooks* (Da Gama); *South Africa's Hall of Fame* by A.P. Cartwright (CNA); *Southern African Literature* by Stephen Gray (David Philip); *Southern Africa at Sport* Ed. R.K. Stent & M. Lee (Cripple Care Assoc.); *Soweto: a City within a City* (Bantu Affairs Admin. Board: West Rand Area); *Soweto: Johannesburg's African City* by Ellen Hellman (SA Institute of Race Relations); *The Speeches of General J.C. Smuts* (Truth Legion); *Speed on Wheels* by Malcolm Campbell (Sampson Low); *The Spirit of Progress* Ed. F. Starck (Felstar); *Spirit of the Vine: Republic of South Africa* Ed. D.J. Opperman (Human & Rousseau); *Springbok Glory* by Louis Duffus (Longmans, Green); *Springbok Record* Comp./Ed. Harry Klein (SA Legion of the British Empire Service League); *Springbok Saga: a pictorial history from 1891* by Chris Greyvenstein (Nelson); *Stamps of South Africa* Ed. Berry, Sheffield, Hagger, Legator (PFSA); *Stamps of the Cape of Good Hope* by G.J. Allis (Gibbons); *Standard Encyclopaedia of Southern Africa* (NASOU); *The State President's Guard* (pamphlet); *The Statesmen* by Terry Eksteen (Nelson); *The Steam Locomotives of the South African Railways* by D.F. Holland (Purnell); *Stories from the Karkloof Hills* by Charles Scott Shaw (Shuter & Shooter); *Story of an African City* by J. Forsyth Ingram (Coester); *The Story of an African Farm* by Olive Schreiner (Penguin); *The Story of Delville Wood: told in Letters from the Front* (Cape Times); *The Story of the Cape to Cairo Railway and River Route from 1887-1922* by Leo Weinthar (Pioneer); *Story of the Johannesburg Stock Exchange (1887-1947)*; *The Story of 'South Africa' Newspaper and its Founder, Told by Others; The Story of the South African Brigade* adapted from John Buchan's *History of the South African Forces in France* (Maskew Miller); *The Strange Ride of Rudyard Kipling* by A.F.J. Wilson (Secker & Warburg); *Strangers in our Midst* by Lucy Bea (Timmins); *Sunflower to the Sun* by Valerie Rosenberg (Human & Rousseau); *Supernature* by Lyall Watson (Hodder & Stoughton); *Tafelberg en die Sweefspoor* by T.V. Bulpin (Tafelberg); *A Taste of South Easter* by Lawrence Green (Timmins); *Tavern of the Seas* by Lawrence Green (Timmins); *The Tavern of the Seas: Die Herberg van die See* Ed. J.F. Craig (United Tobacco Co./Westminster Tobacco Co./Policansky Bros.); *Testament of Youth: an Autobiography of the Years 1900-1924* by Vera Brittain; *Their Majesties the King and Queen and Their Royal Highnesses the Princess Elizabeth and the Princess Margaret in the Union of South Africa, February-April 1947* (SAR & H); *They Built a Theatre, the History of the Johannesburg Repertory Theatre* Ed. A. Hoffman & A. Romain-Hoffman (Donker); *They Came From the Sea: the Story of Port Elizabeth's Dolphins* by M. Rowe (Longmans); *They Seek a Country* by Francis Brett Young (Heinemann); *They were South Africans* by John Bond (OUP); *Thirstland Treks* by C. Birkby (Faber); *The Thirty-Nine Steps* by J. Buchan (Maskew Miller); *This Brutal Glory* by Chris Greyvenstein (Buren); *This is SAA; This was a Man* by P.W. Grobbelaar (Human & Rousseau); *The Thoughts of General Smuts, by his Secretary* by P.B. Blanckenberg (Juta); *Thoughts on South Africa* by Olive Schreiner (Fisher Unwin); *Through Jackson's Eyes* by J.H. Jackson (HAUM); *Tickey: the Story of Eric Hoyland* by T.V. Bulpin (Bulpin); *Timber and Tides: the Story of Knysna and Plettenberg Bay* by Winifred Tapson (Juta); *The Times History of the War in South Africa 1899-1902* Ed. L.S. Amery (Sampson Low); *The Time Shrinkers: the Development of Civil Aviation between Britain and Africa* by David Jones

(Rendel); *The Timetables of History* by Bernard Grun (Thames & Hudson); *Today's News Today* by Eric Rosenthal (Argus); *Too Late for Tears* by Benjamin Bennett (Timmins for Hodder and Stoughton); *Too Late the Phalarope* by Alan Paton (Hamilton); *Total's Book of Southern African Records* Ed. Eric Rosenthal; *To the River's End* by Lawrence Green (Timmins); *Towards the Mountain: an Autobiography* by Alan Paton (David Philip); *Track and Trackless: Omnibuses and Trams in the Western Cape* by P.R. Coates (Struik); *Trader on the Veld* by A. Jackson (Balkema); *Transplanted* by K.A. Carlson (Minerva); *The Transplanted Heart* by Peter Hawthorne (Keartland); *Transvaal Education Department 1876-1976; Transvaal Epic* by Paul Tingay & Jill Johnson (Khenty); *The Transvaal from Within* by Percy James FitzPatrick (Heinemann); *Trekking On* by Deneys Reitz (Faber); *Tribe to Township* by P.L.W. Becker (Panther); *A Trip to South Africa* by J. Salter-Whiter (Pile); *Trooper Peter Halket of Mashonaland* by Olive Schreiner (Unwin); *Try Anything Twice* by Desmond Young (Hamilton); *Turning Wheels* by Stuart Cloete (Collins); *Twenty-Four Inches Apart* by S.M. Moir (Oakwood); *Twenty Thousand Miles in a Flying Boat: my Flight round Africa* by A. Cobham (Harrap); *Twilight over the Tygerberg* by J.P. Duminy (Midgley); *A Twist of Sand* by Geoffrey Jenkins (Collins); *2000 Casualties: a History of the Trade Unions and the Labour Movement in the Union of South Africa* by I.L. Walker & B. Weinbren (SA Trade Union Council); *U Dienswillige Dienaar* by C.J. Langenhoven (Tafelberg); *Union-Castle Chronicle 1863-1953* by Marischal Murray (Longmans, Green); *Union Government Buildings, Pretoria* (Pretoria Pub. Assoc.); *The Union of South Africa: Africa Arsenal* (SA Bureau of Information); *Union of South Africa and the Great War 1914-1918: Official History* (General Staff, Defence HQ, Pretoria); *The Union of South Africa: the Development of its Laws and Constitutions* by H.R. Hahlo & Ellison Kahn (Stevens); *Union Statistics for Fifty Years 1910-1960* (Bureau of Census & Statistics); *Until the Heart Changes: a Garland for Olive Schreiner* by Zelda Friedlander (Tafelberg); *Up for Murder* by Benjamin Bennett (Hutchinson); *Valley of the Vines* by Joy Packer (Ulverscroft); *Van der Merwe: 100 Stories* Comp. A.A. Koenderman (Lorton); *Veld Express* by Harry Zeederberg (Timmins); *Veronica* by Joy Packer (Eyre & Spottiswoode); *Victorian Buildings in South Africa* by D.M. Picton-Seymour (Balkema); *A Victorian Son: an Autobiography* by Stuart Cloete (Collins); *A View from the Ridge* by John Wentzel (David Philip); *Vintage Summer: 1947* by John Arlot (Eyre & Spottiswoode); *Wagon-Tracks and Orchards: Early Days in Sandton* by Juliet Marais Louw (Donker); *The War in South Africa: its cause and conduct* by A. Conan Doyle (Smith Elder); *War Without Glamour — or — Women's War Experiences Written by Themselves 1899-1902* Ed. Emily Hobhouse (Nasionale Pers); *What Every Motorist Ought to Know About the Law* by L. Japhet (Argus); *When the Lion Feeds* by Wilbur Smith (Heinemann); *Where Men Still Dream* by Lawrence Green (Timmins); *Whitaker's Almanac 1981* (Whitaker); *Who's Who in Southern Africa* (Argus); *Wine* by A.C. Hocking (Purnell); *Wine in South Africa* by A.G. Bagnall (SABC); *Wings to the Cape* by J. Godwin (Tafelberg); *With a Show Through Southern Africa* by Charles du Val (Tinsley); *Woman and Labour* by Olive Schreiner (Unwin); *Women's Dress in the Jazz Age* by James Laver (Hamilton); *The World Depression, South Africa and the Gold Standard* by C.G.W. Schumann (Juta); *World Encyclopaedia of Comics* by Maurice Horn (Chelsea House); *The World Atlas of Golf* Ed. Pat Ward-Thomas (Mitchell Beazley); *The World of Nat Nakasa* (Raven Press); *A World of Strangers* by Nadine Gordimer (Jonathan Cape); *Illustrated Story of World War II* (Reader's Digest); *Worthwhile Journey* by Tromp van Diggelen (Heinemann); *Yachting in Southern Africa* by Anthony Hocking (Purnell); *You have been Listening* by Eric Rosenthal (Purnell); *Young Pretoria, 1889-1913* by Lola Dunston.

Bibliography: magazines and periodicals

African Air Travel; Africana Notes and News; African Film News; African Land and Home Journal; African Market; African Pictorial; African Radio Announcer; The African World; African World Annual; Di Afrikaanse Patriot; Agricultural Advertiser and South African Farmer; Agricultural Journal (of the Cape of Good Hope); Agricultural Journal of South Africa; Agricultural Journal of the Union of South Africa; Agricultural News; Arabesque; The Argus; Argus Weekly; Arthur Barlow's Weekly; Automobile; Aviation in Africa, Bandstand; The Bantu World; Bloemfontein Gazette; The Bluestocking; Die Boerevrou; Die Boerevrou & Ons Kleintjie; Boxing South Africa; Die Brandwag; The British Empire; The Builder; The Bulletin of the Adler Museum; Die Burger; Cape Argus; Cape Magazine; Cape Times; Cape Times Annual; The 'Cape Times' South African Hotel Guide; Car; Citizen; Clansman; The Classic; Clink; Comet; Commercial Fishing News; Commercial Opinion; Commercial Review and South African Storekeeper; Contemporary Authors; Counterpoint; The Cricketer; Daily Express; Daily Graphic; Daily Telegraph; De Volksstem; Diamond Fields Advertiser; Digger's News; Drum; Eastern Province Herald; East London Daily Dispatch; The Education Gazette; The Engineer; L'Equipe; Eve at Home; The Executive; Fair Lady; Family Magazine and Mail Order Guide; Farmer; Farmer and Home Companion; Farmer's Gazette; Farmer's Weekly; Farming in South Africa; Fashion and Music Album; Femina; Femina & Woman's Life; Financial Mail; Fletcher and Cartwrights' catalogue; Food Industries of South Africa; Fortnightly Digest of South African Affairs; The Forum; The Friend; The Friend of the Free State; Friend of the Sovereignty & Bloemfontein Gazette; The Furnisher; George and Knysna Herald; Gold Fields News; Guide to Port Elizabeth, 1893; How to Evaluate your Proof Krugerrands; Het Zuid-Westen; Homestead; Homestead Cookery; Home Talk; Die Huisgenoot; Illustrated London News; The Illustrated South African Hotel Guide; The Illustrated Star; Imvo Zabantsundu; The Independent; Inspan; Joscelyn's Catalogue; Die Jongspan; Keesing's Contemporary Archives; The Knobkerrie; Land en Volk; Lantern; Libertas; Licensed Victualler's and Sporting Gazette; Licensed Victualler's Gazette; London Daily Mail; London Morning Chronicle; Mafeking Mail; Man About Town; Medical Journal of South Africa; Milady; Militaria; Morning Post; The Motor; Motor; Motor Age; Motor Parade; Motor Weekly; Motoring in South Africa; The Motorist in South Africa; Mrs Slade's South African Good Housekeeping; The M.T.A. Bulletin; Municipal Affairs; Natal Advertiser; Natal Mercury; Natal Mercury Pictorial; Natal Witness; The New Kruger Millions; News of the World; New Quest; The New State; Nongquai; The Observer (POW); Observer (South Africa); Official South African Municipal Yearbook, 1911; Official Yearbook of the Union of South Africa; Ons Kleintjie; Ons Land; Outlook; The Outspan; The Owl; Pace; Pall Mall Magazine; Performing Arts Council Bulletin; Personality; Phonetic Journal; The Pictorial; Pictorial Times (London); Pleasure Magazine; Post; Pravda; Pretoria News; Public Health; Rand Daily Mail; Rand Young Man's Journal; Rapport; Reader's Digest; Round Table; Royal Automobile Club of South Africa Journal; Sarie Marais; Saturday; Scope; The Sjambok; Social Problems; South Africa; South African Architect and Builder; South African Architect, Engineer and Surveyor's Journal; South African Architectural Record; SABC Bulletin; South African Builder; South African Commercial Advertiser; South African Dancing Times; South African Domestic Monthly; South African Educator; South African Engineer; South African Farm, Road and Seaside; South African Farmer's Advocate; South African Food Review; The South African Grocer; The South African Grocer and General Dealer; South African Grocer's Record and General Dealer's Gazette; South African Handbook; South African Hotel Guide; South African Household Guide; South African Illustrated News; South African Industry and Trade; The South African Lady's Pictorial and Home Journal; South African Law Journal; South African Medical Journal; South African Mining and Engineering Journal; South African Motorist; South African Municipal Magazine; South African Musical Times; South African Nation; South African News; South African Opinion; South African Outlook; S.A. Panorama; South African Photographer; South African Photographic Journal; South African Pictorial; South African Pictorial, Stage and Cinema; South African Railways and Harbours Magazine; South African Review; South African Shopkeeper and Commercial Gazette; South African Storekeeper; South African Trader and Shopkeeper's Journal; South African Treasurer; South African Wheel; South African Woman's Magazine; South African Weekly Standard; S.A. Yachting; The South and East African Yearbook Guide; Speak; The Sphere; Spracklens Mail Order Catalogue; Springbok; Stage and Cinema; Stage, Cinema and Listener-In; The Standard; The Standard and Digger's News; The Star; Statutes of the Union of South Africa; De Strever; Stuttafords Mail Order Catalogue; Sun of South Africa; Sunday Times; The Tatler (London); Tennis S.A. and Squash; Theatre World; Time; The Times (London); Topsport; Touleier; Transvaal Illustrated News; Die Transvaler; Trek; Die Vaderland; The Veld; The Veldt; The Voice; Voice of Labour; Die Volksblad; Voorslag; Vroue Wêreld; The War Illustrated; Warwick Trading Co. Catalogue; Washington Star; Westminster Gazette; Wings; Wisden; Wits' Wits; Woman and Her Affairs; Woman's Domain; Woman's Journal (London); Woman's Outlook; The World; Zero Hour; Zoutpansberg Review and Mining Journal; De Zuid-Afrikaan.

Picture credits

Picture credits for each page read from top to bottom, using the top of the picture as the reference point. Where the tops of two or more pictures are on the same level credits read from left to right.

6 Africana Museum. **10** Africana Museum. **12** Cape Archives; *The Star's* Barnett Collection; South African National Museum of Military History; Cape Archives; South African National Museum of Military History; Cape Archives; Cape Archives; Cape Archives; Africana Museum; Africana Museum; Africana Museum; Africana Museum; Cape Archives; Africana Museum; Africana Museum. **13** South African National Museum of Military History; Cape Archives; *The Sphere*. **14** Cory Library; Killie Campbell Africana Library; Africana Museum. **15** Local History Museum, Durban; De Beers; Killie Campbell Africana Library; Killie Campbell Africana Library; McGregor Museum; Africana Museum. **16** *The Star's* Barnett Collection; Cape Archives. **17** *The Sphere;* Local History Museum, Durban; Africana Museum; Africana Museum; Africana Museum; Ou Pastorie Museum. **18** South African National Museum of Military History. **19** *The Sphere;* Africana Museum; South African Cultural History Museum/Brian Johnson-Barker; South African Cultural History Museum/Brian Johnson-Barker; Africana Museum; South African National Museum of Military History; Cape Archives; Rhodes Memorial Museum and Commonwealth Centre. **20** Local History Museum, Durban; *War Without Glamour — or — Women's War Experiences written by themselves 1899-1902* Ed. Emily Hobhouse (Nasionale Pers Bpk.); *The War in South Africa: its cause and conduct* by Arthur Conan Doyle (Smith, Elder & Co.); *London to Ladysmith via Pretoria* by Winston Churchill (Longmans, Green & Co.); South African Cultural History Museum/John Meek; Africana Museum; Africana Museum; Africana Museum; Africana Museum. **21** Human Sciences Research Council, Archives of the Centre for South African Music, Pretoria; Human Sciences Research Council, Archives of the Centre for South African Music, Pretoria; Human Sciences Research Council, Archives of the Centre for South African Music, Pretoria; Unattributed; Unattributed; Human Sciences Research Council, Archives of the Centre for South African Music, Pretoria; Unattributed; Africana Museum; Africana Museum; Africana Museum; Africana Museum; Africana Museum; Africana Museum; Africana Museum. **22** *South Africa;* South African National Museum of Military History; Stellenbosch Museum. **23** Africana Museum. **24** *The Sphere;* Africana Museum; Killie Campbell Africana Library; *The Pictorial*; *The Pictorial*; Killie Campbell Africana Library. **25** Pretoria Municipal Archives; *Cape Times*; *The Sphere*; Cape Archives; Africana Museum; Africana Museum; Killie Campbell Africana Library. **26** *The Star*, Johannesburg; Africana Museum; *The Star*, Johannesburg; Africana Museum; *Outspan*; *Outspan.* **27** South African Embassy, London/John Meek; South African Rugby Board; South African Rugby Board; South African Library. **28** Africana Museum; Local History Museum, Durban; De Beers/John Meek; De Beers/John Meek; De Beers/John Meek. **29** Africana Museum; Africana Museum; John Meek. **30** Mr Jimmie Lawrence, F.R.N.S. **31** Post Office Museum: Postage Stamps reproduced under Government Printer's Copyright Authority 6607 of 23.5.1980; *The New Kruger Millions*; *The Star*, Johannesburg; Africana Museum; Africana Museum; Africana Museum; Post Office Museum: Postage Stamps reproduced under Government Printer's Copyright Authority 7688 of 15.7.1981. **32** Killie Campbell Africana Library; Killie Campbell Africana Library; Killie Campbell Africana Library; Africana Museum; *Cape Times*; Port Elizabeth Municipal Library. **33** Local History Museum, Durban; Local History Museum, Durban; Local History Museum, Durban; Local History Museum, Durban; Pretoria Municipal Archives; Killie Campbell Africana Library. **34** Africana Museum; South African National Museum of Military History; South African Museum; *The Star*, Johannesburg; Cape Archives; Pretoria Municipal Archives. **35** Imperial War Museum, London; *The Star*, Johannesburg; *The Star*, Johannesburg; *Cape Times*; *Cape Times*. **36** *The Star*, Johannesburg; *Nongquai*; *The Argus*; *The Argus*. **37** *Natal Mercury*; *The Star*, Johannesburg; *The Star*, Johannesburg; Africana Museum. **38** *The Star*, Johannesburg; *The Star*, Johannesburg; Africana Museum; Africana Museum; Africana Museum; Africana Museum; Africana Museum. **39** The Department of Foreign Affairs and Information; *The Star*, Johannesburg; Susan Hart; the Department of Foreign Affairs and Information. **40** Cape Archives. **42** Africana Museum; *The Star's* Barnett Collection; *The Star's* Barnett Collection; Africana Museum; *The Star's* Barnett Collection; *Outspan*. **43** Africana Museum; Africana Museum; Africana Museum; *The Star*, Johannesburg; *The Star*, Johannesburg; Norman Weston. **44** De Beers; De Beers; Mr & Mrs A.J. Burger; De Beers; De Beers; Cape Archives. **45** De Beers; Cape Archives; *Cape Times*; Cape Archives. **46** Cape Archives; Pretoria Municipal Archives; Pretoria Municipal Archives; Pretoria Municipal Archives; Pretoria Municipal Archives; Pretoria Municipal Archives. **47** Pretoria Municipal Archives; Pretoria Municipal Archives; Pretoria Municipal Archives; Pretoria Municipal Archives; Pretoria City Council; Cape Archives. **48** Cape Archives; Cape Archives; Africana Museum; T.V. Bulpin; *Oos, Wes, Tuis Bes, Distrik Ses: Poesie* by Adam Small & Chris Jansen (Human & Rousseau); *South African Illustrated News*. **49** *Cape Times*; John Meek; *Cape Times*; Private Collection: South African National Art Gallery; Africana Museum; Cape Archives. **50** Africana Museum; *The Engineer*; Africana Museum; Africana Museum. **51** Susan Hart; Susan Hart; Susan Hart; Killie Campbell Africana Library; Africana Museum; Mr Nathan Cowan; Local History Museum, Durban. **52** Port Elizabeth Municipal Library; Port Elizabeth Municipal Library; Port Elizabeth Municipal Library; Port Elizabeth Municipal Library; Unattributed; Port Elizabeth Municipal Library. **53** Cape Archives; by courtesy of South African Railways; *Old Fourlegs: the story of the Coelacanth* by J.L.B. Smith (Longmans, Green & Co.); Cape Archives; Africana Museum. **54** *Cape Times*; *The Sphere*; Adler Museum of the History of Medicine, Johannesburg; Pretoria Municipal Archives; Johannesburg Hospital Archives. **55** Adler Museum of the History of Medicine, Johannesburg; Adler Museum of the History of Medicine, Johannesburg; Adler Museum of the History of Medicine, Johannesburg; Adler Museum of the History of Medicine, Johannesburg; Automobile Association of South Africa. **56** *The Star*, Johannesburg; Don MacKenzie Studios; *The Argus*; *The Argus*; *The Argus*; *The Argus*; *Rand Daily Mail*; picture by courtesy of *Fair Lady* & Mrs C. Barnard. **57** *Rand Daily Mail*; Adler Museum of the History of Medicine, Johannesburg; Roy Hallowday, Witwatersrand Medical School; by courtesy of *S.A. Panorama*. **58** Transvaal Education Museum; Transvaal Education Museum; *The Star*, Johannesburg; Transvaal Education Museum; Transvaal Education Museum. **59** *The Star*, Johannesburg; Archives of the University of the Witwatersrand; Archives of the University of the Witwatersrand; Archives of the University of the Witwatersrand. **60** Cape Archives. **62** *The Star's* Barnett Collection; Local History Museum, Durban; Africana Museum. **63** Stuttafords Catalogue; *South Africa;* Stellenbosch Museum. **64** Africana Museum. **65** Africana Museum; Africana Museum; Africana Museum; C.P. Nel Museum, Oudtshoorn; *South Africa*. **66** *South African Architect and Builder*. **67** *Outspan*/Akkersdyk Studios; Dave Shaw/Mr and Mrs D.D. Thomson; Box: J.B. Kramer. **68** *South African Architectural Record*; Dave Shaw; *South African Architectural Record*; *Zero Hour*. **69** Prof. C. Harrop-Allin; Prof. C. Harrop-Allin; Prof. C. Harrop-Allin; *South African Lady's Pictorial*. **70** East London Museum; Local History Museum, Durban; *Australia's Yesterdays* (Reader's Digest). **71** *The Star*, Johannesburg; *Housecraft: Principles and Practice* by Ruth Binnie & Julia Boxall (Pitman & Sons); Africana Museum. **72** J.B. Kramer; *Outspan*; Akkersdyk Studios; *South African Lady's Pictorial*. **73** John Tabraham; John Tabraham; John Tabraham; Box: Joscelyn's Catalogue/Africana Museum. **74** *Mrs Slade's South African Good Housekeeping*; *Housecraft: Principles and Practice* by Ruth Binnie & Julia Boxall (Pitman & Sons); *Homestead Cookery*. **75** J.B. Kramer; *South African Lady's Pictorial*; *Outspan*; Crown Copyright, Science Museum, London; Bloemfontein National Museum; Crown Copyright, Science Museum, London; Crown Copyright, Science Museum, London. **76** *Outspan*; Transvaal Provincial Institute of Architects; *Outspan*. **77** *The Star*, Johannesburg; Jill Johnson; Jill Johnson; *The Star*, Johannesburg. **78** *South African Woman's Magazine*; *South African Woman's Magazine*; *South African Woman's Magazine*; Port Elizabeth Municipal Library; J. Cowie-Shaw. **79** *Outspan*; *South African Architect, Engineer and Surveyor's Journal*; *South African Architect,*

Engineer and Surveyor's Journal; Board of Executors Properties Ltd. **80** Paddy Hartdegen; *Cape Times*; J.B. Kramer. **81** Dr D.J.C. Radford; Tupperware Co.; Tupperware Co.; De Beers; Kimco Studios; Gordon Douglas/Sappi; *South Africa*. **82** By courtesy of South African Railways. **84** *South African Musical Times*; Bensusan Museum of Photography; Bensusan Museum of Photography; Bensusan Museum of Photography; Bensusan Museum of Photography; Bensusan Museum of Photography; Bensusan Museum of Photography; J.B. Kramer. **85** South African Cultural History Museum/John Meek; South African Cultural History Museum/John Meek; South African Cultural History Museum/John Meek; Africana Museum. **86** *South African Lady's Pictorial*; South African Cultural History Museum/John Meek. **87** Africana Museum; Africana Museum; Africana Museum; Africana Museum; *Outspan*. **88** Unattributed; J.B. Kramer; Mr A.J. Woolley; Mr A.J. Wolley; Unattributed; Unattributed; Africana Museum; Africana Museum; J.B. Kramer; J.B. Kramer; J.B. Kramer; J.B. Kramer. **89** J.B. Kramer. **90** *The Star*, Johannesburg; Stellenbosch Museum; Stellenbosch Museum; *The Star*, Johannesburg; Stellenbosch Museum; Africana Museum. **91** *The Star*, Johannesburg; Stellenbosch Museum; Stellenbosch Museum; Africana Museum; Stellenbosch Museum; Africana Museum. **92** *The Star*, Johannesburg; J.B. Kramer; Africana Museum; *The Star*, Johannesburg; South African Cultural History Museum; Africana Museum. **93** *Outspan*; *South African Lady's Pictorial*; *South African Lady's Pictorial*; *Cape Times*; *South African Lady's Pictorial*/Cleghorns; Africana Museum; Africana Museum; Africana Museum. **94** Local History Museum, Durban; Africana Museum; Africana Museum; *Natal Mercury Pictorial*. **95** Africana Museum; Cape Archives; J.B. Kramer. **96** *Pretoria News;* Africana Museum; Africana Museum; Africana Museum; J.B. Kramer. **97** Stuttafords Catalogue; *South African Lady's Pictorial*; South African Cultural History Museum/John Meek; by courtesy of South African Railways; Kellerprinz/TWS. **98** Bensusan Museum of Photography; Cape Archives; Bensusan Museum of Photography; Bensusan Museum of Photography. **99** Cape Archives; Bensusan Museum of Photography; Bensusan Museum of Photography; *The Argus*; J.B. Kramer; J.B. Kramer. **100-101** Duggan-Cronin Collection (McGregor Museum, Kimberley). **102** *Dancing* by Edward Scott (George Bell and Sons); *Dancing* by Edward Scott (George Bell and Sons); *Dancing* by Edward Scott (George Bell and Sons); South African Cultural History Museum; J.B. Kramer; *South African Dancing Times*; Africana Museum. **103** *The Star*, Johannesburg; *South African Musical Times*; painting by C.E. Turner/by courtesy of South African Railways; by courtesy of South African Railways; Unattributed. **104** Africana Museum; Worcester Museum; *The Pictorial*; Local History Museum, Durban. **105** Human Sciences Research Council, Archives of the Centre for South African Theatre, Pretoria; Human Sciences Research Council, Archives of the Centre for South African Theatre, Pretoria; *South Africa*; *South Africa*; *South Africa*; Cape Archives; Human Sciences Research Council, Archives of the Centre for South African Theatre, Pretoria. **106** Port Elizabeth Municipal Library; *The Sphere*; Cape Archives. **107** J.B. Kramer; *Outspan*; *South African Lady's Pictorial*. **108** *The Illustrated South African Hotel Guide*; *The Star*, Johannesburg; Africana Museum; Africana Museum; Mount Nelson Hotel. **109** *The Illustrated South African Hotel Guide*; Royal Hotel; *The "Cape Times" South African Hotel Guide*; *The "Cape Times" South African Hotel Guide*; Cape Archives. **110** J.B. Kramer; Africana Museum; Local History Museum, Durban; *Outspan*. **111** *Seventy Golden Years* by Felix Stark (Felstar Publishing (Pty) Ltd.); Africana Museum; *The Pictorial*; Africana Museum; *The Pictorial*. **112** Africana Museum; *The Star*, Johannesburg; *Milady*; *South African Lady's Pictorial*; Africana Museum. **113** United Tobacco Company Ltd.; United Tobacco Company Ltd.; J.B. Kramer; *Natal Mercury Pictorial*; United Tobacco Company Ltd.; United Tobacco Company Ltd.; Kimberley Mine Museum/John Meek; Kimberley Mine Museum/John Meek; United Tobacco Company Ltd.; J.B. Kramer; United Tobacco Company Ltd.; United Tobacco Company Ltd. **114** Africana Museum; Africana Museum; Africana Museum; South African Breweries. **115** Ohlsson's Cape Breweries Ltd; KWV; Africana Museum; Africana Museum. **116** *Pretoria News*. **118** Cape Archives; Cape Archives; Africana Museum; *Outspan*; Bernberg Museum of Costume; Bernberg Museum of Costume. **119** Africana Museum; Mrs C. Magid; Mrs C. Magid; Mrs C. Magid; Cape Archives. **120** Human Sciences Research Council, Archives of the Centre for South African Theatre, Pretoria. **121** Bernberg Museum of Costume; Bernberg Museum of Costume; Africana Museum; Africana Museum; Human Sciences Research Council, Archives of the Centre for South African Theatre, Pretoria; Africana Museum. **122-123** Mrs C. Magid. **124** Human Sciences Research Council, Archives of the Centre for South African Theatre, Pretoria; Human Sciences Research Council, Archives of the Centre for South African Theatre, Pretoria; *They Built a Theatre, the History of the Johannesburg Repertory Theatre* Ed. Arthur Hoffman and Anna Romain-Hoffman (A.D. Donker); Human Sciences Research Council, Archives of the Centre for South African Theatre, Pretoria; Human Sciences Research Council, Archives of the Centre for South African Theatre, Pretoria; Human Sciences Research Council, Archives of the Centre for South African Theatre, Pretoria; Human Sciences Research Council, Archives of the Centre for South African Theatre, Pretoria; Human Sciences Research Council, Archives of the Centre for South African Theatre, Pretoria. **125** Human Sciences Research Council, Archives of the Centre for South African Theatre, Pretoria; Human Sciences Research Council, Archives of the Centre for South African Theatre, Pretoria; Human Sciences Research Council, Archives of the Centre for South African Theatre, Pretoria; Africana Museum; Africana Museum; Africana Museum; Unattributed; Human Sciences Research Council, Archives of the Centre for South African Theatre, Pretoria; Human Sciences Research Council, Archives of the Centre for South African Theatre, Pretoria; Human Sciences Research Council, Archives of the Centre for South African Theatre, Pretoria; Africana Museum; Africana Museum; Human Sciences Research Council, Archives of the Centre for South African Theatre, Pretoria. **126** Africana Museum; *The Star*, Johannesburg; Unattributed; Africana Museum; Unattributed; Unattributed; Unattributed. **127** Group: *Australia's Yesterdays* (Reader's Digest); Thorn EMI Patents Ltd; *South African Pictorial*; *Outspan*; *South African Pictorial*. **128** James de Villiers; Cape Archives; Human Sciences Research Council, Archives of the Centre for South African Theatre, Pretoria; Human Sciences Research Council, Archives of the Centre for South African Theatre, Pretoria; *Milady*. **129** Human Sciences Research Council, Archives of the Centre for South African Theatre, Pretoria; Civic Theatre; PACT: Human Sciences Research Council, Archives of the Centre for South African Theatre, Pretoria; *Capab Ballet — Kruik Ballet: the past nine years/die afgelope nege jaar 1971-1980* by Alec Beukes (Collectors Press). **130** B. Forda Graham; Human Sciences Research Council, Archives of the Centre for South African Theatre, Pretoria; *The Star*, Johannesburg; René Ahrenson; Eoan Group; Eoan Group; *The Star*, Johannesburg. **131** *The Argus*; *The Star*, Johannesburg; *The Star*, Johannesburg; Mr M. Egnos; Human Sciences Research Council, Archives of the Centre for South African Theatre, Pretoria; *The Star*, Johannesburg. **132** *The Star's* Barnett Collection; Africana Museum; Cape Archives; Cape Archives. **133** Box: Warwick Trading Company Catalogue, Science Museum, London; *South African Pictorial, Stage and Cinema*; *South African Pictorial, Stage and Cinema*. **134** Copyright (c) 1927. Warner Bros. Pictures, Inc. Renewed 1955. Released by United Artists Television. All rights reserved; P.G. Higgins. **135** *Outspan*; Cape Archives; Africana Museum; City Tramways. **136** Africana Museum; Africana Museum; Africana Museum; Human Sciences Research Council, Archives of the Centre for South African Theatre, Pretoria. **137** Local History Museum, Durban; Stellenbosch Museum; *South African Pictorial*; *South African Pictorial*. **138** Kavalier Films. **139** Killarney Film Studios; from Emil Nofal's film *Wild Season*; Mimosa Films; Kavalier Films. **140** Group: *Australia's Yesterdays* (Readers Digest); SABC. **141** Africana Museum; Local History Museum, Durban, Local History Museum, Durban; *Stage and Cinema and Listener-In*. **142** SABC. **143** SABC; SABC; SABC; SABC; *Outspan;* SABC; SABC; *Outspan*. **144** *Cape Times; Rand Daily Mail*; SABC TV/*Cape Times*; SABC TV; SABC TV. **145** *Outspan*; Abe Berry/*The Star*, Johannesburg; SABC TV; SABC TV; SABC TV. **146** Port Elizabeth Municipal Library. **148** *The Star*, Johannesburg; Stellenbosch Museum; Orange Free State Archives. **149** Cape Archives; J.B. Kramer; Port Elizabeth Municipal Library; *The Star*, Johannesburg. **150** Africana Museum. **151** Worcester Museum; *South Africa;* Cape Archives; Unattributed; Pretoria Municipal Archives; East London Museum. **152** Pretoria Municipal Archives; *The Star*, Johannesburg; Africana Museum. **153** Ian Garlick; Pretoria Municipal Archives; Cape Archives; Orange Free State Archives; C.P. Nel Museum, Oudtshoorn; J.B. Kramer; Austin Motor Company (SA) (Pty) Ltd. **154** Ford Motor Company; R.H. Johnston. **155** Orange Free State Archives; R.H. Johnston; *The New State*; Unattributed; East London Museum; R.H. Johnston. **156** *Argus Weekly*; John Meek; R.H. Johnston. **157** Africana Museum; Africana Museum; Africana Museum; R.H. Johnston; R.H. Johnston; R.H. Johnston.**158** Collector Cars UMS (Pty) Ltd/Johan du Plessis; *Motor;* Automobile Association of South Africa; Collector Cars UMS (Pty) Ltd/Johan du Plessis; *M.T.A. Bulletin*. **159** *Motor Age*; *Motor Parade*; Collector Cars UMS (Pty) Ltd/Johan du Plesssis; Mr Verster de Wit; *General Motors*; Mr Verster de Wit. **160-161** David Steele. **162** By courtesy of South African Railways; South African Railways/John Meek; *The Star's* Barnett Collection; by courtesy of South African Railways; Cape Archives. **163** Cape Archives; John Meek; *Cape Times*; by courtesy of South African Railways. **164** By courtesy of South African Railways; National Cultural History and Open-Air Museum (Kruger House). **165** By courtesy of South African Railways; by courtesy of South African Railways; R.L. Cairns; *South African Railways Magazine*; by courtesy of South African Railways; *South African Railways Magazine*; *South African Railways Magazine*. **166-167** A.A. Jorgensen. **168** Port Elizabeth Municipal Library; *The Star*, Johannesburg; *The Star*, Johannesburg; *South African Lady's Pictorial*; Africana Museum. **169** Union-Castle Mail Steamship Co. Ltd. **170** *Cape Times*; Killie Campbell Africana Library; by courtesy of South African Railways; East London Museum. **171** *The Sphere*; *The Sphere*; Union-Castle Mail Steamship Co. Ltd; *The Sphere*. **172** Local History Museum, Durban; *The Star's* Barnett Collection; Africana Museum. **173** Africana Museum; Pretoria Municipal Archives; G. Shields; Unattributed. **174** By courtesy of South African Railways; Dane Gerneke; South African National Museum of Military History; Cape Archives. **175** Africana Museum; South African National Museum of Military History; Mrs C. Magid; by courtesy of South African Railways; by courtesy of South African Railways. **176** *Motor Weekly*; *The Sphere*; *Motor Weekly*; Africana Museum; John Meek; Africana Museum. **177** Press Association/LNA; *African World Annual; African World Annual*; *Aviation in Africa*; *The Sphere*; Central Press Photos Ltd; Africana Museum; Keystone Press Agency Ltd. **178** By courtesy of South African Airways; Africana Museum; G.G. Williams; by courtesy of South African Railways; Local History Museum, Durban; by courtesy of South African Railways. **179** By courtesy of South African Railways. **180** Stellenbosse Heemkring. **182** Cape Archives; Africana Museum; Cape Archives. **183** *South African Domestic Monthly*; *South Africam Domestic Monthly*; *South African Domestic Monthly*; *South African Lady's Pictorial*; *South African Lady's Pictorial*; Box: South African Cultural History Museum; Africana Museum; *South African Lady's Pictorial*. **184** *The Pictorial*; *The Pictorial*; *The Star*, Johannesburg. **185** Stuttafords Catalogue; Stuttafords Catalogue; Stuttafords Catalogue; John Meek; Stuttafords Catalogue; Stuttafords Catalogue; Africana Museum; Stuttafords Catalogue; *The Argus*. **186** Spracklens Catalogue; Unattributed; *Milady*/Maidenform Inc.; *Milady*/Maidenform Inc.; Unattributed. **187** *South African Lady's Pictorial*/Gossard Foundation Garments and Swimwear; *South African Lady's Pictorial*; *South African Lady's Pictorial*/ United Tobacco Company Ltd; Spracklens Catalogue. **188** *South African Lady's Pictorial*; *Cape Times*; Africana Museum; Local History Museum, Durban. **189** Africana Museum; *Outspan*; Box: *Stage and Cinema and Listener-In*. **190** *South African Lady's Pictorial*; Africana Musuem; Mr A.D. Thaw. **191** *South African Lady's Pictorial*; *South African Lady's Pictorial*; Spracklens Catalogue; Spracklens Catalogue; Spracklens Catalogue; *Woman's Journal*, London; *Milady*. **192** *The Star*, Johannesburg; *Outspan;* Africana Museum; *The Star*, Johannesburg; *The Argus*. **193** *Cape Times*; Box: Barbara Brown, Saxon Artists; Foschini; *The Argus*. **194** Cape Archives; Spracklens Catalogue. **195** *Rand Young Man's Journal*; D.A. Cairns; *Man About Town*; *Stage and Cinema*; *Outspan*. **196** *Australia's Yesterdays* (Readers Digest); *South African Lady's Pictorial*; Local History Museum, Durban; Africana Museum. **197** *Cape Times;* Africana Museum; Africana Museum; Africana Museum; *Outlook* /AECI Ltd; *South African Lady's Pictorial;* Cape Archives. **198** *South African Lady's Pictorial*; *Cape Times*; *South African Lady's Pictorial*; *South African Lady's Pictorial*; Africana Museum; Africana Museum. **199** *South African Lady's Pictorial*; *South African Lady's Pictorial*; *Pretoria News*; *Pretoria News*; Africana Museum. **200** Stuttafords Catalogue; Africana Museum; C.P. Nel Museum, Oudtshoorn; Africana Museum; Africana Museum; Africana Museum; Worcester Museum. **201** Africana Museum. **202** Cape Archives; C.P. Nel Museum, Oudtshoorn; Cape Archives; Africana Museum. **203** *The Star's* Barnett Collection; Africana Museum; Africana Museum; Cape Archives; *Milady*; *Milady*. **204** Pretoria Municipal Archives. **206** Newspapers: *Land en Volk, Die Transvaler, Die Volksblad, Imvo, Die Burger*, The Argus Printing and Publishing Company Ltd; D. Boonzaier; Africana Museum. **207** Magazines, first column: *The Veld, The Owl, The South African Review, Milady;* second column: *Huisgenoot, Voorslag, Drum;* third column: *Die Brandwag, Sjambok, Outspan, Fair Lady*; Africana Museum. **208** Africana Museum; Africana Museum; *Cape Times*; *Cape Times*. **209** *Too Late for Tears* by Benjamin Bennett (Howard Timmins for Hodder and Stoughton); *The Argus*; *The Argus*; *The Argus*; *The Star*, Johannesburg; *Pretoria News*. **210** *South African Illustrated News*; *South African Review*: *Book of 50 Famous Cartoons: a unique souvenir of the Anglo-Boer War*; D. Boonzaier; D. Boonzaier; D. Boonzaier; Africana Museum; *Outspan*; Africana Museum. **211** Press Features (Pty.) Ltd; *Rand Daily Mail;* T.O. Honiball; Press Features (Pty.) Ltd; Press Features (Pty.) Ltd; Jackson of *The Argus*, Cape Town. **212** Africana Museum; *Outspan*/Reckitt Household Products; *Cape Times Annual*; Africana Museum; *Cape Times*; *Cape Times;* Africana Museum; *Cape Times; Cape Times Annual*. **213** Ford Motor Company; Local History Museum, Durban; *Milady*/Max Factor; *Cape Times Annual*; *South African Lady's Pictorial*/Lever Brothers; *Milady; Fair Lady*/Elida-Gibbs. **214** Africana Museum; Africana Museum/Lever Brothers; Africana Museum; Africana Museum; *South African Lady's Pictorial*/Lever Brothers; Africana Museum. **215** Africana Museum; Africana Museum/Lever Brothers; Africana Museum; Africana Museum/ Lever Brothers; Africana Museum/Lever Brothers; Africana Museum. **216** *Daily Mail*, London; *Daily Mail*, London; *Daily Mail*, London; Africana Museum. **217** Brigadier John Doyle; *John Buchan: a Biography* by J.A. Smith (Granada Publishing Ltd); *Mark Twain — Himself* by M. Meltzer (Crown Publishers); *John Buchan: a Biography* by J.A. Smith (Granada Publishing Ltd); *The History of the South African Forces in France* by John Buchan (Thomas Nelson and Sons Ltd). **218** South African Library; F. Lafitte; Africana Museum. **219** Africana Museum; Africana Museum; Copyright (c) 1952 by Pauline Smith from *The Little Karoo*. **220** *Jock of the Bushveld* by Percy FitzPatrick (Longmans, Green & Co.); *Jock of the Bushveld* by Percy FitzPatrick (Longmans, Green & Co.); *Jock of the Bushveld* by Percy FitzPatrick (Longmans, Green & Co.); *Jock of the Bushveld* by Percy FitzPatrick (Longmans, Green & Co.); *Fitz: the story of Sir Percy FitzPatrick* by J.P.R. Wallis by permission of Macmillan, London and Basingstoke; *The First South African* by A.P. Cartwright (Purnell); *The First South African* by A.P. Cartwright (Purnell). **221** *Observer*, South Africa; *L'Etoile du Sud* de Jules Verne éd. Hetzel, Hachette; *L'Etoile du Sud* de Jules Verne éd. Hetzel, Hachette; *Meridiana* by Jules Verne (Sampson, Low); the Estate of Sir Henry Rider Haggard; *South Africa;* Africana Museum. **222** Africana Museum; *Maurice Maeterlinck — a study of his life and thought* by W.D. Halls (Oxford, at the Clarendon Press); *Cape Times;* cover photograph of the filmscript *The Guest* by Athol Fugard and Ross Devenish, published by Ad. Donker, 1977. **223** *Supernature* by Lyall Watson (Hodder and Stoughton Ltd/Coronet Books); *Lifetide* by Lyall Watson (Hodder and Stoughton Ltd/Coronet Books); *Die Groot Verlange* by Leon Rousseau (Human & Rousseau Publishers (Pty) Ltd); *The Star*, Johannesburg; *The Star*, Johannesburg. **224** Collection of Valerie Rosenberg; Collection of Valerie Rosenberg; *The Star*, Johannesburg; *The Star*, Johannesburg. **225** Marius Garb; *Herman Charles Bosman as I knew him* by Bernard Sachs (Dial Press); Africana Museum. **226** *Cry, the Beloved Country* by Alan Paton (Longman, Green and Co.); EMI Films; *The Conservationist* by Nadine Gordimer, jacket design by Craig Dodd (Jonathan Cape); Africana Museum; *A Guest of Honour* by Nadine Gordimer, jacket design by Mon Mohan (Jonathan Cape); *Outspan*. **227** *Brolloks en Bittergal* by C.J. Langenhoven (Nasionale Pers Bpk); Human Sciences Research Council, Archives of the Centre for South African Literature, Pretoria; Human Sciences Research Council, Archives of the Centre for South African Literature, Pretoria; Human Sciences Research Council, Archives of the Centre for South African Literature, Pretoria; *Die Rooi Rotte* by C.L. Leipoldt (Nasionale Pers Bpk); *Die Mugu* by Etienne Leroux (HAUM); *The Argus*; *Magersfontein, O Magersfontein* by Etienne Leroux (Human and Rousseau); *The Argus*; verse: reprinted by kind permission of Curtis Brown Ltd, London, on behalf of the Estate of Roy Campbell. **228** *Turning Wheels* by Stuart Cloete (William Collins, Sons and Company Ltd); Africana Museum; D. Boonzaier; Africana Museum; *Home From Sea* by Joy Packer (Eyre Methuen). **229** *To the River's End* by Lawrence Green (Howard Timmins); Africana Museum; *The Lost World of the Kalahari* by Laurens van der Post, illustration by Fredrick Fuchs (Hogarth Press); *Cape Times*; *When the Lion Feeds* by Wilbur Smith (William Heinemann Ltd); *A Twist of Sand* by Geoffrey Jenkins (William Collins, Sons and Company Ltd); *The Golden Keel* by Desmond Bagley (William Collins, Sons and Company Ltd). **230** Africana Museum. **232** Africana Museum; Africana Museum; Pretoria Municipal Archives. **233** *The Star*, Johannesburg; Africana Museum; *The Star*, Johannesburg. **234** Potchefstroom Museum; South African Cultural History Museum; *Springbok Saga* by Chris Greyvenstein (Don Nelson). **235** *Springbok Saga* by Chris Greyvenstein (Don Nelson). **236** *Springbok Saga* by Chris Greyvenstein (Don Nelson); *Cape Times*; *Springbok Saga* by Chris Greyvenstein (Don Nelson). **237** *Springbok Saga* by Chris Grevyenstein (Don Nelson); Akkersdyk Studios; *Topsport*. **238** *Huisgenoot*; *Cape Times;* John Rubython; *Evening Standard*, London. **239** John

Rubython; *Cape Times;* Eugene Labuschagne of *Rapport; Cape Times.* **240** *The Tatler,* London; Africana Museum; *The Tatler,* London. **241** Africana Museum; Africana Museum; *The Tatler,* London; Africana Museum; *Natal Mercury.* **242** *Vintage Summer: 1947* by John Arlott (Eyre and Spottiswoode, London 1967); *Vintage Summer: 1947* by John Arlott (Eyre and Spottiswoode, London 1967). **243** *Vintage Summer: 1947* by John Arlott (Eyre and Spottiswoode, London 1967); *Die Brandwag; Springbok Glory* by Louis Duffus (Longmans, Green & Co.); *Vintage Summer: 1947* by John Arlott (Eyre and Spottiswoode, London 1967). **244** *The Argus:* John Rubython. **245** John Rubython; John Rubython; *The Argus;* John Rubython; John Rubython. **246** Africana Museum. **247** Africana Museum; *S.A. Yachting; S.A. Yachting;* Africana Museum. **248** *Car;* Africana Museum; Gavin Stapleton. **249** Africana Museum; *Cape Times;* Africana Museum; *Personalities in South African Motoring and Aviation* (Knox Printing and Publishing Co.); Africana Museum; John Rubython. **250** John Rubython; Africana Museum; Africana Museum; Africana Museum. **251** *Natal Mercury;* Africana Museum; Africana Museum; Africana Museum. **252** Africana Museum. **253** Africana Museum; *The Argus;* Africana Museum; *Natal Mercury;* Africana Museum. **254** The McGregor Museum, Kimberley; *This Brutal Glory* by Chris Greyvenstein (Buren Publishers (Pty) Ltd); *This Brutal Glory* by Chris Greyvenstein (Buren Publishers (Pty) Ltd). **255** *Boxing South Africa; Boxing South Africa; Boxing South Africa; Boxing South Africa;* Africana Museum. **256** *This Brutal Glory* by Chris Greyvenstein (Buren Publishers (Pty) Ltd). **257** Unattributed; John Rubython; *This Brutal Glory* by Chris Greyvenstein (Buren Publishers (Pty) Ltd); John Rubython; *The Argus.* **258** *The Star,* Johannesburg; *The Star,* Johannesburg; *S.A. Tennis; S.A. Tennis.* **259** John Rubython; *S.A. Tennis; Huisgenoot;* Africana Museum; *The Argus.* **260** Africana Museum. **261** John Rubython; *The Star,* Johannesburg; All-sport Photographic Ltd; All-Sport Photographic Ltd; *The Star,* Johannesburg. **262** Africana Museum. **263** Africana

Museum. **264** Africana Museum. **266** Africana Museum; *African Pictorial.* **267** Local History Museum, Durban; R.H. Johnston; Local History Museum, Durban. **268-269** From *Century of Typewriters Exhibition* at the South African Cultural History Museum, sponsored by Imperial Underwood College of Commerce, Cape Town. **270** *Carnegie Commission Reports.* **271** *The Star's* Barnett Collection; Transvaal Museum Services; Transvaal Museum Services; *The Sphere;* Transvaal Museum Services. **272** Africana Museum. **273** *The Sphere; Illustrated London News* Picture Library. **274** Pretoria Municipal Archives. **275** *Outspan;* Pretoria Municipal Archives. **276** South African Museum. **277** Africana Museum; Africana Museum; Cape Archives; Africana Museum. **278** Rhodes Memorial Museum and Commonwealth Centre; *South Africa;* Pretoria Municipal Archives; D. Boonzaier; Africana Museum; Africana Museum; *South Africa; The Star,* Johannesburg; Africana Museum; *The Star,* Johannesburg; Africana Museum. **280** East London Museum; Fletcher and Cartwrights: Stuttafords Catalogue; Cape Archives; Spracklens Catalogue. **281** Africana Museum. **282** O.K. Bazaars; O.K. Bazaars; O.K. Bazaars; O.K. Bazaars; Greatermans (SA) Ltd. **283** Pick 'n Pay Stores Ltd; Pick 'n Pay Stores Ltd; Pick 'n Pay Stores Ltd; Greatermans (SA) Ltd; Greatermans (SA) Ltd; Greatermans (SA) Ltd. **284** Cape Archives. **285** Johan du Plessis. **286** Africana Museum. **288** *The Pictorial;* Africana Museum; South African National Museum of Military History; Africana Museum. **289** *South Africa; The Pictorial.* **290** *The Star,* Johannesburg; *The Star,* Johannesburg; South African National Museum of Military History. **291** *The Argus; The Argus;* South African National Museum of Military History; South African National Museum of Military History; *The Pictorial; The Pictorial; The Pictorial.* **292** South African Library; *The Pictorial; The Pictorial.* **293** South African National Museum of Military History; South African National Museum of Military History; *The Pictorial; The Pictorial; The Pictorial; The Pictorial.* **294** South African National Mu-

seum of Military History; *My Reminiscences of East Africa* by General von Lettow-Vorbeck (Hurst and Blackett Ltd); South African National Museum of Military History; South African National Museum of Military History. **295** *The Star,* Johannesburg; South African National Museum of Military History; South African National Museum of Military History. **296** South African National Museum of Military History. **297** South African Legion; South African National Museum of Military History; South African National Museum of Military History; South African National Museum of Military History; *The Pictorial.* **298** J.B. Kramer; Africana Museum; *Natal Mercury.* **299** Cape Archives; *Illustrated London News; Cape Times; Cape Times.* **300** South African National Museum of Military History. **301** Dr F.K. Mitchell; Imperial War Museum, London; South African National Museum of Military History; *For Valour* by I.S. Uys. **302** *The Argus.* **303** *Cape Times;* Posters: South African National Museum of Military History; South African National Museum of Military History. **304** Imperial War Museum, London; South African National Museum of Military History; Harry Klein; South African National Museum of Military History; South African National Museum of Military History; Postage Stamps reproduced under Government Printer's Copyright Authority 7688 of 15.7.1981. **305** J.B. Kramer; J.B. Kramer; South African National Museum of Military History; South African National Museum of Military History; Terence McNally; South African National Museum of Military History. **306** Local History Museum, Durban; Local History Museum, Durban; Africana Museum; *Cape Times;* Africana Museum. **307** Tickets: Africana Museum; Posters: South African National Museum of Military History; South African National Museum of Military History; *South African Industry and Trade;* Unattributed. **308** Africana Museum; Local History Museum, Durban; *Cape Times.* **309** Local History Museum, Durban; Yates Wilson/Simonstown Historical Association; *Cape Times;* Local History Museum, Durban; Local History Museum, Dur-

ban. **310** Terence McNally; Terence McNally; Terence McNally; Imperial War Museum, London; *Great Events of the Twentieth Century* (Reader's Digest). **311** South African National Museum of Military History; Postcard: J.B. Kramer; South African National Museum of Military History; South African National Museum of Military History. **312-313** South African National Museum of Military History. **314** South African National Museum of Military History; South African National Museum of Military History; South African National Museum of Military History; Mrs M.G. Watkins. **315** *Cape Times; Outspan; Outspan;* South African National Museum of Military History; South African National Museum of Military History. **316** J.W. Nicholls; J.W. Nicholls; South African National Museum of Military History; J.B. Kramer; J.B. Kramer. **317** J.W. Nicholls; J.W. Nicholls; Newspapers: South African National Museum of Military History; South African National Museum of Military History; South African National Museum of Military History; South African National Museum of Military History. **318** *Cape Times;* Bobby Keartland. **319** *The Star,* Johannesburg; J.B. Kramer; South African National Museum of Military History. **320** Africana Museum; Africana Museum; Africana Museum; South African National Museum of Military History. **321** *South African Lady's Pictorial*/Akkersdyk Studios; Gordon Douglas; with thanks to the General Smuts War Veterans Foundation; *The Sphere;* Africana Museum; Africana Museum; *The Star,* Johannesburg; Africana Museum.

Lines from *The Absent Minded Beggar, The Return* and *Recessional* are taken from *The Definitive Edition of Rudyard Kipling's Verse.*

The Reader's Digest has endeavoured to trace the owners of all copyright material reproduced in *South Africa's Yesterdays.* However, in some instances this has proved impossible, and the editors regret any omissions which may have occurred.

The type used for the body text, captions and chapter headings in this book is Baskerville. The text is set in 9 point, ½ point leaded.

Typesetting and colour separations by Hirt and Carter (Pty) Ltd., Cape Town.

Printed in Hong Kong by South China Printing Co.

®'Reader's Digest' is a registered trademark of the Reader's Digest Association, Inc. of Pleasantville, New York, USA.